Thomas M. K

W9-AOY-726

BT
25
L3
1967

THE IDEA OF REFORM

Its Impact on Christian Thought and Action
in the Age of the Fathers

THE IDEA OF REFORM

Its Impact on Christian Thought and Action in the Age of the Fathers

Francis A. Drexel
LIBRARY

Gift of

Dr. Thomas Keefe

History Department

SAINT JOSEPH'S UNIVERSITY

THE IDEA OF REFORM

Its Impact on Christian Thought and Action
in the Age of the Fathers

GERHART B. LADNER

HARPER TORCHBOOKS
Harper & Row, Publishers
New York, Evanston, and London

Uxori dilectissimae
decennis laboris consorti patientissimae

THE IDEA OF REFORM

Addenda to the Torchbook edition, 1967, copyright © 1967 by
Gerhart B. Ladner.

Copyright © 1959 by the President and Fellows of Harvard College.

Printed in the United States of America.

This book was originally published in 1959 by the Harvard
University Press and is here reprinted by arrangement.

First HARPER TORCHBOOK edition published 1967 by
Harper & Row, Publishers, Incorporated,
49 East 33rd Street, New York, N.Y. 10016.

Library of Congress Catalog Card Number: 59-6159.

CONTENTS

v

PART THREE

MONASTICISM AS A VEHICLE OF THE CHRISTIAN IDEA OF REFORM IN THE AGE OF THE FATHERS

PREFACE

In the past ten years, since the subject of this book was first outlined, the importance of the idea of reform—of what it is and of what it can achieve—has certainly not become smaller. Perhaps the origin and early history of this idea can act as a reminder of what is expected of human beings; because reform originally was so closely related to man's image-likeness to God, it was less violent than revolution and less haphazard than revivals and "responses" of various kinds. Even today one can be sufficiently optimistic to believe that the reform of man remains the hope of man.

While the present volume deals with the idea of reform in the age of the Fathers and its influence on the earliest manifestations of Christian monasticism, successive volumes could profitably describe the continuing life of the idea in the earlier and later Middle Ages, when renovation of Empire, Church reform, and perfection of the whole *Christianitas* were among the dominant aspects of reform ideology.

My debt of gratitude to persons and institutions who have helped me in divers ways during the period of the preparation and writing of this book is very great. The major part of the work was carried out while I was a Member of the Institute for Advanced Study at Princeton (1949–1951) and a Guggenheim Fellow (1950–1951). To the Director of the Institute for Advanced Study, Dr. Robert Oppenheimer, and to its Faculty, especially to Professor Erwin Panofsky and Professor Homer Thompson, as well as to the Secretary General of the John Simon Guggenheim Memorial Foundation, Mr. Henry Allen Moe, go my warmest thanks, likewise to the University of Notre Dame, who gave me leave of absence in the years 1949 to 1951, and in particular to the Rev. Fathers Philip S. Moore, C.S.C., Academic Vice-President, and Thomas T. McAvoy, C.S.C., Chairman of the Department of History.

The unique possibilities of an exchange of ideas between scientists and humanists at the Institute for Advanced Study led to the writing of the methodological Excursuses I, II, and IV. I am extremely grateful to Dr. Robert Oppenheimer, who kindly read Excursuses I and II, and to Dr. Kurt Gödel, who did the same for Excursus IV. I hope that I have profited from their criticisms.

I am very grateful to Professor Herbert Bloch for his reading of the entire manuscript and for important suggestions and kind assistance from which this book has benefited in many ways.

To Professor Werner Jaeger I express my deep gratitude for the very helpful personal interest which he has taken in the book, which in its interpretation of the history of reform may, I hope, not lack a genuine relationship to his studies on the Greek and Christian *paideia* idea.

The history of ideas cannot in practice be separated from the histories of philosophy and theology in the stricter sense. For their exceedingly valuable advice in this respect I am sincerely grateful to Professor Jacques Maritain, who read portions of the book when it was in its beginnings, to Professor Etienne Gilson, and to the Rev. Father Robert Gleason, S.J. Father Gleason was kind enough to read the whole manuscript and I wish to thank him very much also on this occasion for his comments and criticisms.

I owe much to stimulating discussions with two unforgettable scholars and friends, Professor Ernst Robert Curtius and Professor Theodor Ernst Mommsen. I also gratefully acknowledge many helpful suggestions by other friends and colleagues, above all by Professor Ernst Kantorowicz, whose many-sided illuminating works and ideas were never far from my mind in the writing of this book, furthermore by Dom Anselm Strittmatter, O.S.B., Professor Stephan Kuttner, Professor Erwin Panofsky, Professor Harold Cherniss, Professor John Olin, and by my late brother, Dr. George Ladner.

I alone am responsible, of course, for the book's deficiencies.

Finally, very special thanks are due to Fordham University for encouraging this work in every possible way, particularly to the Rev. Father Edwin A. Quain, S.J., former Academic Vice-President, through whom I was enabled to participate in the International Augustinian Congress at Paris in 1954, and to the Rev. Fathers J. Franklin Ewing, S.J., Director of Research Services, and Edward F.

Clark, S.J., Academic Vice-President, for their approval of a generous grant in connection with the preparation of the manuscript for print.

In reading the proofs and in preparing the index I had the intelligent, conscientious, and much appreciated assistance of one of my students, Mr. John W. Hodges.

To Harvard University Press, and especially to Mrs. W. S. Mallory Lash, I wish to express my gratitude for the care and patience spent on the publishing of this book.

The texts quoted in the notes reproduce the spelling (but not punctuation and capitalization) of the editions used, except that in Latin texts "i" is always substituted for "j" and "v" for "u" when it is a consonant. For the Latin Fathers the editions used are, whenever available to me, those given preference in Dom Eligius Dekkers' *Clavis Patrum Latinorum*.

G.B.L.

Scarsdale, New York
August 18, 1959

INTRODUCTION

The history of man can be seen as a sequence of new beginnings. Such a view in fact underlies in one way or another almost all historical interpretation, be it based on the belief in cyclical recurrence or in conversion and redemption, in decline and fall or in *corsi* and *ricorsi*, in progress and evolution or in challenge and response, in rebirth and reform or in revolution. It is not surprising that early Christendom should have impressed its own character on the universal idea of renewal and that specific Christian expressions of it should have had an appreciable influence on subsequent developments in civilization ever since. For Christianity is a great religion of renewal where sin and death are overcome by divine redemption and resurrection.[1] From a Christian point of view the life, death, and revival cycles of nature and their evocations and representations from time immemorial in the rituals and the myths of sacrifice and rebirth are intimations of Christ's death and Resurrection and of the consequent redemption of the universe.[2] But while pre-Christian and Christian renewal ideas do not lack connecting links, there are essential differences; these

[1] See 2 Cor. 5:15 and 17: "And Christ died for all; that they also who live, may not now live to themselves, but unto Him who died for them, and rose again. . . . If then any be in Christ a new creature, the old things are passed away, behold all things are made new." Cf. in general K. Prümm, S.J., *Christentum als Neuheitserlebnis* (Freiburg i. B., 1933).

[2] These cosmic aspects of what might be called the *praeparatio evangelica* idea, in a sense which goes far beyond the title of Eusebius of Caesarea's famous work, were formulated at least as early as Clement of Rome's *Letter to the Corinthians*, also in Theophilus' *Ad Autolycum* and Tertullian's *De resurrectione mortuorum*—see below, p. 133, n. 1—and as recently as Dom Odo Casel's "Mysterientheologie," see, for instance, his essays, collected under the title *Das christliche Kultmysterium*, 2nd ed. (1935). For pre-Christian conceptions of the redemptive enactment of death and resurrection by god, hero, king, especially in the ancient east and in the Greek mysteries, see the survey of modern scholarship in H. Weisinger, *Tragedy and the Paradox of the Fortunate Fall* (Michigan State College Press, 1953); the author in a highly original way tries to demonstrate the continuity between pre-Christian redemptive sacrifice and the even greater results of man's *felix culpa* (see below, pp. 146–147) in the Christian dispensation (his denial of the uniqueness of these results is another matter). For a brief general introduction to Graeco-Roman and late antique oriental mysteries see H. R. Willoughby, *Pagan Regeneration* (Chicago, 1929).

must be determined with particular regard to the Christian idea of reform which has no true equivalent in pre-Christian times.

It will be important also to touch briefly upon the relation between early Christian-mediaeval and modern ideas of renewal and reform. In modern times the term and idea of reform are applied to the renewal and intended improvement of many things, more often however of social entities and of institutions than of individuals. The origins of the Christian idea of reform on the contrary are related to the core of evangelical and Pauline doctrine on the human person: to the experience of its newness in Christ. Scriptural μεταμόρφωσις–reformatio, ἀνακαίνωσις–renovatio, mean personal reformation, renovation toward that image-likeness of man to God (κατ᾽ εἰκόνα καὶ ὁμοίωσιν Θεοῦ, ad imaginem et similitudinem Dei) which according to the Book of Genesis (1:26 f.) had been received by man in creation, but had become impaired through sin. And yet, in spite of the personal, individual character of the Christian idea of reform it became effective as a supra-individual force at a relatively early date, above all, but not exclusively, in monasticism. The crucial initial moments in this process occurred in Late Antiquity and in the earliest Middle Ages or more exactly in the patristic period; they occurred in different forms in the Christian east and west and were followed, especially in the west, by a long series of developments and variations of the idea of reform and of related renewal ideas.

It is common usage among historians to speak of monastic reforms and Church reforms, of imperial and Roman restorations and renovations, of Theodosian, Anglo-Saxon, Carolingian, Byzantine, Ottonian, Twelfth Century Renaissances, of Proto-Renaissances and Pre-Reformations. Are all these manifestations of a tendency toward renewal of the same order or are they heterogeneous? How far is one justified in distinguishing biblical-patristic "reform" or "renovation" not only from pre-Christian but also from other Christian renewal ideas? Especially, what is the relation of reform to baptismal regeneration on the one hand and to the Renaissance idea on the other? Furthermore, what were the structure and dynamics of reform in a society that was Christian at least in intention? How was it possible to seek at the same time the Kingdom of God, not of this world, and to strive for improvement of this world?

If the idea of reform is made the center of the present book, this is done from the conviction that the belief in man's reformation toward his original image-likeness to God (*reformatio* or *renovatio ad imaginem Dei*) was of central importance for early Christian and mediaeval thought and life. This volume will describe the early history of that conception in the patristic age down to the sixth century.[3] It is hoped to show in later studies that the idea persisted and that its reality went far beyond the purely ideological realm. True, the terminology did not always remain the same; but the key terms of *reformatio-renovatio* and *imago* or *similitudo Dei* were never lost, though their scope was extended and their meaning enriched. A few examples from the Middle Ages will confirm this. Such terms were used, for instance, by Gregory the Great when he advocated the manumission of slaves and referred to the original liberty of man, which should thus be reformed;[4] the same formula was later to appear in protection or exemption charters for monasteries, their liberation from all external domination being considered as meritorious as the freeing of slaves.[5] In the early Carolingian age the doctrine of the image of God to which men's minds are to be reformed stands behind Alcuin's hope that a renewal of wisdom and knowledge has actually begun in Charlemagne's empire.[6] In the eleventh century Gregory VII, when he consoles a leader of the Patarian movement who had been mutilated in the Milanese struggle for Church reform, praises the increase of sanctity

[3] The Benedictine and Irish monastic reforms will only occasionally be touched upon in the present volume, since they are of epochal importance for the next, properly mediaeval, phase in the history of reform.

[4] *Epist.* VI, 12, *MGH, Epist.* I, 390 ff.: Cum redemptor noster totius conditor creaturae ad hoc propitiatus humanam voluit carnem adsumere, ut divinitatis suae gratia, disrupto quo tenebamur capti vinculo servitutis, pristinae nos restitueret libertati, salubriter agitur, si homines, quos ab initio natura liberos protulit et ius gentium iugo substituit servitutis, in ea qua nati fuerant manumittentis beneficio libertate reddantur.

[5] See, for instance, Louis VI of France for Cluny, 1113, *Bibliotheca Cluniacensis* (Paris, 1614) 530 (cf. *Recueil des chartes de l'abbaye de Cluny*, edd. A. Bernard and A. Bruel [Collection de documents inédits sur l'histoire de France] V [Paris, 1894] 255, no. 3905): . . . caritas Dei . . . indutus hominem, pristinae libertati hominem restituit et imaginem quae depressa erat reformavit.

[6] Cf. Alcuin, *Expositio in Psalmos penitentiales, PL* C, 574C: . . . imago Dei ad quam reformamur in mente . . . , and *Epist.* CLXXII, *MGH, Epist.* IV, *Karol. Aevi* II, 285: . . . totius sapientiae decus et salutaris eruditionis ornatus . . . renovari incipit.

of the inner man who is renewed from day to day[7] in spite of bodily "diminution": the image of God has become more beautiful regardless of its external form.[8] In the twelfth century St. Bernard of Clairvaux says that the monastic way of life reforms the divine image in man and for this reason is called a second baptism,[9] and at the turn of the same century a Cistercian monk sketches the whole history of monasticism as a series of reforms.[10] Also, St. Bernard and later St. Bonaventure, when they formulate a new mystical theology of the western world, use the old terminology of man's reform to the image and likeness of God and so do St. Thomas Aquinas in his *Summa Theologica* and Vincent of Beauvais in his great encyclopedia.[11] In that age, however, the individual and monastic realizations of the idea of reform had already begun to expand into a new conception of reform of the Church and of Christian society. [2]

[7] Cf. 2 Cor. 4:16.

[8] Gregory VII to the priest Liutprand, 1075, JL 4975, from Landulfus Junior sive de S. Paulo, *Historia Mediolanensis*, ed. C. Castiglioni, in L. A. Muratori, *Rerum Italicarum Scriptores* V, 3 (Bologna, 1934) 478 : . . . integritas quidem corporis tui diminuta est, sed interior homo qui renovatur de die in diem (cf. 2 Cor. 4:16) magnum sanctitatis suscepit incrementum: forma visibilis turpior, sed imago Dei . . . in diminutione iucundior, in turpitudine pulchrior. Cf. my article, "Two Gregorian Letters," *Studi Gregor.* V (1956) 221 ff.

[9] *De praecepto et dispensatione*, 17 (54), PL CLXXXII, 889B f.: . . . praeeminens universis vitae humanae generibus huiuscemodi conversatio professores et amatores suos angelis similes, dissimiles hominibus facit; imo divinam in homine reformat imaginem, configurans nos Christo instar baptismi. Et quasi denique secundo baptizamur. . . .

[10] *Exordium magnum Cisterciense* 10, PL CLXXXV, 1007A f. (with regard to the Cistercian reform): . . . cum . . . nec spes ulla restaurationis uspiam arrideret, omnipotens Deus . . . dum medium silentium tenerent omnia Spiritum Sanctum suum de secretis coelestibus a regalibus sedibus (cf. Wisdom 18:14 and *Introitus, Dominica infra Octavam Nativitatis* [Missale Romanum]) misit in corda quorundam fratrum qui in coenobio quodam degebant quod in Burgundiae partibus situm Molismus vocatur, and *ibid.* 1009C f.: . . . sicut . . . nascente Christo . . . mundus . . . pignus redemptionis novae, reparationis antiquae, felicitatis aeternae suscepit, sic in diebus istis novissimis . . . Deus eiusdem gratiae suae seminarium plantavit in eremo Cisterciensi.

[11] Cf. Bernard of Clairvaux, *De gratia et libero arbitrio* 10, PL CLXXXII, 1018 B f. (Similitudinem divinae imaginis in nobis reformari per Christum); Bonaventure, *Itinerarium mentis in Deum*, 4, 4, *Opera Omnia* V (Quaracchi, 1891) 307: . . . per reformationem imaginis per virtutes theologicas et per oblectationes spiritualium sensuum et suspensiones excessuum efficitur spiritus noster hierarchicus, scilicet purgatus, illuminatus et perfectus; Thomas Aquinas, *Summa Theologica*, I, 93, ed. Forzani, I (Roma 1894) 713 ff.; Vincent of Beauvais, *Speculum doctrinale* I, 9, cf. A. L. Gabriel, O. Praem, *The Educational Ideas of Vincent of Beauvais* (Notre Dame, Ind., 1956), 13 ff.

[12] See below, pp. 277 and p. 423 f.; cf. my article "Erneuerung," *RLAC*, VI (1964), 240 ff.

That an idea of reform existed in the early Christian and later periods is then an abundantly and unambiguously documented fact. What exactly this idea was can emerge only from the study of the historical sources. Nevertheless it is necessary before following the course of the historical idea of reform through time and space to attempt a preliminary definition through distinction from other terms and ideas of renewal. The considerable fluctuations within renewal terminology would make it impossible without a provisional point of reference to class some of these ideas as ideas of reform, others as not.

In studying ideas termed, for instance, *reformatio, renovatio, restauratio, regeneratio*, a historian consciously or unconsciously must measure these terms against preliminary concepts based on his general knowledge of the various forms of renewal ideas including that of reform. Thus only are the terms which occur in the sources classified according to their relevance to the subject matter dealt with, thus only is the linking of terms to ideas initiated. Usually, in historical study, this process of thought is not brought out into the open. To do so is to recognize the existence of a methodological problem of the definition of historical ideas; see Excursus I.

PART ONE

VARIETIES OF RENEWAL IDEOLOGY
AND THE CHRISTIAN IDEA OF REFORM

CHAPTER I

DISTINCTION OF THE IDEA OF REFORM
FROM OTHER IDEAS OF RENEWAL

A definition of the reform idea which may serve as point of reference for a study of the history of that idea in early Christian and subsequent times must be based on quite obvious specific differences between any idea of reform and other representative types of renewal ideology. For the idea of reform is a variant of the more general idea of renewal. The renewal idea itself is more specific than the wider and more general concepts of this kind such as alteration, change, becoming. These concepts do not necessarily imply that emphasis on the relationship between the old and the new in the irreversible process of time which is presupposed in all renewal ideas; even less do they bear the special marks of the reform idea among which the most evident are the notions of reassertion and augmentation of value.

The idea of reform may be considered as essentially Christian in its origin and early development. It is true that adumbrations of the reform idea are not lacking in non-Christian renewal ideology, especially in Greek and Roman literature. Yet such occurrences are of relatively minor significance as compared to the massive importance of the idea in Christian thought;[1] it will therefore be sufficient to refer to them as antecedents or parallels of Christian reform terminology and ideology when occasion arises.[2] Other types of renewal ideas were on the whole of greater prominence and consequence in pre-Christian Antiquity.

The more important of these ancient ideas, most of which survived or reappeared in various transformations and in concomitance with the

[1] In this connection see, for instance, p. 47, n. 61, on the significant absence of the reform idea proper—as distinct from the idea of conversion—from Plato's thought.

[2] Cf., for instance, pp. 40–41, on Seneca's and Pliny the Younger's moral and political use of the term *reformatio* and on the application of reform terminology to Roman legal and institutional ideology by the great jurists of the second and third centuries.

reform idea in the Christian ages, must now be described and distinguished from the idea of reform. The idea of reform must be confronted also with the most relevant fundamentals of Christian renewal ideology.

1. COSMOLOGICAL RENEWAL IDEAS

A first group of renewal ideas other than the idea of reform may be classified as *cosmological*. It includes the theories elaborated in Antiquity about the perpetual cyclical recurrence of identical or similar situations and events. Such theories are rooted in a widespread archaic mentality which attempts to "deny" the relentless course of time by a belief in ever new beginnings;[1] and yet, as early as 500 B.C. Alcmaeon of Croton had recognized that the reason for man's physical death is just his inability to link beginning to end.[2]

Not all cyclical renewal ideas of Antiquity[3] conceive of renewal as a sequence of periodic destructions and restorations of the universe followed by the return of *identical* situations, events, and persons. The interpretation of Heraclitus' doctrine of eternal flux in this sense originates only from the Stoics.[4] Empedocles,[5] Plato,[6] Aristotle,[7] Polybius[8] envisaged cosmic or historical cycles, but these cyclical correspondences are only generic ones. Of the greatest importance for ancient cosmological renewal ideology is the conception of the τέλεος ἐνιαυτός, which first appears in Plato's *Timaeus*.[9] The length of this perfect "world year" is defined by the simultaneous occurrence

[1] See M. Eliade, *Le mythe de l'éternel retour* (Paris, 1949).

[2] Fragm. 2, Diels, *Vorsokratiker* I, 215.

[3] For a cursory survey, also for the survival of these ideas in the Middle Ages, see P. A. Sorokin, *Social and Cultural Dynamics* II (New York, 1937) 315–379, based in part on P. Duhem, *Le système du monde* (reprinted Paris, 1954) and also on L. Thorndike, *History of Magic and Experimental Science* (New York, 1923—); for the ancient and early Christian period in particular see H. Meyer, "Zur Lehre von der ewigen Wiederkunft aller Dinge," *Beiträge zur Geschichte des christlichen Altertums und der byzantinischen Literatur: Festgabe Albert Ehrhard* . . . (Bonn, Leipzig, 1922) 359 ff.

[4] Cf. J. Burnet, *Early Greek Philosophers*, 4th ed. (London, 1948) 158 ff.

[5] Fragms. 17 and 30, Diels, *Vorsokratiker* I, 315 ff. and 325.

[6] *Statesman* 269 ff.; *Laws* 677A.

[7] *De generatione et corruptione* 377 f.; *Metaphysics* XII, 8, 1074B; cf. W. Jaeger, *Aristotle* (Oxford, 1948) 130 ff., on the doctrine, contained in the fragments from *On Philosophy*, that truth returns periodically.

[8] *Histor.* VI, 44 ff. and 57.　　　　[9] *Timaeus* 39D.

of the completions of the eight heavenly revolutions, that is to say, those of the moon, the sun, the five planets then known, and the heaven of fixed stars. Perhaps, already the Pythagoreans, and in any case the Neopythagoreans, expected that the beginning of a new world year would bring about a general renewal of the world.[10] The Stoics linked it to their doctrine of cosmic destruction and renewal through ἐκπύρωσις;[11] according to Seneca[12] the Babylonian priest of the Hellenistic period, Berossus, taught the periodical recurrence not only of conflagrations but also of deluges;[13] Plato himself had known of cataclysmic as well as of fiery upheavals of the universe.[14] It would seem, however, that the Stoics' dogma of *identical* repetition of the same, after an ἐκπύρωσις, owes less to the doctrine of the great world year than to their belief that the cosmic elements, after various transformations and after return to the unity of the primitive divine fire, will again form the same pattern, "so that there will be again Socrates and Plato and every man, with their friends and fellow citizens, sharing the same opinions, meeting the same persons, engaged in the same business, and that there will be restored (ἀποκαθίστασθαι) also every city, village, and countryside: this restoration (ἀποκατά-στασις) to happen not once but often, in fact boundlessly and endlessly."[15] In such terminology the expression ἀποκατάστασις has become a technical term of cosmological renewal; in Christian renewal ideology it will assume further meanings.[16] If the great world year played only a secondary role in Stoic natural philosophy, it was all the more essential to the Roman Neopythagoreans of the late republican and imperial period: a new *magnus annus* was to renovate the whole

---

[10] Cf. E. Zeller, *Die Philosophie der Griechen* I, 1, 6th ed. (Leipzig, 1919) 549 f., 535 f.

[11] *Ecpyrosis* already in Zeno, v. Arnim, *Stoic. Veter. Fragm.* I, 27, fragm. 98; for its connection with the great world year see Arius Didymus, v. Arnim II, 185 f., fragm. 599, and Nemesius, *De natura hominum* 38, v. Arnim II, 190, fragm. 625.

[12] *Naturales quaestiones* III, 29.

[13] Cf. P. Schnabel, *Berossos und die babylonisch-hellenistische Literatur* (Berlin, 1923).

[14] *Timaeus* 22 f. The question of the priority of Greek or of Persian and Indian ideas concerning periodical catastrophes of the world cannot be discussed here; cf. J. Bidez, *Eos ou Platon et l'orient* (Bruxelles, 1945) 82 ff., also Eliade, *Eternel retour*, 167 ff.

[15] Nemesius, *op. cit.*, 38, v. Arnim. Cf. Origen, *Contra Celsum* IV, 68, v. Arnim II, 190, fragm. 626, Alexander of Aphrodisias, *In Aristot. analyt. pr.*, v. Arnim II, 189, fragm. 624, Tatian, *Adversus Graecos* 5, v. Arnim I, 32, fragm. 109.

[16] See below, Part Two, Chapter I and Chapter III, 1.

world and to break the chain of reincarnations.[17] Under Neopythagorean influence, Virgil in his *Fourth Eclogue* found the greatest poetical
expression of ancient cosmological renewal ideology, not without
combining it with the idea of the Golden Age and with vitalistic
renewal ideas:

> Ultima Cumaei venit iam carminis aetas;
> magnus ab integro saeclorum nascitur ordo.
> Iam redit et virgo, redeunt Saturnia regna;
> iam nova progenies caelo demittitur alto.
> Tu modo nascenti puero quo ferrea primum
> desinet ac toto surget gens aurea mundo
> casta fave Lucina; tuus iam regnat Apollo.
> Teque adeo decus hoc aevi, te consule inibit,
> Pollio, et incipient magni procedere menses.[18]

More or less explicit formulations of the world year doctrine and of
the idea of eternal recurrence are found also in Cicero's *Somnium
Scipionis,* [19] in the third century grammarian Censorinus,[20] and in the
interpretation of the *Timaeus* passage mentioned above[21] in Ps.-
Plutarch, *De fato.*[22] Stoic cosmological renewal ideas may have influenced the *Latin Asclepius,* which perhaps dates from the fourth
century and may be derived from a Greek original of the third; the
translator's phrase: *haec enim mundi ⟨re⟩genitura* (or *⟨nova⟩genitura*):
*cunctarum reformatio rerum bonarum et naturae ipsius sanctissima et
religiosissima restitutio*[23] may be influenced by Christian terminology,
but has little relation to Christian ideas of regeneration or reform.

---

[17] Cf. J. Carcopino, *Virgile et le mystère de la IVe Eglogue,* 2nd ed. (Paris, 1943) 84 f. The
idea of reincarnation or metempsychosis itself is not a renewal idea in the proper sense.

[18] *Fourth Eclogue* 4–12. See also *Aeneid* VI, 745 ff., for the interruption of reincarnations
at the turn from one world year to the next.

[19] *De re publica* VI, 21, 23 ff. See P. Boyancé, *Etudes sur le songe de Scipion* (Limoges,
1936) 160 ff.

[20] *De die natali* XVIII, 11.

[21] See p. 10.

[22] *De fato* 3 (569).

[23] *Asclepius* III, 26 a, Scott, *Hermet.* I, 346; cf. the edition by Nock, with French translation by Festugière, *Corp. Hermet.* II, 331, where the reading *genitura* is adhered to. It is
in any case clear from the context that the passage refers to "rebirth"; for the relation to
cosmological renewal, which nevertheless exists, see the commentary of Scott, *Hermet.* III,
177 ff.

The idea of eternal recurrence could be combined with the myth of a Golden Age at the beginning of history, which in Greece first appeared in Hesiod where it had only the vaguest connection with the notion of cyclical return.[24] Later however, for instance, in Virgil's *Fourth Eclogue* the two ideas clearly appear together.[25] The myth of successive ages of decreasing excellence—in Hesiod they are the ages of gold, silver, brass, of the heroes, and of iron—also appears in Indian and Persian sources of the syncretistic period and may be of old-Iranian origin. At first these ages apparently were conceived as purely historical; they also were of the same number as the four Hesiodic metals (not counting Hesiod's age of heroes); later, under the influence perhaps of Hellenized Babylonian astrology, the Mazdaist priests of Asia Minor, Cumont's so-called *mages hellénisés* or *Maguséens*,[26] transformed this conception into that of a planetary world week of seven cosmological and historical ages. Each of these seven ages stood under the ascendency of a planet, as did the seven periods of individual human life, and it was a planet which gave its name to each age as to the days of an ordinary week. Since Saturn was the first and the Sun the last in the sequence,[27] the Golden Age could be conceived of as the return of the age of Saturn, heralded by the still present age of the sun god. Thus Virgil could say in the *Fourth Eclogue*: *redeunt Saturnia regna* and *iam regnat Apollo*.[28]

[24] Hesiod, *Works and Days* 109–201. The only suggestion of a cyclical idea is found in Hesiod's wish to be born if not before then after the end of the last and worst (iron) age (v. 175).

[25] See also *Aeneid* VI, 791 ff., for Augustus as bringer of a new Golden Age. For Hesiod's myth in Ovid see *Metamorphoses* I, 89 ff.

[26] For this whole complex of ideas see F. Cumont, "La fin du monde selon les mages occidentaux," *Rev. hist. rel.* CIII (1931) 29 ff., and J. Bidez and F. Cumont, *Les mages hellénisés* I (Paris, 1938) 131 ff., 218 ff. Cf. also R. Reitzenstein and H. H. Schaeder, *Studien zum antiken Synkretismus aus Iran und Griechenland* (Studien der Bibliothek Warburg VII, Leipzig-Berlin, 1926) Part I/II: "Vom Töpferorakel zu Hesiod," especially 45 ff., where also the most important Indian sources, not discussed by Cumont, are given. For Hesiod and the Golden Age, see also the recent discussion between H. C. Baldry, "Who Invented the Golden Age," *Classical Quarterly*, New Ser. II (1952) 83 ff., "Hesiod's Five Ages," *Jour. Hist. Ideas* XVII (1956) 553 f., J. G. Griffiths, "Archaeology and Hesiod's Five Ages," *ibid.* 109 ff. Cf. R. Eisler, "Metallurgical Anthropology in Hesiod and Plato and the Date of a 'Phoenician Lie'," *Isis* XL (1949) 108 ff.

[27] Cf. Cumont, "Fin du monde" 48 ff., 54 ff.

[28] See Virgil, *Fourth Eclogue* 6–10. The syncretistic series of planetarian gods from Kronos (Saturn) to Helios (Sol or Apollo) which stands behind these Virgilian verses (cf. Carcopino,

In spite of contaminations with cyclical cosmology the Magusean hebdomadal scheme, in which the number of related metals was likewise increased to seven, differs in important respects from the doctrine of the great world year. Instead of eternal recurrence of planetary conjunctions and corresponding recurrent cosmic and historical situations the idea of the great world week envisaged only one succession of planetary ascendencies, each to last a thousand years. After its completion a definitive eschatological renovation of the world would take place, bringing about an eighth age of the heaven of fixed stars, to which the seventh or sun-millennium is only a prelude (to be followed directly by an interlude allowed to the powers of evil).[29] This conception, enriched by Jewish and Early Christian apocalyptic elements, was to become the basis of the chiliastic or millenarian renewal idea which is fundamentally different from that of eternal recurrence.[30] The connecting link between the two conceptions of the world year and the world week is the idea of the Golden Age, the characteristics of which the seventh millennium retains to some extent.

The Hesiodic and Indo-Persian scheme of four or five ages also survived on the historical noncosmical level. In conjunction with the metal myth it appears as the idea of the succession of four world empires[31] in late classical historians from the second century B.C.

Virgile 50 ff., for Virgil's substitution of Apollo for Sol under Neopythagorean and Magusean influence) is different from the sequence of both the official pagan Roman and the Christian order of week days. About Saturday as the first and Sunday as the second day of the Roman week and for Sunday as the first day of the Christian week even before Constantine the Great cf. F. J. Dölger, "Die Planetenwoche der griechisch-römischen Antike und der christliche Sonntag," Ant. u. Chr. VI (1950) 202 ff. See also below, Part Two, Chapter V, 6.

[29] Cf. Cumont, "Fin du monde" 46 f., 56 f., 70 f.: some elements of this conception are found in Origen (Celsus), Contra Celsum VI, 22, GCS, Orig. II, 92, who refers in this connection to the mysteries of Mithras; Lactantius, Divinae institutiones VII, 23–26, CSEL XIX, 655 ff., depends in part on the Ps.-Hystaspes, i.e., indirectly on Magusean sources (cf. also Bidez and Cumont, Mages hellénisés I, 217 ff., and Lactantius' citations from Hystaspes, quoted ibid. II, 364 ff.).

[30] See below, Part One, Chapter I, 3.

[31] Cf. Eduard Meyer, Ursprung und Anfänge des Christentums II (Stuttgart, Berlin, 1921) 189 ff.; idem., Hesiods Erga und das Gedicht von den fünf Menschengeschlechten (Kleine Schriften II, Halle, 1924) 15 ff.; J. W. Swain, "The Theory of the Four Monarchies: Opposition History under the Roman Empire," Class. Philol. XXXV (1940) 1 ff. Meyer and Swain discount a possible connection between Hesiod and the Indian and Persian myths, whereas Reitzenstein and Schaeder, Synkretismus 577 ff., think that Hesiod was dependent on early forms of the latter; see also the article by Griffiths, quoted in n. 26. For the idea of the

to the third century A.D.,[32] in the Book of Daniel,[33] and in Christian commentaries on the latter. The most influential identification of the four world empires was that with the monarchies of the Assyrians (or Babylonians), Persians (or Medes), Macedonians, and Romans, which we find, for instance, in Pompeius Trogus and in St. Jerome.[34] In the Middle Ages this succession scheme was developed in the theory of the so-called *translatio imperii* (transfer of the Roman Empire from one people to another) and of a corresponding *translatio studii* (transfer of wisdom and knowledge).[35] In such conceptions, too, an idea of eternal renewal can be implied, in conjunction, for instance, with the ideology of eternal Rome.[36]

The recurrence idea in its most extreme form, the conception of an eternally cyclical and numerically repetitive renewal of the cosmos and of a cosmologically determined renewal of humanity, was of course essentially incompatible with the rectilinear and chronologically limited Christian view of history[37] and with the Christian approach to the problems of causal determination, contingency, human freedom, and divine predestination. Yet modified in various ways, it did

four world empires see also C. Trieber, "Die Idee der vier Weltreiche," *Hermes* XXVII (1892) 321 ff., and T. E. Mommsen, "St. Augustine and the Christian Idea of Progress," *Jour. Hist. Ideas* XII (1951) 346 ff.

[32] The most important among them was Pompeius Trogus, who wrote in Augustus' time; cf. Swain, "Four Monarchies" 16 ff.

[33] Dan. 2:31 ff. and 7:1 ff.

[34] Jerome, *Comment. in Danielem* 2:31 ff. and 7:1 ff., *PL* XXV, 526 f., 552 ff.; also his translation of the chronological "canon" of Eusebius world chronicle, *GCS, Euseb. VII*, 2nd ed. (cf. Swain, "Four Monarchies" 19 ff.). For ancient and Byzantine identifications of the fourth world empire with Macedon rather than Rome see Swain, "Four Monarchies," and M. V. Anastos, "Political Theory in the Lives of the Slavic Saints Constantine and Methodius," *Harvard Slavic Studies* II (1954) 17 ff.

[35] See now P. van den Baar, *Die kirchliche Lehre der Translatio Imperii Romani* ... (Analecta Gregoriana LXXVIII, Roma, 1956), and W. Goetz, *Translatio Imperii* (Tübingen, 1958), also Anastos, "Political Theory" 22 ff., and for the *translatio studii* E. Gilson, *La philosophie au moyen âge*, 2nd ed. (Paris, 1947) 193 f., E. R. Curtius, *European Literature and the Latin Middle Ages*, trans. W. R. Trask (Bollingen Series XXXVI, New York, 1953) 29, 384 f., H. Grundmann, "Sacerdotium—Regnum—Studium," *Arch. Kult. Gesch.* XXXIV (1951) 8, 13 f.

[36] Cf. below, Part One, Chapter I, 2.

[37] Cf., for instance, Origen, *Contra Celsum* IV, 67 f., V, 20 f. *GCS, Orig.*, I, 337 f., II, 21 ff.; *idem.*, *De principiis* II, 3, 4, *GCS*, Orig. V, 119; Augustine, *De civitate Dei* XII, 14, *Corp. Christ.*, *Ser. Lat.* XLVIII, 369. See also R. Niebuhr, *Faith and History* (New York, 1949) 16, 21.

survive the end of paganism, especially in combination with certain vitalistic and millenarian renewal ideas.[38]

The idea of reform differs from all cosmologic-deterministic renewal ideas through its element of *freedom*.[39]

2. VITALISTIC RENEWAL IDEAS

Vitalistic renewal ideas in the widest sense of the term are founded upon analogies with the reproduction and growth of human life and of life in general. Such are the idea of Renaissance and the idea of evolution; the latter lies on the whole outside the scope of this study—but see the remarks in Excursus IV, 4.

The Renaissance idea, it is true, is not without connection with that of spiritual regeneration[1] and even with that of reform.[2] The remote common roots lie no doubt in very ancient ideas of redemptive sacrificial death and rebirth.[3] The most characteristic trait of the Renaissance idea is at any rate the assumption of rebirth or renewed growth

[38] The most important of these modifications in the early Christian age itself is that of Origen; Origen's adaptation and Augustine's complete rejection of ancient recurrence ideology are well contrasted by H. Meyer, "Ewige Wiederkunft" 368 ff. Origen's idea of periodical *apocatastasis* or restoration of the world will be discussed more fully below, Part Two, Chapter III, 1. Modified ideas of this general type are found also in the Middle Ages and the Renaissance. For the idea of the Golden Age in the early Christian period and its combination with the biblical Paradise see G. Boas, *Essays on Primitivism and Related Ideas in the Middle Ages* (Baltimore, 1948) and below, Part Two, Chapter III, 1.

[39] For the "shortcomings" of the myth of eternal recurrence and of the Golden Age (and to some extent even of the *nostalgie du paradis*) see the excellent remarks of M. Eliade, *Traité des religions* (Paris, 1949) Chapters 10 and 11; cf. also H. de Lubac, S. J., *Catholicisme: Les aspects sociaux du dogme*, 4th ed. (Paris, 1947) 107 ff.

[1] Konrad Burdach and his school, the principal representatives of a trend which W. K. Ferguson, *The Renaissance in Historical Thought* (Boston, New York, 1948) 329 ff., calls "the revolt of the medievalists" against an autonomous concept of the Renaissance, have gone too far in deriving the Italian Renaissance altogether from late ancient, early Christian, and mediaeval ideas of spiritual regeneration; see Burdach's great work *Vom Mittelalter zur Reformation* (Berlin, 1921–1939) and his essay "Sinn und Ursprung der Worte Renaissance und Reformation," *Reformation Renaissance Humanismus*, 2nd ed. (Berlin, Leipzig, 1926). Similarly, the study of F. Heer, "Die 'Renaissance'-Ideologie im frühen Mittelalter," *Mitt. Inst. Öst. Gesch. Forsch.* LVII (1949) 23 ff., which contains much interesting material and some excellent interpretations, does not always sufficiently distinguish between "Renaissance" ideas and the ideology of reform.

[2] Cf. below, p. 23, n. 27.   [3] See Introduction.

or return of vital values in an individual, community or institution, in a nation or in humanity as a whole; this is a quasi-biological revival which has no longer a direct relation to sacrifice. One finds this conception long before the Italian Renaissance, for instance, in the Augustan [4] and Theodosian eras,[5] and all through the Late Roman and

[4] Beside Virgil's *Fourth Eclogue* with its mixed cosmological and vitalistic connotations (cf. below p. 21, n. 20) see, for instance, Horace, *Carmen saeculare* 58: . . . neglecta redire virtus; *idem*, *Ars poetica* 70: Multa renascentur quae iam cecidere cadentque/quae nunc sunt in honore vocabula . . .; Livy, *Histor.* VI, 1: . . . ab secunda origine (i.e., after the destruction by the Gallic invaders) velut ab stirpibus laetius feraciusque renatae urbis; *idem*, *ibid.* III, 9, 1: . . . res Romana in antiquum statum rediit; cf. also *ibid.* XXVI, 41, 22–24, XXIV, 45, 3.

[5] Cf., for instance, Claudian, *De bello Gildonico* 17–27, and especially 208 ff., Koch, 38 f. and above all 44:

. . . adflavit Romam meliore iuventa.
Continuo redit ille vigor seniique colorem
mutavere comae. . . .

See also Claudian, *In Rufinum* I, 50 ff., Koch 12 (of Theodosius as victor over the Furies):

Heu nimis ignavae quas Iuppiter arcet Olympo,
Theodosius terris. En aurea nascitur aetas.
En proles antiqua redit . . .

(dependence on Virgil's *Fourth Eclogue* is here obvious). See furthermore Prudentius, *Contra Symmachum* II, 656 ff., CSEL LXI, 271 (of Rome under Theodosius):

. . . sub quo senium omne renascens
deposui vidique meam flavescere rursus
canitiem : nam cum mortalia cuncta vetustas
imminuat, mihi longa dies aliud parit aevum
quae vivendo diu didici contemnere finem.

See also *ibid.* I, 541 ff., CSEL LXI, 239:

Denique nec metas statuit nec tempora ponit,
imperium sine fine docet, ne Romula virtus
iam sit anus, norit ne gloria parta senectam

(with this cf. Virgil, *Aeneid* I, 287 ff.). See finally Rutilius Namatianus, *De reditu suo e Roma in Galliam Narbonensem* I, 137 ff., Vessereau and Préchac 9:

Quae restant nullis obnoxia tempora metis,
dum stabant terrae, dum polus astra feret.
iliud te reparat quod cetera regna resolvit :
ordo renascendi est crescere posse malis

(cf. again *Aeneid* I, 287 ff., see also C. Pascal, "Una probabile fonte di Rutilio Namaziano," *Graecia Capta* [Firenze, 1905] 163 ff., for possible dependence upon the famous oration in praise of Rome by Aelius Aristides, the Greek rhetor, second century A. D.). Most of the texts cited are discussed by Curtius, *European Literature* 104.

Middle Ages, in connection with the belief in the eternal life and ever-repeated rejuvenation of Rome and with the so-called Roman *Renovatio* idea.[6]

Because the reform ideas of the great Fathers of the late fourth and early fifth century, which this book will study in some detail, stood out against the spirit of the so-called "Theodosian Renaissance," which not a few of them vigorously opposed,[7] it will be well to insert here a few comments on this phase in the history of vitalistic renewal ideas. The occurrence of a vitalistic renewal ideology and Renaissance terminology was neither the reason for the formulation of the concept of a Theodosian Renaissance nor does this term designate more than

---

[6] In general see F. G. Moore, "On Urbs Aeterna and Urbs Sacra," *Trans. Amer. Philol. Ass.* XXV (1894) 34 ff., W. Gernentz, *Laudes Romae* (Rostock, 1918), M. Vogelstein, *Kaiseridee-Romidee und das Verhältnis von Staat und Kirche seit Konstantin* (Historische Untersuchungen VII, Breslau, 1930), especially Excursus III, W. Rehm, *Der Untergang Roms im abendländischen Denken* (Leipzig, 1930), E. Pfeil, *Die fränkische und deutsche Romidee des frühen Mittelalters* (München, 1929), P. E. Schramm, *Kaiser, Rom und Renovatio* (Studien der Bibliothek Warburg XVII, 1 and 2, Leipzig, Berlin, 1929), F. Heer, " 'Renaissance'-Ideologie," E. K. Rand, *The Building of Eternal Rome* (Cambridge, Mass., 1943), W. Paatz, "Renaissance oder Renovatio?," *Beiträge zur Kunst des Mittelalters* (Berlin, 1950) 16 ff. Tibullus, *Carmina* II, 5, 23, seems to have been the first to speak of the *urbs aeterna*, and already the coins of Galba's faction show the legend *Roma renascens*. Dreams of the eternity and of the rebirth, restitution, reparation, renovation of Rome, coupled with Golden Age ideology, determined the official and semiofficial propaganda of the pagan and later of the Christian Empires for many centuries. This well-known fact can nowhere be verified as easily as on the coins. See, for instance, J. Gagé, "Le «Templum Urbis» et les origines de l'idée de «Renovatio»," *Mélanges Franz Cumont* I (Annuaire de l'Institut de Philologie et d'Histoire Orientales et Slaves, Université Libre de Bruxelles, IV, 1, Bruxelles, 1936) 151 ff., H. Mattingly, "Felicium temporum reparatio," *The Numismatic Chronicle and Journal of the Royal Numismatic Society*, Ser. V, XIII (1933) 182 ff., idem, *The Cambridge Ancient History* XII (Cambridge, 1939) 713 ff.: *Appendix on Sources 2: Coins*, P. L. Strack, *Untersuchungen zur römischen Reichsprägung des zweiten Jahrhunderts*, 3 vols. (Stuttgart, 1931–37). It is characteristic of the link which exists between Roman *renovatio* ideology and vitalistic renewal ideas that Constantine the Great used one of the mystical pagan names of Rome, "Flora," in Greek translation: "Anthusa," for Constantinople (cf. V. Burch, *Myth and Constantine the Great* [Oxford, 1927] 76 ff., A. Alföldi, *The Conversion of Constantine and Pagan Rome* [Oxford, 1948] 114), thus connecting his new capital, the second Rome, with the flowering of the first (cf. W. Hartke, *Römische Kinderkaiser* [Berlin, 1951] 298 ff., on the *Floralia*). For the ideology of the "Second Rome," related to that of the *translatio imperii* (see above, p. 15), cf., for instance, F. Dölger, "Rom in der Gedankenwelt der Byzantiner," *Z. Ki. Gesch.* LVI (1937) 1 ff., W. Hammer, "The Concept of a New or Second Rome . . .," *Speculum* XIX (1944) 50 ff., E. H. Kantorowicz, *The King's Two Bodies* (Princeton, 1957) 82f.

[7] Cf. pp. 251–256, for Augustine's rejection of a renewal ideology centered in Rome.

one aspect of the Theodosian age. The modern term "Theodosian Renaissance" is based above all on the evidence of a strong classicist trend in the history of art during the reigns of Theodosius the Great and his sons which produced works of great beauty such as the silver missorium of Theodosius the Great, the Symmachorum-Nicomachorum diptych, and the Stilicho diptych.[8] In literature and thought, too, the "Theodosian Renaissance" thus understood is characterized by a genuine affinity to classical Antiquity, similar in this respect, and perhaps historically not unrelated, to Italian Renaissance humanism.[9] It is eminently represented by the Roman Neopythagorean-Neoplatonic circle of Vettius Agorius Praetextatus, Quintus Aurelius Symmachus, and Virius Nicomachus Flavianus,[10] which forms the milieu of Macrobius' Saturnalia.[11] Among the concerns of these last defenders of paganism and its integral culture were those revisions of the classical authors to which we owe much of what we possess of Roman literature.[12] In one of its aspects then, the age of the "Theodosian Renaissance" prolongs earlier fourth century attempts at a

---

[8] Cf. R. Delbrueck, Die Consulardiptychen und verwandte Denkmäler (Berlin, 1929), especially 28ff., where these works are placed in the historical background here discussed. See also K. Weitzmann and S. Schulz, "Zur Bestimmung des Dichters auf dem Musendiptychon von Monza," Jahrbuch des deutschen archäologischen Instituts XLIX (1934) 128 ff., especially 132 ff., 135 ff. For the classicist character of the imperial portraits around 400 see Delbrueck, Spätantike Kaiserportraits von Constantinus Magnus bis zum Ende des Westreichs (Berlin, Leipzig, 1933). See further J. Kollwitz, Oströmische Plastik der Theodosianischen Zeit (Berlin, 1941). Cf. finally the comprehensive essay by E. Garger, "Zur spätantiken Renaissance," Jahrbuch der kunsthistorischen Sammlungen in Wien, Neue Folge, VIII (1934) 1 ff., where the persistence of the Theodosian Renaissance element through fifth-century art down to the era of Theodoric and Justinian I (paralleled in literature by figures like Apollinaris Sidonius and Ennodius of Pavia [cf. below, pp. 369 f. and 375]) is also traced.

[9] On the possibility of this relation see below, p. 23, n. 27.

[10] On these representatives of "the last pagan revival in the west" see now above all H. Bloch, "A New Document of the Last Pagan Revival in the West," Harv. Theol. Rev. XXXVIII (1945) 199 ff., where most of the older literature is cited.

[11] Macrobius, Saturnalia, ed. F. Eyssenhardt, 2nd ed. (Leipzig, 1893). For Macrobius see P. Courcelle, Les lettres grecques en occident: De Macrobe à Cassidore, 2nd ed. (Paris, 1948).

[12] Cf. Bloch, "Pagan Revival," also idem, review of E. A. Lowe, Codices Latini Antiquiores IV, in Speculum XXV (1950) 279. See also H. Usener, Anecdoton Holderi (Bonn, 1877) 28 ff., E. Lommatzsch, "Literarische Bewegungen in Rom im vierten und fünften Jahrhundert," Zeitschrift für vergleichende Literaturgeschichte, Neue Folge, XV (1904) 177 ff., L. Traube, Einleitung in die lateinische Philologie des Mittelalters (ed. P. Lehmann, Vorlesungen und Abhandlungen von Ludwig Traube, ed. F. Boll, II, München, 1911) 124 f.

revival rather than at a Christianization of pagan civilization, attempts
in which the senatorial aristocracy of the city of Rome played an
important role;[13] in another it continued Constantinian renewal ideas
and especially a Christianized "political" reform ideology in which
the Kingdom of God and the Roman Empire were more or less fused
—Ambrose and Prudentius followed to some extent the tracks of
Eusebius of Caesarea—an ideology which was definitely overcome
only by St. Augustine.[14]

In a recent study on the philological roots of the Renaissance idea,
J. Trier has shown[15] that the metaphorical meaning of *renasci* (*rina-
scita*) is not necessarily "to be reborn," but may be "to grow again,"
the metaphor being taken from the realm of the horticulturist and
forester, from tree life, where the "damage" done by cutting
(pruning) results in new growth, in a "Renaissance." One might add
that *renasci* is thus closely related to *revirescere* ("to grow green again,"
"to grow strong, young again," "to reflourish") and to *reviviscere*
("to revive"), both terms frequently used by Cicero, also to *re-
florescere* ("to blossom again"), found, for instance, in Pliny[16] and in
Silius Italicus.[17] Trier's thesis that the modern as well as the Roman
Renaissance concept originated from the meaning given to *renasci* by
Roman writers *de re rustica* in the widest sense is however convincing
only up to a point. For both in Christian and in non-Christian Latin
mystery language *renasci* and related expressions could, just as
regenerari-regeneratio, be used in the sense of a spiritual rebirth, with

---

[13] Beside Bloch's article cf. especially A. Alföldi, *A Festival of Isis in Rome under the
Christian Emperors of the IVth Century* (Dissertationes Pannonicae, Ser. II, VII, Budapest,
1937), idem, *Die Kontorniaten, ein verkanntes Propagandamittel der stadtrömischen Aristokratie in
ihrem Kampf gegen das christliche Kaisertum* (Budapest, 1942–1943), idem, *A Conflict of Ideas
in the Late Roman Empire: The Clash between the Senate and Valentinian I* (Oxford, 1952); see
furthermore below, pp. 147–150, about the affair of the Altar of Victory. I am much
indebted to Professor Bloch for clarifying in correspondence with me the rather ambiguous
concept of the "Theodosian Renaissance"; the pagan revival trend is, of course, far from
being the only one characteristic of the Theodosian age.

[14] For these developments see below, Part Two, Chapter III, 3, Chapter IV, Chapter
V, 7.

[15] J. Trier, "Zur Vorgeschichte des Renaissance-Begriffs," *Arch. Kult. Gesch.* XXXIII
(1950) 45 ff. (also in: *Holz: Etymologien aus dem Niederwald* [Münster-Köln, 1952]
144 ff.).

[16] *Naturalis Historia* XVIII, 43.

[17] *Punicor.* XV, 741.

connotations which could range all the way from vegetative[18] to cosmological renewal. *Renasci* and *regeneratio* could, for instance, be felt as equivalent to the Greek παλιγγενεσία,[19] and even as related to ἀποκατάστασις.[20] That vitalistic renewal ideas are not exclusively of a vegetative kind can be seen above all from the widespread and ever-recurring myth of the miraculous bird phoenix, who is reborn from his own ashes. Here the connection with cosmological renewal ideology is quite obvious, since according to the myth the life-span of the phoenix corresponds to cosmic periods which vary all the way from the apparent diurnal course of the sun around the earth to the great world year.[21]

[18] For a much more profound interpretation of classical and Christian vegetative renewal symbolism—as it appears, for instance, in the well-known relationship between the paradisiacal trees and the Cross, but also in the motifs of the mandragora and the willow tree—see H. Rahner, S. J., *Griechische Mythen in christlicher Deutung* (Zürich, 1945) 92 ff., 314 ff., 382 ff. Cf. my article "Vegetation Symbolism and the Concept of Renaissance," in *De Artibus Opuscula XL, Essays in Honor of Erwin Panofsky* (New York, 1961), 303 ff.

[19] Cf. below, p. 33. See also R. Newald, "Renatae Litterae und Reformatio," *Hist. Jb.* LXXI (1951) 137 ff.

[20] Cf. above, p. 11. For Virgil's *Fourth Eclogue* in particular see pp. 12–13, and cf. the cosmological interpretation in Servius' commentary to v. 4, ed. G. Thilo, *Servii grammatici qui feruntur in Vergilii Bucolica et Georgica Commentarii* (Leipzig, 1887) 45, also Servius to v. 34, Thilo, *loc. cit.*, 49, where a relation to the *apocatastasis* of the universe is explicitly established. For the combination of vitalistic and cosmological renewal ideas in the *Fourth Eclogue* and for the derivation of the Augustan renewal term *saeculum* (as in Horace's *Carmen saeculare*) from *serere*, to sow, see Nilsson, article "Saeculares ludi," in PW, *RE*, Reihe II, II (I, 2), 1708 and 1697. For Apuleius see below, p. 40, for the Latin *Asclepius* above, p. 12.

[21] For the phoenix myth see J. Hubaux and M. Leroy, *Le mythe du Phénix dans les littératures grecque et latine* (Bibliothèque de philosophie et lettres de l'Université de Liège LXXXII, 1939), with a thorough discussion of the sources such as Herodotus II, 73, Ovid, *Metamorph.* XV, 391 ff., Tacitus, *Annales* VI, 28, Pliny, *Natur. Hist.* X, 2, Ps.-Baruch 6–8, Tertullian, *De resurrectione* 13, Lactantius, *Carmen de ave Phoenice*, Claudianus, *Phoenix*, the *Physiologus*; the authors also deal with renewal ideas connected with other great birds, such as the griphon and the eagle; for the latter's role in Christian renewal ideology according to Ps. 102:5: . . . Renovabitur ut aquila iuventus tua, cf. below, pp. 314–315. Cf. also J. Lassus, "La mosaique du Phénix provenant des fouilles d'Antioche," *Fondation Eugène Piot: Monuments et mémoires publiées par l'Académie des Inscriptions et Belles-Lettres* XXXV (1938) 81 ff.; A. J. Festugière, "Le symbole du Phénix et le mysticisme hermétique," *ibid.* XXXVIII (1941) 147 ff.; D. Levi, *Antioch Mosaic Pavements* I (Princeton, 1947) 253 ff., 351 ff.; C.-M. Edsman, *Ignis Divinus* (Skrifter . . . Vetenskap-Societeten i Lund . . . XXXIV, Lund, 1949) 178 ff. (with important remarks on the relation of the phoenix myth to the Stoic cosmological ideology of *ecpyrosis*, cf. above, p. 11), and now the illuminating chapter "Phoenix" in Kantorowicz, *Two Bodies* 385 ff.

The most typical occurrences of vitalistic renewal ideas are found, of course, in the age which is still called the Renaissance.[22] It is possible that the Italian humanists of the late fifteenth and early sixteenth century who applied the rebirth concept to their own age were influenced not only by Livy and the other Augustans, but also by "Theodosian" poets such as Rutilius Namatianus who had used the term *renasci* in a pregnant meaning.[23] This was the thesis of an erudite study by K. Borinski,[24] which however connected Machiavelli's Renaissance concept too exclusively with the rediscovery of Rutilius Namatianus' poem, whereas Machiavelli's relation to the Augustan authors, to Livy, for instance, must have been at least equally important.[25] In Machiavelli's *History of Florence* the life of the nations is seen as a succession of cycles each of which turns from *virtù* (civic and political excellence) through peace and quiet to disorder and ruin whence new order is born.[26] In a famous chapter of the *Discourses on the First Decade of Livy* Machiavelli discusses the necessity of periodically renovating states and nations by a return to their beginnings (*riduzione verso il principio, rivocare al segno*), so that they may be reborn (e.g.: *che Roma . . . rinascesse*) to new life and new *virtù*.[27]

---

[22] Dante in this respect, too, stands at the threshold of the new age, for instance, in his conception of a *vita nova*. Cf. Kantorowicz, *Two Bodies* 484, where it is said that Dante built up "a doctrine of purely *human* regeneration which was not identical with the doctrine of Christian regeneration—though the one did not need to contradict the other."

[23] See above, p. 17, n. 5.

[24] K. Borinski, "Die Weltwiedergeburtsidee in den neueren Zeiten," *Sitz. Ber. Bayer.*, Philos.-philol. u. hist. Klasse 1919, 1, 1 ff.

[25] See the examples from Livy and Horace quoted above, p. 17, n. 4. Cf. Trier, "Renaissance-Begriff" 159, also Borinski himself in his review article "Politische symbolik des Mittelalters und werden der Renaissance: Anmerkungen und zusätze zu Konrad Burdach: Rienzo und die geistige wandlung seiner zeit," *Zeitschrift für deutsche Philologie* XLVIII (1920) 460.

[26] Machiavelli, *Istorie Fiorentine*, V, 1; also I, 39: antica virtù rinata; I, 31, about the impact of Cola di Rienzo upon Italy: vedendo come Roma era rinata. . . . Cf. Machiavelli's *Discorsi sopra la prima deca di Tito Livio* I, 2, dependent on Polybius' *Histories*, especially VI, 9, 10, that is to say, on his conception of recurrent cycles of political constitutions, which again are related to ancient cyclical cosmology. See also *Discorsi* II, proem, where the scheme of the succession of world empires is transformed into that of a migration of *virtù* from one people to another.

[27] *Discorsi sopra la prima deca di Tito Livio* III, 1. One other possible contact between Machiavelli and an author of the "Theodosian Renaissance" may be mentioned in passing. The ancient source of the Machiavellian terms *ridurre (riduzione) al segno, ritirare al segno, ritornare al segno*—the latter only in a trivial meaning, in the comedy *Clizia* (*Opere*, edd.

The Renaissance idea of spontaneous rebirth[28] is qualified by the explicit reintroduction of an over-arching divine providence in Vico's concept of *ricorso*. Vico's *ricorso* is the first stage of a new cycle of human history and, formally, corresponds to Machiavelli's *riduzione verso il principio*. But Vico abandoned all remnants of the idea of cosmological determination and of the *identical* repetition inherent in such variants of vitalistic renewal ideology. A *ricorso*, such as the Middle Ages, is for him both primitive barbarism and the first phase of an entirely new civilization.[29]

G. Mazzoni and M. Casella [Firenze, 1929] 690); cf. E. W. Mayer, *Machiavelli's Geschichts-auffassung und sein Begriff virtù* (München, Berlin, 1912) 77, n. 1—have, as far as I know, never been ascertained. These expressions must originate in military language. Now, the metaphor *vocare ad signa*, i.e., "to call to the standards (to arms)," occurs in Claudianus' *Panegyricus Manlio Theodoro Consuli* 174 ff., Koch 134, where this philosopher addresses *iustitia* thus:

> . . . Agrestem dudum me, Diva, reverti
> cogis et infectum longi rubigine ruris
> ad tua signa vocas. . . .

Did Machiavelli know these verses? It is interesting also that Theodorus who became consul in 398, returning to the service of the state from philosophical rural solitude, had earlier been one of the transmitters of Platonic wisdom to St. Augustine and also one of his human models in the Cassiciacum period. *De beata vita* (*CSEL* LXIII) is dedicated to him, cf. I, 1–5, *loc. cit.*, 89 ff. (That Augustine considered Theodorus' return to public life as a betrayal of higher ideals is supposed by Courcelle, *Lettres grecques* 126 ff., on the strength of *Confessiones* VII, 9, 13, Skutella 137, but hardly with sufficient reasons; the text does not mention Theodorus and may refer rather to Porphyry; cf. J. J. O'Meara, *The Young Augustine* [London, etc., 1954] 125 f.) *Revocare ad signum* could also be used in a Christian sense: Cassian, *Conlationes* I, 4, 4 (*CSEL* XIII, 10) uses the phrase for recall to the Kingdom of God. For *revocare* see below, p. 46. It may finally be mentioned in this connection that Machiavelli used the phrase *ritirare verso il suo principio* for the renewal of the Church by St. Francis of Assisi and St. Dominic, thus coming close to an ideology of reform; cf. *Discorsi sopra la prima deca di Tito Livio* III, 1.

[28] For other ideological aspects of the Italian Renaissance see J. Huizinga, "Le problème de la Renaissance," *Revue des cours et conférences* XL, 1 (1938–39) 163 ff., 301 ff., 524 ff., 603 ff. (also in *Wege der Kulturgeschichte* [München, 1930]); T. E. Mommsen, "Petrarch's Conception of the 'Dark Ages,'" *Speculum* XVIII (1942) 226 ff.; E. Panofsky and F. Saxl, "Classical Mythology in Mediaeval Art," *Metropolitan Museum Studies* IV (1932–1933) 228 ff.; E. Panofsky, "Renaissance and Renascences," *Kenyon Review* VI (1944) 201 ff.; J. Seznec, *The Survival of the Pagan Gods: The Mythological Tradition and Its Place in Renaissance Humanism and Art*, trans. from the French by Barbara F. Sessions (Bollingen Series XXXVIII, New York, 1953); also my review article in *Traditio* X (1954) 578 ff. For Renaissance theories on historical cycles, on the Golden Age, and on world empires see H. Weisinger, "Ideas of History during the Renaissance," *Jour. Hist. Ideas* VI (1945) 426 ff.

[29] The final version of Vico's main work, *La Scienza Nuova*, was published in 1744 (modern

In order to emphasize the distinctness of the idea of reform from vitalistic renewal ideas, it may be helpful to refer briefly to two modern expressions, one philosophical and one historical, of a vitalistic concept of renewal: to Bergson's principle of *élan vital*[30] and to Toynbee's sequence of challenge and response.[31]

It is characteristic of these antimaterialistic forms of vitalistic renewal ideas that they pass somewhat abruptly from instinctive and unconscious development to mystical transfiguration, so that rational finality recedes into the background.[32] In Bergson's philosophy the intermediate sphere between the infrarational (the biological and social-collective) and the suprarational (the mystical) is thus to some extent lost sight of; the realm of ethics, of human morality, freely oriented towards ends, "vanished into thin air."[33] But this intermediate sphere is inseparable from what we call reform.[34] Arnold Toynbee's spiritual kinship to Bergson is evident and clearly stated by himself.[35] He too has a well-founded, but perhaps somewhat excessive,

critical edition by F. Nicolini, 3rd ed. [Bari, 1942], English translation by T. G. Bergin and M. H. Fisch [Ithaca, N.Y., 1948]; see also the English translation of Vico's *Autobiography* by the same authors [Ithaca, 1944], with a good introduction on Vico).

[30] The idea of an *élan vital*, formulated by Henry Bergson in his *Evolution créatrice*, first published in 1907, has been resumed by him twenty-five years later in *Les deux sources de la morale et de la religion*.

[31] Arnold J. Toynbee, *A Study of History* (Oxford, 1934–54), especially, I, 271 ff., II, 1 ff.

[32] For Bergson's rejection of rational finalism as well as of mechanism in favor of an *élan vital* which tends toward "*une imprévisible création de forme*" see *Evolution créatrice*, 77th ed. (Paris, 1948) 39 ff., especially 45, and *Les deux sources de la morale et de la religion*, 58th ed. (Paris, 1948) 118 f. For his relative disparagement of intellect and rationality—not a necessary but an actual consequence of his fundamental intuitions—and for the resulting radical distinction between static (institutionalized) religion and dynamic religion (mysticism) see *Les deux sources* 222 ff., and, especially, 252 ff.

[33] Cf. Jacques Maritain, "The Bergsonian Philosophy of Morality and Religion," *Ransoming the Time* (New York, 1941) 92 ff.; see also R. Niebuhr, *The Nature and Destiny of Man* (New York, 1949) 37 f.

[34] Recognition of the importance of the intermediate ethical sphere is the key to the thought of Albert Schweitzer, but he in turn does not do full justice to what he calls "super-ethical (self-perfecting) mysticism," i.e., to the contemplative life; see his *Philosophy of Civilization* (New York, 1950) I, Chapter IV: "The Way to the Restoration of Civilization," and II, Chapter XXV: "The Ethic of Self-Devotion and the Ethic of Self-Perfecting."

[35] Cf. Toynbee, *Study* III, 118 f.; 232.

distrust of institutionalism in civilization. The "mechanicalness of mimesis," understood in the sense of uninspired imitation, the "intractability of institutions," the "idolization of an ephemeral institution" or "technique" are for him among the most important causes of the breakdown of civilizations.[36] And the remedy is a "transfiguration," a "palingenesia," which is the mystical continuation of that same vital response which had brought about the genesis and growth of a civilization.[37] In an apparent paradox, but not without deeper consistency, Toynbee considers the concrete cultural phenomenon which is called the Renaissance, and similarly other Renaissances, as "necromantic," artificial ghost raisings of dead cultures by living ones; they are not, therefore, in his view true revivals—except as it were accidentally; he does admit that in the fifteenth–sixteenth century European Renaissance "a springlike outburst of fresh vitality" was associated with "the renaissance of [the] dead antecedent culture" of Greece and Rome.[38] Only this "spring-like outburst" then would correspond to a genuine challenge-response sequence in Toynbee's sense or to a vitalistic renewal concept, whereas the other, "necromantic," component of Renaissance movements, though deprecated by Toynbee, may in fact contain authentic elements of reform, as defined in this book.[39]

The present study is undertaken on the assumption that there is reform which is neither merely response (perhaps because there are evil, hybris, and sin, which are more than challenge) nor sterile return

---

[36] *Ibid*. IV, 119 ff.; 133 ff.; 303 ff.; 423 ff.

[37] *Ibid*. V, 27 ff.; 390 ff.; VI, 149 ff.; 169 ff. For late pagan and early Christian meanings of the term παλιγγενεσία see below, pp. 40 and 50 f. With Toynbee's views compare those of F. S. C. Northrop, *The Meeting of East and West* (New York, 1947) 458 ff. in the chapter on "The Criteria of Cultural Reform," where a synthesis of the "aesthetic" (biological and mystical) and the "theoretic" (scientific and technological) components of man's nature is postulated.

[38] For Toynbee's conception of Renaissances see *Study* IX, 1 ff.; cf. also *ibid*. 4 f., VIII, 97 ff., VI, 49 ff., for his distinction between Renaissance and archaism. For the "new" and the "old" component in the fifteenth–sixteenth century Renaissance, according to Toynbee's view, see *ibid*. IX, 148.

[39] I hope to show in a later volume that the so-called Carolingian Renaissance and other phases of western civilization, dealt with in Toynbee's chapters on Renaissances, are far from being adequately characterized in categories of necromancy and ghost raising or in those of challenge and response.

to a dead past.[40] It will also be found that there are fruitful religious categories of "mimesis" ($X\rho\iota\sigma\tau o\mu\iota\mu\eta\sigma\iota\varsigma$, imitatio Christi)[41] as well as productive sociological ones: to use an expression of Tarde's, there is a logique sociale of imitation;[42] the inventive, quasi-creative elements in history could not survive without their being repeated over and over again. This is a part, especially, of every religious experience[43] and is related again to the repetitive character of sacrifice:

Since human being cannot be preserved
But where dark sacrifice repeats itself.[44]

Contrary to all vitalistic renewal ideas, the idea of reform implies the conscious pursuit of ends. Whether reform be predominantly contemplative or active, its starting point is the element of intention rather than of spontaneity, urge, or response.[45]

In spite of the distinctness of the ideas of reform and rebirth their terminologies can sometimes merge with one another. This is particularly true of terms expressing a "revival"—even in modern English "revival" can have connotations of "reform" as well as of "rebirth."

[40] Cf. J. Maritain's remarks on Toynbee in his On the Philosophy of History (New York, 1957) 171 ff.; in this book Maritain suggests several axiomatic and typological formulae (functional and vectorial laws of history) which are considerably deeper than those advocated by Toynbee, for instance, the latter's law of challenge and response. Maritain's conception, incidentally, of a law of "two-fold contrasting progress" (pp. 43 ff.), i.e., of "degradation" on the one hand and of "revitalization" on the other (p. 46) is not without relation to the idea of reform. See also J. Daniélou, S.J., Essai sur le mystère de l'histoire (Paris, 1953) 236 ff., where P. Daniélou illustrates a conception of ambivalent historical progression similar to that of Maritain by an analysis of St. Gregory of Nyssa's doctrine of $\alpha\kappa o\lambda o\upsilon\theta\iota\alpha$; cf. ibid. 37 on hybris and on renewal through purification.

[41] This is recognized also by Toynbee in his remarks on St. Francis of Assisi and on other saints and reformers, Study IX, 149.

[42] Cf. G. Tarde, Les lois de l'imitation, 2nd ed. (Paris, 1895); idem, La logique sociale (Paris, 1895); idem, Les transformations du pouvoir (Paris, 1899).

[43] See, for instance, Kierkegaard's Repetition, trans. W. Lowrie (Princeton, 1946); cf. F. H. Heinemann, "Origin and Repetition," Review of Metaphysics IV (1950–1951) 201 ff.

[44] Stefan George, Der Stern des Bundes:

Da menschenwesen sich nur dort erhält
Wo sich das dunkle opfer wiederholt.

[45] The phenomenon of reform, especially the element of intention in renewal, is, it would seem, not sufficiently stressed in the otherwise so interesting work of A. L. Kroeber, Configurations of Culture Growth (Berkeley, Los Angeles, 1944).

3. MILLENARIAN RENEWAL IDEAS

A third group of renewal ideas, sometimes combined with those of the first and second groups, may be defined as *messianic-millenarian-utopian*, or more generally as ideas of *absolute* or *total perfection*.

Christian millenarism is the expectation of a thousand years of bliss at the end of, but still within, history.[1] The millennium could be conceived of in a material or in a spiritual manner, but was to be in any case a reign of peace and overflowing blessing. St. Irenaeus[2] is the most important among the early Fathers[3] who on the strength of Apocalypse 20:1-6 ff. expected that at the end of history Christ and His saints would reign on earth for a thousand years, the devil being fettered during that time. One source of this idea is the late Jewish messianic hope which oscillated between political utopia and apocalyptic transcendence,[4] another is oriental-Hellenistic cosmology, the millenarian aspects of which were, about the time of Christ, fused with Jewish messianism. In the tracks of such Jewish-syncretistic speculations[5] the Christian millenarists combined the Magusean

[1] See pp. 13–14 for the connection between world ages and world cycles, between the Golden Age and the millennium. The literature on millenarism (chiliasm) and on the ancient and early Christian division of world history in historical and meta-historical ages (cf. also below, Part Two, Chapter V, 6) is very extensive. I mention only H. Gelzer, *Sextus Julius Africanus* (Leipzig, 1898) 24 ff.; V. Ermoni, "Les phases successives de l'erreur millénariste," *Revue des questions historiques* LXX (1901) 353 ff.; L. Gry, *Le millénarisme dans ses origines et son développement* (Paris, 1904); A. Wikenhauser, "Die Herkunft der Idee des tausendjährigen Reiches in der Johannes-Apokalypse," *Röm. Quart.* XLV (1937) 1 ff.; J. Daniélou, S.J., "La typologie millénariste de la semaine dans le christianisme primitif," *Vigil. Christ.* II (1948) 1 ff.; idem, "La typologie de la semaine au IVe siècle," *Rech.'s sc. rel.* XXXV (1948) 382 ff.; B. Botte, O.S.B., "Prima Resurrectio: Un vestige du millénarisme dans les liturgies occidentales," *Rech.'s théol. a. m.* XV (1948) 5 ff. For the decree of the Congregation of the Holy Office against millenarism of July 21, 1944, see *Acta Apostolicae Sedis* XXXVI (1944) 212; cf. P. Gilleman, S.J., in *Nouv. rev. théol.* LXVII (1945) 847 ff.; J. Huby, S.J., *Mystiques paulinienne et johannique* (Paris, 1946) 226 ff.

[2] *Adversus haereses* V, 28, 3, V, 34 f., 36, Harvey II 402 f., 419 ff.

[3] Such as Ps.-Barnabas, Papias, St. Justin, Tertullian, St. Methodius, St. Victorinus of Pettau, Lactantius, Commodianus.

[4] Cf. W. Bousset, *Die Religion des Judentums im späthellenistischen Zeitalter*, 3rd ed. by H. Gressmann (Tübingen, 1926) 259 ff.; also E. Schürer, *Geschichte des jüdischen Volkes im Zeitalter Jesu Christi*, 4th ed., II (Leipzig, 1907) 579 ff.

[5] Cf. Wikenhauser, "Tausendjähriges Reich" 2 f., and Daniélou, "Semaine dans le christianisme primitif" 3, especially for the idea of the millennium in the *Slavonic Enoch*

seven-millennial world week[6] with the seven days of Genesis 1, with Apocalypse 20 f., and also with Psalm 89:4: "For a thousand years in thy sight are as yesterday which is past" and with the Second Letter of Peter 3:8: ". . . one day with the Lord is as a thousand years and a thousand years as one day." They thus arrived at a conception of history as the succession of six millenniums (corresponding to the six days of creation), to be completed by a seventh millennium of abundance, rest, and peace on earth (identified with the millennium of Apocalypse 20 and corresponding to God's Sabbath, illogically contaminated at times with the idea of the Golden Age, which already Virgil had seen both as a returning first and as a perfecting seventh age).[7] This seventh age was to be followed—after a last onslaught of Satan—by the Last Judgment, the resurrection of the bodies, and by an eighth "ageless age" which is eternity.[8] The great religious and social role of early Christian millenarism and of the fervent expectation of the imminence of the second coming of Christ connected with it is an undeniable fact,[9] however little its spirit may have had in common with that of the Gospels. Origen and the Cappadocians had rejected millenarism,[10] but it was above all its reinterpretation by St. Augustine, his identification of the millennium of Apocalypse 20 (during which the devil is prevented from exercising his full power) with "ordinary" Christian history in the sixth age, which meant a momentous "revirement" of Christian thought important also for the Augustinian doctrine of reform.[11] Nevertheless, millenarism survived in the Middle Ages, especially in connection with the ineradicable belief in the coming of

33, 1 (longer redaction). The text of the *Slavonic Enoch* has not been sufficiently ascertained to permit a decision as to whether the eighth day here symbolizes the beginning of a new cycle of millennia or a final timeless age; see the two different translations by G. N. Bonwetsch. *Abhandl. Gött.*, Philol.-Hist. Klasse, Neue Folge, I, 3 (1896) 31, and *idem*, *Texte u. Untersuch.* XLIV, 2 (1922) 31; for other translations, cf. Wikenhauser, "Tausendjähriges Reich" 3.

[6] See above, pp. 13–14.

[7] See above, p. 13.

[8] For the eighth age, see above, p. 14, and Daniélou, "Semaine dans le christianisme primitif" 3, 7 and 10.

[9] See the remarkable pages in E. Buonaiuti, *Storia del Christianesimo* I (1942) 82 ff.

[10] See, for instance, Origen, *De principiis* II, 11, 2, *GCS*, *Orig.* V, 184 ff.; Gregory Nazianzen, *Carm.* II, I: *De seipso* XXX, 177–180, *PG* XXXVII, 1297.

[11] See p. 231.

a savior-ruler at the end of history.[12] While such ideas did not radically alter the Augustinian "climate" of the earlier mediaeval west, Joachism and its ideological progeny really undid St. Augustine's transformation of early patristic millenarism without exactly returning to the latter.

The Calabrian abbot Joachim of Flora (died 1202) and his followers conceived of a third age of spiritual perfection by applying to history a trinitarian scheme. An ultimate age of the Holy Spirit, corresponding to the sabbatial seventh age of the older tradition, would follow in terrestrial history upon the relatively imperfect ages of the Father (pre-Christian times) and the Son (Church history).[13] Joachimite hopes, prophecies, and anticlerical attacks continued through the later Middle Ages, through the Renaissance and Reformation, and beyond. In religious and secularized forms, the idea of three historical stages, of a third age of perfection, remained consciously and unconsciously a very important element in modern and even recent intellectual history.[14]

---

[12] See the survey given in my article "Erneuerung," to appear in RLAC; F. Kampers, Die deutsche Kaiseridee in Prophetie und Sage (München, 1896); idem, Vom Werdegang der abendländischen Kaisermystik (Leipzig, 1924); E. Sackur, Sibyllinische Texte und Forschungen (Halle, 1898); Rzach, articles "Sibyllen" und "Sibyllinische Orakel," PW, RE, Reihe II, IV (II, 2) 2073–2183; C. Erdmann, "Endkaiserglaube und Kreuzzugsgedanke im 11. Jahrhundert," Z. Ki. Gesch. LI (1932) 384 ff.; W. Meyer, "Der Ludus de Antichristo und über die lateinischen Rythmen," Sitz. Ber. Bayer, Philos.-philol. Klasse, 1882, 1, 1 ff. (also in Gesammelte Abhandlungen zur mittellateinischen Rythmik I [Berlin, 1905] 136 ff.); E. Kantorowicz, Kaiser Friedrich II. (Berlin, 1927) 460–478 and 629 ff., Erg. Bd. (1931) 207 ff. and 251; H. Grundmann, "Die Papstprophetien des Mittelalters," Arch. Kult. Gesch. XIX (1928) 77 ff.; F. Baethgen, "Der Engelspapst," Schriften der Königsberger Gelehrten Gessellschaft, Geisteswiss. Klasse, X, 2 (1933); Burdach, Mittelalter zur Reformation II, 1, 604 ff.

[13] Joachim's trinitarian theology of history also uses and alters a patristic-mediaeval typological division of world history into three ages: ante legem (before Moses), sub lege (from Moses to Christ), sub gratia (after Christ).

[14] For Joachim and Joachism see above all H. Grundmann, Studien über Joachim von Floris (Leipzig, 1927), and idem, Neue Forschungen über Joachim von Fiore (Marburg, 1950); also E. Benz, "Joachim-Studien" I–III, Z. Ki. Gesch. L (1931), LI (1932), LIII (1934), and idem, Ecclesia Spiritualis (Stuttgart, 1934); K. Löwith, Meaning in History (Chicago, 1949) Chapter 8 and Appendix I: "Modern Transfigurations of Joachism"; furthermore the illuminating pages in E. Przywara, S.J., "Die Reichweite der Analogie als katholischer Grundform," Scholastik XV (1940) 339 ff., 508 ff., and in M.-D. Chenu, O.P., "Le dernier avatar de la théologie orientale . . . ," Mélanges Auguste Pelzer (Université de Louvain, Recueil de travaux d'histoire et de philologie, Ser. III, Fasc. XXVI [Louvain, 1947]) 159 ff., especially 162–164; finally M. W. Bloomfield, "Joachim of Flora: A Critical Survey of His Canon, Teachings, Sources, Biography and Influence," Traditio XIII (1957) 249 ff.

Other important perfectionist renewal ideas are those of Utopia, of revolution, and of continuous progress.

The term and concept *Utopia*, taken from Thomas More's novel of that name, is of too late an origin to be of concern to this study, but revolution and progress, though eminently modern ideas, stretch their roots to very ancient times. For the purpose of distinction, it is sufficient to recall a few basic facts.

The term revolution is of astronomical origin, derived from the revolution of the heavens,[15] and therefore not without connection with the idea of cosmic cycles and with the cataclysms (fires or deluges) which were thought to accompany the transition from one world year to the next.[16] The concept of revolution was not applied to social and historical change until the period of transition from the Middle Ages to the Renaissance.[17] There is no doubt that the assumption of a relation between sidereal and terrestrial social revolution was an appreciable element in the ideological background even of the English Glorious Revolution and the Great French Revolution.[18] To posit revolution as the dominant idea in the movement of European history is however to confuse revolution and reform.[19] The former idea is distinguished from the latter by the inherent belief in the possibility of violent, total, and definitive improvement of human destiny.

The idea of progress can be part of many different world views. There can be progress, alternating with decline, in a cyclical and deterministic conception of history. But freedom, spiritual ascent,

---

[15] Cf. Copernicus, *De revolutionibus corporum coelestium* (1543).

[16] See above, pp. 10–12.

[17] See Matteo Villani, *Cronica* IV, 89, ed. Firenze, 1825, vol. II, 285: . . . la subita revoluzione fatta per i cittadini di Siena . . .; IX, 34, vol. IV, 209: . . . il reame de Francia in tanta rivoluzione e traverse . . .; cf. E. Rosenstock-Huessy, *Out of Revolution: Autobiography of Western Man* (New York, 1938) 500, A. Hatto, " 'Revolution': An Enquiry into the Usefulness of an Historical Term," *Mind* LVIII (1949) 502 and 510 ff.

[18] Rosenstock-Huessy, *Revolution* 188, 340 ff.; idem, *Die Europäischen Revolutionen* (Jena, 1931) 7 ff.

[19] This is very evident in Rosenstock's treatment of the Middle Ages and their reforms. See *Revolution* 485: "The nations of the Western world were called into being by five hundred years of clerical revolution"; also pp. 516 ff., Chapter X: "The Revolution of the Holy See." Rosenstock's confusion of reform and revolution leads him to such remarkable statements as "True action is not responsible to so-called ethics" (*Revolution* 721). This is not to deny that there is a grain of truth in Rosenstock's ideas.

and the return of creatures to God can also be conceived as progressive steps. In this sense as well as in other more material respects the idea of reform is an idea of progress. Since the Enlightenment, however, and especially since its alliance with the biological idea of evolution in the nineteenth century, the idea of progress has acquired connotations of continuity, irresistibility, and all-inclusiveness which are lacking in the concept of reform.[20]

As compared with all absolute or total perfectionist renewal ideas the idea of reform, at least in so far as it has preserved essential elements of its earliest Christian origins, is characterized by the belief both in ineradicable terrestrial imperfection and in a *relative perfectibility*[21] the extent of which is unforeseeable.

[20] That belief in progress which until the more recent past was so characteristic of the modern era was strikingly expressed by Spencer, when he said that the ultimate development of the ideal man was logically certain, that progress was not an accident but a necessity and that, civilization being a part of nature and all of a piece with the development of the embryo or the unfolding of a flower, man must become perfect. Cf. Herbert Spencer, *Social Statics* (reprinted New York, 1883) 79 f. For the idea of progress in general see J. Delvaille, *Essai sur l'histoire de l'idée de progrès jusqu'à la fin du XVIIIe siècle* (Paris, 1910); J. B. Bury, *The Idea of Progress* (American edition with introduction by C. A. Beard, New York, 1932); *The Idea of Progress: A Collection of Readings*, selected by J. F. Teggart, revised edition with an introduction by G. H. Hildebrand (Berkeley, Los Angeles, 1949). For Christian thought on progress see E. Dupréel, *Deux essais sur le progrès* (Bruxelles, 1928); Christopher Dawson, *Progress and Religion* (London, 1929); E. Mounier, "Le christianisme et l'idée de progrès," *Progrès technique et progrès moral* (Rencontres internationales, Genève, Paris, 1947) 181 ff.; G. Thils, *Théologie des réalités terrestres* II: *Théologie de l'histoire* (Bruges, Paris, 1949). Cf. also Part Two, Chapter IV on Tertullian, Cyprian, Ambrose, and Part Three, Chapter III, 3, on Vincent of Lérins.

[21] Bury's belief that the defender of the doctrine of original sin must reject the doctrine of perfectibility (*Idea of Progress* 265) is correct only with regard to absolute perfection, not with regard to relative perfectibility. Yet, too comprehensive ideologies of decline and decay could lead to destruction of Christian reform ideology; cf. p. 252, n. 57.

4. The Ideas of Conversion, of Baptismal Regeneration, and of Penance in Their Relation to the Idea of Reform

The ideas of religious conversion and of individual spiritual regeneration through baptism are closely connected, but not identical, with the Christian idea of reform. They may within Christianity be considered as the all-important foundations of the reform idea[1] and yet they are distinct from it, though the terminologies can at times be the same.[2]

Baptismal regeneration is *instantaneous* and *nonrepeatable* since in it the Christian shares in the one death and Resurrection of Christ, which are the fundamental facts of all Christian belief in the renewal of man. The idea of reform on the contrary contains as an essential element multiplicity involving *prolongation* and *repetition*, and the ceaselessly repeated sacrifice of Christ in the sacrament of the altar may perhaps be seen as the exemplary cause and the vivifying center of Christian reform, even though in the age of the Fathers this meaning was not yet very often formulated explicitly, except in the liturgy itself.[3]

Conversion[4] may be prebaptismal, and such it was and is in the case of the conversion of Jews and pagans to Christianity, or postbaptismal, in which case it is closely related to penance. Essentially, postbaptismal as well as prebaptismal conversion is a *unique* experience, but examples of repeated conversions after a "reversion" are not un-

---

[1] See Part Two, Chapter II, of this study. It may be added that in Christianity death and resurrection are the eschatological end terms of all conversion, regeneration, and reform; also, purification of the soul—see below, pp. 91 ff., 294 ff.—may have to be continued in Purgatory (on the Christian and non-Christian religious and ideological background of this continuity, see C.-M. Edsman, *Le baptême de feu* [Acta Seminarii Neotestamentici Upsaliensis IX, Leipzig, Uppsala, 1940]).

[2] See, for instance, p. 135, nn. 13 f., for *reformari* as baptismal regeneration and as conversion.

[3] But see below, p. 98, n. 59, for Gregory of Nyssa and p. 280 f. and 311 for Augustine; for the liturgy see below, p. 294 f. See also below, Part Two, Chapter V, 7, for the role in the history of the reform idea of the doctrine of the ecclesiological Body of Christ, which again is of course closely linked to that of the eucharistic Body of Christ (cf. H. de Lubac, S.J., *Corpus Mysticum*, 2nd ed. [Théologie III, Paris, 1947]).

[4] For the biblical term and concept ἐπιστροφή-*conversio* and the Platonistic origins of the term, see also below, pp. 49 f.

known. In the early Christian period penance too was at first non-repeatable, but by the end of the fourth century, at the latest, this original strictness had begun to give way to a milder practice.[5] While then baptism is the first and foremost sacramental basis of Christian reform, postbaptismal conversion and penance may be indispensable new starts in the long *process* of reform.[6]

There is a vast amount of theological, psychological, and historical literature on conversion[7] and there are dogmatic, canonistic, liturgical, and historical works on the sacraments of baptism and of penance and on pre-Christian ideas of spiritual regeneration or rebirth.[8] But little has been written on the religious roots of the idea and reality of reform, except in so far as it is treated as a part of the doctrine of justification and sanctifying grace in Catholic dogmatics.[9]

Primitive Protestantism had on the whole not much use for a

---

[5] See below, Part Two, Chapter VII, 2.

[6] From the fourth to the sixth century, especially, the term *conversio* was often used for a Christian's turning away from worldly life and also for entry into the monastic life; see below, Part Three, Chapter II, 3.

[7] For the idea of conversion in pagan and Christian Antiquity see A. D. Nock, *Conversion: The Old and the New Religion from Alexander the Great to Augustine of Hippo* (Oxford, 1933); idem, "Conversion and Adolescence," in *Pisciculi F. J. Dölger* 165 ff.; G. Bardy, *La conversion au christianisme durant les premiers siècles* (Paris, 1949); G. Misch, *A History of Autobiography in Antiquity* (Cambridge, Mass., 1951); H. Pinard de la Boullaye, article "Conversion," *DSpir*, fasc. XIV–XV, 2224 ff. See also A. H. Dirksen, C.PP.S., *The New Testament Concept of Metanoia* (Diss., Catholic University of America, Washington, D.C., 1932) and the recent article by Y. M.-J. Congar, O.P., "The Idea of Conversion," *Thought* XXXIII (1958) 5 ff. Cf. below, pp. 49 ff.

[8] For the latter see the remarks above, p. 12 and pp. 16 ff. See also J. Dey, ΠΑΛΙΓΓΕΝΕΣΙΑ (Neutestamentliche Abhandlungen XVII, 5, Münster, 1937). Dey shows that in pagan Graeco-Roman and in Jewish thought the idea of individual spiritual regeneration is much rarer than is often assumed and that on the whole it lacks the ethical element characteristic of the Christian concept of rebirth (Tit. 3 : 5, etc.). In most cases the pre-Christian concept of *palingenesia* concerns cosmology and metempsychosis, though in Apuleius' Isis mysteries (see below, p. 40) there is a slight spiritual overtone and in the famous *Libellus XIII* (*Hermes Trismegistus on Rebirth*) of the *Corpus Hermeticum*, Scott, *Hermet.* I, 238 ff., also Nock and Festugière, *Corp. Hermet.* II, 197 ff., a definite conception of spiritual regeneration; cf. Festugière, *La révélation d'Hermès Trismégiste* IV (Paris, 1954) 216 f., 264, 267. For the rest A. Harnack's *Die Terminologie der Wiedergeburt und verwandter Erlebnisse in der ältesten Kirche* (Texte u. Untersuch. XLII, 2, Leipzig, 1917) is still of great value. Cf. also V. Iacono, "La ΠΑΛΙΓΓΕΝΕΣΙΑ in S. Paolo e nell' ambiente pagano," *Biblica* XV (1934) 369 ff.

[9] See below, pp. 59 ff.

religiously founded idea of repeated reforms; the Reformation[10] seemed to be a unique and final collective conversion. Only later, Protestant reformers saw that it could become necessary to proceed "even to the reforming of the Reformation itself."[11]

[10] The Protestant term "reformation" is, of course, still the early Christian term *reformatio*. Needless to say, Luther first meant to reform the Church, not to break away from it.

[11] Milton, *Areopagitica* (first published, 1655; Everyman's Library edition, 1927) 32: "Now once again by all concurrence of signs, and by the general instinct of holy and devout men . . . God is decreeing to begin some new and great period in this Church, even to the reforming of Reformation itself . . ." (in part quoted by Rosenstock, *Revolution* 362). It is interesting to see that William James treats of "saintliness" as a continuation, as it were, of conversion and as a pragmatically verifiable leaven of civilization, although he does not use the concept of reform. See William James, *Varieties of Religious Experience* (New York, 1902), Lectures XI–XV. Cf. below, pp. 59–61, about the relation between reform and sanctification in Catholic doctrine. For the relation between the reform idea and heretical or sectarian ideologies see, for instance, the remarks below, pp. 162 ff. and 258 ff., on Pelagians and Donatists; also below, p. 252, n. 57, on connections between the ideology of reform and that of decline.

CHAPTER II

DEFINITION OF THE IDEA OF REFORM

On the basis of the distinctions made, the idea of reform may now be defined as the idea of free, intentional and ever perfectible, multiple, prolonged and ever repeated efforts by man to reassert and augment values pre-existent in the spiritual-material compound of the world.

This definition, however, requires two important qualifications. First: its role is that of a provisional conceptual tool only (see above, p. 5), which may not always fit the historical material exactly. Various types of renewal ideas did, of course, mix and blend with the idea of reform.

Second: granted the possibility of defining the idea of reform and of studying and describing it as a historical fact, as a phenomenon essentially Christian in origin and early development, it does not follow implicitly that the idea corresponds to a reality. That it often does not is no serious problem, but whether it ever does is a question whereby the terms contained in the definition are transposed from the history of ideology to that of preterideological existence. Is there possibility at least of spirit besides matter, of value besides indifference, of liberty besides determination, of final besides efficient causality, of relative perfectibility besides the absolute, of multiplicity besides unity; in short, is there possibility of reform besides changelessness and besides other types of renewal and change? No cogent answer can be expected from the historical sources alone. In basing this study on an affirmative answer the author is conscious of certain metahistorical preconceptions which are made explicit in Excursus II.

There are few in any case who would deny that some of the great events which truly transformed history ultimately depended on changes, often only slight and subtle, in the realm of ideas. It is not unreasonable to expect that the idea of reform, because of its content, may have played a particularly important part in historical change.

PART TWO

THE EARLY CHRISTIAN IDEA OF REFORM

CHAPTER I

PRE-CHRISTIAN, BIBLICAL, AND PATRISTIC TERMINOLOGY OF RENEWAL AND REFORM

The early Christian idea of reform is of biblical or more exactly of Pauline origin. A study of its beginnings must be preceded by a survey of the terminology used to express it.[1]

In pre-Christian usage the verb *reformare* itself, which occurs earlier than the noun *reformatio*, did not at first clearly express the reassertion or augmentation of value characteristic of the reform idea. The first occurrence of *reformare* seems to be in Ovid's *Metamorphoses*, where it once refers to a miraculous physical transformation "backward," that is to say, to the undoing of a previous change,[2] and another time to sudden rejuvenation of an old man for one day.[3] *Reformare* thus may be an Ovidian adaptation of the late Greek term μεταμόρφωσις the ideological background of which is in Ovid distinctly cosmological.[4]

---

[1] It is not intended here to make a full terminological study of the origins of *reformare*, *reformatio*, and related expressions, and of their Greek equivalents. Such a study, though interesting and desirable in itself, would be out of proportion with the main scope of this book, which is the history of ideas rather than of terms—and even the treatment of the biblical and patristic *idea* of reform will have to be selective rather than exhaustive. The remarks on the terminological foundations of the reform idea which follow are based in part on the materials of the *Thesaurus Linguae Latinae* and of the Oxford *Lexicon of Patristic Greek*, which is in preparation. I wish to express my gratitude to the Director and staff of the *Thesaurus* Bureau in Munich, and especially to Dr. Lumpe, who compiled for me a list of all *Thesaurus* entries for the words *reformo*, *reformatio*, *renovo*, *renovatio*, *transformo*, *transformatio*, *transfiguro*, *transfiguratio*. Whenever this material has been my source, the fact is noted by the symbol *ThLL*. Similarly, I am greatly indebted to the staff of the *Lexicon of Patristic Greek*, especially to Father B. Krivocheine, for allowing me to consult their files at Oxford in 1954. My use of this material is indicated by the symbol *LPG*. Finally, I have to thank Professor André Grabar of the Collège de France for his kindness in procuring copies of certain entries in D. Lenfant, O.P., *Concordantiae Augustinianae* (Paris, 1656–1665), a work which is not available in America.

[2] Ovid, *Metamorphoses* XI, 254.   [3] *Ibid.* IX, 399.

[4] Cf. the last book of the *Metamorphoses*, also the beginning of Book I. For the use of the term μεταμόρφωσις in Greek literature, see, for instance, Diodorus Siculus, *Bibliotheca Historica* IV, 81, on the metamorphosis of Actaeon.

Reformation is distinguished by the prefix *re-*, signifying directedness toward the past, from the term and concept of transformation, which is basically alteration or change, though it can connote varying degrees of novelty. For transformation, Ovid like Virgil has the term *transformare*, a literal translation of μεταμορφοῦν. Ovid's contemporary Valerius Maximus uses the verb *reformare* for the restoration of Athens by Themistocles after the defeat of Xerxes.[5] About a century later one meets *reformare* and *reformatio* in the *Metamorphoses* of Apuleius, both in the first of the two Ovidian meanings[6] and in the sense of transformation pure and simple.[7] It is clear, therefore, that at least from the middle of the second century A.D. *reformatio* could signify alteration, with or without emphasis on newness, as well as return to a condition of the past. Meanwhile the term had begun also to express an element of value and improvement, originally absent from the strict meaning of both *reformare* and *transformare*. Seneca and Pliny the Younger were, it appears, the first to speak of moral, educational, and political *reformatio*.[8] A little later the great jurists of the Antonine and

---

[5] Valerius Maximus, *Factorum et dictorum memorabilium* VI, 5, *Externa* 2 : Cum . . . ruinas patriae in pristinum habitum reformaret. . . . Cf. K. Burdach, "Sinn und Ursprung der Worte Renaissance und Reformation," *Reformation Renaissance Humanismus*, 2nd ed. (Berlin, Leipzig, 1926) 56.

[6] Apuleius, *Metamorphoses* III, 23, XI, 13, XI, 16. Apuleius in speaking of Lucius' reformation from an ass into a man through the power of Isis and through his initiation into the service of the goddess uses not only the terms *reformare, reformatio*, but also *renatus quodam modo* (*ibid.* XI, 16); cf. R. Reitzenstein, *Die hellenistischen Mysterienreligionen*, 3rd ed. (Leipzig, Berlin, 1927) 39 f., 262 ff., on the close relation between *reformare, renasci*, and kindred terms in Apuleius and other documents of late antique mystery cults and mystical moods, also J. Dey, *ΠΑΛΙΓΓΕΝΕΣΙΑ* (Neutestamentliche Abhandlungen XVII, 5, Münster, 1937) 98 ff. See above, p. 12, on the *Latin Asclepius* and cf. Claudian, *Phoenix* 25, 40 ff., 50 ff., Koch 234 f., where *reformare, redux forma, renasci, mutata melior procede figura*, are all used for the rebirth of phoenix from his own ashes; cf. above, p. 21, and below, p. 140. It will be seen later that in Christendom, too, "reform," "recreation," "renovation," and "rebirth" or "regeneration" are at times used interchangeably, while at other times the terms are distinct from one another.

[7] Apuleius, *Metamorph.* III, 24 f.; XI, 27 and 30. The *ThLL* lists about a dozen other occurrences in Apuleius of *reformare* and *reformatio* in one or the other of the two meanings.

[8] Seneca, *Ad Lucilium Epist.* VI, 6 (58), 26: a reformatione morum; III, 4 (25), 1: Respice aetatem eius iam duram et intractabilem : non potest reformari, tenera finguntur; XV, 2 (94), 51: Pueri ad praescriptum discunt . . . imitari iubentur proposita et ad illa reformare chirographum . . . (*ThLL*). Pliny the Younger, *Panegyricus* 53, 1 : . . . corruptos depravatosque mores principatus parens noster reformet et corrigat; *idem, Epist.* VIII, 12, 1 : literarum iam senescentium reductor ac reformator (quoted by W. Rehm, *Der Untergang*

Severan periods seem to have initiated the application of the term reform to the sphere of legal and institutional improvement.[9] Thus Q. Cervidius Scaevola says of a testator who has changed his will: *non a tota voluntate recessisse videri, sed ab his tantum rebus quas reformasset*[10] and Ulpian speaking about contracts states: *nam si potest res tolli, cur non et reformari ut quodammodo quasi renovatus contractus videatur.*[11]

The Latin New Testament terms which principally shaped the Christian idea of reform in the west are to be found above all in the Epistles of St. Paul. In the early Latin versions ("*Vetus Latina,*" patristic quotations, Vulgate) of the Epistle to the Romans (12:2), the Second Epistle to the Corinthians (3:18), and the Epistle to the Philippians (3:21), *reformari* and *reformare* have served to translate the Greek μεταμορφοῦσθαι and the synonymous μετασχηματίζειν.[12] While the Vulgate has *reformamini* in Rom. 12:2, *transformamur* in 2 Cor. 3:18, *reformabit* in Phil. 3:21, the *Cod. Claromontanus*[13] of the "*Vetus Latina*" ("*Itala*") has *reformamini* in Rom. 12:2, *reformamur* in 2 Cor. 3:18,[14] *transfiguravit* in Phil. 3:21.[15] The testimony of early patristic texts is somewhat different again.[16] So, for instance, St. Cyprian has *transformemini* in Rom. 12:2;[17] Tertullian has *transfigurari*, St. Hilary

---

Roms im abendländischen Denken [Leipzig, 1930] 15). Still without the term *reformare*, Horace, *Carmin.* IV, 15, 12: the age of Augustus *veteres revocavit artes*; Livy, *Histor.* XXXIX, 41: priscos mores revocare; also Suetonius, *Augustus* 24.

[9] However, already the *Res gestae divi Augusti* 8, 5 (ed. J. Gagé [Paris, 1935] 86), without using the word *reformare*, had stated: . . . ⟨e⟩xempla maiorum exolescentia iam . . . re⟨duxi⟩ . . . (in view of διωρθωσάμην in the Greek text and of Suetonius, *Augustus* 31: Annum . . . ad pristinam rationem redegit, one should, perhaps, emend to *redegi* rather than *reduxi*); cf. also Suetonius, *Augustus* 34: leges retractavit, *idem*, *Claudius* 22: exoleta revocavit, Horace, *Epist.* II, 1-3: cum . . . res Italas . . . legibus emendes.

[10] *Digest.* 34, 4, 30, 3 (*ThLL*).

[11] *Digest.* 2, 14, 7, 6 (*ThLL*). About the same time, Solinus, *Collectanea rerum memorabilium*, 1, 47, uses the word *reformavit* in speaking about Augustus' reform of the calendar (*ThLL*).

[12] A Platonic term; cf. *Laws* 903E, 906E.

[13] Ed. C. Tischendorf (Leipzig, 1852).

[14] The Freising fragments have *transformamur* in 2 Cor. 3:18; cf. L. Ziegler, *Italafragmente der paulinischen Briefe* (Marburg, 1876) 95. For other manuscripts cf. Wordsworth and White, *Novum Testamentum* II, 306.

[15] Cf. Wordsworth and White, *Novum Testamentum* II, 483.

[16] For comprehensive lists of early patristic citations of the relevant Pauline texts, see Sabatier, *Bibliorum Versiones* III, and Wordsworth and White, *Novum Testamentum*.

[17] Cf. Sabatier, *Bibliorum Versiones* III, 640; Wordsworth and White, *Novum Testamentum* II, 126.

of Poitiers *transferemur*, Ticonius *commutamur* in 2 Cor. 3:18;[18] Cyprian has *transformavit*,[19] Pelagius *reformabit* in Phil. 3:21 (but Pelagius has *transformavit* where he refers to Phil. 3:21, while commenting on *reformamur* in 2 Cor. 3:18).[20]

In view of such variations, it is all the more necessary to interpret the terms in their context rather than in isolation, and with reference to the definition of "reform," given at the end of Part One. The basic meaning of μεταμορφοῦσθαι and of μετασχηματίζειν is transformation rather than reformation, but it must be noted that in composite verbs μετα- may at times have the meaning of reversal beside that of change. In the Letters of St. Paul at any rate these expressions and their Latin equivalents signify more than mere alteration:[21] in the Epistle to the Romans and in the Second Corinthians the soul's reform from a lower to a higher state is clearly suggested, while the Epistle to the Philippians speaks of the transfiguration of the body from a material to a spiritual condition in the resurrection.[22] Linguistically, the closest Greek equivalents to *reformare-reformatio* are the terms ἀναμορφοῦν-ἀναμόρφωσις which, however, are absent from the New Testament as well as from the Septuagint. This fact may have some bearing on the development of Greek Christian reform terminology and ideology. For even though ἀναμορφοῦν-ἀναμόρφωσις do occur in patristic and Byzantine Greek in the sense of reform,[23] it is the scriptural renewal terms ἀποκαθιστάναι-

---

[18] Sabatier, *Bibliorum Versiones* III, 734; Wordsworth and White, *Novum Testamentum* II, 306.

[19] Wordsworth and White, *Novum Testamentum* II, 483.

[20] Cf. A. Souter, *Pelagius's Exposition of Thirteen Epistles of St. Paul* II (Cambridge, 1926) 410 and 249.

[21] But I cannot follow M. Rule, " 'Transformare' and 'Transformatio,' " *Jour. Theol. Stud.* XII (1911) 413 ff., according to whom in certain liturgical eucharistic texts of early date such terms are equivalent to *praeformare, praefigurare.*

[22] See the following chapter on the reform and renewal ideology of St. Paul. Μεταμορφοῦν-*transfigurare* is also used in Matthew 17:2 and Mark 9:2 for the Transfiguration of Christ on Mount Tabor.

[23] See, for instance, Gregory Nazianzen, *Oratio* VII, 15, *PG* XXXV, 773C, where however baptism rather than reform in general is meant: . . . τῆς νεοκτίστου ψυχῆς ἣν τὸ πνεῦμα δι᾽ ὕδατος ἀνεμόρφωσεν ἄξια τὰ γέρα καρπούμενος (*LPG*)? More important is Cyril of Alexandria, *In Isaiam* 44, 21 f., lib. IV, oratio 2, *PG* LXX, 936B: Οὕτω γὰρ, οὕτω ταῖς ἡμετέραις ἐμπρέπει ψυχαῖς ὁ χαρακτὴρ τῆς ὑποστάσεως τοῦ Θεοῦ καὶ Πατρὸς ἀναμορφοῦντος ἡμᾶς . . . τοῦ ἁγίου Πνεύματος δι᾽ ἁγιασμοῦ πρὸς αὐτόν. Cf. idem, *Homilia paschalis* 10, 4,

ἀποκατάστασις and ἀνακεφαλοῦν-ἀνακεφαλαίωσις on the one hand, and ἀνανεοῦν, ἀνακαινοῦν-ἀνακαίνωσις on the other, which beside scriptural μεταμορφοῦν and μετασχηματίζειν [24] seem to be of the greatest significance for Greek Christian reform ideology.

The terms ἀποκατάστασις, ἀποκαθιστάναι, ἀποκαθιστάνειν are found in the Gospel of St. Matthew (17:11), in that of St. Mark (9:12), and in the Acts of the Apostles (1:6 and 3:21); the Vulgate translation is restitutio, restituere. In the last of these New Testament passages, and later in Origen, ἀποκατάστασις, a term of cosmological connotations,[25] famous in the history of Christian theology as well as of ancient philosophy, has not the meaning of reform, but of eschatological fulfillment and restoration.[26] It is however used in a specific sense of reform, in that of man's pre-eschatological restoration to his origins, ἀποκατάστασις εἰς τὸ ἀρχαῖον, by some of the Greek Fathers, especially by St. Gregory of Nyssa.[27] In Latin patristic literature expressions such as restaurare, reparare, renovare in pristinum are most significant where they stand in contrast to reformare or renovare in melius.[28]

PG LXXVII, 625; cf. In Joannis evangelium II (to John 3:6), PG LXXIII, 245B. For Cyril's doctrine of the role of the Holy Spirit in the reform of man, see below, pp. 79 ff. See also Ps.-Basil of Seleucia (perhaps Proclus of Constantinople), Oratio XXXIX, 2, PG LXXXV, 432B f. (LPG); furthermore Ps.-Dionysius Areopagita, De divinis nominibus 1, 3, PG III, 589C, on God as the ἀνακαινισμός and the ἀναμόρφωσις of fallen man (LPG).

[24] Apart from quotations of the scriptural texts in which μεταμορφοῦν occurs, this term seems to be used relatively rarely by the Greek Fathers in connection with spiritual renewal or reform; its mythological connotations seem to have remained very strong; cf. A. Harnack, Die Terminologie der Wiedergeburt und verwandter Erlebnisse in der ältesten Kirche (Texte u. Untersuch. XLII, 2, 1917) 103. Μετασχηματίζειν, μεταπλάσσειν, μεταστοιχειοῦν, μεταποιοῦν, and similar words, do however appear as characteristic terms of Greek patristic renewal ideology and not infrequently express a true concept of reform; see, for instance, Cyril of Alexandria, In Isaiam 45, 9 f. and 11 f., PG LXX, 961B f. and 965B f. (LPG), idem, Homilia paschalis 10, 4, PG LXXVII, 625C–628A (LPG), idem, In Joannis evangelium II, loc. cit.

[25] See E. Zeller, Die Philosophie der Griechen III, 1, 5th ed. (Leipzig, 1923) 157 f. The concept of ἀποκατάστασις is connected with that of the periodical renewal of the world through fire (ἐκπύρωσις) or other means. See also p. 11. Cf. Lenz, article "Apokatastasis," RLAC I, 510 ff., A. Méhat, "«Apocatastase»," Vigil. Christ. X (1956) 196 ff.

[26] In Matthew 12:13, however, ἀπεκατεστάθη (Vulgate: restituta est) is used for Jesus' healing of a withered hand. See below, p. 142, about St. Hilary of Poitiers' use of the word reformare in his comments on Matthew 12:13.

[27] See below, pp. 76 ff.

[28] See below, pp. 156 ff.

Related to the scriptural ἀποκατάστασις πάντων is the ἀνακεφα-
λαιώσασθαι τὰ πάντα ἐν τῷ Χριστῷ of Ephesians 1:10 (Vulgate: *instaurare omnia in Christo*), which forms the basis of St. Irenaeus'
doctrine of ἀνακεφαλαίωσις (*recapitulatio*).[29]

As to the terms ἀνανεοῦν, ἀνακαινοῦν-ἀνακαίνωσις and their Latin
equivalents *renovare-renovatio*, they are of great importance for the
genesis of both the western and the eastern Christian reform idea.
In pre-Christian Latin *renovare* and *renovatio* are at least as old as
Cicero and were very often used by him, by Livy, and by other
classical and postclassical authors in various senses of renewal: *renovare
bellum, foedus, auspicia, memoriam, gloriam, dolorem*, etc. Yet in the
Epistles to the Ephesians (4:23), to the Colossians (3:10), and to
Titus (3:5), and in the Second Corinthians (4:16), the terms *renovari*
and *renovatio*,[30] which translate ἀνανεοῦσθαι,[31] ἀνακαινοῦσθαι,[32] and
ἀνακαίνωσις, mean a far reaching renewal of the whole nature of
man, a meaning which does not seem to occur in the pre-Christian
usage of *renovare*. The word *novus* itself, in pre-Christian Latin, when
it is not used in a merely temporal sense, often has a pejorative rather
than an ameliorative quality.[33] This shade of meaning survives most
definitely in the terms *innovare* and *innovatio*, which in post-classical
and mediaeval Latin not infrequently, though by no means always,[34]
signify innovation in the sense of inferior novelty and disturbance of
an old tradition.[35] Of the two Greek words for "new"—νέος and
καινός—the second had a more qualitative than temporal character
and could be used in the sense of a better because newer quality;[36]
in Hellenistic Greek νέος however "approximates in meaning to

[29] See below, pp. 68 f.

[30] Most witnesses of the *Vetus Latina* have here the same terms as the Vulgate, but some
of the early Fathers use *innovare* instead (cf. Sabatier, *Bibliorum Versiones* III, 801 and 839).
For *innovare* in a pejorative sense see immediately below.

[31] An old word, found, for instance, in Thucydides.

[32] Equivalent to the classical Greek word.

[33] For instance, in *novus homo, res novae*.

[34] See n. 30, above. See also the Vulgate for Ps. 50:12: spiritum rectum innova in
visceribus meis, cf. below, p. 52, n. 13.

[35] So already Cicero, *Oratio in L. Pisonem* 36, 89: quo te modo ad tuam intemperantiam,
scelerate, innovasti?

[36] See, for instance, the Pseudo-Platonic dialogue *Axiochus* 370E: γέγονα καινός. I owe
this reference to Professor Harold Cherniss.

καινός." [37] St. Paul used both νέος and καινός and their derivatives to express the fundamental renovation of man who becomes a "new man," a "new creature" (καινὴ κτίσις, nova creatura), through Christ. Latin novus and renovare in the Pauline spiritually ameliorative sense therefore seem to be New Testament Graecisms.[38] The Vulgate also translates Old Testament Greek renewal terms such as ἀνακαινίζειν in this sense; see, for instance, Psalm 102:5: Renovabitur ut aquilae iuventus tua, a beautiful formulation of the renewal idea, which was not neglected by theology and liturgy.[39] It will be shown in the next chapter that the terminology of "renovation" in the Epistles to the Ephesians (4:23), Colossians (3:10), and in the Second Corinthians (4:16) is closely related to the reform idea in its most extensive meaning, whereas in the Epistle to Titus (3:5) ἀνακαίνωσις is specifically linked to παλιγγενεσία, baptismal regeneration;[40] μεταμορφοῦν, ἀναμορφοῦν, transformare, reformare, too, can be used in patristic literature in a more specific sense, for the beginning or the end of the whole process of reform: for baptism and for the resurrection.

The renewal terms discussed are the ones which will be encountered most frequently in the study of the reform idea in the patristic age. Other terms, pre-Christian and patristic, such as ἀνακαλεῖν,[41]

---

[37] A. D. Nock, "Notes on Ruler-Cult, I–IV," Jour. Hellen. Stud. XLVIII (1928) 35.

[38] For the idea of "newness" in early Christianity in general, see K. Prümm, S.J., Christentum als Neuheitserlebnis (Freiburg i. B., 1933); Harnack, Wiedergeburt 101 ff., 135 ff. See also E. R. Curtius, European Literature and the Latin Middle Ages, trans. W. R. Trask (Bollingen Series XXXVI, New York, 1953) 251 ff., and J. de Ghellinck, S.J., "Neotericus, neoterici," Arch. Lat. M. Ae. XV (1940) 113 ff., for the late-antique Graecism neoterici (from νεώτεροι), used to distinguish the "modern" writers from the "ancients"; modernus appears only in the late fifth century and, in the late ancient period, on the whole means contemporary rather than novel, cf. W. Freund, Modernus und andere Zeitbegriffe des Mittelalters (Neue Münstersche Beiträge zur Geschichtsforschung IV, Köln, Graz, 1957).

[39] For renewal ideology in the Psalms see below, p. 52; for its influence on the Fathers and the liturgy, below, pp. 80, 312, 314 f. and 295. The motif of the eagle's rejuvenation is related to cosmological and vitalistic renewal ideas, especially to the phoenix myth (cf. above, p. 21, n. 21), but can be transferred to reform ideology (cf. pp. 314 f.).

[40] K. Burdach, "Renaissance und Reformation" 30, goes too far in simply identifying the Pauline terms of "rebirth" and "renovation"-"reform"; see the following section of this chapter.

[41] Cf. Ps.-Dionysius Areopagita, De divinis nominibus 1, 3, PG III, 589B f.: . . . τῶν . . . ἀποπιπτόντων . . . ἀνάκλησίς τε καὶ ἀνάστασις . . . (LPG). It is not always easy to tell whethe the prefix ἀνα- means "again" or "upwards."

ἀναλαμβάνειν, ἀναβιβάζειν, ἀναχαλκεύειν,[42] ἀναστοιχειοῦν,[43] ἀναπλάσσειν, ἀνακτίζειν,[44] ἐπανορθοῦν, κατορθοῦν,[45] revocare,[46] reparare,[47] restaurare,[48] reficere, recreare,[49] corripere, corrigere, emendare[50] are akin to ἀποκαθιστάναι, restituere, and ἀνακεφαλαιοῦν, recapitulare, in that they often stress the reassertion of old values, the regaining of a pristina fortuna, the return to a status pristinus.[51] Though the act of reassertion may itself introduce an element of novelty, and even of betterment,[52] these elements are weaker in such terms than in ἀνανεοῦν, ἀνακαινοῦν, renovare; in this latter term the concept of newness is of greater force than even the eminently retrospective prefix re-. Nevertheless, newness can be

---

[42] Cf., for instance, Cyril of Alexandria, Commentar. in Sophoniam prophetam 44 (3, 16 f.), PG LXXI, 1016D f.: . . . (Christ) τὴν ἀνθρώπου φύσιν ἀναμορφῶν εἰς καινότητα ζωῆς καὶ ἀναχαλκεύων εἰς τὸ ἀπ' ἀρχῆς. . . . Τὸ δὲ ἀνακεφαλαιούμενον ἀναλαμβάνεταί πως καὶ ἀναβιβάζεται πρὸς τὸ ἐν ἀρχαῖς (LPG).

[43] Cf. Cyril of Alexandria, Homilia paschalis 10, 4, PG LXXVII, 625C ff.: . . . εἰς τὸ τῆς ἀφθαρσίας ἀναστοιχειούμενον καύχημα . . . (LPG).

[44] Both expressions are found, for instance, in Athanasius; cf. G. Müller, S.J., Lexicon Athanasianum (Berlin, 1952).

[45] For the penitential-educational meaning of ἐπανόρθωσις in connection with παιδεία in 2 Tim. 3:16 cf. below, p. 60 and p. 313, n. 38. For the patristic use of ἐπανορθοῦν in a wide sense of reform see, for instance, Ps.-Basil of Seleucia (perhaps Proclus of Constantinople), Oratio XXXIX, 4, PG LXXXV, 436B (LPG). For κατορθοῦν cf. the text from John Chrysostom, below, p. 127, n. 54.

[46] Cf., for instance, Ambrose about recall to Paradise, below, p. 144, n. 59, and Augustine on the recall of creation to God, below, pp. 167 ff, and in connection with the reform of man, below, p. 156, n. 13, p. 170, n. 11.

[47] Cf., for instance, Ambrose in connection especially with penance, below, p. 142, n. 53, and with the repair of the human condition, below, p. 143, n. 54, Augustine in connection with penance, below, p. 312, n. 33.

[48] For examples from the liturgy, see below, p. 285, n. 5.

[49] For these two terms see, for instance, Augustine with reference to the resurrection, below, p. 158, n. 17, and in conjunction with the idea of man's reformation, below, p. 312, n. 33.

[50] For corripere, corrigere, emendare see below, pp. 313 and 414 f., in connection with Augustine's and Caesarius of Arles' penitential use of these terms.

[51] See Suetonius, Nero 40: pristinae fortunae restitutionem; idem, Augustus 31: Annum . . . ad pristinam rationem redegit; Curtius Rufus, De rebus gestis Alexandri Magni V, 1, 8: pristinam reparasse fortunam; Ulpian, in Digest 43, 21, 1: reficere est quod corruptum est in pristinum statum restaurare; cf. also Fortuna Redux in inscriptions and on coins.

[52] See Suetonius, Vespasianus 17: restituere in melius.

understood as identity or equivalence of a new condition with a perfect original state; it will be seen that such is often the case in Greek patristic reform ideology.[53] Only the term *reformare*, and to some extent its Greek equivalents ἀναμορφοῦν, μεταμορφοῦν, etc.,[54] can contain the connotations of newness and improvement and those of old goodness in equal strength: in *reformare-reformatio*, especially, the prefix *re-* points toward the previous existence of the constitutive components of a substance or event while *forma* infers their being organized and consolidated toward new shape and "firmness."[55] This synthetic meaning is found above all in *reformare in melius*[56] (corresponding Greek terms are ἀναμορφοῦν εἰς τὸ ἀμείνω[57] or μεταπλάττειν ἐπὶ τὸ ἄμεινον,[58] ἐπὶ τὸ βέλτιον μετακόσμησις[59]) and also in *renovare in melius*:[60] these phrases signify not merely change to the better (as in μεταβάλλειν ἐπὶ τὸ βέλτιον,[61] ἐπὶ τὸ βέλτιον μετάθεσις,[62]

[53] But see below, pp. 64 f., nn. 5 ff., and pp. 72, 143 ff., 230 f., on the conception that the possession of the Kingdom of God is more than return to Paradise, a conception which is found in not a few of the Greek Fathers as well as in the west. For the occurrence of the idea of "reform to the better" in the early Christian east and, more often, in the west, cf. immediately below and above all, p. 87, n. 19, and p. 161, n. 23.

[54] Cf. above, p. 42 f., n. 23.

[55] *Forma* and *firmus* are etymologically connected; Sanscrit: *dhar-*. For this double character of the term *reformare* cf. also F. Delekat, "Reformation, Revolution und Restauration, drei Grundbegriffe der Geschichte," *Zeitschrift für Theologie und Kirche* XLIX (1952) 89.

[56] First occurrence, perhaps, in Tertullian; see below, pp. 134 f. Cf. Virgil, *Aeneid* I, 281 and XI, 426: in melius referre.

[57] So Cyril of Alexandria, *In Isaiam* 45, 9 f., *PG* LXX, 961B f. (*LPG*).

[58] *Ibid.* 45, 11 f., *PG* LXX, 965B f. (*LPG*).

[59] So Basil, *De Sancto Spiritu* XIX, 49, *PG* XXXII, 157B f.; cf. below, p. 80, n. 72. Cf. also Gregory Nazianzen, *Oratio* XL, 7, in sanctum baptisma, *PG* XXXVI, 365C: Ἀλλ' ὥσπερ οὐκ ὄντας ὑπέστησεν, οὕτως ὑποστάντας ἀνέπλασε, πλάσιν θειοτέραν τε καὶ τῆς πρώτης ὑψηλοτέραν.

[60] See below, pp. 156 ff., about St. Augustine's use of this phrase.

[61] See Plato, *Republic* 381B: ἐπὶ τὸ βέλτιόν τε καὶ κάλλιον μεταβάλλειν ἑαυτόν. It is rather significant that this is said of God *per impossibile*. In this connection it is well to recall the illuminating remark of W. Jaeger, *Paideia*, trans. G. Highet, II, (New York, 1943) 237, that Plato's "reform" of old-Greek παιδεία expressly excludes all "progress" of the good, which is an unchangeable norm. This no doubt explains that, while the concept of conversion—a turning about toward the idea of the good (cf. below, p. 49, n. 2)—has Platonic roots, there does not seem to exist a Platonic antecedent of the concepts of personal renewal and reform, which express a combination of new and old values.

[62] Cf. Polybius, *Histor.* I, 35.

πρὸς τὸν ἀμείνονα [βίον][63] or πρὸς τὸ κρεῖττον ἀλλοίωσις,[64] mutare in melius,[65] etc.), but rather improvement on the basis of a return to original perfection, which thus may even be transcended.

[63] See Philo, De Abrahamo 3, 17, Cohn and Wendland IV, 5, about τὸν ἀπὸ χείρονος βίου πρὸς τὸν ἀμείνω μεταβάλλοντα: this corresponds to μετάνοια, cf. below, pp. 49 f.

[64] See Gregory of Nyssa, De perfectione, Jaeger, Greg. Nyss. Opera VIII, 1, 213, there connected however with the phrase ἐπὶ τὸ θειότερον μεταποιούσης

[65] See Tacitus, Histor. I, 50; cf. in melius verti: often in Livy; in melius flectere mentem: Seneca, Hercules furens 1064.

CHAPTER II

THE PAULINE IDEA OF REFORM
AND RELATED SCRIPTURAL CONCEPTS

Conversion from evil to good (ἐπιστρέφειν-ἐπιστροφή), change of mind-repentance (μετανοεῖν-μετάνοια), are according to the New Testament essential conditions for the acceptance of Christ's teaching and for a Christian way of life. 'Επιστροφή and μετάνοια are closely connected with one another in the New as well as in the Old Testament.[1]

In the biblical term ἐπιστροφή the Platonic and Platonist concept of conversion from darkness to light—as in the famous myth of Plato's Republic—is still clearly discernible.[2] The word and ethical concept μετάνοια, too, originated independently from Jewish-Christian terminology,[3] but in the Bible it has an emphatically penitential meaning which is, to say the least, not very strong in the earlier

---

[1] For the New Testament, see, for instance, Luke 17:4: καὶ ἐὰν ... ἑπτάκις ἐπιστρέψῃ πρὸς σὲ λέγων· μετανοῶ, ἀφήσεις αὐτῷ; Acts 26:20: ... τοῖς ἔθνεσιν ἀπήγγελον μετανοεῖν καὶ ἐπιστρέφειν ἐπὶ τὸν θεόν; cf. Acts 3:9, 11:18, 11:21. For the Old Testament (Septuagint), see, for instance, Jer. 38:18 f.: ... ἐπίστρεψόν με, καὶ ἐπιστρέψω ... ὅτι ὕστερον αἰχμαλωσίας μου μετενόησα ... ἐστέναξα ἐφ' ἡμέρας αἰσχύνης ...; Is. 46:8: ... μετανοήσατε οἱ πεπλανημένοι, ἐπιστρέψατε τῇ καρδίᾳ; cf. E. K. Dietrich, Die Umkehr (Stuttgart, 1936). For ἀποστρέφειν in the meaning of conversion see Ez. 3:19 and Acts 3:26.

[2] See Republic 518C–D and cf. above, p. 47, n. 61. It is true that Plato does not use the terms ἐπιστροφή and ἐπιστρέφειν in this sense, but περιαγωγή, περιστρέφεσθαι, and μεταστρέφεσθαι; see also 525C and 532B. Cf. Jaeger, Paideia II, 295 ff., 417 f., n. 77. A. D. Nock, Conversion (Oxford, 1933) 179 f. and 296, n. to pp. 179 f., has roughly sketched the history of the term ἐπιστροφή and its Latin equivalent conversio; while I can not see that ἐπιστροφή is found in Plato in the meaning of conversion, he does show that it occurs in post-Platonic literature from Epictetus to Proclus; see also P. Aubin, "L'image dans l'œuvre de Plotin," Rech.'s sc. rel. XLI (1953) 373 ff.: Appendix I: 'Επιστρέφειν et 'Επιστροφή; earlier examples, which might have influenced the Septuagint, could probably be found.

[3] Thus Werner Jaeger, in Anz. Gött. CLXXV (1913) 589 ff., against E. Norden, in his review of the latter's Agnostos Theos (Leipzig, Berlin, 1913) 134 ff.

occurrences of the term.[4] The combined use of ἐπιστροφή and μετάνοια in the New Testament contains *in nuce* the Christian doctrine of conversion which according to Catholic tradition also includes repentance, amendment, and satisfaction[5] (for conversion, see also above, Part One, Chapter I, 4, and below, pp. 366 ff.).

For Christians, however, conversion taken as an individual or as a collective act could never be more than a preparation. Christianity offered and demanded more: first of all spiritual regeneration, effected through baptism; secondly, lasting or repeated renewal or reform of the inner man as a continuation and a fulfillment of baptismal regeneration.

The concept of rebirth or regeneration appears most clearly in the Gospel of St. John (3:3 and 3:5),[6] the First Letter of St. Peter (1:3 f.)[7] and, especially, in St. Paul's Letter to Titus (3:5), where the term *palingenesia*, rebirth, is used in conjunction with *anakainosis*, renovation.[8] At least in the Gospel of St. John and in the Letter to Titus there is no doubt that rebirth means spiritual regeneration

---

[4] For anticipations of the biblical concept of *metanoia*, cf. Norden, *Agnostos Theos*, and W. Jaeger's review, also K. Latte, "Schuld und Sünde in der griechischen Religion," *Archiv für Religionswissenschaft* XX (1920–1921) 281, n. 1, Nock, *Conversion* 180, A. H. Dirksen, C.PP.S., *The New Testament Concept of Metanoia* (Diss., Catholic University of America, Washington, D.C., 1932) 88 ff., 165–196. Jaeger and Dirksen rightly stress that even in classical and Hellenistic usage the concept of *metanoia* was not purely intellectual, but could also be ethical.

[5] Dirksen, *Metanoia*, gives a very good survey of the traditional Catholic teaching on conversion, and also of the Protestant doctrines; for the latter cf. H. Pohlmann, *Die Metanoia als Zentralbegriff der christlichen Frömmigkeit* (Untersuchungen zum Neuen Testament XXV, 1938). For the Catholic doctrine of conversion as preparation for justification and sanctification in baptism and thereafter, see also Council of Trent, *Sessio VI, Decretum de Justificatione*, cap. 5, Denziger, *Enchir. Symb.* 286, §797.

[6] John 3:3: Ἀμὴν ἀμὴν λέγω σοι, ἐὰν μή τις γεννηθῇ ἄνωθεν, οὐ δύναται ἰδεῖν τὴν βασιλείαν τοῦ θεοῦ. It does not matter much if ἄνωθεν is to be understood temporally or locally, i.e., if it means "again" or "from above". John 3:5: Ἀμὴν ἀμὴν λέγω σοι, ἐὰν μή τις γεννηθῇ ἐξ ὕδατος καὶ πνεύματος, οὐ δύναται εἰσελθεῖν εἰς τὴν βασιλείαν τοῦ θεοῦ.

[7] 1 Peter 1:3 f.: Εὐλογητὸς ὁ θεὸς . . . ἀναγεννήσας ἡμᾶς εἰς ἐλπίδα ζῶσαν δι' ἀναστάσεως Ἰησοῦ Χριστοῦ. . . .

[8] Tit. 3:5: . . . (Christ) οὐκ ἐξ ἔργων τῶν ἐν δικαιοσύνῃ ἃ ἐποιήσαμεν ἡμεῖς, ἀλλὰ κατὰ τὸ αὐτοῦ ἔλεος ἔσωσεν ἡμᾶς διὰ λουτροῦ παλιγγενεσίας καὶ ἀνακαινώσεως πνεύματος ἁγίου. . . . In Matthew 19:28 Christ promises the Apostles: ἐν τῇ παλιγγενεσίᾳ . . . καθήσεσθε καὶ αὐτοὶ ἐπὶ δώδεκα θρόνους; here *palingenesia* is obviously used in an eschatological sense which is distinct from the meaning in Tit. 3:5.

through baptism: "the water" and the "bath" of rebirth are referred to.[9]

The Christian concept of spiritual sacramental regeneration means that each individual Christian must die with Christ, be reborn in Him, and begin a new life following Him. It is therefore very different from the principal forms of pagan and of Jewish rebirth ideology. It differs profoundly from the religious-political ideas about reborn or renewed Rome as well as from the messianic idea of Israel. It also differs from the rebirth ideas of Graeco-Roman and syncretistic mystery religions in which the element of ethical renewal, so essential for the Christian concept, was weak.[10]

Within the New Testament itself the ideas of regeneration and of reform are closely connected with one another, but nevertheless distinct. Where *anakainosis* and related ideas occur in the Letters of St. Paul, they are an extension as it were of the idea of baptismal rebirth. Their meaning is a more general one, expressing the all-embracing renovation or reform brought about, or to be brought about, in man through adherence to Christ not only in, but also after, conversion and baptism. Beside the general term *anakainosis* (renewal, renovation), the more specific ones *kaine ktisis* (new creature) and *metamorphosis* (transformation, reformation) are used in St. Paul's Epistles. The word "reform" expresses the meaning of all these terms best.[11]

The idea of reform as distinct from conversion does not occur in the Gospels or in the Apocalypse except in so far as it is contained in the ideas of regeneration and resurrection. Nor does it occur

---

[9] Cf. the definition of baptism in the *Roman Catechism* P. 2, c. 2, 9.5: *Sacramentum regenerationis per aquam in verbo* (cf. Tit. 3:5 and Eph. 5:26).

[10] For pagan, Jewish, and Christian (Johannine, Petrine, and Pauline) terminology and ideology of regeneration, see the studies mentioned above of J. Dey, *ΠΑΛΙΓΓΕΝΕΣΙΑ* (Neutestamentliche Abhandlungen XVII, 5, Münster, 1937), and of A. Harnack, *Die Terminologie der Wiedergeburt und verwandter Erlebnisse in der ältesten Kirche* (Texte u. Untersuch. XLII, 2, Leipzig, 1917). See also V. Iacono, "La παλιγγενεσία in S. Paolo e nell' ambiente pagano," *Biblica* XV (1934) 369 ff.; Büchsel, article "παλιγγενεσία," *ThWbNT* I, 685 ff.; O. Procksch, "Wiederkehr und Wiedergeburt," *Das Erbe Martin Luthers . . .* (Leipzig, 1928) 1 ff. Cf. also above, pp. 32 f. and 16 ff., for baptismal regeneration on the one hand and "Renaissance" on the other and p. 33, n. 8, for Christian and pagan *palingenesia*; also p. 40, n. 6, for interrelations between all these concepts and terms.

[11] See above, p. 47, and the Introduction.

explicitly in the Old Testament which however, especially in the Psalms, contains general evocations of the renewal of the earth and man by God, such as those in Psalm 103:30:

Thou shalt send forth thy spirit and they shall be created; and thou shalt renew the face of the earth[12]

or in Psalm 50:12:

Create a clean heart in me, o God, and renew a right spirit within my bowels[13]

or in Psalm 102:5:

Who satisfieth thy desire with good things: thy youth shall be renewed like the eagle's.[14]

These verses, of course, were to be incorporated in early Christian renewal ideology.[15]

The greatest contribution, perhaps, of the Old Testament to Christian ideology of reform was through prophecy and "typology." The prophets not only foretold the coming of Christ, but they also are the great exemplars of all authentic reformers within the Church. St. Thomas Aquinas asserted this relationship between prophecy and reform when he said that the faith has already been founded, but that prophecy never was and never will be wanting for the correction of conduct.[16] Furthermore, all through Christian history typology, the *sacramentum futuri*, the mystery of the expectation and anticipation of

---

[12] Ps. 103:30: Emittes spiritum tuum et creabuntur; et renovabis faciem terrae.

[13] Ps. 50:12: Cor mundum crea in me, Deus, et spiritum rectum innova in visceribus meis.

[14] Ps. 102:5: Qui replet in bonis desiderium tuum: Renovabitur ut aquilae iuventus tua. In this Psalm verse and in its Christian applications the eagle symbol does not remain on the cosmological-vitalistic plane which, otherwise, it often shared with the phoenix; cf. above, p. 21, and below, p. 134.

[15] See, for instance, below, pp. 80, 295, 312, n. 33, 314 f.

[16] Thomas Aquinas, *In Matthaeum* 11 (Venezia, 1775) 135: . . . iam fides fundata est. . . . Sed ad corrigendos mores numquam deficit nec deficiet prophetia. This text is quoted by Y. M.-J. Congar, O.P., *Vraie et fausse reforme dans l'église* (Unam Sanctam XX, Paris, 1950) 219; see the whole chapter "Prophètes et réformateurs," *ibid.* 196 ff. For prophetic ideology of conversion and renewal see, for instance, Jeremiah's Lamentations 5:21: "Convert us, o Lord, to thee and we shall be converted; renew our days as from the beginning"; cf. below, p. 408, n. 28.

Christ and the Church in the Old Testament,[17] acted as a stimulus for further reform in the spirit of the Gospel: the sequence of creation, Incarnation and reform is a fundamental pattern in early Christian and mediaeval historical consciousness and theology of history (see below, pp. 170 ff.).

It remains true however that for St. Paul, as for Christianity in general, prophecy and typology constitute only one, and perhaps not even the most important, aspect of the comprehensive reformation of mankind.[18] The Pauline doctrine of reform or renovation must now be studied from those texts in the Letters to the Romans (12:2), to the Ephesians (4:23), to the Colossians (3:10), and in the Second Letter to the Corinthians (3:18) which have already been discussed from the terminological point of view in the preceding chapter.

In the Letter to the Romans the Apostle warns Christians not to be conformed to this world, but to be transformed or reformed in accordance with the renovation of their minds.[19]

In the Letter to the Ephesians Christ is called a peacemaker between Jews and Gentiles, creating out of the two one new man.[20] He has taught his followers to put off the old man, to be spiritually renewed, and to put on the new man created according to God.[21]

In the Letter to the Colossians St. Paul writes that those regenerated through baptism, that is to say, those buried with Christ and risen in

[17] See, for instance, J. Daniélou S.J., *Sacramentum Futuri: Etudes sur les origines de la typologie biblique* (Paris, 1950).

[18] See, for instance, 1 Cor. 13:2, 13:8 ff., 14:39 f., where prophecy, as everything else, is referred to charity.

[19] Rom. 12:2: καὶ μὴ συσχηματίζεσθε τῷ αἰῶνι τούτῳ, ἀλλὰ μεταμορφοῦσθε (Vulgate: *reformamini*) τῇ ἀνακαινώσει τοῦ νοός . . . Cf. Rom. 8:29 about God predestinating men to be συμμόρφους τῆς εἰκόνος τοῦ υἱοῦ αὐτοῦ. Phil. 3:20 f.: . . . ὃς μετασχηματίσει τὸ σῶμα τῆς ταπεινώσεως ἡμῶν σύμμορφον τῷ σώματι τῆς δόξης αὐτοῦ, refers to the resurrection of man rather than to his reform in this life. Similarly, μετεμορφώθη is used in Matthew 17:2 and Mark 9:2 for the Transfiguration of Christ on Mount Tabor.

[20] Eph. 2:14 ff.: Αὐτὸς γάρ ἐστιν ἡ εἰρήνη ἡμῶν, ὁ ποιήσας τὰ ἀμφότερα ἕν . . . ἵνα τούς. . . . δύο κτίσῃ ἐν αὐτῷ εἰς ἕνα καινὸν ἄνθρωπον. . . .

[21] Eph. 4:21 ff.: εἴ γε αὐτὸν ἠκούσατε καὶ ἐν αὐτῷ ἐδιδάχθητε, καθώς ἐστιν ἀλήθεια ἐν τῷ Ἰησοῦ, ἀποθέσθαι ὑμᾶς κατὰ τὴν προτέραν ἀναστροφὴν τὸν παλαιὸν ἄνθρωπον τὸν φθειρόμενον κατὰ τὰς ἐπιθυμίας τῆς ἀπάτης, ἀνανεοῦσθαι (Vulgate: *renovamini*) δὲ τῷ πνεύματι τοῦ νοὸς ὑμῶν καὶ ἐνδύσασθαι τὸν καινὸν ἄνθρωπον τὸν κατὰ θεὸν κτισθέντα ἐν δικαιοσύνῃ καὶ ὁσιότητι τῆς ἀληθείας.

Him,[22] should strip themselves of the old man and put on the new, him who is renewed unto knowledge according to the image of his creator.[23]

This last passage receives its best elucidation from the parallel ones in the Second Letter to the Corinthians. There it is said in the third chapter that Christians, beholding (mirroring) the glory of the Lord with open face, are reformed or transformed according to the same image from glory to glory as by the spirit of the Lord.[24] In the following chapter Christ is called the image of God[25] and a few verses later the Apostle speaks of the divine illumination of our hearts which is to make known the glory of God in the face of Christ.[26] A little later again, St. Paul says that though our outward man is decomposed continually the inner man is renewed day by day[27] and in chapter five he closes this sequence of thought with the words:

If then any be in Christ a new creature, the old things are passed away, behold all things are made new.[28]

In the Letters to the Colossians and the Corinthians the renovation of the inner man is reformation to the image of God. This linking of reform and image-likeness to God was to remain essential for the Christian reform idea.[29] The conception of image-likeness to God is

[22] Col. 2:12: συνταφέντες αὐτῷ ἐν τῷ βαπτίσματι, ἐν ᾧ καὶ συνηγέρθητε . . .; ibid. 3:1: Εἰ οὖν συνηγέρθητε τῷ Χριστῷ, τὰ ἄνω ζητεῖτε. . . .

[23] Col. 3:9 f.: . . . ἀπεκδυσάμενοι τὸν παλαιὸν ἄνθρωπον σὺν ταῖς πράξεσιν αὐτοῦ καὶ ἐνδυσάμενοι τὸν νέον τὸν ἀνακαινούμενον (Vulgate: novum eum qui renovatur) εἰς ἐπίγνωσιν κατ' εἰκόνα τοῦ κτίσαντος αὐτόν. . . .

[24] 2 Cor. 3:18: ἡμεῖς δὲ πάντες ἀνακεκαλυμμένῳ προσώπῳ τὴν δόξαν Κυρίου κατοπτριζόμενοι τὴν αὐτὴν εἰκόνα μεταμορφούμεθα (Vulgate: transformamur) ἀπὸ δόξης εἰς δόξαν, καθάπερ ἀπὸ Κυρίου πνεύματος. To Col. 3:9 f. and 2 Cor. 3:18 see also 1 Cor. 15:49 (quoted p. 55, n. 34).

[25] Ibid. 4:4: . . . τὸν φωτισμὸν τοῦ εὐαγγελίου τῆς δόξης τοῦ Χριστοῦ, ὅς ἐστιν εἰκὼν τοῦ θεοῦ.

[26] Ibid. 4:6: . . . ὁ θεὸς ὁ εἰπών· ἐκ σκότους φῶς λάμψαι, ὃς ἔλαμψεν ἐν ταῖς καρδίαις ἡμῶν πρὸς φωτισμὸν τῆς γνώσεως τῆς δόξης τοῦ θεοῦ ἐν προσώπῳ ['Ιησοῦ] Χριστοῦ.

[27] Ibid. 4:16: . . . εἰ καὶ ὁ ἔξω ἡμῶν ἄνθρωπος διαφθείρεται, ἀλλ' ὁ ἔσω ἡμῶν ἀνακαινοῦται (Vulgate: renovatur) ἡμέρᾳ καὶ ἡμέρᾳ.

[28] Ibid. 5:17: . . . ὥστε εἴ τις ἐν Χριστῷ, καινὴ κτίσις· τὰ ἀρχαῖα παρῆλθεν, ἰδοὺ γέγονεν καινά. For all these passages cf. E. B. Allo, O.P., Saint Paul: Seconde Épître aux Corinthiens (Paris, 1937) 98 f.

[29] For good accounts of Old Testament and New Testament doctrine of the image of God, see G. Söhngen, "Die biblische Lehre von der Gottebenbildlichkeit des Menschen,"

based, of course, on Genesis 1:26, where God says: "Let us make man to our image and likeness," which is then taken up in the following verse: "And God created man to His own image: to the image of God He created him."[30] Yet St. Paul makes here an important distinction between Christ, who is the image of God,[31] and man who is reformed (as he was created) only *according to* or *in* the image of God,[32] a distinction which again was lasting. The creational image-likeness of man to God, after Genesis 1:26, must have been inseparable in the Apostle's thought from the second biblical account of the creation of man in Genesis 2:7, where it is said that "the Lord God formed man of the slime of the earth and breathed into his face the breath of life, and man became a living soul."[33] In the First Letter to the Corinthians Paul quotes Genesis 2:7 and says that the "choic" and "psychic" Adam—the man of the earthen body and the living soul—came first and that only the "second man," the "last Adam" of the life-giving spirit, that is to say, Christ, came from heaven and is heavenly.[34] Thus it is clear that the image-likeness of Genesis 1:26 cannot be on the same plane as Christ's image relation to the Father, that only the last or second, not the first, Adam is truly divine. Paul seems to have referred God's image in man to his soul—this became

Münchener Theologische Zeitschrift II (1951) 52 ff., and especially W. Hess, O.S.B., "Imago Dei (Gn 1, 26)," *Benediktinische Monatsschrift* XXIX (1953) 371 ff. For an interpretation in scholastic terms of St. Paul's concept of the image, see J. M. Bover, S.J., " 'Imaginis' Notio apud B. Paulum," *Biblica* IV (1923) 174 ff.

[30] Septuagint: καὶ εἶπεν ὁ θεός: ποιήσωμεν ἄνθρωπον κατ᾽ εἰκόνα ἡμετέραν καὶ καθ᾽ ὁμοίωσιν ... καὶ ἐποίησεν ὁ θεὸς τὸν ἄνθρωπον. κατ᾽ εἰκόνα θεοῦ ἐποίησεν αὐτόν. ... Vulgate: et ait: Faciamus hominem ad imaginem et similitudinem nostram. ... Et creavit Deus hominem ad imaginem suam: ad imaginem Dei creavit illum. ...

[31] 2 Cor. 4:4. See also Col. 1:15. In 1 Cor. 11:7 man (ἀνήρ), as distinct from woman, is characterized as εἰκὼν καὶ δόξα θεοῦ ὑπάρχων; perhaps the use of ὑπάρχων instead of ὤν is significant.

[32] Col. 3:10; 2 Cor. 3:18.

[33] Gen. 2:7 (Septuagint): καὶ ἔπλασεν ὁ θεὸς τὸν ἄνθρωπον, χοῦν ἀπὸ τῆς γῆς· καὶ ἐνεφύσησεν εἰς τὸ πρόσωπον αὐτοῦ πνοὴν ζωῆς, καὶ ἐγένετο ὁ ἄνθρωπος εἰς ψυχὴν ζῶσαν.

[34] 1 Cor. 15:45-49: ... οὕτως καὶ γέγραπται· " ἐγένετο " ὁ πρῶτος " ἄνθρωπος " Ἀδὰμ " εἰς ψυχὴν ζῶσαν " (Gen. 2:7), ὁ ἔσχατος Ἀδὰμ εἰς πνεῦμα ζωοποιοῦν. ἀλλ᾽ οὐ πρῶτον τὸ πνευματικόν, ἀλλὰ τὸ ψυχικόν, ἔπειτα τὸ πνευματικόν. ὁ πρῶτος ἄνθρωπος ἐκ γῆς χοϊκός, ὁ δεύτερος ἄνθρωπος ἐξ οὐρανοῦ. οἷος ὁ χοϊκός, τοιοῦτοι καὶ οἱ χοϊκοί, καὶ οἷος ὁ ἐπουράνιος, τοιοῦτοι καὶ οἱ ἐπουράνιοι. καὶ κάθως ἐφορέσαμεν τὴν εἰκόνα τοῦ χοϊκοῦ, φορέσομεν (or φορέσωμεν, exhortative rather than futuric; this seems preferable, cf. Allo's commentary, quoted p. 54, n. 28) καὶ τὴν εἰκόνα τοῦ ἐπουρανίου.

in any case the prevalent patristic tradition[35]—whereas Christ, *the image of God*, in His divinity is spirit, and man can become a heavenly, a spiritual image only through Him.[36] The passage from the First Corinthians perhaps implied Paul's rejection of the widespread *Anthropos* and Adam mysticism of the New Testament period and certainly stands in opposition to all syncretistic speculations about a primal heavenly man who was conceived of as either identical with, or the prototype of, the ancestor of humanity[37] and at the same time as its savior.[38]

The idea of a pre-existent divine *Anthropos* is found, for instance, in the Hermetic Poimandres,[39] in certain gnostic writings,[40] in Philo,[41]

[35] See below, pp. 85 ff.

[36] In this respect, see also G. Kittel, article "εἰκών," ThWbNT, II, 394 f.

[37] Cf. C. H. Kraeling, *Anthropos and Son of Man: A Study in the Religious Syncretism of the Hellenistic Orient* (Columbia University Oriental Studies XXV, New York, 1927). This book gives an excellent survey and on the whole a sound evaluation of the much disputed Iranian and Indian derivation of essential trends in syncretistic, Hellenized Jewish, and New Testament thought. The main works of the "Iranian-Indian" school are W. Bousset, *Hauptprobleme der Gnosis* (Göttingen, 1907), W. Bousset, *Die Religion des Judentums im späthellenistischen Zeitalter*, 3rd ed. by H. Gressmann (Tübingen, 1926), R. Reitzenstein, *Die hellenistischen Mysterienreligionen*, 3rd ed. (Leipzig, Berlin, 1927), idem, *Das iranische Erlösungsmysterium* (Bonn, 1921), R. Reitzenstein and H. H. Schaeder, *Studien zum antiken Synkretismus aus Iran und Griechenland* (Studien der Bibliothek Warburg VII, Leipzig, Berlin, 1926). See the critical remarks of J. de Menasce, "The Mysteries and the Religion of Iran," *The Mysteries: Papers from the Eranos Yearbooks* II (Bollingen Series XXX, 2, New York, 1955) 135 ff., and of G. Quispel, "Der gnostische Anthropos und die jüdische Tradition," *Eranos-Jahrbuch* XXII (1954) 195 ff. Cf. also M. Jonas, *Gnosis und spätantiker Geist* I (Forschungen zur Religion und Literatur des Alten und Neuen Testaments LI [Neue Folge XXXIII] Göttingen, 1934).

[38] A good account of the identifications of "Urmensch" and savior in these myths is given by E. Käsemann, *Leib und Leib Christi* (Beiträge zur historischen Theologie IX, Tübingen, 1933) 50 ff.

[39] *Poimandres* 12–15 (*Corpus Hermeticum* I), Scott, *Hermet*. I, 120 ff., cf. *Notes, ibid*. II, 1 ff., *Addenda* (B. A. S. Ferguson), *ibid*. IV, 354 ff. See also Nock and Festugière, *Corp. Hermet*. I, *Traité* I, pp. 10 ff. Cf. Reitzenstein, *Poimandres* (Leipzig, 1904) with edition on pp. 328 ff.; Reitzenstein and Schaeder, *Synkretismus* 8 ff. and 154 ff. (edition); Kraeling, *Anthropos* 42 ff.

[40] Cf. Bousset, *Gnosis* 160 ff.; Reitzenstein and Schaeder, *Synkretismus* 26, 104 ff.; Kraeling, *Anthropos* 38 ff.

[41] See H. A. Wolfson, *Philo* I (Cambridge, Mass., 1947) 310, E. Bréhier, *Les idées philosophiques et religieuses de Philon d'Aléxandrie*, 3rd ed. (Etudes de philosophie médiévale III, Paris, 1950) 121 ff., and cf. below, p. 57, n. 47; cf. also Reitzenstein, *Mysterienreligionen* 347; Bousset-Gressmann, *Judentum* 352 f.

and later in Manicheeism.[42] Related conceptions of a "greater" Adam occur, for instance, in Naassene[43] and Mandean[44] sources, and in late Jewish literature down to the Adam Kadmon of the Cabala.[45] Essential characteristics of these figures may ultimately originate in the Iranian myth of the god-man Gayomart,[46] though this factor must not be stressed too much at the cost of Hellenic (Platonist-Stoic) and Jewish elements. All these ideas were in any case fundamentally incompatible with the Christian teaching of the single Incarnation of God in man which took place not before, but within, the earthly course of the human race. For Paul and for the whole New Testament only Christ is Son of God and Son of Man at the same time.[47]

---

[42] See Kraeling, *Anthropos* 17 ff., with further literature.

[43] For these, cf., especially, Reitzenstein and Schaeder, *Synkretismus* 104 ff.; Kraeling, *Anthropos*, 47 ff.

[44] Cf. Kraeling, *Anthropos* 55 ff., with further literature.

[45] Bousset-Gressmann, *Judentum* 352 ff.; Kraeling, *Anthropos* 128 ff.

[46] *Gayo* (= ζωή, *vita*)-*Maretan* (= *mortalis*). See, especially, Bousset, *Gnosis* 202 ff.; Reitzenstein and Schaeder, *Synkretismus* 18 ff., 214 ff.; Kraeling, *Anthropos* 85 ff.

[47] Cf. Allo, *Corinthiens* 426 ff., to 1 Cor. 15:45 ff., on the divergence of Paul's thought from all *Anthropos* speculation. It is impossible to tell with certainty whether the Apostle intended to refute such theories explicitly. (Allo points rightly to the late origin of Jewish Adam mysticism; cf. also H. L. Strack and P. Billerbeck, *Kommentar zum Neuen Testament erläutert aus Talmud und Midrasch* III [München, 1926] 477 f.) Did Paul have Philo in mind? In the latter's thought, the pre-existent "ideal" man, more Platonistic than Iranian in character, overlaps with the "generic" heavenly man, who with the "generic" earthly man forms the historical Adam (cf. the valuable dissertation of B. A. Stegmann, *Christ, the "Man from Heaven"* [The Catholic University of America New Testament Studies VI, Washington, D. C., 1927], who however seems to draw too sharp a distinction between Philo's conceptions of "generic" and "ideal"; see also below, p. 175). In any case, neither Philo's ideal man nor his generic man have anything in common with St. Paul's idea of Christ. (E. Käsemann, *Leib Christi* 137 ff., in part following H. Schlier, *Christus und die Kirche im Epheserbrief* [Tübingen, 1930], seems greatly to overrate Gnostic influence on St. Paul's Christology and anthropology, and, especially, on 2 Cor. 3:18 and Col. 3:10.) It is quite certain that for the Apostle, Christ, the second Adam, did not exist, as man, before the first Adam (1 Cor. 15:46). That Paul intended to make this clear is recognized also by Bousset and Gressmann, *Judentum* 353, and to some extent even by Reitzenstein, *Erlösungsmysterium* 107 ff., and *Mysterienreligionen* 244 ff.; cf. Kraeling, *Anthropos* 161. There is also no need to explain the designation "Son of Man," so often used in the Synoptic Gospels and in the Gospel of St. John by Christ for Himself (for instance, Matthew 8:20, 9:6, 10:23, 11:19, 12:8, 12:40, 13:41, 16:27 f., 17:9, 24:27, 30, 37, 44, 25:31, 26:2, John 1:51, 3:13 f., 5:27, 6:27, 54, 62, 8:28, 12:23, 13:31) and attributed to Christ also in the Acts of the Apostles (7:56) and in the Apocalypse (1:13, 14:14), as an echo of the *Anthropos* idea. It was surely essential for Christ's own message, and for the testimony of the Apostles, that the Son of God was also Son of Man. Jesus most probably knew and

In this connection, it must also be noted that St. Paul, while he sees a great difference between εἰκών and κατ' εἰκόνα, uses only the word image, εἰκών, not similitude, ὁμοίωσις. He obviously does not know of a distinction between the terms image and likeness[48] —such a difference, in fact, had hardly been envisaged in the book of Genesis itself.[49] A distinction was soon to appear however in patristic

considered as prophetic of His Incarnation Daniel 7 : 13 : "And lo, one like the son of man came with the clouds of heaven, and he comes even to the Ancient of days: and they presented him before him" (thus the Septuagint, cf. also Dan. 10 : 16; the Hebrew and Aramaean texts have "like a man"); perhaps he knew also the similar but richer vision in the apocryphal *Enoch* I, especially 46, 1 ff., 48, 1 ff., 62, 7 ff. (this is the "Ethiopic Enoch" the Aramaeic original of which probably dates from the beginning of the first century B.C.; ed. and trans. J. Flemming and L. Radermacher, *GCS* V; also R. H. Charles, *Apocrypha and Pseudoepigrapha of the Old Testament* [Oxford, 1913]). In how far the terminology of these texts was influenced by the *Anthropos* idea is not of relevance here (cf. for the problem Kraeling, *Anthropos* 130 ff.; R. Otto, *Reich Gottes und Menschensohn* [München, 1934] 141 ff., 335 ff.).

[48] Similarly James 3 : 9 in speaking of the image-likeness of man to God uses only *one* term, namely καθ' ὁμοίωσιν..

[49] Many modern exegetes consider that the two expressions צֶלֶם (εἰκών, imago, image) and דְּמוּת (ὁμοίωσις, similitudo, likeness) form a hendiadys. See M. Hetzenauer, O.C., *Commentarius in Librum Genesis* (Gratz, Wien, 1910) 17 ff.; A. Dillman, *Die Genesis*, 6th ed. (Leipzig, 1892) 31; E. Palis, article "Adam (Histoire)," *DBibl* I, 171; G. v. Rad. article "εἰκών," *ThWbNT* II, 389. Certain modern exegetes interpret the term "likeness" in Gen. 1 : 26 as a "weakening" specification of the term "image," the latter being understood as a physical effigy: the sense of Gen. 1 : 26 then would be that man is a physical image of God, but not substantially equal, only similar to Him. Cf. P. Humbert, *Etudes sur le récit du paradis et de la chute dans la Genèse* (Mémoires de l'Université de Neuchâtel, Neuchâtel, 1940) 153 ff., L. Koehler, "Die Grundstelle der Imago-Dei-Lehre," *Theologische Zeitschrift* IV (1948) 16 ff. (where the image relation is referred to man's upright posture— for classical and patristic roots of this interpretation, see, for instance, my article "The Philosophical Anthropology of St. Gregory of Nyssa," *Dumb. Oaks Pap.* XII [Cambridge, Mass., 1958]), K. L. Schmidt, "Homo Imago Dei im Alten und Neuen Testament," *Eranos-Jahrbuch* XV (1947) 166 ff., Hess, "Imago Dei" 377 f. As far as a physical image-likeness between God and man is concerned, such interpretations, however well supported philologically, must be carefully qualified in view of the nonanthropomorphic concept of God in the book of Genesis; here the interpretation of Gen. 1:26 ff. by G. v. Rad, *Genesis: A Commentary*, trans. J. H. Marks (Philadelphia, 1961) 55 ff., seems to fall short, cf. rather B. Vawter, C. M., *A Path through Genesis* (New York, 1956) 44 f.; there is little doubt that "the Hebrew author . . . saw man's similarity to God at least partially fulfilled in his having been created to rule over the earth" (Vawter, *Genesis* 45) and that this rulership was seen founded on man's spiritual rather than on his physical nature (Hess, "Imago Dei" 383 f.). The full conception of human image-likeness to God through the higher, the rational, part of the soul, through spirit rather than body, seems however to have been only a later, and especially a Christian, realization (cf. Vawter, *Genesis*, and below

thought and this too was to have important consequences for the development of the idea of reform.[50]

The Pauline reformation of man to the image of God then consists in the true knowledge of *the* image of God, Christ, such knowledge to include the practice of Christian virtues, the whole life according to Christ. This reform leads to a complete renovation of the inner man which amounts to a new creation of man. Thus in the Epistles of St. Paul the concept of reform-renovation is seen as a continuation of rebirth in baptism and at the same time as a *repetition* as it were of the *creation* of man.[51] This doctrine is an essential part of the New Testament. In Catholic tradition, as reassumed by the Council of Trent, it is an element of the doctrine of justification and sanctification. Justification, which must be preceded by conversion,[52] is impossible without baptismal regeneration;[53] and justification in

pp. 85 ff.). K. Barth, *Die kirchliche Dogmatik* III, 1 (Zollikon, Zürich, 1945) 204 ff., and III, 2 (1948) 390 f., as well known, propounds the ingenious but untraditional view that man's image-likeness to God is the analogy between the personal human "I-thou" relationship (especially, between man and woman, the Church and Christ) and the interpersonal life in the Trinity; on this point, see also p. 238, n. 48; E. Brunner, *Der Mensch im Widerspruch* (Zürich, 1941), and *Dogmatics* II, trans. by O. Wyon (Philadelphia, 1952), and similarly D. Cairns, *The Image of God in Man* (New York, 1953), hold that man's image-likeness to God is, since Adam's fall, a mere "point of contact" or a mere "formal" relation of responsibility to God and fellow man. Brunner and Cairns as well as Barth, following early Protestantism, oppose the Catholic tradition that man's original image-likeness to God is related to the rational part of his soul, that this rationality is a value, and that it has not been completely destroyed by original sin. See on the contrary the emphasis on the rationality of the "image" to be found already in early Christian liturgical prayers, as pointed out in the important study by W. Dürig, *Imago: Ein Beitrag zur Terminologie und Theologie der Römischen Liturgie* (Münchener Theologische Studien II, 5, München, 1952) 117 ff.

[50] See below, pp. 83 ff. Most Catholic and Protestant theologians are in agreement today concerning the introduction of this distinction into Christian theology by Irenaeus (see below, Part Two, Chapter III, 2), who in this respect developed rather than merely continued scriptural thought; see the good survey of opinions in Dürig, *Imago* 82 ff., and cf. especially H. M. Somers, S.J., "The Riddle of a Plural (Genesis 1, 26)," *Folia* IX (1955) 63 ff., also R. McL. Wilson, "The Early History of the Exegesis of Gen. 1, 26," *Stud. Patr.* I, 420 ff., and Hess, "Imago Dei" 390.

[51] Cf. R. C. Trench, *Synonyms of the New Testament*, 9th ed. (reprinted Grand Rapids, Mich., 1948) 64 f.

[52] See above, pp. 32 ff.

[53] Council of Trent, *Sessio VI, Decretum de Iustificatione*, cap. 4, (Denzinger, *Enchir. Symb.* 285 §796): (justification is a) translatio ab eo statu, in quo homo nascitur filius primi Adae, in statum gratiae et "adoptionis filiorum" (Rom. 8:15) Dei per secundum Adam Iesum

baptism does not only mean remission of sins, but also "sanctification and renovation of the inner man," [54] in which the justified are "renewed day by day" (2 Cor. 4:16), in which they grow and are more fully justified (whence the term "second justification"). [55] For, as St. Paul himself had written to Timothy: ". . . continue thou in those things which thou hast learned. . . . All scripture inspired of God is profitable to teach, to reprove, to correct (πρὸς ἐπανόρθωσιν), to instruct (πρὸς παιδείαν) in justice, that the man of God may be perfect, furnished to every good work" (cf. 2 Tim. 3:14 and 16 f.). [56]

Christum Salvatorem nostrum; quae quidem translatio post Evangelium promulgatum sine lavacro regenerationis aut eius voto fieri non potest, sicut scriptum est: "Nisi quis renatus fuerit ex aqua et Spiritu Sancto, non potest introire in regnum Dei" (John 3:5).

[54] *Ibid.* cap. 7 (Denzinger, *Enchir. Symb.* 287 §799): . . . iustificatio . . . non est sola peccatorum remissio sed et sanctificatio et renovatio interioris hominis. . . .

[55] *Ibid.* cap. 10 (*loc. cit.*, 289 f. §803): Sic ergo iustificati et "amici Dei" ac "domestici" (John 15:15, Eph. 2:19) facti, "euntes de virtute in virtutem" (Ps. 83:8), "renovantur" (ut Apostolus inquit) "de die in diem" (2 Cor. 4:16), hoc est, "mortificando membra carnis" (Col. 3:5) suae et "exhibendo ea arma iustitiae" (Rom. 6:13, 19) in sanctificationem per observationem mandatorum Dei et Ecclesiae: in ipsa iustitia per Christi gratiam accepta, "cooperante fide bonis operibus" (James 2:22), crescunt atque magis iustificantur, sicut scriptum est: "Qui iustus est, iustificetur adhuc" (Apoc. 22:11), et iterum: "Ne verearis usque ad mortem iustificari" (Eccli. 18:22) et rursus: "Videtis quoniam ex operibus iustificatur homo et non ex fide tantum" (James 2:24). Hoc vero iustitiae incrementum petit sancta Ecclesia, cum orat: "Da nobis, Domine, fidei, spei et caritatis augmentum" (cf. *Missale Romanum*, Collect for the thirteenth Sunday after Pentecost). Cf. J.-M. Lagrange, O.P., *Saint Paul: Epître aux Romains* (Paris, 1916) 140 f., about St. Paul's conception of justification as an initial act, whereas sanctification develops continually (second justification); also F. Prat, S.J., *La théologie de saint Paul*, 22nd ed., II (Paris, 1937) 302, J. Huby, S.J., *Mystiques paulinienne et johannique* (Paris, 1946) 40, 73 f. Furthermore, J. van der Meersch, article "Grâce (habituelle ou sanctifiante)," *DThC* VI, 1604 ff., J. Rivière, article "Justification," *ibid.* VIII, especially 2074. As well known, the doctrine of justification and sanctification (sanctifying grace) is one of the principal points of difference between Catholics and Protestants. Early Protestant doctrine, at least, cannot place much weight on the Pauline idea of postbaptismal renovation-reformation (see above, pp. 33 f.). This can still be seen, for instance, in J. Behm's article "ἀνακαινόω," *ThWbNT* III, 454 f. A Lutheran revision of Protestant *imago* and reform ideas, which comes much closer to the Catholic (especially the original Augustinian) tradition is found in F. K. Schumann, "Imago Dei," *Imago Dei: Beiträge zur theologischen Anthropologie . . . Gustav Krüger . . . dargebracht* (Giessen, 1932) 167 ff.

[56] For ἐπανόρθωσις and its Vulgate translation, *corripere*, in patristic reform ideology cf. above, p. 46, and below, p. 313. The verses from 2 Tim. establish a substantial link between the Greek concept of *paideia* (cf. Jaeger's *Paideia*) and Christian ideology of reform. For

In St. Paul and in Catholic theology, rebirth in baptism includes the germs of all later acts of reform; [57] it is the beginning, not the end, of the road for a Christian, nor does it exclude the possibility of relapses. Permanent or repeated renewal of the soul is necessary [58] and is made possible through the presence of the Holy Ghost in the soul. [59] This "multiple" renewal, which has found specific dogmatic formulations in the doctrines of postbaptismal sanctification and of penance, [60] is expressed also in the more general idea of the reform of man to the image of God. This idea too concerned first and foremost the individual, but in addition it proved eminently well adapted to reach beyond personal spiritual renewal and to meet universal needs in given historical situations. This so to speak "historical" aspect of the Christian idea of reform was never fixed dogmatically to the same extent as personal sanctification and penance, though in a sense the reform idea is a facet also of the doctrine of the Church as the Body of Christ: perennial and essentially immutable it, nevertheless, needs reform for its life and growth. [61] In the history of the reform idea itself

paideia in Greek patristic thought see W. Jaeger, Paideia II, 414, n. 39a, idem, Humanism and Theology (Aquinas Lecture, Marquette University, Milwaukee, 1943) 63, idem, Two Rediscovered Works of Ancient Christian Literature: Gregory of Nyssa and Macarius (Leiden, 1954) 12 f., 32 ff., 70 ff., especially 108 ff., idem, "Von Affen und wahren Christen," Varia Variorum 161 ff., especially 164; for Augustine and the connotations of reform in his conception of doctrina christiana see below, pp. 373 ff.

[57] Sanctification is contained already in baptism and justification (cf. 1 Cor. 6:11, where ἡγιάσθητε is the middle term between ἀπελούσασθε and ἐδικαιώθητε), reform-renovation in baptismal rebirth (cf. Titus 3:5).

[58] See 1 Cor. 10:12; 2 Tim. 2:19; Rom. 5:2; cf. F. Amiot, L'enseignement de saint Paul, 2nd ed., I (Paris, 1938) 318.

[59] See above, p. 54 to 2 Cor. 3:18; also Rom. 8:2, 8:14 ff., Eph. 3:16, Rom. 5:5. Cf. Amiot, Saint Paul I, 296 f., 302 ff., 318 f.

[60] Council of Trent, Sessio XIV, Doctrina de Sacramento Poenitentiae cap. 2 (Denzinger, Enchir. Symb. 313 §895): . . . "Per baptismum" enim "Christum induentes" (Gal. 3:27) nova prorsus in illo efficimur creatura, plenam et integram peccatorum omnium remissionem consequentes: ad quam tamen novitatem et integritatem per sacramentum poenitentiae sine magnis nostris fletibus et laboribus, divina id exigente iustitia, pervenire nequaquam possumus.

[61] For the doctrine of the Church's growth toward quantitative and qualitative plenitude, see Eph. 1:22 f., Col. 3:11, 1 Cor. 15:28 f., and Eph. 3:17 f., 4:12 f.; cf. Amiot, Saint Paul II, 8 f., 29, I, 232 f. For the relation of the Christian reform idea to the doctrine of the Body of Christ, both ecclesiological and eucharistic, see also above, p. 32, and below, pp. 98, 268 ff., 280 f., 294 f., 311.

the dogmatically "undefined" aspect of reform prevailed and the idea, while it always remained basically personal, gradually assumed the character also of supraindividual, communal renovation. The idea of the reform of man to the image and likeness of God became the inspiration of all reform movements in early and mediaeval Christianity.

CHAPTER III

THE IDEA OF REFORM IN GREEK CHRISTIAN THOUGHT OF THE PATRISTIC PERIOD

In attempting to follow the course of an idea as complex as that of reform through the wide realms of patristic literature one cannot strive for anything like completeness in the selection of authors and texts.[1] The present chapter on eastern Christian patristic thought will be restricted to the Greek Fathers, except for a few remarks on St. Ephraem, and to the discussion of three aspects of the history of the reform idea which seem to be of great significance both in the eastern and, in a different way, in the western tradition.[2] These three facets of the idea of reform are: the return to Paradise, the recovery of man's lost image-likeness to God, and the representation on earth of the heavenly Basileia.[3]

1. THE RETURN TO PARADISE

And the Lord God had planted a Paradise of pleasure from the beginning; wherein he placed man whom he had formed.

After Adam and Eve had disobeyed God's command by eating from the tree of knowledge of good and evil God sent man

out of the Paradise of pleasure to till the earth from which he was taken. And he cast out Adam and placed before the Paradise of pleasure Cherubims, and a flaming sword, to keep the way to the tree of life.

---

[1] Some patristic terms of reform ideology have been touched upon in Chapter II of Part Two.

[2] For the latter, see Chapters IV and V of Part Two.

[3] Compare with this the corresponding sections on "Innocence and Reform," on "The Image of God in Man," and on the "Civitas Dei," in Chapter V, 1, 3, and 7 of Part Two.

These verses of the Book of Genesis[4] encompass man's original felicity and his subsequent exile and misery which resulted from original sin. Man's attempts to reform his post-paradisiac condition could therefore be conceived of as a return to Paradise.

This conception was first of all eschatological, envisaging in various ways man's sojourn after death in a Paradise the localization of which remained somewhat uncertain, but which ever since patristic times could be thought of in two ways: either as terrestrial, though separated from the inhabited earth, or as outside (above) the earth, as heavenly.[5] Early Christian speculation on an extraterrestrial, supraterrestrial Paradise appealed to the authority of Holy Scripture itself. In Genesis 2:7 f. it is said that God created man from earth and then placed him in Paradise; this was often considered as an inference that Paradise is not on earth. According to Luke 23:42 f., when the good thief had "said to Jesus: 'Lord, remember me when thou shalt come into thy kingdom,'" the Savior replied: "Amen, I say to thee, this day thou

---

[4] Gen. 2:8 and 3:23 f., Douay translation; similarly, the Vulgate, Gen. 2:8, has: *paradisum voluptatis a principio*, and Gen. 3:23: *de paradiso voluptatis*; the Septuagint translation has: ἐκ τοῦ παραδείσου τῆς τρυφῆς in Gen. 3:23, but παράδεισον ἐν Ἐδέμ κατὰ ἀνατολάς in Gen. 2:8. The Hebrew "Eden" was, perhaps, meant as a geographical name and instead of "in the beginning" one should, perhaps, understand "down in the east" with the Septuagint and the Greek Fathers; cf., for instance, the translation of the Old Testament by R. A. Knox, I (New York, 1948) 3, n. 1.

[5] Cf. H. R. Patch, *The Other World according to Descriptions in Medieval Literature* (Cambridge, Mass., 1950) 80 ff., 134 ff., and J. Daniélou, S.J., " Terre et paradis chez les pères de l'église," *Eranos-Jahrbuch* XXII (1953) 433 ff. See also the extensive study of Ildefonse Ayer de Vuippens, O.M. Cap., "Où plaça-t-on le paradis terrestre?," *Etudes Franciscaines* XXXVI (1924), 117 ff., 371 ff., 561 ff., XXXVII (1925) 21 ff., 113 ff. (reprinted in book form under the title *Le paradis terrestre au troisième ciel* [Paris, 1925]). This study however suffers from the author's too rigid thesis that Paradise and Kingdom of God were *generally* kept distinct from one another by the Fathers. This is surely an exaggeration; see also p. 65, n. 6, and cf. the review of E. Peterson, in *Theologische Literaturzeitung*, LII (1927) 78 ff. It seems that P. Ildefonse did not sufficiently consider that if a Father speaks of Paradise in one place and of the Kingdom in another this often does not in the least mean that he wanted to distinguish the two conceptions from one another. Cf. the articles of P. Bernard, "ciel," *DThC* II, 2, 2474 ff., of J, Jeremias, "παράδεισος," *ThWbNT* V, 763 ff., and of H. Leclercq," "paradis," *DACL* XIII, 2, 1578 ff., the latter, especially, for representations of Paradise in early Christian art. See furthermore L. Atzberger, *Die christliche Eschatologie in den Stadien ihrer Offenbarung im Alten und Neuen Testament* (Freiburg i. B., 1890), idem, *Geschichte der christlichen Eschatologie in der vornicänischen Zeit* (ibid., 1896), J. Feldmann, *Paradies und Sündenfall* (Münster, 1913), H. Bietenhard, *Die himmlische Welt im Urchristentum und Spätjudentum* (Tübingen, 1951) 161 ff.

shalt be with me in Paradise." This Gospel text has always been crucial with respect to the exegetical problem whether the Kingdom of Heaven, the Kingdom of God, should be identified with, or distinguished from, Paradise. Some Fathers did hold that the former is superior to the latter.[6] Regardless of this particular question it is certain that in the early Christian period the ideas of paradisiac and heavenly bliss easily coalesced. That the early Christians could think of after-life as taking place in a Paradise-like, that is to say, in a garden-like, region is illustrated, for instance, by the *Passion of Perpetua and*

[6] See below, pp. 72 ff., on Origen, and especially pp. 143 ff., on St. Ambrose, though even these Fathers do not always make this distinction (cf. p. 145, n. 61). Of the other references given by P. de Vuippens few support his thesis. So, for instance, Paulinus of Nola clearly does *not* distinguish the *regnum coeleste* from Paradise: the good thief (Luke 23 : 42 f.) according to him obtains access to both; cf. *Carm.* XXXI, 133 f., *CSEL* XXX, 312. Very interesting in this respect is St. Ephraem's *Eighth Hymn on Paradise*; see the Latin translation and commentary in E. Beck, O.S.B., *Ephraems Hymnen über das Paradies* (Studia Anselmiana XXVI, Roma, 1951) 77 ff. For Ephraem, Paradise is identical with the Kingdom of Heaven, in which the just will dwell for ever only after the resurrection of their bodies; this is why Ephraem assumes that the soul of the good thief of Luke 23:43, whose body (as that of all other men) will not rise until the end of times, cannot be truly in Paradise, but only in a Pre-Paradise. On the other hand, already Clement of Alexandria can say of redeemed man: ὁ ἐκ τοῦ παραδείσου πέσων μείζων ὑπακοῆς ἆθλον οὐρανοὺς ἀπολαμβάνει (*Protrepticus* XI, 111, 3, *GCS, Clem. Alex.* I, 2nd ed., 79, 11, 5 f.). Among the Greek Fathers, St. John Chrysostom seems to come closest to St. Ambrose in emphasizing that the Kingdom of God, which because of Christ's redemptive sacrifice on the Cross will be open to man after the resurrection of the bodies, is something better even than Paradise; see *In Genesim sermo VII*, 5, *PG* LIV, 614 (on the occasion of a reference to Luke 23 : 42 f.): οὐ γὰρ εἰς παράδεισον ἐπαγγέλλεται εἰσαγαγεῖν ἡμᾶς ὁ Θεός, ἀλλ' εἰς αὐτὸν τὸν οὐρανὸν οὐδὲ βασιλείαν παραδείσου, ἀλλὰ βασιλείαν οὐρανῶν ἐκήρυξεν. . . . 'Απώλεσας μὲν γὰρ παράδεισον, ἔδωκε δέ σοι ὁ Θεὸς τὸν οὐρανόν . . . τοῦ Θεοῦ πρὸς μείζονα ἀεὶ τιμήν ἡμᾶς ἀνάγοντος. This whole problem is connected with that of the relation between the seventh and the eighth (metahistorical) world ages—cf. above, pp. 28 f, and below, pp. 222 ff.—and with the question, not yet clearly answered by the Fathers, whether the just have the full beatific vision of God between their death and the resurrection of their bodies (cf. below, p. 230). The Fathers seem to depend here to some extent on Jewish late ancient distinctions, found in the Old Testament Apocrypha and Pseudepigrapha and in Rabbinical literature, of an only provisional beatitude of the just immediately after death and of a final beatitude after the coming of the Messiah and the Last Judgment; on these Jewish views, see H. L. Strack and P. Billerbeck, *Kommentar zum Neuen Testament erläutert aus Talmud und Midrasch* IV, 2 (München, 1928) 799 f., Exkurs 29: "Diese Welt, die Tage des Messias und die zukünftige Welt" (especially pp. 804–815, 816–821, 968 ff.) and *ibid.* IV, 2, 1016 ff., Exkurs 31: "Sche'ol, Gehinnom und Gan 'Eden" (especially pp. 1032 ff., 1118 ff., 1130 ff.); see also Th. Zahn, *Das Evangelium des Lucas* (Kommentar zum Neuen Testament III, 2 [Leipzig, 1913]), 703 ff., on distinctions between Paradise and Kingdom at the time of Jesus.

Felicitas[7] and by certain paintings in the Catacombs, reliefs on sarcophagi,[8] and mosaics in basilicas. But heaven could be conceived also as a holy city, the heavenly Jerusalem (Apocalypse 21),[9] or as a succession of planetary and superplanetary spheres.[10] Even those Fathers who distinguished the supreme Kingdom of God from Paradise might place the latter in a lower sphere of heaven, perhaps, the third heaven of St. Paul's rapture. On the other hand, as already suggested, there also existed a strong tradition which placed Paradise not in heaven, but in some normally inaccessible part of the earth,[11] which might become the goal of man's search and in a literal as well as metaphorical way the object of his dreams. This tradition is both "geographical"[12] and visionary and not infrequently reminiscent of the Elysium,[13] the Golden Age,[14] the millennium.[15] It reaches from visions and journeys or pilgrimages of early Christian eastern

[7] Ed. C. J. M. J. van Beek, *Flor. Patr.* XLIII. For the identification of Paradise and heaven in early Christian inscriptions see, for instance, C. Mohrmann, *Die altchristliche Sondersprache in den Sermones des hl. Augustinus* I (Nijmegen, 1932) 132.

[8] Cf. H. U. v. Schoenebeck, "Die christlichen Paradeisossarkophage," *Rivista di Archeologia Cristiana* XIV (1937) 289 ff.

[9] Cf. de Vuippens, "Paradis terrestre," R. Knopf, "Die Himmelsstadt," *Neutestamentliche Studien G. Heinrici zu seinem 70. Geburtstag* . . . (Untersuchungen zum Neuen Testament VI, Leipzig, 1914) 231 ff. See also below, pp. 242 ff.

[10] See L. Gry, "Séjours et habitats divins d'après les apocryphes de l'ancien testament," *Revue des sciences philosophiques et théologiques* IV (1910) 694 ff., H. Schlier, *Christus und die Kirche im Epheserbrief* (Tübingen, 1930) Chapter 1: "Die Himmelfahrt des Erlösers."

[11] Cf. F. Kampers, *Mittelalterliche Sagen vom Paradies und vom Holze des Kreuzes Christi* (Köln, 1897) 46 ff., 56 ff. Some phases of this tradition from St. Augustine to Dante are now conveniently found in the paper of C. S. Singleton, "Stars over Eden," *Annual Report of the Dante Society [of America]* LVII (1957) 1 ff.

[12] For geographical identifications of Paradise down to Christopher Columbus cf., for instance, L. Olschki, *Storia letteraria delle scoperte geografiche* (Firenze, 1937); also A. Graf, *Miti, leggende e superstizioni del Medio Evo* (Torino, 1925): "Il mito del Paradiso terrestre."

[13] For the Homeric Elysium and other Greek, Roman, and Celtic abodes of the blest, see, for instance, A. Rüegg, *Die Jenseitsvorstellungen vor Dante und die übrigen literarischen Voraussetzungen der "Divina Commedia"* I (Einsiedeln, Köln, 1945) and Graf, *Miti*.

[14] See above, Part One, Chapter I, 1.

[15] The influence of millenarian ideas on the conception of Paradise was to remain a permanent factor. In the early Christian period, Irenaeus (see below, p. 69) and also Tertullian may be mentioned, and especially Ephraem who transferred the characteristics of the millennium (extraordinary fertility, etc.) to his description of a "Pre-Paradise" (concerning which see also above, p. 65, n. 8); cf. Beck, *Ephraems Hymnen über das Paradies* 113 f.

hermits (*Historia monachorum*)[16] and from mediaeval Irish literature such as the *Voyages of Bran* and *St. Brendan*, the *Visions of Adamnan* and *Tundal*,[17] to Dante's terrestrial Paradise on the mountain of Purgatory, which in the *Divine Comedy*, *Purgatorio* XXVIII ff., forms the transition from Purgatory to the astral-celestial and supracelestial *Paradiso*.

The foregoing remarks have, it is hoped, cleared the way for discussion of that aspect of the idea of return to Paradise which has the most immediate bearing upon the history of reform ideology in general. The early Christian age not only knew of a Paradise in which man had dwelt at the beginning and to which he may return after death, but also believed in the possibility of a mystical anticipation of such return during man's terrestrial life. For Paradise was not an exclusively "archeological" and eschatological idea; neither was the mystical return idea identical with "quests" for Paradise as those mentioned above or even with Dante's vision of the terrestrial and celestial Paradise (though there did of course exist some relationship between the visionary and the mystical ideas of the return).[18] The fountainhead of early Christian mysticism, in so far as it was centered around pre-eschatological return to Paradise, was the Second Letter to the Corinthians (12:2 ff.), where St. Paul had told of his rapture to the third heaven and to Paradise through which he experienced an anticipation in this life of the mysteries beyond it.[19] Though the full

---

[16] See R. Reitzenstein, *Historia Monachorum und Historia Lausiaca* (Göttingen, 1916) 173 ff.

[17] See Rüegg, *Jenseitsvorstellungen* I, 314 ff. For the ascetic elements in early Christian and mediaeval ξενιτεία and *peregrinatio* see H. Frh. v. Campenhausen, *Die asketische Heimatlosigkeit im altkirchlichen und frühmittelalterlichen Mönchtum* (Sammlung gemeinverständlicher Vorträge und Schriften aus dem Gebiet der Theologie und Religionsgeschichte CXLIX, Tübingen, 1930); cf. also below, p. 241, n. 10.

[18] For the deep significance of Dante's clear distinction between a terrestrial and a celestial Paradise—which makes his idea of return to Paradise quite different from patristic conceptions eastern or western—see now the Dante chapter in E. H. Kantorowicz, *The King's Two Bodies* (Princeton, 1957) 451 ff.

[19] See A. Stolz, O.S.B., *The Doctrine of Spiritual Perfection*, trans. from the German, *Theologie der Mystik*, by A. Williams, O.S.B. (St. Louis, London, 1938) 13 ff., 24 ff., where the great importance of this text for Christian mystical experience is rightly stressed (cf. also below, p. 78). Dom Anselm Stolz' book is altogether an excellent introduction to the conception of man's mystical return to Paradise. It does not matter much in this connection whether St. Paul's rapture to the third heaven and to Paradise was one mystical experience or whether they were two; for the prevalence of the first opinion in the patristic period and for the identification of Paradise with the third heaven by many Fathers, see de Vuippens, "Paradis terrestre."

extent of St. Paul's rapture was considered as more or less exceptional by most later mystical writers, the aspiration for a spiritual return even before death to man's original paradisiac state became an important part of early Christian ideology of reform.[20]

The author of the so-called *Epistle of Barnabas* (probably of the first half of the second century) writes:

The Lord says: Behold, I shall make the last things like the first.[21]

This passage, which is one of the earliest postapostolic testimonies for the conception that renewal through Christ is also a return of the world to its creational integrity, is not an exact scriptural quotation, but it is very close to Apocalypse 22:13: "I am Alpha and Omega, the first and the last, the beginning and the end."[22] As the context shows, Ps.-Barnabas must have had in mind also St. Paul's comprehensive, and not merely eschatological, doctrine of the reformation of the image of God in man and of Christ as the second Adam.[23]

Half a century later this line of thought has become even more explicit in the doctrine of recapitulation of St. Irenaeus, who speaks of

the Word of God recapitulating into Himself that which was formed by Him (that is to say, reassuming the creation of man in body and soul through the Incarnation).[24]

---

[20] Needless to say, hope for the "return to Paradise" is a wide-spread motif all through the history of religions. In this respect see the studies of Mircea Eliade, especially the illuminating article "The Yearning for Paradise in Primitive Tradition," *Diogenes* III (1953) 28: even in "primitive" shamanic mysticism, "just as among the saints and the Christian theologians, mystic ecstasy is a return to Paradise, expressed by . . . the recovery of the primordial state of man."

[21] Ps.-Barnabas, *Epistola* 6, 13, *Flor. Patr.* I, 42: Λέγει δὲ Κύριος· '' Ἰδού, ποιῶ τὰ ἔσχατα ὡς τὰ πρῶτα.''

[22] See also Apoc. 1:8 and 21:6.

[23] Ps.-Barnabas, *Epist.* 6, 11 f., *Flor. Patr.* I, 42: Ἐπεὶ οὖν ἀνακαινίσας ἡμᾶς ἐν τῇ ἀφέσει τῶν ἁμαρτιῶν, ἐποίησεν ἡμᾶς ἄλλον τύπον, ὡς παιδίων ἔχειν τὴν ψυχήν, ὡς ἂν δὴ ἀναπλάσσοντος αὐτοῦ ἡμᾶς (this is followed by quotation of Gen. 1:26 and 1:28); and *ibid.* 6, 14, *Flor. Patr.* I, 42 f.: Ἴδε οὖν, ἡμεῖς ἀναπεπλάσμεθα . . . ὅτι αὐτὸς ἐν σαρκὶ ἔμελλεν φανεροῦσθαι. . . .

[24] Irenaeus, *Adversus haereses* III, 31, 1, Harvey II, 121: Nos autem . . . corpus sumus de terra acceptum et anima accipiens a Deo spiritum. . . . Hoc itaque factum est Verbum Dei, suum plasma in semetipsum recapitulans. . . .

Part of this recapitulation (ἀνακεφαλαίωσις)[25] is man's return to
Paradise at the end of time[26] of which Irenaeus heard the "presbyters"
speak: the saints will be found worthy to enter heaven (that is to say,
the Kingdom of God) or Paradise or the resplendent city (the heavenly
Jerusalem).[27] While this text probably has millenarian connotations[28]
and as a whole is certainly eschatological, there is no doubt that
Irenaeus also knew of another signification of the term Paradise, in
which it means the spiritual state of the Christian in this terrestrial
life, even before the end of all things: *spirituales tanquam in paradiso
Dei plantati*.[29] This condition he apparently did not identify with St.
Paul's exceptional rapture to Paradise, which he does mention on
other occasions.[30] In those happy early days of Christendom Irenaeus

---

[25] Cf. A. d'Alès, "La doctrine de la récapitulation en saint Irénée," *Rech.'s sc. rel.* VI
(1916) 185 ff., K. Prümm, S.J., "Göttliche Planung und menschliche Entwicklung nach
Irenäus Adversus Haereses," *Scholastik* XIII (1938) 206 ff., *idem*, "Zur Terminologie und
zum Wesen der christlichen Neuheit bei Irenäus," *Pisciculi F. J. Dölger* 192 ff., J. Daniélou,
S.J., "Saint Irénée et les origines de la théologie de l'histoire," *Rech.'s sc. rel.* XXXIV
(1947) 227 ff., J. Lawson, *The Biblical Theology of Saint Irenaeus* (London, 1948) 140 ff.,
J. Quasten, *Patrology* (Westminster, Md., 1951) 295 ff. J. Daniélou, S.J., *Sacramentum
Futuri* (Paris, 1950) 3 ff., especially 21 ff., stresses the elements of novelty and amelioration
beside that of restoration in Irenaeus' concept of recapitulation and in Greek patristic
ideology of the return to Paradise. It is quite true that these elements are found already in
St. Paul (see above, pp. 53 ff, and cf. Stolz, *Perfection* 26 f.) and therefore also in the
Greek and eastern Fathers—see, for instance, Ephraem, *Carm. Nisibena* LXIX, 10 ff.,
quoted by Beck, *Ephraems Hymnen über das Paradies* 131: Melius est hoc ultimum (i.e., the
Incarnation) quam illud in initio (i.e., creation). The idea of "reform to the better" was
however to be expressed more strongly and more explicitly by St. Augustine; cf. below,
pp. 156 ff.

[26] Cf. also Tertullian, *De monogamia* 5, *PL* II, 984D ff., where man's return to Paradise is
linked up with Christ as Alpha and Omega and as Second Adam.

[27] *Adv. haeres.* V, 36, 1, Harvey, II, 427 f.: ὡς οἱ πρεσβύτεροι λέγουσι τότε καὶ οἱ μὲν
καταξιωθέντες τῆς ἐν οὐρανῷ διατριβῆς ἐκεῖσε χωρήσουσιν, οἱ δὲ τῆς τοῦ παραδείσου τρυφῆς
ἀπολαύσουσιν, οἱ δὲ τὴν λαμπρότητα τῆς πόλεως καθέξουσιν· πανταχοῦ γὰρ ὁ Σωτὴρ ὁραθήσεται,
καθὼς ἄξιοι ἔσονται οἱ ὁρῶντες αὐτόν.

[28] On millenarism, see above, pp. 27 ff.

[29] *Adv. haeres.* V, 10, 1 f., Harvey II, 345 f.: . . . homines, si quidem per fidem profecerint in melius et assumserint spiritum Dei . . . erunt spirituales tanquam in paradiso
Dei plantati. . . . Et . . . in pristinam veniunt hominis naturam, eam quae secundum
imaginem et similitudinem facta est Dei. Note that here *proficere in melius* remains after all
a return to the *pristina natura*.

[30] *Adv. haeres.* V, 5, 1, Harvey, II, 331.

still could define the return to Paradise simply and without qualification as membership in the Church, for he says:

The Church is planted as a Paradise in this world.[31]

Similarly, for the author of the *Epistle to Diognetus* those who love God rightly "have been made a Paradise of delight"[32] and for Origen baptism can mean entry into Paradise, namely into the Church.[33] Comparisons between the Church and Paradise still play a considerable role in the fourth century, in St. Ephraem's *Hymns on Paradise*.[34]

Nevertheless,· ever since the development of a Christian *gnosis* in the School of Alexandria in the second and third centuries, the conception of a pre-eschatological Paradise had become increasingly mystical and ascetic rather than applicable to Christian life in general: Paradise is now often a key term for the end of a process of spiritual purification of the soul through which a true Christian must pass in order to be reformed in such a way that the original integrity and innocence of Adam before the fall is restored in him. Clement of Alexandria in distinguishing *gnosis* from ordinary knowledge says that the Lord and Savior, who is the Light, is Himself the content of true *gnosis* and this *gnosis* of Christ is the spiritual Paradise, the good earth, since we have been transferred and transplanted from the old life and are now planted in Him.[35]

In Alexandrian theology, spiritual reform on earth is bound up in a very special way with eschatology: this fusion is centered in the concept of restoration, ἀποκατάστασις, which is a scriptural term and idea,[36] but in patristic literature can also be a Christian trans-

---

[31] *Adv. haeres*, V, 20, 2, Harvey, II, 379 : Plantata est enim ecclesia paradisus in hoc mundo.

[32] *Epistola ad Diognetum*, XII, 1, Bihlmeyer, *Apostol. Väter* I, 149: . . . . οἱ γενόμενοι παράδεισος τρυφῆς (cf. Gen. 2:15). H. I. Marrou, in his commented edition and translation, *A Diognète* (Sources chrétiennes XXXIII, Paris, 1951) 80 f., 235, refers here to *Psalms of Solomon* 14, 2.

[33] Origen, *Selecta in Genesim*, PG XII, 100B.

[34] Cf. Beck, *Ephraems Hymnen über das Paradies* 51 ff., where Latin translations of the Syriac *Hymns on Paradise* are given. See especially the *Sixth Hymn on Paradise* 8 ff.: Congregatio sanctorum (that is to say, the Church) similis est paradiso, etc.

[35] Clement of Alexandria, *Stromata* VI, 1, 2, 4, *GCS*, *Clem. Alex.* II, 2nd ed., 423: ἡ γνῶσις δὲ ἡμῶν καὶ ὁ παράδεισος ὁ πνευματικὸς αὐτὸς ἡμῶν ὁ σωτὴρ ὑπάρχει, εἰς ὃν καταφυτευόμεθα μετατεθέντες καὶ μεταμοσχευθέντες εἰς τὴν γῆν τὴν ἀγαθὴν ἐκ βίου τοῦ παλαιοῦ . . . φῶς οὖν ὁ κύριος καὶ γνῶσις ἡ ἀληθής, εἰς ὃν μετετέθημεν.

[36] See above, Part Two, Chapter I.

formation of pagan cosmological and eschatological renewal ideology.[37] Already in Clement it is often difficult to say whether he speaks of higher knowledge ($\gamma\nu\hat{\omega}\sigma\iota\varsigma$) and of perfection ($\tau\epsilon\lambda\epsilon\acute{\iota}\omega\sigma\iota\varsigma$) and restoration ($\dot{a}\pi o\kappa a\tau\acute{a}\sigma\tau a\sigma\iota\varsigma$) in this life or beyond.[38] In Origen, the one is altogether not essentially different from the other.

For Origen the great eschatological reestablishment, the final restoration, *apocatastasis*, of a state of bliss after the end of the world, meant also the return of all men to a spiritual condition or at least to a fully spiritualized corporeality, which was their original status, the only one good in itself. He seems to have thought of all lesser forms of corporeal life as an occasion for evil and as a punishment consequent upon the fall, though not as evil in itself, since sin and evil result from the will. The possibility of evil—just because it is a necessary corollary of the creaturely freedom which God has desired to grant—cannot however be permanent; neither therefore can punishment be eternal. This doctrine of Origen's was obviously hard to reconcile first of all with the account of man's creation in the body, "of the slime of the earth," according to Gen. 2:7. If furthermore on Origen's premises it was only logical to conclude that full spiritualization can and must set an end to the existence of evil and punishment after death, such a conclusion was bound to impair fatally the fulness of man's moral responsibility which was part of that very spiritual freedom which Origen had meant to safeguard. An additional difficulty was his view that the final *apocatastasis* was to be preceded by numerous cycles of corruption and restoration. In fact, his system is so replete with dynamic spiritualty that it will always be hard to decide whether for

[37] See above, Part One, Chapter I, 1.

[38] Clement of Alexandria, *Stromata* VII, 10, 56, 7 ff., *GCS, Clem. Alex.* III, 41 f.: $\tau a\chi\epsilon\hat{\iota}a$ $\tau o\acute{\iota}\nu\nu\nu$ $\epsilon\dot{\iota}\varsigma$ $\kappa\acute{a}\theta a\rho\sigma\iota\nu$ $\dot{\eta}$ $\gamma\nu\hat{\omega}\sigma\iota\varsigma$ $\kappa a\grave{\iota}$ $\dot{\epsilon}\pi\iota\tau\acute{\eta}\delta\epsilon\iota o\varsigma$ $\epsilon\dot{\iota}\varsigma$ $\tau\grave{\eta}\nu$ $\dot{\epsilon}\pi\grave{\iota}$ $\tau\grave{o}$ $\kappa\rho\epsilon\hat{\iota}\tau\tau o\nu$ $\epsilon\dot{\upsilon}\pi\rho\acute{o}\sigma\delta\epsilon\kappa\tau o\nu$ $\mu\epsilon\tau a\beta o\lambda\acute{\eta}\nu$. $^{\prime\prime}O\theta\epsilon\nu$ $\kappa a\grave{\iota}$ $\rho a\delta\acute{\iota}\omega\varsigma$ $\epsilon\dot{\iota}\varsigma$ $\tau\grave{o}$ $\sigma\upsilon\gamma\gamma\epsilon\nu\grave{\epsilon}\varsigma$ $\tau\hat{\eta}\varsigma$ $\psi\upsilon\chi\hat{\eta}\varsigma$ $\theta\epsilon\hat{\iota}\acute{o}\nu$ $\tau\epsilon$ $\kappa a\grave{\iota}$ $\ddot{a}\gamma\iota o\nu$ $\mu\epsilon\tau o\iota\kappa\acute{\iota}\zeta\epsilon\iota$ $\kappa a\grave{\iota}$ $\delta\iota\acute{a}$ $\tau\iota\nu o\varsigma$ $o\dot{\iota}\kappa\epsilon\acute{\iota} o\upsilon$ $\phi\omega\tau\grave{o}\varsigma$ $\delta\iota a\beta\iota\beta\acute{a}\zeta\epsilon\iota$ $\tau\grave{a}\varsigma$ $\pi\rho o\kappa o\pi\grave{a}\varsigma$ $\tau\grave{a}\varsigma$ $\mu\upsilon\sigma\tau\iota\kappa\grave{a}\varsigma$ $\tau\grave{o}\nu$ $\ddot{a}\nu\theta\rho\omega\pi o\nu$ $\ddot{a}\chi\rho\iota\varsigma$ $\ddot{a}\nu$ $\epsilon\dot{\iota}\varsigma$ $\tau\grave{o}\nu$ $\kappa o\rho\upsilon\phi a\hat{\iota} o\nu$ $\dot{a}\pi o\kappa a\tau a\sigma\tau\acute{a}\sigma\eta$ $\tau\hat{\eta}\varsigma$ $\dot{a}\nu a\pi a\acute{\upsilon}\sigma\epsilon\omega\varsigma$ $\tau\acute{o}\pi o\nu$, $\tau\grave{o}\nu$ $\kappa a\theta a\rho\grave{o}\nu$ $\tau\hat{\eta}$ $\kappa a\rho\delta\acute{\iota}a$ $\pi\rho\acute{o}\sigma\omega\pi o\nu$ $\pi\rho\grave{o}\varsigma$ $\pi\rho\acute{o}\sigma\omega\pi o\nu$ $\dot{\epsilon}\pi\iota\sigma\tau\eta\mu o\nu\iota\kappa\hat{\omega}\varsigma$ $\kappa a\grave{\iota}$ $\kappa a\tau a\lambda\eta\pi\tau\iota\kappa\hat{\omega}\varsigma$ $\tau\grave{o}\nu$ $\Theta\epsilon\grave{o}\nu$ $\dot{\epsilon}\pi o\pi\tau\epsilon\acute{\upsilon}\epsilon\iota\nu$ $\delta\iota\delta\acute{a}\xi a\sigma a$. $\dot{E}\nu\tau a\hat{\upsilon}\theta a$ $\gamma\acute{a}\rho$ $\pi o\upsilon$ $\tau\hat{\eta}\varsigma$ $\gamma\nu\omega\sigma\tau\iota\kappa\hat{\eta}\varsigma$ $\psi\upsilon\chi\hat{\eta}\varsigma$ $\dot{\eta}$ $\tau\epsilon\lambda\epsilon\acute{\iota}\omega\sigma\iota\varsigma$. . . . It would seem that A. Mayer, O.S.B., *Das Gottesbild im Menschen nach Clemens von Alexandrien* (Studia Anselmiana XV, Roma, 1942), referring to C. Bigg, *The Christian Platonists of Alexandria*, 2nd ed. (Oxford, 1913) 106, posits too sharp a contrast between Clement and the other Greek Fathers when he asserts that Clement never envisaged a restoration of creational integrity (Mayer, *Gottesbild* 76 f.), though it is true that he did not go as far in this respect as Origen; see also below, p. 86, n. 12, with regard to the relation between $\epsilon\dot{\iota}\kappa\acute{\omega}\nu$ and $\dot{o}\mu o\acute{\iota}\omega\sigma\iota\varsigma$.

him the end of all things in God was really *the* end or only one of many successive ends. Even though his *apocatastasis* doctrine is based on the scriptural rather than on the pagan term ἀποκατάστασις, he was not free from the influence of the ancient cosmology of eternal recurrence, however much he rejected the Stoic belief in the identity of successive worlds.[39]

In the great book of his youth, *De principiis*, Origen says that after their death the souls of the saints will first enter Paradise which will serve as a place of instruction (*auditorium vel schola animarum*) from which they will rise through the various spheres of heaven to the Kingdom of Heaven and to God Himself.[40] Yet, at the consummation of the world, when the end will become as the beginning, when God

---

[39] See Origen, *De principiis* II, 3, 1 ff., especially 4, *GCS*, *Orig.* V, 113 ff., especially 119, and cf. Augustine's much more radical rejection of all cyclical world views in *De civitate Dei* XII, 14, *Corp. Christ.*, *Ser. Lat.* XLVIII, 369. For Origen in general see now the comprehensive survey and full bibliography in Quasten, *Patrology* II, 37 ff. For Origen's conception that corporeality is not evil in itself, but a result of the mutability of created spirits, which had led them to their fall, at the same time a punishment for drawing away from God and a paedagogical trial conducive to the restoration of "pure" spirituality, see J. Daniélou, *Origène* (Paris, 1948) 215 f. See also G. Bürke, S.J., "Des Origenes Lehre vom Urstand," *Z. kath. Theol.* LXXII (1950) 10 ff., 14 ff.: against Gnostic depreciation of matter and corporeality Origen identified "pure" spirituality and a completely "spiritualized" materiality; Bürke ("Urstand" 38) therefore believes that the reproach of an over-spiritualization of Christian doctrine, so often directed against Origen, is unjustified. It is hard, however, in view of *De principiis* III, 5, 3, *GCS*, *Orig.* V, 273, to agree with Bürke's minimizing of Origen's considerations regarding repeated falls and redemptions; for a well-balanced view of this problem, see E. Gilson, *La philosophie au moyen âge*, 2nd ed. (Paris, 1947) 58, also *idem*, *History of Christian Philosophy in the Middle Ages* (New York, 1954) 40 ff.

[40] *De principiis* II, 11, 6, *GCS*, *Orig.* V, 190, 2: Puto enim quod sancti quique discedentes ex hac vita permanebunt in loco aliquo in terra posito quem paradisum dicit scriptura divina, velut in quodam eruditionis loco et, ut ita dixerim, auditorio vel schola animarum. . . . Si qui sane mundus corde et purior mente et exercitatior sensu fuerit, velocius proficiens cito et ad aëris locum ascendet et ad caelorum regna perveniet per locorum singulorum, ut ita dixerim, mansiones, quas Graeci quidem σφαίρας, id est globos, appellaverunt, scriptura vero divina caelos nominat. . . . See the more pointed distinction between Paradise and Kingdom of God in St. Ambrose, below, p. 143. That Origen thought that Paradise was on this earth of ours is not very probable; more likely he was thinking of that scriptural *terra bona et terra viventium* which he places above the firmament and under the supernal heavens in *De principiis* II, 3, 6, *GCS*, *Orig.* V, 123 and 126, where he also says: . . . videtur quasi iter quoddam sanctorum profectibus aperiri ab illa terra ad illos coelos, ut non tam permanere in illa terra quam habitare videantur, transituri scilicet, cum in id quoque profecerint, ad haereditatem regni caelorum.

will be all in all (cf. 1 Cor. 15:27), He "will restore that state which rational nature possessed when there was no need of eating from the tree of knowledge of good and evil": thus the *apocatastasis* is identical with the condition of Paradise before the fall.[41]

For the end is always like the beginning.

These words are part of Origen's great hymnic praise of the consummation and restoration of all things in the sixth chapter of the first book of *De principiis*.[42] This sentence, often repeated by Origen (though with slight variations),[43] is superficially reminiscent of several passages in the Apocalypse and similar to the text from Pseudo-Barnabas already quoted. The deviation from the Apocalypse is here even more marked than in Ps.-Barnabas: the Lord of the Apocalypse had not said "the end is always like the beginning," but "I am the beginning and the end."[44] Again it would appear that, with all his emphatic denial of the recurrence of identical events, Origen could not shake off completely the ideology of cyclical return. What he does deny is that there will be worlds which are alike in every respect, that, for instance, another Adam and another Eve will do the same things which they did before, or that another Great Flood will occur, in sum that, in many cycles of many ages, souls will have to act out a repetitious and predetermined course; he rather holds that the souls are directed by their free intentions.[45] He thus wishes to safeguard man's full spiritual freedom. Yet, as far as the ἀποκατάστασις

---

[41] *De principiis, loc. cit.*, III, 6, 3, *GCS, Orig.* V, 284: Si ergo finis ad principium reparatus et rerum exitus conlatus initiis—(the original Greek equivalent for *reparare* and the following *restituere* was probably ἀποκαθιστάναι or the like)—restituet illum statum, quem tunc habuit natura rationabilis, cum de ligno sciendi bonum et malum edere non egebat, ut amoto omni malitiae sensu et ad sincerum purumque deterso solus qui est unus Deus bonus . . . in omnibus ipse sit omnia (cf. 1 Cor. 15:27).

[42] *De principiis* I, 6, 2, *GCS, Orig.* V, 79, 22: Semper enim similis est finis initiis.

[43] See preceding note; furthermore, *De principiis* II, 1, 1, *GCS, Orig.* V, 107, 9; *In Joannem* XIII, 37, *GCS, Orig.* IV, 262, 35; *Contra Celsum* VIII, 72, *GCS, Orig.* II, 289, 8.

[44] See Apoc. 22:13; 1:8; 21:6.

[45] Origen, *De principiis* II, 3, 4, *GCS, Orig.* V, 119: Iam vero qui indissimiles sibi mundos ac per omnia pares aliquando evenire confirmant, nescio quibus id possint adserere documentis. Si enim per omnia similis mundo mundus dicitur, erit ut iterum Adam vel Eva eadem faciant quae fecerunt; idem iterum ⟨erit⟩ diluvium. . . . Non enim cursu aliquo in eosdem se circulos post multa saecula revolvente aguntur animae, ut hoc aut illud vel agant vel cupiant, sed quocumque proprii ingenii libertas intenderit, illo gestorum suorum dirigunt cursum.

πάντων is concerned, he imposes, as it were, on God a mere reduction of the world to that same spiritualized state which he posits as the initial one. In this respect as in others Origen remained under the strong influence of Platonism.[46]

Origen linked his eschatology to his conception of man's pre-eschatological anticipations of the Kingdom of God, of Paradise, and of heaven:

We travel toward perfection, if stretching forth ourselves to the things that are before, we forget those that are behind (Phil. 3:13);[47] the Kingdom of God being in us (cf. Luke 17:21),[48] the final height (ἀκρότης) will be at hand for those who ceaselessly progress toward the Kingdom . . . God will be all in all. . . .

But this will happen only if we give up sin, so that even now God can dwell in us as in a spiritual Paradise.[49] The man who has no idol set up in his heart, that is to say, he who is not diverted from God by such things as unbelief, hypocrisy, wickedness, intemperance, can be built up into a temple of God and can become a Paradise of God.[50] The

---

[46] Compare with this mental attitude that of St. Ambrose and of St. Augustine, discussed below, pp. 142 ff. and pp. 153 ff.

[47] For the importance of this Pauline text in Gregory of Nyssa's mystical reform ideology see below, p. 105.

[48] For other significant Greek patristic applications of Luke 17:21 see below, pp. 100 and 114.

[49] See De oratione 25, 2 f., GCS, Orig. II, 358 f.: ὁδεύομεν δὲ ἐπὶ τὴν τελειότητα ἐὰν τοῖς ἔμπροσθεν ἐπεκτεινόμενοι τῶν ὄπισθεν ἐπιλανθανώμεθα (cf. Phil. 3:13). Τῇ οὖν ἐν ἡμῖν βασιλείᾳ τοῦ Θεοῦ ἡ ἀκρότης ἀδιαλείπτως προκόπτουσιν ἐνστήσεται ὅταν πληρωθῇ τὸ παρὰ τῷ ἀποστόλῳ εἰρημένον ὅτι ὁ Χριστὸς πάντων αὐτῷ τῶν ἐχθρῶν ὑποταγέντων παραδώσει τὴν βασιλείαν τῷ Θεῷ καὶ Πατρὶ ἵνα ᾖ ὁ Θεὸς τὰ πάντα ἐν πᾶσι (cf. 1 Cor. 15:24 ff.) . . . Εἰ τοίνυν θέλομεν ὑπὸ Θεοῦ βασιλεύεσθαι μηδαμῶς βασιλευέτω ἡ ἁμαρτία ἐν τῷ θνητῷ ἡμῶν σώματι (cf. Rom. 6:12). . . , ἀλλὰ νεκρώσαντες τὰ μέλη τὰ ἐπὶ τῆς γῆς καρποφορῶμεν τοὺς καρποὺς τοῦ Πνεύματος (cf. Col. 3:5, John 15:8 and 16, Gal. 5:22), ἵνα ὡς ἐν παραδείσῳ πνευματικῷ κύριος ἡμῖν ἐμπεριπατῇ (cf. Gen. 3:18; 2 Cor. 6:16; Lev. 26:12; Deut. 23:14). . . . The distinction, observed in De principiis (cf. p. 72, n. 40) between Paradise and the heavenly Kingdom of God, is not made in De oratione.

[50] See In Jerem., homil. I, 136, GCS, Orig. III, 16, 4 ff. (with reference to Jer. 1:10 and the prophet's task to root up and to destroy, to build and to plant): . . . οὐκ ἔστι δύναμις . . . δύναμις ἐκριζοῦσα, εἴ τις ἀπιστία, εἴ τις ὑπόκρισις, εἴ τις πονηρία, εἴ τις ἀκολασία; οὐκ ἔστι κατασκάπτουσα, εἴ που εἰδωλεῖον ᾠκοδόμηται εἰς τὴν καρδίαν; ἵνα ἐκείνου κατασκαφέντος οἰκοδομηθῇ ναὸς τοῦ Θεοῦ καὶ δόξα τοῦ Θεοῦ εὑρεθῇ ἐν τῷ ἀνοικοδομηθέντι ναῷ καὶ γένηται οὐκ ἄλσος, ἀλλὰ φυτεία παράδεισος τοῦ Θεοῦ, ὅπου ὁ ναὸς τοῦ Θεοῦ ἐν Χριστῷ Ἰησοῦ. . . . Cf. Bürke, "Urstand" 27.

Kingdom of the Heavens and the land of the living have been promised for the end; but in those whose "conversation is in heaven" (cf. Phil. 3:20) God rests and resides even now. If they are as perfect as the Apostles had been, then they are celestial beings, they have in fact become the "heavens" which "shew forth the glory of God" (Ps. 18:1).[51]

The greatest of the orthodox continuators of Origen's thought, St. Gregory of Nyssa, made eschatological concepts, such as that of *apocatastasis*, restoration and return, even more fruitful for the idea of terrestrial reform. It must be noted in this connection that Gregory with all his dependence on Origen does not accept to its full extent his eschatological doctrine of *apocatastasis* or at least not the doctrine traditionally labelled with Origen's name. While Gregory did hold that the ultimate end of all evil would also include the ceasing of punishment after death and the conversion of sinners in hell to God, he did not believe in a purely spiritual state of man before and after his life in the body nor in eternally or at least repeatedly recurrent cycles of corruption and spiritual restoration of the soul.[52] Gregory himself used the term *apocatastasis*, first, as synonymous with *anastasis*,[53]

---

[51] *In Genes.*, *homil.* I, 12, *GCS*, *Orig.* VI, 14 f.: Ex hoc ergo considera, quanta sit magnitudo hominis . . . , qui habet honorem coeli, propter quod et coelorum ei promittitur regnum. Habet et terrae honorem, quoniam quidem in terram bonam et terram vivorum fluentem lac et mel ingredi sperat (cf. Exod. 33:3). . . . *Ibid.* 13, *loc. cit.*, 15 f.: Quod enim dicit: "coelum mihi sedes" (Is. 66:1), ita digne de Deo intelligitur, ut sciamus quia in his, quorum in coelis est conversatio (cf. Phil. 3:20), Deus requiescit et residet. . . . Et propterea perfecti quique coelestes facti vel coeli effecti, enarrant gloriam Dei, sicut in Psalmo dixit (cf. Ps. 18:1). Propterea denique et apostoli, qui erant coeli, mittuntur ad enarrandum gloriam Dei. . . . See also *Commentary to the Gospel of St. Matthew* XII, 14 GCS X, I, 97, 13 ff.: τάχα δὲ καὶ ἑκάστη ἀρετὴ οὐρανοῦ ἐστι βασιλεία, καὶ πᾶσαι ἅμα βασιλεία τῶν οὐρανῶν· ὡς κατὰ τοῦτο ἤδη ἐν βασιλείᾳ εἶναι οὐρανῶν τὸν κατὰ τὰς ἀρετὰς βιοῦντα. . . .

[52] See Gregory of Nyssa, *De hominis opificio* 28, *PG* XLIV, 229B ff. Cf. Daniélou, *Origène* 282 f.; also *idem*, "L'apocatastase chez saint Grégoire de Nysse," *Rech.'s sc. rel.* XXX (1940) 328 ff., *idem*, *Platonisme et théologie mystique*: *Essai sur la doctrine spirituelle de saint Grégoire de Nysse*, 2nd ed. (Théologie II, Paris, 1953), furthermore introduction by J. Laplace, S.J., to *Grégoire de Nysse: La création de l'homme* (i.e., *De hominis opificio*), trans. J. Laplace, notes by J. Daniélou (Sources chrétiennes VI, Paris, 1943) 64 ff.

[53] He also uses the phrase εἰς τὸ ἐξ ἀρχῆς σχῆμα ἀναπλάσσειν in this connection; see *Oratio catechetica* 8, Srawley 42.

as signifying the general resurrection of mankind, both in body and spirit, which is but man's return to Paradise,[54] and secondly, in the sense of the reformation of man in this life on earth.[55] When, for instance, in his second sermon On the Lord's Prayer, Gregory says that God will restore (ἀποκαταστήσει) to his heavenly fatherland (οὐρανίῳ πατρίδι) that man who flees vice with the intention of becoming similar to God, he also asserts that this restoration (though it is consummated only in the resurrection) is very real already on this earth: "you are entitled to be in heaven immediately, because you have seized God with your mind."[56] The most striking illustration of the pre-eschatological restoration of a spiritual Paradise in man's soul occurs in the twelfth chapter of Gregory's treatise On Virginity. There Gregory speaks of "the restoration to its original condition" (ἡ εἰς τὸ ἀρχαῖον ἀποκατάστασις) of the divine image in man, which implies that man must become "that which the protoplast" (i.e., Adam) "was in the first beginnings of his life. . . ."[57] And he continues:

It is indeed possible for us to return to the original beatitude, if we now will

---

[54] See De hominis opificio 17, PG XLIV, 188C: Ἡ δὲ τῆς ἀναστάσεως χάρις οὐδὲν ἕτερον ἡμῖν ἐπαγγέλλεται ἢ τῆς εἰς τὸ ἀρχαῖον τῶν πεπτωκότων ἀποκατάστασιν. Ἐπάνοδος γάρ τίς ἐστιν ἐπὶ τὴν πρώτην ζωὴν ἡ προσδοκωμένη χάρις τὸν ἀποβληθέντα τοῦ παραδείσου πάλιν εἰς αὐτὸν ἐπανάγουσα. Cf. De anima et resurrectione, PG XLVI, 148A, In Ecclesiasten, homilia 1, PG XLIV, 633C, In Psalmos 5, PG XLIV, 581A. Already St. Eustathius had spoken of apocatastasis to Paradise (without Origenist connotations) in connection with Christ's words to the good thief (Luke 23:42 f., see also pp. 64 f. and pp. 144 ff.), cf. De engastrimytho contra Origenem 18, PG XVIII, 652: . . . τῇ ἀρχαιοτάτῃ τοῦ παραδείσου πάλιν ἀποκαθιστῶσα νόμῃ. . . .

[55] See also Gregory Nazianzen, in connection with baptism, Oratio XL, in sanctum baptisma, 8, PG XXXVI, 368C; in connection with penitential reconciliation cf. Apostolic Constitutions II, 41, 2 and 4, VIII, 9, 3, 5 and 10, VIII, 10, 14, Funk, Didascal. et Constit. Apostol. I, 131, 486, 488, 490, and for reform in general ibid. II, 56, 4, Funk I, 159.

[56] De oratione dominica, oratio II, PG XLIV, 1145A ff.: Ὁδὸς δὲ ἡ πρὸς τὸν οὐρανὸν τὴν ἀνθρωπίνην φύσιν ἀνάγουσα οὐδεμία τίς ἐστιν ἄλλη εἰ μὴ φυγὴ καὶ ἀποστάσις τῶν περιγείων κακῶν· τῆς δὲ φυγῆς τῶν κακῶν ἐπίνοια οὐκ ἄλλη μοί τις εἶναι δοκεῖ πλὴν τῆς πρὸς τὸν Θεὸν ὁμοιώσεως . . . ἔξεστί σοι εὐθὺς ἐν τῷ οὐρανῷ εἶναι τὸν Θεὸν ἐν τῇ διανοίᾳ λαβόντι . . . (for "flight and assimilation" see Plato's Theaetetus 176A f., cf. p. 83, n. 3) and ibid. 1148C: [God] ἀποκαταστήσει σε τῇ οὐρανίῳ πατρίδι. . . .

[57] De virginitate 12, Cavarnos, in Jaeger, Greg. Nyss. Opera VIII, 1, 302: Εἰ οὖν αὕτη ἐστὶν ἡ ἐπίνοια τῆς τοῦ ζητουμένου εὑρέσεως ἡ τῆς θείας εἰκόνος εἰς τὸ ἀρχαῖον ἀποκατάστασις . . . ἐκεῖνο γενώμεθα ὃ ἦν παρὰ τὴν πρώτην ἑαυτοῦ ζωὴν ὁ πρωτόπλαστος.

run backward on the same road which we had followed when we were
ejected from Paradise together with our forefather [Adam]. . . .[58]

We must, therefore, act

as those who have become strangers from their homes: after they have turned
back (ἐπιστρέφωσιν) in the direction whence they started, they leave that
place first which they had reached last when setting forth. Since then in the
separation from paradisiac life marriage is the last step, reason leads those who
sever all other ties on behalf of Christ to leave behind first marriage, the last
station as it were; then to withdraw from the hard work of the soil in which
man was placed after sin; next to take off the carnal cloaks, the "coats of skin"
(Gen. 3:21), that is to say, to divest themselves of the wisdom of the flesh and
to renounce all the secrets of shamefulness (2 Cor. 4:2) . . .; also to repel
the illusion of taste and sight and to have as counsellor no longer the venom-
spitting serpent, but the precept of God only. . . . And if it be allowed to
speak daringly, a man might thus again be caught up from the world which
lies in evil into Paradise, in which also Paul arrived. . . .[59]

This passage contains a whole outline of man's potential return to
Paradise even in this life, or more exactly, of the spiritual restoration
(*apocatastasis*) of Paradise in the Christian who desires to come as
close to God as possible. It describes a way of spiritual purification and
of renunciation of all things which, though they are not bad in themselves, are less good than the purely spiritual: to give up marriage as
well as the most common type of work and to restrict the exercise of
the faculties of the senses. The advice to withdraw from agricultural

---

[58] *Ibid.* 12, Cavarnos, in Jaeger, *Greg. Nyss. Opera* VIII, 1, 302: Δι' ἧς τοίνυν ἀκολουθίας
ἔξω τοῦ παραδείσου γεγόναμεν τῷ προπάτορι συνεκβληθέντες καὶ νῦν διὰ τῆς αὐτῆς ἔξεστιν
ἡμῖν παλινδρομήσασιν ἐπανελθεῖν ἐπὶ τὴν ἀρχαίαν μακαριότητα.

[59] *Ibid.* 13, VIII, 1, 303 f.: . . . ὥσπερ οἱ τῶν οἰκείων ἀποξενωθέντες, ἐπειδὰν ἐπιστρέφωσιν,
ὅθεν ὡρμήθησαν, πρῶτον ἐκεῖνον καταλείπουσι τὸν τόπον ᾧ τελευταῖον προϊόντες ἐνέτυχον.
Ἐπεὶ οὖν τοῦ χωρισμοῦ τῆς ἐν τῷ παραδείσῳ ζωῆς τὸ τελευταῖον ὁ γάμος ἐστί, τούτου πρῶτον
καταλιπεῖν ὥσπερ τινὰ σταθμὸν ἔσχατον τοῖς πρὸς τὸν Χριστὸν ἀναλύουσιν ὑφηγεῖται ὁ λόγος·
εἶτα τῆς περὶ τὴν γῆν ταλαιπωρίας ἀναχωρῆσαι ᾗ ἐνιδρύνθη μετὰ τὴν ἁμαρτίαν ὁ ἄνθρωπος·
ἐπὶ τούτῳ ἔξω τῶν τῆς σαρκὸς προκαλυμμάτων γενέσθαι, τοὺς δερματίνους χιτῶνας, τουτέστι
τὸ φρόνημα τῆς σαρκὸς ἀποδυσαμένους. Καὶ πάντα ἀπειπαμένους τὰ κρυπτὰ τῆς αἰσχύνης . . .
τήν τε κατὰ γεῦσιν καὶ ὄψιν ἀπάτην ἀπώσασθαι σύμβουλόν τε μηκέτι τὸν ἰοβόλον ὄφιν, ἀλλὰ τὴν
ἐντολὴν τοῦ Θεοῦ μόνην ἔχειν. . . . Καὶ εἰ χρὴ τολμήσαντα εἰπεῖν, τάχα οὕτως ἄν τις ἀπὸ τοῦ
κόσμου τούτου, ὃς ἐν τῷ πονηρῷ κεῖται, ἁρπαγείη πάλιν εἰς τὸν παράδεισον, ἐν ᾧ καὶ Παῦλος
γενόμενος. . . . For the role of the "garments of skin" of Gen. 3:21 in the ideology of
reform, see p. 176.

work is particularly noteworthy—one need only think of the role which such work played in later Byzantine monasticism [60] and also in the mediaeval development of Benedictine monasticism. Gregory of Nyssa certainly did not mean to contradict Pachomian and Basilian monastic practice, which beside various crafts and chores included agricultural work. His words rather reflect the biblically founded patristic view that the work of the soil is a consequence of original sin and more especially the attitude of St. Basil who stressed the spiritual value of manual work, but at the same time kept the monks outside the ordinary social-economic patterns, be it those of the land-owners and peasants or of the city dwellers; above all, monastic work must not be detrimental and disturbing to the ascetic way of life. [61]

The end of the Gregorian text refers to the aim of this virginal and ascetic life: it is St. Paul's rapture to Paradise (2 Cor. 12:2 ff.), which for Gregory is the Paradise of creation as well as St. Paul's third heaven, [62] the Paradise of the good thief as well as the celestial Jerusalem. [63] Gregory seems to have been one of the first theologians to envisage Paul's rapture as a model of mystical experience accessible on principle, though in proper gradation, to all Christians striving for perfection. [64]

How meditation on the creational Eden of the Book of Genesis could literally lead to a renovation of man in the sense of a visionary and mystical return to Paradise, becomes strikingly evident from the *Paradise Hymns* of Gregory of Nyssa's contemporary, the Syrian St. Ephraem. It is the poring over the Genesis account of Paradise which "projected" Ephraem "from the bosom of the book into the bosom

---

[60] Cf. J. Leroy, O.S.B., "La vie quotidienne du moine studite," *Irénikon* XXVII (1954), 37 ff.

[61] See Basil, *Regulae fusius tractatae* XXXVIII, *PG* XXXI, 1016D ff.; cf. S. Giet, *Les idées et l'action sociales de saint Basile* (Paris, 1941) 143 ff. See also *Regulae fusius tractatae* V, 1 f., *PG* XXXI, 920C ff., and VI, 1 f., *PG* XXXI, 925A ff.; cf. Dom David Amand (de Mendieta), *L'ascèse monastique de saint Basile* (Maredsous, 1948) 109 ff. St. Benedict, as well known, considered manual, but not agricultural, work as essential; cf. the *Rule of St. Benedict* 41 and 48, Linderbauer 51 and 55 ff.

[62] *Explicatio apologetica . . . in Hexaemeron*, *PG* XLIV, 121D.

[63] *In Christi resurrectionem, oratio I*, *PG* XLVI, 617A ff. For these identifications cf. E. F. Sutcliffe, S.J., "St. Gregory of Nyssa and Paradise," *The Ecclesiastical Review* LXXXIV (Ninth Series, vol. IV, 1931) 337 ff.

[64] See *In Canticum Canticorum, homil.* v, *PG* XLIV, 860 A–C.

of Paradise.'' [65] Because he has meditated on Paradise, he has become drunk with its perfumes and has been ecstatically lifted above himself, has been renewed and transfigured.[66]

That such renewal had been made possible through redemption by Christ [67] and was brought about in man by the presence in his soul of the Holy Spirit together with the other two divine persons was self-evident scriptural truth for Ephraem [68] as for all of the Fathers. The role of the Holy Spirit in this respect was stressed most strongly by St. Basil the Great and by St. Cyril of Alexandria, in full awareness however that man's sanctification in and by the Holy Ghost is received also by and in the Son, that it comes from the Father and at the same time consists in participation in the divine essence which is one in the three persons.[69]

[65] Beck, *Ephraems Hymnen über das Paradies* 40, Fifth Paradise Hymn 3 : Et . . . perveni ad illam lineam in qua scripta est narratio paradisi, illa me portavit et proiecit e sinu libri in sinum paradisi.

[66] Beck, *Ephraems Hymnen über das Paradies* 49, Sixth Paradise Hymn 4 : Extulit me (paradisus) quia sensi eum, ditavit me quia meditatus sum de eo. Oblitus sum paupertatem meam quia inebriavit me odoribus suis et tanquam "non ego" factus sum quia renovavit me.

[67] See also Fourth Paradise Hymn and Carmina Nisibena 39, 7 (Beck, *Ephraems Hymnen über das Paradies* 33 ff.) for Adam's return to Paradise through Christ.

[68] Cf. Beck, *Die Theologie des hl. Ephraem in seinen Hymnen über den Glauben* (Studia Anselmiana XXI, Roma, 1949) 101, Hymn 80, on Faith, 2 : Ex Patre per Filium fluit veritas quae omnes vivificat per Spiritum.

[69] See above all P. Galtier, S.J., *Le Saint Esprit en nous d'après les pères grecs* (Analecta Gregoriana, Ser. Theol., XXXV A 4, Roma, 1946), very important also for the early Alexandrians and the two Cappadocian Gregories; cf. H. du Manoir de Juaye, S.J., *Dogme et spiritualité chez saint Cyrille d'Alexandrie* (Etudes de théologie et d'histoire de la spiritualité II, Paris, 1944) 221 ff., 236 ff., and on the other hand B. Fraigneau-Julien, "L'inhabitation de la Sainte Trinité dans l'âme selon saint Cyrille d'Alexandrie," Rev. sc. rel. XXX (1956) 135 ff., who follows Petau, Scheeben, and de Régnon rather than Galtier and du Manoir in interpreting Greek patristic thought as attributing a proper hypostatic character to the Holy Spirit's sanctifying inhabitation in man. See furthermore J. Gross, *La divinisation du chrétien d'après les pères grecs* (Paris, 1938) 153 ff. for St. Irenaeus, 210 ff. for St. Athanasius, 241 ff. for St. Basil, 250 f. for St. Didymus the Blind; for Origen and Cyril of Alexandria, cf. A. Lieske, S.J., *Die Theologie der Logosmystik bei Origenes* (Münster, 1938) 141 ff. and 218 f.; for Basil and Gregory of Nyssa the important pages in W. Jaeger, *Two Rediscovered Works of Ancient Christian Literature: Gregory of Nyssa and Macarius* (Leiden, 1954) 99 ff. (Professor Jaeger promises a special study on Gregory's concept of sanctification by the Holy Spirit); cf. finally R. Leys, S.J., *L'image de Dieu chez saint Grégoire de Nysse* (Museum Lessianum, Sect. Theol. XLIX, Bruxelles, Paris, 1951) 97, n. 1, and the article of Charlier on Cyril quoted below, p. 81, n. 76. For the theological problem in general, see C. Journet, *L'église du verbe incarné* II (Paris, 1951) 358 ff.: Excursus II: "Présences de la Trinité à elle-même et au monde" (including a discussion of the relation between created and uncreated grace, a relation of great relevance for the trinitarian aspects of sanctification).

In the wonderful praises through which Basil in *De Sancto Spiritu*
extols the full divinity of the Holy Spirit there is not lacking the
affirmation of His deifying power by which hearts are raised up, progress is perfected, a heavenly and angelic conversation in God is
achieved, and finally God-likeness is reached as the goal of all desires—
Θεὸν γενέσθαι.[70] It is not surprising then to read in the same
treatise that it is through the Holy Ghost that there occurs that
apocatastasis to Paradise[71] which, as was seen, can begin already in
this life. Basil indeed refers Psalm 103:30: "Thou shalt send forth
thy spirit, and they shall be created: and thou shalt renew the face
of the earth," not only to that revival (ἀναβίωσις) which is the
resurrection of the bodies, but also to the renewal (ἀνακαινισμός)
of man's terrestrial condition, to the transformation even here and
now of his sinful state to a better one (ἐπὶ τὸ βέλτιον μετακόσμησις),
to a change (μεταβολή) which already makes him part of the heavenly
"republic" (πολιτεία).[72] Cyril of Alexandria, not without reason
called σφραγὶς τῶν πατέρων,[73] expresses the role of the divine sancti-
fier in the reform of man in terms of a restoration of Adam's πρώτη
χάρις and even more often in terms of the recovery of our lost
image-likeness to God.[74] If, as Cyril says, Christ reforms man to His

---

[70] Basil, *De Spiritu Sancto* 9, 23, PG XXXII, 109B ff.: (the Holy Spirit) καρδιῶν
ἀνάβασις, χειραγωγία τῶν ἀσθενούντων, τῶν προκοπτόντων τελείωσις . . . αἱ πνευματοφόροι
ψυχαὶ ἐλλαμφθεῖσαι παρὰ τοῦ Πνεύματος, αὐταί τε ἀποτελοῦνται πνευματικαὶ καὶ εἰς ἑτέρους
τὴν χάριν ἐξαποστέλλουσιν. Ἐντεῦθεν μελλόντων πρόγνωσις, μυστηρίων σύνεσις, κεκρυμμένων
κατάληψις, χαρισμάτων διανομαί, τὸ οὐράνιον πολίτευμα, ἡ μετὰ ἀγγέλων χορεία, ἡ ἀτελεύτητος
εὐφροσύνη, ἡ ἐν Θεῷ διαμονή, ἡ πρὸς Θεὸν ὁμοίωσις, τὸ ἀκρότατον τῶν ὀρεκτῶν: Θεὸν γενέσθαι.
For those aspects of deification ideology which are more closely connected with the recovery of man's lost image-likeness see the following chapter.

[71] *Ibid.* 15, 36, PG XXXII, 132B: Διὰ Πνεύματος Ἁγίου ἡ εἰς παράδεισον ἀποκατάστασις· ἡ
εἰς βασιλείαν οὐρανῶν ἄνοδος· ἡ εἰς υἱοθεσίαν ἐπάνοδος. . . .

[72] *Ibid.* 19, 49, PG XXXII, 157B f. See also Gregory of Nyssa, *De instituto christiano,*
Jaeger, *Greg. Nyss. Opera* VIII, 61 f.: Ὅταν γὰρ μισήσῃ μὲν ἡ ψυχὴ τὸ ἁμαρτάνειν, οἰκειώσῃ
δὲ ἑαυτὴν τῷ Θεῷ κατὰ δύναμιν τῇ τῆς ἀρετῆς πολιτείᾳ καὶ δέξηται μεταποιηθεῖσα τῷ βίῳ τὴν
τοῦ Πνεύματος εἰς ἑαυτὴν χάριν, καινὴ γέγονεν ὅλη καὶ ἀνεκτίσθη.

[73] By Anastasius Sinaita, *Viae dux adversus Acephalos* 7, PG LXXXIX, 113D (quoted by
Galtier, *Saint Esprit* 217).

[74] Cyril of Alexandria, *In Joannis evangelium* XI, 10, PG LXXIV, 541C f.: Ἐπειδὴ γάρ
ἐστι τῆς τοῦ Μονογενοῦς οὐσίας εἰκὼν ἀκραιφνὴς τὸ Πνεῦμα αὐτοῦ . . . , τοὺς οἷσπερ ἄν ἐνυπ-
άρξαι συμμόρφους ἀποτελεῖ τῇ τοῦ Πατρὸς εἰκόνι, τοῦτ' ἔστι τῷ Υἱῷ. . . . Ἀνανεοῦσθαι
τοιγαροῦν καὶ ἀναπλάττεσθαί πως εἰς εἰκόνα τὴν πρώτην τὴν ἀνθρώπου φύσιν ἐρωτᾷ διὰ μετουσίας
τοῦ Πνεύματος, ἵνα τὴν πρώτην ἐκείνην ἀμφιεσάμενοι χάριν καὶ τὴν πρὸς αὐτὸν ἀνακομισάμενοι
μόρφωσιν ἀμείνους τε ἤδη καὶ δυνατώτεροι τῆς ἐν τῷδε τῷ κόσμῳ βασιλευούσης ἁμαρτίας
εὑρισκώμεθα. . . .

own image through the Holy Spirit, this is a return to the πρώτη εἰκών and thus approximation to a God-likeness which Christ possesses to the ultimate degree of substantial identity: it is truly a return to high origins, a journey backward and upward to that which was in the beginning.[75] All this is closely connected with Cyril's Trinitarian orthodoxy. Since we are reformed in and toward Christ and the Holy Spirit and at the same time toward creational God-likeness, it necessarily follows that all three persons in the Trinity are equally divine: otherwise our reform would not be a true ἀνακαινισμός toward God, not scriptural new creation, but an inferior καινουργία.[76]

[75] Cyril of Alexandria, De Sanctissima Trinitate, dial. III, PG LXXV, 808B f. : Ἀναμορφοῖ γὰρ ἡμᾶς διὰ τοῦ Πνεύματος εἰς ἰδίαν εἰκόνα Χριστός. . . . Ἀναστοιχειούμεθα γὰρ εἰς εἰκόνα τὴν πρώτην, ἀκριβεῖ σημάντρῳ κατασφραγιζόμενοι τῷ Υἱῷ, πρὸς τὸ τῇδε ἔχειν, ὅς ἐστι καὶ χαρακτὴρ καὶ ὁμοίωσις τοῦ Πατρὸς καὶ οὐχ ἕτερος παρ' αὐτὸν κατά γε τὸ ἐν οὐσίᾳ ταυτόν.

[76] Cyril expresses this in the following ad absurdum argumentation against those who do not believe in the essential unity of the divine Trinity, ibid., PG LXXV, 808B f.: Ἀνακαινισμὸς γὰρ οὐ τί που κατὰ τὰς Γραφάς, καινουργία δὲ μᾶλλον τὰ καθ' ἡμᾶς, ἀναφοίτησιν μὲν οὐδαμῶς τὴν εἰς τὸ ἄνω λάχοντα καὶ ἀναδρομὴν οὐκ ἔχοντα τὴν εἰς ὅπερ ἦν ἐν ἀρχαῖς. . . . If Christ was not fully divine: Τί δὴ οὖν ἄρα διὰ Χριστοῦ πεπλουτήκαμεν, . . . αὐτήν, ὡς ἔοικεν, ἐκλελῃστευμένοι τὴν πρὸς Θεὸν ὁμοίωσιν . . . , εἴπερ ἐστὶν ἡμῶν ἡ πᾶσα μακαριότης ἕν γε τῷ καθ' ὁμοίωσιν γενέσθαι Θεοῦ; see also De Sanctissima Trinitate, dial. VII, PG LXXV, 1089A f. In the recent article by N. Charlier, C.SS.R., "La doctrine sur le Saint-Esprit dans le «Thesaurus» de saint Cyrille d'Alexandrie," Stud. Patr. II, 187 ff., many other texts concerning the reformation of man by the Holy Spirit are cited. Cf. also W. J. Burghardt, S.J., The Image of God in Man according to Cyril of Alexandria (Catholic University of America Studies in Christian Antiquity XIV, Washington, D.C., 1957) 65 ff. and 118, concerning Cyril's views on sanctification and on reform through Christ and the Spirit as return to and increase of Adam's blissful condition. The Cappadocians and Cyril of Alexandria stress the role of the Holy Spirit in man's deifying reform chiefly in order to prove against those who denied the divinity of the Third Person that He who is able to deify must be Himself fully divine; cf. Galtier, op. cit., passim. It can be seen how in the problems of Trinitarian subordinationism (be it Origenist, Arian or Pneumatomachian) both theological and anthropological doctrines are at stake (see also below, p. 96). Some Platonizing Christian theologians in fact went far beyond Basil or Cyril. They tried to strengthen the Trinitarian dogma above all by attempting to demonstrate that the doctrine of the Holy Spirit could explain how the One God could generate a second hypostasis which is not inferior to Him. The Third Person, the mutual spiration of divine love, could be construed as maintaining divine unity. See, for instance, Synesius, Hymn II (IV) 95 ff., Terzaghi, Synes. Cyren. Hymni 29 f. :

ὠδῖνα Πατρός	αὐτὰ μάτηρ,	αὐτὰ πρόχυσις	Πατρὸς ἀθανάτου
γόνιμον βούλαν	αὐτὰ γνωτά,	εὕρετο βλάσταν.	πρόχυσιν πάλι Παῖς
μεσάταν ἀρχάν	αὐτὰ θυγάτηρ	ἔστη δὲ μέσα	εὕρετο βλάσταν.
Ἁγίαν Πνοίαν,	. . .	Θεὸς ἔκ τε Θεοῦ	μονὰς εἶ τριὰς ὤν,
κέντρον γενέτου	ἵνα γὰρ προχυθῇ	διὰ Παῖδα Θεόν	μονὰς ἅ γε μένει
κέντρον δὲ κόρου.	ἐπὶ Παιδὶ Πατήρ,	καὶ διὰ κλεινάν	καὶ τριὰς εἶ δή.

A mystical theology such as that developed by the Greek Fathers may fall short of the individual experiences of the mystic, but it may transcend them through its supra-individual significance. It can under certain circumstances quicken the heartbeat of a whole civilization. The mystical reform ideas of the Greek and eastern Fathers—centered around the key concepts of the return to Paradise, of divine resemblance and assimilation, and of the Kingdom of God—were to become forces which molded the sacral culture of the Byzantine world. Within this culture the moral and sociative aspects of reform were lifted up to, but also to a large degree absorbed in, the overpowering light of the mystical ideal. The fact that Greek and eastern patristic thought could conceive of reform as a *return* to the paradisiac state of innocence must not be understood, of course, in the sense that the eastern Christians were in any way unaware of the tremendous novelty of the Christian dispensation. But they conceived of this very newness as making possible the *restoration* of that newness which was man's part on the first glorious day of his creation.[77]

See also *Hymn* I (III) 210 ff., Terzaghi, *Synes Cyren. Hymni* 13. Both these hymns must date from the period of transition between Synesius' Neoplatonic and his Christian persuasion (cf. C. Lacombrade, *Synésios de Cyrène* [Paris, 1951] 170 ff., 198). See furthermore, Gregory Nazianzen, *Oratio* XXIII, 8, *PG* XXXV, 1160 f.: [Τριὰς] πρώτη γὰρ ὑπερβαίνει δυάδος σύνθεσιν, ἵνα μήτε στένῃ μένῃ ἡ θεότης, μήτε εἰς ἄπειρον χέηται; also *Oratio* XXIX, 2, *PG* XXXVI, 76B f.: . . . μονὰς ἀπ᾽ ἀρχῆς εἰς δυάδα κινηθεῖσα μέχρι τριάδος ἔστη. See finally, Marius Victorinus, *De Trinitate, hymnus* III, *PL* VIII, 1146B: Tu, Spiritus Sancte, connexio es: connexio autem est quidquid connectit duo; ita, ut connectas omnia, primo connectis duo, esque ipsa tertia complexio duorum; atque ipsa complexio nihil distans uno, unum cum facis duo; cf. E. Benz, *Marius Victorinus und die Entwicklung der abendländischen Willensmetaphysik* (Stuttgart, 1932) 129 ff.; also Marius Victorinus, *De Trin., hymn.* I, 3, *PL* VIII, 1139: Adesto, sancte Spiritus, Patris et Filii copula; cf. Benz, *Marius Victorinus* 128 ff., and *ibid.* 394, about Augustine's use of the terms *copula, copulare* for the Holy Ghost, in *De Trinitate* XV, 21, 41, *PL* XLII, 1089, and VIII, 10, 14, *PL* XLII, 960. See on the other hand below, p. 213, on Augustine's non-numerical conception of the divine Trinity. For modern eastern Christian attempts to overcome dualism through Trinitarian doctrine see, for instance, S. Boulgakof, *Le Paraclet*, trans. C. Andronikof (Paris, 1946) 62, 72 f., A. van der Mensbrugghe, *From Dyad to Triad* (London, 1935). On Christian-Platonistic premises the Holy Spirit could also be understood as bringing creation back to God, as reforming creation, which had been the formative work of the Logos. See Marius Victorinus, *De Trin., hymn.* III, *PL* VIII, 1144B: Tu esse cunctis praestas, tu Filii formam, tu Spiritus reformationem: o beata Trinitas; cf. Benz, *Marius Victorinus* 134, also on the related Plotinizing ternary *status-progressio-regressus* in Victorinus. Cf. below, pp. 197 ff., on Augustine's trinitarian reform ideology.

[77] The hope for a return to Paradise, not only in the eschatological, but also in the preeschatological sense, was not lacking in western thought. Yet, as will be seen later, other and rather different aspects of the idea of reform were to gain greater importance in the west.

2. The Recovery of Man's Likeness to God

Whatever the original relationship between the Hebrew terms used for "image" and "likeness" in Genesis 1:26,[1] it was a fateful event in the history of ideas when the Septuagint chose the word ὁμοίωσις (literally: likening) rather than ὁμοίωμα (that which is like) or ὁμοιότης (being alike) for the translation of the second of these two terms. For, the word ὁμοίωσις connotes an element of action which allows, if it does not require, the signification of "assimilation" alongside that of "likeness" or resemblance.[2] Furthermore, before being used by the Greek translators of the Old Testament ὁμοίωσις had already had a long history in Greek philosophic-religious thought. It was bound up with the conception of the assimilation of man to God. I quote only Plato's words from the *Theaetetus* about ὁμοίωσις θεῷ κατὰ τὸ δυνατόν,[3] which together with similar Platonic and Platonist phrases remained an ever-present substratum also of Christian divine-human resemblance ideology in the Greek-speaking world.[4]

Under these circumstances it is not surprising that a distinction and even an antithesis of εἰκών (image) and ὁμοίωσις (likeness) was developed in early Christian Greek exegesis of Genesis 1:26.[5] As far as known the heretical Valentinian gnostics were the first to do so.[6] According to St. Irenaeus they said that man was made κατ᾽ εἰκόνα in so far as he is "material" though not corporeal, καθ᾽ ὁμοίωσιν in so far as psychical. While even the material man of the "image" (identical

---

[1] See above, pp. 58 f.

[2] Cf. the remarks of I. Hausherr, S.J., "L'imitation de Jésus-Christ dans la spiritualité byzantine," *Mélanges Cavallera* 232 f., where the gradual fading of the distinction between such terms as ὁμοίωμα and ὁμοίωσις, μίμημα and μίμησις is also discussed. See also below, pp. 94 f., about Gregory of Nyssa's use of these terms.

[3] *Theaetetus* 176A f. Cf. also *Republic* X, 12, 613A.

[4] See the excellent study by H. Merki, O.S.B., *'ΟΜΟΙΩΣΙΣ ΘΕΩ: Von der platonischen Angleichung an Gott zur Gottähnlichkeit bei Gregor von Nyssa* (Paradosis VII, Freiburg, Schweiz, 1952), in the future see also Merki's article "Ebenbildlichkeit," to appear in *RLAC*.

[5] For the exegetical problem and patristic interpretations of Gen. 1:26 see now H. M. Somers, S.J., "The Riddle of a Plural (Genesis 1:26)," *Folia* IX (1955) 63 ff., and R. McL. Wilson, "The Early History of the Exegesis of Gen. 1:26," *Stud. Patr.* I, 420 ff.

[6] Cf. A. Struker, *Die Gottesebenbildlichkeit des Menschen in der altchristlichen Literatur der ersten zwei Jahrhunderte* (Münster, 1913) 55 ff.; also Wilson, *op. cit.*, 429 f.

with the "earthen" man of Genesis 2:7) was made of invisible substance, he was not consubstantial (ὁμοούσιος) with God; but once he had become psychical and a "likeness" through the breath of God he had received the spirit of life (πνεῦμα ζωῆς) as his substance.[7]

The Valentinians then valued ὁμοίωσις higher than εἰκών. This trait was taken over by Irenaeus himself, and later, perhaps through Irenaeus, by Clement of Alexandria and by Origen.

Irenaeus differs in this respect from the heretical gnosis chiefly in that for him man was created in a true body and not in some quasi-immaterial matter. He too however holds that resemblance to God comes through the spirit in the soul, whereas he refers the image rather to the flesh, that is to say, to the man formed from earth according to Genesis 2:7.[8] The apparent paradox that the corporeal part of man should be according to the image of God, Irenaeus explains beautifully from the fact of the Incarnation:

In previous times man, it is true, was said to have been made according to the image of God, but he was not shown as such. For the Word according to Whose image man was made was still invisible. Therefore also man easily lost the likeness. But when the Word of God was made flesh He confirmed both: for on the one hand He truly showed the image by becoming what His image was; on the other hand He firmly established (κατέστασε) the likeness (or assimilation: ὁμοίωσις) by the coassimilation of man (συνεξομοιώσας τὸν ἄνθρωπον) to the invisible Father through the visible Word.[9]

Thus man, body and soul, could be created in the image of God because God was to become man, body and soul. At the same time

[7] See Irenaeus, Adv. haeres., I, 1, 10, Harvey I, 49. Cf. also Clement of Alexandria, Excerpta ex Theodoto 50–54, GCS, Clem. Alex. III, 123 ff.

[8] Adv. haeres. V, 6, 1, Harvey II, 333 f. : . . . perfectus autem homo commixtio et adunitio est animae assumentis spiritum Patris et admixta ei carni quae est plasmata secundum imaginem Dei . . . Cum autem spiritus hic commixtus animae unitur plasmati . . . spiritalis et perfectus homo factus est: et hic est qui secundum imaginem et similitudinem factus est Dei. Si autem defuerit animae spiritus, animalis est vere qui est talis . . . imaginem quidem habens in plasmate, similitudinem vero non assumens per spiritum. . . .

[9] Ibid. V, 16, 2, ed. Harvey II, 368: Ἐν τοῖς πρόσθεν χρόνοις ἐλέγετο μὲν κατ' εἰκόνα Θεοῦ γεγονέναι τὸν ἄνθρωπον, οὐκ ἐδείκνυτο δέ. Ἔτι γὰρ ἀόρατος ἦν ὁ Λόγος οὗ κατ' εἰκόνα ὁ ἄνθρωπος ἐγεγόνει. Διὰ τοῦτο δὴ καὶ τὴν ὁμοίωσιν ῥᾳδίως ἀπέβαλεν. Ὁπότε δὲ σὰρξ ἐγένετο ὁ Λόγος τοῦ Θεοῦ τὰ ἀμφότερα ἐπεκύρωσε· καὶ γὰρ καὶ τὴν εἰκόνα ἔδειξεν ἀληθῶς αὐτὸς τοῦτο γενόμενος ὅπερ ἦν ἡ εἰκὼν αὐτοῦ· καὶ τὴν ὁμοίωσιν βεβαίως κατέστησε συνεξομοιώσας τὸν ἄνθρωπον τῷ ἀοράτῳ Πατρί. . . .

the Incarnation was not only the assumption of manhood by God, but also the assimilation of manhood to God with and through Christ.

Clement and Origen too distinguish εἰκών and ὁμοίωσις, but in a sense which differs somewhat from that of Irenaeus.

Clement, after an exposé of the Platonic doctrine of assimilation, asks:

Is it not thus that some of ours understand κατ' εἰκόνα, as having been received by man immediately according to creation, καθ' ὁμοίωσιν, however, to be his future destiny according to perfection?[10]

In another famous passage of the Stromata, where in the tracks of Philo he consciously and elaborately weaves together biblical, Platonic, and Stoic concepts of assimilation to God and followership of God, Clement says that the human mind is the image of the image of God which is Christ, the divine Word, whereas ὁμοίωσις—likeness or assimilation—is to follow God, which means leading a virtuous life.[11]

For Clement then not only the relation of ὁμοίωσις but also the image relation between man and God is purely spiritual, an epochal doctrine later taken up by Origen, Gregory of Nyssa, Ambrose,

---

[10] Clement of Alexandria, Stromata II, 22 (131, 6), GCS, Clem. Alex. II, 185: . . . ἢ γὰρ οὐχ οὕτως τινὲς τῶν ἡμετέρων τὸ μὲν κατ' εἰκόνα εὐθέως κατὰ τὴν γένεσιν εἰληφέναι τὸν ἄνθρωπον, τὸ καθ' ὁμοίωσιν δὲ ὕστερον κατὰ τὴν τελείωσιν μέλλειν ἀπολαμβάνειν ἐκδέχονται. See also the distinction between μίμησις-εἰκών and γνῶσις-ὁμοίωσις in Stromata IV, 6 (30, 1 ff.), GCS, Clem. Alex. II 261.

[11] Ibid. V, 14 (94, 5 ff.), GCS, Clem. Alex. II, 388: (after reference to Gen. 2:7 and Gen. 1:26): . . . εἰκὼν μὲν γὰρ Θεοῦ Λόγος θεῖος καὶ βασιλικὸς ἄνθρωπος ἀπαθής, εἰκὼν δ' εἰκόνος ἀνθρώπινος νοῦς. Ἑτέρῳ δ' εἰ βούλει παραλαβεῖν ὀνόματι τὴν ἐξομοίωσιν, εὕροις ἂν παρὰ τῷ Μωυσεῖ [τὴν] ἀκολουθίαν ὀνομαζομένην θείαν· φήσι γὰρ· "Ὀπίσω Κυρίου τοῦ Θεοῦ ὑμῶν πορεύεσθε καὶ τὰς ἐντολὰς αὐτοῦ φυλάξατε" (Deut. 13:4). Ἀκόλουθοι δ', οἶμαι, καὶ θεραπευταὶ Θεοῦ πάντες οἱ ἐνάρετοι. Ἐντεῦθεν οἱ μὲν Στωϊκοὶ τὸ τέλος τῆς φιλοσοφίας τὸ ἀκολούθως τῇ φύσει ζῆν εἰρήκασι, Πλάτων δὲ ὁμοίωσιν Θεῷ (cf. Plato, Theaetetus 176B). Clement then gives several other quotations from Plato, especially Laws 716B ff., about the "old saying" that like agrees with like, measure with measure, and about God who ought to be our measure in all things. On this conception, see the somewhat sketchy article by A. Schneider, "Der Gedanke der Erkenntnis des Gleichen durch Gleiches in antiker und patristischer Zeit," Beiträge zur Geschichte der Philosophie des Mittelalters, Erg. Bd. II (Münster, 1923) 65 ff., and also A.-J. Festugière, Contemplation et vie contemplative selon Platon, 2nd ed. (Paris, 1950) 127, Merki, ΟΜΟΙΩΣΙΣ 22 and 121, R. Arnou, Le désir de Dieu dans la philosophie de Plotin (Paris, s.a.) 143 ff. For Philo as the direct source of Clement's combination of biblical, Platonic, and Stoic motifs in the text quoted above see the excellent remarks of W. Völker, Fortschritt und Vollendung bei Philo von Alexandrien (Texte u. Untersuch. XLIX, 1, Leipzig, 1938) 333, and idem, Der wahre Gnostiker nach Clemens Alexandrinus (Texte u. Untersuch. LVII, Leipzig, 1952) 579 ff.

Augustine, in fact by almost all of the Fathers. Yet ὁμοίωσις nevertheless differs from εἰκών. The latter is the state or condition of primitive creational integrity, the former was given to man at the time of creation as a disposition still to be fulfilled. After the fall and through redemption ὁμοίωσις (or ἐξομοίωσις) has become a "process" which begins with rebirth in baptism and ends in the reformation of the earthly man into a heavenly one—only thus fulfilling man's creation according to the image and likeness.[12] Combining the terminology of Philo and St. Paul, Clement also calls this process imitation (μίμησις) of God or of Christ.[13] Origen stresses the imitation and followership of *Christ* even more than Clement had done and thus is an important figure in the perpetuation of Christ-centered piety[14] to which he contributed so much also through his mystical ideas of a

---

[12] Clement of Alexandria, *Paedagogus* I, 12, 98, 2 f., *GCS, Clem. Alex.* I, 148 f.: . . . καί μοι δοκεῖ αὐτὸς οὗτος πλάσαι μὲν τὸν ἄνθρωπον ἐκ χοός, ἀναγεννῆσαι δὲ ὕδατι, αὐξῆσαι δὲ Πνεύματι, παιδαγωγῆσαι δὲ ῥήματι εἰς υἱοθεσίαν καὶ σωτηρίαν ἁγίαις ἐντολαῖς κατευθύνων, ἵνα δή, τὸν γηγενῆ εἰς ἅγιον καὶ ἐπουράνιον μεταπλάσας ἐκ προσβάσεως ἄνθρωπον, ἐκείνην τὴν θεϊκὴν μάλιστα πληρώσῃ φωνήν· "Ποιήσωμεν ἄνθρωπον κατ᾿ εἰκόνα καὶ καθ᾿ ὁμοίωσιν ἡμῶν" (Gen. 1 : 26). Καὶ δὴ γέγονεν ὁ Χριστὸς τοῦτο πλῆρες ὅπερ εἴρηκεν ὁ Θεός, ὁ δὲ ἄλλος ἄνθρωπος κατὰ μόνην νοεῖται τὴν εἰκόνα. Ἡμεῖς δὲ . . . πληρώσωμεν τὸ θέλεμα τοῦ Πατρός, ἀκούωμεν τοῦ Λόγου καὶ τὸν σωτήριον ὄντως ἀναμαξώμεθα τοῦ σωτῆρος ἡμῶν βίον. . . . Also *ibid.*, III, 12, 101, 1, *loc. cit.*, 291: Δὸς δὲ ἡμῖν τοῖς σοῖς ἑπομένοις παραγγέλμασιν τὸ ὁμοίωμα πληρῶσαι τῆς εἰκόνος . . . Cf. also Völker, *Clemens* 112 f., 532 f., 579 ff. Clement does not always make a strict distinction between εἰκών and ὁμοίωσις, as Dom A. Mayer, *Gottesbild* 22 ff., has shown. Nevertheless it is necessary to stress that for Clement too the ὁμοίωσις *potentially* existed already in Adam (in spite of Mayer, *Gottesbild*, 76 f.). For Clement's conception of image-likeness see also E. F. Osborn, *The Philosophy of Clement of Alexandria* (Cambridge, 1957) 88 ff.

[13] For the origins of Christian μίμησις ideology see Michaelis, article "μίμησις," *ThWbNT* IV, 666 ff., J. M. Nielen, "Die Kultsprache der Nachfolge und Nachahmung Gottes und verwandter Bezeichnungen im neutestamentlichen Schrifttum," *Heil. Überlief.* 59 ff., A. Heitmann, O.S.B., *Imitatio Dei: Die ethische Nachahmung Gottes nach der Väterlehre der zwei ersten Jahrhunderte* (Studia Anselmiana X, Roma, 1940), E. J. Tinsley, "The *Imitatio Christi* in the Mysticism of St. Ignatius of Antioch," *Stud. Patr.* II, 553 ff. Following St. Paul (1 Cor. 11:1, Eph. 5:1, etc.) and Philo, patristic thought begins to place the concept of *mimesis* on the high level of assimilation to God and followership of God, whereas Plato had accorded it at best a relative dignity (cf. my article "The Concept of the Image in the Greek Fathers and the Byzantine Iconoclastic Controversy," *Dumb. Oaks Pap.* VII [Cambridge, Mass., 1953] 1 ff.). For Philo, see Völker, *Philo* 333 f., for Clement, Völker, *Clemens* 582 ff.

[14] See W. Völker, *Das Vollkommenheitsideal des Origenes* (Beiträge zur historischen Theologie, Tübingen, 1931) 215 ff. For St. Athanasius, St. Basil, etc., and for the later Byzantine writers, see Hausherr, "Imitation" 231 ff. Cf. below, p. 91.

bridal union between the soul and Christ[15] and of the birth and growth of Christ in the heart of man.[16] Yet, the imitation of Christ is ultimately conceived by Origen as instrumental imitation of the divine Logos and as directed toward the Father.[17] It will be seen later that this conception played a certain role also in Eusebius' ideology of imperial "Logomimesis."[18]

As to the distinction of "image" and "likeness," it remained relatively sketchy in Clement's writings in comparison with the much more extensive treatment of this matter by Origen.[19]

In *De principiis* III, 6, Origen ponders over a discrepancy between Genesis 1:26 and Genesis 1:27. While according to the former verse God had said, "Let us make man in our image and likeness," the term "likeness" no longer occurs in the latter verse where God is only said to have made man in the image of God. Origen says:

Now the fact that He . . . was silent about the likeness points to nothing else but this, that man received the honor of God's image in his first creation, whereas the perfection of God's likeness was reserved for him at the consummation. The purpose of this was that man should acquire it for himself by his

---

[15] Especially in his *Commentary to the Canticle*; cf. Völker, *Origenes* 100 ff., Lieske, *Origenes* 61 ff.

[16] Cf. Völker, *Origenes* 99 f., H. Rahner, S.J., "Die Gottesgeburt: Die Lehre der Kirchenväter von der Geburt Christi in den Herzen der Gläubigen," *Z. kath. Th.* LIX (1935) 333 ff., Lieske, *Origenes* 67 ff.

[17] See, for instance, *De oratione* 22, 4, GCS, Orig. II, 348: Πᾶν οὖν ἔργον αὐτοῖς καὶ λόγος καὶ νόημα ὑπὸ τοῦ μονογενοῦς Λόγου μεμωρφομένα κατ' αὐτὸν μεμίμηται τὴν εἰκόνα "τοῦ Θεοῦ τοῦ ἀοράτου" (cf. Col. 1:15 [Rom. 8:29, 2 Cor. 3:18]) καὶ γέγονε "κατ' εἰκόνα τοῦ κτίσαντος" (cf. Col. 3:10) . . . ὡς εἶναι ἐν αὐτοῖς "τὴν εἰκόνα τοῦ ἐπουρανίου" (cf. 1 Cor. 15:49) καὶ αὐτοῦ ὄντος εἰκόνος Θεοῦ. Cf.Völker, *Origenes* 101 f., 217, and the review of H.-C. Puech, "Un livre récent sur la mystique d'Origène," *Rev. hist. et philos. rel.* XIII (1933) 524 f.; also Lieske, *Origenes, passim.*

[18] See below, pp. 120 ff., 131 f.

[19] I cannot agree with Dom H. Merki, 'ΟΜΟΙΩΣΙΣ 61, when he considers the homoiosis-motif as secondary in Origen's works. See the similar criticism in the book of H. Crouzel S.J., *Théologie de l'image de Dieu chez Origène* (Théologie XXXIV, Paris, 1956) 261, n. 1, which gives a comprehensive account of Origen's image and assimilation doctrine. (Cf. now also his summary of the book in his article "L'image de Dieu dans la théologie d'Origène," *Stud. Patr.* II, 194 ff.) P. Crouzel shows that Origen, just as Clement before him, is not always consistent in his distinction of εἰκών and ὁμοίωσις; see his book, pp. 179, 217 ff., and especially 221 f., for the question whether Origen conceived of ὁμοίωσις as a mere restoration of the εἰκών or as a progressive development; the answer to the question probably lies in the merely potential existence of the ὁμοίωσις in creation.

own earnest efforts to imitate God, so that, while the possibility of attaining perfection was given to him in the beginning through the honor of the "image," he should in the end through the accomplishment of these works obtain for himself the perfect "likeness."

Origen then refers to John 17:24 and 21:

"Father, I will that, where I am, they also may be with me," and, "as I and thou art one, so they may be one in us." Here indeed the "likeness" seems, if we may say so, to make an advance and from being something similar to become "one thing"; for this reason, undoubtedly that in the consummation or end God is "all in all."[20]

In his *First Homily to Genesis* Origen develops the consoling thought that even though sinful man has given up his image relation to God and taken on an image relation to the Devil he can be "transformed" or "reformed" to a "likeness" (*ad similitudinem*) with the image of God, Christ. For were not some of the Apostles more like images of the Devil than of God? And yet, in following the image of God, Christ, they became similar to Him.[21]

How is such assimilation possible? Only through God's grace. If

[20] Origen, *De principiis* III, 6, 1, GCS, *Orig.* V, 280 f.: Hoc ergo quod dixit "ad imaginem Dei fecit eum" et de similitudine siluit, non aliud indicat nisi quod imaginis quidem dignitatem in prima conditione percepit, similitudinis vero ei perfectio in consummatione servata est: scilicet, ut ipse sibi eam propriae industriae studiis ex Dei imitatione conscisceret, quo possibilitate sibi perfectionis in initiis data per imaginis dignitatem in fine demum per operum expletionem perfectam sibi ipse similitudinem consummaret. . . . Ipse quoque Dominus in evangelio haec eadem . . . futura designat dum ipse hoc a Patre discipulis suis impetrare dignatur dicens: "Pater volo ut ubi ego sum et isti mecum sint" et "sicut ego et tu unum sumus, ita et isti in nobis unum sint" (John 17:24 and 21). In quo iam videtur ipsa similitudo, si dici potest, proficere et ex simili unum iam fieri, pro eo sine dubio quod in consummatione vel fine omnia et in omnibus Deus est (cf. 1 Cor. 15:28). See also *Contra Celsum* IV, 30, GCS, *Orig.* I, 299; *Comment. in Epist. ad Rom.* IV, 5, PG XIV, 978B.

[21] Origen, *In Genesim, homil.* I, 13, GCS, *Orig.* VI, 18 ff.: Et nemo desperet, videns similitudinem suam magis esse cum diabolo quam cum Deo, posse se iterum recuperare formam imaginis Dei quia non venit Salvator vocare iustos sed peccatores in poenitentiam (cf. Luke 5:32, Matthew 10:3). Matthaeus publicanus erat et utique imago eius diabolo similis erat, sed veniens ad imaginem Dei, Dominum et Salvatorem nostrum, et sequens eam transformatus est ad similitudinem imaginis Dei . . . Paulus ipsius imaginis Dei persecutor erat. Ut autem potuit decorem eius et pulchritudinem contueri, visa ea in tantum ad eius similitudinem reformatus est ut diceret: "An documentum quaeritis eius qui in me loquitur Christus?" (2 Cor. 13:3).

Moses and the Psalmist call men gods, if St. John says *similes illi erimus*, this means that men are *capaces Dei*, but only by grace and by participation; nobody is similar to God through his own power or by his own nature (*vel in potentia vel in natura*).[22] But man must do all in his power through his imitation or followership of Christ to create the necessary conditions for his assimilation to God.[23] For though man is *logikos*, being made in the image of the Image of God, in the image of the Logos,[24] he must still attain that which truly makes him an image of the Image, namely "likeness."[25]

St. Athanasius differs from St. Irenaeus, Clement, and Origen in that he does not adopt their distinction between the terms εἰκών and ὁμοίωσις of Genesis 1:26.[26] Similitude with God is for him simply the content of the image.[27] The rare use of the former concept in his

---

[22] Origen, *In Exodum*, homil. VI, 5, GCS, Orig. VI, 196 f. (with reference to Ex. 15, 11: Τίς ὅμοιος σοι ἐν θεοῖς κύριε): ... deos illos dicit qui per gratiam et participationem Dei dii appellantur. De quibus et alibi scriptura dicit: "Ego dixi: dii estis" (Ps. 81:6). ... Sed hi, quamvis capaces sint Dei et hoc nomine donari per gratiam videantur, nullus tamen Deo similis invenitur vel in potentia vel in natura. Et licet Joannes apostolus dicat: "Filioli, nondum scimus quid futuri sumus, si autem revelatus nobis fuerit"— de Domino scilicet dicens—"similes illi erimus" (1 John 3:2), similitudo tamen haec non ad naturam sed ad gratiam revocatur. ... See below, pp. 194 f., for St. Augustine's use of these same scriptural passages.

[23] Origen, *In Lucam*, homil. *VIII*, GCS, Orig. IX, 56: Translation of St. Jerome: Si considerem Dominum Salvatorem imaginem esse invisibilis Dei et videam animam meam factam ad imaginem conditoris ut imago esset imaginis—neque enim anima mea specialiter imago est Dei, sed ad similitudinem imaginis prioris effecta est—tunc videbo quoniam in exemplum eorum qui solent imagines pingere et uno, verbi causa, vultu regis accepto ad principalem similitudinem exprimendam artis industriam commodare, unusquisque nostrum ad imaginem Christi formans animam suam aut maiorem ei aut minorem ponit imaginem vel obsoletam vel sordidam aut claram atque lucentem et respondentem ad effigiem imaginis principalis. ... Greek Fragment: Ὅτι εἰκών ἐστι τοῦ Θεοῦ τοῦ ἀοράτου, οὐ γενομένη εἰκών, ἀλλὰ κατ᾽ εἰκόνα προυπάρχουσαν αὐτῆς. Ἕκαστος δὲ ἡμῶν τὴν ἑαυτοῦ ψυχὴν τελειῶν καὶ προάγων ἐπὶ μακαριότητα οἷον εἰκόνα τοῦ Χριστοῦ ἀνατίθησιν ἤτοι μιμουμένην τὸν πρωτότυπον τὸν Υἱὸν τοῦ Θεοῦ τὴν εἰκόνα τοῦ Θεοῦ.

[24] See In Joannem II, 3, 20, GCS, Orig. IV, 55: Ὁ γὰρ ἐν ἑκάστῳ λόγος τῶν λογικῶν τοῦτον τὸν λόγον ἔχει πρὸς τὸν ἐν ἀρχῇ Λόγον, πρὸς τὸν Θεὸν ὄντα Λόγον Θεόν, ὃν ὁ Θεὸς Λόγος πρὸς τὸν Θεόν· ὡς γὰρ αὐτόθεος καὶ ἀληθινὸς Θεὸς ὁ Πατὴρ πρὸς εἰκόνα καὶ εἰκόνας τῆς εἰκόνος (διὸ καὶ κατ᾽ εἰκόνα λέγονται εἶναι οἱ ἄνθρωποι, οὐκ εἰκόνες), οὕτως ὁ αὐτόλογος πρὸς τὸν ἐν ἑκάστῳ λόγον.

[25] Cf. Lieske, *Origenes* 102 ff., 131 ff.

[26] Cf. R. Bernard, *L'image de Dieu d'après saint Athanase* (Théologie XXV, Paris, 1952) 27 ff., Merki, ΟΜΟΙΩΣΙΣ 141.

[27] Athanasius, *Oratio contra gentes* 2, PG XXV, 5C–D.

anthropology[28] would seem to reflect the terminology of his theological and Trinitarian doctrine which rejected the term ὅμοιος κατ' οὐσίαν as too weak to express the "consubstantiality" (the ὁμοούσιος) of the Son with the Father and at the same time opposed the pretension of any essential resemblance between God and man.[29]

St. Gregory of Nyssa[30] continues, clarifies, and completes both Origen's and Athanasius' anthropological views. As Athanasius, he does not make a distinction between the εἰκών and the ὁμοίωσις of Genesis 1:26,[31] but he develops all the more strongly and originally the significance of that similitude to God which was contained in the creational divine image in man and must be restored in him. He likes to repeat with slight variations a memorable sentence:

The definition of human beatitude is the assimilation to God.[32]

[28] Cf. Bernard, Image 28 f.

[29] Cf. Bernard, Image 114 ff. and 29.

[30] The following characterization of Gregory of Nyssa's role in the history of the idea of reform owes much to several recent important works on the great Cappadocian mystic: J. Daniélou, S.J., Platonisme et théologie mystique: Doctrine spirituelle de saint Grégoire de Nysse, 2nd ed. (Paris, 1953), A. Lieske, S.J., "Die Theologie der Christusmystik Gregors von Nyssa," Z. kath. Th. LXX (1948) 129 ff., R. Leys, S.J., L'image de Dieu chez saint Grégoire de Nysse (Museum Lessianum, Sect. Théol. XLIX, Bruxelles, Paris, 1951), see now also his article "La théologie spirituelle de Grégoire de Nysse," Stud. Patr. II, 495 ff., furthermore Merki, 'ΟΜΟΙΩΣΙΣ, J. Gaïth, La conception de la liberté chez Grégoire de Nysse (Paris, 1953), W. Völker, Gregor von Nyssa als Mystiker (Wiesbaden, 1955), W. Jaeger, Two Rediscovered Works of Ancient Christian Literature: Gregory of Nyssa and Macarius (Leiden, 1954), the latter study based on the recent edition of Gregory's ascetical works by W. Jaeger, J. P. Cavarnos, and Virginia Callahan, Gregorii Nysseni Opera VIII, 1: Gregorii Nysseni Opera Ascetica (Leiden, 1952). Professor Jaeger's book is particularly illuminating with regard to the continuity between Christian and pre-Christian ascesis including such ideas as purification, spiritual combat, and—as the ascetic's goal—assimilation with and contemplation of God. From this point of view, one might not unreasonably consider Christian and especially Greek Christian reform ideology as the heir of the ideology of paideia (for which see W. Jaeger, Paideia I–III, trans. by G. Highet [New York, 1939–1944], idem, Rediscovered Works 108 ff., idem, "Von Affen und wahren Christen," Varia Variorum 161 ff.

[31] On this point, which has been clarified by Merki, 'ΟΜΟΙΩΣΙΣ, see below, pp. 94 f., especially n. 43.

[32] Gregory of Nyssa, In Psalmos 1, PG XLIV, 433C: . . . ὅρος ἐστὶ τῆς ἀνθρωπίνης μακαριότητος ἡ πρὸς τὸ θεῖον ὁμοίωσις. . . . See also ibid. 12, PG XLIV, 557C: ῎Ιδιος δὲ χαρακτὴρ ἀνθρώπου ἡ πρὸς τὸ θεῖον ὁμοίωσις, De beatitudinibus, or. I, PG XLIV, 1200C: . . . ἡ δὲ τοῦ μακαρισμοῦ κοινωνία τοῖς ἀνθρώποις διὰ τῆς πρὸς τὸν Θεόν ἐστιν ὁμοιώσεως . . . In Cantica Canticorum, hom. IX, PG XLIV, 960D f.: Πέρας γὰρ τῆς ἐναρέτου ζωῆς ἡ πρὸς τὸ θεῖόν ἐστιν ὁμοίωσις. . . . Cf. Merki, 'ΟΜΟΙΩΣΙΣ 105–110.

Combining the ideas of similitude and imitation, he explains:

By way of interpreting, therefore, through a definition the notion of Christianity we shall say that Christianity is the imitation of the divine nature. . . . For the first making of man was according to the imitation of God's likeness (ὁμοιότητος) . . . and the promise of Christianity is that man will be brought back to the original happiness (εἰς τὴν ἀρχαίαν εὐκληρίαν). If then originally man was God's likeness (ὁμοίωμα), our definition will probably not miss the mark if we declare that Christianity is an imitation of divine nature.[33]

Again, how is such assimilation and imitation possible? This question Gregory answers even more thoroughly and deeply than Origen, perhaps, because in his doctrine the process of assimilation is more fully (though not wholly) freed from the element of cyclical recurrence which was part of their common Neoplatonic inheritance.

Even more than for the earlier Greek Fathers man's reformation or re-assimilation to the image of God is for Gregory first and last purification, the restoration of purity (καθαρότης).[34] In working out the idea of the reform of man to the image and likeness of God the Greek Fathers ever so often described this process as the cleaning of a painting, spoiled but not completely ruined by the application of wrong colors and especially by the accumulation of dirt and dust.[35] In his Thirteenth Homily to Genesis Origen had said that the divine image cannot be seen as long as the "house" of the human soul is filled with uncleanness and rubbish.[36] The Son of God is the painter of this

---

[33] Gregory of Nyssa, De professione christiana, Jaeger, Greg. Nyss. Opera VIII, 1, 136: Οὐκοῦν ὡς ἄν τις ὅρῳ τοῦ χριστιανισμοῦ τὴν διάνοιαν ἑρμηνεύσειεν, οὕτως ἐροῦμεν, ὅτι χριστιανισμός ἐστι τῆς θείας φύσεως μίμησις. . . . Ἥ τε γὰρ πρώτη τοῦ ἀνθρώπου κατασκευή κατὰ μίμησιν τῆς τοῦ Θεοῦ ὁμοιότητος ἦν . . . καὶ ἡ τοῦ χριστιανισμοῦ ἐπαγγελία ἐστὶ τὸ εἰς τὴν ἀρχαίαν εὐκληρίαν ἐπαναχθῆναι τὸν ἄνθρωπον.

Εἰ δὲ τὸ ἀρχαῖον Θεοῦ ὁμοίωμα ὁ ἄνθρωπος ἦν, τάχα οὐκ ἔξω τοῦ σκοποῦ τὸν ὁρισμὸν πεποιή-μεθα μίμησιν θείας φύσεως τὸν χριστιανισμὸν εἶναι ἀποφηνάμενοι.

[34] For the pre-Christian Greek tradition of the idea of purity and purification of the mind, see Jaeger, Rediscovered Works 27; cf. J. Trouillard, La purification plotinienne (Paris, 1955). See also Jaeger, Rediscovered Works 32 f., for the way in which the Greek concepts of τελειότης and ἀρετή were incorporated in patristic thought and ibid. 80 for the mixture of Platonic and Stoic terms which have served Gregory for his own terminology.

[35] See Ladner, "Image," especially, p. 25, n. 58, where the topoi of God as painter of the divine image in the soul and of the cleansing of the latter are discussed at greater length. See furthermore E. R. Curtius, European Literature, Excursus XXI.

[36] Origen, In Genesim, homil. XIII, 4, GCS, Orig. VI, 119, 17 f.: Haec in te videri non poterat, donec domus tua sordida erat immunditiis et ruderibus repleta.

image, but man can paint over it "the image of the earthly" (1 Cor. 15:49). The vices are so many colors which cover the original painting. Therefore, man must implore God that he delete all these wrong colors so that the image will shine again in its creational splendor.[37] Athanasius gives a somewhat different turn to the same idea when he says that an image ruined by dirt can be renewed only if the one after whom it had been made—Christ in the case of the divine image in man—is present again.[38] Gregory of Nyssa in his treatise *On Virginity* says that "the godlike beauty of the soul, made in imitation of its prototype," namely God, is now like "iron blackened by the rust of evil." He also uses the comparison (Plotinian in its terminology) of a man who slips and falls into the mud, with which he is then covered to such an extent that he can no longer be recognized. Reason counsels such a man to wash himself with clean water.[39] He goes on

---

[37] *Ibid.*, GCS, *Orig.* VI, 119, 24 ff.: Filius Dei est pictor huius imaginis (i.e., of the image of Gen. 1:26). Et quia talis et tantus est pictor, imago eius obscurari per incuriam potest, deleri per malitiam non potest. Manet enim semper imago Dei, licet tu tibi ipse superducas "imaginem terreni" (cf. 1 Cor. 15:49). Istam picturam tu tibi ipse depingis. Cum enim te libido fuscaverit, induxisti unum colorem terrenum; si vero et avaritia aestuas, miscuisti et alium. . . . Et sic per singulas quasque malitiae species . . . hanc imaginem terreni . . . tu tibi ipse depingis. . . . Cf. also Gregory of Nyssa, *De hominis opificio* 5, PG XLIV, 137; *De perfectione*, Jaeger, *Gregor. Nyss. Opera* VIII, 1, 195 f.; *De professione christiana*, Jaeger, *Gregor. Nyss. Opera* VIII, 1, 137, continuation of the text quoted, p. 91, n. 33.

[38] Athanasius, *De incarnatione* 14, PG XXV, 120: Ὡς γὰρ τῆς γραφείσης ἐν ξύλῳ μορφῆς παραφανισθείσης ἐκ τῶν ἔξωθεν ῥύπων πάλιν χρεία τοῦτον παραγενέσθαι οὗ καί ἐστιν ἡ μορφὴ ἵνα ἀνακαινισθῆναι ἡ εἰκὼν δυνηθῇ ἐν τῇ αὐτῇ ὕλῃ—διὰ γὰρ τὴν εἰκόνος γραφὴν ἡ αὐτὴ καὶ ὕλη ἐν ᾗ καὶ γέγραψαι οὐκ ἐκβάλλεται, ἀλλ' ἐν αὐτῇ ἀνατυποῦται—κατὰ τοῦτο καὶ ὁ πανάγιος τοῦ Πατρὸς Υἱὸς εἰκὼν ὢν τοῦ Πατρὸς παρεγένετο ἐπὶ τοὺς ἡμετέρους τόπους ἵνα τὸν κατ' αὐτὸν πεποιημένον ἄνθρωπον ἀνακαινίσῃ. . . .

[39] Gregory of Nyssa, *De virginitate*, ed. Cavarnos, in Jaeger, *Greg. Nyss. Opera* VIII, 1, 299 f.: Πᾶν γὰρ κτίσμα Θεοῦ καλὸν . . . · ἀλλ' ἐπειδὴ . . . εἰσεφθάρη τῇ ζωῇ τῶν ἀνθρώπων ἡ τοῦ ἁμαρτάνειν ἀκολουθία . . . καὶ τὸ θεοειδὲς ἐκεῖνο τῆς ψυχῆς κάλλος τὸ κατὰ μίμησιν τοῦ πρωτοτύπου γενόμενον οἷόν τις σίδηρος κατεμελάνθη τῷ τῆς κακίας ἰῷ, οὐκέτι τηνικαῦτα τῆς οἰκείας αὐτῷ καὶ κατὰ φύσιν εἰκόνος τὴν χάριν διέσωζεν, ἀλλὰ πρὸς τὸ αἶσχος τῆς ἁμαρτίας μετεμορφώθη. Ὅθεν τὸ μέγα καὶ τίμιον τοῦτο ὁ ἄνθρωπος, ὡς ὑπὸ τῆς γραφῆς ὠνομάσθη (cf. 2 Peter 1:4), ἐκπεσὼν τῆς οἰκείας ἀξίας οἷον πάσχουσιν οἱ ἐξ ὀλισθήματος ἐγκατενεχθέντες βορβόρῳ καὶ τῷ πηλῷ τὴν μορφὴν ἑαυτῶν ἐξαλείψαντες ἀνεπίγνωστοι καὶ τοῖς συνήθεσι γίνονται, οὕτω κἀκεῖνος ἐμπεσὼν τῷ βορβόρῳ τῆς ἁμαρτίας ἀπώλεσε μὲν τὸ εἰκὼν εἶναι τοῦ ἀφθάρτου Θεοῦ, τὴν δὲ φθαρτὴν καὶ πηλίνην εἰκόνα διὰ τῆς ἁμαρτίας μετημφιάσατο ἢν ἀποθέσθαι συμβουλεύει ὁ λόγος οἷόν τινι ὕδατι τῷ καθαρῷ τῆς πολιτείας ἀποκλυσάμενον ὡς ἂν περιαιρεθέντος τοῦ γηΐνου καλύμματος πάλιν τῆς ψυχῆς φανερωθείη τὸ κάλλος. Cf. Plotinus, *Ennead* I, 6, 5: οἷον εἴ τις δὺς εἰς πηλὸν ἢ βόρβορον τὸ μὲν ὅπερ εἶχε κάλλος μηκέτι προφαίνοι, τοῦτο δὲ ὁρῷτο,

to an allegorical interpretation of the parable of the lost drachma in Luke 15:9, in which he largely follows Origen.[40] He considers the drachma as a symbol of the image of God in man, not really lost, but only hidden by uncleannesses of the flesh, which must be swept out and purged by concentrating one's whole life on this purpose. In a passage already quoted in part he adds that the meaning of the finding of the sought-for coin is the restoration to its original paradisiac state of the divine image covered by carnal dirt.[41]

Beside painting metaphors, similes from the art of the sculptor are related to these ideas of purification. In the tracks of Plotinus, Gregory of Nyssa compares the progress of man's soul to the making of an image of stone: the first step is separation from the rock of brute matter; then follows a long process of carving out and polishing with finer and finer instruments until the work of the artist becomes similar to the image in his thought. The removal of material by the sculptor is thus another symbol of purification, of spiritualization, of the assimilation of man to God.[42]

It was stated above that Origen and Clement had conceived of

ὁ παρὰ τοῦ πηλοῦ ἢ βορβόρου ἀπεμάξατο. See Daniélou, *Platonisme* 224 ff.; Merki, ΟΜΟΙ-ΩΣΙΣ 115 ff.; M. Aubineau, S.J., "Le thème du «bourbier» dans la littérature grecque profane et chrétienne," *Rech.'s sc. rel*, XLVII (1959) 185 ff. For the rust metaphor, see also Gregory of Nyssa, *De beatitudinibus*, oratio VI, PG XLIV, 1272A.

[40] Origen, *In Genesim*, homil. XIII, 4, GCS, *Orig*. VI, 119, 8 ff. For a detailed comparison of this text and the Gregorian one, quoted in n. 41, see Merki, ΟΜΟΙΩΣΙΣ 149 ff.

[41] Gregory of Nyssa, *De virginitate* 12 Cavarnos, in Jaeger, *Greg. Nyss. Opera* VIII, 1, 301 f.: Διὰ δὲ τῆς ζητουμένης δραχμῆς τὴν εἰκόνα πάντως τοῦ βασιλέως αἰνίσσεται, τὴν οὐχὶ παντελῶς ἀπολομένην, ἀλλ᾽ ὑποκεκρυμμένην τῇ κόπρῳ. Κόπρον δὲ χρὴ νοεῖν, ὡς οἶμαι, τὴν τῆς σαρκὸς ῥυπαρίαν, ἧς ἀποσαρωθείσης καὶ ἀποκαθαρθείσης διὰ τῆς ἐπιμελείας τοῦ βίου ἔκδηλον τὸ ζητούμενον γίνεσθαι. . . . Εἰ οὖν αὕτη ἐστὶν ἡ ἐπίνοια τῆς τοῦ ζητουμένου εὑρέσεως ἡ τῆς θείας εἰκόνος εἰς τὸ ἀρχαῖον ἀποκατάστασις τῆς νῦν ἐν τῷ τῆς σαρκὸς ῥύπῳ κεκαλυμμένης, ἐκεῖνο γενώμεθα, ὃ ἦν παρὰ τὴν πρώτην ἑαυτοῦ ζωὴν ὁ πρωτόπλαστος (for the continuation of this text, see above, pp. 76 f., nn. 57–59).

[42] *De hominis opificio* 30, PG XLIV, 253C: Οἶον δὲ ἐπὶ τῶν λιθογλύφων ἔστιν ἰδεῖν. Πρόκειται μὲν γὰρ τῷ τεχνίτῃ ζῴου τινος εἶδος ἐν λίθῳ δεῖξαι· τοῦτο δὲ προθέμενος πρῶτον μὲν τὸν λίθον τῆς συμφυοῦς ὕλης ἀπέρρηξεν· εἶτα περικόψας αὐτοῦ τὰ περιττὰ προήγαγέ πως διὰ τοῦ πρώτου σχήματος τῇ μιμήσει τῇ κατὰ πρόθεσιν . . . πάλιν ἐπεργασάμενος προσήγγισε πλέον τῇ ὁμοιότητι τοῦ σπουδαζομένου. Εἶτα τὸ τέλειον καὶ ἀκριβὲς εἶδος ἐγχειρουργήσας τῇ ὕλῃ εἰς πέρας τὴν τέχνην προήγαγε. . . . See also the longer exposition of the same thought in Gregory's *In Psalmos* 11, PG, XLIV, 531D–544. For the dependence on Plotinus—clearly established by Daniélou, *Platonisme* 46 and Merki, ΟΜΟΙΩΣΙΣ 113 f.—see *Ennead* I, 6, 9. Cf. E. Panofsky, *Idea* (Studien der Bibliothek Warburg V, Leipzig, Berlin, 1924) 14 f., 5 f., 8 ff.; also Ladner, "Image," especially 12.

ὁμοίωσις as the perfection of the original image of God in man; also that Gregory had considered ὁμοίωσις as the realization of what existed already in the εἰκών. When Gregory refers to Genesis 1:26 he uses interchangeably not only "image" and "likeness," but also the "static" terms ὁμοίωμα (that which is alike) or ὁμοιότης (being alike) and the "dynamic" term ὁμοίωσις (which literally means becoming alike), thus stressing man's creational resemblance to God as the foundation in divine grace of all human, but divinely assisted, efforts to become similar to Him again.[43]

[43] See, for instance, De virginitate 12, Cavarnos, in Jaeger, Greg. Nyss. Opera VIII, 1, 300: Οὐ γὰρ ἡμέτερον ἔργον οὐδὲ δυνάμεως ἀνθρωπίνης ἐστὶ κατόρθωμα ἡ πρὸς τὸ θεῖον ὁμοίωσις, ἀλλὰ τοῦτο μὲν τῆς τοῦ Θεοῦ μεγαλοδωρεᾶς ἐστιν, εὐθὺς ἅμα τῇ πρώτῃ γενέσει χαρισαμένου τῇ φύσει τὴν πρὸς αὐτὸν ὁμοιότητα. Here the creational image-likeness (ὁμοιότης) is clearly the basis for all later assimilation (ὁμοίωσις), and both are gifts of God's grace (cf. the text from Origen, quoted p. 89, n. 22). For the use of ὁμοίωμα, ὁμοιότης beside ὁμοίωσις in Gregory of Nyssa, see also the texts from De hominis opificio 30, PG XLIV, 253C, and De professione christiana, Jaeger, Greg. Nyss. Opera VIII, 136, quoted above, pp. 91, 93, nn. 33, 42 and the text from De beatitudinibus, oratio VI, quoted below, p. 101, n. 67. For the relation between εἰκών and ὁμοίωσις according to Gregory of Nyssa and for the fact that both concepts move on the supranatural plane of grace, see Leys, Image 116 ff., 97 ff., 135 f., and above all Merki, ΌΜΟΙΩΣΙΣ part II, also H. de. Lubac, S.J., Surnaturel: Etudes historiques (Théologie VIII, Paris, 1946) where it is shown that on the whole the Greek Fathers emphasized more strongly than the Latins that already in the original condition of man both the fulness of grace and natural perfection were present (which does not mean that they were incapable of distinguishing the natural and the supranatural from one another; cf. de Lubac, Sur-naturel, 365 ff., Leys, Image, 99 ff.). This difficult problem need not be further discussed here, except for the reminder that it is, perhaps, related to the fact that in Greek Christian reform ideology the return to Paradise is comparatively more important than the reformatio ad melius (see above, pp. 67–82). Dom Hubert Merki, in his valuable study ΌΜΟΙΩΣΙΣ, which with exemplary philological method traces especially the ancient pagan roots of the patristic homoiosis concept, has firmly established the equivalence in Gregory's doctrine of εἰκών and ὁμοίωσις, both in creation and in reformation. He also convincingly refutes (pp. 165 ff., Appendix a) recent attempts (by E. v. Ivanka, "Die Autorschaft der Homilien Εἰς τὸ Ποιήσωμεν . . . ," Byz. Z. XXXVI [1936] 46 ff., and by Leys, Image 130 ff.) to save the authenticity of the two homilies Εἰς τὸ Ποιήσωμεν ἄνθρωπον κατ' εἰκόνα ἡμετέραν καὶ ὁμοίωσιν, In verba "Faciamus hominem secundum imaginem et similitudinem nostram" ascribed to Gregory of Nyssa (PG XLIV, 257 ff.), which clearly make the same sharp distinction between εἰκών and ὁμοίωσις which is found in Irenaeus, Clement, and Origen; see above, pp. 84 ff. (Merki was not aware of the fact that the homilies which go under the name of St. Basil and under the title De structura hominis [PG XXX, 9 ff.] constitute a longer and modified version of those entitled In verba "Faciamus . . . ," ascribed to Gregory; cf. S. Giet, "Saint Basile a-t-il donné une suite aux homélies de l'héxaméron?," Rech.'s sc. rel. XXXIII [1946] 317 ff., David Amand [de Mendieta], O.S.B., "Les états de texte des homélies pseudo-basiliennes sur la création de l'homme," Rev. bén. LIX [1949] 3 ff., J. Daniélou, S.J., "La chronologie des sermons de Grégoire de Nysse," Rev. sc. rel.

Similarity thus even more than the "image" is the dominant relation which links man to God in the thought of Gregory of Nyssa as well as in that of most of the Greek Fathers with the one great exception of Athanasius.[44] The image relation is important to them chiefly because it contains the relation of resemblance. This is no doubt due to the influence of Platonism which never completely shook off the conception of an image as something inferior or second best if compared to its archetype.[45] The dialectic of like and unlike on the other hand, as it appears in Plato's late dialogues,[46] must have been congenial to Christian thinkers who desired to make use of Platonic formulations in order to illustrate the closest possible relation between the creature man and the creator God. For it had been one of the main concerns of Platonism to show that, while it is impossible for man to speak of like without unlike, of same without other, of one without many, of being without nonbeing, this fact does not destroy the positive meaning of a concept such as likeness.[47]

What has been called the "agonal" character of Platonic dialectics, the status of the Platonic "logos" as an "in-between" (μεταξύ),[48] could be fitted to the Christian doctrine of the assimilation of man to

XXIX [1955] 346 ff.; Giet and Daniélou believe that the shorter recension of the homilies [i.e., In verba, "Faciamus . . ."] is based on notes taken after homilies given by Basil). Merki, perhaps, stresses too strongly the static character, which ὁμοίωσις, just as εἰκών, can have in Gregory's terminology, though he admits that the equivalence of both concepts is in part due to the dynamic component of ὁμοίωσις, which Gregory can transfer even to the εἰκών. Merki does not discuss the occasional use of the truly static terms ὁμοιότης and ὁμοίωμα by Gregory and their distinctness from the more dynamic ὁμοίωσις (see also p. 83). He is right in asserting that Gregory is the first among the Fathers to attribute to man the ὁμοίωσις Θεῷ, in the fullest Christian meaning of the term, not only at the end but also at the beginning of his history; but this does not mean that this ὁμοίωσις is necessarily static, cf. below, p. 98.

[44] See above, p. 89 f.

[45] For this very complex matter, see, for instance, E. Cassirer, "Eidos und Eidolon," Vorträge der Bibliothek Warburg 1922–1923 I (1924) 1 ff., H. Wilms, ΕΙΚΩΝ (Münster, 1935), also Ladner, "Image."

[46] Especially, in the Parmenides 132D and 148 and in the Sophist 259. Cf. La Touche Godfrey, "Plato's Doctrine of Participation," Hermathena LXIII (1944) 4, also J. Stenzel, Zahl und Gestalt bei Platon und Aristoteles, 2nd ed. (Leipzig, Berlin, 1933) 154, H. Cherniss, "Parmenides and the 'Parmenides' of Plato," Amer. Jour. Philol. LIII (1932) 124 ff.

[47] The transcendence of the divine nevertheless remains in Platonism as well as in Christianity. For Plotinus see P. Aubin, "L'«image» dans l'œuvre de Plotin," Rech.'s sc. rel. XLI (1953) 348 ff.

[48] E. Przywara, S.J., Analogia Entis; Metaphysik I (München, 1932) 67 ff.

the Word of God, Christ[49]—even though it might not be easy to avoid making the divine Logos Himself a μεταξύ, as Origen's subordination-ism[50] and later Arianism were to demonstrate.

Though overcome during the Arian struggles on the level of Trini-tarian dogmatics, Platonist-Origenist doctrines of this general type did indeed influence in some degree, though terminologically more than substantially, even the anthropology of a fighter against Arianism such as Gregory. It does look at first glance as if Gregory had taught that the Logos of God, and in Him God Himself, could be encompassed by the pure or purified, the virtuous, soul; but this first impression is deceptive, as the sequel will soon show.[51] The doctrine in question is couched in one of the most significant metaphors in Greek patristic assimilation ideology, that of the soul as a polished mirror in which God Himself can be seen even in this life.[52] Sources of this metaphor are to be found in Holy Scripture: in the "Sixth Beatitude" of the Sermon on the Mount (Matthew 5:8), where Christ said:

Blessed are the clean of heart; for they shall see God

and, more important for reform ideology, in one of the crucial Pauline texts, 2 Cor. 3:18:

But we all beholding (κατοπτριζόμενοι, that is to say, mirroring) the glory

---

[49] See Gregory of Nyssa, Contra Eunomium I, Jaeger, Greg. Nyss. Opera I, 275, about man as μεθόριος between the divine and the earthly; cf. Merki, 'ΟΜΟΙΩΣΙΣ 94 and W. Jaeger, Nemesios von Emesa (Berlin, 1914), for the relation to the old idea of συνδεσμός.

[50] Cf. Lieske, Origenes 178 ff., for the way in which this subordinationism is rooted in the Origenist close tie-up between the Logos and a quasi-eternal, quasi-necessary creation: beside being eternally generated by the Father, the Logos is also eternally mediator between God and this creation, thus He becomes somehow dependent on the latter and consequently is not quite on the same level as the Father; in this respect Origen was strongly influenced both by Neoplatonism and by Philo. See also Crouzel, Image 112 ff. For Origen's latent subordinationism, for its relation to Arianism, and for the way in which the great Cappa-docians overcame this whole trend of thought see E. v. Ivanka, Hellenisches und Christliches im frühbyzantinischen Geistesleben (Wien, 1948) 24 ff.

[51] Origen, though he held that man can be like God only through grace (see p. 89, n. 22), had seen this grace as a necessary consequence, so to speak, of the Logos' mediatorship between God and the God-seeking soul (see preceding note); cf. the discussion of the difference between Origen and Gregory also in this respect, by Lieske, "Gregor" 63, 145 ff., 315 ff. See also above, pp. 79 ff., about Cyril of Alexandria's even less Origenist conception of the great role of the Holy Spirit in the sanctification and reformation of man.

[52] Cf. Daniélou, Platonisme 223 ff., Leys, Image 39 ff., Merki, 'ΟΜΟΙΩΣΙΣ 153 ff.

of the Lord with open face are transformed into the same image from glory to glory as by the Spirit of the Lord,[53]

a verse which could be interpreted by Origen in the sense of the deifying vision of God in the soul.[54] Platonic and Neoplatonic sources also contributed to this conception. With regard to Gregory of Nyssa it has been pointed out that he probably knew the (Pseudo-)Platonic *First Alcibiades*, in which self-knowledge of the soul is made dependent on the soul's seeing itself in its most divine part—that which has to do with wisdom and knowledge—as in a mirror.[55] Gregory was however not concerned so much with self-knowledge of the soul as with the knowledge of God in the soul.[56] His aim was the vision of God which makes man similar to God: for it was old Greek and old Christian tradition that to assert that man can see God is only another way of expressing the God-likeness of man.

St. Athanasius had already said that it is through his own purity that man sees the image of the Father, that is to say, the Word of God, in whose image he was made. This holds true for the first man, Adam, and for the mind of all men, who are his descendents: if the mind does not follow the bent of the body, it is carried upward and rejoices in the sight of God and is ever renewed in the desire for Him. For it is the meaning of the "Sixth Beatitude" (Matthew 5:8) that

The soul's purity is capable of mirroring God through itself.[57]

This is the burden also of Gregory of Nyssa's thought.[58] Assimilation to God, God-likeness regained, enables man to see God, while it is the vision of God which makes man God-like, which deifies

---

[53] Cf. above, p. 54.

[54] Origen, *In Joannem* XXXII, 27, 17, *GCS, Orig.* IV, 472, 27 ff. (quoted by Crouzel, *Image* 233).

[55] *Alcibiades I* 132 f.; cf. H. Cherniss, *The Platonism of Gregory of Nyssa* (University of California Publications in Classical Philology XI, 1, Berkeley, 1930) 40. Cf. also Plotinus, *Ennead* IV, 3, 11; 5, 7; VI, 2, 22.

[56] Already Plotinus, *Ennead* V, 3, 9, used the idea in the sense that man in contemplating the θειότατον of his soul can reach the divine νοῦς.

[57] Athanasius, *Oratio contra gentes* 2, *PG* XXV, 8B: Ἱκανὴ δὲ ἡ τῆς ψυχῆς καθαρότης ἐστὶ τὸν Θεὸν δι' ἑαυτῆς κατοπτρίζεσθαι. . . . Cf. *ibid*. 8, *PG* XXV, 16. See also the excellent introduction of P. T. Camelot, O.P., to his translation, *Contre les paiens—Sur l'incarnation du Verbe* (Sources chrétiennes XVIII, Paris, 1946) 49 ff.

[58] It is possible that in his mirror metaphors (see immediately below) Gregory is directly dependent on Athanasius; cf. Merki, ὉΜΟΙΩΣΙΣ 156 ff.

him.[59] Greek patristic doctrine of deification (θεοποίησις) or divinization (θέωσις), through as well as on account of the vision (θεωρία) of
God, continues the old Greek belief that to be is to know and
vice versa.[60] If the vision of God is the ultimate aim of man's reform through purification and assimilation to God, it is on the other
hand the mirror view of God in the purified soul which divinizes him.
In spite of this relation of convertibility or even identity one might
say that ὁμοίωσις and θεωρία correspond to those two stages of
spiritual ascent which ever since Philo, Clement of Alexandria, and
Origen were known as πρᾶξις and as θεωρία, the latter an aspect of
true γνῶσις.[61] In this tradition, which was maintained by the Cappadocians and elaborately systematized by their contemporary Evagrius

[59] In a profound sequence of thought Gregory of Nyssa, *Oratio catechetica* 37, Srawley
141 ff., fits the eucharistic sacrament into the doctrine of spiritual image-likeness, assimilation, vision, and deification. Since man is a corporeal-spiritual compound, not only his
soul but also his body must become united with his Savior. Christ's body and blood, which
during His life on earth were replenished by bread and wine as ours, have the power to
blend with our bodies under the guise of bread and wine which we can assimilate to
ourselves. Thus the God-Man, transforming (μεταστοιχειώσας) the nature of the visible
elements, "mingled (κατέμιξεν) Himself with our mortal nature in order that by communion with His godhead humanity might at the same time be deified (συναποθεωθῇ)"
(Srawley 151 f., translation by Srawley, *The Catechetical Oration of St. Gregory of Nyssa*
[London, 1917] 11 f.).

[60] For the Greek patristic doctrines of deification or divinization and of the vision of God,
see A. Harnack, *Die Terminologie der Wiedergeburt und verwandter Erlebnisse in der ältesten
Kirche* (Texte u. Untersuch. XLII, 2 [1917]), Gross, *Divinization*, Mme. Lot-Borodine, "La
doctrine de la 'déification' dans l'église grecque jusqu'au XIe siècle," *Rev. hist. rel.* CV–CVI
(1932) 18 ff., CVIII (1933) 34 ff., with the review article by Y. M.–J. Congar, O.P., "La
déification dans la tradition spirituelle de l'orient . . . ," *Vie spir.* XLIII, 2 (1935), Suppl., 91
ff., Stolz, *Perfection*, K. Prümm, S.J., *Christentum als Neuheitserlebnis* (Freiburg, 1933) 253 ff.,
J. Maréchal, S.J., *Etudes sur la psychologie des mystiques* II (Museum Lessianum, Sect. Philos.
XIX, Bruxelles, Paris, 1937) 91 ff., Appendix I: "Vers la théologie mystique du Pseudo-
Denys. Points de comparaison dans la mystique grecque du IVe siècle"; also R. Arnou,
article "Platonisme des pères," *DThC* XII, 2, 2381 ff., and the cooperative article "Con-
templation," in *DSpir*, fasc. XIII and XIV–XV, especially J. Lebreton, fasc. XIII, 1654 ff.
P. Maréchal's and Mme. Lot-Borodine's studies are especially important for the relation
between deification and vision of God and for its ancient Greek background, e.g. the
Socratic-Platonic doctrine that to know the good is to be good (a doctrine which is connected with the conception of the understanding of like by like, cf. above p. 85, n. 11).
See also Leys, *Image* 51–57.

[61] For the Greek philosophical origins of the distinction between the contemplative βίος
θεωρητικός and the active βίος πρακτικός or πολιτικός see, for instance, Festugière,
Contemplation 17 ff., 45 ff.; also W. Jaeger, "Über Ursprung und Kreislauf des philo-
sophischen Lebensideals," *Sitz. Ber. Preuss.*, Philos.-Hist., Klasse, 1928, no. XXV, 390 ff.,

Ponticus, the πρακτικὴ (φιλοσοφία) is man's God-assisted ethical *agon* against vice and for virtue,[62] a struggle which is purgative and in a sense even illuminative and leads him to *apatheia* and *homoiosis*, whereas the θεωρητική includes the illuminative and the unitive stages of the God-man relationship and therefore is first φυσική, in the sense of an understanding of creation in God as well as of detachment from creation for God's sake, and then θεολογική, in the sense of the most intimate experience of God possible in this life.[63]

But how can man see God? In his interpretation of the "Sixth

idem, *Aristotle* (Oxford, 1948) 67–98, 242 f., 397, R. Arnou, article "Contemplation," *DSpir*, fasc. XIII, 1716 ff., idem, *ΠΡΑΞΙΣ* et *ΘΕΩΡΙΑ*: *Etude de détail sur le vocabulaire et la pensée des Ennéades de Plotin* (Paris, 1921), idem, *Désir de Dieu* 233 ff. For the first blending of philosophical and scriptural motifs concerning the active and the contemplative life in the School of Alexandria see also below, p. 331, and cf. Völker, *Philo*, especially 176 ff., 270 f., idem, *Clemens* 303 ff., 316 ff., 403 ff., idem, *Origenes* 193 ff., Daniélou, *Origéne* 297 f., I. Lemaître, "La contemplation chez les grecs et autres orientaux chrétiens," *Rev. ascét. myst.* XXVI (1950) 142. For the relation between γνῶσις and θεωρία in Clement and Origen cf. T. Camelot, O.P., *Foi et gnose: Introduction à l'étude de la connaissance mystique chez Clément d'Aléxandrie* (Etudes de théologie et d'histoire de la spiritualité III, Paris, 1945), Völker, *Origenes* 93 ff., idem, *Clemens* 303 ff., 403 ff., Lemaître, "Contemplation" 121 ff., J. Daniélou, I. Lemaître, R. Roques, and M. Viller, in the cooperative article "Contemplation," *DSpir*, fasc. XIII f., 1787–1911; for γνῶσις and θεωρία in Cyril of Jerusalem as well as in the School of Alexandria see A. A. Stephenson, S.J., "St. Cyril of Jerusalem and the Alexandrian Christian Gnosis," *Stud. Patr.* I, 142 ff.

[62] This, of course, includes the Pauline "day by day" reformation of man according to 2 Cor. 4:16 (cf. above, p. 54, n. 27) which is beautifully expounded, for instance by Origen in his *Commentary to the Epistle to the Romans* (text quoted below, p. 166, n. 41), but was to receive even stronger emphasis by St. Augustine (see below, pp. 165 f).

[63] Beside the antithesis of πρᾶξις and θεωρία Philo, Clement, and Origen knew a threefold gradation of the Christian life. See, for instance, Philo, *Legum Allegor.* I, 17, 57, Cohn and Wendland I, 75: . . . ἡ δὲ ἀρετὴ καὶ θεωρητική ἐστι καὶ πρακτική· καὶ γὰρ θεωρίαν ἔχει ὁπότε καὶ ἡ ἐπ' αὐτὴν ὁδὸς φιλοσοφία διὰ τῶν τριῶν αὐτῆς μερῶν, τοῦ λογικοῦ, τοῦ ἠθικοῦ, τοῦ φυσικοῦ, καὶ πράξεις . . . , Clement, *Stromata* I, 28, 176, 1, *GCS, Clem. Alex.* II, 108, on ἡ ἠθικὴ πραγματεία (subdivided in τὸ ἱστορικὸν καὶ τὸ . . . νομοθετικόν, with regard to the Pentateuch and in correspondence with the scriptural senses, cf. pp. 333 f., n. 18), ἡ φυσικὴ θεωρία, and τὸ θεολογικὸν εἶδος, ἡ ἐποπτεία, Origen, *In Canticum Canticorum*, Prologue, *PG* XIII, 73: *ethica, physica, theorice*. Cf. Daniélou, *Platonisme* 18, and *Origène* 298, where P. Daniélou points to the equivalence of this division with the modern terminology of the three mystical ways, the purgative, illuminative, and unitive. For Gregory of Nyssa cf. Daniélou, *Platonisme* 148 ff., 18 ff. While Origen at times used θεολογία instead of θεωρία Gregory of Nyssa favored θεογνωσία over θεολογία and θεωρία; cf. Daniélou, *Platonisme* 189 f., Leys, "Théologie spirituelle" 497; for the origins of the concept of theology see also J. de Ghellinck, S.J., *Le mouvement théologique du XIIe siècle*, 2nd ed. (Museum Lessianum, Sect. Histor. X, Bruges, Bruxelles, Paris, 1948) 90 ff., Appendix I: "A propos des sens du mot «Theologia»." The Alexandrian terminology recurs almost unchanged in Evagrius

Beatitude" Gregory of Nyssa starts from the impasse created by the apparent contradiction between Christ's promise "they shall see God" (Matthew 5:8) and St. John's words "No man hath seen God at any time" (John 1:18), St. Paul's "whom no man hath seen, nor can see" (1 Tim. 6:16) and the "you cannot see my face: for, no man can see me and live" of Exodus 33:20. Must not a man be driven to despair, if the highest felicity is held out as a hope *and* denied by Holy Scripture itself?[64] It is no full consolation to say that God, though invisible by nature, is visible by his "energies" or actions (ἐνεργείαις), as they appear through his works in the created world.

Rather, it appears to me, does the magnificence of this Beatitude suggest something else to those who are able to grasp that the desired [good] can be seen. . . .[65]

Has not Scripture told us: ". . . the Kingdom of God is within you" (Luke 17:21)?[66]

There is . . . in you a measure of the perception of God, that namely, which can be contained by you . . . ,

a "copy" (μίμημα) of God, a godlike "figure" (χαρακτήρ), which

Ponticus, for instance, *Practicus* I, 1, *PG* XL, 1221D (cf. Lemaître, "Contemplation" 141, and Lemaître, Roques, Viller, article "Contemplation," *DSpir*, fasc. XIII f., 1775 ff.) as πρακτική, φυσική, θεολογική. For Evagrius, the recovery of whose works is one of the great achievements of recent patristic scholarship, see, beside the older contributions of Reitzenstein, *Historia Monachorum* 124 ff., and W. Bousset, *Apophthegmata* (Tübingen, 1923) part III, the studies and editions of Frankenberg, Gressmann, Hausherr, Marsili, Draguet, Muyldermans, and Viller, cited in the bibliography of J. de Ghellinck, S.J., *Patristique et moyen âge* III (Museum Lessianum, Sect. Histor. IX, Bruges, Bruxelles, Paris, 1948) 215 ff. For the origin of the combination of the *praxis-theoria* antithesis with more complicated gradations, cf. Festugière, *Contemplation* 43, 58, 165 f., and 233, with regard to Plato's hierarchy of the sensible, the moral, the physico-mathematical, the dialectical and the theoretical, and Jaeger, *Aristotle* 82 (see also the references to this book, p. 99, n. 61). See above all Aristotle, *Eth. Nicom.* X, 7, 1177, I, 2 ff., 1095 ff., II, 1 f., 1103 f. (for the antithesis of theory and praxis), and *Metaphys.* VI, 1, 1026A (for the division of theoretical knowledge in φυσική, μαθηματική, θεολογική).

[64] *De beatitudinibus*, oratio VI, *PG* XLIV, 1264D: 'Ὁρᾷς τὸν ἵλιγγον ᾧ ψυχὴ πρὸς τὸ βάθος τῶν ἐν τῷ λόγῳ θεωρουμένων συνέλκεται; Εἰ ζωὴ ὁ Θεός, ὁ μὴ ἰδὼν αὐτὸν τὴν ζωὴν οὐ βλέπει· τὸ μὴ δύνασθαι ἰδεῖν Θεὸν οἱ θεοφόροι τῶν προφητῶν τε καὶ ἀποστόλων διαμαρτύρονται. Εἰς τί τοῖς ἀνθρώποις ἡ ἐλπὶς περιΐσταται; . . .

[65] *Ibid.*, *PG* XLIV, 1269B: 'Ἀλλ' οὐ πρὸς τοῦτο βλέπει μόνον τοῦ μακαρισμοῦ ἡ διάνοια τὸ ἔκ τινος ἐνεργείας τὸν ἐνεργοῦντα δύνασθαι τοιοῦτον ἀναλογίσασθαι . . . , ἀλλ' ἕτερόν μοι δοκεῖ ἡ τοῦ μακαρισμοῦ μεγαλοφυΐα τοῖς δυναμένοις δέξασθαι κατιδεῖν τὸ ποθούμενον τὴν συμβουλὴν ὑφηγεῖσθαι. [66] *Ibid.* 1269C.

when cleansed from vices will recuperate the similitude (ὁμοιότης) with the divine archetype.[67]

Therefore, who looks at himself sees in himself the object of his desire (namely, God). And thus the pure in heart is made blessed, because in looking at his own purity he sees the archetype in the image. For as those who see the sun in a mirror, even though they do not look straight at the sky see it no less in the mirror's radiance than those who look at the disc of the sun itself, thus . . . also you, though too weak for the perception of the light [itself], have in yourselves the sought-for [good] if you direct your course backward to the grace of the image which was created in you in the beginning.[68]

Similarly, in his *Fifteenth Homily on the Canticle*, Gregory interprets verse 2 of chapter six—"I to my beloved, and my beloved to me"— as expressing the conformation (συμμεμορφῶσθαι) to Christ of the soul which recovers (ἀπολαβοῦσα) its own beauty, the first bliss of our nature which it possessed in accordance with its being made to the image and likeness of the true and only beauty.

And it is as in the case of a mirror: if it is made in accordance with good workmanship and suitable for use, then it will show in itself, on its pure surface, exactly the figure (τὸν χαρακτῆρα) of the face which appears in it. Thus also the soul, after it has been made suitable for use and has thrown off all material blemish, again begins to express in itself the pure form of the unmixed beauty. A living mirror, endowed with free will, the soul therefore can say: "Since I look with my entire circle at the face of the Beloved, the whole beauty of His form is seen in me."[69]

---

[67] *Ibid.* 1269D–1272A f.: Τὸ γάρ σοι χωρητὸν τῆς τοῦ Θεοῦ κατανοήσεως μέτρον ἐν σοί ἐστιν. . . . Τῶν γὰρ τῆς ἰδίας φύσεως ἀγαθῶν ὁ Θεὸς ἐνετύπωσε τῇ σῇ κατασκευῇ τὰ μιμήματα. . . . Ἀλλ᾽ ἡ κακία τῷ θεοειδεῖ χαρακτῆρι περιχυθεῖσα ἄχρηστον ἐποίησέ σοι τὸ ἀγαθόν. . . . Εἰ οὖν ἀποκλύσειας πάλιν δι᾽ ἐπιμελείας βίου τὸν ἐπιπλασθέντα τῇ καρδίᾳ σου ῥύπον, ἀναλάμψει σοι τὸ θεοειδὲς κάλλος . . . καὶ ὁ ἔνδον ἄνθρωπος . . . πάλιν ἀναλήψεται τὴν πρὸς τὸ ἀρχέτυπον ὁμοιότητα. . . .

[68] *Ibid.* 1272B: Οὐκοῦν ὁ ἑαυτὸν βλέπων ἐν ἑαυτῷ τὸ ποθούμενον βλέπει· καὶ οὕτω γίνεται μακάριος ὁ καθαρὸς τῇ καρδίᾳ ὅτι πρὸς τὴν ἰδίαν καθαρότητα βλέπων ἐν τῇ εἰκόνι καθορᾷ τὸ ἀρχέτυπον. Ὥσπερ γὰρ οἱ ἐν κατόπτρῳ ὁρῶντες τὸν ἥλιον, κἂν μὴ πρὸς αὐτὸν τὸν οὐρανὸν ἀποβλέψωσιν ἀτενές, οὐδὲν ἔλαττον ὁρῶσι τὸν ἥλιον ἐν τῇ τοῦ κατόπτρου αὐγῇ τῶν πρὸς αὐτὸν ἀποβλεπόντων τοῦ ἡλίου τὸν κύκλον, οὕτω . . . καὶ ὑμεῖς, κἂν ἀτονῆτε πρὸς κατανόησιν φωτός, ἐὰν ἐπὶ τὴν ἐξ ἀρχῆς ἐγκατασκευασθεῖσαν ὑμῖν χάριν τῆς εἰκόνος ἐπαναδράμητε, ἐν ἑαυτοῖς τὸ ζητούμενον ἔχετε.

[69] *In Canticum Canticorum*, homil. *XV*, PG XLIV, 1093D–1096A: Καὶ οἷον ἐπὶ τοῦ κατόπτρου γίνεται, ὅταν τεχνικῶς τε καὶ καταλλήλως τῇ χρείᾳ κατεσκευασμένον ᾖ, ἐν καθαρᾷ τῇ ἐπιφανείᾳ δι᾽ ἀκριβείας ἐν ἑαυτῷ δείξει τοῦ ἐπιφανέντος προσώπου τὸν χαρακτῆρα, οὕτως

However much such texts[70] depend on Neoplatonic formulations,[71] the Christian distinctness of Gregory's thought is nevertheless maintained. For while it is true that the purified soul is again similar to God because it sees nothing but Him and that it can now see God because it is again similar to Him, this vision of God in the soul is strictly speaking no longer in the soul at all.[72]

The lost resemblance to God is recovered in the soul, but it is in no way contained by it. It is rather recovered in and through purification itself, the impulse for which comes from God Himself and the exercise of which is aided by God. For this is the central point of Gregory's doctrine of purification and assimilation and reformation: the object of all such aspirations and actions, the vision of God, is *one and the same* with the unceasing desire for Him.[73]

ἑαυτὴν ἡ ψυχὴ προσφόρως τῇ χρείᾳ κατασκευάσασα καὶ πᾶσαν ὑλικὴν ἀπορριψαμένην κηλίδα καθαρὸν τοῦ ἀκηράτου κάλλους ἐν ἑαυτῇ τὸ εἶδος ἀνετυπώσατο. Λέγει οὖν τὴν φωνὴν ταύτην τὸ προαιρετικόν τε καὶ ἔμψυχον κάτοπτρον ὅτι "Ἐπειδὴ τῷ κύκλῳ ἐγὼ ὅλῳ τὸ τοῦ ἀδελφιδοῦ πρόσωπον βλέπω, διὰ τοῦτο ὅλον τῆς ἐκείνου μορφῆς τὸ κάλλος ἐν ἐμοὶ καθορᾶται."

[70] See also In Canticum Canticorum, homil. II, PG XLIV, 805D, homil. III, 824C, homil. IV, 833B ff., homil. V, 868B ff.; De mortuis, PG XLVI, 509B ff.; De vita Mosis, Daniélou 44; De hominis opificio 12, PG XLIV, 161C f.; De virginitate 11, Cavarnos, in Jaeger, Greg. Nyss. Opera VIII, 1, 295 ff.; De anima et resurrectione, PG XLVI, 89C. Cf. Daniélou, Platonisme 223 ff.

[71] See above, p. 97.

[72] For the following, see—in addition to the texts referred to, nn. 73 ff., 85 ff.—Daniélou, Platonisme 321, 324, and 188, H. v. Balthasar, Présence et pensée: Essai sur la philosophie religieuse de Grégoire de Nysse (Paris, 1942) 81 ff., E. v. Ivanka, "Vom Platonismus zur Theorie der Mystik," Scholastik XI (1936) 163 ff., especially 188, and idem, Geistesleben 49 ff., Leys, Image 32 ff.

[73] See De vita Mosis, Daniélou 107 ff.: . . . ὡς ἐν τούτῳ ὄντος τοῦ ἀληθῶς ἰδεῖν τὸν Θεόν· ἐν τῷ μὴ λῆξαί ποτε τῆς ἐπιθυμίας τὸν πρὸς αὐτὸν ἀναβλέποντα. . . . Οὕτως οὖν πληροῦται τῷ Μωϋσεῖ τὸ ποθούμενον δι' ὧν ἀπλήρωτος ἡ ἐπιθυμία μένει: παιδεύεται γὰρ . . . ὅτι τὸ θεῖον κατὰ τὴν ἑαυτοῦ φύσιν ἀόριστον οὐδενὶ περιειργόμενον πέρατι. . . . Οὐκ ἄρα περίληψίς τις τῆς ἀορίστου φύσεως νομισθήσεται· τὸ δὲ ἀπερίληπτον καταληφθῆναι φύσιν οὐκ ἔχει. Ἀλλὰ πᾶσα πρὸς τὸ καλὸν ἡ ἐπιθυμία, ἡ πρὸς τὴν ἄνοδον ἐκείνην ἐφελκομένη, ἀεὶ τῷ δρόμῳ τοῦ πρὸς τὸ καλὸν ἱεμένον συνεπεκτείνεται. Καὶ τοῦτό ἐστιν ὄντως τὸ ἰδεῖν τὸν Θεὸν τὸ μηδέποτε τῆς ἐπιθυμίας κόρον εὑρεῖν. Ἀλλὰ χρὴ πάντοτε βλέποντα δι' ὧν ἐστι δυνατὸν ὁρᾶν πρὸς τὴν τοῦ πλέον ἰδεῖν ἐπιθυμίαν ἐκκαίεσθαι. Καὶ οὕτως οὐδεὶς ὅρος ἂν ἐπικόπτοι τῆς πρὸς τὸν Θεὸν ἀνόδου τὴν αὔξησιν διὰ τὸ μήτε τοῦ καλοῦ τι πέρας εὑρίσκεσθαι μήτε τινὶ κόρῳ τὴν πρόοδον τῆς πρὸς τὸ καλὸν ἐπιθυμίας ἐκκόπτεσθαι. For Gregory's belief (which corresponds to the conviction of the Greek Fathers in general) that not even Moses could see God in His nature or essence see ibid. 102 ff.; for the different attitude of Augustine, see below, pp. 191 f. The problem of the possibility of an immediate or essential vision of God according to the Greek Fathers has been largely clarified by P. Maréchal, Etudes II, 109 and 178, who has shown that they denied it because

Who desires to see God, sees Him whom he desires by always following Him and the vision of His face is the ceaseless journey toward Him. . . .[74]

. . . to progress forever in seeking, and never to pause on the road up, this is truly to enjoy the desired. . . .[75]

The aim and the way to perfection emerge as identical. Assimilation to God means the attainment of the vision of God, but this vision is itself the desire for Him. For since God exceeds all understanding of creatures, to see Him means to want to see Him more.[76]

Thus Gregory on this highest level of his mystical speculation once more returns to that convertibility or identity relation between *homoiosis* and *theoria*, between deification and vision of God, which had been apparent also on the lower planes of his conception of the recovery of divine image-likeness.[77] Whether or not he here goes beyond his predecessors, such as Origen and Basil,[78] it is certain that in this most sublime sameness of desire and fulfilment the experience of θεωρία or, to use the more specifically Gregorian term, of

they conceived of it as comprehensive or total. His explanation corresponds better with the relevant texts, especially of Gregory of Nyssa, than those of H. Koch, "Das mystische Schauen beim hl. Gregor von Nyssa," *Theologische Quartalschrift* LXXX (1898) 405 (against F. Diekamp, *Die Gotteslehre des hl. Gregor von Nyssa* [Münster, 1896]) and of Völker, *Gregor* 205 f., who assert that Gregory held that an immediate, though not a comprehensive, vision of God is possible.

[74] *In Canticum Canticorum*, homilia XII, PG XLIV, 1025D f.: . . . ὁ ἰδεῖν τὸν Θεὸν ἐπιθυμῶν ἐν τῷ ἀεὶ αὐτῷ ἀκολουθεῖν ὁρᾷ τὸ ποθούμενον καὶ ἡ τοῦ προσώπου αὐτοῦ θεωρία ἐστὶν ἡ ἄπαυστος πρὸς αὐτὸν πορεία. . . .

[75] *Ibid.*, PG XLIV, 1037B: . . . ὅτι τὸ ἀεὶ προκόπτειν ἐν τῷ ζητεῖν καὶ τὸ μηδέποτε τῆς ἀνόδου παύεσθαι, τουτέστιν ἡ ἀληθὴς τοῦ ποθουμένου ἀπόλαυσις τῆς πάντοτε πληρουμένης ἐπιθυμίας ἑτέραν ἐπιθυμίαν τοῦ ὑπερκειμένου γεννώσης. Some of the terms of the three last-quoted texts are found in Plotinus (e.g. πόθος, πορεία, ἐπιθυμία) and so is their basic idea, however much Gregory has transposed it in a Christian key. See Plotinus, *Ennead* V, 6, 5: . . . καὶ τοῦτ' ἔστι νοεῖν κίνησις πρὸς ἀγαθὸν ἐφειμένου ἐκείνου· ἡ γὰρ ἔφεσις τὴν νόησιν ἐγέννησε καὶ συνυπέστησεν αὐτῇ· ἔφεσις γὰρ ὄψεως ὅρασις. Cf. Arnou, *Désir de Dieu* 100 ff., idem, ΠΡΑΞΙΣ et ΘΕΩΡΙΑ 1 f. However, Gregory also could express the idea in the purely Pauline terms of Phil. 3 : 12 ff.; see below, p. 105.

[76] H. Koch, in the brilliant article, "Mystisches Schauen," quoted above, n. 73 (from p. 102), 410 ff., discusses the Philonic and Plotinian anticipations of Gregory's conception; as so often, Philo in all probability was Gregory's immediate source. Koch, "Mystisches Schauen," 416 and Völker, *Gregor* 196 ff., have indicated that this whole ideology is the source of Ps.-Dionysius' later formulations of *docta ignorantia*.

[77] See above, p. 98.

[78] On this point see the somewhat divergent views of Daniélou, *Platonisme*, *passim*, and of Völker, *Gregor* 204 ff., 231 ff.

θεογνωσία[79] is no longer contained by the relatively ordinary categories of luminous vision or knowledge; the light in which God dwells is so dazzling that it can be experienced only as darkness, in a complete surrender to divine transcendence.[80] This is a conception of mystical union in which Gregory of Nyssa is one of the great initiators and through which he anticipates Ps.-Dionysius and many later Christian mystics.[81]

Even ecstasis then is for Gregory not merely a status in which the body is temporarily left behind—which it may have been for Origen[82] —or in which human individuality is absorbed as far as possible in the One—as it had been for Plotinus.[83] Even though the mystic has a firm stand on the rock which is Christ,[84] his condition is not στάσις in the ordinary sense, it is κίνησις, movement, τόνος, a tension that never slackens, προκοπή, unceasing progress.[85] The soul does not truly stand still at any time. The desire for God is never fulfilled, the

[79] Cf. p. 99, n. 63.

[80] For Gregory of Nyssa's γνόφος doctrine, see Daniélou, Platonisme 17 ff., 175 ff., 190 ff. See also ibid. 222 ff. for the related doctrine of the spiritual senses, which had been first developed by Origen; cf. K. Rahner, S.J., "Le début d'une doctrine des cinq sens spirituels," Rev. ascét. myst. XIII (1932) 113 ff.

[81] Völker, Gregor 209, n. 2, rightly stresses the fact that Gregory of Nyssa's and the Ps.-Dionysius' mystical darkness is also an excess of light. Cf. also idem, Kontemplation und Ekstase bei Pseudo-Dionysius Areopagita (Wiesbaden, 1958) 210 ff., and H.-C. Puech, "La ténèbre mystique chez le Pseudo-Denys l'Aréopagite et dans la tradition patristique," Etudes carmélitaines XXIII, 2 (1938) 33 ff. ; these two authors hold different views concerning Gregory's and the Ps.-Dionysius' conceptions of the mystical "night of the soul."

[82] For this problem see Puech, "Mystique d'Origène," 526 ff., with reference to Völker, Origenes 134 ff.

[83] Cf. Arnou, Désir de Dieu 245 ff., E. Bréhier, La philosophie de Plotin (Paris, 1928) 62 ff.

[84] See Gregory of Nyssa, De vita Mosis, Daniélou 109 ff. (with reference to Ex. 33:21 f. and 1 Cor. 10:4); cf. Maréchal, Etudes II, 107.

[85] De vita Mosis, Daniélou 110: Τοῦτο δὲ τὸ πάντων παραδοξότατον, πῶς τὸ αὐτὸ καὶ στάσις ἐστὶ καὶ κίνησις. Ὁ γὰρ ἀνιὼν πάντως οὐχ ἵσταται καὶ ὁ ἑστὼς οὐκ ἀνέρχεται: ἐνταῦθα δὲ διὰ τοῦ ἑστάναι τὸ ἀναβῆναι γίνεται. Τοῦτο δέ ἐστιν ὅτι ὅσῳ τις πάγιός τε καὶ ἀμετάθετος ἐν τῷ ἀγαθῷ διαμένει, τοσούτῳ πλέον τὸν τῆς ἀρετῆς διανύει δρόμον. See also ibid. 105: Ποθοῦσα γὰρ διὰ τῶν ἤδη κατειλημμένων μὴ καταλιπεῖν τὸ ὕψος τὸ ὑπερκείμενον, ἄπαυστον ποιεῖται τὴν ἐπὶ τὰ ἄνω φοράν, ἀεὶ διὰ τῶν προηγνυσμένων τὸν πρὸς τὴν πτῆσιν τόνον ἀνανεάζουσα. Μόνη γὰρ ἡ κατ' ἀρετὴν ἐνέργεια καμάτῳ τρέφει τὴν δύναμιν, οὐκ ἐνδιδοῦσα διὰ τοῦ ἔργου τὸν τόνον, ἀλλ' ἐπαύξουσα. Cf. again In Canticum Canticorum, homil. XII, PG XLIV, 1037B: τὸ ἀεὶ προκόπτειν ἐν τῷ ζητεῖν . . . , τουτέστιν ἡ ἀληθὴς τοῦ ποθουμένου ἀπόλαυσις. . . . Cf. Maréchal, Etudes II, 108 ff., Daniélou, Platonisme 305 f., v. Ivanka, Geistesleben 49 f., Völker, Gregor 186 ff., also for the idea of προκοπή in Philo and the Alexandrians.

happiness of man cannot—especially on this earth—consist in anything but to seek God in ever greater heights. This for Gregory is the true resolution—Christian and at the same time Greek—of the antinomies of rest and motion, of like and unlike, of unity and multiplicity, of being and becoming, of eternity and change.

To recapitulate: for Gregory reform even on earth was the return to a spiritual Paradise in the soul and the recovery of the image-likeness to God, which had been possessed by Adam in Paradise. Gregory speaks of examples of such mystical restorations: Abraham, Moses, David and, above all, St. Paul.[86] The Apostle's ecstasis "in the body . . . or out of the body . . ." was an ascent to the third heaven, a return to Paradise. But even the blissful stillness of the highest immobile heaven cannot be grasped as mere stability by human minds. This, according to Gregory, is signified by St. Paul's words in Phil. 3:13 f.: "Brethren, I do not count myself to have apprehended. But one thing I do: forgetting the things that are behind, and stretching forth myself to those that are before, I press towards the mark, to the prize of the supernal vocation of God in Christ Jesus."[87] To this Gregory remarks:

It is clear that even after that third heaven which he alone knew . . . and even after the ineffable hearing of the mysteries of Paradise he still goes toward higher regions and never stops the ascent and never makes the good which he has grasped the end of his desire. He thus teaches us, I believe, that with regard to that blessed nature of goodness ($\tau\hat{\omega}\nu$ $\dot{\alpha}\gamma\alpha\theta\hat{\omega}\nu$) much means always that which is found; but infinitely more than that which is ever grasped is that which lies above it. And this happens continuously to him who participates [in God], so that there is increase of ever better things for those who participate through the whole eternity of aeons ($\alpha\dot{\iota}\dot{\omega}\nu\omega\nu$ $\dot{\alpha}\ddot{\iota}\delta\iota\dot{\omega}\tau\eta\tau\iota$). . . . And neither

---

[86] See In Cantic. Cantic., homil. VIII, PG XLIV, 940C–941C.

[87] Cf. ibid. 940C–D. The Pauline text is so often used by Gregory in this sense, that P. Daniélou, Platonisme 291 ff., has formed a Gregorian technical term, épectase (antithetical to mere ecstase), out of the Pauline ἐπεκτείνεσθαι (to stretch forth). Yet, as Völker, Gregor 231 ff., rightly remarks, Origen and Basil had preceded Gregory of Nyssa in using this term with the same meaning, and it is found also in Gregory Nazianzen. Already Philo, De posteritate Caini 4, 13, Cohn and Wendland II, 3, had said: καὶ ἐπιτείνων οὐκ ἀνήσει τὸν πόθον (quoted by Koch, "Mystisches Schauen" 411); cf. also Crouzel, Image 57, and J. Giblet, L'homme image de Dieu dans les commentaires littéraux de Philon d'Alexandrie (Sylloge Excerptorum e Dissertationibus . . . in Sacra Theologia vel in Iure Canonico . . . XVII, Louvain, 1949).

does he who ascends ever stand still, for he exchanges one beginning for another, nor is the beginning of ever better things ever perfected in itself. . . .[88]

So there is no end. The return to Paradise, the recovery of the lost resemblance to God, even the face-to-face vision of God in heaven, they all are as drops in the ocean of His unfathomable being.[89] Here the κατὰ τὸ δυνατόν of Platonic assimilation ideology,[90] hovering at the brink of an abyss of divine light, has become almost, but not quite, a κατὰ τὸ ἀδύνατον.[91] Origen's idea of ever-repeated spiritual declines and restorations—even if he should have thought them never completed—was less tantalizing and less sublime than this conception of mystical desire.

The mystical recovery of the lost resemblance to God, as conceived by Gregory of Nyssa and the Greek Fathers in general, is certainly reform. In fact, it is the most far-reaching reform conceivable. For, it amounts to deification—τὸ ἀκρότατον τῶν ὀρέκτων: Θεὸν γενέσθαι, as St. Basil said.[92] It would be quite wrong to assume that this ideal was so highly individualistic that it could not or did not influence civilization (see above, p. 82). But it is true that it influenced civilization in a way that is very different from that to which the west has

---

[88] In Cant. Cant., homil. VIII, PG XLIV, 940D–941C: . . . δῆλον ὅτι καὶ μετὰ τὸν τρίτον οὐρανὸν ἐκεῖνον ὃν αὐτὸς ἔγνω μόνος . . . καὶ μετὰ τὴν ἄρρητον τῶν τοῦ παραδείσου μυστηρίων ἀκρόασιν, ἔτι ἐπὶ τὸ ἀνώτερον ἵεται καὶ οὐ λήγει τῆς ἀναβάσεως οὐδέποτε τὸ καταλαμβανόμενον ἀγαθὸν ὅρον τῆς ἐπιθυμίας ποιούμενος, διδάσκων, οἶμαι, διὰ τούτων ἡμᾶς ὅτι τῆς μακαρίας ἐκείνης τῶν ἀγαθῶν φύσεως πολὺ μέν ἐστι τὸ ἀεὶ εὑρισκόμενον, ἀπειροπλάσιον δὲ τοῦ πάντοτε καταλαμβανομένου τὸ ὑπερκείμενον. Καὶ τοῦτο εἰς τὸ διηνεκὲς γίνεται τῷ μετέχοντι ἐν πάσῃ τῇ τῶν αἰώνων ἀϊδιότητι διὰ τῶν ἀεὶ μειζόνων τῆς ἐπαυξήσεως τοῖς μετέχουσι γινομένης (the combination of ἀϊδιότης and αἰών here no doubt means eternity, though in other texts αἰών often signifies only a very long period of time; cf. Excursus III). Καὶ οὔτε ὁ ἀνιὼν ποτε ἵσταται, ἀρχὴν ἐξ ἀρχῆς μεταλαμβάνων, οὔτε τελεῖται περὶ ἑαυτὴν ἡ τῶν ἀεὶ μειζόνων ἀρχή.

[89] See Völker, Gregor 199, who quotes Gregory of Nyssa, Contra Eunomium I, 364, Jaeger, Greg. Nyss. Opera, p. 128, 10 f.: . . . καθάπερ τι πέλαγος ἀχανὲς ἡ τῆς θείας φύσεως θεωρία. For the Greek patristic conception that even in the beatific vision of God in heaven the desire for God can never be sated, because the essence of God is incommensurable with man's nature, see Maréchal, Etudes II 109 ff., 132, and cf. above, pp. 102 f., n. 73.

[90] See the famous text from the Theaetetus, quoted above, p. 83.

[91] To some extent this is true, of course, for all Christian as compared to Platonic thought. See, for instance, J. Meifort, Der Platonismus bei Clemens Alexandrinus (Heidelberger Abhandlungen zur Philosophie und ihrer Geschichte XVII, Tübingen, 1928) 69 ff., 81 ff.

[92] Basil, De Spiritu Sancto 9, 23, PG XXXII, 109C; cf. above, p. 80, n. 70.

become accustomed.[93] If reform in its most spiritualized form in the mystic's soul and even in the bliss of heaven is mainly something negative, though negative in the very high sense of never-ending purification and of purest desire for the incommensurable majesty of God, it is understandable that on the lower levels of terrestrial life reform will also express itself in a negative rather than in a positive way: in withdrawal from the world, rather than in penetration of the world, or at least in a relatively disconnected juxtaposition of the mystical and the profane. For the Greek and eastern Christians of the patristic era and their Byzantine successors the Kingdom of God was emphatically in man, but at the same time the Empire of the Basileus-Autokrator was around them and the question arose, even then, if and to what extent the two could be integrated.

3. BASILEIA

Ἐλθέτω ἡ βασιλεία σου: "Thy Kingdom come" (Matthew 6:10). What is this Kingdom of God or Kingdom of the Heavens, for which Christ said men should pray and of which he spoke so many times? Where is it and when may it be expected?

. . . for the Kingdom of Heaven is at hand (Matthew 4:17).

For lo, the Kingdom of God is within you (Luke 17:21).

And the good seed are the children of the Kingdom. And the cockle are the children of the wicked one. . . . Even as cockle therefore is gathered up and burnt with fire: so shall it be at the end of the world. . . . Then shall the just shine as the sun in the Kingdom of their Father (Matthew 13:38, 40, 43).

The Kingdom of God then is near, or in a sense already in existence, and it will come with all its power—δυνάμει (Mark 8:39)—at the end of the world.

This doubleness of terrestrial immanence and eschatological tran-

---

[93] See below, pp. 131 f. This is not to say that the western Fathers and later western theologians did not have a conception of the deification of man by the grace of God. St. Augustine himself had it, though in a manner somewhat different from that of the Greek Fathers; cf. pp. 194 ff.; see also the interesting texts gathered by E. H. Kantorowicz, "Deus per naturam, Deus per gratiam," *Harv. Theol. Rev.* XLV (1952) 253 ff. As so often in such comparisons, the difference is one of degree; perhaps it would be better to say that the west, especially since Augustine, added a new dimension to the Christian doctrine of human-divine relations by stressing aspects which the east had left relatively undeveloped.

scendence of the Kingdom of God has been one of the great paradoxes of Christendom.[1] At bottom it is only another aspect of the immanent-transcendent doubleness which has been observed in studying the ideas of man's return to Paradise and of the recovery of his lost likeness to God. Yet a peculiar problem arose from the concept of kingship (βασιλεία). Christ's conception of the Kingdom was clearly directed against Jewish-Hellenistic political-religious expectations of a messianic Kingdom, expectations in which the *ethos* of the Prophets had given way to a combination of apocalyptic and soteriological ideas. And still the fact that the highest religious reality, the power of God in and beyond the world, could be expressed in "royal" terms must lead to further search for the relation between divine and human kingship. This relation was basically antithetical—Christ had said

My Kingdom is not of this world (John 18:36)

and

Render therefore to Caesar the things that are Caesar's and to God the things that are God's (Matthew 22:21)—

but it was not necessarily hostile. Even in the midst of persecutions by Jews and pagans the earliest Christians had seen in rulers a representation of the kingly power of God. St. Peter and St. Paul themselves had laid the foundation for this attitude:

Be ye subject therefore to every human creature for God's sake: whether it be to the king as excelling or to governors as sent by him. . . . Honor all men. Love the brotherhood. Fear God. Honor the king (1 Peter 2:13 ff.).

---

[1] O. Cullmann, *Königsherrschaft Christi und Kirche im Neuen Testament* (Theologische Studien X, Zollikon–Zürich, 1946) 11, and less definitely K. L. Schmidt, article *"βασιλεία," ThWbNT* I, 586 ff., are of the opinion that in the New Testament the βασιλεία Θεοῦ is of a purely eschatological character. This is hardly tenable, in spite of the fact, pointed out, for instance, by A. v. Gall, *ΒΑΣΙΛΕΙΑ ΤΟΥ ΘΕΟΥ* (Heidelberg, 1926) 474 f., and by A. Feuillet, P.S.S., "La venue du règne de Dieu . . . ," *Rech.'s sc. rel.* XXXV (1948) 547, that in the crucial text Luke 17:21: . . . ἰδοὺ γὰρ ἡ βασιλεία τοῦ Θεοῦ ἐντὸς ὑμῶν ἐστιν the present tense is inconclusive, since in the Aramaean the copula is as a rule not expressed. For Cullmann's strict distinction of the Kingdom of God and the Kingdom of Christ see below, p. 115, n. 28. Since in Luke 17:21 Christ speaks of the Pharisees, ἐντὸς ὑμῶν probably does not mean *in* you (in your soul), but *in the midst* of you, cf. M.-J. Lagrange, O.P., *Evangile selon saint Luc*, 4th ed. (Paris, 1927) 460 f., Schmidt, article *"βασιλεία," ThWbNT* I, 587; yet, the Fathers were soon to interpret this verse in the sense that the Kingdom of God can be in man's soul, see below, p. 114.

Let every soul be subject to higher powers (ἐξουσίαις): for there is no power but from God: and those that are, are ordained of God (Rom. 13:1).

For princes (ἄρχοντες) are not a terror to the good work, but to the evil. . . . For he (the ruler) is God's minister (διάκονος) to thee for good . . . (Rom. 13:3 f.).

St. Paul, therefore, desires that prayers be said for all men, also

for kings, and for all that are in high stations . . . (1 Tim. 2:2),

for God wants all to be saved. This admonishment is heeded even by such an outspoken enemy of the Roman Empire as Tertullian when he says:

For we invoke the eternal God for the well-being of the emperors, the true God, the living God. . . .[2]

Along two converging lines, then, could terrestrial human kingship be made congruent with the Kingdom of God in man on earth: every man is a king, if the Kingdom of God is in him; the ruler is a man, but one who represents the Kingdom in a special way by taking the lead in its realization. Man who has recovered his lost resemblance with God and has thus returned to Paradise becomes a king as Adam was. The ruler, on the other hand, who wants to be a true king must first of all reform himself as man.[3]

This in rough outline is the theory of the relationship between man and king in Greek Christendom. In it, the Old Testament teaching of Adam as ruler over the earth (Gen. 1:28) as well as the Platonic concept of the kingly philosopher are clearly discernible beside the New Testament doctrine of the Kingdom of God. The practical application of the theory was vitiated by two factors inherent, perhaps, in the re-transfer down to earth of the concept of Basileia, after it had been

---

[2] Tertullian, *Apologeticum* 30, 1, *Corp. Christ.*, *Ser. Lat.* I, 141.

[3] This last idea is particularly characteristic of Eusebius of Caesarea, cf. below, pp. 119 ff. For the various meanings of scriptural Kingdom of God terminology in the Greek Fathers see G. W. H. Lampe, "Some Notes on the Significance of ΒΑΣΙΛΕΙΑ ΤΟΥ ΘΕΟΥ, ΒΑΣΙΛΕΙΑ ΧΡΙΣΤΟΥ, in the Greek Fathers," *Jour. Theol. Stud.* XLIX (1948) 58 ff. For early Christian and mediaeval ideology of the Kingdom of God in man in general and in the ruler in particular see, for instance, my article "Image" 33, n. 64, E. Kantoro-wicz, *Kaiser Friedrich II.* (Berlin, 1927) 233 ff., also Erg. Bd. (1931), and *idem*, "Kaiser Friedrich II. und das Königsbild des Hellenismus," *Varia Variorum* 171 ff., Struker, *Gottesebenbildlichkeit*.

raised to heaven.[4] First, the "royal" road to individual perfection, as practiced in certain forms of asceticism and mysticism, could lead away from the realization of interpersonal love. Secondly, the representation of the Kingdom of God in the kingdom of the terrestrial Basileus could become form rather than substance.

At the end of the second century, Athenagoras of Athens testifies both to the ruler quality of man in general, connected with his image relation to God, and to the special representation of God the Father and the Son in the Roman Emperors, Marcus Aurelius and his son Commodus: they master, he says, the whole world, having received their empire ($\beta\alpha\sigma\iota\lambda\epsilon\iota\alpha$) from above, for "the heart of the king is in the hand of the Lord" (Prov. 21:1).[5]

In Clement of Alexandria the interest for the royal dignity of man is stronger than that for rulership in the political sense, but the two nevertheless emerge as interrelated.

The "royal and authentic entry" into justice goes through "the door of the Lord" (Ps. 117:20) in "gnostic piety."[6] Who enters thus

... is the gnostic, according to the image and likeness: he imitates God ... not omitting anything that leads toward receiving resemblance [with Him]. He is continent, patient, lives justly, rules over the passions ($\beta\alpha\sigma\iota\lambda\epsilon\dot{\upsilon}\omega\nu$ $\tau\hat{\omega}\nu$ $\pi\alpha\theta\hat{\omega}\nu$), and gives away a share of what he has, a benefactor ($\epsilon\dot{\upsilon}\epsilon\rho\gamma\epsilon\tau\hat{\omega}\nu$) in word and deed.[7]

---

[4] The transfer of imperial imagery into the spheres of Christian theology, anthropology, and spirituality, of course, continued. For the homilies of Ps.-Macarius of Egypt, for instance, see J. Stiglmayr, S.J., "Bilder und Vergleiche aus dem byzantinischen Hofleben in den Homilien des Makarius," *Stimmen aus Maria Laach* LXXX (1911) 414 ff.

[5] Athenagoras, *Supplicatio pro Christianis* 18, ed. E. J. Goodspeed, *Die ältesten Apologeten* (Göttingen, 1914) 332 f.: Ἔχοιτε ἀφ' ἑαυτῶν καὶ τὴν ἐπουράνιον βασιλείαν ἐξετάζειν· ὡς γὰρ ὑμῖν πατρὶ καὶ υἱῷ πάντα κεχείρωται, ἄνωθεν τὴν βασιλείαν εἰλήφοσι—βασιλέως γὰρ ψυχὴ ἐν χειρὶ Θεοῦ, φησὶ τὸ προφητικὸν πνεῦμα (Prov. 21:1)—οὕτως ἑνὶ τῷ Θεῷ καὶ τῷ παρ' αὐτοῦ Λόγῳ Υἱῷ νοομένῳ ἀμερίστῳ πάντα ὑποτέτακται. ...

[6] *Stromata* I, 7, 38, 6 f., GCS, *Clem. Alex.* II 25: ... ἐὰν δὲ τὴν βασιλικήν τε καὶ αὐθεντικὴν εἴσοδον ζητῇς, ἀκούσῃ. "αὕτη ἡ πύλη τοῦ Κυρίου, δίκαιοι εἰσελεύσονται ἐν αὐτῇ" (Ps. 117:20). Πολλῶν τοίνυν ἀνεῳγμένων πυλῶν ⟨ἡ⟩ ἐν δικαιοσύνῃ αὕτη ἦν ἐν Χριστῷ, ἐν ᾗ μακάριοι πάντες οἱ εἰσελθόντες καὶ κατευθύνοντες τὴν πορείαν αὐτῶν ἐν ὁσιότητι γνωστικῇ (cf. 1 *Clem. ad Cor.* 48, 4 f., Bihlmeyer, *Apostol. Väter* I, 61).

[7] *Stromata* II, 19, 97, 1, GCS, *Clem. Alex.* II, 166: Οὗτός ἐστιν ὁ κατ' εἰκόνα καὶ ὁμοίωσιν, ὁ γνωστικός, ὁ μιμούμενος τὸν Θεὸν καθ' ὅσον οἷόν τε, μηδὲν παραλιπὼν τῶν εἰς τὴν ἐνδεχομένην ὁμοίωσιν, ἐγκρατευόμενος, ὑπομένων, δικαίως βιούς, βασιλεύων τῶν παθῶν, μεταδιδοὺς ὧν ἔχει, ὡς οἷός τέ ἐστιν, εὐεργετῶν καὶ λόγῳ καὶ ἔργῳ.

For indeed a divine effigy (ἄγαλμα) resembling (προσεμφερές) God is the soul of a just man, in which through obedience of the precepts the leader of all mortals and immortals is consecrated and set up as king and progenitor of the good, as true law and ordinance, eternal Word, one Savior to each singly and to all in common.[8]

Thus Clement's "gnostic," the Christian who has the higher knowledge, is perfectly just because he rules over his passions like a king and hence like the ideal Hellenistic ruler is *euergetes*,[9] a benefactor. He has in his soul the image (χαρακτήρ) of the glory of the highest King (παμβασιλέως καὶ παντοκράτορος), in other words, of the Oneborn, the Logos, Christ

who impresses upon the gnostic the perfect vision according to His image, so that he already is, as it were, the third divine image.[10]

Image-likeness, assimilation with God, the vision of God, these are familiar concepts of biblical and Platonist origin (discussed in the preceding chapter as to their bearing upon the ideology of reform). In connection with the Basileia-ideology the rule over the passions is of special significance. This is one of the primary virtues of the Christian gnostic, which leads to justice and lawfulness and thus also produces right relationship to others. Clement devotes a whole chapter of the *Stromata* to the exposition of the gnostic's ἀπάθεια.[11]

---

[8] *Stromata* VII, 3, 16, 5, GCS, Clem. Alex. III, 12: Μάλιστα γὰρ ἄγαλμα θεῖον καὶ Θεῷ προσεμφερὲς (cf. Tragicorum Graecorum Fragmenta Adesp. 117, ed. A. Nauck, 2nd ed. [Leipzig, 1889] 863) ἀνθρώπου δικαίου ψυχή, ἐν ᾗ διὰ τῆς τῶν παραγγελμάτων ὑπακοῆς τεμενίζεται καὶ ἐνιδρύεται ὁ πάντων ἡγεμὼν θνητῶν τε καὶ ἀθανάτων, βασιλεύς τε καὶ γεννήτωρ τῶν καλῶν, νόμος ὢν ὄντως καὶ θεσμὸς καὶ Λόγος αἰώνιος, ἰδίᾳ τε ἑκάστοις καὶ κοινῇ πᾶσιν εἷς ὢν σωτήρ.

[9] Already Ptolemy III (died 225 B.C.) had been surnamed Euergetes. Jesus Himself, perhaps, criticized the conventional identification of kingship and goodness, when He said: "The kings of the gentiles lord it over them; and they that have power over them are called beneficent (εὐεργέται)" (Luke 22:25). Clement of Alexandria's interest was concentrated not in the king, but in "royal" man.

[10] *Stromata* VII, 3, 16, 6, GCS, Clem. Alex., III, 12: Οὗτος ὁ τῷ ὄντι μονογενής, ὁ τῆς τοῦ παμβασιλέως καὶ παντοκράτορος Πατρὸς δόξης χαρακτήρ, ἐναποσφραγιζόμενος τῷ γνοστικῷ τὴν τελείαν θεωρίαν κατ᾽ εἰκόνα τὴν ἑαυτοῦ, ὡς εἶναι τρίτην ἤδη τὴν θείαν εἰκόνα τὴν ὅση δύναμις ἐξομοιουμένην πρὸς τὸ δεύτερον αἴτιον. . . . Note here how image-likeness to God and vision of God are considered as one and the same thing (cf. above, pp. 98, 103); also how the concept of the "third image," which in Plato's *Republic* 597 ff., had served to depreciate works of art, is used to enhance man, the image of the Logos, who is the image of God the Father (cf. above, p. 87).

[11] *Stromata* VI, 9, GCS, Clem. Alex. II, 467 ff.

This word and the whole terminology appertaining to it give evidence of the Stoic (beside the Platonic) element in Clement's adaptation of Greek thought to the Christian faith.[12] The *apatheia* concept was to remain characteristic of Greek asceticism and mysticism,[13] but, significantly enough, was to be opposed by St. Augustine[14] as detrimental to the realization that man cannot be perfect by himself and to the full practice of charity.

For Clement, as for Philo before him, Moses was the true paragon of the royal philosopher, of the wise man, who because self-controlled and just is a king, and of the king who is lawful and wise.[15] Clement thought it certain that the very concept of the king-philosopher had been received by Plato directly or indirectly from the great mouthpiece of the Old Law of God.[16] It is with regard to Moses that Clement defines the various kinds of the royal office, of which the first is

that according to God and His Holy Son by whom the good things of the earth as well as those beyond and the bliss of perfection are directed. . . . The second idea or form (εἶδος) of kingship (βασιλείας) is that according to the purely rational and divine type of government which for ruling makes use only of the passionate-spirited (θυμοειδεῖ) part of the soul. . . .

There follow a third type, in which the *thymoeides* is abused in the

---

[12] For Stoic *apatheia* see v. Arnim, *Stoic. Veter. Fragm.* III, fragm. 443–455, especially p. 109, fragm. 448; for the Christianization of the concept by Clement, who connects *apatheia* with martyrdom and with the eucharistic sacrifice, and by Origen cf. Völker, *Clemens* 535 f., 559 ff., idem, *Origenes* 153 ff. For pagan and Christian *apatheia* see also G. Bardy, article "Apatheia," *DSpir*, vol. I, 727 ff.

[13] For the quite un-Stoic meaning of Christian *apatheia* in Gregory of Nyssa see Daniélou, *Platonisme* 50 ff., 99 ff., and above all Gaïth, *Liberté* 60 ff. See also Evagrius of Pontus, *Centuriae (Problemata prognostica)* II, 6, Frankenberg 133 : Ἡ ψυχὴ ἡ ἐργαζομένη, ἥτις χαρίτι τοῦ Θεοῦ εὐοδώθη καὶ τοῦ σώματος ἀφώρισται, ἐν ἐκείνοις τοῖς τόποις τῆς γνώσεως ἔσται, ὅπου αἱ τῆς ἀπαθείας πτέρυγες αὐτὴν καταντᾶν ποιήσουσιν. Cf. ibid. I, 11, Frankenberg 57 : Πάντες ὅσοι τὰ νῦν σώματα πνευματικὰ κέκτηνται, βασιλεύουσι ἐν τοῖς γενομένοις αἰῶσιν· ὅσοι δὲ ἐν σώμασιν ἐργάταις συνέχονται, ἐν τοῖς μέλλουσιν αἰῶσι βασιλεύσουσιν. See, furthermore, Diadochus Photicus, *One Hundred Gnostic Chapters* (Κεφάλαια γνωστικά Ρ') 98, ed. and trans. E. des Places, S.J., *Diadoque de Photicé: Œuvres spirituelles* (Sources Chrétiennes V bis, Paris, 1955) 160.

[14] See below, p. 160; also *ibid.*, n. 21, for St. Jerome's opposition to what he considered to be Evagrius' conception of *apatheia*.

[15] Philo, *De vita Mosis* II, 1 ff., Cohn and Wendland IV, 200 ff.; Clement of Alexandria, *Stromata* I, 24, 158, 1 ff., *GCS, Clem. Alex.* II, 99 ff.

[16] *Stromata* I, 25, 165, *GCS, Clem. Alex.* II, 103; II, 5, 20, 1 ff., *GCS, Clem. Alex.* II, 123 ff.

sense of lust for domination, and a fourth in which *epithymia*, the "appetitive-desirous" part of the soul, here greed, prevails. But these two are not good or true types of kingship.[17]

King, therefore, is he who rules according to the laws, who possesses the understanding to rule over willing [subjects]. Such is the Lord [Christ] who receives those who believe in Him and through Him. For, God handed over and subjected everything to Christ, our King. . . .[18]

But if Christ is the true King, then true Christians are kings through him. Had not Plato said that whoever had royal understanding, whether a ruler or a private citizen, could rightly be called royal?[19]

Just as wise men are wise through wisdom and the law-abiding are law-abiding through law, so are Christ's Christians royal through Christ the King.[20]

Clement goes on to speak of the royal and political man as of the law animate (νόμος ἔμψυχος).[21] This term[22] had become one of the

[17] *Stromata* I, 24, 158, 2 ff., GCS, *Clem. Alex.* II, 99 f.: Τοῦ δὲ βασιλικοῦ τὸ μὲν θεῖον μέρος ἐστίν, οἷον τὸ κατὰ τὸν Θεὸν καὶ τὸν ἅγιον Υἱὸν αὐτοῦ, παρ' ὧν τά τε ἀπὸ γῆς ἀγαθὰ καὶ τὰ ἐκτὸς καὶ ἡ τελεία εὐδαιμονία χορηγεῖται . . . Δεύτερον δέ ἐστιν εἶδος βασιλείας μετὰ τὴν ἀκραιφνῶς λογικὴν καὶ θείαν διοίκησιν τὸ μόνῳ τῷ θυμοειδεῖ τῆς ψυχῆς εἰς βασιλείαν συγχρώμενον (exemplified by Hercules and Alexander). . . . Τρίτον δὲ τὸ ἑνὸς ἐφιέμενον τοῦ νικῆσαι μόνον καὶ καταστρέψασθαι (exemplified by the Persians). . . . Τετάρτη δὲ ἡ πασῶν κακίστη ἡ κατὰ τὰς ἐπιθυμίας τάττεται βασιλεία (exemplified by Sardanapalus). . . .

[18] *Ibid.* 159, 5 f., GCS, *Clem. Alex.* II, 100: Βασιλεὺς τοίνυν ἐστὶν ὁ ἄρχων κατὰ νόμους ὁ τὴν τοῦ ἄρχειν ἑκόντων ἐπιστήμην ἔχων, οἷός ἐστιν ὁ Κύριος τοὺς εἰς αὐτὸν καὶ δι' αὐτοῦ πιστεύοντας προσιέμενος. Πάντα γάρ παρέδωκεν ὁ Θεὸς καὶ πάντα ὑπέταξεν Χριστῷ τῷ βασιλεῖ ἡμῶν (there follows quotation of Phil. 2 : 10 f.).

[19] *Stromata* II, 4, 18, 2, GCS, *Clem. Alex.* II, 122, quoting Plato's *Statesman* 259A f.: . . . "ὥστε ἡ τοῦ ἀληθινοῦ βασιλέως ἐπιστήμη βασιλική, καὶ ὁ ταύτην κεκτημένος, ἐάν τε ἄρχων ἐάν τε ἰδιώτης ὢν τυγχάνῃ, πάντως κατά γε τὴν τέχνην αὐτὴν βασιλικὸς ὀρθῶς προσαγορευθήσεται."

[20] *Stromata* II, 4, 18, 3 f., GCS, *Clem. Alex.* II, 122: Ὡς γὰρ οἱ σοφοὶ σοφίᾳ εἰσὶ σοφοὶ καὶ οἱ νόμιμοι νόμῳ νόμιμοι (cf. Plato[?], *Minos* 314C), οὕτως [οἱ] Χριστῷ βασιλεῖ βασιλικοὶ Χριστοῦ ⟨οἱ⟩ χριστιανοί.

[21] *Ibid.* II, 4, 18, 4, GCS,*Clem. Alex.* II, 122: Ὅ τε Ἐλεάτης ξένος τὸν βασιλικὸν καὶ πολιτικὸν ἄνδρα νόμον ἔμψυχον ἀποφαίνεται. There is no such phrase in Plato's *Politicus*; Stählin in the edition of Clement's *Stromata*, GCS, *Clem. Alex.* II, 104, rightly refers to Philo, *De vita Mosis* I, 28, 162 and II, 4, Cohn and Wendland IV, 159 and 201.

[22] For the related *topoi* of the animate law and the animate image (ἄγαλμα ἔμψυχον) cf. W. Bousset, *Kyrios Christos* (Göttingen, 1921) 150 ff., 200 ff., 244 ff., A. Steinwenter, "ΝΟΜΟΣ ΕΜΨΥΧΟΣ," *Anz. Wien*, Philos.-histor. Klasse, LXXXIII, 1946 (1947) 250 ff., also the works cited in the following note and E. H. Kantorowicz, *The King's Two Bodies* (Princeton, 1957) 127 ff.

key concepts of Hellenistic kingship.[23] It is used for Moses, the law-giver, and for the king also by Philo.[24] Clement, still in the same context, applies it to the perfect Christian, not to the king in particular, for he adds:

Such is the one who fulfils the law, "doing the will of the Father" (Matthew 21:31). . . .[25]

Clement of Alexandria's ideology of kingship remains on the whole centered more about Platonic than about biblical ideas; just as for Plato so for Clement true wisdom and kingship are one and the same thing. This Platonic inheritance is of importance not only for Greek Christian spirituality, it also helped in shaping Christian political thought in the Greek-speaking east, from Clement to Origen, Eusebius, Justinian, and beyond. Nevertheless, ever since Origen scriptural texts emerge as fundamental.

Origen repeatedly quotes and expounds the word of the $\beta \alpha \sigma \iota \lambda \epsilon \iota \alpha$ $\Theta \epsilon o \hat{v}$ $\dot{\epsilon} \nu \tau \dot{o} s$ $\dot{v} \mu \hat{\omega} \nu$ (Luke 17:21) and there is no doubt that he places this Kingdom of God in the soul of man.[26] He also makes the

---

[23] Cf. L. Delatte, Les traités de la royauté d'Ecphante, Diotogène et Sthénidas (Liège, Paris, 1942), E. R. Goodenough, "The Political Philosophy of Hellenistic Kingship," Yale Classical Studies I (1928) 53 ff., Kantorowicz, "Königsbild," 169 ff., idem, "Deus per naturam, Deus per gratiam," 253 ff.

[24] See the references to Philo, p. 113, n. 21.

[25] Stromata II, 4, 19, 1, GCS, Clem. Alex. II, 122: $To\iota o\hat{v}\tau os$ $\delta \dot{\epsilon}$ $\dot{o}$ $\pi \lambda \eta \rho \hat{\omega} \nu$ $\mu \dot{\epsilon} \nu$ $\tau \dot{o} \nu$ $\nu \dot{o} \mu o \nu$ "$\pi o\iota \hat{\omega} \nu$ $\delta \dot{\epsilon}$ $\tau \dot{o}$ $\theta \dot{\epsilon} \lambda \eta \mu \alpha$ $\tau o\hat{v}$ $\Pi \alpha \tau \rho \dot{o} s$" (Matthew 21:31). In Stromata I, 26, 167, 3, GCS, Clem. Alex. II, 104, Clement follows Philo, De vita Mosis I, 162 (cf. p. 113, n. 21) in speaking of Moses as animate law: $M \omega \upsilon \sigma \hat{\eta} s$ $\delta \dot{\epsilon}$ $\sigma \upsilon \nu \epsilon \lambda \dot{o} \nu \tau \iota$ $\epsilon \dot{\iota} \pi \epsilon \hat{\iota} \nu$ $\nu \dot{o} \mu o s$ $\ddot{\epsilon} \mu \psi \upsilon \chi o s$ $\mathring{\eta} \nu$ $\tau \hat{\omega}$ $\chi \rho \eta \sigma \tau \hat{\omega}$ $\lambda \dot{o} \gamma \omega$ $\kappa \upsilon \beta \epsilon \rho \nu \dot{\omega} \mu \epsilon \nu o s$. In Clement the concept of the royal man as $\nu \dot{o} \mu o s$ $\ddot{\epsilon} \mu \psi \upsilon \chi o s$ is fused with that of his image-likeness to God. He, therefore, also speaks of man as $\ddot{\epsilon} \mu \pi \nu o \upsilon s$ $\epsilon \dot{\iota} \kappa \dot{\omega} \nu$ or $\ddot{\alpha} \gamma \alpha \lambda \mu \alpha$ $\ddot{\epsilon} \mu \psi \upsilon \chi o \nu$ (Protrepticus X, 98, 2 f., GCS, Clem. Alex. I, 71), terms which are dependent both on the Bible and on Hellenistic ruler worship: see, for instance, the famous inscription for Ptolemy V Epiphanes on the Rosetta Stone. (For further texts and bibliography see the article of E. H. Kantorowicz, quoted p. 109, n. 3, and my article "Imago".)

[26] See, for instance, In Genesim, homil. XIII, 4, GCS, Orig. VI, 119, 5: Adest enim Verbum Dei et haec nunc eius est operatio, ut de anima unius cuiusque vestrum removeat terram et aperiat fontem tuum. Intra te enim est et non extrinsecus venit, sicut et regnum Dei intra te est . . .; also De oratione 25, 1 ff., GCS, Orig. II, 356 ff., especially 356, 30–357, 7: . . . $\delta \hat{\eta} \lambda o \nu$ $\ddot{o} \tau \iota$ $\dot{o}$ $\epsilon \dot{\upsilon} \chi \dot{o} \mu \epsilon \nu o s$ "$\dot{\epsilon} \lambda \theta \epsilon \hat{\iota} \nu$ $\tau \dot{\eta} \nu$ $\beta \alpha \sigma \iota \lambda \epsilon \iota \alpha \nu$" $\tau o\hat{v}$ $\Theta \epsilon o\hat{v}$ $\pi \epsilon \rho \dot{\iota}$ $\tau o\hat{v}$ $\tau \dot{\eta} \nu$ $\dot{\epsilon} \nu$ $\alpha \dot{\upsilon} \tau \hat{\omega}$ $\beta \alpha \sigma \iota \lambda \epsilon \iota \alpha \nu$ $\tau o\hat{v}$ $\Theta \epsilon o\hat{v}$ $\dot{\alpha} \nu \alpha \tau \epsilon \hat{\iota} \lambda \alpha \iota$ $\kappa \alpha \dot{\iota}$ $\kappa \alpha \rho \pi o \phi o \rho \hat{\eta} \sigma \alpha \iota$ $\kappa \alpha \dot{\iota}$ $\tau \epsilon \lambda \epsilon \iota \omega \theta \hat{\eta} \nu \alpha \iota$ $\epsilon \dot{\upsilon} \lambda \dot{o} \gamma \omega s$ $\epsilon \dot{\upsilon} \chi \epsilon \tau \alpha \iota$ . . . $\pi \alpha \rho \dot{o} \nu \tau o s$ $\alpha \dot{\upsilon} \tau \hat{\omega}$ $\tau o\hat{v}$ $\Pi \alpha \tau \rho \dot{o} s$ $\kappa \alpha \dot{\iota}$ $\sigma \upsilon \mu \beta \alpha \sigma \iota \lambda \epsilon \dot{\upsilon} o \nu \tau o s$ $\tau \hat{\omega}$ $\Pi \alpha \tau \rho \dot{\iota}$ $\tau o\hat{v}$ $X \rho \iota \sigma \tau o\hat{v}$ $\dot{\epsilon} \nu$ $\tau \hat{\eta}$ $\tau \epsilon \tau \epsilon \lambda \epsilon \iota \omega \mu \dot{\epsilon} \nu \eta$ $\psi \upsilon \chi \hat{\eta}$. . . . See also the texts quoted from Origen, Athanasius, Gregory of Nyssa, Cyril of Alexandria, etc., by Lampe, "$BA\Sigma I\Lambda EIA$" 63.

following important comment to Matthew 18:23 on the Kingdom of Heaven:

For, He Himself is the King of the Heavens; and since He Himself is Wisdom itself (αὐτοσοφία) and Justice itself (αὐτοδικαιοσύνη) and Truth itself (αὐτοαλήθεια) how could He ever not be the Kingdom itself (αὐτοβασιλεία). . . .

And if you inquire what this is: "theirs is the Kingdom of Heaven" (cf. Matthew 5:3 and 10), you may say that "theirs" means Christ, in so far as He is the Kingdom itself and rules as King in the thought of every man who is no longer ruled by sin. . . .[27]

Just as with Origen's idea of Paradise, so it is also with his conception of the Kingdom of God: the spiritualized immanent aspect and the eschatological-transcendent are merged into one another. Even before the *apocatastasis* of all things the Kingdom of God itself *is* Christ Himself and therefore those who possess the Kingdom *are* Christ even on earth.[28] This one might say is the doctrine of the Church as

[27] Origen, *Commentary to the Gospel of St. Matthew*, XIV, 7, GCS, Orig. X, 289: Αὐτὸς γάρ ἐστιν ὁ βασιλεὺς τῶν οὐρανῶν, καὶ ὥσπερ αὐτός ἐστιν ἡ αὐτοσοφία καὶ ἡ αὐτοδικαιοσύνη καὶ ἡ αὐτοαλήθεια οὕτω μήποτε καὶ ἡ αὐτοβασιλεία. . . . Κἂν ζητῇς δὲ πῶς "αὐτῶν ἐστιν ἡ βασιλεία τῶν οὐρανῶν" (cf. Matthew 5:3) δύνασαι λέγειν ὅτι αὐτῶν ἐστιν ὁ Χριστός, καθὸ αὐτοβασιλεία ἐστίν, βασιλεύων καθ᾽ ἑκάστην ἐπίνοιαν αὐτοῦ τοῦ μηκέτι βασιλευομένου ὑπὸ τῆς ἁμαρτίας. . . . Compare with this the texts from St. Cyprian and St. Ambrose, quoted below, p. 145, n. 62. R. Frick, *Die Geschichte des Reich-Gottes-Gedankens in der alten Kirche bis zu Origenes und Augustin* (Beihefte zur Zeitschrift für die neutestamentliche Wissenschaft VI, Giessen, 1928) 101, 124, n. 2, 136, quotes these texts without, however, noting the significant differences between Origen on the one hand and Cyprian and Ambrose on the other. Lampe, ΒΑΣΙΛΕΙΑ 72, quotes Origen's "remarkable conception of Christ as himself the βασιλεία," but without further comments.

[28] For patristic identifications and distinctions of the Kingdom of Christ and the Kingdom of God, see Lampe, ΒΑΣΙΛΕΙΑ 68 ff. According to Cullmann, *Königsherrschaft Christi*, already the New Testament made a distinction. But this seems doubtful in spite of 1 Cor. 15:28: "And when all things shall be subdued unto Him, then the Son also Himself shall be subject unto Him . . . ," especially in view of Apoc. 11:15: ". . . The kingdom of the world is become our Lord's and His Christ's, and He shall reign for ever and ever . . ." (cf. v. Gall, ΒΑΣΙΛΕΙΑ 478 ff., and K. L. Schmidt, article "βασιλεία," ThWbNT I, 581 f., 590 ff., where the author also discusses the concept of αὐτοβασιλεία). Patristic views on the relationship between Kingdom of God and Kingdom of Christ are bound up with the development of Trinitarian doctrine (cf. Lampe, ΒΑΣΙΛΕΙΑ). So, for instance, Origenist subordinationist tendencies could lead Evagrius Ponticus to the conception of an ascending hierarchy from Χριστοῦ βασιλεία to βασιλεία τῶν οὐρανῶν and to βασιλεία Θεοῦ (cf. S. Marsili, O.S.B., *Giovanni Cassiano ed Evagrio Pontico* [Studia Anselmiana V, Roma, 1936] 93 f., 107 f., 161 f.; see also Origen, *De oratione* 25, GCS, Orig. II, 356 ff.);

the Body of Christ, expressed in terms of the Kingdom of God, and in a famous passage at the end of his work *Against Celsus* Origen did in fact identify the Church with the Christian's fatherland.[29] However, Origen's terminology of αὐτοβασιλεία has a second meaning which seems to be related to his attitude toward the universal political "Kingdom" of his time, the Roman Empire.

In his refutation of Celsus, who was appalled by the threat to Roman political life if all citizens should adopt the Christian way of thinking, Origen considers such a hypothetical but not improbable event from the point of view of a Christian. He states his belief that in this case the enemies of the empire would be destroyed by Christian prayers or by the direct intervention of God.[30]

---

characteristically, Cassian, who is otherwise so strongly influenced by Evagrius, did not follow him in this respect (cf. Marsili, *Cassiano* 108, 161 f.); see also Ambrose, *De fide* III, 12, *PL* XVI, 633 ff., and V, 12, *PL* XVI, 705 ff., and *De Abraham* II, 9, 66, *CSEL* XXXII, 1, 621, where he speaks of the *regnum Trinitatis*. Occasional distinctions between the Kingdom of Heaven and the Kingdom of God, as in St. Isidore of Pelusium and St. Maximus the Confessor—cf. Lampe, *ΒΑΣΙΛΕΙΑ* 59—seem to be of a more accidental nature.

[29] *Contra Celsum* VIII, 75, *GCS*, *Orig.* II, 292: Ἡμεῖς δὲ ἐν ἑκάστῃ πόλει ἄλλο σύστημα πατρίδος κτισθὲν Λόγῳ Θεοῦ ἐπιστάμενοι τοὺς δυνατοὺς λόγῳ καὶ βίῳ ὑγιεῖ χρωμένους ἄρχειν ἐπὶ τὸ ἄρχειν ἐκκλησιῶν παρακαλοῦμεν. . . . A little later in the same text Origen speaks of the καλῶς ἄρχοντες ἐν τῇ ἐκκλησίᾳ τῆς κατὰ Θεὸν πατρίδος and repeats: λέγω δὲ τῆς ἐκκλησίας. See also *Epistola ad Diognetum* V, 4 ff. – VI, 1, an equally famous text, Bihlmeyer, *Apostol. Väter* I, 144: . . . παράδοξον ἐνδείκνυνται τὴν κατάστασιν τῆς ἑαυτῶν πολιτείας. Πατρίδας οἰκοῦσιν ἰδίας, ἀλλ' ὡς πάροικοι . . . πᾶσα ξένη πατρίς ἐστιν αὐτῶν, καὶ πᾶσα πατρὶς ξένη . . . ἐπὶ γῆς διατρίβουσιν ἀλλ' ἐν οὐρανῷ πολιτεύονται . . . ὅπερ ἐστὶν ἐν σώματι ψυχή, τοῦτ' εἰσὶν ἐν κόσμῳ χριστιανοί. Likewise, Clement of Alexandria, *Paedagogus* II, 1, 6, 2, *GCS*, *Clem. Alex.* I, 157, speaks of the Kingdom of God as of the heavenly Church and in *Stromata* IV, 8, 66, 1, *GCS*, *Clem. Alex.* II, 278, he says that of this heavenly Church the one on earth is the image. For the interchangeable use in patristic literature of the terms Kingdom of God and City of God in their relation to the concepts of the Church and the soul see below, pp. 245 ff.

[30] *Contra Celsum* VIII, 68, *GCS*, *Orig.* II, 284 f.: Celsus, referring to Homer, *Iliad* II, 204 f.: "εἷς κοίρανος ἔστω, εἷς βασιλεύς . . . ," had challenged the Christian disregard of terrestrial rulership, alleged by him: "ὡς ἂν τοῦτο λύσῃς τὸ δόγμα, εἰκότως ἀμύνεταί σε ὁ βασιλεύς. Εἰ γὰρ τὸ αὐτό σοι ποιήσειαν ἅπαντες, οὐδὲν κωλύσει τὸν μὲν καταλειφθῆναι μόνον καὶ ἔρημον, τὰ δ' ἐπὶ γῆς ἐπὶ τοῖς ἀνομωτάτοις τε καὶ ἀγριωτάτοις βαρβάροις γενέσθαι, καὶ μήτε τῆς σῆς θρησκείας μήτε τῆς ἀληθινῆς σοφίας ἐν ἀνθρώποις ἔτι καταλείπεσθαι κλέος." Origen replies: . . . καὶ τὸ αὐτό γε ποιείτωσάν μοι ἅπαντες, τὸ μὲν Ὁμηρικὸν καταλύοντες δόγμα, τὸ δὲ θεῖον περὶ βασιλέως τηροῦντες καὶ τὸ "τὸν βασιλέα τιμᾶτε" (1 Peter 2:17) φυλάττοντες. . . . Εἰ γὰρ, ὡς λέγει Κέλσος, τὸ αὐτό μοι ποιήσειαν ἅπαντες, δηλονότι καὶ οἱ βάρβαροι τῷ Λόγῳ τοῦ Θεοῦ προσελθόντες νομιμώτατοι ἔσονται καὶ ἡμερώτατοι· καὶ πᾶσα μὲν θρησκεία καταλυθήσεται, μόνη δὲ ἡ Χριστιανῶν κρατήσει, ἥτις καὶ μόνη ποτὲ κρατήσει τοῦ Λόγου

And indeed, if the Kingdom of God can exist in the hearts of men, why should not even the most pagan and hostile empire, Rome, the new Babylon, be reformed in its convictions and actions and become a Kingdom of God on earth—or to use the terminology of Clement, at least a second εἶδος βασιλείας, representing divine government?[31]

For, Origen's formulation of Christ's *autobasileia* not only asserts that the Kingdom of God is Christ Himself, but also that Christ is kingship itself, the essence as it were of all rulership; not only that those who possess the Kingdom of Heaven are Christ-like, but also that Christ *qua* essence of kingship is identical with them.[32] But, if this

ἀεὶ πλείονας νεμομένου ψυχάς. See also *Contra Celsum* VIII, 70, GCS, *Orig.* II, 286 f: Ἀλλ' οἱ καθ' ὑπόθεσιν Κέλσου πάντες ἂν πεισθέντες Ῥωμαῖοι εὐχόμενοι περιέσονται τῶν πολεμίων ἢ οὐδὲ τὴν ἀρχὴν πολεμήσονται, φρουρούμενοι ὑπὸ θείας δυνάμεως.... Similar ideas are found already in the Apologetes. For both the Apologetes and Origen cf. E. Peterson, *Der Monotheismus als politisches Problem*, reprinted in *Theologische Traktate* (München, 1951) 45 ff., T. E. Mommsen, "St. Augustine and the Christian Idea of Progress," *Jour. Hist. Ideas* XII (1951) 357 ff., P. de Francisci, *Arcana Imperii* III, 2 (Milano, 1948) 52–62, and for all the texts referred to in nn. 29 and 30 the excellent commentary of H. I. Marrou to *A Diognète* (Sources chrétiennes XXXIII, Paris, 1951) 119–176.

[31] For Clement see above, p. 112. Cf. below, pp. 122 f. The empirical, pagan, Roman Empire, of course, remained a manifestation of demoniac power also for Origen; in this connection see his interpretations of the Gospel verse about the tribute money (Matthew 22:15 ff., etc.), discussed by Crouzel, *Image* 193 ff., and in my article "Image" 21 f., 33 f.

[32] For the concept of *autobasileia* cf. Frick, *Reich-Gottes-Gedanke* 10, 124 n. 2, 136, Schmidt, article "βασιλεία," *ThWbNT* I, 591, idem, *Le problème du christianisme primitif* (Paris, 1938) 82 and 86, idem, *Die Polis in Kirche und Welt* (Basel, 1939) 39 f. See also below, p. 145, n. 62, for the superficially similar texts in Cyprian, and in Ambrose. The term αὐτοβασιλεία belongs together with such expressions as αὐτὸ ἀγαθόν (Plato, *Republic* VI, 507B, VII 540A), αὐτοάνθρωπος (Aristotle, *Eth. Nic.* I, 4, 1096a 34 f.), αὐτοσωκράτης (Plotinus, *Ennead* I, 4), αὐτοουσία (*Ennead* VI, 8, 12), αὐτογή (*Ennead* VI, 7, 11), αὐτοθεός (Origen, *In Joann.* II, 2, GCS, *Orig.* VI, 54, 1, 32), αὐτολόγος (*idem, Contra Celsum* VI, 63, GCS, *Orig.* II, 133); cf. Crouzel, *Image* 96, 106, and 123, for other occurrences in Origen of such expressions as αὐτοαγαθόν, αὐτοθεός, αὐτολόγος, αὐτοσοφία, αὐτοαλήθεια. In all these cases αὐτο- indicates essence. However, the idea of sovereignty inherent in such terms as αὐτοεξούσιος, endowed with free will, αὐτοκρατής, ruling by oneself, is not too far removed from the concept of essence of rulership as expressed by the word αὐτοβασιλεία, especially since according to the tradition of the philosopher-king (see above, pp. 112 ff.) rule over oneself and God-like independence from passions are among the prerequisites of true rulership (cf. also Eusebius, *Tricennial Oration* 5, GCS, *Euseb.* I, 203 ff.; for Synesius, see below, pp. 122 f., n. 42). The resulting ideological synthesis is probably present in the term αὐτοκράτωρ, used to translate *imperator* in the official title of the Eastern Roman Emperor before Heraclius officially adopted the Basileus title; even later *autokrator* remained the title of the principal and

is so, must not a Christian empire strive and claim to represent the *autobasileia* of Christ, that is to say, imitate Christ's rule over the world, though such a claim may somewhat obscure the fact that the Kingdom of God is also the ecclesiological Body of Christ? Will not the terrestrial Basileia be potentially identical with the heavenly one or at least similar to it in the manner of the Platonist-Christian image-archetype relationship according to which the image is no longer truly inferior in so far as its very existence means its assimilation, its return, to its origin? Origen did not ask these questions explicitly, but they were answered in the affirmative after the actual Christianization of the empire by Origen's spiritual descendent, Eusebius, and by a whole tribe of like-minded Christian "imperialists."

With the end of persecution and with the Christianization of the Roman Empire, the conception of the βασιλεία Θεοῦ remained no longer concentrated in eschatological renewal and preparation for it, as it necessarily had remained even for Origen.[33] Renovation of the empire, accompanied by age-old traditions of ruler worship and of the eternal rejuvenation of Rome, became one aspect of Christian reform ideology. This imperial idea of Christian reform is inseparable from the Constantinian-Theodosian age,[34] but it is not simply identical

---

actually reigning Basileus (cf. above all the two articles by F. Dölger, "Das byzantinische Mitkaisertum in den Urkunden," *Byz. Z.* XXXVI [1936] 123 ff., and "Die Entwicklung der byzantinischen Kaisertitulatur und die Datierung von Kaiserdarstellungen in der byzantinischen Kleinkunst," *Studies Presented to D. M. Robinson* II [1953] 985 ff. [both reprinted in F. Dölger, *Byzantinische Diplomatik* (Ettal, 1956) 102 ff. and 130 ff.], where the older studies by L. Bréhier, E. Stein, and G. Ostrogorsky are discussed). In this connection see the interesting historical discussion of the titles and concepts of βασιλεύς, αὐτοκράτωρ and τύραννος in Synesius, *De regno* 17, Terzaghi, *Synes. Cyrenen. Opuscula* 38 ff., with preference significantly given to the αὐτοκράτωρ title; see also John Lydus, *De magistratibus populi Romani* I, 3 f., ed. R. Wuensch (Leipzig, 1903) 9 f.

[33] There is still another aspect of Origen's views on these matters, where he anticipates later patristic doubts concerning the value of the Church's rapid expansion; see the texts quoted below, p. 252, n. 57.

[34] Cf. above, pp. 18–20. The "imperial" ideology of Christian reform continued to a large extent pagan ideas about the ruler as savior, liberator, benefactor, reformer of mankind. For rich material on the origin and development of the ideology of ruler worship see de Francisci, *Arcana Imperii*. In recent years the importance especially of Hellenistic monarchical ideology for late antique, early Christian, and mediaeval thought and its expression in literature, art, and life of Church and state has been more fully realized. A survey of most of the relevant works by E. R. Goodenough, L. Delatte, W. Schubart, A. Steinwenter, N. H. Baynes, J. Straub, A. Alföldi, H. P. L'Orange,

with the vitalistic and cosmological renewal ideas then current. The Christian element in the Constantinian-Theodosian, and later in the Byzantine and western mediaeval, idea of empire was too strong to be absorbed by the ancient ideology of recurrence and rebirth (which nevertheless continued to form a part of its background). The "Christian empire" was to live on as an important conception *sui generis* in the history of reform, of special significance also for the west in the Carolingian age and in the Ottonian-Salian era.

In the Christian east the conception that the Christian empire by its very existence is close to the Kingdom of God was most deeply ingrained. It is true that political theory continued to demand the highest virtues from the emperor and expected him to represent to the highest degree that which every Christian ought to be; everywhere in mediaeval Christendom a ruler who did not live and act as a Christian could come to be considered as a tyrant, as *rex iniustus*, and lose his claim to rule. But this did not alter the fact that in the normal exercise of his functions the Christian king and emperor, in the east even more than in the west, was *ipso facto* considered as a minister of God on earth and that he saw himself and his actions in this light.

The history of the early Christian empire is rich in pronouncements concerning reform of the empire or specific reforms brought about by the emperors. Eusebius,[35] no doubt also Constantine himself, and later emperors and imperial theorists, conceived of the task of restoring and conserving the Roman Empire, including Christianization and maintenance of orthodoxy, as part of the reform of mankind and used typical reform *termini* in expressing this idea. Thus in his *Church History*, Eusebius characterizes the era of Constantine as one of

and others, may be found in the study of E. H. Kantorowicz, "Königsbild" 169 ff. See also A. D. Nock, "Notes on Ruler-Cult, I–IV," *Jour. Hellen. Stud.* XLVIII (1928) 21 ff., M. P. Charlesworth, "Some Observations on Ruler-Cult, Especially in Rome," *Harv. Theol. Rev.* XXVIII (1935) 5 ff., H. U. Instinsky, "Kaiser und Ewigkeit," *Hermes* LXXVII (1942) 313 ff. Cf. now L. Cerfaux and J. Tondriau, *Un concurrent du christianisme : Le culte des souverains dans la civilisation gréco-romaine* (Tournai, 1957); *The Sacral Kingship* (VIIth Internat. Congress for the History of Religions, Rome, 1955 = Studies in the History of Religions [Supplements to *Numen*] IV, Leiden, 1959); A. Michel, *Die Kaisermacht in der Ostkirche (843–1204)* (Darmstadt, 1959).

[35] See, in general, H. Berkhof, *Die Theologie des Eusebius von Caesarea* (Amsterdam, 1939) 53 ff.; further literature below, pp. 123 f., n. 44.

renovation[36] and purification[37] and links it to the reformation of man through Christ.[38] In keeping with the close relation between reform and imitation ideology (see above, pp. 86–91), he also never tires in defining Constantine's, the great renewer's, role as that of an imitator of the deity.

In the texts paraphrased hereunder it is important that the emperor's imitation of Christ as conceived by Eusebius is formulated as imitation of the divine Logos: Constantine rules for the Logos just as the Logos Himself rules for the Father. This Eusebian conception of imperial

[36] *Historia ecclesiastica* X, 1, 3, *GCS, Euseb.* II, 2, 856: ... τὸν τέλειον ... καὶ πανηγυρικὸν τῆς τῶν ἐκκλησιῶν ἀνανεώσεως λόγον κατατάξομεν ... , *ibid.* X, 4, 18, II, 2, 868: ... ὡς ἀνθεῖν ὁσημέραι καὶ νεάζειν διὰ παντὸς τοῦ βίου ... , *ibid.* X, 4, 55 f., II, 2, 878: ... θαυμάτων δὲ θαυμασιώτερα ... τὰ τῆς ἐνθέου ... καὶ λογικῆς ἐν ψυχαῖς οἰκοδομῆς ἀνανεώματα. See also *Tricennial Oration* 17, 5, *GCS, Euseb.* I, 255, where Eusebius after speaking of the destruction wrought by the last great persecution says that now Christ has renewed in an even better form the destroyed churches (... τὰ πάσης ἐλπίδος ἀφῃρημένα δευτέρας ἠξίωσεν πολὺ κρείττονος τῆς ἔμπροσθεν ἀνανεώσεως καὶ ἀνενεώσατο ...) See furthermore *Historia ecclesiastica* IX, 9, 10 f., *GCS, Euseb.* II, 2, 832, about the inscription on the famous statue of Constantine on the Roman Forum, concerning the liberation and restoration of Rome: τῇ ἀρχαίᾳ ἐπιφανείᾳ καὶ λαμπρότητι ἐλευθερώσας ἀποκατέστησα. The "salutary sign" which the statue of the emperor held in the right hand was probably the same as the one which Constantine saw in his famous vision and which made him win his victory over Maxentius (in spite of H. Grégoire, "La statue de Constantin et le signe de la croix," *L'Antiquité classique* I [1936] 135 ff., and of A. Piganiol, *L'empereur Constantin* [Paris, 1932] 67 ff.; for the problem see A. Alföldi, "Hoc signo victor eris," *Pisciculi F. J. Dölger* 7 f., P. Franchi de' Cavalieri, *Constantiniana* [Studi e Testi CLXXI, Città del Vaticano, 1953] 24 ff., 93 ff., n. 105 ff., K. Aland, "Die religiöse Haltung Kaiser Konstantins," *Stud. Patr.* I, 588 f.). For the "imperialization" of the Cross itself in Byzantium, see J. Gagé, "Σταυρὸς νικοποιός: La victoire impériale dans l'empire chrétien," *Rev. hist. et philos. rel.* XIII (1933) 370 ff., A. Grabar, *L'empereur dans l'art byzantin* (Publications de la Faculté des Lettres de l'Université de Strasbourg LXXV, 1936) 32 ff., 239 ff. See also the recent article by J. Deér, "Das Kaiserbild im Kreuz," *Schweizer Beiträge zur allgemeinen Geschichte* XIII (1955) 48 ff., on imperial portraits in the center of crosses in Byzantium (and in the west as well).

[37] *Historia ecclesiastica* X, 4, 60, *GCS, Euseb.* II, 2, 879 f.: [Christ] αὐτὰς δὴ οὖν πρώτας τὰς τῶν ἀνωτάτω βασιλευόντων ψυχὰς προελόμενος, τῶν μὲν ... τυράννων τὴν οἰκουμένην ἅπασαν δι᾽ αὐτῶν τῶν θεοφιλεστάτων ἐκαθήρατο, εἶτα δὲ ... αὖθις ... τὰς ... ἐρρυπωμένας ψυχὰς ὕλης τε παντοίας καὶ χώματος ἀσεβῶν ἐπιταγμάτων συμπεφορημένας ὄρυξι καὶ δικέλλαις ταῖς πληκτικαῖς τῶν μαθημάτων διδασκαλίαις ἐξεκαθήρεν. ...

[38] *Ibid.* X, 4, 56 ff., *GCS, Euseb.* II, 2, 878 f., where Eusebius boldly jumps from man's creation according to the image of God and his corruption through sin to his recovery under Constantine; cf. especially X, 4, 59, II, 2, 879: ἀλλ᾽ ὅ ... Λόγος ὁ θεοφεγγὴς καὶ σωτήριος τὴν κατ᾽ ἀξίαν δίκην τῶν ἁμαρτημάτων ὑποσχοῦσαν αὖθις ἐξ ὑπαρχῆς ἀνελάμβανεν, Πατρὸς παναγάθου φιλανθρωπίᾳ πειθόμενος—a sentence which is followed directly by the reference to the emperor, quoted in the preceding note.

Christomimesis, dependent as it is on Origenist Logos theology (see above, pp. 87 and 96), was to remain the basis of "political theology" in the Christian east. The significance of these interrelations will be seen more fully at the end of this chapter.

Why was the earthly Basileia of Constantine an imitation of the heavenly one? The divine Logos, who had fashioned man according to the image and likeness of God and had made him, alone among all earthly creatures, capable of ruling and of being ruled, had renewed (ἀνανεούμενος) this seed laid in creation through His Gospel of the heavenly Kingdom. Now Constantine has become a participant in the Kingdom of God already on earth, shaping through truly royal virtues a copy (μίμημα) of the Kingdom beyond in his soul.[39] Thus the βασιλεύς, friend of God, who bears the image of the supernal βασιλεία, can be said to govern the affairs of the world with and through the Word of God in imitation of the Almighty.[40] The emperor's relationship to God is seen as an imitation of the relation between the divine Logos and the Father: just as the Logos rules together (συμβασιλεύων) with the Father from and in infinity, so Constantine rules over the earth for many years; just as the Savior

[39] *Tricennial Oration* 4–5, *GCS, Euseb.* I, 203 f.: Ὡς δὲ τὸν κατ᾽ εἰκόνα Θεοῦ καὶ ὁμοίωσιν ἐν ἀνθρώπου ψυχῇ χαρακτῆρα Λόγος ... βασιλικόν τε τουτοὶ τὸ ζῷον ἀπειργάζετο, μόνον τῶν ἐπὶ γῆς βασιλεύειν καὶ βασιλεύεσθαι [τοῦτ᾽ εἰδέναι] ἀναδείξας προμελετᾶν τε καὶ προδιδάσκεσθαι ἐνθένδε τῆς οὐρανίου βασιλείας τὴν ἐπηγγελμένην ἐλπίδα ..., τὰ δ᾽ αὐτοῦ γεωργῶν σπέρματα καὶ τὰς ἄνωθεν ἀνανεούμενος χορηγίας οὐρανίου μεθέξειν βασιλείας τοῖς πᾶσιν εὐηγγελίζετο ..., ἐπλήρου τε ἀρρήτῳ δυνάμει τὴν σύμπασαν ὅσην ἥλιος ἐφορᾷ τοῦ κηρύγματος, τῷ τῆς κατὰ γῆν βασιλείας μιμήματι τὴν οὐράνιον ἐκτυπούμενος ἐφ᾽ ἣν καὶ σπεύδειν τὸ πᾶν τῶν ἀνθρώπων παρορμᾷ γένος, ἀγαθὴν ἐλπίδα ταύτην προβεβλημένος. Ἧς ὁ μὲν τῷ Θεῷ φίλος (i.e., Constantine) ἐντεῦθεν ἤδη μεθέξει ταῖς ἐμφύτοις τῷ Θεῷ κοσμηθεὶς ἀρεταῖς καὶ τὰς ἐκεῖθεν ἀπορροίας τῇ ψυχῇ καταδεδεγμένος καὶ λογικὸς μὲν ἐκ τοῦ καθόλου γεγονὼς Λόγου. ... Ἀτὰρ δὴ καὶ βασιλεὺς ἀληθεῖ Λόγῳ χρηματίσειεν ⟨ἂν⟩ οὗτος ὁ τῆς ἐπέκεινα βασιλείας τὸ μίμημα βασιλικαῖς ἀρεταῖς τῇ ψυχῇ μεμορφωμένος.

[40] *Tricennial Oration* 1, 6, *GCS, Euseb.* I, 199: ... παρ᾽ οὗ καὶ δι᾽ οὗ (that is to say, through the Logos, the Son of God) τῆς ἀνωτάτω βασιλείας τὴν εἰκόνα φέρων ὁ τῷ Θεῷ φίλος βασιλεὺς κατὰ μίμησιν τοῦ κρείττονος τῶν ἐπὶ γῆς ἁπάντων τοὺς οἴακας διακυβερνῶν ἰθύνει. Similarly *ibid.* 3, 5, I, 201; 7, 12, I, 215; 5, 4, I, 204, where the metaphor of the passionless soul as the mirror of God (see above, pp. 96 f.) is applied to Constantine, who is therefore the true philosopher-king: ... νικητὴς ἐτύμως ὁ τὴν νίκην τῶν καταπαλαιόντων θνητὸν γένος παθῶν ἀράμενος, ὁ πρὸς τὴν ἀρχέτυπον τοῦ μεγάλου βασιλέως ἀπεικονισμένος ἰδέαν καὶ ταῖς ἐξ αὐτῆς τῶν ἀρετῶν αὐγαῖς ὥσπερ ἐν κατόπτρῳ τῇ διανοίᾳ μορφωθείς, ἐξ αὐτῶν δὲ ἀποτελεσθεὶς σώφρων, ἀγαθός, δίκαιος, ἀνδρεῖος, εὐσεβής, φιλόθεος. Ἀληθῶς δὴ καὶ μόνος φιλόσοφος βασιλεὺς οὗτος ... ὁ τῆς μονάρχου δυνατείας τὸ σεβάσμιον πρόσημα. ...

orders the supernal Kingdom for His Father, so the emperor makes his subjects on earth fit for it; just as the one opens the doors of the Father's Kingdom to those who leave this world, so the other after having purged this terrestrial kingdom of godless error calls all pious men into the mansions of the empire (εἴσω βασιλικῶν οἴκων).[41] It would indeed be hard to imagine a closer representation of the heavenly in the terrestrial Basileia, of the Kingdom of God in the Roman Empire, renewed by Christ and Constantine.[42] It is not sur-

[41] Ibid. 2, 1 ff., GCS, Euseb. I, 199: Ὁ μέν γε τοῦ Θεοῦ μονογενὴς Λόγος τῷ αὐτοῦ Πατρὶ συμβασιλεύων ἐξ ἀνάρχων αἰώνων εἰς ἀπείρους καὶ ἀτελευτήτους αἰῶνας διαρκεῖ· ⟨ὁ⟩ δὲ τούτῳ φίλος ταῖς ἄνωθεν βασιλικαῖς ἀπορροίαις χορηγούμενος . . . , μακραῖς ἐτῶν περιόδοις τῶν ἐπὶ γῆς κρατεῖ. Εἶθ' ὁ μὲν τῶν ὅλων σωτὴρ τὸν σύμπαντα οὐρανόν τε καὶ κόσμον τήν τε ἀνωτάτω βασιλείαν εὐπρεπῆ τῷ αὐτοῦ Πατρὶ παρασκευάζει· ὁ δὲ τούτῳ φίλος αὐτῷ τῷ μονογενεῖ καὶ σωτῆρι Λόγῳ τῶν ἐπὶ γῆς τοὺς ὑποχειρίους προσάγων ἐπιτηδείους πρὸς τὴν αὐτοῦ βασιλείαν καθίστησιν. . . . Καὶ ὁ μὲν τῶν ὅλων σωτὴρ τὰς οὐρανίους πύλας τῆς τοῦ Πατρὸς βασιλείας τοῖς ἐνθένδε ἐκεῖσε μεθισταμένος ἀναπετάννυσιν. Ὁ δὲ ζήλῳ τοῦ κρείττονος πάντα ῥύπον ἀθέου πλάνης τῆς κατὰ γῆν βασιλείας ἀποκαθηράμενος χοροὺς ὁσίων καὶ εὐσεβῶν ἀνδρῶν εἴσω βασιλικῶν οἴκων εἰσκαλεῖται. . . .

[42] In the latter part of the fourth century the pagan Themistius (cf. V. Valdenberg, "Les discours politiques de Thémistios dans leur rapport avec l'antiquité," Byzantion I [1924] 557 ff., J. A. Straub, Vom Herrscherideal in der Spätantike [Forschungen zur Kirchen- und Geistesgeschichte XVIII, Stuttgart, 1939] 160 ff., 168 f., de Francisci, Arcana Imperii III, 2, 114 ff., and now especially G. Downey, "Education and Public Problems As Seen by Themistius," Trans. Amer. Philol. Ass. LXXXVI [1955] 291 ff., and idem, "Themistius and the Defence of Hellenism in the Fourth Century," Harv. Theol. Rev. L [1957] 259 ff., also idem, "Education in the Christian Roman Empire . . .," Speculum XXXII [1957] 48 ff.) has the same conception of βασιλεία; see Oratio XI, Dindorf 170: . . . οὗ (i.e., Διός) γέννημα ἱερὸν καὶ εἰκὼν ἡ ἐπὶ τῆς γῆς βασιλεία. The topos of the βασιλεύς as νόμος ἔμψυχος (cf. above, p. 113) also plays a great role in his thought (cf. Orat. V, VIII, XVI, and XIX, Dindorf 76, 141, 259, and 277) and is related to the idea of reform; cf. Orat. XIX, Dindorf 277: animate law must set right, correct (ἐπανορθοῦν) the rigid letter of the laws. Reform by the king is truly a μεταμόρφωσις βασιλικώτερα, for it transforms souls; cf. Orat. VII, Dindorf 115, 7–24, also Orat. XIII, Dindorf 204, 14 ff. It is interesting to see how Themistius tries to blend Hellenistic political ideas with Christian imperial ideology (which itself owed not a little to pre-Christian thought), for instance, in his use of Proverbs 21:1: ". . . the heart of the king is in the hand of the Lord . . ." (cf. Orat. VII, XI, and XIX, Dindorf 107, 175, and 278; for all this cf. now Downey, "Themistius and Hellenism" 262 ff.). See also Orat. IX, Dindorf 151, where Plato and Aristotle are said to initiate the emperor mystically to the οὐρανοῦ βασιλεία, and Orat. XVIII, Dindorf 267, where this mystique royale is strikingly evident in the description of the royal soul which gazes up to the All-King and draws great things from heaven for the benefit of the terrestrial βασιλεία. Conversely, Themistius' younger contemporary, the Christianized Hellenist Synesius, Bishop of Cyrene (cf. the character sketch by C. H. Coster, "Synesius a Curialis of the Time of the Emperor Arcadius," Byzantion XV [1940–1941] 10 ff.) attempted to set up a Christian "mirror of princes" for Arcadius, the great Theodosius'

prising, therefore, that Eusebius assigns to Constantine also the Christ-like and priestly function of offering up his own "kingly soul" and the souls of his subjects, whose "good shepherd" he is, to the All-King.[43]

The distinction between the Christian empire and the Church was to say the least not clearly defined in Eusebius' world view[44] and, as

son, in Platonic and Neopythagorean terms. See his *De regno* 8, Terzaghi, *Synes. Cyren. Opuscula* 18 (cf. the French translation and commentary by C. Lacombrade, *Le discours sur la royauté de Synésios de Cyrène à l'empereur Arcadios* [Paris, 1951], with important remarks [pp. 95 ff.] also on Themistius): ... προνοίας βασιλικῆς καὶ κηδεμονίας ἔμφρονος, ἣν ὁ Θεὸς αὐτὸς ἑαυτὸν ἐν τοῖς νοητοῖς στήσας ἀρχέτυπον δίδωσιν εἰκόνα τῆς προνοίας καὶ ἐθέλει τὰ τῇδε τετάχθαι κατὰ μίμησιν ὑπερκόσμιον. See also *De regno* 9, Terzaghi, *Synes. Cyren. Opuscula* 20, where Synesius varies the topos of the ἄγαλμα ἔμπνουν (cf. above, p. 114, n. 25) in the sense that Arcadius must show himself worthy of his dignity and thus give life to the image which Synesius paints of him. The empire's reform and the emperor's "self-reform" are characteristically conceived of by Synesius as a return to "ancient goodness"; see *De regno* 18, Terzaghi 42, where Synesius invites Arcadius to restore his kingship ἐς τὸ ἀρχαῖον πρᾶγμα ... and then goes on to explain: Ἀνάγκη γὰρ, κεκολασμένων τῶν βίων καὶ σωφροσύνης ἐπανελθούσης, συνεπανελθεῖν μὲν αὐτῇ τὰ παλαιὰ καλά, τῶν δὲ ἐκ τῆς ἐναντίας μερίδος ἀντιμετάστασιν πάντων γενέσθαι. Καὶ σύ, βασιλεῦ, τῆς ἐπαναγωγῆς τῶν ἀγαθῶν ἄρξαιο καὶ ἀποδοίης ἡμῖν λειτουργὸν τῆς πολιτείας τὸν βασιλέα. This is the political application of that ἀποκατάστασις εἰς τὸ ἀρχαῖον which one meets in a mystical and eschatological sense, for instance, in Gregory of Nyssa; cf. above, pp. 75–77, and below, p. 124, n. 45. For the emperor's and the imperial court's "enactment" of the heavenly *Basileia* on earth in Byzantium, of which Constantine VII Porphyrogenetus' *De caerimoniis* is the incomparable document, cf., for instance, O. Treitinger, *Die oströmische Kaiser- und Reichsidee nach ihrer Gestaltung im höfischen Zeremoniell*, 2nd ed. (Darmstadt, 1956), especially 153.

[43] *Tricennial Oration* 2, 5, GCS Euseb., I, 200: ... τὴν δ' αὐτῷ τῷ βασιλεῖ τῶν ὅλων προσφιλῆ καὶ χαρίεσσαν θυσίαν, αὐτὴν δηλαδὴ τὴν αὐτοῦ βασιλικὴν ψυχὴν καὶ τὸν νοῦν τὸν θεοπρεπέστατον ἀφιερῶν αὐτῷ. ... Τοῦτο δὴ μέγιστον ἱερεῖον πρὸ τῶν ἁπάντων καλλιερεῖ βασιλεύς, θύει δ' ἅτε ποιμὴν ἀγαθὸς ... τῶν ὑπ' αὐτῷ ποιμαινομένων λογικῶν θρεμμάτων τὰς ψυχὰς τῇ αὐτοῦ γνώσει καὶ εὐσεβείᾳ προσάγων. See also *ibid.* 5, 5, I, 204 f., about the Emperor's prayers for his people and his own στερρὸν ἦθος καὶ γνησίαν ψυχῆς παίδευσιν. Similarly Gregory Nazianzen, *Oratio* IV, *contra Julianum* I, 35, PG XXV, 561B: τὸ βασίλειον ἱεράτευμα τὸ πολλῷ πόνῳ καὶ πολλοῖς ἱδρῶσι συναυξηθέν.

[44] For Constantine the Great's own conception of Church and Empire cf. H. Dörries, "Das Selbstzeugnis Kaiser Konstantins," *Abhandl. Gött.*, Philol.-Histos. Klasse, Folge III, XXXIV (1954) 286 ff., and J. Straub, "Kaiser Konstantin als ἐπίσκοπος τῶν ἐκτός," *Stud. Patr.* I, 678 ff. For the role allotted to the Church in Eusebius' world view see F. E. Cranz, "Kingdom and Polity in Eusebius of Caesarea," *Harv. Theol. Rev.* XLV (1952) 47 ff., where most of the more important recent studies on Eusebius are utilized; cf., for instance, N. H. Baynes, "Eusebius and the Christian Empire," *Mélanges Bidez* (Annuaire de l'Institut de Philologie et d'Histoire Orientales) II (Bruxelles, 1934) 13 ff., Peterson, *Monotheismus*, H.-G. Opitz, "Euseb von Caesarea," *Z. neutest. Wiss.* XXXIV (1935) 1 ff., H.

well known, the political and the ecclesiastical order of Christian life were to remain closely interwoven, if not lacking in distinctness, throughout the course of Byzantine history.[45] For in eastern Christendom the ascetic and mystic and the ruler shared between them as it were true kingship.[46] Reformed in the royal image of God, they represented two different but equally high orders of mankind. Thus

Eger, "Die ersten Ansätze zu einer politischen Theologie in der christlichen Kirche," *Deutsche Theologie* II (1935) 272 ff., and *idem*, "Kaiser und Kirche in der Geschichtstheologie Eusebs von Caesarea," *Z. neutest. Wiss.* XXXVIII (1939) 97 ff., Berkhof, *Theologie des Eusebius*, Straub, *Herrscherideal*; in addition, see de Francisci, *Arcana Imperii* III, 2, especially 93 ff., H. Berkhof, *Kirche und Kaiser* (Zollikon, Zürich, 1947), K. M. Setton, *Christian Attitude towards the Emperor in the Fourth Century* (New York, 1941) 47 ff.; also the important article of Straub, mentioned at the beginning of this note. A very significant result of the study of Cranz is the demonstration that Eusebius' conceptualizations of the Ecclesia in terms of the Kingdom and of the Heavenly City merge into one another. As will be seen later (below, pp. 244 ff.), this is characteristic of Greek patristic thought which never developed a *Civitas Dei* concept as significant as that of Augustine. See also the comparison of Eusebius and Augustine in F. E. Cranz, "De civitate Dei XV, 2, . . ." *Speculum* XXV (1950) 220 ff.

[45] This is not to deny that Byzantine religious life should not be seen as altogether stifled by "caesaropapism." (For the doubtful usefulness of this term with regard to the Christian east cf. Michel, *Kaisermacht in der Ostkirche* (843–1204) 2, 83, 127; also L. Wenger, "Canon in den römischen Rechtsquellen und in den Papyri," *Sitz. Ber. Wien*, Philos.-hist. Klasse CCXX, 2 [1942]; R. Janin, A. A., "L'empereur dans l'église byzantine," *Nouv. rev. théol.* LXXVII [1955] 49 ff., where the term "theocracy" is rightly suggested as preferable to "caesaropapism.") At least before the progressive "desiccation" due to the Schism the deepest layers of doctrine and spirituality were not overmuch affected by the emperor's dominant position in the Church except through the admittedly ever present danger of his adoption of a new heresy (cf. my article "Image" 21). The nonpolitical Gregory of Nyssa, for instance, in his funeral orations for an empress and for a princess could thus use the Basileia concept in a purely eschatological sense, connecting it with the return to Paradise and with the *apocatastasis* idea. See his *Oratio in funere Pulcheriae*, PG, XLVI, 869A: . . . ἔνθεν τὸ φυτὸν ἀνεσπάσθη, ἀλλὰ τῷ παραδείσῳ ἐνεφυτεύθη, ἐκ βασιλείας εἰς βασιλείαν μετέστη, followed (*ibid.* 877 f.) by Gregory's usual characterizations of death and resurrection as ἀνάπλασις, as τῷ ἐξ ἀρχῆς βίῳ ἀποκατάστασις, as εἰς τὸ ἀρχαῖον ἀναστοιχείωσις. See also *Oratio funebris de Placilla*, PG XLVI, 889C: Κατέλιπε βασιλείαν γηΐνην, ἀλλὰ τὴν οὐράνιον κατέλαβεν. Cf. Setton, *Emperor* 87.

[46] The great significance for Greek ascetic thought of the idea of the Kingdom of Heaven in us, according to Luke 17:21—cf. above pp. 107, 114—is still evident in the works of Symeon the New Theologian, the great eleventh-century monastic reformer; see K. Holl, *Enthusiasmus und Bussgewalt beim griechischen Mönchtum* (Leipzig, 1898) 92 ff. The parallelism between "king" and "monk" emerges also from the fact that an angelic character could be attributed to both; for the angelic king and "body politic" see now E. H. Kantorowicz, *Two Bodies*, especially 8 f.; for the concept of the monk's angelic life, which could be extended to priest and ordinary Christian, see below, pp. 126, 288, n. 20, 326.

on the one hand monks rather than secular priests came to be considered the spiritual rulers of the Christian conscience while so-called canonical or public ecclesiastical penance receded into the background; [47] on the other hand the emperors not infrequently asserted a quasi-sacerdotal position in the Church [48] and generally had it understood that the value of all acts of reform in Church and empire flowed directly from the fact that they were put into effect by, or on the command of, the emperor. [49]

There was one great exception to the eastern Christian development of Basileia ideology here described: the thought and life of St. John

[47] On penance, see also below, pp. 303–315. Cf. Holl, *Enthusiasmus*, especially 166 ff., 312 ff.; J. Hörmann, *Untersuchungen zur griechischen Laienbeicht* (Donauwörth, 1913). Both authors show how popular admiration of ascetic heroism, together with the increasingly impractical severities of canonical penance, made the monks the principal confessors in Greek Christendom from the fifth to the thirteenth century. Yet, as Hörmann, *Laienbeicht* 226 ff., rightly stresses, the fact that not a few of these monks were at the same time priests must also be taken into consideration. Cf. also M. Viller, S.J., "Exemplar ideale monasticum et sacerdotale in oriente graeco usque ad saeculum nonum," *Commentarium pro Religiosis* VIII (1927) 206 ff. I. Hausherr, S.J., *Direction spirituelle en orient autrefois* (Orientalia Christiana Analecta CXLIV [1955] 105 ff.).

[48] This is true especially for Constantine the Great, Justinian I, and the iconoclastic emperors; the well-known facts need hardly special discussion here; cf. the rich material in de Francisci, *Arcana Imperii* III, 2, and in Michel, "Kaisermacht," *passim*, also C. Toumanoff, "Caesaropapism in Byzantium and Russia," *Theol. Stud.* VII (1946) 213 ff. (for the term "caesaropapism" see, however, p. 124, n. 45), and the same author on the relation between the emperor and the Church in Byzantium in his illuminating study "Christian Caucasia between Byzantium and Iran . . . ," *Traditio* X (1954) 109 ff.

[49] This is very clearly evident from the tone, for instance, of Justinian's legislation; see in particular the famous constitution *Deo auctore*, C. 1, 17, 1, §7: . . . si aliquod in veteribus legibus vel constitutionibus . . . non recte scriptum inveniatis, et hoc reformetis. . . . Cum enim lege . . . regia . . . omne ius omnisque potestas populi Romani in imperatoriam translata sunt potestatem . . . , quid possit antiquitas nostris legibus abrogare? . . . nostrae electioni hoc adscribatur; also the constitution *Tanta*, C. 1, 17, 2, §18: . . . quia ideo imperialem fortunam rebus humanis Deus praeposuit, ut possit omnia quae noviter contingunt et emendare et componere et modis et regulis competentibus tradere; both texts are quoted and discussed also by de Francisci, *Arcana Imperii* III, 2, 204 ff. See also Constantine Porphyrogenitus, *De administrando imperio*, ed. G. Moravcsik, with English trans. by R. J. H. Jenkins (Magyar-Görög Tanulmányok XXIX, Budapest, 1949) 46, where the emperor advises his son to study ὅσα ἐν τῇ καθ' ἡμᾶς πολιτείᾳ ἀλλὰ καὶ ἐν πάσῃ τῇ 'Ρωμαίων ἀρχῇ κατά τινας χρόνους ἐκαινοτομήθη. . . . The law codification of Justinian, of course, was to influence articulate expressions of the relationship between legislation and reform many times, in many places, and in many ways. The legal aspects of the reform idea I hope to discuss more fully in a later volume. Meanwhile see below, Part Two, Chapter VII, 1, on the early stages of the renewal of Canon Law.

Chrysostom.[50] He too had taken his start from the ascetic tradition according to which the monk was the true king and his way of life similar to that of the angels. This is the gist of two of his early treatises, *Comparison of a King with a Monk* and *Against the Enemies of the Monks*.[51] A change of attitude however is evident already in his six books *On the Priesthood*, which strike the key note of his life work as a great priestly orator and preacher in Antioch and as a reforming Patriarch of Constantinople. The priest's soul, just because he lives and works in the midst of the world's storms and dangers, must be stronger and purer even than the monk's, who stays as it were in a safe port. The dignity of the priesthood is now extolled over all merely terrestrial things and compared to the pure ministry of the angels; for, the priest's throne is set up in heaven and stands on a higher plane than all human rulership.[52]

While for St. Basil the thought that man cannot be saved if he does not work for his neighbour's salvation had become the great justifica-

---

[50] See A. Puech, *St. Jean Chrysostome et les mœurs de son temps* (Paris, 1891), Chrysostomus Baur, O.S.B., *Der heilige Johannes Chrysostomus und seine Zeit*, 2 vols. (München, 1929–1930), also L. Meyer, "Perfection chrétienne et vie solitaire dans la pensée de saint Jean Chrysostome," *Rev. ascét. myst.* XIV (1933) 232 ff., idem, *Saint Jean Chrysostome, maître de perfection chrétienne* (Paris, 1933).

[51] John Chrysostom, *De comparatione regis et monachi* 1, PG XLVII, 388: Οὐκοῦν ὁ μὲν βασιλεὺς πόλεσι, καὶ χώραις, καὶ πολλοῖς ἐφέστηκεν ἔθνεσι. . . . ὁ δὲ Θεῷ δεδωκὼς ἑαυτόν, καὶ τὸν μονήρη βίον ᾑρημένος, θυμοῦ, καὶ φθόνου, καὶ φιλαργυρίας, καὶ ἡδονῆς, καὶ τῶν ἄλλων ἄρχει κακῶν . . . ὥστε δικαιότερον ἄν τις τοῦτον βασιλέα καλέσειεν ἢ τὸν ἁλουργίδι καὶ στεφάνῳ λαμπόμενον καὶ καθήμενον ἐπὶ θρόνου χρυσοῦ. Even in this early work, which greatly praises the monk as the Christian philosopher, the Platonic-Alexandrian-Eusebian conception of the king-philosopher is no longer in evidence; the comparison is all in favor of the monk. *Adversus oppugnatores vitae monasticae* III, 11, PG XLVII, 366: Ἀλλ' ἐν τοῖς μοναστηρίοις . . . μόνοι κάθηνται ἐν λιμένι καὶ γαλήνῃ καὶ ἀσφαλείᾳ πολλῇ, καθάπερ ἐξ οὐρανοῦ τὰ τῶν ἄλλων ἐπισκοποῦντες ναυάγια· καὶ γὰρ πολιτείαν οὐρανῷ πρέπουσαν εἵλοντο καὶ ἀγγέλων οὐδὲν χεῖρον διάκεινται. Ὥσπερ οὖν ἐν ἐκείνοις (i.e., in the angels) οὐκ ἔστιν ἀνωμαλία τις . . . , οὕτω δὴ καὶ ἐνταῦθα (i.e., in the monasteries) . . . πάντα αὐτοῖς κοινά . . . καὶ τί θαυμαστόν, ὅπου γε καὶ αὐτὴ ἡ ψυχὴ μία πᾶσι καὶ ἡ αὐτή (cf. Acts 4:32). The "angelic life" of the monks is praised also in Chrysostom's *De virginitate* X, 11, PG XLVII, 540 (cf. L. Meyer, "Perfection" 243); for his "monastic" treatises cf. now R. Carter, "Saint John Chrysostom's Rhetorical Use of the Socratic Distinction between Kingship and Tyranny," *Traditio* XIV (1958) 367 ff.

[52] See *De sacerdotio* III, 1 and 4, PG XLVIII, 641 f., for the comparison between priest and angel; *ibid.* III, 4 and 7, and VI, 6–8, PG XLVIII, 642, 645 and 682 ff., for the fact that the priest needs greater strength and purity than the monk; *ibid.* III, 5 f., XLVIII, 643 f., for the superiority of the priestly over the kingly office. On the latter point see also *In illud* "*Vidi Dominum sedentem in solio excelso*" (Is. 6:1), homil. V, 1, PG LVI, 130 ff.,; *ibid.*, homil. IV, 4, LVI, 126.

tion of the coenobitical as against the hermitical ideal of monasticism,[53] St. John Chrysostom explicitly re-applied this scriptural principle to the entire Church, transcending the sphere of the ascetic quest for perfection.[54] His pastoral and homiletic efforts among the Christians of such great cities as Antioch and Constantinople were all founded on and centred in the conviction that, apart from the privilege of marriage, the Christian who lived in the world had the same obligations as the monk.[55] At the same time the great bishop

[53] See below, pp. 342 f., for the only gradual development of Basil's conception of the coenobitical life from more general ascetic ideals.

[54] De sacerdotio VI, 10, PG XLVIII, 686: . . . οὐδὲ γὰρ αὐτὸς τοῦτο πιστεύειν ἔχω, ὅτι σώζεσθαι ἔνεστι τὸν οὐδὲν εἰς τὴν τοῦ πλησίον κάμνοντα σωτηρίαν. . . . This is said with respect to the question whether or not to become a priest rather than a monk, though especially at this stage of his life John Chrysostom dreaded the possibility of becoming an unworthy priest; see the immediately following chapters of Book VI. See also De S. Babyla contra Julianum et gentiles 8, PG L, 545: Τὸν γὰρ ἀγαθὸν ἄνδρα πρὸς τὸ κοινωφελὲς ἅπαντα πράττειν χρὴ καὶ τὸν τῶν ἄλλων βίον κατορθοῦν (cf. L. Meyer, "Perfection" 252).

[55] In Matthaeum, homil. VII, 7, PG LVII, 81 f.: Καὶ γὰρ πάντα ἡμῖν τὰ τῶν νόμων κοινὰ πρὸς τοὺς μοναχούς ἐστι πλὴν τοῦ γάμου. The whole chapter is important for John Chrysostom's conviction and emphatic assertion that it is neither necessary to go into the wilderness (τὰ ὄρη καταλαμβάνειν) in order to become a perfect Christian nor excusable not to be one under the pretext of not being a monk (cf. L. Meyer, Chrysostome 192 ff., where it is shown that the ideal of the angelic life could be extended by Chrysostom from the monk and priest to every true Christian). The Christian who lives in the world must obey 1 Cor. 7:29 f.: ". . . it remaineth that they also who have wives be as if they had none . . . and they that buy, as though they possessed not; and they that use this world, as if they used it not," which John Chrysostom interprets here and elsewhere in the sense that the marital relationship should not be dominated by sex alone, that children should not be degraded by bad example, that possessions should not become a source of avarice or greed or dissipation. Cf. in this connection D. Gorce, "Mariage et perfection chrétienne d'après saint Jean Chrysostome," Etudes carmélitaines XXI, 1 (1936) 245 ff. In his homil. VII, in Epist. ad Hebraeos, 4, PG LXIII, 67 f., Chrysostom says that the Beatitudes of the Sermon on the Mount are not reserved for the monks; for, again, in accordance with 1 Cor. 7:29, it is possible for people who have wives and possessions to be virtuous, if such is their will. See also In Epist. ad Romanos, homil. XXVI, 4, PG LX, 643, where the saint once more denies that Christians must live in monasteries in order to be good; the true "philosophy" can and should be followed also by the ordinary citizen; only thus will cities truly become cities, only thus would the pagans be "reformed" (ὀρθῶσαι): if they see that every Christian reforms his own life (τὸν βίον διόρθου τὸν σαυτοῦ). In spite of all these assertions by John Chrysostom it remains true that with the exception of the priesthood the monastic way of life is more perfect also in his view than life in the world; see, for instance, De inani gloria et de educandis liberis 19, Schulte 8; see also De virginitate, passim, PG XLVIII, 533 ff. Yet, at least after he had become a bishop, he more than even St. Basil wanted the monks to be examples and apostles of Christian life within the cities rather than in deserts; cf. L. Meyer, "Perfection" 253 ff., 260 ff.

must have felt, in spite of all disappointments and notwithstanding his continuous laments over the prevailing corruption,[56] that it was not impossible to reform the Christian society of his time, to bring about a fair measure of perfection in the Church as a whole.

He believed that

one man who burns with zeal is sufficient to set straight a whole people.[57]

To the whole Church of his day, not only to the monks, he held up as a model the age of the Apostles, "when there was one soul and one heart in all" (cf. Acts 4:32).[58] Similarly, he applied the sculptor and painter metaphors, which an Origen or Gregory of Nyssa had used to describe the process of ascetic formation or reformation,[59] to the moral betterment of ordinary Christians and to the education of their children.[60] Also, in his famous Address on Vainglory and the Right

[56] Cf. the literature quoted, p. 126, n. 50.

[57] Homil. I de statuis ad populum Antiochenum 12, PG XLIX, 34: . . . ἀρκεῖ εἷς ἄνθρωπος ζήλῳ πεπυρωμένος ὁλόκληρον διορθώσασθαι δῆμον (quoted by A. Puech, Chrysostome 319).

[58] In Epist. I ad Corinthios, homil. XXXVI, 4 f., PG LXI, 312 f. In the apostolic age, he says, the Church was heaven (cf. above, pp. 69 f., for the same idea in St. Irenaeus), but now we have only the symbols without the substance. In the early work Adversus oppugnatores vitae monasticae, he had applied the text from the Acts of the Apostles only to the monks, whereas later, In Epist. I ad Corinthios, homil. VI, 4, PG LXI, 52 f., he says that if Christian society would live in conformity with the apostolic way of life, the whole οἰκουμένη would be converted, even without miracles. See also In Acta Apostolorum, homil. XI, 2 f., PG LX, 96 ff., where he compares such life to heaven on earth and expresses confidence that it can be realized by all Christians, not only by the monks; cf. below, pp. 129 f., n. 62. See below, pp. 342 f., 359 ff., for the application of Acts 4:32 ff. to the monastic way of life by Basil the Great, Cassian, Augustine.

[59] See above, pp. 91 ff.

[60] De inani gloria et de educandis liberis 22, Schulte 9: Ἕκαστος τοίνυν ὑμῶν τῶν πατέρων καὶ τῶν μητέρων, καθάπερ τοὺς ζωγράφους ὁρῶμεν τὰς εἰκόνας καὶ τὰ ἀγάλματα μετὰ πολλῆς τῆς ἀκριβείας ἐξασκοῦντας, οὕτω τῶν θαυμαστῶν τούτων ἀγαλμάτων ἐπιμελώμεθα. Προθέντες γὰρ οἱ ζωγράφοι τὸν πίνακα καθ᾽ ἑκάστην ἡμέραν αὐτὸν ἐπιχρίουσι πρὸς τὸ δέον. Οἱ δὲ λιθοξόοι τῶν λίθων καὶ αὐτοὶ τὸ αὐτὸ πράττουσι τὸ μὲν περιττὸν περιαιροῦντες, τὸ δὲ ἐνδέον προστιθέντες. Οὕτω δὴ καὶ ὑμεῖς· καθάπερ ἀγαλμάτων τινῶν κατασκευασταὶ πρὸς τοῦτο τὴν σχολὴν ἅπασαν ἔχετε τὰ θαυμαστὰ ἀγάλματα τῷ Θεῷ κατασκευάζοντες, καὶ τὸ μὲν περιττὸν ἐξαιρεῖτε, τὸ δὲ ἐνδέον προστίθετε καὶ καθ᾽ ἑκάστην αὐτὰ περισκοπεῖτε τὴν ἡμέραν, ποῖον ἀπὸ φύσεως ἔχει πλεονέκτημα, ὥστε αὐτὸ αὔξειν, ποῖον ἀπὸ φύσεως ἐλάττωμα, ὥστε αὐτὸ περιαιρεῖν. Cf. the English translation with commentary by M. L. W. Laistner, Christianity and Pagan Culture in the Later Roman Empire (Ithaca, N. Y., 1951) 75; also idem, "Pagan Schools and Christian Teachers," in Liber Floridus: Mittellateinische Studien, Paul Lehmann gewidmet (Erzabtei St. Ottilien, 1950) 53 ff. See also the general moral use of the painter metaphor in Catechesis II ad illuminandos 3, PG XLIX, 235. Similarly, the doctrine of man as the image

Way for Parents to Bring Up Their Children, he speaks of a child's soul as of a city in which the King of the universe intends to dwell and God's earthly representative in this city is not the emperor, but the child's father.[61]

Nothing could be less "Eusebian" than this conception of the Kingdom of God on earth and it is not surprising that John Chrysostom perished as a martyr for Christian ethical principles in resistance to an unholy alliance of corrupt Church dignitaries with the irresponsible heirs of the Constantinian-Theodosian Empire. Chrysostom's heroic effort to reform the urban society of the nascent Byzantine Empire can hardly be called successful. It is true that he had admirers and followers, who probably perpetuated his influence to some extent, and that the immense body of his oratorical work, from which his character still speaks with amazing immediacy, became a permanent inspiration to Christian ethics and eloquence. Yet he was unable to change the course of eastern Christendom, whose culminations remained monastic and imperial. John Chrysostom had tried to reform the "Polis" within the "Basileia,"[62] and in this he had

---

and likeness of God is applied to practical charity when John Chrysostom in one of his many homilies directed against the neglect of the poor insists that the most wretched beggar is created according to that image and likeness; cf. *In Epist. I ad Corinthios, homil.* XXI, 5, PG LXI, 176–179 (quoted by Baur, *Chrysostomus* I, 313, cf. also the excellent remarks of L. Meyer, *Chrysostome* 206, about apostolic charity—man's love for his neighbour—as the principal content of image-likeness to God according to Chrysostom). See, furthermore, *In Epist. ad Philippenses, homil.* XII, PG LXII, 269 ff., where verse 14 of ch. 3 is interpreted not in Gregory of Nyssa's sense as never-ending mystical desire, but rather as never-ending ethical struggle (cf. L. Meyer, *Chrysostome* 138 ff.).

[61] *De inani gloria* . . . 23 and 28, Schulte 9 ff.: Νόμισον εἶναι βασιλεὺς πόλιν ἔχων ὑπήκοον τὴν τοῦ παιδὸς ψυχήν· πόλις γάρ ἐστιν ὄντως ἡ ψυχή. . . . Οὐ γὰρ ἄνθρωπός τις, ἀλλ' αὐτὸς ὁ τῶν ὅλων βασιλεὺς ταύτην μέλλει τὴν πόλιν οἰκεῖν ἐὰν κατασκευασθῇ. See also, *ibid.* 25, Schulte 10, where John Chrysostom says that the child's soul-city can be easily directed, because of its newness, while it is more difficult, though not impossible, to reform older people.

[62] See *In Acta Apostolorum, homil.* XI, 3, PG LX, 96 ff. (with regard to the apostolic community of goods): Πείσθητέ μοι μόνον καὶ κατὰ τάξιν καθορθώσομεν τὰ πράγματα καὶ . . . πιστεύω ὅτι ταχέως εἰς ταύτην ἡμᾶς ἄξομεν τὴν πολιτείαν. Cf. E. Troeltsch, *The Social Teaching of the Christian Churches* I (trans. from *Die Soziallehren der christlichen Kirchen und Gruppen* by O. Wyon, Halley Stewart Publications I, London, New York, 1931) 127: "Chrysostom . . . would like . . . to turn Constantinople and Antioch into a communistic fellowship of love like the monastic life"; for the patristic period Troeltsch's work is based largely on I. Seipel, *Die wirtschaftsethischen Lehren der Kirchenväter*

failed.[63] Soon St. Augustine was to transpose the Polis-Civitas concept to an altogether different plane which lay outside the sociopolitical realities of the Christian empire.[64] Furthermore, while the great Patriarch of Constantinople had tried to reassert the ideals of the Gospel in Christian society at large, the even greater Bishop of Hippo in one of the practical realizations of his reform ideology undertook a "monastization" of his clergy, thus setting an example which proved to be of great and lasting consequence in the history of Christianity in the west.[65]

In spite of St. Augustine it took several centuries, even in the west, before the inherent pre-eminence of the priestly office over any lay status, and be it that of the emperor or the monk, was able thoroughly

(Theologische Studien der Leogesellschaft XVIII, Wien, 1907); see Seipel 99 ff. for Chrysostom; both Seipel and Troeltsch stress the "ideal" character of Chrysostom's advocation of an extension of monastic community of possessions to Christian society as a whole; but it would seem that Chrysostom believed that his ideal might some day, and even soon ($\tau \alpha \chi \epsilon \omega s$) be fulfilled; see also A. Puech, *Chrysostome* 77–92 and 320, S. Giet, "La doctrine de l'appropriation des biens chez quelques-uns des pères," *Rech.'s sc. rel.* XXXV (1948) 75 f.

[63] For the rest, Chrysostom's misgivings with regard to the Christian world at large—though not his all-inclusive reform attitude—were shared by most of the Fathers of the turn of the fourth century, in the east especially by his older contemporary, St. Basil, who, for instance, just as Chrysostom, inveighed against the existence of excessive wealth and poverty in a Christian society and against the callousness of the rich. See his *Homil. in divites*, PG XXXI, 277 ff., his *Homil. in Ps. XIV, contra foeneratores*, PG XXIX, 264 ff., and the *Homil. in illud Lucae* 12, 18, PG XXXI, 261 ff. A fuller treatment of this matter can be found in Y. Courtonne, *Saint Basile: Homélies sur la richesse* (Paris, 1935), and in Sr. Margaret M. Fox, *The Life and Times of St. Basil the Great as Revealed in His Works* (Catholic University of America Patristic Studies LVII, Washington, D.C., 1939). For St. Augustine see the books of van der Meer and Frend, quoted in Excursus V; cf. below, pp. 251 f., on St. Jerome. As to St. Ambrose, he depends largely on St. Basil also in his ethical-social views. See his *De Nabuthae* 5 (21 ff.), 13 (56), 3 (12), CSEL XXXII, 478 ff., 500 f., 474; *De Tobia*, CSEL XXXII, 517 ff. (against usury). Cf. R. Thamin, *Saint Ambroise et la morale chrétienne au IVe siecle* (Paris, 1895) 282 ff., M. R. P. McGuire, *S. Ambrosii De Nabuthae: A Commentary, with an Introduction and Translation* (Catholic University of America Patristic Studies XV, Washington, D.C., 1927), L. M. Zucker, *S. Ambrosii, De Tobia: A Commentary, with an Introd. and Trans.* (Catholic University of America Patristic Studies XXXV, Washington, D.C., 1933). See McGuire 4 ff. and Zucker 10 for Ambrose's dependence on Basil. McGuire 5, n. 3, as well as A. Dirking, *S. Basilii Magni de Divitiis et Paupertate Sententiae quam Habeant Rationem cum Veterum Philosophorum Doctrina* (Münster, 1911), and O. Stählin, *Clemens Alexandrinus: Quis Dives Salvetur* (Leipzig, 1908), have rightly noted the role of an ancient *topos* in these attacks against wealth; but from the use of *topoi* we must not always infer that the situations to which they are applied were not real.

[64] See below, Part Two, Chapter V, 7.

[65] See below, Part Three, Chapter II, 2.

to penetrate and upset an order which the east maintained in hallowed stability in spite of St. John Chrysostom and in spite of the mystical exaltation of the ecclesiastical hierarchy by Ps-Dionysius the Areopagite.[66] One might perhaps add that only the west, in making the priest's apostolic mission supreme within the Church, fully realized the impulse toward societal reform which the Church had received from Christ and the Apostles—an impulse which then, and only then, could be extended also to lay society in a contrapuntal movement between clerical and lay reform.

A brilliant recent study[67] touches upon a deep difference between the Christian east and west, in stating that "in Byzantium the imperial *Christomimetes* ceaselessly and ex officio follows the tracks of his divine 'co-king,' as in the west only a Saint Francis," and in asking "how it came that . . . $\mu\iota\mu\eta\sigma\iota\varsigma$ meant something different in the east and in the west." The answer to the question lies, perhaps, in the direction indicated in this chapter. Except possibly for the latest phase of the Byzantine Empire, the emperor was not in any real way the $\mu\iota\mu\eta\tau\dot\eta\varsigma$ $X\rho\iota\sigma\tauo\hat\upsilon$ of St. Paul, his $\mu\iota\mu\eta\sigma\iota\varsigma$ was certainly not the *Christum sequi* of St. Francis.[68] His *Christomimesis* continued as it were a subordinationist Logos-God relationship of the Origenist type;[69] not unlike Clement

---

[66] For Ps.-Dionysius, see below, pp. 348 f. For the exaltation of the ruler's reforming function even in western patristic thought, see, for instance, Aponius (early fifth century), *In Canticum Canticorum*, eds. G. (H.) Bottini and G. (J.) Martini (Roma, 1843) 202: "Nam in tantum religiosissimi reges vices Dei agentes in terris caput Christianae plebis esse noscuntur, ut si quando morbo haereticae contagionis aut persequutionis ecclesiae corpus coeperit infirmari, ipsorum auctoritate ad pristinam sanitatem reformetur." For the role which the conception of the ruler as vicar of God played in this connection, see, for instance, M. Maccarrone, *Vicarius Christi* (Lateranum, Nova Series, XVIII, 1–4, Roma, 1952), especially 41 ff., on Aponius, and the important remarks in E. H. Kantorowicz, *Two Bodies* 87 ff., 159 ff., on the different meanings of the terms *vicarius Dei* and *vicarius Christi* and on their history, furthermore W. Dürig, "Der theologische Ausgangspunkt der mittelalterlichen liturgischen Auffassung vom Herrscher als Vicarius Dei," *Hist. Jb.* LXXVII (1958) 174 ff. For Aponius, see also T. E. Mommsen, "Aponius and Orosius on the Significance of the Epiphany," *Studies A. M. Friend* 96 ff.

[67] Kantorowicz, "Königsbild" 182 and 184.

[68] For the attempts of the late Byzantine emperors to imitate Christ in his humanity see the remarks of Treitinger, *Reichsidee* 128 and 153 f.; Treitinger's interpretation of this development, however, needs revision. Cf. also Michel, *Kaisermacht in der Ostkirche* 10 ff., for the fact that from the middle-Byzantine period onward the imperial dignity was seen as generally sacramental in mystical assimilation to the $X\rho\iota\sigma\tauo\varsigma$ rather than as specifically sacerdotal or quasi-sacerdotal.

[69] See above, pp. 87 and 96.

of Alexandria's royal gnostic[70] the emperor was, through the divine Logos, a "third image" of God the Father, συμβασιλεύων[71] with the δεύτερος Θεός rather than συμπαθής with Christ.[72] An eastern Christian ruler might exchange the Basileia for the monastery, but only the west knew the "Franciscan" kingship of St. Louis IX.

In addition to a much more variegated development of the monarchical idea the west as already suggested knew societal categories of reform on a much larger scale than the east. In this latter western development the scriptural idea of the heavenly Jerusalem, the Polis of God, was one of the most important influences. Not that the concept of the Holy City was absent from, or unimportant in, Greek Christendom or that the idea of the *Regnum Dei* was not essential also for western Christians. Yet, the idea of the heavenly city, of the *Civitas Dei*, especially in its Augustinian formulation, was much more important for the history of reform in the Christian west than in the east. It is justifiable, therefore, to treat of the origin and development of the Polis-Civitas ideology in the section which is devoted to St. Augustine's City of God.[73]

[70] See above, pp. 110 ff.

[71] For the conception of the συμβασιλεία of the terrestrial ruler with Christ, see L. Bréhier, *Les institutions de l'empire byzantin* (Le monde byzantin II, Paris, 1949) 64, Kantorowicz, "Königsbild" 182 and n. 76, Toumanoff, "Christian Caucasia" 118. The idea is derived in part from the ancient belief in θεοὶ σύνθρονοι (cf., for instance, E. H. Kantorowicz, ΣΥΝΘΡΟΝΟΣ ΔΙΚΗΙ, American Journal of Archaeology XVII [1953] 65 ff.); also, Christ Himself is συμβασιλεύων with the Father (see, for instance, the text from Eusebius, quoted above, p. 122, n. 41); especially, if the trinitarian συμβασιλεία is understood in a slightly subordinationist sense (see above, p. 96, n. 50), the extension to the ruler is easily understandable. Cf. the well-known objection of the *Libri Carolini* I, 1, *MGH*, *Leges* III, *Concil.* II, Suppl., 8 ff., against the συμβασιλεία formula, used by the Byzantine rulers at the Second Council of Nicaea of 787.

[72] Similarly, it is hardly by accident that according to Ps.-Dionysius Areopagita, *De coelesti hierarchia* 3, 3 and 12, 3, *PG* III, 168A and 293B, the mystic strives for deification through imitation of God (θεομιμησίᾳ) rather than Christ; see also the texts quoted by W. Völker, *Kontemplation und Ekstase bei Pseudo-Dionysius Areopagita* (Wiesbaden, 1958) 56 ff.

[73] See below, Part Two, Chapter V, 7.

CHAPTER IV

THE IDEA OF REFORM IN LATIN PATRISTIC THOUGHT BEFORE ST. AUGUSTINE

In its interpretation of scriptural terminology and ideology of renovation and reform Greek patristic thought emphasized above all the restoration of the creational integrity of the universe and of man and the terrestrial representation of original God-nearness in a present world order upheld by the ruler and by the monk.

In Latin patristic thought one is first of all struck by certain peculiarities of the terminology of reform which, though slight in themselves, are of some weight if held together with the ideological development that was to culminate in St. Augustine.

The great role of Tertullian in the formulation of Latin Christian thought is well known. This process included both reception and modification of Greek thought. Thus Tertullian quite often uses the term *reformare* in the sense of return to a previous condition. In a brilliantly written chapter of his *De resurrectione mortuorum* he argues from the recurrence and preservation of all things in nature to the resurrection of the bodies—*universa conditio recidiva est.*

The universal condition is one of recurrence. . . . There is nothing that does not repeat itself; all things return to the state from which they departed. . . . This whole reversible order of things is therefore evidence for the resurrection of the dead. . . . [1]

To designate this general repetitiousness of the universe he finally uses the term *reformare*,[2] which in his as well as in Minucius

---

[1] Tertullian, *De resurrectione mortuorum* 12, 6 f., *Corp. Christ.*, *Ser. Lat.* II, 935: . . . universa conditio recidiva est. . . . Nihil non iterum est; omnia in statum redeunt cum abscesserint. . . . Totus igitur hic ordo revolubilis rerum testatio est resurrectionis mortuorum. . . . See also Clemens Romanus, *1 Cor.* 24, Bihlmeyer, *Apostol. Väter* 49; Theophilus of Antioch, *Ad Autolycum* I, 13, Otto, *Corp. Apologet.* VIII, 36 ff.; Minucius Felix, *Octavius* 34, 11, *Flor. Patr.* VIII, 77 f.

[2] Tertullian, *De resurrectione mortuorum* 13, 1, *Corp. Christ.*, *Ser. Lat.* II, 936 (*ThLL*). See also *Apologeticum* 48, 8, *Corp. Christ.*, *Ser. Lat.* I, 167 (*ThLL*).

Felix'[3] and later in St. Ambrose's[4] terminology also can refer to the resurrection itself.[5] The supreme exemplar and prototype of the resurrection was for Tertullian,[6] as for not a few Christian writers after him, a renewal symbol which contained and transcended cosmological and vitalistic connotations: the fabulous bird phoenix who since ancient times had been believed to die periodically and to arise rejuvenated from his ashes.[7]

All this is part of the terminological and ideological tradition of the return of all things to their beginnings which was seen to be characteristic also for Greek patristic thought.[8] But, in a few instances, Tertullian goes beyond the merely restorative conception of the term and concept of reform. He seems in fact to have been the first to use the phrase *in melius reformare*.[9] In his early apologetic work *Ad nationes*

---

[3] Minucius Felix, *Octavius* 34, 9, *Flor. Patr.* VIII, 77: *reformari*, beside *reparari* (ThLL).

[4] Ambrose, *De sacramentis* II, 6, 17, ed. and trans. B. Botte, O.S.B., *Ambroise de Milan: Des sacrements, Des mystères* (Sources chrétiennes XXV) 67: . . . quia et mors finis est peccatorum et resurrectio naturae est reformatio.

[5] Tertullian, *De resurrectione mortuorum* 55, 12, *Corp. Christ., Ser. Lat.* II, 1003, ll. 49 f., and *ibid.* 26, 7, II, 954, l. 27; cf. *Apologeticum* 18, 3, *Corp. Christ., Ser. Lat.* I, 118, l. 16 (ThLL).

[6] *De resurrectione mortuorum* 13, 1, *Corp. Christ., Ser. Lat.* II, 936: . . . accipe plenissimum atque firmissimum huius spei specimen . . . illum dico alitem orientis peculiarem . . . qui semetipsum libenter funerans renovat, natali fine decedens atque succedens, iterum phoenix ubi nemo iam, iterum ipse qui non iam, alius idem . . . Deus etiam in scripturis suis [posuit]: "Et florebis enim" inquit "velut phoenix" (cf. Ps. 91:13 according to the Vulgate: Iustus ut palma [another meaning of Greek φοίνιξ] florebit).

[7] In view of the cosmological and vitalistic aspects of the phoenix myth it is not surprising that its two most important literary formulations occur in the Constantinian and Theodosian ages: Lactantius' *De ave Phoenice* and Claudianus' *Phoenix*. For the myth of the phoenix cf. above, p. 21, n. 21; for the related one of the eagle's rejuvenation and for its transformations in Christian renewal ideology see below, pp. 314 ff.

[8] Tertullian, whose dependence on St. Irenaeus is well known, stands in that tradition also when he links up man's return to Paradise with Christ as *alpha* and *omega*; cf. above, pp. 68 ff., 73.

[9] For related but not identical pre-Christian Greek and Latin terminology of change to the better see above, pp. 47 f., especially for Philo's πρὸς τὸν ἀμείνω βίον μεταβάλλειν in the sense of μετάνοια. While Greek Christian writers do speak of change to the better, they do not very often combine old and new goodness as in the Latin *reformare* or *renovare in melius*, but even in equivalent terminology rather keep the two apart, emphasizing more strongly either the restorative or the progressive element (cf. above, pp. 47 f., and above all below, pp. 161 f.).

he speaks of a pagan who objected to the Christian virtue of his wife: *mulieri non permisit in melius reformari*.[10] In his *Apologeticum* he uses the word *reformare* in a similar way when he says that Christians were to receive a "fuller grace" than the Jews had had and that this was to be brought about through reform and illumination by Christ.[11]

The phrase *in melius reformare* reappears in a very significant manner in Tertullian's relatively late, but still pre-Montanist, treatise *Adversus Hermogenem*. This gnostic heretic had posited matter as coeternal with God and in his radical dualism apparently also had involved himself in contradictions concerning the possibility of God's "reformative" operation on formless matter. It is part of Tertullian's refutation of Hermogenes to stress that matter, created out of nothing and good in itself as all creatures of God, nevertheless can be "reformed to something better": *Si bona fuisset materia semper, quare non desiderasset in melius reformari?*[12]

Tertullian also uses the term *reformari* for baptismal rebirth,[13] while Minucius Felix says that his friend Octavius has reformed Caecilius to the true religion, that is to say, has converted him.[14] But, this does not mean that the process of reform is completed by conversion and baptism; quite the contrary: *Fiunt, non nascuntur christiani*.[15] This famous sentence of Tertullian's implies that a Christian must become through his postbaptismal life that which he is through baptism. It has been ingeniously pointed out that *nasci* and *fieri* here correspond to the Greek and Roman concepts of φύσις

---

[10] *Ad nationes* I, 4, 12, *Corp. Christ.*, *Ser. Lat.* I, 15 (*ThLL*). See also *Apologeticum* 21, 31 (*Vulgata*), *Corp. Christ.*, *Ser. Lat.* I, 128, note to l. 155: . . . ad bonum quis reformatur (*ThLL*).

[11] *Apologeticum* 21, 6 f., I, 123 (*ThLL*). See also *De monogamia* 17, 5, *Corp. Christ.*, *Ser. Lat.* II, 1253; through Christ a Christian should have become better than Adam was.

[12] *Adversus Hermogenem* 37, 4, *Corp. Christ.*, *Ser. Lat.* I, 429 (*ThLL*). It is interesting to compare chapters 12–43 of Tertullian's work with Augustine's much clearer views, expressed in *De Genesi ad litteram*, on the *formatio* of created matter as a *revocatio* to God; see below, pp. 167 ff.

[13] *De anima* 41, 4, Waszink 57; cf. *De baptismo* 3, 1, *Corp. Christ.*, *Ser. Lat.* I, 278.

[14] Minucius Felix, *Octavius* 1, 5, *Flor. Patr.* VIII, 12: . . . Caecilium . . . ad veram religionem reformavit (*ThLL*).

[15] Tertullian, *Apologeticum* 18, 4, *Corp. Christ.*, *Ser. Lat.* I, 118; cf. *De testimonio animae* 1, 7, *Corp. Christ.*, *Ser. Lat.* I, 176.

(natura) and ἄσκησις (exercitatio):[16] to the contrast of nature—
which is renewed instantaneously in baptism—and of ethical-mystical
ascesis—which includes the whole process of purification and of
assimilation to God, a process which constitutes such an important
part especially of Greek, but not exclusively of Greek, Christian
reform ideology.[17]

St. Cyprian, who just as the Greek Fathers could conceive of the
Church as paradisi instar,[18] on two occasions comes close to Tertullian's phraseology of reformatio in melius. In his treatise Ad Donatum
when speaking of the culmination of Christian life in the resurrection,
he says:

. . . [that life] can be neither abolished nor extinguished, it can only be
formed to the better with the return of the body (in melius corpore redeunte
formari).[19]

In De mortalitate he teaches that death is not an exitus, rather a transitus
. . . ad aeterna transgressus:

Who would not speed toward the better, who would not greatly desire to be
changed and reformed toward the form of Christ . . . ?[20]

An important aspect of Tertullian's and Cyprian's reform ideology
concerns the problem of the relationship between truth and tradition.
Tertullian in his De praescriptione haereticorum[21] answers the challenge
of heretics who claim that it is the Church herself who had altered the
teaching of the Lord and of the Apostles. He uses the juridical concept

---

[16] See E. Bickel, "Fiunt, non nascuntur christiani," Pisciculi F. J. Dölger 54 ff., where
the author also shows that that other famous Tertullianean dictum about the anima naturaliter
christiana (Apologeticum 17, 6, Corp. Christ., Ser. Lat. I, 117) does not stand in real opposition
to the sentence here discussed.

[17] See above, pp. 60 f., about the connection of these Greek patristic reform ideas with
the ancient Greek ideas of paideia and ascesis.

[18] Cyprian, Epist. LXXIII, 10, CSEL III, 785.

[19] Cyprian, Ad Donatum 15, CSEL III, 16 (ThLL). See also ibid. 4, III, 6, the combination
of "newness" and "reparation" in baptism: . . . in novum me hominem nativitas secunda
reparavit . . . ; cf. Epist. LXXIV, 5, CSEL III, 803: . . . in baptismo . . . sanctificatus . . . et
in novum hominem spiritaliter reformatus.

[20] Cyprian, De mortalitate 22, CSEL III, 310 f. (ThLL). Cyprian did not ignore the idea of
return to Paradise (see Ad Demetrianum 26, CSEL III, 370: . . . hic [Christus] ad paradisum
reduces facit, hic ad caelorum regna perducit) nor that of reform in pristinum through
penance (Epist. XXV, CSEL III, 538 [ThLL]).

[21] Tertullian, De praescriptione haereticorum, Corp. Christ., Ser. Lat. I, 185 ff.

of *praescriptio* (objection of the accused, which if sustained leads to the dismissal of the law suit) in asserting that the heretics can appeal neither to Holy Scripture nor to apostolic tradition, since neither the one nor the other are rightfully theirs.[22] They do not belong to them, because scriptural and apostolic teaching, as represented by the apostolically founded Churches, is much older than all heresies; at the same time, since truth always antedates a mere semblance (*similitudo*), a mere image (*imago*) of truth, the relatively late appearance of heresies is sufficient to discredit them. The priority (*principalitas*) of truth stands against the posteriority (*posteritas*) of falsehood.[23] Tertullian's argument, that truth is in all cases (*in omnibus*)[24] older than falsehood, is extremely formalistic; it did not prevent Tertullian from becoming a heretic himself; the step from ultraconservatism to revolt is not a very wide one.[25] Yet Tertullian did grapple sincerely with the undeniable fact that truth can be both old and new. In his *De virginibus velandis*, written after *De praescriptione*, but probably before he left the Catholic Church definitely, to adhere openly to what he considered the progressive and yet old truth of the Montanist Paraclete,[26] he formulated a doctrine of truth in its relation to tradition, or more exactly to custom (*consuetudo*) and progress (*proficere*), which was to have a great though not unproblematic future. In *De virginibus velandis* Tertullian wants to prove that the practice of veiling virgins is wholesome, however old contrary custom might be. For only the *regula fidei* is immobile and irreformable, whereas discipline and way of life (*conversatio*) admit of "the newness of correction." This continuous reform is the work of the Holy Ghost.

What therefore is the Paraclete's administration but the direction of discipline, the unveiling of the scriptures, the reform of understanding, the

---

[22] Cf. J. K. Stirnimann, *Die Praescriptio Tertullians im Lichte des römischen Rechts und der Theologie* (Paradosis III, Freiburg in der Schweiz, 1949); J. Quasten, *Patrology* II (Westminster, Md., 1953) 269.

[23] Cf. Stirnimann, especially 96 ff., 99 ff.

[24] Tertullian, *De praescriptione haereticorum* 29, 5, *Corp. Christ.*, *Ser. Lat.* I, 210: Sed enim in omnibus veritas imaginem antecedit, post rem similitudo succedit.

[25] K. Adam, *Der Kirchenbegriff Tertullians* (Forschungen zur christlichen Literatur-und Dogmengeschichte VI, 4, Paderborn, 1907) especially 121 ff., illustrates Tertullian's development from *De praescriptione* to Montanism.

[26] For the date of *De virginibus velandis*, see Quasten, *Patrology* II, 307.

progress to better things? . . . Those who have received Him put truth before custom.[27]

And above all:

Our Lord Christ has called Himself truth (cf. John 14:6), not custom.[28]

This last sentence was taken up by Cyprian[29] and received an impressive formulation at the Carthaginian Council of September 1, 256:

In the Gospel the Lord said: "I am the truth." He did not say: I am the custom.[30]

Through St. Augustine[31] this formula was destined finally to enter into the reform ideology of Gregory VII and Urban II and to be codified by St. Ivo of Chartres and Gratian.[32]

It will be seen later how Cyprian's conception of the relationship between custom and truth, between renewal and tradition, was

[27] Tertullian, De virginibus velandis 1, 3-7, Corp. Christ., Ser. Lat. II, 1209 ff.: Regula quidem fidei una omnino est, sola immobilis et irreformabilis . . . cetera iam disciplinae et conversationis admittunt novitatem correctionis. . . . Quae est ergo Paracleti administratio, nisi haec, quod disciplina dirigitur, quod scripturae revelantur, quod intellectus reformatur, quod ad meliora proficitur? . . . Hunc qui receperunt, veritatem consuetudini anteponunt.

[28] Tertullian, De virginibus velandis, 1, 1, Corp. Christ., Ser. Lat. II, 1209: . . . virgines nostras velari oportere . . . hoc exigere veritatem cui nemo praescribere potest, non spatium temporum non patrocinia personarum, non privilegium regionum. Ex his enim fere consuetudo initium ab aliqua ignorantia vel simplicitate sortita in usum per successionem corroboratur et ita adversus veritatem vindicatur. Sed Dominus noster Christus veritatem se (cf. John 14:6), non consuetudinem, cognominavit.

[29] Cyprian, Epist. LXXIV, 9, CSEL III, 806 f.: Nam consuetudo sine veritate vetustas erroris est. . . . Quam veritatem nobis Christus ostendens in evangelio dicit: "Ego sum veritas" (John 14:6).

[30] Sententiae LXXXVII episcoporum, ed. H. v. Soden, Nachr. Gött., Philol.-Histor. Klasse, 1909, 262 f.: Sentence 30, by Bishop Libosus of Vaga: In evangelio Dominus: "Ego sum," inquit, "veritas" (cf. John 14:6). Non dixit: Ego sum consuetudo. Itaque veritate manifesta cedat consuetudo veritati, ut etsi in praeteritum quis in ecclesia haereticos non baptizabat, nunc baptizare incipiat. See also Sentences 77 and 63, and cf. H. Koch, "Die karthagische Ketzertaufsynode vom 1. September 256," Internationale kirchliche Zeitschrift XIII (1923) 73 ff.

[31] Augustine, De baptismo III, 6, 9, CSEL LI, 203: In evangelio Dominus: "Ego sum," inquit, "veritas." Non dixit: Ego sum consuetudo.

[32] Cf. my article "Two Gregorian Letters: On the Sources and Nature of Gregory VII's Reform Ideology," Studi Gregor. V (1956) 221 ff. In general, see A. van Hove, Commentarium Lovaniense in Codicem Iuris Canonici I, III: De Consuetudine . . . (Malines, Roma, 1933) 23-32, important also for the relation between Christian and Roman Law concepts of consuetudo.

bound up with the contemporary controversy over the baptism of heretics, with attempts to reform by rebaptizing.[33] In this Cyprianic controversy Pope Stephen I enunciated his famous dictum: *Nihil innovetur nisi quod traditum est*,[34] a sentence which at first sight seems to emphasize tradition almost to the exclusion of reform, but actually takes account of both ideas.[35] For the principle of tradition and a concept of renewal which stresses the superiority of truth over custom are like the obverse and reverse of a single coin. They supplement one another. The essential question is whether or not a custom is in conformity with the truth and its truthful tradition.[36] If it is, it should not be tampered with, if it is not, it should be reformed. This reform need not be an innovation, which would violate tradition, in the sense of Stephen I's objections to Cyprian on the particular question then debated, it may rather be the undoing of such innovations in favor of customs which are in accordance with truth and tradition.

In the Constantinian Period, both Arnobius and Lactantius use the expression *in melius reformare*: Arnobius, when he blames the pagans for refusing to reform to the better their opinions concerning their

[33] See below, pp. 304 f. In keeping with the distinction between renewal which is in accordance with truth, and therefore good, and renewal which is contrary to truth, and therefore bad, Cyprian also could use renewal terms such as *convertere* and *reformare* in a pejorative sense. In *De habitu virginum* 15, *CSEL* III, 198, speaking about feminine cosmetics, he says with reference to Gen. 1:26 . . . et audet quisquam mutare et convertere quod Deus fecit! Manus Deo inferunt quando id quod ille formavit reformare et transfigurare contendunt, nescientes quia opus Dei est omne quod nascitur, diaboli quodcumque mutatur.

[34] Contained in Cyprian's *Epist.* LXXIV, *CSEL* III, 1, 799. Cf. F. J. Dölger, "Nihil innovetur nisi quod traditum est," *Ant. u. Chr.* I (1929) 79 ff.

[35] A. d'Alès, *La théologie de saint Cyprien* (Paris, 1922) 380 ff.: Appendix I: "Le rescrit du pape saint Etienne," interprets Stephen's elliptic sentence as if the Pope had meant to assert an absolute contrast between tradition and renewal, but this is hardly correct. *Innovare*, as used here, has the same meaning as *renovare* and similar terms in the renewal of conciliar canons—see below, pp. 298 ff.—that is to say, it signifies a self-renewing tradition. This conception of continuity between oldness and newness is found also in late patristic sources, among papal documents, for instance, in the letters of Gelasius I, cf. W. Freund, *Modernus und andere Zeitbegriffe des Mittelalters* (Neue Münstersche Beiträge zur Geschichtsforschung IV, Köln, Graz, 1957) 8 ff.

[36] So already Cyprian himself, cf. text cited p. 138, n. 29, and *Epist.* LXXIV, 10, *CSEL* III, 808 (cf. d'Alès 72 ff. for Cyprian's views on *traditio* and *consuetudo*), and especially Augustine, with reference to the Cyprianic baptismal controversy, in *De baptismo* III, 9, 12, *CSEL* LI, 204: Si autem veritas id aperuerit esse retinendum, quod illa consuetudo praescripserat, manifestum erit nec illam frustra fuisse institutam adque roboratam.

gods,[37] Lactantius in connection with his chiliastic expectation of a seventh millennium of bliss at the end of history.[38] While he conceives of the consequences of the protoplasts' fall in the biblical manner,[39] Lactantius also adopted the ancient idea of the Golden Age which for him was a postparadisiac era in which man still worshipped the true God and was just toward his fellow man.[40] Lactantius, a truly transitional figure in the history of the reform idea, is a representative of the Constantinian combination of Christian and ancient renewal ideas when he says that in a sense the Golden Age has returned already with the coming of Christ.[41] He is also the great fourth century poet of the phoenix; the cosmological and vitalistic restorative symbolism of this fabulous bird fits the imperial renewal ideology of the Constantinian and Theodosian ages at least as well as it does the doctrine of the resurrection which it was thought to symbolize since the third century if not earlier.[42] Lactantius, however, qualifies his concept of a Christian Golden Age by calling it a semblance (*species*), because

---

[37] Arnobius, *Adversus nationes* IV, 23 f., *CSEL* IV, 160: . . . si aperire oculos mentis et veritatem propriam intueri . . . vultis . . ., miseriarum omnium causas . . . ex huiusmodi reperietis opinationibus fluere, quas habetis antiquitus de diis vestris et quas in melius reformare ante oculos posita veritate renuistis (*ThLL*). Cf. also *ibid*. II, 66, *CSEL* IV, 101 f., against those who condemn Christianity because of its novelty.

[38] Lactantius, *Divinae institutiones* VII, 14, *CSEL* XIX, 628 f.: Sciant igitur philosophi . . . nondum sextum millesimum annum esse conclusum: quo numero expleto consummationem (i.e., the seventh millennium, cf. *Divinae institutiones* VII, 14, XIX, 630) fieri necesse est et humanarum rerum statum in melius reformari (*ThLL*). Lactantius also uses *reformare* in connection with penance (*ibid*. VI, 24 [9], XIX, 573 [*ThLL*]), for the rebirth of the phoenix (see below), etc.

[39] *Divinae institutiones* II, 12 ff., *CSEL* XIX, 157 ff.; cf. *Epitome* 22 (27), *CSEL* XIX, 694 f.

[40] *Divinae institutiones* V, 5, XIX, 413 ff.; cf. *Epitome* 20 (25), XIX, 691 ff.

[41] *Divinae institutiones* V, 7 (2), XIX, 419: Rediit ergo species illius aurei temporis, et reddita quidem terrae, sed paucis assignata iustitia est. . . . The seventh millennium also has characteristics of the Golden Age; cf. above pp. 14 and 27.

[42] Cf. Lactantius, *De ave Phoenice* 61 and 63, *CSEL* XXVII, 139:

Ut reparet lassum spatiis vergentibus aevum

. . . .

Cumque renascendi studio loca sancta reliquit.

See also 105 f., *CSEL* XXVII, 143:

Inde reformatur qualis fuit ante figura
Et Phoenix ruptis pullulat exuviis.

Already Tertullian (cf. above, p. 134, n. 6) and the early Catacomb painters had seen a

even now justice is assigned to a very few only and, on second thought, he even denies the existence of a Golden Age in his time.[43] The real superiority of Christianity lies for him in the recognition that a virtuous life amidst evil and suffering is of greater value than even a return to primaeval bliss and innocence.[44] This idea too had pre-Christian as well as Christian roots;[45] above all, it foreshadows Augustine's views on the relation between innocence and reform.[46]

St. Hilary of Poitiers in his *De Trinitate* has a beautifully concentrated synthesis of the Pauline doctrine of the reform of the divine image in man.[47] He also offers interesting indirect confirmation of the

symbol of the resurrection of the body in the phoenix. Perhaps, there is an allusion to the resurrection also in the last verse of Lactantius' poem (*CSEL* XXVII, 147):

Aeternam vitam mortis adepta bono.

V. 61 (Ut reparet . . . aevum) is typical of the political-religious ideology of the Constantinian age (see above, p. 20 and pp. 118 ff.). G. Boas, *Essays on Primitivism and Related Ideas in the Middle Ages* (Baltimore, 1948) 33 ff., has noted the dependence of Lactantius in his *Divine Institutions* on both the Genesis account of Paradise and on the Golden Age ideology. J. Hubaux and M. Leroy, *Le mythe du Phénix dans les littératures grecque et latine* (Bibliothèque de philosophie et lettres de l'Université de Liège LXXXII, 1939), have discussed the biblical and extrabiblical sources of Lactantius' poem on the phoenix.

[43] See above, p. 140, n. 41, and *Divinae institutiones*, V, 7 (10), *CSEL* XIX, 420 f.: . . . quamvis sit hominibus missa iustitia, tamen aureum saeculum non esse dicatur, quia malum non sustulit, ut retineret diversitatem quae sacramentum divinae religionis continet sola.

[44] *Ibid.* V, 7 (8), XIX, 420: Si enim virtus est malis ac vitiis fortiter repugnare, apparet sine malo ac vitio nullam esse virtutem. Quam Deus ut absolutam perfectamque redderet, retinuit id quod erat ei contrarium cum quo depugnare posset. . . .

[45] See Boas, *op. cit.*, 37, also A. O. Lovejoy and G. Boas, *Primitivism and Related Ideas in Antiquity* (Baltimore, 1935) 164, 268, and 274, with references to Plato and Seneca.

[46] See below, Part Two, Chapter V, 1.

[47] Hilary of Poitiers, *De Trinitate* XI, 49, *PL* X, 432B ff.: Nostra haec itaque lucra sunt et nostri profectus, nos scilicet conformes efficiendi gloriae corporis Dei (cf. Rom. 8:29). Caeterum unigenitus Deus, licet et homo natus sit, non tamen aliud quam Deus omnia in omnibus est (cf. Eph. 4:6). . . . Noster autem ille homo (i.e., Christ as man) in id proficit. Caeterum nos in hominis nostri conformem gloriam proficiemus et in agnitionem Dei renovati ad creatoris imaginem reformabimur, secundum apostoli dictum: "Exuti veterem hominem . . . et induti novum, eum qui innovatur in agnitionem Dei secundum imaginem eius qui creavit eum" (Col. 3:9 f.). Consummatur itaque homo imago Dei. Namque conformis effectus gloriae corporis Dei in imaginem creatoris excedit secundum dispositam primi hominis figurationem. Et post peccatum veteremque hominem in agnitionem Dei novus homo factus, constitutionis suae obtinet perfectionem, agnoscens Deum suum et per id imago eius: et per religionem proficiens ad aeternitatem et per aeternitatem creatoris sui imago mansurus (*ThLL*).

fact that Greek *apocatastasis* can be equivalent to reform in the restorative sense, when he refers to Christ's healing of the withered hand on a Sabbath day according to Matthew 12:13. While the Greek Gospel text says of the hand: ἀπεκατεστάθη ὑγιής, "it was restored to health," Hilary on at least three occasions,[48] uses the word *reformare* in this connection (whereas the Vulgate has: *restituta est sanitati*).

St. Ambrose's indebtedness to the Greek Fathers and to Philo directed his thought to a considerable extent. Just for this reason a comparison between his terms and ideas of reform and theirs will be fruitful; beside general similarities it will show significant differences.

In his book *On Abraham*, which, as his other small monographs on the Old Testament, draws heavily on Philo, Ambrose speaks of Abraham relinquishing his country.[49] Just as Philo[50] he sees in this an allegory of the striving for perfect purification of the mind and of followership of God who for Ambrose of course is Christ.[51]. However, Ambrose adds, we must understand Abraham's migration as a symbol not yet of perfection, but rather only of progress toward it.

For as yet the mind, which in first man fell, reforms itself in Abraham and therefore collects itself gradually and increasingly.[52]

This text is important both from the terminological and the ideological point of view. The word *reformare* is here clearly related to "progress" rather than to "return."[53] At the same time, the concept of reform does not, as it so often does in the Greek Fathers and in other texts of St. Ambrose himself, lead directly to the recovery of man's image-

---

[48] See *Tractatus in Ps. CXXXIX*, 4, *PL* IX, 818A: Aridam manum reformat; cf. *Commentarius in Matthaeum* 12, 7 and 15, 8, *PL* IX, 986B and 1005B (*ThLL*).

[49] Ambrose, *De Abraham* II, *CSEL* XXXII, 1, 564 ff.

[50] See Philo's *De Abrahamo* as well as his *De migratione Abrahami*.

[51] Ambrose, *De Abraham* II, 1, 3 and 2, 5, *CSEL* XXXII, 1, 566 f.

[52] *Ibid.* II, 2, 5, XXXII, 1, 568 (*ThLL*). The corresponding text in Philo, *De migratione Abrahami* 27, 150, Cohn and Wendland II, 297, does not use the term and concept of reform, but rather the contrast of unsettledness and settledness of the mind: νῦν μὲν γὰρ τὰ θεωρήματα αὐτῷ ὡς ἂν ἄρτι ἀρχομένῳ τῆς θείας θεωρίας πλαδᾷ καὶ σαλεύει· ὅταν δ'ἤδη παγέντα κραταιότερον ἱδρυθῇ, δυνήσεται τὸ δελεάζον καὶ κολακεῦον ὡς ἐχθρὸν . . . διαζεῦξαι.

[53] With regard to penance, however, and with reference to Matthew 4:17, Ambrose can say : . . . fracta animae tuæ ossa conectat et soliditate reparata in pristinas vires reformet ac discissos artus . . . restituat (*Expositio Psalmi CXVIII* 21, 5, *CSEL* LXII, 476 [*ThLL*]).

likeness to God.[54] Ambrose here rather stresses a preliminary character of reform; he has in mind the reformative road to that vision of
God of which he speaks a little later in the same work [55] and which
for him as for the Greeks remains the final goal and content of reformation toward God-likeness.[56]

Similarly, St. Ambrose's conception of man's return to Paradise is
not quite like that of the Greek Fathers, though he follows them in
several essential respects. For him, as for most of them, Paradise is
not on our earth but in a heavenly place: there Adam, after his body
had been formed on earth from earth, was placed by God; his situation
there was exalted indeed, even as that of the sun in heaven, but still one
of expectation of the coming of the Kingdom of Heaven.[57] The conception that Paradise, though supraterrestrial, is nevertheless inferior
to the Kingdom of Heaven, the Kingdom of God, and as it were a
stepping stone to it, is familiar also to some of the Greek Fathers,
adumbrated by Clement of Alexandria, developed in a spiritual
manner by Origen and later in a more scriptural way by St. John
Chrysostom.[58] Yet Ambrose has greatly elaborated upon this idea,
especially in his application of it to the pre-eschatological reformation
of man. In his *Letter LXXI*, to Horontianus, he allegorically interprets
the whole economy of salvation in terms of the history of the soul of

---

[54] See, for instance, Ambrose, *Expositio Evangelii Lucae* VII, 234, CSEL XXXII, 4, 387:
. . . periit Adam et in illo omnes perierunt. Homo igitur et in illo homine qui perierat
reformatur, et ille ad similitudinem Dei factus et imaginem divina patientia et magnanimi-
tate reparatur.

[55] Ambrose, *De Abraham* II, 3, 9, CSEL XXXII, 1, 570.

[56] See Ambrose, *De Isaac vel anima* 8, 79, CSEL XXXII, 1, 698 f.: quod enim videtur non
debet dissonare ab eo qui videt, quoniam conformes nos Deus imaginis voluit esse filii sui
(cf. Rom. 8:29) . . . solem nisi sanus et vigens oculus non aspicit nec bonum potest
videre nisi anima bona. Fiat ergo bonus qui vult videre Dominum et quod est bonum.
Huius boni similes simus et secundum id operemur quae bona sunt.

[57] Ambrose, *De paradiso* 1, 5, CSEL XXXII, 1, 267: In hoc ergo paradiso hominem Deus
posuit quem plasmavit (cf. also *ibid.* 4, 24, to Gen. 2:15, XXXII, 1, 280). . . . Posuit
autem eum in paradiso sicut solem in caelo expectantem regnum cælorum. . . .
See the studies of J. E. Niederhuber, *Die Eschatologie des hl. Ambrosius* (Forschungen zur
christlichen Literatur- und Dogmengeschichte VI, 3, Paderborn, 1907) 54 ff., and especially
Die Lehre des hl. Ambrosius vom Reiche Gottes auf Erden (same series IV, 3–4, 1904), also C.
Morino, *Il ritorno al Paradiso di Adamo in S. Ambrogio* (Città del Vaticano, 1952).

[58] See above, p. 65, n. 6, and p. 72, n. 40. Compare Origen's conception of Paradise
as *auditorium vel schola animarum* with Ambrose's preliminary paradisiacal *habitacula* or
promptuaria (after *IV Esdras* 7:32); cf. Niederhuber, *Eschatologie* 67 and 69 ff.

man. This history is a return to Paradise, but it is also more. After its exile from Paradise, Ambrose says, humanity was erring to and fro, until Christ, when He allowed Himself to be taken prisoner in the garden, *in paradiso*, also gave Himself up so to speak to man who through and in Him was caught up to Paradise: *ut exsulem in se susciperet et veterem reformaret gratiam.*[59] This "reform" of the lost "grace of old" was necessary if the Kingdom of God was to be attained by man in the end. It is in this sense that Ambrose interprets the good thief's request for the Kingdom and Christ's answer (Luke 23:42 f.):

Christ in his answer did not refer to the Kingdom, but with good reason. "This day thou shalt be with me in Paradise" (Luke 23:43), that is to say, first it is necessary to reform that which was lost, then to confer that which is to be added as increase, so that one may arrive through Paradise to the Kingdom, not through the Kingdom to Paradise.[60]

And Ambrose goes on to assert (somewhat unbiblically, perhaps) that those who have worked much for Christ deserve a greater reward than the last hour convert: power in the Kingdom of God rather than mere rest in Paradise.[61] In fact, the Kingdom of God,

---

[59] Ambrose, *Epistola LXXI, ad Horontianum,* 3 f., *PL* XVI, 1295B f.: . . . Christus . . . transivit in paradisum ubi se capiendum dedit, passus est in Golgotha. Omnes isti processus animae nostrae sunt, per quos exercitata gratiam piae institutionis invenit. Nam posteaquam exclusa de paradiso conditio humana in Adam et Eva in castello relegata est, vagari coepit huc atque illuc . . . sed tempore complacito sibi exaninivit se Dominus Jesus, ut exsulem in se susciperet et veteri reformaret gratiae. Itaque inventam recurso anfractu erroris revocavit ad paradisum . . . ; see also *ibid.* 8, *PL* XVI, 1296B.

[60] *Ibid.* 8, XVI, 1296C: Christus non de regno respondit, sed ad causam. "Hodie mecum eris in paradiso" (Luke 23:43), id est, reformandum est ante quod amissum est, postea conferendum id quod augendum est, ut per paradisum ad regnum perveniatur, non per regnum ad paradisum.

[61] *Ibid.* 9, XVI, 1297A. This conception is based on Ambrose's doctrine of a "first" and a "second" Kingdom of God, see *Expositio evangelii Lucae* V, 61, *CSEL* XXXII, 4, 206; cf. below, p. 230, n. 28. The perfectly just, the saints, immediately after their death pass through the testing fire of individual judgment and through Paradise into the "first Kingdom of Heaven"; the "second Kingdom of Heaven" for them, too, will not become actual until after the resurrection of the bodies; the souls of the less perfect but still good Christians after their purification by fire spend the period before the Last Judgment in the *promptuaria* of Paradise (see above, p. 143, n. 58), whereas those who have committed serious sins, and those who are damned, must remain in the fire, the former temporarily, the latter for ever; cf. Niederhuber, *Eschatologie* 32 ff. In *Expositio evangelii Lucae* V, 61, Ambrose goes on to interpret the text in John 14:2 about the many mansions in the house of the Father as a *processus mansionum* according to merit, and uses this significant comparison: nam et intra

both in heaven and in man's soul, is nothing less than Christ Himself.[62]

In St. Ambrose's *Letter XLV*, to Sabinus, Paradise is an altogether spiritual entity, the abode of virtues in the principal, the rational, part of the soul.[63] Because of the fall, we are in perpetual danger of lapsing from this Paradise. Yet

the Lord came to reform the grace of nature, and even to increase it, so that where there was a superabundance of sin, there would be a superabundance of grace.[64]

The "grace of nature," the grace of original paradisiac innocence, has

hoc saeculum multi in imperio Romano sunt, sed maiorem imperii gratiam qui propiores imperatori sunt consequuntur. Ambrose, however, does not always make a sharp distinction between Paradise and Kingdom of God. In *De bono mortis* 12, 53, *CSEL* XXXII, 1, 748, he says: Ibimus eo ubi paradisus iocunditatis est . . ., ubi et latro ipse regni caelestis consortio gratulatur. . . . According to *Expositio Evangelii Lucae* X, 121, *CSEL* XXXII, 4, 500, the good thief's entry into paradise makes him partake also of the Kingdom: . . . vita est enim esse cum Christo quia ubi Christus ibi regnum. Cf. also Augustine, *Sermo Mai* XIX, 2, Morin, *Aug. Serm.*, *Miscell. Agost.* I, 309: Quidquid potest dulce habere ista vita, non est paradisus, non est caelum, non est regnum Dei, non est societas angelorum, non est consortium illorum civium supernae Hierusalem (quoted in part by Christine Mohrmann, *Die altchristliche Sondersprache in den Sermones des hl. Augustin* I [Nijmegen, 1932] 132).

[62] *Sermo II, de natali Domini veniente*, 3, *PL* XVII, 627B: Regnum coelorum non nisi Christus est Dominus, qui regnat in coelis, and *Expositio in evangelium Lucae* V, 112, *CSEL* XXXII, 4, 228 (to Luke 17:21): . . . advertimus in nobis regnum caeleste solidari, cum Christus . . . intra nostrorum secreta regnat animorum; *ibid.* 115, XXXII, 4, 230: Regnum meum Christus est. These texts are superficially reminiscent of Origen's conception of Christ as *autobasileia* (see above, pp. 115 ff.). See also Cyprian, *De dominica oratione* 13, *CSEL* III, 276: Potest vero . . . et ipse Christus esse regnum Dei quem venire cotidie cupimus, cuius adventus ut cito nobis repraesentetur optamus. Nam cum resurrectio ipse sit, quia in ipso resurgimus, sic et regnum Dei potest ipse intellegi, quia in illo regnaturi sumus. Bene autem regnum Dei petimus, id est regnum caeleste, quia est et terrestre regnum. Sed qui renuntiavit iam saeculo, maior est et honoribus eius et regno. Et ideo qui se Deo et Christo dicat, non terrena, sed caelestia regna desiderat. The essential difference between these texts and Origen's *autobasileia* text lies in the fact that here the Kingdom is Christ Himself, whereas for Origen Christ is kingship itself; cf. above, p. 115.

[63] Ambrose, *Epist.* XLV, *ad Sabinum* 3, *PL* XVI, 1191C: . . . paradisum . . . non terrenum . . . non in solo aliquo sed in nostro principali quod animatur et vivificatur animae virtutibus et infusione spiritus Dei. In *De paradiso*, too, Ambrose has the spiritual conception of Paradise beside the historical one; cf. 3, 12 *CSEL* XXXII, 1, 272: Est ergo paradisus terra quaedam fertilis, hoc est anima fecunda. . . .

[64] *Epist.* XLV, *ad Sabinum*, 15, *PL* XVI, 1193C. At times Ambrose simply contrasts grace and nature; cf. *Expositio Psalmi CXVIII* 14, 42, *CSEL* LXII, 327: dedit gratiam, reformavit naturam.

not only been restored, but has also been augmented by Christ: with St. Paul (Rom. 5:20) Ambrose calls it now a "superabundant grace."

The reform of man then is both return to Paradise and attainment of a much higher state which, even if Adam had not sinned, he could never have reached by himself. For Christ's redemptive act has raised man to an altogether new plane on which he is not only creature, but also the adopted son of God.[65] Further, the *gratia naturae*, reformed and augmented by Christ, has become a perpetual *gratia renovationis* which operates through the Holy Spirit in the sacraments.[66] This is the background of the great doctrine of *felix culpa* which St. Ambrose seems to have been the first to have formulated clearly in several of his works and which above all is expressed in the beautiful *Exultet* hymn of the Holy Saturday liturgy.[67] Man's original sin, terrible as it

[65] *Expositio in Evangelium Lucae* V, 61, *CSEL* XXXII, 4, 206: Plus est enim Dei esse filium quam possidere terram et consolationem mereri (cf. Matthew 5:4 f.); for the continuation of this text see pp. 144 f., n. 61.

[66] *Apologia prophetae David* I, 14, 66, *CSEL* XXXII, 2, 345, commenting upon Ps. 50 as prophetic of the sacraments: . . . quoniam de mysteriis dicit lectio et futurae gratia renovationis exprimitur, Spiritus Sancti infusio postulatur. Cf. *De Helia et ieiunio* 22, 84 f., *CSEL* XXXII, 2, 464: . . . nemo enim nisi per aquam et Spiritum ascendit in regnum caelorum (cf. John 3:5). . . . Et vos potestis ascendere si sacramenti gratiam consequamini. . . . Et quanta gratia renovaris, o homo! ⟨Purgaris⟩ et non exureris, sanaris et non doles, reformaris et non dissolveris, ictum mortis non excipis et resurgis. See also *Epist. LXXVI, ad Irenaeum* 14, *PL* XVI, 1318B, where Ambrose comments upon the Epistle to the Ephesians and speaks of *renovari per gratiam sacramentorum*.

[67] See *De Iacob* I, 6, 21, *CSEL* XXXII, 2, 18: Facta est mihi culpa mea merces redemptionis, per quam mihi Christus advenit . . . fructuosior culpa quam innocentia . . . ubi superabundavit peccatum, superabundavit et gratia; *Explanatio Psalmi XXXIX*, 20, *CSEL* LXIV, 225: Felix ruina quae reparatur in melius; *De institutione virginis* XVII, 104, *PL* XVI, 346A: Amplius nobis profuit culpa quam nocuit: in quo redemptio quidem nostra divinum munus invenit; *Expositio in Evangelium Lucae* II, 41, *CSEL* XXXII, 4, 64: Plus igitur, Domine Iesu, iniuriis tuis debeo quod redemptus sum, quam operibus quod creatus sum. Non prodesset nasci, nisi redimi profuisset. The most famous and beautiful formulation of the doctrine is that in the great *Exultet* hymn of the Holy Saturday liturgy: . . . nihil enim nobis nasci profuit nisi redimi profuisset. . . . O certe necessarium Adae peccatum quod Christi morte deletum est. O felix culpa quae talem ac tantum meruit habere redemptorem . . . . Following the late Cardinal Mercati's suggestions in *Paralipomena Ambrosiana con alcuni appunti sulle benedizioni del cereo pasquale* (Studie e Testi XII, II, Roma 1904) 36 ff., Dom B. Capelle, O.S.B., "L'Exultet' pascal, oeuvre de saint Ambroise," *Miscellanea Giovanni Mercati* I (Studi e Testi CXXI, Città del Vaticano, 1946) 219 ff., has made a strong case for Ambrosian authorship of the *Exultet* (cf. also Myrtilla Avery, "The Relation of Saint Ambrose to the 'Exultet' Hymn," *Studies in Art and Literature for Belle da Costa Greene* [Princeton, 1954] 374 ff.); but see the opposite views of Dom M. Huglo, O.S.B.,

was in itself and in its consequences, was nevertheless to lead him to his highest possibilities: such was God's plan of salvation.

While some of the Greek Fathers had pointed to the superiority of the eschatological Kingdom of Heaven over the "archeological" and eschatological Paradise, none of them seems to have emphasized as strongly as St. Ambrose the fact that even the pre-eschatological reform by Christ of the Paradise of innocence in man's soul must result in a "superabundant" augmentation of the *gratia naturae*.[68] Through this doctrine St. Ambrose contributed essential elements to the history of the idea of reform in the west where that idea was to include many aspects supplementary to a mere return—even to a return to Paradise.[69]

Apart from the development of formal doctrines, different mental attitudes are here involved. In the case of St. Ambrose his opposition to an ideology of mere return became evident on a lesser level in his famous controversy with Symmachus of the year 384 concerning the restoration of the Altar of Victory in the Curia of the Roman Senate, desired by the pagan senatorial aristocracy.[70] It is true that in certain

"L'auteur de l'*Exultet pascal*," *Vigil. Christ.* VII (1953) 79 ff., and of Dom B. Fischer, O.S.B., "Ambrosius der Verfasser des österlichen Exultet?," *Archiv für Liturgiewissenschaft* II (1952) 61 ff. These two learned Benedictines, not quite convincingly in my opinion, ascribe the *Exultet* hymn to an unknown author who followed the Gallican rite. For the survival of the doctrine of *felix culpa* in early modern times, see A. O. Lovejoy, "Milton and the Paradox of the Fortunate Fall," in his *Essays in the History of Ideas* (Baltimore, 1948) 277 ff.

[68] In this connection, see H. de Lubac, S.J., *Surnaturel* (Paris, 1946), for the history of the concept "supranatural." P. de Lubac, however, does not seem to consider that root of the concept which is found in the superabundant grace of Rom. 5:20 and was developed by St. Ambrose.

[69] St. Jerome is in this respect closer to the Greek Fathers, when he repeatedly characterizes the ideal Christian life—the virginal life and especially that of the monks in the desert—as paradisiacal. See, for instance, *Epist.* XIV, *ad Heliodorum monachum*, 10, CSEL LIV, 60: Infinita heremi vastitas terret? Sed tu paradisum mente deambula . . .; *Epist.* XXII, *ad Eustochium* 19, CSEL LIV, 169: Eva in paradiso virgo fuit: post pellicias tunicas (cf. Gen. 3:21, see pp. 77 and 176) initium nuptiarum. Tua regio paradisus. Serva quod nata es . . .; *Epist.* XXXIX, *ad Paulam de morte Blesillae*, 4, LIV, 302: . . . in Iesu vero . . . per quem paradisus est apertus mortem gaudia prosequuntur. . . .

[70] Of the more recent literature on this episode cf. J. R. Palanque, *Saint Ambroise et l'empire romain* (Paris, 1933) 118 ff., 129 ff., 222, 277 ff., 510, 536, J. Wytzes, *Der Streit um den Altar der Viktoria* (Paris, 1936), L. Malunovicz, *De ara Victoriae in curia Romana quomodo certatum sit* (Wilno, 1937), H. Bloch, "A New Document of the Last Pagan Revival in the West," *Harv. Theol. Rev.* XXXVIII (1945) 214 ff. In 393 an ephemeral restoration of the

respects Ambrose was more subject to the religious-political atmosphere of the Theodosian age than a Jerome or Augustine and above all somewhat closer to the Eusebian ideology of "imperial" reform. So, for instance, in his interpretation of Psalm 45:10 he saw Christian Rome as the true fulfillment of the Augustan *pax Romana*,[71] whereas Augustine commenting on the same Psalm verse was to stress that after the Christianization of the Empire wars were still being waged, even on a larger scale than before, and that only those who recognize that all strength is from God are beyond all terrestrial struggles.[72] Yet where the essence of Christianity was at stake, as in the affair of the Altar of Victory, Ambrose was as single-minded as a Chrysostom or an Augustine.[73]

altar actually took place under the pagan emperor Eugenius whose rise and fall were shared by Symmachus' friend Virius Nicomachus Flavianus (for him see above, p. 19), then the leader of the pagan party in Rome. Theodosius, after his victory over Eugenius, removed the altar, but it seems that the statue of the goddess Victoria remained untouched (Malunovicz 104 ff., cf. the review of Palanque, in *Rev. hist. ecclés.* XXXV [1939] 298; earlier authors must be corrected accordingly). About 404, shortly before Symmachus' death, the incident had in any case still enough actuality to move the most brilliant of the early Christian poets, Prudentius, to write a poem in refutation of paganism and in the form of a reply to Symmachus; see his *Contra Symmachum, CSEL* LXI (also edited and translated into French with commentary by M. Lavarenne, *Prudence* III [Paris, 1948]); on Prudentius see below, p. 370.

71 Ambrose, *Explanatio Psalmi XLV*, 21, *CSEL* LXIV 344: ... in exortu ecclesiae potestatem Romani imperii toto orbe diffudit et dissidentium mentes terrarumque divortia donata pace composuit. Didicerunt omnes homines sub uno terrarum imperio viventes unius Dei omnipotentis imperium fideli eloquio confiteri.

72 Augustine, *Enarr. in Ps. XLV*, c. 13 (v. 10), *Corp. Christ.,* Ser. Lat. XXXVIII, 527 f.: ... sunt adhuc bella, sunt inter gentes pro regno, inter sectas, inter Judaeos, paganos, christianos, haereticos, sunt bella, crebrescunt bella. ... Quando autem nos Dominus suscipit, numquid inermes dimittit? Armat nos, sed aliis armis, evangelicis, veritatis, continentiae, salutis, spei, fidei, caritatis. Cf. E. Peterson, *Der Monotheismus als politisches Problem,* reprinted in *Theologische Traktate* (München, 1951) 95 ff., T. E. Mommsen, "St. Augustine and the Christian Idea of Progress," *Jour. Hist. Ideas* XII (1951) 346 ff., 363 ff.

73 For the famous clash between Ambrose and Theodosius himself after the dreadful massacre in the Hippodrome of Thessalonica see, for instance, Palanque, *Ambroise* 227 ff., H. v. Campenhausen, *Ambrosius von Mailand als Kirchenpolitiker* (Arbeiten zur Kirchengeschichte XII, Berlin, Leipzig, 1929) 236 ff. In spite of certain deficiencies of Theodosius' character—he was hardly the ideal Christian ruler of Ambrose's funeral oration, *De obitu Theodosii oratio, CSEL* LXXIII, 369 ff. (cf. O. Seeck, *Geschichte des Untergangs der antiken Welt* V [Berlin, 1913] 170 ff.)—the great qualities of this emperor both as a ruler and as a man must not be forgotten. He had utterly unshakable faith in the truth of his Catholic religion, as he proved for instance in the greatest crisis of his later reign, the battle of

Symmachus had bolstered his argument for restoration and public support of the cult of Victory by making *Roma* herself defend this rite because of its antiquity.[74] Ambrose's *Roma* replies:

I do not blush, in my protracted age, to be converted together with the whole world. It is certainly true that no age is too late for thorough instruction. Let rather old age blush if it cannot amend itself. Not maturity of years, but of morals (cf. Wisdom 4:8 f.) is praiseworthy. There is nothing shameful in passing to better things. . . .[75]

And there is more:

But the rite of the elders, he (i.e., Symmachus) says, must be preserved. Yet, how if everything has thereafter progressed to the better? The world itself, which had first grown together in a tender orb through the forcing together of the elemental seeds in the void or still lay in the confused horror and darkness of the yet unfinished work [of creation], did it not afterwards, in the clear separation of heaven, sea, and earth, receive the forms of the things through which it appears more beautiful . . .?[76]

Here Ambrose's conception of the formative improvement of an originally unformed creation is noteworthy; this idea, foreshadowed in western Christendom already by Tertullian,[77] was to be developed

---

Fluvius Frigidus against Eugenius and Arbogast, where everything seemed to be lost. He also possessed a sort of magnanimous humility in repenting and repairing his faults. We may believe St. Ambrose, when he said: *Dilexi virum,* "I loved the man" (cf. *De obitu Theodosii oratio* 33 ff., *CSEL* LXXIII, 388 f.). Above all, Theodosius finally seems to have accepted Ambrose's principle that even the Christian Emperor was a son of the Church, and as such in, not above, the Church, especially not in matters of doctrine and morals. That most of Ambrose's episcopate fell under the reign of Theodosius may in part explain the saint's relative optimism with regard to the Christian Roman Empire. For Theodosius' religious policy cf. also W. Ensslin, "Die Religionspolitik des Kaisers Theodosius d. Gr.," *Sitz. Ber. Bayer.,* Philos.-Histor. Klasse, 1953, 2 (1953), Bloch, "Pagan Revival," 223 n. 56.

[74] Q. Aurelius Symmachus, *Relatio* III, 9, *MGH, AA* VI, 1, 282.

[75] Ambrose, *Epist.* XVIII, 7, *PL* XVI, 1015A: Non erubesco cum toto orbe longaeva converti. Verum certe est quia nulla aetas ad perdiscendum sera est. Erubescat senectus, quae emendare se non potest. Non annorum canities est laudata, sed morum (cf. Wisdom 4:8 f.). Nullus pudor est ad meliora transire. . . .

[76] *Ibid.* 23, *PL* XVI, 1020B: "Sed maiorum," inquit, "servandus est ritus." Quid quod omnia postea in melius profecerunt? Mundus ipse, qui vel primum coactis elementorum per inane seminibus tenero orbe concreverat vel confuso adhuc indigesti operis caligabat horrore, nonne postea distincto coeli, maris terrarumque discrimine rerum formas, quibus speciosus videtur, accepit?

[77] See above, p. 135.

much more fully by St. Augustine.[78] The tenor of Ambrose's refutation of Symmachus asserts progress, understood in a Christian way, against the exaltation of a *status quo* merely on the strength of its antiquity.[79]

Let them say, then, that all things should have stayed in their beginnings, that they dislike a world, once covered with darkness, because it now shines in the splendor of the sun. And how much more pleasing is it to have driven out the darkness of the mind than that of the body, to see the radiance of faith break forth than that of the sun ! In sum the primaeval condition of the world and of all things has changed, so that it may be succeeded by the old age of a venerable mature faith. Let those who are disturbed about it blame the harvest because fertility comes late. . . . Now our harvest is the faith of the minds, the grace of the Church is the harvest of the merits, which from the origin of the world flourished in the saints, but [only] in this last age spread among the peoples, so that all would realize that the faith of Christ has not stolen into unprepared minds. . . .[80]

In his controversy with Symmachus who still hoped for the renovation of pagan *Roma aeterna* Ambrose stands against a Rome ideology which was fundamentally cosmological and vitalistic.[81] Ambrose's progressive Christian Rome idea, linked to his ideology of reform in general, amounts to a vindication of Christ's "I am Alpha and Omega, the first and the last, the beginning and the end" (Apoc. 22:13) against a merely human claim "For my end is my beginning"—whether this end be Symmachus' ancestral Rome or an Origenist *apocatastasis*.[82]

---

[78] See below, pp. 167 ff.

[79] Cf. J. Straub, "Christliche Geschichtsapologetik in der Krise des römischen Reiches," *Historia* I (1950) 54, for interesting references to old-Roman antecedents of the persuasion, also found in Tertullian, Cyprian, and Arnobius (see above, pp. 136 ff., pp. 138 f., and pp. 139 f.), that antiquity is not in itself a value: especially Tacitus, *Annales* XI, 24: . . . omnia . . . quae nunc vetustissima creduntur nova fuere . . . Inveterascet hoc quoque et quod hodie exemplis tuemur inter exempla erit.

[80] Ambrose, *Epist.* XVIII, 28 f., *PL* XVI, 1021A f.: Dicant igitur in suis omnia manere debuisse principiis; mundum tenebris obductum, quia splendore solis illuxerit, displicere. Et quanto gratius est animi tenebras depulisse quam corporis fideique iubar emicuisse quam solis. Ergo et mundi sicut omnium rerum primaeva mutarunt, ut venerabilis canae fidei sequeretur senectus. Quos hoc movet, reprehendant messem quia sera fecunditas est. . . . Ergo et messis nostra fides animorum est, ecclesiae gratia meritorum vindemia est, quae ab ortu mundi virebat in sanctis, sed postrema aetate se diffudit in populos, ut adverterent omnes non rudibus animis irrepsisse fidem Christi. . . .

[81] See above, p. 18, and below, pp. 254 f.

[82] See above, pp. 73 f.

If Ambrose too readily perhaps applied his conception of progress through Christianity to the Christian Roman Empire,[83] he at least did not go as far as Eusebius and his spiritual descendents in extolling the terrestrial Basileia of Constantine or his successors as the actual representation of the celestial one.[84] If there was such a representation on earth, it was in every man and in the Church; in the Church more truly than in the Empire there lives the image of God and model of man which is Christ:

For we are all by spiritual grace anointed to the kingship and priesthood of God.[85]

But in the Church I know of one image, that is the image of the invisible God, of which God said: "Let us make man to our image and likeness" (Gen. 1:26), that image of which it is written that Christ is "the brightness of His glory and the figure of His substance" (Hebr. 1:3). In this image I see the Father, since the Lord Jesus Himself said: "He that seeth me, seeth the Father also" (cf. John 14:9). . . . The Church is God's, it may certainly not be adjudged to Caesar, because the temple of God cannot be Caesar's law court. This is said with all honor to the emperor and nobody can deny it. For what is more honorable than that the emperor should be called son of the Church? . . . For, the emperor is within the Church, not above the Church. . . .[86]

---

[83] See above, p. 148, n. 71, and cf. T. E. Mommsen, "Augustine" 366 ff., also Peterson, *Monotheismus* 95 ff. Yet while recognizing Ambrose's overoptimism one must still distinguish between the exaltation of the Rome idea as such (the claim of eternity by an essentially unchanged Rome), which Ambrose did not accept, and the ideology of the Christianization of Rome and of Christian progress to which he adhered. The idea that the Roman Empire of Augustus and its peace served as a preparation for the coming of Christ can be found not only in Ambrose, Prudentius, and Orosius (for the latter cf. T. E. Mommsen, "Aponius and Orosius," 104 ff.), but also in such nonimperialistic authors as John Chrysostom, Cyril of Alexandria, and Leo the Great (some material in Peterson, *Monotheismus*). Prudentius' argumentation against Symmachus (cf. above, p. 148, n. 70) was similar to that of Ambrose, though contaminated somewhat more strongly with "Theodosian Renaissance" ideology; see the texts quoted above, p. 17, n. 5, also *Contra Symmachum* I, 506 ff., CSEL LXI, 238.

[84] Cf. above, p. 122.

[85] Ambrose, *De mysteriis* 6, 30, PL XVI, 415B: . . . omnes enim in regnum Dei et in sacerdotium ungimur gratia spiritali (quoted by R. Frick, *Die Geschichte des Reich-Gottes-Gedankens in der alten Kirche bis zu Origenes und Augustin* [Beihefte zur Zeitschrift für die neutestamentliche Wissenschaft VI, Giessen, 1928] 118 f., and by Niederhuber, *Reich Gottes* 80).

[86] Ambrose, *Sermo contra Auxentium de basilicis tradendis* 32, PL XVI, 1059D f. (with reference to the incident of the tribute money of Matthew 22:17 ff.): Sed in ecclesia unam imaginem novi, hoc est imaginem Dei invisibilis, de qua dixit Deus: "Faciamus hominem

This courageous attitude, epochal in the history of "Church-state relations," was, it is true, to usher in new problems which were to become typical for western Christendom. Even though St. Ambrose himself has shown on at least one occasion that not only statesmen but also ecclesiastics can overstep their bounds,[87] there can be no doubt that he contributed not a little to the Church's defence of the freedom of the spirit. Together with St. Augustine and St. Cyprian he was to become a model for the great Church reform of the age of St. Gregory VII in his rejection of mere oldness and in his opposition to a whole "mystique" of restoration which could be detrimental to true reform.

ad imaginem et similitudinem nostram" (Gen. 1:26), illam imaginem de qua scriptum est, quia Christus "splendor gloriae et imago substantiae eius" (Hebr. 1:3). In ista imagine Patrem cerno, sicut dixit ipse Dominus Jesus: "Qui me videt, videt et Patrem" (John 14:9). . . . *Ibid.* 35 f., *PL* XVI, 1061A f.: . . . Ecclesia Dei est, Caesari utique non debet addici, quia ius Caesaris esse non potest Dei templum. Quod cum honorificentia imperatoris dictum nemo potest negare. Quid enim honorificentius quam ut imperator ecclesiae filius esse dicatur. . . . Imperator enim intra ecclesiam, non supra ecclesiam est. . . . Cf. Niederhuber, *Reich Gottes* 84 n. 4 (to *Apologia prophetae David* I, 17, 82): "In der Sache besteht zwischen dem 'Reiche Gottes' und der 'Kirche Christi' kein Unterschied." The last quoted famous sentence of Ambrose is all the more remarkable if compared with the likewise well-known utterance of his older contemporary, Optatus, Bishop of Mileve in North Africa, who tried to justify his appeal to the state's power against the Donatists; cf. *De schismate Donatistarum* III, 3, *CSEL* XXVI, 73 f.: Non enim respublica est in ecclesia, sed ecclesia in republica, id est in imperio Romano . . . ubi et sacerdotia sancta sunt et pudicitia et virginitas quae in barbaris gentibus non sunt et si essent tuta esse non possent.

[87] On the occasion of the burning of the Synagogue of Callinice, when he insisted on the impunity of the culprits; cf. v. Campenhausen, *Ambrosius* 231 ff., 274 f., Palanque, *Ambroise* 205 ff., H. Berkhof, *Kirche und Kaiser* (Zollikon, Zürich, 1947) 90 ff., 172 ff. Ensslin, "Theodosius" 60 ff., does not discuss the questionable aspects of Ambrose's action.

CHAPTER V

ST. AUGUSTINE AND THE DIFFERENCE BETWEEN THE REFORM IDEAS OF THE CHRISTIAN EAST AND WEST

1. INNOCENCE AND REFORM

The reform doctrine of the Greek Fathers envisaged the possibility of man's return to a condition of integrity and innocence corresponding to that of Adam in Paradise before his fall and characterized by the recovery of his original similarity to God. This doctrine was rooted deeply in that of the Incarnation of Christ which at least since the fourth century was to Greek Christians the most important dogma of all. Perhaps it might be said that in the event and effect of the Incarnation they saw more clearly that the God-Man had remained God than that He had become man. Among the inexhaustible meanings of the Incarnation they stressed above all the fact that because God had become man and yet remained God, every man participating in the God-Man could reestablish in himself the original God-likeness of the human race. As compared with the deep absorption in the mysteries of God's Incarnation and man's deification, the redemptive act of Christ crucified was not, perhaps, always felt or expressed with the same poignancy which it had in Holy Scripture or which is found in the documents of the times of persecution[1] and which it was to regain in western Christendom not least through the influence of St. Augustine.[2]

Where the Passion and Crucifixion stand in the center of theology

[1] In this connection, see Dom Odo Casel, O.S.B., "Art und Sinn der ältesten christlichen Osterfeier," *Jahrbuch für Liturgiewissenschaft* XIV (1938) 1 ff., on the great changes which in the fourth century occurred in the Easter liturgy, which in the first three centuries had been centered as much in the Passion as in the Resurrection of Christ.

[2] This comparison between eastern and western Christendom is a generalization not of absolute but of relative validity; see also p. 107, n. 93, and below, p. 155, n. 9. For the following, cf. O. Scheel, *Die Anschauung Augustins über Christi Person und Werk* (Tübingen, Leipzig, 1901), especially 274 ff., 284 ff.; Scheel too has seen that in Christ's work of salvation the Greek considered more His Incarnation and Augustine more His Passion.

and spirituality as much if not more than Nativity-Epiphany and
Resurrection, there the idea of the reform of man must move away,
imperceptibly at first, from the concepts of recapitulation, *apocatastasis*, and purification which had been so characteristic of the reform
doctrines of Irenaeus, Origen, and Gregory of Nyssa, and to some
extent of the Greek Fathers in general. Christ's suffering on the
Cross, if realized in its fulness, must mean infinitely more than any
reduction of man or of the whole universe to their beginnings. To
assert the consummation of the divine self-sacrifice in a historically
testified Crucifixion was a claim without precedent, which in a sense
went beyond the belief in the Incarnation and Resurrection for which
parallel claims might be found in paganism.[3] If God really was crucified as man, man could never again be quite the same. If he did not
want to remain much less than Adam, he must become much more.

The Greek Fathers did not of course ignore the far reaching consequences of Redemption for the conception of man's reformation.[4]
Already to Origen the Crucifixion had been the fulfillment of Christ's
whole Gospel[5] and the imitation of Christ could be conceived by him
literally or metaphorically as martyrdom, as a reliving of Christ's
Passion.[6] For Gregory Nazianzen the fact ($\pi\rho\hat{\alpha}\gamma\mu\alpha$) of the Cross of
Christ is superior to all human reasoning ($\lambda\acute{o}\gamma os$)[7] and St. Gregory
of Nyssa says that man cannot be renewed without being crucified,
without dying with Christ.[8] And yet, with few exceptions, the

[3] Leaving aside the Far East, one might refer to the role of divine or semi-divine heroes
in Graeco-Roman religion.

[4] Cf., for instance, V. Lossky, *Essai sur la théologie mystique de l'orient* (Paris, 1944)
especially 146–150 (Greek liturgy of Good Friday and of the feast of the Exaltation of the
Cross, but see also below, pp. 290 ff., on the Greek liturgy).

[5] See Origen, *Commentary to St. Matthew*, XII, 18 f., *GCS*, *Orig.* X, 109 ff., quoted by
W. Völker, *Das Vollkommenheitsideal des Origenes* (Beiträge zur historischen Theologie VII,
Tübingen, 1931) 102.

[6] Cf. Völker, *Origenes* 218 ff., A. Lieske, *Die Theologie der Logosmystik bei Origenes*
(Münster, 1938) 124 f. But see also pp. 87 and 96, for the central place of Logos-mysticism
in Origen's thought.

[7] Gregory Nazianzen, *Oratio XXXII*, 26, *PG XXXVI*, 204C.: . . . $\tau\grave{o}\nu$ $\sigma\tau\alpha\upsilon\rho\grave{o}\nu$ $\tau o\hat{\upsilon}$
$X\rho\iota\sigma\tau o\hat{\upsilon}$ $\pi\rho\hat{\alpha}\gamma\mu\acute{a}$ $\tau\iota$ $\lambda\acute{o}\gamma o\upsilon$ $\kappa\rho\epsilon\hat{\iota}\tau\tau o\nu$. Cf. also *idem*, *Oratio XXIX*, 21, *PG XXXVI*, 104A.
Cf. J. Plagnieux, *Saint Grégoire de Nazianze théologien* (Paris, 1952) 193, who draws
attention to these texts.

[8] For Gregory of Nyssa see the texts discussed by J. Gaïth, *La conception de la liberté chez
Grégoire de Nysse* (Paris, 1953) 158 f., 162 f., 172 ff.

realization of Christ's suffering is not expressed by the Greek Fathers with the same immediacy, force, and frequency as it is by St. Augustine.[9]

A text from Augustine's *Enarration to Psalm XXXVII*, for instance, contains the well-known concepts of the renewal of the old man and of the desire and imitation of Christ; but everything is referred here in the most explicit manner to the Savior's Passion and Crucifixion:

We know, for the Apostle has said so, "that our old man is crucified with Him" (Rom. 6:6). But we should not be freed from oldness, if He had not been crucified in weakness. For He came for this purpose, that we should be renewed in Him: because it is by desiring Him and by imitating His Passion, that we are renewed.[10]

---

[9] This, I believe, is true in spite of the undoubted existence of a theory and practice of μίμησις Χριστοῦ in the Christian east, for which see, especially, I. Hausherr, S.J., "L'imitation de Jésus-Christ dans la spiritualité byzantine," *Mélanges Cavallera* 231 ff. The most striking example discussed by P. Hausherr are the meditations on the Cross and the Passion by the Syrian Monophysite Abbot Isaias (died 488), written in Greek. For the development of "private" devotion to the Crucifixus and the crucifix in the Christian east (beside the "public" triumphal and eschatological conception of the Cross) see E. Peterson, "La croce e la preghiera verso oriente," *Ephem. Liturg.* LIX (1945) 52 ff. See also the important hypothesis of A. Grillmaier, S.J., *Der Logos am Kreuz* (München, 1956), concerning a synthesis of the human and the divine in representations of Christ crucified of the type of the famous crucifixion in the Laurentiana Codex of the Syrian monk Rabulas (of the year 586). As to Augustine, it need hardly be recalled that his early works, the so-called philosophical dialogues, do not yet express full realization of Christ's suffering and its consequences; see, for instance, the doctrine of the purification of the soul in *De quantitate animae* 33, 70 ff., *PL* XXXII, 1073 ff., with its strongly Platonist character.

[10] *Enarr. in Ps. XXXVII*, 27, *Corp. Christ., Ser. Lat.* XXXVIII, 400: Scimus dicente apostolo "quia vetus homo noster confixus est cruci cum illo" (Rom. 6:6). Non autem careremus vetustate, nisi crucifigeretur in infirmitate. Ad hoc enim venit, ut renovemur in illo: quia desiderando eum et passionem eius imitando renovamur. For Augustine's emphasis on the suffering of Christ, see M. Pontet, *L'exégèse de saint Augustin prédicateur* (Paris, 1944), especially 355 ff. Cf. also Augustine's *Epist.* CLXXVII, 9 ff., *CSEL* XLIV, 678 ff., where he bases his doctrine of grace against the Pelagians on the *scandalum crucis*. For a significant difference in the interpretation of the very shape of the Cross by Augustine on the one hand and by Gregory of Nyssa and other Greek Fathers on the other see my article "St. Gregory of Nyssa and St. Augustine on the Symbolism of the Cross," *Studies A. M. Friend* 88 ff. While for Gregory the Cross is a visual symbol of the four principal extensions of the universe and of its unity in Christ, it is for Augustine a symbol of the four invisible dimensions of Christ's charity. At the same time, Augustine's cross symbolism is closer than Gregory's to the human image of the Redeemer stretched out in endurance of the crucifixion; see *Epistola* LV, 14, 25, *CSEL* XXXIV, 2, 196 f.: Itaque etiam longitudo qua totum corpus extenditur, ipsam tolerantiam significat unde longanimes dicuntur qui tolerant.

And yet, granted that it is because of Christ's redemptive act on the Cross that man can be renewed at all, to what form can he be reformed except to that which God meant him to have in the beginning, which was lost by Adam's transgression? Must not every reform, even the redemption of man by Christ in His Crucifixion and Resurrection, be a *renovatio in pristinum*, or in Greek terms lead to an ἀποκατάστασις εἰς τὸ ἀρχαῖον?[11] This is the gist of a question which Augustine asks and answers in the sixth book of *De Genesi ad litteram*.[12] Many things, Augustine says, are renewed not to their pristine state but to something better and such *renovatio in melius* presupposes a previous inferior condition. There is no doubt in Augustine's mind that this holds true also for Adam. The protoplast died because of his sin: he was then able to lose the immortality which he had received from God. St. Paul had spoken antithetically of the animate earthly first Adam and of the spiritual heavenly Adam, Christ. Only if Adam had not sinned would God have changed his merely animate body into a spiritual one which could no longer lose immortality.[13] Augustine's view sharply contrasts, for instance, with that of Origen for whom

[11] And in fact Greek spirituality saw it in this way. See below, pp. 291 f., on the Greek liturgy of Easter, in which the Passion and Resurrection of Christ symbolize the reopening of Paradise, just as does His Incarnation.

[12] Augustine, *De Genesi ad litteram* VI, 20 ff., *CSEL* XXVIII, 1, 194 ff.

[13] *De Genesi ad litteram* VI, 20 ff., *CSEL* XXVIII, 1, 194 ff.: Hic occurrit alia quaestio quomodo renovemur si non ad hoc per Christum revocamur quod in Adam prius eramus. Quamquam enim multa non in pristinum sed in melius renoventur, ab inferiore tamen statu quam quo erant antea renovantur. Unde ergo ille filius mortuus erat et revixit, perierat et inventus est (cf. Luke 15:32), unde illi profertur stola prima (cf. Luke 15:22), si non inmortalitatem recipit quam perdidit Adam? Quomodo autem perdidit inmortalitatem si corpus habuit animale? Neque enim animale corpus sed spiritale erit, cum corruptibile hoc induerit incorruptionem et mortale hoc induerit inmortalitatem (cf. 1 Cor. 15:53). Nonnulli his angustiis coartati, ut et illa constet sententia qua exemplum de animali corpore (cf. 1 Cor. 15:44) hinc datum est ut diceretur "Factus est primus homo Adam in animam viventem, [novissimus Adam in spiritum vivificantem]" (1 Cor. 15:45), et ista renovatio receptioque inmortalitatis non absurde dicatur in pristinum futura, in illud scilicet quod Adam perdidit, putaverunt prius quidem hominem fuisse corporis animalis, sed dum in paradiso constitutus est eum fuisse mutatum sicut nos quoque resurrectione mutabimur . . . (21, p. 194 f.). Sed si ita est, frustra conamur paradisum et illas arbores earumque fructus praeter figuratam significationem prius accipere ad rerum gestarum proprietatem . . . (22, p. 195, l. 27). Quomodo ergo [corpus Adam] inmortale si animale? . . . (23, p. 196, ll. 8 ff.): Verum est quidem quod non moreretur [Adam] etiam corpore nisi peccasset . . . [corpus] animale tamen posset esse ante peccatum et post vitam iustitiae, cum Deus vellet, fieri spiritale.

the body of Adam at its first creation was as spiritualized as the bodies of all men will be after their resurrection.[14]

How therefore (Augustine asks) are we said to be renewed, if we do not receive that which the first man through whom all die has lost? Clearly, we do receive it in one way and do not receive it in another. [On the one hand] then we do not [yet] receive the immortality of a spiritual body which [first] man did not yet have, but we do receive justice from which man has lapsed through sin. [On the other hand], accordingly, we shall be renewed from the oldness of sin not into the pristine animalic body in which Adam was, but into a better one, that is to say, into a spiritual body . . . a spiritual body, into which Adam had not yet been changed, but was to be changed, if he had not in sinning deserved death also of his animalic body. . . .[15]

---

[14] See above, pp. 71-74. For the body's "spirituality" in the beginning and at the end of all things according to Origen, especially according to his De principiis, cf. also G. Bürke, S.J., "Des Origenes Lehre vom Urstand," Z. kath. Theol. LXXII (1950) 19-21. It is not impossible that Origen assumed that Adam's "earthen" body in Gen. 2:7 already corresponded to man's fallen condition (cf. Bürke, "Urstand" 25 ff.). Perhaps Gregory of Nyssa's doctrine of a "double creation," or more exactly his hypothesis that "first man," the man of the image (Gen. 1:26), was created spiritual and that the man of the material body (Gen. 2:7), though not posterior in time, was created only in foresight of the fall (see below, p. 175) is dependent on such views of Origen. Another verse of the book of Genesis, 3:21, where God makes the protoplast wear "garments of skin" (χιτῶνες δερμάτινοι) after the fall, is considered by Origen and Gregory of Nyssa as definitely symbolic of the change of man's condition to materiality or mortality; for Origen see In Leviticum, homil. VI, 2, GCS, Orig. VI, 362, and Selecta in Genesim, PG XII, 93 ff.; for Gregory of Nyssa, see the ample references in J. Daniélou, S.J., Platonisme et théologie mystique: Doctrine spirituelle de saint Grégoire de Nysse, 2nd ed. (Théologie II, Paris, 1953) 60 ff., and my article "The Philosophical Anthropology of Saint Gregory of Nyssa," Dumb. Oaks Pap. XII (Cambridge, Mass., 1958). Gregory seems to consider even the body which Adam received according to Gen. 2:7 as spiritualized (see De anima et resurrectione, PG XLVI, 108A) so that only the clothing with garments of skin after the fall would have brought about the body's materiality. For the symbolism of the χιτῶνες δερμάτινοι in general, see below, p. 176, n. 27.

[15] De Genesi ad litteram VI, 24, CSEL XXVIII, 1, 196 f.: Quomodo ergo . . . renovari dicimur si non hoc recipimus quod perdidit primus homo in quo omnes moriuntur? Hoc plane recipimus secundum quendam modum et non hoc recipimus secundum quendam modum. Non itaque inmortalitatem spiritalis corporis recipimus quam nondum habuit homo, sed recipimus iustitiam ex qua per peccatum lapsus est homo. Renovabimur ergo a vetustate peccati non in pristinum corpus animale in quo fuit Adam, sed in melius, id est in corpus spiritale, cum efficiemur aequales angelis Dei (cf. Matthew 22:30) apti caelesti habitationi, ubi esca quae corrumpitur non egebimus. Renovabimur ergo spiritu mentis nostrae secundum imaginem eius qui creavit nos (Eph. 4:23), quam peccando Adam perdidit. Renovabimur autem etiam carne cum hoc corruptibile induet incorruptionem ut sit spiritale corpus, in quod nondum mutatus sed mutandus erat Adam nisi mortem etiam corporis animalis peccando meruisset. Denique non ait apostolus: Corpus quidem mortale propter peccatum, sed: "Corpus mortuum propter peccatum" (cf. Rom. 8:10).

For the impossibility to die is one thing . . . , the possibility not to die another and according to this latter mode was man created immortal. . . .[16]

Because of original sin, it is true, we shall not until the end be renewed *in melius* to a spiritual body, which is no longer Adam's *pristinum corpus animale*: this will happen in the resurrection. Even now, however, are we being renewed to the image of the Creator, though not according to our body, but *spiritu mentis nostrae* (Eph. 4:23). This is the image-likeness to God in the rational soul, which though it was not completely lost, was greatly impaired in the very moment in which Adam forfeited the gift of immortality through his disobedience.

The passages from *De Genesi ad litteram* quoted above,[17] if taken by themselves, would make it appear that Augustine applied a Christian's *renovatio in melius* only to his ultimate resurrection and not to his life on earth; for that which is renewed even before the end of all things —the image of God in the soul—Adam had already had, though he lost it. Thus it would seem that as far as man's terrestrial life is concerned his reformation is still equivalent to his return to the innocence of Adam in which he had represented the image of God.[18] In his anti-Pelagian period, however, Augustine definitely transcended such views. This development of his thought is evident in the last chapter of *De civitate Dei* and above all in *De correptione et gratia*.

[16] *Ibid.* VI, 25, XXVIII, 1, 197: Illud (i.e., corpus) quippe ante peccatum et mortale secundum aliam et inmortale secundum aliam causam dici poterat: id est mortale quia poterat mori, inmortale quia poterat non mori. Aliud est enim non posse mori, sicut quasdam naturas inmortales creavit Deus, aliud est autem posse non mori, secundum quem modum primus homo creatus est inmortalis. . . . Mortalis ergo erat conditione corporis animalis, inmortalis autem beneficio conditoris. Si enim corpus animale, utique mortale quia et mori poterat, quamvis et inmortale ideo quia et non mori poterat. Neque enim inmortale, quod mori omnino non possit, erit nisi spiritale, quod nobis futurum in resurrectione promittitur.

[17] See, for a similar statement, also *Contra Faustum Manichaeum* XXIV, 2, *CSEL* XXV, 1, 723: Ergo totus ille homo, id est, et interiore et exteriore sui parte, inveteravit propter peccatum et poenae mortalitatis addictus est. Renovatur autem nunc secundum interiorem hominem, ubi secundum sui creatoris imaginem reformatur, exuens se iniustitiam, hoc est veterem hominem, et induens iustitiam, hoc est novum hominem. Tunc autem cum resurget corpus spiritale quod seminatur animale, etiam exterior percipiet caelestis habitudinis dignitatem: ut totum quod creatum est recreetur et totum quod factum est reficiatur illo recreante qui creavit et reficiente qui fecit.

[18] See also *De Genesi ad litteram* XI, 40, *CSEL* XXVIII, 1, 375, where the Church is called *paradisus* as it often is in the Greek Fathers.

Here he takes up the distinction made in *De Genesi ad litteram* between *posse non mori* and *non posse mori* and now extends it to that between *posse non peccare* and *non posse peccare* and to that between *bonum posse non deserere* (*perseverantiae potestas*) and *bonum non posse deserere* (*felicitas perseverantiae*).[19] In each of these distinctions the second member of the antithesis is of far greater weight than the first. Even on earth the saints predestined for the Kingdom of God receive a grace which is superior to that possessed by Adam in Paradise: for even though they have free will like Adam and even though they are tempted much more strongly than he, the elect of God cannot lose the gift of perseverance in the good, whereas Adam with all his great privileges had actually fallen into the one decisive sin.

Greater indeed is the freedom required in the midst of so many and so great temptations which did not exist in Paradise; such freedom must be protected and strengthened by the gift of perseverance if it is to conquer this world with all its loves, terrors, and errors: this the martyrdoms of the saints have taught us.

How is it possible at all? Only *interpellante Christo, ne deficiat fides eorum.*[20]

[19] *De correptione et gratia* 12, 33, *PL* XLIV, 936: Quapropter bina ista quid inter se differant diligenter et vigilanter intuendum est: posse non peccare et non posse peccare, posse non mori et non posse mori, bonum posse non deserere et bonum non posse deserere. . . . Prima ergo libertas voluntatis erat posse non peccare, novissima erit multo maior non posse peccare; prima immortalitas erat posse non mori, novissima erit multo maior non posse mori; prima erat perseverantiae potestas bonum posse non deserere, novissima erit felicitas perseverantiae bonum non posse deserere. Cf. *De civitate Dei* XXII, 30, 49 ff., *Corp. Christ., Ser. Lat.* XLVIII, 863 f.

[20] *De correptione et gratia* 12, 34 f., *PL* XLIV, 937: Primo itaque homini qui in eo bono quo factus fuerat rectus acceperat posse non peccare, posse non mori, posse ipsum bonum non deserere, datum est adiutorium perseverantiae non quo fieret ut perseveraret, sed sine quo per liberum arbitrium perseverare non posset. Nunc vero sanctis in regnum Dei per gratiam Dei praedestinatis non tale adiutorium perseverantiae datur, sed tale ut eis perseverantia ipsa donetur. . . . Pro his igitur interpellante Christo, ne deficiat fides eorum, sine dubio non deficiet usque in finem. . . . Maior quippe libertas est necessaria adversus tot et tantas tentationes, quae in paradiso non fuerunt, dono perseverantiae munita atque firmata, ut cum omnibus amoribus terroribus erroribus suis vincatur hic mundus: hoc sanctorum martyria docuerunt . . . (see also the remainder of this chapter). These distinctions with regard to Adam's condition before the fall and to the perseverance of the Christian elect, is not yet found in Augustine's *Enchiridion* or *De fide spe et caritate*, which was written c. 421, that is to say, between *De Genesi ad litteram* (c. 401–415) and *De correptione et gratia* (c. 426–427); cf. *Enchiridion* 104 (28), *PL* XL, 281.

Augustine's insistence on the fact that the superiority of Christian renovation over paradisiac innocence is closely connected with the trials and moral decisions to be faced in human life leads away from the Christianized ideal of *apatheia*, as it is found in Greek patristic and eastern monastic thought as a step toward mystical experience.[21] On Augustinian premises a Christian's reformation in this world, and away from this world toward God, can be compared with his return to Paradise only in a sense which is less comprehensive and forceful than that of most of the Greek Fathers.[22] As to St. Paul's extraordinary rapture to the third heaven and to Paradise, it seems that St. Augustine considered it even more exceptional than the Greek Fathers had done. This different view is connected with his ideas on the assimilation of

[21] See *De civitate Dei* XIV, 8 f., especially 9, *Corp. Christ.*, *Ser. Lat.* XLVIII, 428 : Quocirca illa quae ἀπάθεια Graece dicitur (quae si Latine posset inpassibilitas diceretur), si ita intellegenda est (in animo quippe non in corpore accipitur) ut sine affectionibus vivatur quae contra rationem accidunt mentemque perturbant bona plane et maxime optanda est, sed nec ipsa huius est vitae. . . . Porro, si ἀπάθεια illa dicenda est, cum animum contingere omnino non potest ullus affectus, quis hunc stuporem non omnibus vitiis iudicet esse peiorem ? . . . Cf. also Jerome, *Epist.* CXXXIII, *ad Ctesiphontem, adversus Pelagium*, 3, *CSEL* LVI, 246, where he condemns Evagrius Ponticus' conception of *apatheia*: . . . quam nos inpassibilitatem vel inperturbationem possumus dicere, quando numquam animus ulla cogitatione et vitio commovetur: et—ut simpliciter dicam—vel saxum vel Deus est.

[22] Augustine's position is thus poles apart from Origenist *apocatastasis* ideology, and even from its more moderate Cappadocian version. It is interesting that the Cappadocians' younger contemporary, Evagrius Ponticus, though otherwise a continuator of Origenist thought, uses the term νοῦ κατάστασις (J. Muyldermans, " Evagriana," *Muséon* XLIV [1931] 51, Lemaître, article "Contemplation," in *DSpir*, fasc. XIV–XV, 1830 f.) rather than ἀποκατάστασις for that freeing of the mind from passion, which leads to mystical experience. It may be recalled also that during Augustine's life time Theodore of Mopsuestia, then the leading exegete and theologian of the School of Antioch, set down his doctrine of two *catastases*, which one can hardly fail to recognize as directed against the remnants of the Origenist idea of *apocatastasis*. Theodore distinguished two *catastases* or "conditions" of man: the first, constituting the life of unredeemed man after the fall, the second, which is not simply a return to integrity, beginning only with the coming of Christ; cf. R. Devreesse, *Essai sur Théodore de Mopsueste* (Studi e Testi CXLI, Città del Vaticano, 1948) 89 f., 100 f.; see also E. v. Ivanka, *Hellenisches und Christliches im frühbyzantinischen Geistesleben* (Wien, 1948) especially 79, n. 12 (Ivanka combines the traditional view of Theodore as a forerunner of Nestorianism and spiritual relative of Pelagius with an interesting attempt to derive his anthropology from Aristotelianism; for Theodore see now also F. A. Sullivan, S.J., *The Christology of Theodore of Mopsuestia* [Analecta Gregoriana LXXXII, Ser. Theol., Sectio B, n. 29, Roma, 1956], against Mons. Devreesse's assertion of the orthodoxy of Theodore's authentic teaching).

man to God and on the vision of God, in which he also diverges from the latter.

While these ideas will be studied in a later section, it is necessary to recall here that a terminology and ideology of renewal to the better was formulated also by some of the Greek Fathers,[23] not however exactly in the Augustinian manner. For the Greeks renewal to the better could and often did remain restorative.[24] So, for instance, when St. Basil speaks of the μετακόσμησις ἐπὶ τὸ βέλτιον of sinners, there is little doubt from the context that this ἀνακαινισμός, this change (μεταβολή) from passion-bound earthly life to citizenship in heaven (οὐράνιος πολιτεία) is identical with return to paradisiac bliss.[25] Where on the other hand the progress of the new over the old dispensation is stressed most strongly in Greek thought, it is conceived as ceaseless mystical progress, which does not end even in heaven,[26] rather than in the Augustinian way as a greater grace toward perseverance in earthly sufferings and temptations and toward rest in God after terrestrial life.[27] So, for instance, Gregory of Nyssa consoles those who are distressed about the mutability of human beings: there is, he says, also an increase in the good, ἐν τοῖς ἀγαθοῖς αὔξησις, an alteration to the better, πρὸς τὸ κρεῖττον ἀλλοίωσις, a remaking toward the divine, ἐπὶ τὸ θειότερον μεταποιεῖν; true perfection means

[23] For Greek patristic terminology and ideology of renewal to the better see also above, pp. 64 f., nn. 5 f., in connection with the return to Paradise and the possession of the Kingdom of God and below, p. 230, in connection with the superiority of the easterly and dominical "eight" over the sabbatical "seven." For Greek and Augustinian ideas on the divine image in man and assimilation to God see pp. 83 ff. and 185 ff., respectively. The view, held by Clement of Alexandria, Origen, and not a few other Greek Fathers, that in the reformation of man the ὁμοίωσις is something to be added to the εἰκών—see above, pp. 85 ff.—expresses in a sense the idea of renewal to the better; yet, it must be remembered that the similarity to God was for them at least potentially, and for Gregory of Nyssa explicitly, present already in the image.

[24] And this in spite of Greek patristic realization of the novelty and superiority of the Christian dispensation, a realization which had from earliest times been alive in typological exegesis and also had not been absent from Irenaeus' doctrine of recapitulation; cf. J. Daniélou, S.J., Sacramentum Futuri: Etudes sur les origines de la typologie biblique (Paris, 1950) 3 ff., 21 ff.

[25] See Basil, De Spiritu Sancto 19, 49, PG XXXII, 157B f.

[26] See pp. 105 ff.

[27] For Augustine's conception of the heavenly fulfillment of man's quest for God (satiabitur) see below, p. 190, n. 16.

never to stop that increase to the better, never to set limits to the extent of perfection.[28]

The subtle differences between Greek and Augustinian thought on anthropological renewal are repeated in a much more massive form in the conflict between Pelagianism and Augustinianism. For Pelagius, apart from his heretical one-sidedness, was in some, though not in all, respects closer to the Greeks than Augustine.

Generally speaking Pelagianism, in its beginnings at least, was one of the symptoms of the necessity for reform in the Church at the turn of the fourth century. Pelagius[29] was of the same mind as his opponents, St. Jerome and St. Augustine, or as St. John Chrysostom, in looking askance at the numerous and superficial conversions made as a consequence of the Christianization of the Roman Empire. Just as the orthodox Fathers he was particularly incensed about the abuse of wealth in contemporary society. But, in his exaggeration of the truth that faith must bear fruit in good works, he was carried beyond the spirit of the New Testament into a rigorous moralism and moralistic optimism which was alien to authentic Christianity. His assertion that man, since he must not sin, must have it in his own power not to

---

[28] See, for instance, Gregory of Nyssa, De perfectione, Jaeger, Greg. Nyss. Opera VIII, 1, 213: Οὐδὲ γὰρ μόνον πρὸς τὸ κακὸν ὁ ἄνθρωπος τῇ τροπῇ χρῆται ... τὸ κάλλιστον τῆς τροπῆς ἔργον ἡ ἐν τοῖς ἀγαθοῖς ἐστιν αὔξησις, πάντοτε τῆς πρὸς τὸ κρεῖττον ἀλλοιώσεως ἐπὶ τὸ θειότερον μεταποιούσης τὸν καλῶς ἀλλοιούμενον. ... Μὴ τοίνυν λυπείσθω ὁ βλέπων ἐν τῇ φύσει τὸ πρὸς τὴν μεταβολὴν ἐπιτήδειον, ἀλλὰ πρὸς τὸ κρεῖττον διὰ παντὸς ἀλλοιούμενος καὶ ἀπὸ δόξης εἰς δόξαν μεταμορφούμενος (cf. 2 Cor. 3:18) οὕτω τρεπέσθω, διὰ τῆς καθ' ἡμέραν (cf. 2 Cor. 4:16) αὐξήσεως πάντοτε κρεῖττων γινόμενος καὶ ἀεὶ τελειούμενος καὶ μηδέποτε πρὸς τὸ πέρας φθάνων τῆς τελειότητος. Αὕτη γάρ ἐστιν ⟨ἡ⟩ ὡς ἀληθῶς τελειότης τὸ μηδέποτε στῆναι πρὸς τὸ κρεῖττον αὐξανόμενον μηδέ τινι πέρατι περιορίσαι τὴν τελειότητα. For Gregory of Nyssa's conception of spiritual progress (προκοπή) see also p. 104, and W. Jaeger, Two Rediscovered Works of Ancient Christian Literature: Gregory of Nyssa and Macarius (Leiden, 1954) 86 ff., W. Völker, Gregor von Nyssa als Mystiker (Wiesbaden, 1955) 186 ff. Gregory at times combines even this idea of ceaseless progress with that of the return to Paradise; see In Canticum Cantic., homil. IX, PG XLIV, 968 D: (to Cant. 4:13 ff.): ... καὶ οὐδὲ ἐν τούτοις ἔστη· ἀλλ' εἰς τοσοῦτον ἔφθασε τῆς ἐπὶ μεῖζον αὐξήσεως ὡς ἐκ τοῦ στόματος αὐτῆς βλαστάνειν παράδεισον. ...

[29] On Pelagius see the work of G. de Plinval, Pélage (Lausanne, 1943) and the same author's Essai sur le style et la langue de Pélage (Fribourg, 1947), also the recent important study by T. Bohlin, Die Theologie des Pelagius und ihre Genesis (Uppsala Universitets Årsskrift, Acta Universitatis Upsaliensis, 1957:9), which stresses Pelagius' use of Origen's Commentary to the Epistle to the Romans in Rufinus' translation. (Bohlin's work became known to me only while this book was in the press.)

sin was an all too easy equation. In estimating man's natural power
for goodness so highly Pelagianism must limit the role of God's grace
in the process of man's conversion and reformation.[30] The Pelagian
doctrine of *impeccantia*, that is to say, the teaching that a man does not
have to commit sin if he wills not to do so[31]—for sin is not hereditary,
only imitative[32]—implied among other things that physical death
cannot be a punishment for sin. For every man, good or bad, must
die: death is and always was natural. Perhaps Pelagius himself and
certainly later Pelagians such as Julian of Eclanum believed that
Adam too would have died even had he not transgressed.[33] In this
they differ from St. Augustine's doctrine that Adam was granted
immortality and would have remained immortal had he obeyed God,[34]
but even more from those Greek Fathers who held that Adam had a
spiritual, a "resurrectional," body before his sin.[35] On the other
hand, St. Jerome was not far from the truth if he threw together in
one condemnation Pelagius' *impeccantia* and the Origenist concept of
apatheia in the form in which he encountered it in the doctrine of
Evagrius Ponticus. The deifying conquest of all passions and the
necessarily successful effort to be virtuous as conceived by Evagrius
and Pelagius, respectively, can be regarded as two different aspects of
man's own power to reform himself.[36] Augustine on the other hand

---

[30] I believe this remains true in spite of Bohlin's analysis of the dialectic relationship
between Pelagius' conceptions of the grace of creation, the grace of revelation, and the
grace of forgiveness through baptism.

[31] The term *impeccantia* may have been coined by St. Jerome, but Pelagius in any case
admitted that it corresponded to his doctrine; cf. Plinval, *Pélage* 222 f., 389 ff.

[32] Cf. Augustine, *De peccatorum meritis et remissione et de baptismo parvulorum* I, 9, 9 ff.,
CSEL LX, 1, 10.

[33] See Julian of Eclanum, in Augustine, *Contra secundam Iuliani responsionem imperfectum
opus* VI, especially 27, *PL*, XLV, 1568: . . . [Adam] procul dubio non iniquitatis sed
naturae mortalis fuit . . ., and Augustine *ibid*. 37, XLV, 1595: Quia scilicet corporis
mortem non vultis peccato primi hominis tribuere sed naturae: quam sic in illo homine
primo dicitis institutam, ut sive peccaret sive non peccaret moriturus esset.

[34] See above, p. 156, n. 13.

[35] See above, p. 71, and below, p. 176.

[36] For Evagrius, see above, pp. 99 f., n. 63. Plinval, *Pélage* 273, in blaming St. Jerome for
confusing Origenist *apatheia* (in its Evagrian simplification) and Pelagian *impeccantia*, does
not consider, perhaps, that the former as the latter is based on the belief that it is "vir-
tuosity" in virtue, attainable to all, which leads man back to his inheritance, in other words,
makes the divine image in man again similar to God. To Jerome such a conception of
perfection in this world meant no longer assimilation to God, but the pretension of possible

showed that man, though he has free will, has not the power to use it to the good, if God does not gratuitously give him the grace to do so, thus adding *libertas* to *liberum arbitrium*.[37]

The importance of Pelagianism as a catalyst of fourth century Christendom must not be underestimated. It started out as a reform movement and tried to prove the necessity and the possibility of an individual and social life in accordance with Christian morality. In its deviation, it represented both a danger signal and one of the two great temptations in the history of the reform idea: to believe that man can reform himself and the world on his own. The other was the temptation of that slothful frivolity which believes that trusting God means relaxing one's own efforts. St. Augustine in his struggle against Pelagianism—the last of his great intellectual battles—in fact fought against both these temptations. While he opposed the Pelagian view that for him who is without personal sin, especially for innocent children, baptism is not a necessary prerequisite for salvation,[38] he equally

equality with God. See *Dialogus adversus Pelagianos*, Prologue 1, *PL* XXIII, 518, where he speaks not only of the Pelagians, but also of Cicero, Origen, Evagrius, etc.: quorum omnium ista sententia est posse ad perfectionem, et non dicam ad similitudinem, sed aequalitatem Dei, humanam virtutem et scientiam pervenire . . .; cf. also *Epist.* CXXXIII, *ad Ctesiphontem*, 1, *CSEL* LVI, 242; *In Jeremiam* II, 1 *CSEL* LIX, 74: . . . qui opinione virtutum cotidie corruunt in superbiam et Deo se similes arbitrantur, ut aequalitatem, quam impia Arrianorum heresis in Filio negat, cunctis hominibus tribuant. That Pelagius knew content and terminology of Greek assimilation doctrine, without having penetrated however the higher mystical meaning which it had attained, for instance, in Origen and Gregory of Nyssa can be seen from his letter to Demetrias. Cf. *Epist. ad Demetriadem* 2–8, *PL* XXX, 17 ff.: after having asserted man's ability to choose the good rather than the bad on the strength of his being created according to the image and likeness of God (*ibid.* 2, XXX, 18A f.), he states: Est enim, inquam, in animis nostris naturalis quaedam, ut ita dixerim, sanctitas, quae par velut in arce animi praesidens exercet mali bonique iudicium . . . (*ibid.* 4, XXX, 20B). In order to define the function of God's law in the ethical process of human nature's return from the darkness of sin to its original splendor, he uses the metaphors of the removal of rust and of filing out and polishing (*ibid.* 8, XXX, 24C), metaphors which the Greeks had applied in a more mystical sense to the purification of the soul (see above, pp. 92–93).

[37] It will suffice here to refer to the admirable pages in E. Gilson, *Introduction à l'étude de saint Augustin*, 3rd ed. (Etudes de philosophie médiévale XI, Paris, 1949) 204 ff.; see also the texts, quoted above, p. 159, nn. 19 f.

[38] Cf. Augustine, *De peccatorum meritis et remissione et de baptismo parvulorum* I, 30, 58, *CSEL* LX, 1, 57. Here Augustine objects to the Pelagians who interpreted John 3:5: . . . *nisi quis renatus fuerit ex aqua et Spiritu Sancto non potest introire in regnum Dei*, as follows: . . . ad hoc parvuli baptizandi sunt, ut sint etiam cum Christo in regno Dei . . ., quamvis

strongly objected to those who claimed that the baptized Christian is by necessity wholly a son of God for ever. In a text of *De peccatorum meritis et remissione*, for instance, which is very important for his conception of reform and its distinctness from baptismal regeneration, Augustine appeals to 2 Corinthians 4:16: ". . . though our outward man is corrupted, yet the inward man is renewed day by day" and shows that baptism must be supplemented by daily efforts of reform.[39]

et sine baptismo . . . salutem vitamque aeternam habituri sint, quoniam nullo peccati vinculo obstricti sunt. See also Augustine, *De gratia Christi et de peccato originali* II, 21, 24, *CSEL* XLII, 182 f., where after quoting Pelagius' statement: *Baptisma unum tenemus quod isdem sacramenti verbis in infantibus quibus etiam in maioribus dicimus esse celebrandum*, he makes the following objection: . . . tamquam infantibus remissio peccatorum verborum sonitu diceretur, non rerum ageretur effectu.

[39] *De peccatorum meritis et remissione* . . . II, 7, 9, *CSEL* LX 1, 79 ff.: Non enim advertunt eo quosque fieri filios Dei (cf. 1 John 3:9) quo esse incipiunt in novitate spiritus et renovari in interiore homine secundum imaginem eius qui creavit eos (cf. Col. 3:10). Non enim ex qua hora quisque baptizatur omnis vetus infirmitas eius absumitur, sed renovatio incipit a remissione omnium peccatorum et in quantum quisque spiritalia sapit qui iam sapit. Cetera vero in spe facta sunt, donec etiam in re fiant. . . . Nam in baptismo quamvis tota et plena fiat remissio peccatorum, tamen si continuo tota et plena etiam hominis in aeternam novitatem mutatio fieret . . ., si in ipso animo qui est homo interior perfecta in baptismo novitas fieret, non diceret apostolus: "Etsi exterior homo noster corrumpitur, sed interior renovatur de die in diem" (2 Cor. 4:16). Profecto enim qui de die in diem adhuc renovatur, nondum totus est renovatus. Et in quantum nondum est renovatus, in tantum adhuc in vetustate est. Proinde ex hoc quod adhuc in vetustate sunt, quamvis iam baptizati, ex hoc etiam adhuc sunt filii saeculi . . . apostolus explicat quid sit exui veterem hominem et indui novo . . . (cf. Eph. 4:22 ff.). Et hoc ut faciant iam baptizatos fidelesque adhortatur; quod adhuc monendi non essent si hoc in baptismo iam perfecte factum esset: et tamen factum est sicut et salvi facti sumus. Cf. E. J. Carney, O.S.F.S., *The Doctrine of St. Augustine on Sanctity* (Washington, D.C., 1945) 93, and the literature cited there. See also *De perfectione iustitiae hominis* XVIII, 39, *CSEL* XLII, 40 f.: . . . sine . . . infirmitate nondum sumus, donec illa renovatione quae fit de die in diem (cf. 2 Cor. 4:16)—quoniam secundum ipsam ex Deo nati sumus—infirmitas tota sanetur . . ., cuius reliquiis in homine interiore manentibus, quamvis de die in diem minuantur in proficientibus, "si dixerimus quia peccatum non habemus, nos ipsos seducimus . . ." (1 John 1:8). . . . Sed intellegendum arbitror quia renovatio perficienda videt et cognoscit, infirmitas vero absumenda nec videt nec cognoscit eum (that is to say, Christ). . . . [Homo] sanctificat enim se non per se ipsum, sed credendo in illum et invocando illum qui sanctificat sanctos suos, cuius sanctificationis perfectio, quae nunc proficit et crescit de die in diem, omnes infirmitatis reliquias ablatura est. Cf. also *Sermo* CCCLXVI (of doubtful authenticity), *PL* XXXIX, 1646 ff., where Ps. 22 is interpreted as *reformationis hominis mysterium continens*: it is referred to baptism and its effects: per aquam refectionis Christi coeperis esse idoneus. Augustine had expressed himself similarly already in his anti-Donatist *De baptismo* IV, 15, 22, *CSEL* LI, 248: Unde multi post baptismum proficientes, et maxime qui infantes vel baptizati sunt, quanto magis eorum intellectus serenatur et inluminatur, dum interior homo renovatur de

Such reassertion of the Pauline doctrine on the reformation of man[40] was, of course, not neglected by the Greek Fathers—one needs only refer to Origen.[41] Nevertheless, however important "practical" reform was to them, it was "overshadowed" completely by the luminous darkness of "theoria."[42]

St. Augustine established that balance between God's grace and

die in diem (cf. 2 Cor. 4:16), priores suas opiniones . . . abiciunt, nec tamen ideo non accepisse baptismum existimantur . . ., sed in eis et sacramenti integritas honoratur et mentis vanitas emendatur. . . . See also *Sermo* CLXIX, 15, 18 *PL* XXXVIII, 926, all the more significant, as it is directed against the Pelagians and at the same time interprets Phil. 3:13 in a sense very different from the *epectasis* idea of Gregory of Nyssa (cf. above, p. 105 and n. 87): Adhuc sequor, adhuc proficio, adhuc ambulo, adhuc in via sum, adhuc me extendo, nondum perveni. . . . Perfecti et non perfecti: perfecti viatores, nondum perfecti possessores. . . . Videtis quia viatores sumus. Dicitis: "Quid est ambulare?" Breviter dico: "Proficere," ne forte non intelligatis et pigrius ambuletis. Proficite, fratres mei, discutite vos semper sine dolo. . . . Semper tibi displiceat quod es, si vis pervenire ad id quod nondum es. . . . Si autem dixeris: "Sufficit," et peristi. Semper adde, semper ambula, semper profice. Noli in via remanere, noli retro redire, noli deviare. . . . See finally *Enchiridion* 64 (17), *PL* XL, 262 and *Sermo* CCCLI, 3, *PL* XXXIX, 1537 ff. (perhaps, not authentic), with regard to the necessity of postbaptismal penance (cf. below, pp. 303–315). Augustine's terminology is, however, somewhat fluctuating; so, for instance, he says in his unfinished *Exposition of Romans* 19, *PL* XXXV, 2102, that strictly speaking penance is not renewal (*renovatio*) but healing (*curare*): . . . quia renovatio in baptismo est, ubi quidem operatur poenitentia sed tanquam in fundamento. Cf. E. Dinkler, *Die Anthropologie Augustins* (Forschungen zur Kirchen-und Geistesgeschichte IV, Stuttgart, 1934) 127 ff., and especially 169 ff., about Augustine's conception of the Christian life as a struggle in which the remission of sin by baptism is only the beginning of further progress through divine grace; also O. Scheel, "Zu Augustins Anschauung von der Erlösung durch Christus," *Theologische Studien und Kritiken* LXXVII (1904) 401 ff., 491 ff.

[40] Cf. above, Part Two, Chapter II.

[41] Origen, *Commentar. in Epistulam ad Romanos* V, 8, *PG* XIV, 1042A ff.: . . . (to Col. 3: 9 ff.) neque enim putes quod innovatio vitae, quae dicitur semel facta, sufficiat; sed semper et quotidie, si dici potest, ipsa novitas innovanda est . . . (to 2 Cor. 4:16) sicut enim vetus semper veterascit et de die in diem vetustior efficitur, ita et novus hic semper innovatur et nunquam est quando non innovatio eius augescat. Intuere denique eos qui in fide proficiunt et quotidie in virtutibus enitescunt quomodo semper bonis operibus adiciunt meliora et honestis actibus honestiora conquirunt. . . . Et vide si non . . . huiusmodi hominem quotidie dixeris innovari, sicut econtrario . . . si quis vetus effici coeperit proficiet in peius et quotidie vetustior et semetipso deterior invenietur. In novitate ergo vitae ambulemus (cf. Rom. 6: 4) ostendentes nosmetipsos ei qui nos cum Christo suscitavit quotidie novos et, ut ita dixerim, pulchriores decorem vultus nostri in Christo tanquam in speculo colligentes et in ipso gloriam Domini speculantes in eandem imaginem transformemur (cf. 2 Cor. 3:18). . . .

[42] For *praxis* and *theoria* in their relation to the idea of reform cf. above, pp. 98 f., 103 f., and below, pp. 330 ff.

man's will, between mystery and ethos, which was to become the theological substratum of all Christian reform movements in the west for a thousand years. He did so by stressing the role of the divine reformer Christ over that of man the reformer and, on the other hand, by insisting on the necessity of continuous reform in human life. As will be seen presently he also held that the divine Creator anticipated divine reformation even in the very "lightning stroke" (ictus) of creation. On principle then Augustine overcame the Origenist remnants of Platonism's spiritualistic depreciation of creation and also its reverse, creature man's spiritual pride, manifest in Pelagianism, and a latent, though not inherent, danger in all mysticism.

2. CREATION, FORMATION, REFORMATION

Not only was reform for Augustine more than return to the creational integrity of Adam in Paradise, but creation itself, in so far as it was a process of formation, included a nontemporal act of conversion toward God to which all temporal historical reformation is related.

The very first day of creation in St. Augustine's interpretation of the first chapter of Genesis[1] already manifests the fundamental principle which he sees at work in the whole economy of salvation: creation itself is unthinkable without God's immediate recall of his creatures to Himself and their conversion toward Him. When God in the beginning created heaven and earth, they were not yet our heaven and

[1] The following analysis is based above all on the last two books of the Confessiones (written about the year 400) and on De Genesi ad litteram libri XII (401–415); these works contain the fullest and ripened expression of Augustine's thought on these matters. The fine study of Christopher J. O'Toole, C.S.C., The Philosophy of Creation in the Writings of St. Augustine (Catholic University of America Philosophical Studies LXXXI, Washington, D.C., 1944) analyzes Augustine's exegesis of Genesis 1, as found in the two works named and also in the two earlier books De Genesi contra Manichaeos and De Genesi ad litteram imperfectus liber and in his other writings. (In the following pages the title De Genesi ad litteram always refers to De Genesi ad litteram libri XII.) Cf. E. Gilson, Introduction à l'étude de saint Augustin, third ed. (Paris, 1949) 256 ff., A. C. Pegis, "The Mind of St. Augustine," Mediaeval Studies VI (1944) 34, F. Cayré, Initiation à la philosophie de saint Augustin (Paris, 1947) 176 ff., J. de Blic, S.J., "Le processus de la création d'après saint Augustin," Mélanges Cavallera 179 ff., J. Pépin, "Recherches sur les sens et les origines de l'expression caelum caeli dans le livre XII des Confessions de s. Augustin," Arch. Lat. M. AE. XXIII (1953) 185 ff.

our earth, but the realm of spirit (*caelum caeli*),[2] a spiritual matter, still inchoate and unformed, and the realm of matter in the ordinary sense of the term, physical matter, still without order and form, even to the point of invisibility (*terra invisibilis et incomposita*)[3]—the former understood as a world of pure spirit, as close to God as creatures can be, and ultimately to be identified by Augustine with the angels, the latter almost nothing, a condition of existence as far removed from God as anything that is at all can be.[4] But without any lapse of time, for time had not yet been created,[5] God recalled ([*creaturam*] *revocante ad se creatore*) both created spirit and brute matter to Himself by giving

[2] Ps. 113:16: caelum caeli Domino, terram autem dedit filiis hominum (quoted by Augustine in *Confessiones* XII, 2); cf. also Ps. 67:33 f.; Deut. 10:14.

[3] The Latin version of Gen. 1:1–2, quoted and used by Augustine in *Confessiones* XII f. and in *De Genesi ad litteram*, reads: In principio fecit Deus caelum et terram. Terra (autem) erat invisibilis et inconposita, et tenebrae erant super abyssum et spiritus tuus superferebatur super aquas (or *aquam*). This corresponds exactly to the Septuagint (ἡ δὲ γῆ ἦν ἀόρατος καὶ ἀκατασκεύαστος) and differs considerably from the Vulgate, the text of which has no relation to Augustine's interpretation.

[4] *Confessiones* XII, 7, 7–9, 9, Skutella 298 f.: Tu eras et aliud nihil unde fecisti caelum et terram, duo quaedam, unum prope te, alterum prope nihil. . . . Sed illud caelum caeli tibi, Domine; terra autem quam dedisti filiis hominum cernendam atque tangendam non erat talis qualem nunc cernimus et tangimus. Invisibilis enim erat et inconposita et abyssus erat super quam non erat lux. . . . Terra autem ipsa quam feceras informis materies erat quia invisibilis erat et inconposita et tenebrae super abyssum. . . . Nimirum enim caelum caeli, quod in principio fecisti, creatura est aliqua intellectualis, quamquam nequaquam tibi, Trinitati, coaeterna, particeps tamen aeternitatis tuae. . . . See also *De Genesi ad litteram* I, 1, *CSEL* XXVIII, 1, 3 ff. An explicit identification of spiritual matter (i.e., of the *caelum caeli* or "first" heaven of Gen. 1:1) with the angels is found, for instance, in *De Genesi ad litteram* II, 8, *CSEL* XXVIII, 1, 43 (cf. quotation, p. 179, n. 33, below); see also *De Genesi ad litteram liber imperfectus* 5, *CSEL* XXVIII, 1, 472. It may be that, in his interpretation of *caelum* and *terra* of Gen. 1:1, Augustine utilized the Manichaean dualistic conception of the universe and transformed it in a Christian way for his exegetical purpose; cf. *Confessiones* V, 10, 20, Skutella 92 f., where Augustine says that to the Manichaeans *terra* was a metaphor for the substance of evil; for the Christian Augustine the "first" earth is not evil, but it is chaotic and *prope nihil*. A further influence upon Augustine's cosmogony may have come from the concept of the invisible and formless "receptacle" (ὑποδοχή), the "mother" and "nurse" of all creation, of Plato's *Timaeus* 49–51. At any rate, J. Pépin, in his important study "*Caelum caeli*," quoted above, has pointed to possible Platonic, Neoplatonic, Philonian, and Origenian sources for Augustine's conception of a spiritual, but originally formless, *caelum caeli*. He has also shown that at the stage of the *Confessiones* this highest heaven was not yet identified by Augustine with the angelic realm, but rather with that of the ideas (in a Platonic sense), and that the later identification with the angels is connected with several other changes in Augustine's interpretation of the first verses of Genesis.

[5] See below, p. 181.

them form. If even the spiritual *caelum caeli* needed conversion to God in order to be truly formed, then all the more physical matter, nearly non-existent in its unformed state, had to be converted to God in order to assume form. And the creative act by which the initial recall and conversion were effected were the words "Let there be light" (*Fiat lux*).[6] They signify the role in creation of the divine Logos Christ, of the Word who is Light and through illumination forms the created light of the spirit and all other creatures, the Word through and in whom later also the great reformation of man was to come.[7]

Since for a Christian the spiritual heaven, the formless earth, and all the rest of the work of creation are made and formed out of nothing, Augustine does not here speak of reform. For unlike the Neoplatonists he did not believe that the world was an emanation from God; if he had shared this view, which implied a certain "estrangement" of God from Himself, he might have conceived also of the creational movement of turning to God as a return or reform. But within an act of *creatio ex nihilo* there can be no *reformatio* because there had been no *forma*, there can only be *formatio* of a still *informis creatura*; this *formatio* consists in *revocatio* to God of a creature which, when it was drawn out of nothingness, found itself outside of God and in *conversio* of that creature to Him.[8]

And yet, if one looks at Augustine's world view as a whole, this

---

[6] Gen. 1:3 (transl. R. Knox, *The Old Testament* I [New York, 1948] 1).

[7] *De Genesi ad litteram* I, 2 f., CSEL XXVIII, 1, 5 ff.: Et quomodo dixit Deus "Fiat lux" (Gen. 1:3)? Utrum temporaliter, an in Verbi aeternitate? . . . aeternum est quod ait Deus "Fiat lux". . . . Et quod est lux ipsa quae facta est? Utrum spiritale quid an corporale? Si enim spiritale, potest ipsa esse prima creatura . . . quae primo caelum appellata est, cum dictum est "in principio fecit Deus caelum et terram," ut quod dixit Deus "Fiat lux et facta est lux" eam revocante ad se creatore conversio eius facta atque inluminata intellegatur. . . . *Ibid.* I, 4, XXVIII, 1, 7 f.: An cum primum fiebat informitas materiae sive spiritalis sive corporalis, non erat dicendum "Dixit Deus: Fiat," quia formam Verbi . . . non imitatur inperfectio, cum . . . informitate quadam tendit ad nihilum, sed tunc imitatur Verbi formam . . . cum et ipsa pro sui generis conversione ad id quod vere ac semper est, id est, ad creatorem suae substantiae, formam capit et fit perfecta creatura? Ut in eo quod scriptura narrat "Dixit Deus: Fiat" intellegamus Dei dictum incorporeum in natura Verbi eius coaeterni revocantis ad se inperfectionem creaturae, ut non sit informis sed formetur secundum singula quae per ordinem exequitur. . . . See also *Confessiones* XIII, 2–5, Skutella 329 ff.

[8] Both the influence of Neoplatonism and Augustine's transformation of it are clearly visible here. See the account of the "*Selbsthypostasierung*" of the νοῦς and of the world soul through "progression" (πρόοδος) and "conversion" (ἐπιστροφή) according to Plotinus in

revocatio-conversio must be considered the archetype of all later *reformatio*. The Pauline concept of *reformatio-renovatio*, as was seen above,[9] means a new creation which is primarily an overcoming of sin and evil, a victory from which alone all further improvements can flow. But in Christianity sin and evil are only an absence of good;[10] they are in a sense the remnants in the created world of the precreational nothing. Reform therefore is a second turning to God from nothingness, starting with a new recall, a new conversion,[11] this time to the creational condition of formation, lifted up however to an even higher plane through regeneration in Christ, which became possible only through Incarnation and Redemption, and continued in a ceaseless process of reform, *de die in diem* (2 Cor. 4:16), until the ultimate return of all creation to God.[12]

E. Benz, *Marius Victorinus und die Entwicklung der abendländischen Willensmetaphysik* (Stuttgart, 1932) 210 ff.; cf. also R. Arnou, article "Platonisme des pères," *DThC* XII, 2 (Paris, 1935) 2355 ff. This ideology is even more fully developed in Proclus; cf. his *Elements of Theology*, ed. E. R. Dodds (Oxford, 1933). Cf. also Pépin, "*Caelum caeli*" 245 ff. Even though the Neoplatonists (as also Augustine) use the terminology of conversion and not of reform when speaking of the origin of the world, their ἐπιστροφή is neither the simple Platonic turning about of the soul (cf. Plato's *Republic* 518C ff.) nor the Augustinian *conversio*, but rather the return of the "engendered," i.e. the "emanated," to the "engendering," i.e. the principle of "emanation" (Plotinus, *Ennead* V, 1, 6, cf. Benz, *Marius Victorinus* 219). Neoplatonic ἐπιστροφή applies equally to inner-divine life and to the return and reformation of creation toward God—and this close link up was to remain characteristic of patristic thought wherever it is radically Platonist. See p. 96, n. 50, for Origen's linking of the generation of the Son to creation; for Marius Victorinus: his dependence on Plotinus, his influence on Augustine, and his relationship to Origen, see Benz, *Marius Victorinus*, also P. Henry, S.J., *Plotin et l'occident* (Louvain, 1934) 44 ff. and 94 ff. The undeniable influence of Neoplatonism upon St. Augustine and its importance for his conversion led P. Alfaric, *L'évolution intellectuelle de saint Augustin* (Paris, 1918) to the exaggerated thesis that in Cassiciacum Augustine was converted to Neoplatonism rather than to Christianity; for correction see the studies quoted below, n. 12.

[9] See Part Two, Chapter II.

[10] This was recognized by Augustine only after a long struggle; see especially *Confessiones* III, 7 and VII, 12.

[11] The terms *convertere* and *revocare* appear very often in the *Confessiones*, in relation to the reformation of man. For *revocare*, cf. *Confessiones* I, 14, 23, V, 12, 22, VI, 16, 26, VII, 6, 8, VIII, 4, 9, Skutella 18, 95, 122, 132, 159. See also *Confessiones* IV, 16, 31, Skutella 76: . . . quia . . . aversi sumus, perversi sumus. Revertamur . . ., ut non evertamur. . . .

[12] Ever since 386, a few months before his conversion, Augustine had begun to study and to discover for himself St. Paul; cf. *Confessiones* VII, 21, 27, Skutella 150. This discovery followed very shortly upon that of the Neoplatonists (cf. Henry, *Plotin* 63 ff., idem, *La vision d'Ostie* [Paris, 1938] 15 ff., W. Theiler, *Porphyrios und Augustin* [Halle, 1933], P. Courcelle,

In the last book of the *Confessiones*, which has been somewhat neglected by modern interpreters, Augustine himself establishes the connection between the *creatio-formatio* of the beginning and the *reformatio* of man to the image of God, a connection of capital importance for his ideology of reform.

For among us, too, in His Christ did God make "heaven" and "earth," namely those who are spiritual and those who are carnal in His Church. And our "earth," before it had received the form of doctrine, was "invisible and unordered," and we were covered by the darkness of ignorance. . . . But because your "spirit moved over the waters" (Gen. 1:2), your mercy did not abandon our misery, and you said: "Be light made" (Gen. 1:3). "Do penance: for the Kingdom of heaven is at hand" (Matthew 3:2). Do penance: Be light made.[13]

Les lettres grecques en occident. De Macrobe à Cassiodore, 2nd ed. [Bibliothèque des Ecoles Françaises d'Athènes et de Rome CLIX, Paris, 1948] 159 ff., J. J. O'Meara, *The Young Augustine* [London, New York, Toronto, 1954] 131 ff.) and upon the somewhat earlier hearing of St. Ambrose's sermons, which contained Christianized Neoplatonic as well as Greek patristic ideas (see P. Courcelle, *Recherches sur les Confessions de saint Augustin* [Paris, 1950] 93 ff., and cf. C. Boyer, S.J., *Christianisme et néo-platonisme dans la formation de saint Augustin*, 2nd ed. [Rome, 1953] 107 ff., O'Meara, 116 ff., and now G. A. McCool, S.J., "The Ambrosian Origin of St. Augustine's Theology of the Image of God in Man," *Theol. Stud.* XX (1959) 62 ff. Augustine, in 386, read books of the *Platonici* in translation by Marius Victorinus, at about the same time he heard with great emotion of Victorinus' conversion to Christianity some years earlier (*Confessiones* VIII, 2, 3 ff., Skutella 154 ff.). It is interesting in this connection that contrary to Augustine Victorinus interpreted the Pauline doctrine of *reformatio-renovatio* in the Greek patristic sense (see above, pp. 68–82) of "return to the beginning" (*Comment. in Epist. ad Ephes.* 1, 23, *PL* VIII, 1250C, cf. Benz *Marius Victorinus* 118 ff.); he also conceived of the Holy Spirit as the agent of this *reformatio* (cf. p. 82, n. 76), which, however, for him as for most of the Greek Fathers remained equivalent to a *regressus* (*De Trinitate hymnus* III, *PL* VIII, 1144A, cf. Benz, *Marius Victorinus* 131–134, and above, p. 82). Though Victorinus does not seem to owe much to the Greek Fathers, the structure of his doctrine is on the whole closer to theirs than Augustine's thought is to his. Concerning Victorinus' relationship to Greek patristic thought, Benz 422, has shown that he and Origenes developed Plotinian ideas independently from one another and differently; in particular, Victorinus does not make any use of the specifically Origenist *apocatastasis* ideology (incorrectly termed "recapitulation" ideology by Benz). Victorinus' conception that the soul, once alienated from God, must experience materiality, sensuality, sin, and evil in order to learn how to scorn them and thus gladly to return to God (see *Comment. in Epist. ad Ephes.* 1, 4, *PL* VIII, 1239B f. and 1241A f., also *Comment. in Epist. ad Galat.* 4, 19, *PL* VIII, 1184B, cf. Benz 124), is however very similar to the view of Gregory of Nyssa (cf. Gaïth, *Liberté* 137 ff.) whom Victorinus antedates.

[13] *Confessiones* XIII, 12, 13, Skutella 337: . . . quia et apud nos in Christo suo fecit Deus caelum et terram, spiritales et carnales ecclesiae suae. Et terra nostra ante quam acciperet formam doctrinae, invisibilis erat et incomposita, et ignorantiae tenebris tegebamur. . . .

Penance, conversion overcome formless darkness and thus correspond to the *Fiat lux* which formed primaeval matter.[14] They must be carried forward continuously through nonconformity with this world and through reform in newness of mind according to St. Paul (Rom. 12:2).[15] For, the course of Christian history is fulfillment of all earlier unfoldings of creation.[16] Just as the creation of the first "heaven" and first "earth," so every one of the subsequent works of creation is repeated, as it were, on a higher plane in the new dispensation: the division of the waters above and below the firmament in the election of souls, the solidity of the firmament in the authority of Holy Scripture, the congregation of the waters under the firmament in the conspiracy of the unbelievers, the emergence of our earth out of the sea in the zeal of the faithful, the splendor of the sidereal lights in the spiritual gifts of the saints, the life force of the animals in the ascetic strength of the human soul, and, finally, the creation of man according to the image and likeness of God in his reformation to the same image and likeness.[17]

It is very significant also that Augustine in accordance with the account of the Book of Genesis sees God's first creative act directed

---

Sed quia Spiritus tuus superferebatur super aquam (cf. Gen. 1:2), non reliquit miseriam nostram misericordia tua et dixisti: "Fiat lux" (Gen. 1:3). "Paenitentiam agite: appropinquavit enim regnum caelorum" (Matthew 3:2). Paenitentiam agite: Fiat lux.

[14] *Ibid.*, *loc. cit.:* . . . et displicuerunt nobis tenebrae nostrae et conversi sumus ad te et facta est lux.

[15] *Ibid.* XIII, 13, 14, Skutella 338: Adhuc et ille (i.e., St. Paul) . . . nondum se arbitratur conprehendisse et quae retro oblitus in ea quae ante sunt extenditur (cf. Phil. 3:12 ff.), et ingemescit gravatus et sitit anima eius ad Deum vivum . . . (cf. Ps. 41:2 f.) dicens: "Nolite conformari huic saeculo, sed reformamini in novitate mentis vestrae" (Rom. 12:2). . . .

[16] *Ibid.* XIII, 34, 49, Skutella 369: Ubi autem coepisti praedestinata temporaliter exequi, ut occulta manifestares et inconposita nostra conponeres. . . . For the temporal unfolding of created life in general see pp. 181 ff.

[17] *Ibid.* (continuation of text quoted in the immediately preceding note): . . . et iustificasti inpios et distinxisti eos ab iniquis, et solidasti auctoritatem libri tui inter superiores qui tibi dociles essent et inferiores qui eis subderentur, et congregasti societatem infidelium in unam conspirationem ut apparerent studia fidelium, ut tibi opera misericordiae parerent distribuentes etiam pauperibus terrenas facultates ad adquirenda caelestia. Et inde accendisti quaedam luminaria in firmamento verbum vitae habentes sanctos tuos et spiritalibus donis praelata sublimi auctoritate fulgentes . . ., et deinde fidelium animam vivam per affectus ordinatos continentiae vigore formasti, atque inde tibi soli mentem subditam . . . renovasti ad imaginem et similitudinem tuam. . . .

equally toward corporeal matter (*terra*) and toward the realm of pure spirit (*coelum*). Conversion and formation which give both the realm of the spirit and that of matter their true function in creation, must correspond furthermore to the order which is adequate to each kind of creature: *pro sui generis conversione . . . ad creatorem suae substantiae formam capit et fit perfecta creatura . . ., ut . . . formetur secundum singula quae per ordinem exequitur.*[18] It is not surprising then that for St. Augustine the aim of reformation, too, is not spiritualization pure and simple, but rather an order in which spirit and matter both have their place though that of spirit will always be the higher.

In St. Augustine's conception, the chain of formative and reformative principles and acts, which extends from the first to the last day of the world's history, could and can be broken only by sin, not by any other descent from a spiritual to a material condition. Yet, just as for the Greek Fathers so for Augustine the double account of man's creation in the Book of Genesis (1:26–28 and 2:7) presented a problem. He too believed that the man of Gen. 1:26, created according to the image and likeness of God, was essentially rational and spiritual.[19] What then is to be thought about the corporeal man of Gen. 2:7, who is shaped out of the slime of the earth, and what about human bisexuality which is already mentioned in Gen. 1:27 and then again in Gen. 2:22, when Eve is created? Some, Augustine says, believe that the body of man was made only *postea*, that is to say, after the six days of creation described in Gen. 1; but this is impossible because Gen. 1:27 already tells us: "male and female he created them," an obvious reference to the body.[20]

---

[18] Cf. *De Genesi ad litteram* I, 4, *CSEL* XXVIII, 1, 7 f., as quoted p. 169, n. 7.

[19] See, for instance, *De Genesi ad litteram* III, 20, *CSEL* XXVIII, 1, 86: . . . in eo factum hominem ad imaginem Dei in quo inrationalibus animantibus antecellit. Id autem est ipsa ratio vel mens vel intellegentia . . . (followed by quotation of Col. 3:10). See also *ibid.* VII, 22 and 24, XXVIII, 1, 220 and 223, where man's creation according to the image and likeness of God is called *secundum animam* or *in anima*; cf. below, p. 183, n. 43.

[20] *De Genesi ad litteram* III, 22, *CSEL* XXVIII, 1, 88 f.: Nonnulli autem etiam hoc suspicati sunt nunc interiorem hominem factum, corpus autem hominis postea, cum ait scriptura "Et finxit Deus hominem de limo terrae" (Gen. 2:7), ut quod dictum est "fecit" ad spiritum pertineat, quod autem "finxit" ad corpus. Nec adtendunt masculum et feminam nonnisi secundum corpus fieri potuisse. . . . Ac ne quisquam putaret solum spiritum hominis factum . . . , fecit illum, inquit, masculum et feminam . . . (Gen. 1:27), ut iam etiam corpus factum intellegatur. See also *ibid.* VI, 7, XXVIII, 1, 178, *De civitate Dei* XIV, 24, *Corp. Christ.*,

In order to understand the way in which Augustine solved this difficulty it is necessary to discuss more fully his interpretation of the biblical narration of creation in general, and in particular his famous theory of the *rationes seminales* or *causales*.[21] This theory serves Augustine in integrating the two creations of man related in Gen. 1 and 2, and, beyond that, forms an important part of his attempts to reconcile the simultaneity of creation with the six-day-work and with the post-creational development and history of the world.

Gregory of Nyssa had been the first to make a similar attempt. In his *Homilies on the Hexaemeron*, intended to supplement the *Homilies on the Hexaemeron* of his brother, St. Basil,[22] he did not take the six days of creation literally, but spoke of the sources (ἀφορμαί), causes (αἰτίαι), potencies (δυνάμεις), and of the seminal power (σπερματικὴ δύναμις), instituted by God in the first instantaneous creative impulse whence all the various works of the six-day-creation and their subsequent developments were to make their appearance according to an ordered and necessary temporal succession. This seems to be the earliest clear occurrence in hexaemeral literature of the concept of a "seminal power" or "reason" which Gregory and later Augustine could find in ancient philosophy.[23] As to Gregory's

---

Ser. Lat. XLVIII, 446 ff., where Augustine explains that the body's bisexuality led to irrational lust only after the fall. Cf. p. 157, n. 14, and below, p. 176, about the way in which Gregory of Nyssa identified, not the bisexual body as such, but actual sexuality and materiality with the χιτῶνες δερμάτινοι which Adam and Eve received from God after their sin of disobedience.

[21] The expression *seminales rationes* occurs in *De Genesi ad litteram* IX, 17, *CSEL* XXVIII, 1, 291, but terms such as *causales rationes* or *causae primordiales* are more frequently used. For the theory of the seminal reasons, see, in addition to the works mentioned p. 167, n. 1, H. Meyer, *Geschichte der Lehre von den Keimkräften von der Stoa bis zum Ausgang der Patristik nach den Quellen dargestellt* (Bonn, 1914), for Augustine pp. 122 ff., M. McKeough, O. Praem., *The Meaning of the Rationes Seminales in St. Augustine* (Diss., Faculty of Philosophy, Catholic University of America, Washington, D.C., 1926), and above all C. Boyer, S.J., "La théorie augustinienne des raisons séminales," in *Miscell. Agost.* II 795 ff.; also P. Galtier, S.J., "Saint Augustin et l'origine de l'homme," *Gregorianum* XI (1930) 5 ff., and R. Capdet, "Les raisons causales d'après saint Augustin," *Bulletin de littérature ecclésiastique* IV (1949).

[22] Cf. now E. Corsini, "Nouvelles perspectives sur le problème des sources de l'Hexaéméron de Grégoire de Nysse," *Stud. Patr.* I, 94 ff.

[23] See Gregory of Nyssa, *Explicatio apologetica . . . in Hexaemeron*, *PG* XLIV, 72B f.: . . . ἡ ἀρχὴ τῆς κοσμογονίας ὑποτίθεται ὅτι πάντων τῶν ὄντων τὰς ἀφορμὰς καὶ τὰς αἰτίας καὶ τὰς δυνάμεις συλλήβδην ὁ Θεὸς ἐν ἀκαρεῖ κατεβάλλετο καὶ ἐν τῇ πρώτῃ τοῦ θελήματος ὁρμῇ ἡ ἑκάστου τῶν ὄντων οὐσία συνέδραμεν. . . . Τῇ δὲ συγκαταβληθείσῃ δυνάμει τε καὶ σοφίᾳ πρὸς τὴν τελεί-

famous theory of man's "double creation," in a God-like mind and in an animate body,[24] it is easy to recognize the influence both of Philo and of Origen[25] who had somehow connected corporeality with the fall of the angels and of man, and in general with a lapse from original pure spirituality. Only that in this respect, too, Gregory modified Origen's extremely spiritualistic doctrine by pointing out that saving graces are attached to the fact that man was created as a spiritual-corporeal composite. God created man as a sexual-corporeal being, in foresight of the loss of his immortality through sin. The bisexual body is conceived of by Gregory as means for the perpetuation

ωσιν ἑκάστου τῶν μορίων τοῦ κόσμου εἱρμός τις ἀναγκαῖος κατά τινα τάξιν ἐπηκολούθησεν. . . . Ibid 77D: . . . τῇ μὲν δυνάμει τὰ πάντα ἦν ἐν πρώτῃ τοῦ Θεοῦ περὶ τὴν κτίσιν ὁρμῇ, οἰονεὶ σπερμα- τικῆς τινος δυνάμεως πρὸς τὴν τοῦ παντὸς γένεσιν καταβληθείσης, ἐνεργείᾳ δὲ τὰ καθ' ἕκαστον οὔπω ἦν. De hominis opificio 29, PG XLIV, 236A–240B: . . . ὥσπερ ἐν τῷ σίτῳ φαμὲν ἢ ἐν ἑτέρῳ τινὶ τῶν σπερμάτων ἅπαν ἐμπεριειλῆφθαι τῇ δυνάμει τὸ κατὰ τὸν στάχυν εἶδος, τὸν χόρτον . . . τὸν καρπὸν . . . καὶ οὐδὲν τούτων ἐν τῷ τῆς φύσεως λόγῳ προϋπάρχειν ἢ προγίνεσθαί φαμεν τῇ φύσει τοῦ σπέρματος, ἀλλὰ τάξει μέν τινι φυσικῇ· τὴν ἐγκειμένην τῷ σπέρματι δύναμιν φανεροῦσθαι . . . κατὰ τὸν αὐτὸν λόγον καὶ τὴν ἀνθρωπίνην σπόραν ὑπειλήφαμεν ἔχειν ἐν τῇ πρώτῃ τῆς συστάσεως ἀφορμῇ συνεσπαρμένην τὴν τῆς φύσεως δύναμιν. . . . Καὶ γὰρ καὶ τῶν καρπῶν τὰς ἐντερίωνας καὶ τὰς τῶν ῥίζων ἀποσπάδας οὐ νεκρωθείσας τῆς ἐγκειμένης τῇ φύσει ζωτικῆς δυνάμεως τῇ γῇ καταβάλλομεν. . . . Ὅπερ οὐχ οἷόν τε ἦν γινέσθαι μή τινος φυσικῆς δυνάμεως συνεντεθείσης. . . . Though Gregory does not seem to use the term λόγος σπερματικός itself, the way in which he combines the expressions δύναμις σπερματική and φύσεως λόγος would indicate that he was familiar with the concept of "seminal reasons." For Plotinus' λόγοι σπερματικοί and γεννητικοί cf. Ennead II, 3, 16 f. and Ennead IV, 4, 16; for Stoic λόγοι σπερματικοί cf. Preisigke, article "Logos (Psychologie, Metaphysik)," PW, RE XIII, 1, 1055 ff. For the related concept of δύναμις ζωτική (possibly Posidonian), which also occurs in Gregory's De hominis opificio 29 (see above), cf. p. 221, n. 28. Philo, De opificio mundi 13, 43 f., Cohn and Wendland I, 13 f., has the concept of οὐσίαι or λόγοι σπερματικοί, but only with reference to the emergence of fruits from seeds. For a more detailed discussion of the differences between Philo's and Gregory's interpretations of the Genesis account of creation, see my article "Anthropology." In general, cf. F. E. Robbins, The Hexaemeral Literature: A Study of the Greek and Latin Commentaries on Genesis (Chicago, 1912), and above all Meyer, Keimkräfte 7 ff. for the Stoics, 26 ff. for Philo, 55 ff. for Plotinus, 102 ff. for Origen, 108 ff. for Gregory of Nyssa, and also 80 ff. about Justin's altogether different conception of the λόγος σπερματικός as presence of the divine Logos in the world; see furthermore R. Leys, S.J., L'image de Dieu chez saint Grégoire de Nysse (Museum Lessianum, Sect. Théol. XLIX, Bruxelles, Paris, 1951) 82 ff.

[24] See Gregory of Nyssa, De hominis opificio 16, PG XLIV, 181B: Οὐκοῦν διπλῆ τίς ἐστιν ἡ τῆς φύσεως ἡμῶν κατασκευή.

[25] For Gregory's "double creation" doctrine, and especially for his view that man's creation in the image and likeness of God was creation of the πλήρωμα of the human race, cf. my article quoted above, n. 23, which also deals with Philo's conception of the stages of man's creation and with Origen's anticipation of Gregory's πλήρωμα doctrine.

of the human race through propagation until the day of the general resurrection and the ἀποκατάστασις πάντων.[26] Even the body, however, was at first spirit-like, as it will be again after its resurrection. Only after the original sin had actually been committed, did man assume his passible and passionate, coarsely corporeal condition. This fatal alteration Gregory, as already mentioned (above, p. 157, n. 14), saw allegorically expressed in Gen. 3:21 by the "tunics of skin" (χιτῶνες δερμάτινοι), those hides or furs of dead animals, in which God clothed Adam and Eve after their fall.[27]

[26] For Origen, cf. also above, pp. 71 ff., and for both Gregory and Origen, pp. 75 ff. For Gregory's theory concerning the creation of man's material body in foresight of the fall and concerning the beneficial effects of this corporeality, of sexuality, bodily death, and time, cf. p. 206; the principal texts are in De hominis opificio 16 ff., 22, PG XLIV, 177D ff.; cf. Gaïth, Liberté 54 and 172 ff.

[27] For all this, cf. my article "Anthropology," also J. Daniélou, "La résurrection des corps chez Grégoire de Nysse," Vigil. Christ. VII (1953) 154 ff. On the original spirit-likeness of man's body according to Gregory of Nyssa, see, for instance, De anima et resurrectione, PG XLVI, 108A; also De oratione dominica, orat. V, PG XLIV, 1184B, and In Cant. Cant., homil. XI, PG XLIV, 1005B, about the χιτῶνες or ἐνδύματα φωτοειδεῖς or λαμπρά, "resplendent vestments," "tunics of light," which man wore before he had to put on the "tunics of skin" (χιτῶνες δερμάτινοι) of Gen. 3:21; on the latter, see also Oratio catechetica 8, Srawley 43, ll. 5 ff., De anima et resurr., PG XLVI, 148C ff., De mortuis, PG XLVI, 521D. True, the creational body was bisexual, while the resurrectional body will be neither male nor female; but in Paradise sexuality was not yet operative and man's mode of propagation could have been a spiritual, an angelic one, see De hominis opificio 17, PG XLIV, 188 f.; similarly, Augustine, De civitate Dei XIV, 24 (see pp. 173 f., n. 20), who, however, insists that even before the fall man, though eminently rational, did not possess a spiritual body (cf. De civitate Dei XIII, 23, Corp. Christ., Ser Lat. XLVIII, 405 ff., Epist. CXLIII, 6, CSEL XLIV, 256). Both Gregory of Nyssa (Oratio catechetica 8, Srawley 43) and Augustine (Confessiones VII, 18, XIII, 15, 16, Skutella 147, 340, Enarr. in Ps. CIII, serm. I, 8, Corp. Christ., Ser. Lat. XL, 1479 f., Contra secundam Iuliani responsionem imperfectum opus IV, 37, PL XLV, 1357) can interpret the tunicae pelliceae of Gen. 3:21 as man's mortality, which was in fact the most usual patristic interpretation; yet, for Gregory the χιτῶνες δερμάτινοι signify more comprehensively the entire post-paradisiac condition of brute corporeality (cf. De anima et resurrectione, PG XLVI, 148C f., De mortuis, ibid. 521D–524D). On patristic exegesis of Gen. 3:21 and pagan parallels, see P. Wendland, "Das Gewand der Eitelkeit," Hermes LI (1916) 481 ff., J. Quasten, "A Pythagorean Idea in Jerome," Amer. Jour. Philol. LXIII (1942) 207 ff., idem, "Theodore of Mopsuestia on the Exorcism of the Cilicium," Harv. Theol. Rev. XXXV (1942) 209 ff., L. Spitzer, "Additional Note on 'Wool and Linen' in Jerome," Amer. Jour. Philol. LXIV (1943) 98 f., W. J. Burghardt, S.J., "Cyril of Alexandria on 'Wool and Linen,'" Traditio II (1944) 484 ff. On "garments of light" in and alongside patristic anthropology cf., for instance, Daniélou, Platonisme 57, G. P. Wetter, Phos (Skrifter . . . K. Humanistiska Vetenskaps-Samfundet i. Uppsala XVII, 1, 1915) 172 ff., A.-J. Festugière, O.P., La révélation d'Hermes Trismégiste III (Paris, 1953) 144 ff.

Contrary to Gregory of Nyssa, Augustine does not account for man's body by God's anticipation of Adam's sin. In his view the creation of the body is not in any sense connected with the fall.[28] Another difference between Augustine's and Gregory's exegesis of the first chapters of the Book of Genesis is found in the role allotted by Augustine to the angelic vision of the six-day-work, which will be touched upon presently. The principal similarity between Gregory's *Hexaemeron* and Augustine's interpretation of Genesis is the one already referred to, which concerns creation, before time, of seminal potencies, causes, or reasons. While this similarity does not prove an otherwise improbable dependence of Augustine on Gregory,[29] it does constitute an interesting partial anticipation of Augustine's thought by Gregory.

As in the Gregorian so in the Augustinian exegesis of the Genesis account of creation the work of the six days has aspects both of succession and of simultaneity, but this succession, though of a causal nature, is not temporal in the ordinary sense, for God is and acts in eternity not in time. Augustine emphasizes the simultaneity of creation and repeatedly quotes Ecclesiasticus 18:1: *Qui vivit in aeternum, creavit omnia simul.*[30] Certainly the creation of corporeal as well as of spiritual unformed matter could not result in the beginning of time. For time is dependent on movement; where there is no form, there,

---

[28] See Augustine's implicit criticism of such views in *De civitate Dei* XIV, 26, *Corp. Christ.*, *Ser. Lat.* XLVIII, 449 f., where he asserts that in sinless man propagation was or would have been both sexual and rational; similarly Thomas Aquinas, *Summa Theologica* I, 9. 98, a. 2, who even explicitly rejects, with reference to this Augustinian text, Gregory of Nyssa's linking of man's bisexual condition to God's foresight of his fall; cf. A. H. Armstrong, "Platonic Elements in St. Gregory of Nyssa's Doctrine of Man," *Dominican Studies* I (1948) 113 ff.

[29] There is no evidence that Augustine has used Gregory of Nyssa's works. See B. Altaner, "Augustinus, Gregor von Nazianz und Gregory von Nyssa," *Rev. bén.* LXI (1951) 62. Augustine did use the Latin translation of Basil's *Hexaemeron* by Eustathius, cf. Altaner, "Augustinus und Basilius der Grosse," *Rev. bén.* LX (1950) 17 ff., but Basil's work does not contain the specific ideas discussed here; see also Altaner, "Augustinus und Origenes," *Hist. Jb.* LXX (1951) 15 ff., especially 33 ff., and *idem*, "Augustins Methode der Quellenbenützung," *Sacr. Erud.* IV (1952) 5 ff.; Meyer, *Keimkräfte* 212 ff., refers to Marius Victorinus and to Cicero and Seneca as to probable transmitters to Augustine of the Neoplatonic and Stoic conceptions of "seminal reasons."

[30] See, for instance, *De Genesi ad litteram* IV, 33, V, 3 and 17, VI, 3 and 6, CSEL XXVIII, 1, 133, 141, 160, 173, 178.

Augustine says, movement and temporal change also cannot be, because there can be no transformation of one condition into another. As to the formation of spiritual and of corporeal matter, there is a great difference between these two divine acts. Through the divine command *Fiat lux*,[31] spiritual matter was instantaneously (*sine ullo lapsu*) recalled and converted to God and thus received a form which for ever transcends the vicissitudes of time.[32] This formed and timeless spiritual matter in Augustine's exegesis is the work of the first day, that is to say, the light created by the words *Fiat lux*. This first created light, which in fact is the first day itself, was identified by Augustine, from the time when he wrote his twelve book commentary *De Genesi ad litteram* (401–415), with the angels. The first day is not a temporal day, but the mode of angelic existence. It is quite otherwise with corporeal matter. It is formed by God in the mode of ordered succession which corresponds to the days from the second to the sixth in the Genesis narrative. These days, too, are not in themselves temporal, though they contain the causes of all temporal succession to come; in themselves these days constitute a fivefold repetition of the first "angelic" day. In other words, they signify the taking cognizance by the angels of the creation-formation of the other creatures.[33]

---

[31] Cf. above, p. 169, n. 7.

[32] For the timelessness of unformed matter, both spiritual and corporeal, and for the immediate turning of spiritual matter to God, whereby it transcends time, see *Confessiones* XII, 12, Skutella, 302 f.: . . . duo reperio quae fecisti carentia temporibus, cum tibi neutrum coaeternum sit: unum quod ita formatum est, ut sine ullo defectu contemplationis, sine ullo intervallo mutationis, quamvis mutabile, tamen non mutatum, aeternitate atque inconmutabilitate perfruatur; alterum quod ita informe erat ut ex qua forma in quam formam vel motionis vel stationis mutaretur, quo tempori subderetur, non haberet. See also *ibid.* XII, 9, Skutella 299 f.: . . . (spiritual matter) valde mutabilitatem suam prae dulcedine felicissimae contemplationis tuae cohibet et sine ullo lapsu ex quo facta est inhaerendo tibi excedit omnem volubilem vicissitudinem temporum. Ista vero informitas, terra invisibilis et inconposita, nec ipsa in diebus numerata est. Ubi enim nulla species, nullus ordo nec venit quicquam nec praeterit; et ubi hoc non fit, non sunt utique dies nec vicissitudo spatiorum temporalium. See, furthermore, *De Genesi ad litteram* V, 5, *CSEL* XXVIII, 1, 145: Factae itaque creaturae motibus coeperunt currere tempora: unde ante creaturam frustra tempora requiruntur quasi possint inveniri ante tempora tempora. Motus enim si nullus esset vel spiritalis vel corporalis creaturae . . ., nullum esset tempus omnino. . . .

[33] For the identity of formed spiritual matter with the realm of the angels, i.e., with first created light, and with the first day of creation and for the fact that every creature exists primarily in the word of God, secondarily in angelic knowledge, and thirdly in itself

The original *ictus condendi*,[34] the primitive stroke or moment of creation and formation, thus includes above all the entire work of the six days: the creation and formation-illumination of heaven and earth on the first day unfolds rather than proceeds on the following days of creation. God did not need days in order to create nor did "He who does not feel the labor . . . require a pause" (that is to say, the seventh day of rest) after having created.[35] But, creatures are somehow bound to succession. Once Augustine had identified the creation of the *caelum caeli* and its formation as *lux* with the realm of the angels, he found that even the most spiritual, the angelic creatures, if they want to know creation not only in its causes or ideas in the Word of God (*causae* or *rationes aeternae*), but also in its effects, that is to say, in each emerging creature, must know it in the order of succession. The first manner of knowing is a *cognitio diurna*, a day or noon vision. The cognition through effects is dimmer (*cognitio vespertina*), but the angels immediately refer it back to God, to a new morning as it were. These different kinds of angelic vision or knowledge Augustine saw symbolized in Gen. 1, by the days, evenings, and mornings of the six-day work, and in the morning of the seventh day which has no evening.[36]

see, for instance, *De Genesi ad litteram* II, 8, *CSEL* XXVIII, 1, 43: An . . . primo die quo lux facta est conditionem spiritalis et intellectualis creaturae lucis appellatione intimari— in qua natura intelleguntur omnes sancti angeli atque virtutes . . ., cetera vero, quae infra sunt, ita creantur ut prius fiant in cognitione rationalis creaturae ac deinde in genere suo. . . . Conditio vero caeli prius erat in Verbo Dei . . ., deinde facta est in creatura spiritali, hoc est in cognitione angelorum . . ., deinde quod caelum factum est, ut esset iam ipsa caeli creatura in genere proprio. Sic et discretio vel species aquarum atque terrarum, sic naturæ lignorum et herbarum, sic luminaria caeli, sic animantia orta ex aquis ac terra. While Augustine here puts his opinion in the form of a hypothesis, he is more definite in *De civitate Dei* XI, 9, *Corp. Christ.*, *Ser. Lat.* XLVIII, 328 ff.; cf. O'Toole, *Creation* 39 f., Pépin, "*Caelum caeli*" 213 f., 220 ff., 223 ff. See, furthermore, *De Genesi ad litteram* V, 5, *CSEL* XXVIII, 1, 146: In his vero quae iam ex informitate formata sunt . . ., primum factus est dies. Oportebat enim ut primatum creaturae obtineret illa natura quae creaturam per creatorem, non creatorem per creaturam posset agnoscere.

[34] See below, p. 183, n. 42.

[35] *De catechizandis rudibus* 17, 28, *PL* XL, 331: Poterat enim omnipotens et uno momento temporis omnia facere. Non autem laboraverat, ut requiesceret . . ., sed ut significaret quia post sex aetates mundi huius septima aetate tanquam septimo die requieturus est in sanctis suis, quia ipsi in illo requiescent . . . (cf. below, pp. 222 ff.). . . . Nam quod ad ipsum attinet, pausationem non quaerit, quia laborem non sentit.

[36] See *De Genesi ad litteram* IV, 24, *CSEL* XXVIII, 1, 123 f., a text in which the repetition of day, evening, and morning of the following day according to the Hexaemeron account of Gen. 1 is interpreted as angelic day, evening, and morning cognition: . . . sancti angeli

Augustine has only a first and very slight adumbration of the scholastic distinction between *aevum* (*aeviternitas*) and *aeternitas* and does not yet apply the term *aevum* to the angelic mode of life.[37] Yet, his thought on the angels anticipates scholastic angelology: angels are not coeternal with God, since they are created by Him, but stand halfway between God's eternity and man's temporality. Ever since the defection of the rebellious angels, the angels of light adhere to God without change, but as creatures they are, nevertheless, changeable and, therefore, must for ever refer their existence and knowledge back to the eternal morning and noonday of God, the uncreated Light of His Word.[38]

. . . procul dubio universam creaturam . . . in ipso Verbo Dei prius noverunt, in quo sunt omnium, etiam quae temporaliter facta sunt, aeternae rationes . . ., ac deinde in ipsa creatura . . . eamque (i.e., cognitionem) referentes ad illius laudem in cuius incommutabili veritate rationes . . . principaliter vident. Ibi ergo tamquam per diem . . ., hic autem tamquam per vesperam, sed continuo fit mane, quod in omnibus sex diebus animadverti potest, quia non remanet angelica scientia in eo quod creatum est (cf. also *De civitate Dei* XI, 29, *Corp. Christ., Ser. Lat.* LXVIII, 349: . . . angeli . . . creaturam melius . . . in sapientia Dei . . . quam in ea ipsa sciunt, ac per hoc et se ipsos ibi melius quam in se ipsis. . . . Ibi ergo tamquam in diurna cognitione, in se ipsis autem tamquam in vespertina . . .); see, furthermore, *De Genesi ad litteram* IV, 32, *CSEL* XXVIII, 1, 129, where the angelic mind is said to know *simul omnia . . . nec ideo tamen sine ordine quo adparet conexio praecedentium sequentiumque causarum.* See, finally, *ibid.* IV, 26, XXVIII, 1, 125: Huius ergo diei, cuius et vespera et mane secundum supra dictam rationem accipi potest, sexta repetitione consummata est universa creatura . . . unde inciperet septimus, vesperam non habiturus, quia Dei requies non est creatura. . . . For the *rationes aeternae*, christianized Platonic ideas, see also *De diversis quaestionibus LXXXIII*, quaest. 46: *De ideis* 2, *PL* XL, 30, where they are placed in the mind of God. For the transformation of the Platonic ideas from independent entities into thoughts of God, see my article, "Image" 7 and 23, n. 23, with bibliography, in addition R. M. Jones, "Ideas as the Thoughts of God," *Class. Philol.* XXI (1926), and above all H. A. Wolfson, *The Philosophy of the Church Fathers* I (Cambridge, Mass., 1956) 257 ff.

[37] See Excursus III.

[38] See *De civitate Dei* XII, 16, *Corp. Christ., Ser. Lat.* XLVIII, 371 f.: Sicut ergo dicimus creatum tempus, cum ideo semper fuisse dicatur, quia omni tempore tempus fuit: ita non est consequens ut, si semper fuerunt angeli, ideo non sint creati, ut propterea semper fuisse dicantur, quia omni tempore fuerunt, et propterea omni tempore fuerunt, quia nullo modo sine his ipsa tempora esse potuerunt. Ubi enim nulla creatura est, cuius mutabilibus motibus tempora peragantur, tempora omnino esse non possunt; ac per hoc, etsi semper fuerunt, creati sunt nec, si semper fuerunt, ideo creatori coaeterni sunt. Ille enim semper fuit aeternitate inmutabili; isti autem facti sunt; sed ideo semper fuisse dicuntur, quia omni tempore fuerunt, sine quibus tempora nullo modo esse potuerunt; tempus autem, quoniam mutabilitate transcurrit, aeternitate inmutabili non potest esse coaeternum. Ac per hoc, etiamsi inmortalitas angelorum non transit in tempore nec praeterita est, quasi iam

This doctrine makes it possible for St. Augustine to "locate" the creational order of succession, which for God is no succession at all and on the other hand transcends man's temporal mode of knowledge, in the angelic mind. It will be seen later that "human" time, though objectively related to change and movement, would not exist in St. Augustine's opinion without the subjectivity of man's mind. Similarly, "hexaemeral" succession according to Augustine exists as quasi-temporal succession in the minds of the angels, who are only quasi-eternal.

While transition from eternity to time thus begins with the angels, that is to say, with the first day, time in the strict sense begins with the completion of instantaneous and simultaneous though six-partite creation.

There is a definite "cut," therefore, in Augustine's exegesis between the "Hexaemeron" and those things which, though owing their existence to the Creator, were to make their actual appearance not during, but only after, the six days of the Genesis account. Such are all living bodies; according to Augustine they were created at first only in their seminal reasons, and these *rationes seminales* constitute the *ad extra* aspect, so to speak, of their *rationes aeternae*, which are in the Word of God.[39] Augustine applies the principle of the unfolding of *rationes seminales* not to creation as a whole, as Gregory of Nyssa

---

non sit, nec futura, quasi nondum sit: tamen eorum motus, quibus tempora peraguntur, ex futuro in praeteritum transeunt et ideo creatori, in cuius motu dicendum non est vel fuisse, quod iam non sit, vel futurum esse, quod nondum sit, coaeterni esse non possunt. See also *Confessiones* XII, 11, 12, Skutella 301: . . . nec illa creatura tibi coaeterna est, cuius voluptas tu solus es, teque perseverantissima castitate hauriens mutabilitatem suam nusquam et numquam exerit, et te sibi semper presente, ad quem toto affectu se tenet . . ., nulla vice variatur nec in tempora ulla distenditur . . . ; *ibid*. XII, 12, 15, Skutella 302: . . . quamvis mutabile, tamen non mutatum . . . ; *ibid*. XII, 15, 21, Skutella 307: . . . inest ei tamen ipsa mutabilitas, unde tenebresceret et frigesceret, nisi amore grandi tibi cohaerens tamquam semper meridies luceret et ferveret ex te. Cf. Pépin, "*Caelum caeli*" 190; but see above, p. 168, n. 4, for Pépin's demonstration that in the *Confessiones* the spiritual creatures of the *caelum caeli* are not yet identified with the angels. On the other hand, I cannot follow Pépin 196, when he asserts that the quasi-eternity of the *caelum caeli* of *Confessiones* XII is replaced by real temporality of the angels in *De civitate Dei* XII; in my opinion Augustine envisaged a half-way house between eternity and time in both works. See also Excursus III.

[39] For the *rationes aeternae* see above, pp. 180 f., n. 36; for literature on the *rationes seminales*, cf. above, p. 174, n. 21.

had done, but only to the living among material creatures; his use of
the seed metaphor is thus less radically metaphorical than Gregory's
and also than that of Plotinus and the Stoics. Augustine's theory of the
merely potential, "seminal," creation of plants and animals is founded
largely upon Gen. 2:5 and Gen. 2:19 (in the old Latin version, used
by him).[40] While his interpretation especially of the second of these
scriptural passages is, perhaps, somewhat forced, he could indeed
read in Gen. 2:5 that God had made "every plant of the field before
it sprang up in the earth and every herb of the ground before it grew."
It is true that this last mentioned sentence hardly does justice to
the Hebrew original,[41] but Augustine on the strength of his Latin
translation was certainly of the opinion that not only individual plants
and animals but also all their various species had made their actual
visible appearance only after the simultaneity of the "Hexaemeron,"
that is to say, within temporal succession, and it is only natural that

[40] For the initial seminal or causal creation of plants according to St. Augustine, see *De
Genesi ad litteram*, V, 1 ff., *CSEL* XXVIII, 1,137 ff., especially V, 4, XXVIII, 1, 144: Causaliter
ergo tunc (refers to Gen. 1:11 f. and 2:5) dictum est produxisse terram herbam et lignum,
id est producendi accepisse virtutem. In ea quippe iam tamquam in radicibus, ut ita dixerim,
temporum facta erant quae per tempora futura erant . . . ; also V, 5, XXVIII, 1, 146:
Tertio [die, cf. Gen. 1:11] species maris et terrae, atque in terra potentialiter, ut ita dicam,
natura herbarum atque lignorum. Sic enim terra ad Dei verbum ea produxit, antequam
exorta essent (cf. Gen. 2:5), accipiens omnes numeros eorum, quos per tempora exereret
secundum suum genus. For the "seminal" creation of animals, see *ibid*. V, 5, XXVIII, 1,
146 f.: . . . aquarum natura . . . produxit . . . natatilia et volatilia (cf. Gen. 1:20 ff.),
et haec potentialiter in numeris qui per congruos temporum motus exererentur . . . ,
terrestria similiter animalia (cf. Gen. 1:24 f.) tamquam ex ultimo elemento mundi ultima
nihilominus potentialiter, quorum numeros tempus postea visibiliter explicaret; also *ibid*.
VI, 5, XXVIII, 1, 175: Non itaque hic diceretur: "Et finxit Deus adhuc de terra omnes
bestias agri et omnia volatilia caeli" (Gen. 2:19 [*Vetus Latina*]), nisi quia iam terra pro-
duxerat omnes bestias agri sexto die et aqua omnia volatilia caeli quinto die. Aliter ergo
tunc, id est potentialiter atque causaliter, sicut illi operi conpetebat, quo creavit omnia
simul . . . , aliter autem nunc, sicut ea videmus, quae per temporalia spatia creat, sicut
usque nunc operatur. Here Augustine's argument hinges somewhat artificially on the *adhuc*
of the *Vetus Latina*. From the merely exegetical point of view, Augustine's interpretation
of Gen. 2:5 is likewise not the only possible one; cf. Boyer, "Raisons séminales"
799.

[41] See, for instance, the modern translation of Gen. 2:5 by R. A. Knox, *The Old
Testament* I (New York, 1948) 2: "But no woodland shrub had yet grown, no wild plant
yet sprung up. . . ." See also G. v. Rad, *Das erste Buch Mose, Genesis Kapitel* 1–12, 9 (Göttingen, 1950) 58, J. Chaine, *Le Livre de la Genèse* (Lectio Divina III, Paris, 1951) 31, B. Vawter,
C.M., *A Path through Genesis* (New York, 1955) 50; cf. Boyer, "Raisons séminales," 799,
and below Excursus IV, 4.

he extended this view also to the body of man, formed by God from earth according to Gen. 2:7. As everything else, so the body of man was created by God in the timeless *ictus condendi*,[42] but contrary to man's spiritual part, which was created actually within the six-day-work in God's image and likeness (Gen. 1:26), his body was created then only in its seminal reason and was to make its actual appearance, which corresponds to its formation from earth (Gen. 2:7), only in time.[43] Yet, to repeat it, there is no indication that Augustine considered the seminal reason of Adam's body as created only in foresight of the fall or the human body itself as a necessary evil; the intention of his exegesis seems to be that of integrating the narratives of man's creation in Gen. 1:26 f. and in Gen. 2:7, of harmonizing rather than of depreciating man's "double creation" in spirit and body. In Augustine's beautifully unified vision of all creation the sixfold unfolding of the first day in the quasi-eternal angelic mind blends with the evolution of the seminal reasons of the living creatures which are

[42] This beautiful expression is used, without special reference to man, but with regard to creation in general in De Genesi ad litteram IV, 33, CSEL XXVIII, 1, 132: Quapropter quam facilis ei efficacissimus motus est, tam facile condidit omnia . . ., ut hoc, quod nunc videmus temporalibus intervallis ea moveri ad peragenda quae suo cuique generi competunt, ex illis rationibus insitis veniat, quas tanquam seminaliter sparsit Deus in ictu condendi, cum "dixit et facta sunt, mandavit et creata sunt" (Ps. 32:9). The phrase in ictu condendi is no doubt derived from in ictu temporis, which occurs, for instance, in Aulus Gellius, Noctes Atticae 14, 1, 27, and is used also by Augustine (Epist. CXXXVII, 2, 8, CSEL XLIV, 106). Similarly, Ambrose, Hexameron III, 11, 47, CSEL XXXII, 1, 90 f.: Hoc enim in singulis privilegium natura tenuit in reliquum, quod sub ictu mundi surgentis accepit.

[43] See De Genesi ad litteram VI, 3, CSEL XXVIII, 1, 173: . . . non est dubium hoc quod homo de limo terrae fictus est eique formata uxor ex latere iam non ad conditionem qua simul omnia facta sint pertinere . . ., sed ad eam operationem quae fit iam per volumina saeculorum qua usque nunc operatur . . .; ibid. 5, XXVIII, 1, 176: Aliter ergo tunc ambo et nunc aliter ambo: tunc scilicet secundum potentiam per Verbum Dei tamquam seminaliter mundo inditam cum creavit omnia simul (Ecclesiasticus 18:1) . . ., ex quibus omnia suis quaeque temporibus iam per saeculorum ordinem fierent; nunc autem secundum operationem praebendam temporibus qua usque nunc operatur, et oportebat iam suo tempore fieri Adam de limo terrae eiusque mulierem ex viri latere. For Augustine's view that the creation of the soul, i.e., of man in his image-likeness to God (Gen. 1:26), probably took place actually, not only seminally, already in the first timeless ictus condendi see De Genesi ad litteram VII, 24, XXVIII, 1, 222 f.: Illud ergo videamus utrum forsitan verum esse possit, quod certe humanae opinioni tolerabilius mihi videtur, Deum in illis primis operibus, quae simul omnia creavit, animam etiam humanam creasse, quam suo tempore membris ex limo formati corporis inspiraret, cuius corporis in illis simul conditis rebus rationem creasse causaliter. . . . Nam neque illud quod dictum est "ad imaginem suam" nisi in anima, neque illud quod dictum est "masculum et feminam" nisi in corpore recte intelligimus.

below the angels.[44] Creation was from its very start also formation which took place through the conversion of both spiritual and material creatures to God. In the realm of living, but subangelic, creatures this formation was to be developed in time through the actualization of *rationes seminales* such as that of Adam's body; the reformation of man, therefore, was not to be an undoing as it were of bodily creation but rather a continuation of creation in its entirety. For Augustine that reform of the inner man which was made possible by Incarnation and Redemption was not a return only to the spiritual aspect of creation but the completion and elevation of a spiritual-corporeal compound.

It can be understood from these premises why and how in the doctrine of St. Augustine the forms of things constitute a sort of vindication of the sensible material aspects of the created world and can help in converting man, in reforming him toward God. When man becomes involved in sensible and sensual things, he can be led beyond them by their aesthetic and intelligible forms.[45] This, in fact, happened

Credatur ergo, si nulla scripturarum auctoritas seu veritatis ratio contradicit, hominem ita factum sexto die ut corporis quidem humani ratio causalis in elementis mundi, anima vero iam ipsa crearetur, sicut primitus conditus est dies, et creata lateret in operibus Dei, donec eam suo tempore sufflando, hoc est inspirando (cf. Gen. 2 : 7), formato ex limo corpori insereret. For Augustine's uncertainties concerning the original relation between soul and body and the origin of succeeding souls see, for instance, Gilson, *Augustin* 272 ff., and O'Toole, *Creation* 87 ff., 92 ff. For contacts between Augustine's doctrine of the *rationes seminales* and modern theories of evolution see Excursus IV, 4.

[44] See especially *De Genesi ad litteram* V, 5, *CSEL* XXVIII, 1, 146: In his vero, quae iam ex informitate formata sunt evidentiusque appellantur creata vel facta vel condita, primum factus est dies: oportebat enim, ut primatum creaturae obtineret illa natura, quae creaturam per creatorem, non creatorem per creaturam posset agnoscere. This *dies*, this *natura*, is identical with the realm of the angels (see above, pp. 168, 180 f.). The text goes on to characterize briefly the following days of the "Hexaemeron"—see above, pp. 181 ff., for the creation of plants and animals in their *rationes seminales* on the third, fifth and sixth days—and then resumes (XXVIII, 1, 147): Hunc omnem ordinem creaturae ordinatae dies ille (i.e., the angelic mind) cognovit; et per hanc cognitionem sexies quodammodo praesentatus tamquam sex dies exhibuit. . . .

[45] See *De libero arbitrio* II, 163, *CSEL* LXXIV, 77: Quoquo enim te verteris, vestigiis quibusdam, quae operibus suis inpressit, loquitur tibi et te in exteriora relabentem ipsis exteriorum formis intro revocat, ut, quidquid te delectat in corpore et per corporeos inlicit sensus, videas esse numerosum et quaeras unde sit et in te ipsum redeas . . .; and, above all, *ibid*. II, 167, *CSEL* LXXIV, 78: Transcende . . . ut numerum sempiternum videas; iam tibi sapientia de ipsa interiore sede fulgebit et de ipso secretario veritatis, quae si adhuc languidiorem aspectum tuum reverberat, refer oculum mentis in illam viam ubi ostendebat hilariter. Memento sane distulisse te visionem quam fortior saniorque repetas. Note the word *revocare* which is used also in connection with creation-formation (see

in the life of St. Augustine himself, as almost every page of his *Confessions* demonstrates.[46]

St. Augustine's views on these matters were of momentous importance for the history of reform in the west. They were an essential influence within an ideological trend which maintained the supremacy of the spiritual and, nevertheless, evinced sufficient interest in the material world to allow for the gradual emergence and the frequent repetition of attempts at including ever larger areas of human terrestrial life in the idea and reality of reform. Other factors played their role in this process, but it would not be difficult to demonstrate that the Augustinian ideological impulse here described had abiding and recurrent strength. It was certainly not to a small part thanks to it that by the end of the Middle Ages the west had achieved a considerably greater measure of integration between individual and supraindividual reform than the Christian east.

Augustine's version of the patristic doctrine of the divine image in man also played its role in this process—inseparably bound up as it is with his conception of memory as the soul's consciousness of itself, of the world, and of God.

3. THE IMAGE OF GOD IN MAN

Everything in the universe has according to St. Augustine some likeness to God. There are vestiges of Him in every part of inorganic nature, to an even higher degree in organic and animate creatures,[1] and finally there is the divine resemblance in man.

---

above, p. 168), and observe the function of created forms and numbers as "relays" on the road to the absolute; cf. pp. 212 ff. and see this page on the Augustinian doctrine of the *vestigia Dei*, also p. 214, n. 3, where the text from *De libero arbitrio* II, 163 ff., is quoted more fully.

[46] For the all-important antithesis of *forma-reformatio* and *deformitas* in the *Confessiones*, see, for instance, VII, 8, 12, Skutella 136 f.: . . . et placuit in conspectu tuo reformare deformia mea . . .; IX, 6, 14, Skutella 190: Munera tua tibi confiteor, Domine Deus meus, creator omnium, et multum potens formare (variant: reformare) nostra deformia . . .; X, 27, 38 Skutella 237: . . . et in ista formosa quae fecisti deformis inruebam; XI, 30, 40, Skutella 292: Et stabo atque solidabor in te, in forma mea, veritate tua . . .; XII, 16, 23, Skutella 309: . . . et non avertar donec . . . colligas totum quod sum a dispersione et deformitate hac et conformes atque confirmes in aeternum, Deus meus, misericordia mea (cf. Ps. 58:18).

[1] For Augustine's doctrine of the *vestigia Dei* see *De Trinitate* XI, 1, 1, *PL* XLII, 985; *De libero arbitrio* II, 163, *CSEL*, LXXIV, 77; cf. Gilson, *Augustin* 282 f., also *idem, La*

Nevertheless it must be observed that for St. Augustine similarity is far from being the most essential characteristic of *man's* image relation to God; the scriptural concept of "likeness" has for him a lower rank than that of "image"—and this has a bearing on his conception of reform and its difference from Greek Christian reform ideology.

St. Augustine's clearest definition of the biblical terms of "image" (*imago*) and "likeness" (*similitudo*) is to be found in his *Questions on the Heptateuch* and can be held together with questions 51 and 74 of his book *On Diverse Questions*. We read that where there is an image there is also similitude, but not vice versa. In order to become an image, similitude must originate from that which it resembles; the image relationship requires that the image is somehow produced or begotten by that which is reproduced in it—as the reflection in a mirror by the object which is reflected, the portrait by its model, a son by his father, Christ by God. Some people, says St. Augustine, referring, perhaps, to Origen and in any case to Greek patristic tradition, have held that *similitudo* is more than *imago*, that it is reserved for that man who will be reformed by the grace of Christ. But Augustine says expressly that he does not share this view.[2] He does admit of course

---

philosophie de saint Bonaventure (Paris, 1924) 386 f. A secularized version of this conception can still be found in Shakespeare's famous verses in *As You Like It*, II, 1:

    . . . tongues in trees, books in the running brooks
    Sermons in stones, and good in every thing.

[2] *Quaestiones in Heptateuchum* V, 4 (to Deut. 4:16), *CSEL* XXVIII, 3, 371 f.: Quid intersit inter similitudinem et imaginem, quaeri solet. Sed hic non video quid interesse voluerit, nisi . . . similitudinem dixerit, si . . . fiat statua vel simulacrum habens effigiem humanam, non tamen alicuius hominis exprimantur liniamenta . . .: hanc enim imaginem dici nemo dubitaverit (this evidently means that only a "true likeness" is an "image," whereas an effigy which shows no resemblance with its model is a mere "similitude"); secundum quam distinctionem omnis imago etiam similitudo est, non omnis similitudo etiam imago est. Following a new line of thought, Augustine continues: Unde si gemini inter se similes sint, similitudo dici potest . . ., non imago. Si autem patri filius similis sit, etiam imago recte dicitur, ut sit pater prototypus unde illa imago expressa videatur, quarum aliae sunt eiusdem substantiae sicut filius, aliae non eiusdem sicut pictura. Unde illud quod in Genesi scriptum est "Fecit Deus hominem ad imaginem Dei" (Gen. 1:27), manifestum est ita dictum ut non eiusdem substantiae sit imago quae facta est: si enim eiusdem esset, non facta sed genita diceretur. Sed quod non addit "et similitudinem," cum superius (Gen. 1:26) dictum esset "Faciamus hominem ad imaginem et similitudinem nostram," quibusdam visum est similitudinem aliquid amplius esse quam imaginem, quod homini reformando per Christi gratiam postea servaretur. Miror autem si non propterea postea imaginem solam voluit commemorare, quia, ubi imago, continuo et similitudo est.

that there are degrees of similarity between an image and its prototype
or original. This is especially true in the case of the image relation
between God and man: it is part of the reformation of that image that
it become more and more similar to God.[3] But he does not hold with
some of the Greek Fathers (for instance, Clement and Origen) that
likeness to God was given to man only potentially in creation to be
perfected later;[4] on the contrary, the creational image of God in man
included full likeness.[5]

If equality, the perfection of similarity, is considered then the concepts of image and likeness overlap as Augustine takes great pains to
demonstrate.[6] In a certain sense, as just noted, similitude can be a

[3] See *De civitate Dei* XI, 26, *Corp. Christ.*, *Ser. Lat.* XLVIII, 345: Et nos quidem in nobis
tametsi non aequalem, immo valde longeque distantem neque coaeternam et . . . non
eiusdem substantiae cuius Deus est, tamen qua Deo nihil sit in rebus ab eo factis natura
propinquius, imaginem Dei, hoc est illius summae Trinitatis, agnoscimus, adhuc reformatione
perficiendam, ut sit etiam similitudine proxima. The emphasis here seems to be on *proxima*
rather than on *similitudine*, and, though this is here not especially stated, the *imago* no doubt
already contains the *similitudo* (see end of preceding note). Augustine also knows the
Irenaean conception (cf. above, p. 84) that Christ, by the very fact of becoming similar
to us, *reformat nos ad similitudinem Dei*; see *Sermo* CXCIV, 3, *PL* XXXVIII, 1016.

[4] For Clement and Origen cf. above, pp. 85-88. Augustine does not mention anyone
in particular. He may have had in mind Greek patristic views, perhaps also Paulinus of
Nola; cf. the latter's *Epist.* XXIV, 9, *CSEL* XXIX, 209.

[5] See the end of the text, quoted p. 186, n. 2. As was seen above, pp. 90 ff., for Gregory
of Nyssa, too, image and likeness were both in the possession of man from the beginning;
yet for him and for the Greek Fathers in general the image relation was important chiefly
because it contains the superior relation of similitude, whereas for Augustine that *similitudo*
which is not at the same time *imago*, is definitely on a lower plane; see, for instance, the
beginning of the text, quoted p. 186, n. 2, and cf. below, n. 6.

[6] For the following see *De diversis quaestionibus* LXXXIII, *quaestio* LXXIV (to Col. 1:14 f.),
PL XL, 85 f.: Imago et aequalitas et similitudo distinguendae sunt. Quia ubi imago, continuo
similitudo, non continuo aequalitas; ubi aequalitas, continuo similitudo, non continuo
imago; ubi similitudo, non continuo imago, non continuo aequalitas. Ubi imago, continuo
similitudo, non continuo aequalitas: ut in speculo est imago hominis, quia de illo expressa
est, est etiam necessario similitudo, non tamen aequalitas . . . (with this relative depreciation
of the similarity of the mirror image to its model compare the high evaluation of the mirror
relationship of the human soul to God in Gregory of Nyssa, above, pp. 96 f.). Ubi aequalitas,
continuo similitudo, non continuo imago: velut in duobus ovis paribus . . ., imago . . .
non est, quia neutrum de altero expressum est. Ubi similitudo, non continuo imago, non
continuo aequalitas: omne quippe ovum omni ovo . . . simile est . . . nec imago tamen eius est,
quia de illo expressum non est, nec aequale. . . . Sed ubi dicitur "non continuo," utique
intelligitur quia esse aliquando potest. . . . The main example for this possibility: *In Deo
autem . . . [Filius] non solum . . . imago eius, quia de illo est, et similitudo, quia imago, sed etiam
aequalitas. . . .*

wider concept than image. Two eggs may be alike and even equal without one being an image of the other. In other respects the image concept is wider than that of likeness. An image can range all the way from complete equality with its prototype, as in the Son of God as Image of God the Father,[7] to disastrous though remediable dissimilitude, as resulted for the image of God in man from original sin.[8] A truly similar image in any case has higher rank than mere likeness. In particular, while a certain resemblance to God can be seen even in the purely corporeal world—this is what Augustine calls the vestigia Dei[9] —only man has an image relation to God through and in his intellect, his rational soul.[10] This can never be completely lost in spite of original

[7] Augustine, as many other Fathers, points to the scriptural distinction between Christ, who is the image of God, and man, who is usually only said to be made and reformed in or according to the image of God (cf. above, pp. 55, 88 ff.). See, for instance, De diversis quaestionibus LXXXIII, quaest. LI, 4, PL XL, 33: Neque inscite distinguitur quod aliud sit imago et similitudo Dei, qui etiam Filius dicitur, aliud "ad imaginem et similitudinem Dei" sicut hominem factum accipimus; see also Retractiones I, 25, 52, CSEL XXXVI, 122, where Augustine acknowledges that Paul once calls man outright imago et gloria Dei (1 Cor. 11:7): sed dicitur etiam "ad imaginem Dei," quod unigenitus non dicitur, qui tantummodo "imago" est, non "ad imaginem."

[8] See Confessiones VII, 10, 16, Skutella 141: . . . et inveni longe me esse a te in regione dissimilitudinis . . . . Cf. E. Gilson, "Regio dissimilitudinis de Platon à Saint Bernard de Clairvaux," Mediaeval Studies IX (1947) 108 ff. (with bibliography on the problem), G. Dumeige, "Dissemblance," DSpir III, 1330 ff. See also below, p. 189, n. 12.

[9] Cf. above, p. 185, n. 1.

[10] De Trinitate XI, 5, 8, PL XLII, 991: Non sane omne quod in creaturis aliquo modo simile est Deo, etiam eius imago dicenda est, sed illa sola qua superior ipse solus est (i.e., man); De diversis quaestionibus LXXXIII, quaest. LI, 2, PL XL, 33: Quare cum homo possit particeps esse sapientiae secundum interiorem hominem, secundum ipsum ita est ad imaginem, ut nulla natura interposita formetur et ideo nihil sit Deo coniunctius. . . . Cf. Gilson, Augustin 282. See also the important passages in De diversis questionibus LXXXIII, quaest. LI, 3 f., loc. cit., 33 f., where Augustine interprets the image as the mind, and as the "inner man," using in part the same words as in quaestio LXXIV, whereas it is left open by him whether or not the likeness (again considered as inferior to the image, cf. above, p. 187, n. 5) might be understood as caetera hominis: for, even the "external man," the body, particeps dicitur similitudinis Dei, non solum quia vivit . . ., sed amplius quod ad mentem convertitur se regentem quam illustrat sapientia . . ., et . . . quia tale est ut ad contemplandum coelum sit aptius. . . . The last-mentioned reference to the upright posture and heavenward gaze of man as part of man's image-likeness to God is a wide-spread patristic topos (see, for instance, Gregory of Nyssa, De hominis opificio 8, PG XLIV, 144B; for the ancient origins of the topos and for Gregory's development of it, which may in part depend on Posidonius [not so according to Reinhardt], cf. K. Gronau, Poseidonios und die jüdisch-christliche Genesis-exegese [Leipzig, Berlin, 1914] 161, 288 f., K. Reinhardt, Poseidonios [München, 1921] 260,

sin,[11] but it can become more and more dissimilar to God through individual sins and imperfections. The road back from such dissimilarity is for Augustine identical with the process of reform of the image of God in man;[12] but even so, in this life the reformation

idem, Kosmos und Sympathie [München, 1926] 144 ff., *idem*, article "Poseidonios," in PW, *RE* XLIII [XXII, 1] 714 ff., 723 f., E. v. Ivanka, "Die Quellen von Cicero, De natura deorum II 45–60 [Poseidonios bei Gregor von Nyssa]," *Egyetemes Philologiai Közlöny: Archivum Philologicum* LIX [1935] 14; also the translation of Gregory's treatise *De hominis opificio* by J. Laplace, S.J., and J. Daniélou, S.J., *Grégoire de Nysse: La création de l'homme* [Sources chrétiennes VI, Paris, 1943] 19 ff. and 106 ff., and my article "Anthropology" 68). Augustine refers to this *topos* only in a tentative way and attaches a warning that such a conception must not lead to a materialistic idea of God. In general, his view is that the likeness is part of the image and that man is an image of God resembling Him in so far as he is a spiritual being. For the intellectual character of the image see also the following texts: Imago Dei intus est, non est in corpore (*Enarr. in Ps. XLVIII*, 11, *Corp. Christ., Ser. Lat.* XXXVIII, 574); . . . ad imaginem Dei nos . . . factos nec alibi quam in ipso intellectu (*Enarr. in Ps. LIV*, 3, *ibid.* XXXIX, 657); ergo intellegimus habere nos aliquid ubi imago Dei est, mentem scilicet atque rationem (*Enarr. in Ps. XLII*, 6, XXXVIII, 479); cf. also above, pp. 173 and 183, nn. 19 and 43.

[11] The impossibility of completely destroying the image is most clearly pointed out in the *Retractationes*, where Augustine corrects earlier inexact formulations. See, for instance, *Retractationes* I, 25, 68, *CSEL* XXXVI, 126 f. (to *De diversis quaestionibus* LXXXIII, *quaest.* LXVII, 4, *PL* XL, 67: . . . homo cum iam signaculo imaginis propter peccatum amisso remansit tantummodo creatura): Quod non ita est accipiendum quasi totum amiserit homo quod habebat imaginis Dei. Nam si omnino non amisisset, non esset propter quod diceretur "Reformamini in novitate mentis vestrae" (Rom. 12:2) et "in eandem imaginem transformamur" (2 Cor. 3:18). Sed rursus, si totum amisisset, nihil maneret unde diceretur "Quamquam in imagine ambulat homo, tamen vane conturbatur" (Ps. 38:7). See also *Retractationes* II, 50, 3, *CSEL* XXXVI, 160 (to *De Genesi ad litteram* VI, 27, *CSEL* XXVIII, 1, 199): non sic accipiendum est tamquam [imago] in eo nulla remanserit, sed quod tam deformis ut reformatione opus |haberet. In *Enarr. in Ps. CXXIX*, 1, *Corp. Christ., Ser. Lat.* XL, 1890, Augustine speaks of the image as "worn out" (*detrita*), not as lost. See also *In Johannis evangelium tractatus* XL, 9, *Corp. Christ., Ser. Lat.* XXXVI, 355: Moneta Dei sumus, nummus a thesauro oberravimus. Errore detritum est quod in nobis fuerat impressum; venit qui reformet, quia ipse formaverat; quaerit et ipse nummum suum . . . "Reddite Caesari quae Caesaris sunt et Deo quae Dei sunt" (Matthew 22:21). Cf. Pontet, *Augustin prédicateur* 517, J. Heijke, C. S. Sp., "The Image of God according to St. Augustine . . . ," *Folia* X (1956) 8 f.

[12] See *Enarr. in Ps. CXLVI*, 14, *Corp. Christ., Ser. Lat.* XL, 2132: (bad men) iacent in dissimilitudine sua exterminantes in se similitudinem Dei. Dissimiles facti recesserunt, reformati redeant. See also *Enarr. in Ps. LXXV*, 3, *Corp. Christ., Ser. Lat.* XXXIX, 1039: Vide ex quanta parte dissimilis es. . . . Factus enim es, o homo, ad imaginem Dei. Per vitam vero perversam et malam perturbasti in te et exterminasti in te imaginem conditoris tui. Factus dissimilis adtendis in te et displices tibi: iam ex eo coepisti similis fieri quia hoc tibi displicet quod displicet et Deo. The expression *exterminare* must not be taken too literally; see preceding note.

of the image's similarity to God can be no more than a beginning.[13]

For St. Gregory of Nyssa, the greatest speculative mind of the
Christian east between Origen and Ps.-Dionysius the Areopagite, the
goal of all assimilation of man to God had been the attainment of a
vision of God in the soul which in reality is identical with the soul's
ceaseless journey toward the infinite height and depth of God.[14] This
is genuine Christian mysticism which is found also in St. Augustine.
Yet Augustine makes a much sharper distinction than the Greek
Fathers between man's capacity to see God in this life and in the next.
For Gregory of Nyssa, for instance, the reform of man had been purification of the soul which would thus mirror God more and more
clearly; a resulting vision of God is not excluded even on earth, but it
is never total or completed, not even in heaven.[15] For Augustine,
on the one hand, the desire to see God *sicuti est*, will be fully satisfied
(*satiabitur*) in heaven;[16] on the other hand, while he considers the

---

[13] See, for instance, *De spiritu et littera* 22, 37, *CSEL* LX, 190 f. (to 1 John 3:2 [*Vetus
Latina*]: Dilectissimi, filii Dei sumus, et nondum apparuit quod erimus. Scimus quia cum
apparuerit, similes ei erimus; quoniam videbimus eum sicuti est): Haec similitudo nunc
incipit reformari (followed by references to 2 Cor. 4:16 and 1 Cor. 13:11 f.).

[14] See above, Part Two, Chapter III, 2.

[15] See above, pp. 102 ff.

[16] In *Epist.* CXLVII (*De videndo Deo liber*), 26, *CSEL* XLIV, 299 f., he adapts in this sense
Ps. 102:5 (Qui replet in bonis desiderium tuum): Tunc quippe satiabitur in bonis desider-
ium eorum. See also *Sermo* CXCIV, 3, *PL* XXXVIII, 1017: Nam qui sunt illi sapientiae
scientiaeque thesauri, quae illae divitiae divinae (cf. Col. 2:2 f.), nisi quia sufficiunt nobis?
Et quae illa multitudo dulcedinis (cf. Ps. 30:20), nisi quia satiat nos? Ostende ergo nobis
Patrem et sufficit nobis (cf. John 14:8) . . . "Satiabor, dum manifestabitur gloria tua"
(Ps. 16:15 [*Vetus Latina*]) . . . Convertens nos ostendet nobis faciem suam et salvi erimus
(cf. Ps. 79:4) et satiabimur et sufficiet nobis. If Augustine in *Sermo* CCCLXII, 28, 29, *PL*
XXXIX, 1632 f., speaks of the *insatiabilis satietas* of the blessed in heaven, he does so only
to refute in a priceless way those who in his own time (and at any time) fear that the
continuous praise of God might be rather monotonous an occupation for the saints: Sed nolite
. . . carnali cogitatione contristari quia, si forte aliquis vestrum steterit et dixerit quotidie:
"Amen et Alleluia," taedio marcescet et in ipsis vocibus dormitabit et tacere iam volet et
propterea putet sibi esse aspernabilem vitam et non desiderabilem, dicentes vobismetipsis:
"Amen et Alleluia semper dicturi sumus? Quis durabit?" Dicam ergo, si potero, quantum
potero. Non sonis transeuntibus dicemus "Amen et Alleluia," sed affectu animi. Quid est
. . . Amen? Quid Alleluia? Amen est: verum, Alleluia: Laudate Dominum. . . . Amen
utique dicemus, sed insatiabili satietate. Quia enim non deerit aliquid, ideo satietas. Quia
vero illud, quod non deerit, semper delectabit, ideo quaedam, si dici potest, insatiabilis
satietas erit. . . .

possibility of a mystical foretaste on earth of the beatific vision in heaven, he makes it clear that such a privilege, if granted to a very few (*aput perpaucos*), must still remain *magis in fide . . . per speculum in enigmate et ex parte in aliqua visione*.[17] It is hard to say how far Augustine applied this limitation also to Moses and St. Paul and to other great saints; for he did believe that at least Paul and Moses, in momentary rapture, saw God in His nature (*substantia*). One thing is certain: Augustine did not think that the terrestrial condition of even the holiest man warrants the expectation of a vision of the fulness of God this side of heaven.[18]

For, we shall see God, in so far as we shall be similar to Him (cf. 1 John 3:2), since also now we do not see Him, in so far as we are dissimilar. . . . But, who would be so utterly out of his mind as to say that we are or shall be similar to God through our body? In the inner man, therefore, is the similitude. . . . And the more we progress in His knowledge and in charity, the more similar shall we become to Him. . . . And still, how ever high a man may be

---

[17] *De consensu evangelistarum* I, 5, *CSEL* XLIII, 8.

[18] For Augustine's doctrine of the vision of God, see above all J. Maréchal, S.J., *Etudes sur la psychologie des mystiques* II (Museum Lessianum, Sect. Philos., XIX, Bruxelles, Paris, 1937) 145 ff.: "La vision de Dieu au sommet de la contemplation d'après saint Augustin," especially 165 ff. Augustine, *Epist.* CXLVII (*De videndo Deo liber*), 13, 31 f., *CSEL* XLIV, 305 f., and *De Genesi ad litteram* XII, 27, *CSEL* XXVIII, 1, 420 ff., interprets Num. 12:8 (*Vetus Latina*), where God's appearance to Moses is defined as taking place *per speciem* (for Augustine's understanding of this term see Dom C. Butler, O.S.B., *Western Mysticism*, 2nd ed. [London, 1951] LIII f.) *non per aenigmata . . .: et gloriam (claritatem) Domini vidit*, in the sense that Moses, while still alive, could see God *sicuti est* (1 John 3:2), because in his rapture, comparable to that of St. Paul (according to 2 Cor. 12:2), he did not longer live *vita ista, qua mortaliter vivitur in istis sensibus corporis* (*De Genesi ad litteram* XII, 27, *CSEL* XXVIII, 1, 422). In view of such texts, the attempt of E. Hendrikx, O.E.S.A., *Augustins Verhältnis zur Mystik* (Würzburg, 1936), to prove that Augustine was not a mystic, is not convincing; cf. also M. Olphe-Galliard, article "Contemplation," *DSpir*, fasc. XIV–XV, 1920. It remains true, however, that an essential vision of God on earth was considered quite exceptional by Augustine (see also Gilson, *Augustin* 40 f., and F. Cayré, A.A., *La contemplation augustinienne*, 2nd ed. [Paris, 1954] 193 ff.). Without limiting it on principle, Augustine never names anyone except Moses and Paul as having possessed it, whereas for the Greeks it was the great goal of all mystical experience, though according to them it could be had, even in heaven, not in final attainment, but only in never ending pursuit; on this latter point, cf. Maréchal, *Etudes* II, 109 and 178: the Greeks could not imagine any vision of God as "satiating," because essential vision to them meant comprehensive vision, whereas in the western tradition there can be a true, though not full, vision of God even in this life, with fulfillment in the beatific vision in heaven; cf. also above, pp. 102 f., n. 73, and p. 190, n. 16.

[spiritually] borne up in this life, he will be far removed from the perfection of similitude which would be apt for a vision of God . . . from face to face (cf. 1 Cor. 13:12).[19]

Augustine's conception of divine transcendence, not only with regard to the body, but also with regard to soul and mind, is more severe and sober, though not more sublime, than Greek patristic equations of the soul's God-finding and God-seeking.

But is, perhaps, the God [of the mind] some such thing as the mind (*animus*) itself is? For it is true that God can be seen only by the mind. And yet, He cannot be seen in the same way as the mind. For that mind seeks something which is God . . . , a certain unchangeable truth, a substance without deficiency. Such even the mind itself is not: it waxes weaker or stronger, it knows and ignores, it remembers and forgets, it now wills a certain thing and now wills it not. . . . Seeking, therefore, my God in visible and corporeal things and not finding Him there, seeking His substance in myself, as if He was some thing such as I, and still not finding, I perceive that God is something above the soul. That I may touch Him, therefore, "I meditated these things and poured out my soul above me" (Ps. 41:5). When would my soul attain that which is sought above my soul, if my soul were not poured above itself? For, if it remained in itself, it would see nothing but itself and if it saw itself would indeed not see its God.[20]

[19] *Epist.* XCII, 3, *CSEL* XLIV, 438 f.: In tantum ergo videbimus in quantum similes erimus (cf. 1 John 3:2), quia et nunc in tantum non videmus in quantum dissimiles sumus. . . . Quis autem dementissimus dixerit corpore nos vel esse vel futuros esse similes Deo? In interiore igitur homine ista similitudo est . . . (there follows a reference to Col. 3:10). Et tanto efficimur similiores illi, quanto magis in eius cognitione et caritate proficimus . . . (this is followed by a reference to 2 Cor. 4:16), ita sane ut in hac vita quantuscumque provectus sit, longe absit ab illa perfectione similitudinis quae idonea erit ad videndum Deum . . . "facie ad faciem" (1 Cor. 13:12). See also *De civitate Dei* XI, 26, quoted p. 187, n. 3, and the text from *Enarr. in Ps. XLIX*, 2, quoted below, p. 195, n. 27.

[20] *Enarr. in Ps. XLI*, 7 f., *Corp. Christ.*, *Ser. Lat.* XXXVIII, 465: Sed numquid aliquid tale Deus ipsius est qualis est animus? Non quidem videri Deus nisi animo potest. Nec tamen ita ut animus videri potest. Aliquid enim quaerit animus iste, quod Deus est. . . . Aliquam quaerit incommutabilem veritatem, sine defectu substantiam. Non est talis ipse animus: deficit, proficit; novit, ignorat; meminit, obliviscitur; modo illud vult, modo non vult. . . . Quaerens ergo Deum meum in rebus visibilibus et corporalibus, et non inveniens, quaerens eius substantiam in meipso, quasi sit aliquid qualis ego sum, neque hoc inveniens, aliquid super animam esse sentio Deum meum. Ergo, ut eum tangerem, "haec meditatus sum et effudi super me animam meam" (Ps. 41:5, the Vulgate reads: "Haec recordatus sum et effudi in me animam meam"). Quando anima mea contingeret quod super animam meam quaeritur, nisi anima mea super seipsam effunderetur? Si enim in seipsa remaneret, nihil aliud quam se videret, et cum se videret, non utique Deum suum videret.

Even though the Neoplatonic background of patristic thought, and in particular Augustine's own indebtedness to Platonism, are clearly perceptible also in his ideas on man's image-likeness to God,[21] it is alone the sacrifice of Christ which in his view can reform the image of God in us. Having the Neoplatonists in mind he censures those proud men who believe that they can be purified by their own virtue, so that they can contemplate God and adhere to Him. These people, he says, scoff at the Christians who on earth have only their faith, while they claim that some amongst them were touched (in momentary ecstasy) by the light of the unchangeable truth. But what good is such remote vision of the fatherland to those who scorn the Cross through which alone we can actually be carried home? Vain are all "sacrilegious similitudes," all "magical consecrations"; what counts is only the one sacrifice which is the death of Him who was God and man.[22]

[21] See, for instance, the Plotinian metaphor of the divine sealing ring's impression in the wax of man's soul, which appears in the text quoted on p. 194, n. 22. Cf. furthermore, p. 188, n. 8 (article by Gilson).

[22] See *De Trinitate* IV, 12, 15, *PL* XLII, 897: Nequaquam igitur per sacrilegas similitudines et impias curiositates et magicas consecrationes animae purgantur et reconciliantur Deo . . . ; *ibid.* 13, 18, XLII, 900: Superbi autem homines, quibus Christus, quia mortuus est, viluit . . . , et istam mortem reddunt cum hominibus conditioni aerumnosae naturae . . . ; *ibid.* 13, 18–14, 19, XLII, 901: Et cum de mortibus sacrificiorum suorum multum praesumant . . . , non intelligunt ne ipsos quidem superbissimos spiritus honoribus sacrificiorum gaudere potuisse, nisi uni vero Deo, pro quo coli volunt, verum sacrificium deberetur neque id posse rite offerri nisi per sacerdotem sanctum et iustum. . . . Quis ergo tam iustus et sanctus sacerdos quam unicus Filius Dei . . . ?; *ibid.* 15, 20, XLII, 901 f.: Sunt autem quidam qui se putant ad contemplandum Deum et inhaerendum Deo virtute propria posse purgari: quos ipsa superbia maxime maculat. . . . Hinc enim purgationem sibi isti virtute propria pollicentur quia nonnulli eorum potuerunt aciem mentis ultra omnem creaturam transmittere et lucem incommutabilis veritatis quantulacumque ex parte contingere: quod christianos multos ex fide interim sola viventes nondum potuisse derident. Sed quid prodest superbienti et ob hoc erubescenti lignum conscendere de longinquo prospicere patriam transmarinam? Aut quid obest humili de tanto intervallo non eam videre in illo ligno ad eam venienti, quo dedignatur ille portari? See also the distinction between "perverse" and "true" assimilation to, and imitation of, God in *Enarr. in Ps. LXX*, *sermo* II, 6 f., *Corp. Christ.*, *Ser. Lat.* XXXIX, 964 ff.: Et homo se extollit . . . , audit serpentem suggerentem: "Gustate et eritis sicut dii" (Gen. 3:5). Homines sicut dii: "Deus quis similis tibi" (Ps. 70:19). . . . Ego autem, ait Adam miser et in Adam omnis homo, cum volo esse perverse similis tibi, ecce quid factus sum . . . , et clamo ad te quia cecidi abs te. Et unde abs te cecidi? Cum quaero esse perverse similis tibi. Quid enim? Deus nonne ad suam similitudinem nos vocat? . . . Qui . . . bene vult inimico suo, Deo similis est, nec ista superbia, sed obedientia est. Quare? Quia ad imaginem Dei facti sumus. . . . Non ergo aliquid alienum est, si imaginem Dei tenemus in nobis: utinam eam

When therefore Augustine, as Plotinus and Gregory of Nyssa before him,[23] compares man's purification to the work of a sculptor, the sculptor is no longer the spiritual nature of man himself, but God Himself.

We, therefore, . . . must after a fashion resculpt [the image] and reform it. But, who would be able to do this, except if he were the artist who shaped it? We could deform the image of God in us, but we cannot reform it.[24]

For Augustine, too, man's reassimilation to God, his reformation, is deification.[25] Scriptural texts, such as Ps. 81:6: *Ego dixi: dii estis*, John 1:12: *Dedit enim eis potestatem filios Dei fieri*, and 1 John 3:2: . . . *filii Dei sumus*, he interprets, just as Origen and others had done before him,[26] in the sense of deification not by nature but through grace and adoption. But he insists more strongly than the

---

per superbiam non amittamus. . . . Ut ergo boni simus, Deo indigemus; ut bonus sit Deus, nobis non indiget. . . . Ut autem homo sit aliquid, convertit se ad illum a quo creatus est. Recedendo enim frigescit, accedendo fervescit; recedendo tenebrescit, accedendo clarescit. . . . Ergo quisquis ita vult esse similis Deo, ut ad illum stet . . ., non ab illo recedat; ei cohaerendo signetur tamquam ex anulo cera, illi affixus habeat imaginem eius . . ., vere custodit similitudinem et imaginem ad quam factus est. Porro autem, si perverse voluerit imitari Deum, ut, quomodo Deus non habet a quo formetur, non habet a quo regatur . . ., quid restat . . . nisi ut recedens ab eius calore torpescat, recedens a veritate vanescat, recedens ab eo, quod summe atque incommutabiliter est, in deterius mutatus deficiat. Hoc diabolus fecit: imitari Deum voluit, sed perverse. . . .

[23] See above, p. 93, n. 42.

[24] *Sermo* XLIII, 3, 4, *PL* XXXVIII, 255: Hoc ergo unde bestias antecedimus (i.e., reason through which we are made according to the image of God) maxime in nobis excolere debemus et resculpere quodam modo et reformare. Sed quis poterit, nisi sit artifex qui formavit? Imaginem in nobis Dei deformare potuimus, reformare non possumus. See also *Enarr. in Ps.* VI, 5, *Corp. Christ.*, *Ser. Lat.* XXXVIII, 30, where man's conversion to God is at one and the same time man's "resculpting" of his spirit and the "conversion" of God Himself to man: "Convertere, Domine, et erue animam meam" (Ps. 6:5). Convertens se orat ut ad eam (i.e., man's soul) convertatur et Deus, sicut dictum est: "Convertimini ad me et convertar ad vos, dicit Dominus" (Zach. 1:3). . . . Dum autem nos convertimus, id est, mutatione veteris vitae resculpimus spiritum nostrum, durum sentimus et laboriosum ad serenitatem et tranquillitatem divinae lucis a terrenarum cupiditatum caligine retorqueri. Et in tali difficultate dicimus: "Convertere, Domine" id est, adiuva nos, ut perficiatur in nobis conversio quae te paratum invenit. . . .

[25] See, especially, the important article by P. V. Capánaga, O.R.S.A., "La deificación en la soteriología agustiniana," in *Aug. Mag.* II, 745 ff.

[26] See above, p. 89, n. 22, text from Origen's *Sixth Homily to Exodus*, where the same biblical texts are quoted as in Augustine's *Enarr. in Ps. XLIX*, quoted in the following note.

Greek Fathers on the fact that deification by grace on earth is not yet the glory of heaven, except *in spe*.[27] A deification doctrine of the Greek type was certainly far from Augustine's mind when he wrote:

"And see that I am God" (Ps. 45:11), that is: Not you but I am God. I did create, I recreate; I did form, I reform; I did make, I remake. If you could not make yourself, how can you remake yourself?[28]

Augustine developed a fuller doctrine of divine grace, justification, and sanctification than the Greek Fathers;[29] the appertaining terminology was to become more dominant in western theological thought than that of θέωσις-*deificatio*.[30]

It is, perhaps, against the background of his doctrine of sanctification, of reformation by grace, that Augustine's famous sentence *Crede ut intelligas*, which was to have such a great fortune in later centuries,

[27] *Enarr. in Ps. XLIX*, 2, *Corp. Christ.*, *Ser. Lat.* XXXVIII, 575 f.: Videte . . . quibus dicat: "Ego dixi: dii estis . . ." (Ps. 81:6). Manifestum est . . . quia homines dixit deos ex gratia sua deificatos, non de substantia sua natos. Ille enim iustificat, qui per semetipsum non ex alio iustus est, et ille deificat, qui per seipsum non alterius participatione Deus est. Qui autem iustificat, ipse deificat, quia iustificando filios Dei facit. "Dedit enim eis potestatem filios Dei fieri" (John 1:12). Si filii Dei facti sumus, et dii facti sumus: sed hoc gratiae est adoptantis, non naturae generantis. Unicus enim Dei Filius et cum Patre unus Deus. . . . Ceteri, qui fiunt dii, gratia ipsius fiunt, non de substantia eius nascuntur. . . . "Dilectissimi, filii Dei sumus et nondum apparuit quid erimus" (1 John 3:2). Ergo sumus in spe, nondum in re. "Scimus . . . autem quoniam cum apparuerit, similes ei erimus, quoniam videbimus eum sicuti est" (1 John 3:2). Unicus similis nascendo, nos similes videndo. Non enim ita similes ut ille, qui hoc est, quod ille, a quo genitus, est; nos enim similes, non aequales; ille, quia aequalis, ideo similis. . . . See also above, p. 187, n. 6.

[28] *Enarr. in Ps. XLV*, 14, *Corp. Christ.*, *Ser. Lat.* XXXVIII, 528: "Et videte quoniam ego sum Deus" (Ps. 45:11). Hoc est: non vos, sed ego sum Deus. Ego creavi, ego recreo; ego formavi, ego reformo; ego feci, ego reficio. Si non potuisti facere te, quomodo potes reficere te?

[29] A comprehensive study of patristic terminology and doctrine of sanctification (ἁγιασμός-*sanctificatio*) does not seem to exist; for the Greek Fathers and especially for Cyril of Alexandria, see above, pp. 79–80, and the study of P. Galtier, S.J., *Le Saint Esprit en nous d'après les pères grecs* (Analecta Gregoriana, Ser. Theol. XXV A 4, Roma, 1946); for St. Augustine, cf. Carney, *Sanctity*, and A. Turrado, O.E.S.A., "La inhabitación de la Sᵐᵃ Trinidad en los justos según la doctrina de San Agustín," in *Aug. Mag.* I, 583 ff.

[30] On the survival of deification terminology also in the mediaeval west, both in the weaker Augustinian and in the stronger Greek sense, see, for instance, the article of E. H. Kantorowicz, "Deus per naturam, Deus per gratiam," *Harv. Theol. Rev.* XLV (1952) 253 ff.

receives its fullest significance. For Augustine, there is only one thing that really can help us to understand higher truth and to see God, and that is that faith which is the beginning of God's grace:[31]

Every man wants to understand, there is none who does not. Not all men want to believe. A man says to me: I wish to understand, so that I may believe. I answer: Believe, so that you may understand.[32]

While there are several formulations of the *Crede ut intelligas* in Augustine's writings,[33] this particular one is quoted here from *Sermo* XLIII, because it directly follows the text just cited about the reform of the image of God in man, not by man but by God.[34]

Now it will also be realized more fully how the "overlapping" of the concepts of image and similitude discussed earlier[35] affects Augustine's doctrine of the divine image and likeness in man. Man will always have less than that perfect resemblance or equality to God which exists only in Christ;[36] but he also will always remain an image which, though not generated by God, still is the highest of all creatures made by God, except for the angels, and therefore will contain relations of resemblance to Him which cannot be found in mere similarity as it exists between creatures or in the vestiges of God in creation. This divine image-likeness is imperishable and therefore redeemable and "reformable"; but on earth this process of reform is essentially one of faith, hope and charity—not yet of that charity which can exist without faith and hope as an intellectual vision of God's essence in heaven,

[31] See *De diversis quaestionibus ad Simplicianum* I, quaestio 2, 2, PL XL, 111: Incipit autem homo percipere gratiam ex quo incipit Deo credere. . . .

[32] *Sermo* XLIII, 3, 4, *PL* XXXVIII, 255: Omnis homo vult intelligere, nemo est qui nolit. Credere non omnes volunt. Dicit mihi homo: Intelligam, ut credam. Respondeo: Crede, ut intelligas.

[33] See, for instance, *De libero arbitrio* II, 17, *CSEL* LXXIV, 41; *In Johannis evangelium tractatus* XXIX, 6, *Corp. Christ.*, *Ser. Lat.* XXXVI, 286 f.; *Epist.* CXX, I, 3, *CSEL*, XXXIV, 706; *Sermo* CXVIII, 1, *PL* XXXVIII, 672; cf. Gilson, *Augustin* 36 ff. Augustine's *Crede ut intelligas* is based on Is. 7:9, which in the Vulgate reads: "Si non credideritis, non permanebitis," but in the version used by Augustine: "Nisi credideritis, non intelligetis"; cf. his *De doctrina christiana* II, 12, 17, *Flor. Patr.* XXIV, 27.

[34] See above, p. 194, n. 24.

[35] See pp. 186–188.

[36] Cf. also the end of the text, quoted, p. 195, n. 27: . . . nos enim similes, non aequales, ille, quia aequalis, ideo similis.

when "we shall be like to Him" (1 John 3:2). Augustine's *imago* is less than Greek ὁμοίωσις, though more than Augustinian *similitudo*.

How little Augustine's view of terrestrial man as image of God is circumscribed by a concept of similitude in the Greek sense can be seen in his work *On the Trinity* where he develops a deep and subtle doctrine concerning the way in which the soul is an image of the Triune God.[37] He discusses several psychological ternaries or trinities analogous to the divine Trinity. Here it suffices to recall that on the highest level of the human soul, where it is truly according to the image of God, memory (*memoria*), which stands for the mind's consciousness (see below), corresponds to the Father, knowledge (*intelligentia*) to the Son, and love (*amor*) to the Holy Spirit. While this Trinitarian analogy also applies to the mind's relation to the corporeal world and to itself,[38] it receives its true meaning only in the right relation between man and God.

Now this trinity in the mind is not for that reason the image of God that

---

[37] The best analyses of the relevant parts of *De Trinitate* are to be found in M. Schmaus, *Die psychologische Trinitätslehre des hl. Augustinus* (Münster, 1927), in A. Gardeil, O.P., *La structure de l'âme et l'expérience mystique*, 2nd ed., I (Paris, 1927) 21 ff., in Gilson, *Augustin* 286 ff., and in Benz, *Marius Victorinus* 364 ff.; see also H. Kusch, "Studien über Augustinus," *Festschrift Franz Dornseiff zum 65. Geburtstag* (Leipzig, 1953) 124 ff., where the author, perhaps, goes somewhat too far in attempting to demonstrate that Trinitarian analogies between God and His image, man, form the background also of *Confessiones* II to IV and X to XIII; in the future cf. H. Merki, O.S.B., article "Ebenbildlichkeit," *RLAC*.

[38] Augustine begins the discussion of the psychological trinities at the end of *De Trinitate* VIII, *PL* XLII, 960, with an analysis of human love: Ecce tria sunt: amans et quod amatur et amor (*De Trinitate* VIII, 10, 14, XLII, 960). But a short cut from human love to the Triune God is impossible; Augustine, therefore, turns to the structure of the mind as an image of God, and in Books IX to XIV expounds its trinitarian character. In Book XV, before stating his doctrine on the divine Trinity, he recapitulates his previous analyses, book by book, a recapitulation which may be briefly summarized as follows: In Book IX, Augustine finds that there is in man as the image of God *quaedam trinitas . . ., id est mens et notitia, qua se novit, et amor, quo se notitiamque suam diligit* (cf. *De Trinitate* XV, 3, 5, *PL* XLII, 1060). In Book X, this trinity of the mind is defined in more general terms as *memoria, intelligentia*, and *voluntas* (cf. *PL* XLII, 1060). In Book XI, it is shown that the trinitarian structure of the mind applies to sense perception of corporeal things—*ex corpore scilicet quod videtur, et forma quae inde in acie cernentis imprimitur, et utrumque copulantis intentione voluntatis*—which is referred back to the mind's *memoria, informatio*, and *intentio voluntatis* (cf. *PL* XLII, 1060). In Books XII to XIV, the trinitarian structure of the mind is considered from the point of view of *scientia, fides* and finally of *sapientia*, that *sapientia hominis vera* in which there is the fullest analogy between the trinity in the reformed image of God, i.e. the mind renewed by God, and the Trinity in God (cf. *PL* XLII, 1060 f.).

the mind remembers, knows, and loves itself, but because it also can remember, know, and love Him by whom it is made. . . .[39]

Those who, remembering, are converted to the Lord from that deformity in which, through worldly cupidities, they were conformed to this world, are reformed by Him; they heed the Apostle's words "And be not conformed to this world, but be reformed to the newness of your mind" (Rom. 12:2), so that that image may begin to be reformed by Him through whom it was formed. For it cannot reform itself as it could deform itself. He (i.e., St. Paul) also says elsewhere: "And be renewed in the spirit of your mind: And put on the new man, who according to God is created in justice and holiness of truth" (Eph. 4:23 f.). When he says: created "according to God," this is expressed in another place by the words "to the image of God" (Gen. 1:27). But, in sinning [man] lost justice and holiness of truth; therefore, the image has become deformed and discoloured: [yet] he recovers it, when he is reformed and renewed. . . . Still elsewhere he (i.e., Paul) named the image even more openly . . . : "stripping yourselves," he said, "of the old man with his deeds, put on the new man, who is renewed in the knowledge of God according to the image of Him who created him" (cf. Col. 3:9 f.). . . . That renovation and reformation of the mind, then, takes place according to God or according to the image of God. . . .[40]

Indeed, this renovation does not occur in the one moment of conversion itself, as that baptismal renovation occurs through the remission of all sins. . . . Of this fact the apostle most clearly spoke when he said: "but though our

---

[39] *De Trinitate* XIV, 12, 15, *PL* XLII, 1048: Haec igitur trinitas mentis non propterea Dei est imago quia sui meminit mens et intelligit ac diligit se, sed quia potest etiam meminisse et intelligere et amare a quo facta est. . . .

[40] *De Trinitate* XIV, 16, 22, *PL* XLII, 1053 f.: Qui vero commemorati convertuntur ad Dominum ab ea deformitate, qua per cupidates saeculares conformabantur huic saeculo, reformantur ex illo, audientes apostolum dicentem: "Nolite conformari huic saeculo, sed reformamini in novitate mentis vestrae" (Rom. 12:2), ut incipiat illa imago ab illo reformari a quo formata est. Non enim reformare se ipsam potest, sicut potuit deformare. Dicit etiam alibi: "Renovamini spiritu mentis vestrae et induite novum hominem, eum qui secundum Deum creatus est in iustitia et sanctitate veritatis" (cf. Eph. 4:23 f.). Quod ait "secundum Deum" creatum, hoc alio loco dicitur "ad imaginem Dei" (Gen. 1:27). Sed peccando iustitiam et sanctitatem veritatis amisit; propter quod imago deformis et decolor facta est; hanc recipit cum reformatur et renovatur. . . . Alibi quoque apertius etiam imaginem nominavit . . . : "Expoliantes vos," inquit, "veterem hominem cum actibus eius induite novum hominem, qui renovatur in agnitione Dei secundum imaginem eius qui creavit eum" (cf. Col. 3:9 f., the Vulgate differs here slightly). . . . Fit ergo ista renovatio reformatioque mentis secundum Deum vel secundum imaginem Dei. . . .

outward man is corrupted, yet the inward man is renewed day by day" (2 Cor. 4:16). . . .[41]

But the image which is renewed in the mind unto the knowledge of God (cf. Rom. 12: 2, Col. 3:10), not outward but inward day by day (cf. 2 Cor. 4:16), will be perfected itself by the vision [of God], which then, after the Judgement, will be "face to face," but now advances "through a glass in a dark manner" (1 Cor. 13:12). It must be understood that it is because of that perfection that it was said: "we shall be like to Him, because we shall see Him as He is" (1 John 3:2). . . .[42]

These texts from the fourteenth book of *De Trinitate* will serve to recapitulate Augustine's doctrine on the reformation of man's image-likeness to God; at the same time they demonstrate very clearly his closeness to those crucial Pauline formulations of the reform idea,[43] which constitute the basis of all Christian reform terminology and ideology.

Augustine's Trinitarian analogies are much richer than their terms would at a first glance reveal. *Memoria*, as already mentioned, stands for the mind in so far as it is conscious of the external world, of itself, and of God, *intelligentia* for the act of knowledge which is generated, as it were, by that mind, and *amor* or *voluntas* or *intentio* for the connecting link between the mind's consciousness and the act and content of its knowing. Thus the mind (*memoria*) is the first member of the psychological trinity (just as the Father is the First Person in the divine Trinity); thought (*intelligentia*), the second, is engendered by the first (just as the Son is by the Father), and love or will (*amor*,

---

[41] *Ibid.* XIV, 17, 23, PL XLII, 1054: Sane ista renovatio non momento uno fit ipsius conversionis, sicut momento uno fit illa in baptismo renovatio remissione omnium peccatorum. . . . De qua re apostolus apertissime locutus est, dicens: "Et si exterior homo noster corrumpitur, sed interior renovatur de die in diem" (2 Cor. 4:16). . . .

[42] *Ibid.* XIV, 19, 25, PL XLII, 1056: Imago vero quae renovatur in spiritu mentis in agnitione Dei (cf. Rom. 12:2, Col. 3:10), non exterius, sed interius de die in diem, ipsa perficietur visione quae tunc erit post iudicium ad faciem, nunc autem proficit per speculum in aenigmate (cf. 1 Cor. 13:12). Propter cuius perfectionem dictum intelligendum est: "Similes ei erimus, quoniam videbimus eum sicuti est" (1 John 3:2). . . . For the texts quoted pp. 198 f., nn. 39 ff., see also Cayré, *Contemplation* 182 ff.

[43] See above, pp. 53–54. See also Augustine, *Enarr. in Ps. CXLII*, 7, Corp. Christ., Ser. Lat. XL, 2068 (to Ps. 103:30: "Emittes spiritum tuum et creabuntur et renovabis faciem terrae"): Si qua igitur in Christo nova creatura vetera transierunt (cf. 2 Cor. 5:17). In spiritu suo vetera transierunt, in spiritu tuo nova facta sunt.

voluntas) is the bond which guarantees the unity and mutual coherence of our mind and its thought (just as the Holy Spirit is the mutual love between the First and Second Person in the Trinity).[44]

Augustine fully realizes the imperfections of all such analogies. And yet, how can we understand God and our relation to Him except by analogies? Augustine refers 1 Cor. 13:12: *Videmus nunc per speculum in aenigmate*, directly to the divine image and likeness in man. *In speculo nisi imago non cernitur . . . Nomine aenigmatis . . . similitudinem [voluit intelligi]*. Because man's vision of God can on earth be only a mirror image, Augustine has tried to understand the Triune God through His image and likeness in man.[45]

The quest for the vision of God cannot be but image-like, for it is an image's quest. The soul must turn toward God who has made it and thus become consciously aware of its character as divine image; to be with God is to realize fully this image relation: to remember Him, to

---

[44] See, especially, *De Trinitate* XV, 21, 41, *PL* XLII, 1089, where among other things Augustine expounds the mutual bond of love or will between the mind and its thought which exists in analogy to the love between the Father and the Son.

[45] See *De Trinitate* XV 8, 14, *PL* XLII, 1067 f.: Quale sit et quod sit hoc speculum si quaeramus, profecto illud occurrit, quod in speculo nisi imago non cernitur. Hoc ergo facere conati sumus, ut per imaginem hanc, quod nos sumus, videremus utcumque a quo facti sumus tanquam per speculum. . . . In the immediately following sentences Augustine comments on the crucial Pauline reform-text: "Nos autem revelata facie gloriam Domini speculantes in eamdem imaginem transformamur de gloria in gloriam tanquam a Domini Spiritu" (2 Cor. 3:18). "Speculantes," he rightly says, does not here have its usual meaning of "observing from a watch tower" (*specula*), but it signifies "seeing through a mirror" (κατοπτρίζομενοι in the Greek original, to which Augustine refers). This indicates the relatively obscure nature of the divine image in man and of his vision of God. However, through the great "transformation," through man's progressive reform to that same image or glory, *de forma in formam mutamur atque transimus de forma obscura in formam lucidam . . . natura [humana] in rebus creatis excellentissima, cum a suo creatore ab impietate iustificatur, a deformi forma formosam transfertur in formam . . . de gloria creationis in gloriam iustificationis . . .*, and finally: *de gloria fidei in gloriam speciei, de gloria qua filii Dei sumus, in gloriam qua similes ei erimus quoniam videbimus eum sicuti est* (cf. 1 John 3:2). . . (see also Cayré, *Contemplation* 173 ff.). *De Trinitate* XV, 9, 16, *PL* XLII, 1069: Proinde, quantum mihi videtur, sicut nomine speculi imaginem voluit intelligi, ita nomine aenigmatis, quamvis similitudinem, tamen obscuram et ad perspiciendum difficilem. Cum igitur speculi et aenigmatis nomine quaecumque similitudines ab apostolo significatae intelligi possint, quae accomodatae sunt ad intelligendum Deum, eo modo quo potest, nihil tamen est accomodatius quam id quod imago eius non frustra dicitur. Once more attention is drawn to the very different conception of similitude and mirror-image in the Greek Fathers; see, for instance, above, pp. 96 f.

know Him, and to love Him—it is in other words the reformation of
the image of God in man.[46]

In St. Augustine's conception of reform, all members of the
psychological ternaries are equally important—and this must be so,
since together they correspond to the Triune God. But, while the
Augustinian combination of *intelligentia* and of *amor-voluntas* in the sanctification of man is easily understandable and corresponds to the way
in which Augustine sees the sanctifying roles of Christ and the
Holy Spirit "as coalescing into a single action,"[47] the place of *memoria*
in this scheme is not quite so obvious. It is indeed very remarkable
and very significant that in Augustine's highest psychological ternary
the analogon to the First Person of the Trinity is memory. In the concept of memory, as here understood by St. Augustine, there is hardly
any trace left of the Platonic doctrine of recollection (ἀνάμνησις),
which Augustine had transformed into a doctrine of divine illumination
in an earlier phase of his spiritual development. This development had
begun at the latest with the writing of *De magistro*,[48] where the fact
that the act of knowing is, as it were, the recovery of truth—see
Plato's *Meno*[49]—is not explained as in Platonism by the preexistence
of the soul, but by the presence in the soul of Christ, the Teacher and
Truth.[50] In the book on the Trinity, memory, as has been seen, is not
directed solely toward the past; on the contrary, Augustine says expressly that memory is also the condition in which the mind is present
to itself.[51] In this sense, memory is the basic condition of a rational

---

[46] This last sentence is a paraphrase of Gilson, *Augustin* 296, last line, to 297, first lines.

[47] See Carney, *Sanctity* 86; cf. the literature quoted there 84 ff. See above, pp. 79–81,
for Greek patristic views on sanctification by man's participation in the divine Trinity,
especially by the inhabitation in him of the three divine persons. For the relationship between created and uncreated grace in the Fathers, cf. above, p. 79, n. 69; see also,
Augustine, *De Trinitate* XV, 8, 14, *PL* XLII, 1067 f. (continuation of the text quoted p. 200,
n. 45, still to 2 Cor. 3:18): Quod vero adiunxit "tanquam a Domini Spiritu," ostendit
gratia Dei nobis conferri tam optabilis transformationis bonum.

[48] See Augustine, *De magistro*, *PL* XXXII, 1193 ff.   [49] *Meno* 82 ff.

[50] For the entire process of elaboration of the Augustinian doctrine of illumination, see
Gilson, *Augustin* 94 ff., 103 ff.; R. Jolivet, "La doctrine augustinienne de l'illumination,"
Mélanges augustiniens publiés à l'occasion du XVe centenaire de saint Augustin (Paris, 1931)
52 ff., especially 77 ff., 115 ff., 125 ff.

[51] *De Trinitate* XIV, 11, 14, *PL* XLII, 1048: Quapropter sicut in rebus praeteritis ea
memoria dicitur qua fit ut valeant recoli et recordari, sic in re praesenti quod sibi est mens
memoria sine absurditate dicenda est, qua sibi praesto est ut sua cogitatione possit intelligi
et utrumque sui amore coniungi.

creature and a fitting analogon to God the Father who created everything in that Beginning which according to Augustine's exegesis of Gen. 1:1 is His Word, while His Spirit moved over the waters (Gen. 1:2). Memory thus comprises here the entire width and depth of the mind which learns how to know itself and how to direct its will toward the right kind of love.[52] This is why in the psychological trinities it stands before knowledge and before love. Already in his *Confessions*, the concept of memory, though on the whole applied to the past only,[53] had become a psychological focus through which conversion is initiated, reformation gained out of time and multiplicity. Memory of sin and of God, memory as distraction and as consciousness, is the bridge between the timeless perfection of the Triune Creator and the temporal and multiple nature of the imperfect creature man.[54] Augustine's

---

[52] See *Confessiones* XIII, 5, 6, Skutella 331 f.; *De Genesi ad litteram* I, 6, *CSEL* XXVIII, 1, 10. Even more explicitly than the Greeks (cf. above pp. 79 ff.) Augustine thus maintains the operation of the whole Trinity in the sanctification, in the reformation of man. He does not adopt the numerical explanation of the Trinitarian mystery, given by more extreme Christian Platonists such as Marius Victorinus and Synesius (cf. above, pp. 81 f., n. 76); on the contrary, he rejects it (cf. below, p. 213).

[53] But see *Confessiones* X, 8, 14, Skutella 219: . . . (in the memory) similitudines rerum . . . alias atque alias et ipse contexo praeteritis, atque ex his etiam futuras actiones et eventa et spes, et haec omnia rursus quasi praesentia meditor.

[54] See the famous long invocation of the power of memory in *Confessiones* X; cf. for instance, X, 8, 12, Skutella 217: . . . et venio in campos et lata praetoria memoriae, ubi sunt thesauri innumerabilium imaginum de cuiuscemodi rebus sensis invectarum . . .; *ibid.* 8, 14, Skutella 219: Intus haec ago in aula ingenti memoriae meae. Ibi enim mihi caelum et terra et mare praesto sunt. . . . Ibi mihi et ipse occurro meque recolo . . .; *ibid.* 8, 15, Skutella 220: Magna ista vis est memoriae, magna nimis, Deus meus, penetrale amplum et infinitum. . . . Et eunt homines mirari alta montium et ingentes fluctus maris et latissimos lapsus fluminum et Oceani ambitum et gyros siderum, et relinquunt se ipsos— (this is the famous passage which Petrarch read on top of Mont Ventoux, see *Familiar.* IV, 1, ed. V. Rossi, *Le Familiari* I [Firenze, 1933] 159)—nec mirantur quod haec omnia cum dicerem non ea videbam oculis, nec tamen dicerem nisi . . . intus in memoria mea viderem . . .; *ibid.* 24, 35, Skutella 236: Ecce quantum spatiatus sum in memoria mea quaerens te, Domine, et non te inveni extra eam. . . . Nam ex quo didici te, non sum oblitus tui . . .; *ibid.* 30, 41, Skutella 239: Sed adhuc vivunt in memoria mea . . . talium rerum imagines (i.e., memories of his sins) . . .; *ibid.* 30, 42, Skutella 240: Augebis, Domine, magis magisque in me munera tua, ut anima mea sequatur me ad te. . . . For St. Augustine's doctrine of memory, see also A. N. Kertész, O.F.M. Conv., *Doctrina S. Augustini de memoria mentis* (Roma, 1944), J. Chaix-Ruy, *Saint Augustin: Temps et histoire* (Paris, 1956) 10 ff., 19 ff., and furthermore M. Moreau, "Mémoire et durée," *Rev. ét.'s aug.* I (1955) 239 ff.

theory of memory therefore is related to his theory of time, which again is connected with his theory of number, and these, too, constitute important aspects of patristic reform ideology.

4. TIME

How can we experience time if it is continuously passing? This is the problem of time in Augustine's *Confessions*.[1] The past of a thing no longer exists even in the immediately following instant and the future does not yet exist.[2] The present, indivisible as it is—otherwise it would be part past and part future—is so closely "crowded in" by past and future that Augustine exclaims almost in despair: *praesens autem non habet spatium*.[3] If then we nevertheless experience and measure time, we can do so only by means of memory and expectation which are in our soul: memory of the past and expectation of the future.[4]

---

[1] *Confessiones*, especially Book XI, Skutella 263 ff. For this chapter, see also Excursus IV, 2.

[2] *Confessiones* XI, 15, 18, Skutella 276: Praeteritum enim iam non est et futurum nondum est.

[3] *Ibid*. XI, 15, 20, Skutella 277 f.: Si quid intelligitur temporis, quod in nullas iam vel minutissimas momentorum partes dividi possit, id solum est, quod praesens dicatur; quod tamen ita raptim a futuro in praeteritum transvolat, ut nulla morula extendatur. Nam si extenditur, dividitur in praeteritum et futurum: praesens autem nullum habet spatium. Cf. *ibid*. XI, 27, 34, Skutella 288: . . . praesens nullum habet spatium; also *ibid*. XI, 21, 27, Skutella 281, XI, 28, 37, Skutella, 291. See further *De civitate Dei* XIII, 11, *Corp. Christ., Ser. Lat.* XLVIII, 393: Ita etiam in transcursu temporum quaeritur praesens nec invenitur, quia sine ullo spatio est, per quod transitur ex futuro in praeteritum. This conception of the impossibility to perceive past, future, or present in themselves must be traditional. It is found also in Eusebius' *Tricennial Oration* 6, 3, *GCS, Euseb*. I, 206, though there is no sharp distinction here between αἰών and χρόνος (concerning this point, see pp. 443 ff.): Αἰὼν δ' ὁ σύμπας ἀγήρως καὶ ἀτελεύτητος οὔτ' ἀρχὴν οὔτε περιγραφὴν θνητῶν λογισμοῖς πεφυκὼς ὁρᾶσθαι, ἀλλ' οὐδ' ἐκ μέσου κέντρου λαμβάνεσθαι οὐδὲ τὸ νῦν αὐτοῦ λεγόμενον ἐφιεὶς τοῖς ἐθέλουσι περιδράττεσθαι, μήτι γε τὸ μέλλον ἢ τὸ παρῳχηκὸς τοῦ χρόνου· τὸ μὲν γὰρ οὐκ ἔστιν ὁ δὴ παρῆλθεν, τὸ δὲ μέλλον οὔπω πάρεστιν, δίο οὐδ' ἔστιν, τὸ δέ γε νῦν αὐτοῦ λεγόμενον ἅμα νοήματι καὶ φωνῇ λόγου θᾶττον διαδιδράσκει. Οὐκ ἔστιν δ' ὅλως αὐτοῦ ἐπιλαβέσθαι ὡς ἐστῶτος. Ἡ γὰρ μέλλοντα προσδοκᾶν ἢ παρελθόντα συνορᾶν ἀνάγκη· ἅμα γάρ ἐννοίᾳ διολισθάνων φεύγει. Οὕτως ὁ σύμπας αἰὼν οὐ φέρει θνητῶν λογισμοῖς καθυποτάττεσθαι, ἀλλ' ἀναίνεται τὴν παρὰ τούτοις δουλείαν. Eusebius, however, is far from developing a psychological theory of time such as that of Augustine.

[4] Cf. the entire chapters XI, 27 and XI, 28. In the *Confessiones*, *memoria* does not, as in *De Trinitate*, signify the whole consciousness of the self-knowing mind, but the latter is divided according to its "chronological" aspects of which *memoria* in the sense of memory of the past is one.

. . . it seemed to me that time is nothing else but a *distension*; but of what I do not know and it would be strange if it was not a distension of the mind itself.[5]

In you, my mind, do I measure the times. . . . In you, I say, do I measure the times. I measure as present the very impression (*affectionem*) which the things which pass away have had on you and which remains after they have passed away; when I measure the times, I measure that impression and not the things which have passed away so that it could take place.[6]

These passages are of the greatest importance for the right understanding of Augustine's theory of time. Does he mean to say that time is itself a distension of the mind or only that time is measured in the mind? The latter view, though held by some modern interpreters,[7] must, I believe, be qualified. For after having said that he measures his times in his mind, Augustine interprets his own statement in the sense that things which pass through the mind affect it and that it is this "affection" or impression in the mind which is measured when time is measured. Time then, it seems, can be a certain aspect of the mind: the mind between memory and expectation. Augustine in fact knows of two different kinds of time: that time which together with space belongs to all created existence and that time which is specifically human because it belongs only to the soul.[8] Of the two, it is not the first or physical, but the second or psychological time which is most

---

[5] *Confessiones* XI, 26, Skutella 287: . . . mihi visum est nihil esse aliud tempus quam distentionem, sed cuius rei nescio, et mirum si non ipsius animi . . .; cf. already XI, 23, 30, Skutella 285: Video igitur [tempus] quandam esse distentionem.

[6] *Ibid.* XI, 27, 36, Skutella 290. In te, anime meus, tempora metior. . . . In te, inquam, tempora metior. Affectionem quam res praetereuntes in te faciunt et, cum illae praeterierint, manet, ipsam metior praesentem, non ea quae praeterierunt ut fieret; ipsam metior, cum tempora metior. . . .

[7] So by H. A. Wolfson, *The Philosophy of Spinoza* I (Cambridge, Mass., 1934) 342 f., who, however, probably was misled by the *CSEL* edition of the *Confessiones*, where the sentence from XI, 27, quoted in the preceding note reads: tempora *mea* metior; the editor, P. Knöll, relied too much on the Cod. Sessorianus which has that reading; cf. Skutella's introduction to his edition; see also the edition and French translation by P. de Labriolle (Collection des Universités de France . . ., Association Guillaume Budé, Paris, 1937). Also, the phrase *et mirum si non ipsius animi* in *Confessiones* XI, 26 can hardly be interpreted as if Augustine had said, "I marvel if it be not of the mind itself," but rather in the sense of "if I am not mistaken, it is of the mind itself" or more literally "it would be strange if it was not of the mind itself."

[8] See, for instance, *De libero arbitrio* II, 167, *CSEL* LXXIV, 78, where Augustine says of craftsmen and artists: corpus suum per locos et tempora movent, animum vero per tempora.

important to Augustine and in the *Confessiones*, especially, he is almost exclusively concerned with it.

From the texts quoted above and from those to be discussed presently three principles emerge as fundamental in Augustine's theory of time, whether it be physical or psychological: first, time though a distension is not a material extension; second, time is not the same as motion or change in general; and third, while both time and change exist also outside the soul, there is a time which does not: this "human" psychological time is the way in which the soul copes with change.[9]

The first principle: time as such is immaterial, is implied in the fact that the present which alone *is* (past having gone, future not having come) cannot be grasped, is not extended, has in fact no "space" between past and future.[10] The distension which is time has, therefore, nothing to do with material extension. Here an interesting transformation of Augustine's sources of the concept of *distentio* can be observed. The term *distentio* occurs once in the Old Testament (Ecclesiastes 8:16), as a translation of the term περισπασμός of the Septuagint, and there denotes the multiple distraction of life on earth. Yet it is well known that Augustine also knew of the Greek philosophical terms διάστασις and διάστημα, which have a long history. For the Stoics and for Philo διάστημα signified an interval or an extension of movement and referred to the measurable space units traversed by a moving body.[11] This definition is akin to the Aristotelian definition of time as the "number of motion in respect of the before and after."[12] St. Basil and his brother St. Gregory of Nyssa used the Stoic and Plotinian *diastema* or *diastasis* in the sense of temporal and spatial extension

---

[9] Gilson, *Augustin* 254 f., stresses the psychological character of Augustinian time; on the other hand he seems to consider the concept of *distentio animi* only as a metaphor (p. 253). J. Chaix-Ruy in his valuable book *Saint Augustin: Temps et histoire* (Paris, 1956) rightly stresses the fact that time, together with space and movement, are for Augustine "le fondement ontologique de la création" (p. 103, cf. p. 3), but he does not, perhaps, do full justice to the privileged character which psychological time had for Augustine.

[10] See the texts quoted p. 203, n. 3. Augustine's insistence in *De quantitate animae* 5, 9, *PL* XXXII, 1040 f., upon the fact that the soul has no spatial extension, even though memory can include objects of vast size, is related to this principle.

[11] Cf. H. Leisegang, *Die Begriffe der Zeit und Ewigkeit im späteren Platonismus* (Beiträge zur Geschichte der Philosophie des Mittelalters XIII, 4, Münster, 1913); H. v. Balthasar, S.J., *Présence et pensée: Essai sur la philosophie religieuse de Grégoire de Nysse* (Paris, 1942) 6 f., n. 1.

[12] Aristotle, *Physics* IV, 11, 220A; *De caelo* I, 9, 279A. Cf. J. F. Callahan, *Four Views of Time in Ancient Philosophy* (Cambridge, Mass., 1948) 38 ff.

proper to creatures,[13] Gregory also in the more literal sense of an interval constituting the "difference" as it were between creatures and eternity. In his treatise *De hominis opificio* Gregory deals at length with time as a delay (ἀναβολή) which keeps man from the goal of his desire: eternity. But as everything else in creation, so time, too, was created for a good reason. Since as a result of his fall man was to propagate himself in a material, that is to say, sexual manner, God ordained the time necessary for the achievement of the fulness (πλήρωμα) of the human race. Let us, therefore, not be impatient but use the delay in such a way that we shall not be excluded from eternity.[14] Though Gregory does not differ from Augustine concerning the use to be made of time and its relative value for that purpose,[15] it is evident that for him even human time remains a physical rather than a psychological fact.[16] Already Plotinus, however, had referred the term *diastasis* to

---

[13] See Basil, *Adversus Eunomium* I, 21, PG XXIX, 560B: Χρόνος δέ ἐστι τὸ συμπαρεκτεινό-μενον τῇ συστάσει τοῦ κόσμου διάστημα (quoted also by S. Giet in his edition and translation of Basil's *Hexaemeron* [Sources chrétiennes XXVI, Paris, 1949] 104, n. 2). Cf. Gregory of Nyssa, *Contra Eunomium* 1, 341 ff., Jaeger, *Greg. Nyss. Opera* I, 122 ff., especially 370, loc. cit., 129, on τοὺς αἰῶνας καὶ τὸν ἐν τούτοις τόπον οἷόν τι χώρημα δέκτικον τῶν γινομένων. Here the ages and the *diastema* appertaining to them are quasi-spatial and the dependence on the Platonic concept of the χώρα, "background" of the formed world (*Timaeus* 52 f.), is evident. See also J. F. Callahan, "Greek Philosophy and the Cappadocian Theology," *Dumb. Oaks Pap.* XII (1958) 29 ff., idem, "Basil of Caesarea: A New Source for St. Augustine's Theory of Time," *Harvard Studies in Classical Philology* LXIII (1958) 437 ff.

[14] See *De hominis opificio* 22, PG XLIV, 205B ff. (cf. the translation of J. Laplace, S.J. [Sources chrétiennes VI, Paris, 1943], with introduction by J. Daniélou, S.J.). Cf. Gaïth, *Liberté* 168 ff. For Gregory's interrelated conceptions of time, corporeality, sexuality, and death, cf. also p. 176, n. 26.

[15] This is true also for his conviction that the temporal as well as the spatial and in general non-unified condition of the entire world reveals the harmony of parts in a whole, of opposites which tend toward unity. See for instance, *De hominis opificio* 13, PG XLIV, 165A ff., for the alternation of sleep and waking hours which leads to a continuous renewal of the human body. See also *In Ps.* 3, PG XLIV, 440 f., where the multiform universe is compared to a musical harmony (cf. Leys, *Image* 66, v. Balthasar, *Présence* 12 ff.), much in the same way in which Augustine was to speak of the world as a *pulcherrimum carmen etiam ex quibusdam quasi antithetis* (*De civitate Dei* XI, 18, Corp. Christ., Ser. Lat. XLVIII, 337; cf. also *Epist.* CXXXVIII, I, 5, CSEL XLIV, 130: *magnum carmen*); in general see L. Spitzer, "Classical and Christian Ideas of World Harmony," *Traditio* II (1944) 409 ff., III (1945) 307 ff.

[16] Gaïth, *Liberté* 168 ff., and Callahan, "Greek Philosophy," *Dumbarton Oaks Papers* XII, 56, seem to view Gregory's idea of time too much in the light of Augustine. I do not find in Gregory a truly psychological conception of time. *Contra Eunomium* I, 370 f., and II, 459, Jaeger, *Greg. Nyss. Opera* I, 129 f. and 344 f., and the other passages, interpreted in a psychological sense by Gaïth and Callahan, do not in my opinion express such a meaning.

the soul by calling time a *diastasis*, an extension, of the life of the universal or world soul.[17] While Augustine could not accept this idea unchanged, as for him the existence of a world soul was to say the least very doubtful,[18] he may still have made use of this Plotinian psychological approach in preference to the Aristotelian and Stoic cosmological outlook on time. Ever since his earliest writings he had emphasized the immateriality of the soul which has no dimensions or extension;[19] it was natural for him to locate human time in it.

With regard to the second principle: nonidentity of time and change, I mention in passing the famous text of the *Confessions* in which Augustine rejects the possibility that time be identical with the motions of the heavenly bodies.[20] Why not rather call all motion time, he asks. If the motion of the stars were to cease and were to be replaced by the turning of a potter's wheel, would this then be time?[21] It is true that without physical change, of which motion is an essential part, time would not exist,[22] but nowhere does Augustine admit an identity of time and change.

[17] Plotinus, *Ennead* III, 7, 11: Εἰ οὖν χρόνον τις λέγοι ψυχῆς ἐν κινήσει μεταβατικῇ ἐξ ἄλλου εἰς ἄλλον βίον ζωὴν εἶναι, ἆρ' ἂν δοκοῖ τι λέγειν. Cf. Callahan, *Time* 134 ff.

[18] See especially Augustine, *Retractationes* I, 10, 4, *CSEL* XXXVI, 54 ff.; cf. Gilson, *Augustin* 274.

[19] See *De quantitate animae* 3, also 13 f., and 32, *PL* XXXII, 1037 f., 1047 ff., 1071 ff. (cf. translation by J. M. Colleran, C.SS.R. [Ancient Christian Writers IX, Westminster, Maryland, 1950] 17, 39 ff., 93 ff.). See also *Epist.* CLXVI, 1, 4, *CSEL* XLIV, 550 ff.: (corporeal things have length, breadth, depth, etc.) per loci spatium . . . (whereas the soul) per totum . . . corpus, quod animat, non locali diffusione, sed quadam vitali intentione porrigitur . . .; for *intentio*, see below, pp. 209–211.

[20] This had been expressly denied already by Plotinus, *Ennead* III, 7, 8, also by Basil, who according to Callahan, "Basil" 440 ff., was Augustine's source.

[21] *Confessiones* XI, 23, 29 f., Skutella 283 ff.: Audivi a quodam homine docto quod solis et lunae ac siderum motus ipsa sint tempora et non annui. Cur enim non potius omnium corporum motus sint tempora? An vero si cessarent caeli lumina et moveretur rota figuli, non esset tempus quo metiremur eos gyros et diceremus aut aequalibus morulis agi aut, si alias tardius alias velocius moveretur, alios magis diuturnos esse, alios minus? . . . Nemo ergo mihi dicat caelestium corporum motus esse tempora, quia et cuiusdam voto, cum sol stetisset—(Joshua commanding the sun to stand still before Jericho [Jos. 10:12 ff.])—ut victoriosum praelium perageret, sol stabat, sed tempus ibat: per suum quippe spatium temporis, quod et sufficeret, illa pugna gesta atque finita est.

[22] *De civitate Dei* XI, 6, *Corp. Christ.*, *Ser. Lat.* XLVIII, 326: . . . tempus sine aliqua mobili mutabilitate non est . . . quis non videat quod tempora non fuissent, nisi creatura fieret, quae aliquid aliqua motione mutaret, cuius motionis et mutationis cum aliud atque aliud, quae simul esse non possunt, cedit atque succedit, in brevioribus vel productioribus morarum intervallis tempus sequeretur? That God is *creator temporum et ordinator* (*ibid.* XI, 6,

All the more important is the third principle of Augustine's theory of time which concerns above all psychological time; it demands a more detailed exposition of his views on the relationship between time and the soul or mind.

It is, Augustine says, not the time to come (*tempus futurum*) itself which we can measure in our mind and rightly call long or short, for the future is not yet here; the length of the future is rather our expectation which reaches out a certain length into the future. Nor is it the past (*praeteritum tempus*) itself which is strictly speaking long or short, for the past exists no longer; the length of the past is rather that memory which covers the length of the past.[23] It is the mind which contains past, present, and future, for it expects (*expectat*) the future, concentrates upon (*adtendit*) the present, and remembers (*meminit*) the past.[24] Every action of human life, from the time it is first planned to its final completion, extends over a certain length of time. Action begins with expectation in which its future course is mapped out; but as it proceeds, it becomes shorter in expectation and the part already performed sinks back into memory, while concentration upon the present exists as medium through which what was to come is drawn into the past.[25]

XLVIII, 326), that he made man *in tempore* (*ibid*. XII, 15, XLVIII, 369), does not conflict with Augustine's psychological theory of human time, because—as was seen above, p. 181—the entire act of creation, including that of man, was carried out in one and the same timeless moment and only with this moment time began; the six-day-work is contained for Augustine in the angelic mind, which, even if not strictly eternal, is not by nature temporal, though it can move and thus produce time; cf. above, p. 180 and *De civitate Dei* XII, 16, *Corp. Christ. Ser. Lat.* XLVIII, 372: . . . eorum (i.e., angelorum) motus quibus tempora peraguntur. . . .

[23] *Confessiones* XI, 28, 37, Skutella 291: Non igitur longum tempus futurum, quod non est, sed longum futurum longa expectatio futuri est; neque longum praeteritum tempus, quod non est, sed longum praeteritum longa memoria praeteriti est.

[24] *Ibid*.: Sed quomodo minuitur aut consumitur futurum, quod nondum est, aut quomodo crescit praeteritum, quod iam non est, nisi quia in animo, qui illud agit, tria sunt? Nam et expectat et adtendit et meminit, ut id, quod expectat, per id, quod adtendit, transeat in id, quod meminerit. Quis igitur negat futura nondum esse? Sed tamen iam est in animo expectatio futurorum. Et quis negat praeterita, iam non esse? Sed tamen adhuc est in animo memoria praeteritorum. Et quis negat praesens tempus carere spatio, quia in puncto praeterit? Sed tamen perdurat attentio, per quam pergat abesse quod aderit.

[25] *Ibid*. XI, 28, 38, Skutella 291: . . . antequam incipiam, in totum expectatio mea tenditur; cum autem coepero, quantum ex illa in praeteritum decerpsero, tenditur et memoria mea et distenditur vita huius actionis (i.e., the recitation of a verse) meae in

The frightening sensation of the instability and elusiveness of time hovers over page after page of Augustine's *Confessions* and vibrates through all his works.[26] In his desperate or hopeful search for eternal truth, in his contemptuous or serene rejection of impermanent satisfactions, he could have said with one of his modern commentators: "*Le temps est un effritement progressif.*"[27] How then can time be a fulcrum of reform? Only if the soul becomes fully conscious that time is part of its own life and if it thus conquers it.[28]

But because thy mercy is better than lives (Ps. 62:4), behold, my life is a distension and [yet] "thy right has received me" (Ps. 62:9) in my Lord who being the Son of Man is the mediator between thee, who are the One, and us, who are many in many things and through many things (cf. Luke 10:42). And I may thus apprehend through Him in whom I am also apprehended and may be gathered up from my old days, following the One, forgetting the past, not distended toward the things which are of the transitory future, but stretched forth toward those which are before (i.e., toward eternal life, cf. Phil. 3:12–14). Not then, according to a distension, but according to an intention,[29] do I follow [thee] "to the prize of the supernal vocation" (Phil.

memoriam, propter quod dixi, et in expectationem, propter quod dicturus sum; praesens tamen adest attentio mea, per quam traicitur, quod erat futurum, ut fiat praeteritum. Quod quanto magis agitur et agitur, tanto breviata expectatione prolongatur memoria, donec tota expectatio consumatur, cum illa actio finita transierit in memoriam . . . hoc in tota vita hominis, cuius partes sunt omnes actiones hominis, hoc in toto saeculo filiorum hominum, cuius partes sunt omnes vitae hominum. For further texts, see M. Moreau, "Mémoire et durée," *Rev. ét.'s aug.* I (1955) 239 ff.

[26] See, for instance, *Enarr. in Ps. XXXVIII*, 7, *Corp. Christ.*, *Ser. Lat.* XXXVIII, 409: Momentis transvolantibus cuncta rapiuntur, torrens rerum fluit. . . . Isti ergo dies non sunt: ante abeunt paene, quam veniant; et cum venerint, stare non possunt. . . . Nihil de praeterito revocatur. Quod futurum est, transiturum exspectatur. Nondum habetur, dum non venit; non tenetur, dum venerit. "Numerum" ergo "dierum meorum qui est" (Ps. 38:5): non istum, qui non est, et, quod me difficilius et periculosius perturbat, et est et non est: nec esse possumus dicere, quod non stat, nec non esse, quod venit et transit. . . .

[27] Pontet, *Augustin prédicateur* 313.

[28] For this double aspect of the Augustinian view of time, see the continuation of the text from *Enarr. in Ps. XXXVIII* just quoted, to the end of the sermon (cf. p. 236 f., n. 42). In general, see Pontet, *Augustin prédicateur*, as well as the equally important older book of J. Guitton, *Le temps et l'éternité chez Plotin et saint Augustin* (Paris, 1933), and the essay by H.-I. Marrou, *L'ambivalence du temps de l'histoire chez saint Augustin* (Montréal, Paris, 1950); also H. de Lubac, S.J., *Catholicisme: Les aspects sociaux du dogme* (Paris, 1947) 110 ff., and Chaix-Ruy, *Temps*, passim.

[29] For *intentio*, see also *Epist.* CLXVI, 1, 4, quoted p. 207, n. 19.

3:14) where "I hear the voice of thy praise" (Ps. 25:7) and contemplate thy delight which neither comes nor passes.[30]

"Behold, my life is a distension." The life of the soul takes place in a temporal form, the succession of past, present, future is part of the soul. This temporal order in the soul is a necessity for man if he is to integrate change and multiplicity into wholeness even of the lowest kind and into even relative permanence. The order of time injects a first element of stability into the awesome flux, the dread mutability of the many things.

The times are not empty (non vacant), they do not roll idly through our senses, they perform wonderful works in our mind. . . .[31]

For what is the character of the good things of creation?

You have only granted them to be parts of things which do not exist all at the same time (simul). Yet, in receding and succeeding they all bring about the whole of which they are parts.[32]

If therefore our senses were capable of comprehending the entire universe (totum), they would concur in the transitoriness of the present

---

[30] Confessiones XI, 29, 39, Skutella 292: Sed quoniam melior est misericordia tua super vitas (cf. Ps. 62:4), ecce distentio est vita mea et me suscepit dextera tua in Domino meo (cf. Ps. 62:9) mediatore filio hominis inter te unum et nos multos, in multis per multa (cf. Luke 10:42 [Vetus Latina]), ut per eum adprehendam in quo et adprehensus sum et a veteribus diebus colligar sequens unum praeterita oblitus; non in ea quae futura et transitura sunt, sed in ea quae ante sunt, non distentus, sed extentus, non secundum distentionem, sed secundum intentionem sequor ad palmam supernae vocationis (cf. Phil. 3:12 ff.) ubi audiam vocem laudis (cf. Ps. 25:7) et contemplor delectationem tuam nec venientem nec praetereuntem. The latter half of this text is largely made up of fragments from Phil. 3:12-14 (not, however, according to the Vulgate, but according to an older version), verses which play such a great role also in Gregory of Nyssa's mystical anthropology (cf. above, p. 105); but Gregory stresses the ceaselessness of the search for God, Augustine the contrast between temporal distentio and intentio toward eternity; cf. also Dinkler, Anthropologie 234–239, Chaix-Ruy, Temps 48 ff., G. Quispel, "Time and History in Patristic Christianity," Man and Time: Papers from the Eranos Yearbooks III (Bollingen Series XXX, 3, New York, 1957) 85 ff. See, in addition, Confessiones X, 29, 40, Skutella 238: Per continentiam quippe colligimur et redigimur in unum a quo in multa defluximus. The Augustinian ascending movement from distendere to extendere-intendere-colligere is noted also by A.-M. la Bonnardière, "Marthe et Marie, figures de l'église d'après saint Augustin," Vie spir. LXXXVI (1952) 415 ff.

[31] Confessiones IV, 8, 13, Skutella 63: Non vacant tempora nec otiosa volvuntur per sensus nostros; faciunt in animo mira opera.

[32] Ibid. IV, 10, 15, Skutella 65: Tantum dedisti eis quia partes sunt rerum quae non sunt omnes simul, sed decedendo ac succedendo agunt universum cuius partes sunt.

and would take pleasure from the succession of things in time, for only through it is it possible to conceive of the whole (omnia).[33] For the lower forms of beauty (infima pulchritudo) are brought to completion in the procession of time through the soul; and it is thus that God allows terrestrial integration to imitate to some extent the realm of permanence.[34]

But much better than these [created things, however beautiful] is He who made all things and He is God who does not pass away, because there is nothing which succeeds Him.[35]

If you, too, want to be, you must transcend time.[36]

Time then remains a distension of the soul which is a consequence of multiplicity and change. But if it is a distraction from eternity, it is also an occasion for the righting of one's intention toward eternity: "Not then according to a distension, but according to an intention do I follow thee."[37] It is a "wearing away" of the soul's life on earth, past becoming longer, while future becomes shorter; but it is also a frame of reference constituted by memory and anticipation within

---

[33] Ibid. IV, 11, 17, Skutella 66 f.: Sed si ad totum comprehendendum esset idoneus sensus carnis tuae, ac non et ipse in parte universi accepisset pro tua poena iustum modum, velles ut transiret quidquid existit in praesentia, ut magis tibi omnia placerent. . . . Ita semper omnia, quibus unum aliquid constat, et non sunt omnia simul ea, quibus constat: plus delectant omnia quam singula, si possint sentiri omnia.

[34] De musica VI, 14, 44, PL XXXII, 1186: . . . quoniam rerum transitu completur infima pulchritudo et, quod in illa imitatur constantiam, a summo Deo per animam traicitur. For the meaning of this text and Augustine's revision of it in the Retractationes, see below, p. 221, n. 28. Cf. the text from De diversis quaestionibus LXXXIII, quaest. XLIV, p. 238, n. 45. The conception of time as an imitation or sign (vestige) of eternal constancy is no doubt derived from Plato, Timaeus 37D. See also Augustine's De Genesi ad litteram imperfectus liber 13, CSEL XXVIII, 1, 487: ut signum, id est quasi vestigium, aeternitatis tempus adpareat; Enarr. in Ps. IX, c. 7, Corp. Christ., Ser. Lat. XXXVIII, 61: Quid est "saeculum saeculi" (cf. Ps. 9:6), nisi cuius effigiem et tamquam umbram habet hoc saeculum? Vicissitudo enim temporum sibi succedentium . . . aeternitatis quaedam imitatio est (in part quoted also by R. Gillet, O.S.B., "Temps et exemplarisme chez Saint Augustin," Aug. Mag. II, 940), for the context, see Excursus IV, 2.

[35] Confessiones IV, 11, 17, Skutella 67: Sed longe his melior qui fecit omnia et ipse est Deus noster et non discedit, quia nec succeditur ei.

[36] In evangelium Johannis tractatus XXXVIII, 10, Corp. Christ., Ser. Lat. XXXVI, 343 f.: Ut ergo et tu sis, transcende tempus . . . (quoted also by Callahan, Time 187).

[37] See also Sermo CCLV, 6, PL XXXVIII, 1188 ff. (concerning Luke 10:42, on Martha and Mary): . . . unum nos extendat, ne multa distendant et abrumpant ab uno . . .; cf. below, pp. 212 ff., on number, and pp. 335 ff., on the contemplative life in monasticism

which man may strive for reformation; far from being brute irrational change it is an order which points beyond itself to eternal truth.

And Christ, who is that truth, has accepted this temporal order in becoming man, in order to absorb all men finally into His eternity:

For your sake, He has become temporal, so that you may become eternal.[38]
Finally, there came the fulness of time, and He also came who was to free us from time.[39]

Therefore,

entrust to the truth whatever there is in you that comes from the truth and you will not lose anything; and what is rotten in you will bloom again (*reflorescent*) and your languors will be healed and the fluctuations of your existence will be reformed and renewed (*fluxa tua reformabuntur et renovabuntur*) and will be drawn together toward you rather than to drag you down whither they descend: but they will become stable with you and permanent unto God who is ever stable and permanent.[40]

Had St. Augustine considered time to be merely a form of physical change, he would hardly have given it so much thought nor struggled with the problem as strenuously as he did. Because for good or for evil human time is an "affection" of the soul, the idea of time is intimately related to that of reform.

5. NUMBER

For St. Augustine, number as well as time is an element of reform. Numbers belong to the realm of creation and they have a special

[38] *In Johannis epist. ad Parthos tract.* II, 10, *PL* XXXV, 1994: Propter te factus est temporalis, ut tu fias aeternus (quoted by de Lubac, *Catholicisme* 114).

[39] *In Johannis evangelium tractatus* XXXI, 5, *Corp. Christ.*, *Ser. Lat.* XXXVI, 296: Denique ubi venit plenitudo temporis, venit et ille qui nos liberaret a tempore (quoted by de Lubac, *Catholicisme* 114); cf. Gal. 4: 4.

[40] *Confessiones* IV, 11, 16, Skutella 66: Veritati commenda quidquid tibi est a veritate, et non perdes aliquid et reflorescent putria tua et sanabuntur omnes languores tui et fluxa tua reformabuntur et renovabuntur et constringentur ad te et non te deponent quo descendunt, sed stabunt tecum et permanebunt ad semper stantem ac permanentem Deum. See also the texts quoted above, p. 210, n. 30. For the relation between Augustine's doctrine of time, expressed in all these texts, and P. Teilhard de Chardin's conception of the "cone of time" see Excursus IV, 2.

function in leading man back to God. Yet numbers differ from time in that they are not only below the soul and in the soul, but also above it.

In studying Augustine's doctrine of numbers it is important first of all to realize that it is not directly connected with his teaching on the Trinity. The vestiges and images of the Triune God in nature and man, as Augustine sees them, are made to correspond to the so-called appropriations (attributes or activities) of the Divine Persons without any emphasis on three as number. God is to Augustine above all One God. He is simply Being transcending all quantity as well as quality. There are not really numbers in Him: the Three Persons in God are not numerical in the ordinary sense. The Trinity is a mystery:

One says . . . Three Persons not in order to pronounce on it, but in order not to be silent concerning it.[1]

The realm of number is within the realm of creation and re-creation, of formation and reformation. In the philosophic dialogues, written during the period immediately following his conversion to Christianity, such as De ordine, De quantitate animae, De musica, De magistro, De libero arbitrio, Augustine expressed his doctrine of numbers more largely in the terms of Platonism than later on when he wrote his great theological works such as De civitate Dei. There number speculation

---

[1] Cf. De Trinitate V, 8, 9, PL XLII, 917: . . . tantamque vim esse eiusdem substantiae in Patre et Filio et Spiritu Sancto, ut quidquid de singulis ad se ipsos dicitur, non pluraliter in summa, sed singulariter accipiatur. Quemadmodum enim Pater Deus est, et Filius Deus est et Spiritus Sanctus Deus est, quod secundum substantiam dici nemo dubitat: non tamen tres deos, sed unum Deum dicimus eam ipsam praestantissimam Trinitatem; ibid. V, 9, 10, XLII, 918: . . . cum quaeritur quid tres, magna prorsus inopia humanum laborat eloquium. Dictum est tamen: tres personae, non ut illud diceretur, sed ne taceretur. See also In Johannis evangelium tractatus XXXIX, 4, Corp. Christ., Ser. Lat. XXXVI, 346 f.: Est ibi aliquid ineffabile, quod verbis explicari non possit, ut et numerus sit et numerus non sit . . . Deus nec recedit a numero, nec capitur numero. Unde dictum est: "Magnus Dominus noster et magna virtus eius, et sapientiae eius non est numerus" (Ps. 146:5); cf. Ursula Grossmann, "Studien zur Zahlensymbolik des Frühmittelalters," Z. kath. Theol. LXXVI (1954) 22. While Augustine uses the conception of the human will or love as a copula between the mind (memory) and its thought (intelligence) in analogy with the operation of the Holy Spirit in the divine Trinity (see De Trinitate XIV, 6, 8, PL XLII, 1042, XV, 21, 41, XLII, 1089, VIII, 10, 14, XLII, 960, cf. Benz, Marius Victorinus 394 f., see also De doctrina christiana I, 5, 5, Flor. Patr. XXIV, 6: In patre unitas, in filio aequalitas, in spiritu sancto unitatis aequalitatisque concordia . . .), there is no indication that he considered the fact, that in God there are three in one, as an ultimate solution of the problems of dualism

is anchored above all in a few striking biblical passages, for instance, Wisdom 11:21 and Isaias 40:26, where it is said of God *Omnia in mensura et numero et pondere disposuisti* and *qui profert numerose saeculum*.[2] But it is equally characteristic of Augustine's earlier and later works that he sees the world built up from numbers which are direct manifestations of divine wisdom. The realm of numbers is not instituted by man, it is rather that part of the eternal truth which acts as the all-inclusive order of spiritual as well as of corporeal creation. This order is unchangeable—nobody can change the fact that three times three is nine—and accessible to human reason which takes delight in it.[3] Augustine's most systematic exposé of different kinds of numbers and

---

(cf. above, pp. 81 f., n. 76, for Marius Victorinus, Gregory Nazianzen, Synesius), though he could in his early period argue from it against the absolute dualism of the Manicheans (cf. *De moribus Manichaeorum* II, 11, 24, *PL* XXXII, 1355, see also Grossmann, "Zahlen-symbolik" 23). For the synthetic role of the three on the lower numerical level see *De musica* I, 12, 20–22, especially 12, 22, *PL* XXXII, 1096: . . . duo principia numerorum (i.e., one and two) sibimet copulata totum numerum faciunt atque perfectum (i.e., three). . . . Magna haec ergo concordia est in prioribus tribus numeris . . . ista concordia quanto est arctior atque coniunctior, tanto magis in unitatem quamdam tendit et unam quiddam de pluribus efficit. . . .

[2] Se *De civitate Dei* XII, 19, quoted below, p. 456, n. 3; Is. 40:26 in the Augustinian version differs from the Vulgate, but is an exact translation from the Septuagint; note also the reference to Plato's demiurge *mundum numeris fabricantem* (see *Timaeus* 35A).

[3] See *De doctrina christiana* II, 38, 56, *Flor. Patr.* XXIV, 44: . . . numeri disciplina . . . non . . . ab hominibus instituta, sed potius indagata atque inventa. Non enim . . . quisquam potest efficere, cum voluerit, ut ter terna . . . non sint novem . . .; similarly, *De moribus Manichaeorum* II, 11, 24, *PL* XXXII, 1355: Ratio aliqua numerorum violari et commutari nullo pacto potest nec ulla natura qualibet violentia effecerit, ut post unum, qui sequitur numerus, non duplo ei concinat. See, furthermore, *De libero arbitrio* II, 164 ff., *CSEL* LXXIV, 77 f.: Intuere caelum et terram et mare et quaecumque in eis vel desuper fulgent vel deorsum repunt vel volant vel natant: formas habent, quia numeros habent. . . . Et omnium quidem formarum corporearum artifices homines in arte habent numeros, quibus coaptant opera sua . . ., donec illud, quod formatur foris, ad eam, quae intus est, lucem numerorum relatum . . . placeat . . . per interpretem sensum interno iudici supernos numeros intuenti. . . . Transcende . . . et animum artificis, ut numerum sempiternum videas; iam tibi sapientia de ipsa interiore sede fulgebit et de ipso secretario veritatis: quae si adhuc languidiorem aspectum tuum reverberat, refer oculum mentis in illam viam, ubi ostendebat hilariter. Memento sane distulisse te visionem, quam fortior saniorque repetas; *ibid.* II, 171, LXXIV, 79 f.: Si ergo quicquid mutabile aspexeris vel sensu corporis vel animi consideratione capere non potes, nisi aliqua numerorum forma teneatur, qua detracta in nihil recidat, noli dubitare, ut ista mutabilia non intercipiantur, sed dimensis motibus et distincta varietate formarum, quasi quosdam versus temporum peragant, esse aliquam formam aeternam et incommutabilem. For the relation between form and number, see also above, pp. 184, n. 45.

numerical ratios and harmonies,[4] of a whole hierarchy of numbers, is contained in his *De musica*,[5] from which therefore most of the texts quoted in this section are taken.

In *De musica* we find, for instance, the following statement:

. . . all measure and limit must be rightly preferred to immoderateness and endlessness. . . . Two movements then which have some numerical relation to one another are to be preferred to those which do not have it. This . . . is manifest and consistent: for movements of the first kind are connected by a certain limit and measure which exists in numbers, whereas those which lack this measure truly are not related to one another by any ratio (*aliqua ratione*).[6]

Through numbers sheer diversity is ordered and directed toward unity.[7] But how exactly does the limiting and unifying power of numbers operate? What is the relation of numbers to infinity?

. . . do you see that all those rational movements, that is to say, those which have a relation of numerical measure to one another, can go through numbers

---

[4] G. Finaert, A.A., and F.-J. Thonnard, A.A., in their edition and translation of *De musica* (Œuvres de Saint Augustin VII, Bibliothèque Augustinienne, Paris, 1947) often translate *numerus* by *harmonie*. While the term "number" is adhered to here, the reader should remember that Augustine often means a numerical relation. The paramount role of number in Augustine's *De musica* is, as well known, due to the fact that this work is a treatise on rhythmic and metric.

[5] For analyses of *De musica*, see F. Amerio, "Il '*De Musica*' di S. Agostino," *Didaskaleion*, N.S. VIII, 3 (1929) 1 ff., H. Edelstein, *Die Musikanschauung Augustins nach seiner Schrift "De Musica"* (Diss. Freiburg i. B., Ohlau i. Schl., 1929), W. Hoffmann, *Philosophische Interpretation der Augustinusschrift de arte musica* (Diss. Freiburg i.B., Marburg, 1931); see also H. Davenson (H.-I. Marrou), *Traité de la musique selon l'esprit de saint Augustin* (Les Cahiers du Rhône, Série Blanche, II, Neuchâtel, 1942). For Augustine's conception of number according to *De musica* cf. also P. M. Vélez, "El numero Agustiniano," *Religion y Cultura* XV (1931) 139 ff.

[6] *De musica* I, 9, 15, PL XXXII, 1092 (the dialogue form has not been preserved in the following quotation): . . . omnem mensuram et modum immoderationi et infinitati (or *informitati*, Finaert and Thonnard, *De musica* 59, n. 2) recte anteponi. . . . Duo igitur motus, qui ad sese . . . habent aliquam numerosam dimensionem, iis, qui eam non habent, anteponendi sunt. Et hoc manifestum est atque consequens: illos enim certus quidam modus atque mensura, quae in numeris est, sibimet copulat, qua qui carent non utique sibi aliqua ratione iunguntur. Augustine goes on to distinguish "irrational" from "rational" numbers, the latter being defined within narrower limits than would correspond to the modern technical use of these terms (cf. Finaert and Thonnard 492 f., n. 17; see also H.-I. Marrou, *Saint Augustin et la fin de la culture antique* [Paris, 1938] 253 ff.); Augustine also speaks of "rational" numbers in a higher sense (*numeri rationis, numeri sapientiae, numeri rationales et intellectuales*) in *De musica*, see below, p. 219.

[7] This proposition is elaborated in detail in *De ordine* II, 18, 47–19, 51, CSEL LXIII, 179 ff.

to the infinite, if not a certain "reasonable ratio" (*certa ratio*) would check them and recall them to some limit and form? . . . For there is this power in number that every time a number is pronounced it is finite, but if a number is not uttered, number is infinite.[8]

Individually numbers are finite, but taken all together they are infinite; this infinity of numbers can be comprehended only by God.[9] Nevertheless, it is possible to find order not only in numerical ratios,[10] but also within the infinite progress of numbers itself. This Augustine tries to prove by an investigation of the decadic structure of arithmetic, by asking for the reason why

. . . although . . . number progresses to infinity, men have made certain articulations in numbering by which they return again to one, which is the beginning of numbers. For in numbering we progress from one to ten and from there we return to one. And if you wish to pursue the decadic framework and thus progress, then the progression will be from ten to twenty, thirty, forty, till hundred . . .

and so on.[11] That "the first articulation should be at ten" Augustine explains by the fact that ten is the sum of the two "principles" of number, namely one and two (not themselves numbers in the strict sense), and of three and four, the two basic numbers, odd and even.[12]

---

[8] *De musica* I, 11, 18, *PL* XXXII, 1094: . . . videsne omnes istos rationabiles motus, id est qui ad sese habent aliquam numerorum dimensionem, in infinitum posse per numeros pergere, nisi rursus eos certa ratio coercuerit et ad quemdam modum formamque revocaverit? . . . Namque ista vis numero inest, ut omnis dictus finitus sit, non dictus autem infinitus.

[9] See the famous text in *De civitate Dei* XII, 19 and the similar one in *Enarr. in Ps. CXLVI*, 11, both cited and discussed in Excursus IV, 3.

[10] See above, n. 8, and cf. below, p. 218, n. 18.

[11] *De musica* I, 12, 19, *PL* XXXII, 1094 f.: . . . ut quamvis per infinitum . . . numerus progrediatur, articulos quosdam homines in numerando fecerint, a quibus ad unum rursus redeant, quod est principium numerorum. In numerando enim progredimur ab uno usque ad decem, atque inde ad unum revertimur: ac si denariam complicationem persequi velis, ut hoc modo progrediaris, decem viginti triginta quadraginta usque ad centum est progressio; si centenariam, centum ducenta trecenta quadringenta in mille est articulus, a quo redeat. Quid iam opus est ultra quaerere. Cf. A. Schmitt, "Mathematik und Zahlenmystik," in *Aurelius Augustinus*, edd. M. Grabmann and J. Mausbach (Festschrift der Görres-Gesellschaft zum 500. Todestage des heiligen Augustinus, Köln, 1930) 362 f.

[12] *De musica* I, 12, 20–26, especially 12, 26, *PL* XXXII, 1098. See also Grossmann, "Zahlensymbolik" 25.

All this is part of elementary Graeco-Roman arithmology which Augustine probably encountered above all in the lost works of Varro.[13] This same arithmology had found an even more elaborate illustration half a century earlier in Eusebius' *Tricennial Oration*.[14] But while there the sacredness of Constantine's thirty year jubilee is enhanced by the unifying qualities of the numbers three and ten,[15] Augustine, when he connects arithmology with number symbolism, not surprisingly remains within his non-political frame of reference. In this sense, he interprets the number ten as a synthesis of the Trinitarian spiritual three and of the corporeal elemental and cosmic four.[16]

Augustine's number symbolism, based as it is on an arithmology of

[13] Cf. Marrou, *Augustin* 260 f., idem, *Histoire de l'éducation dans l'antiquité* (Paris, 1948) 249 f., Edelstein, *Musikanschauung* 69 f., 84 f. See also A. Delatte, *Etudes sur la littérature pythagoricienne* (Bibliothèque de l'Ecole des Hautes Etudes, Sciences historiques et philologiques CCXVII, Paris, 1915) 215 on the conception of the ten as a limit and means of articulation of the realm of numbers in the Neopythagorean tradition, as represented, for instance, by Anatolius, Περὶ δεκάδος . . . , ed, J.-L. Heiberg, *Annales internationales d'histoire*, Congrès de Paris 1900, Section V: *Histoire des Sciences* (Paris, 1901) 29 and 39 f., and by Ps.-Jamblichus, *Theologoumena arithmetices*, ed. V. de Falco (Leipzig, 1922) 79 ff. and 86 f. (excerpt from Anatolius); cf. also Jamblichus, *In Nicomach. Arithm. Introd.*, ed. H. Pistelli (Leipzig, 1894) 88, and Theo of Smyrna, *Expositio rerum mathematicarum ad legendum Platonem utilem*, ed. E. Hiller (Leipzig, 1878) 106.

[14] Eusebius, *Tricennial Oration* 6, 5 ff., GCS, Euseb. I, 207 ff. It does not seem to have been noticed so far that Eusebius' conception of the decadic structure of the realm of numbers (ibid. 14 ff., GCS, Euseb. I, 210) is exactly the same as Augustine's in *De musica*, and no doubt is dependent on the "Pythagorean" sources mentioned, which also Philo, *De decalogo* 7, 27, Cohn and Wendland IV, 274, *De opificio mundi* 15, 47, Cohn and Wendland I, 15, and later Lydus, *De mensibus* III, 4, ed. R. Wuensch (Leipzig, 1898) 38 knew and used.

[15] Eusebius, *Tricennial Oration* 6, 13 f., GCS, Euseb. I, 210.

[16] See *De doctrina christiana* II, 16, 25, Flor. Patr. XXIV, 31 f.: Porro autem denarius numerus creatoris atque creaturae significat scientiam. Nam trinitas creatoris est, septenarius autem numerus creaturam indicat propter vitam et corpus. Nam in illa tria sunt, unde etiam toto corde, tota anima, tota mente diligendus est Deus (Matthew 22:37). In corpore autem quattuor manifestissima apparent quibus constat elementa. In hoc ergo denario, dum temporaliter nobis insinuatur, id est quater ducitur (reference to the forty days fast of Moses, Elias, and of Christ Himself, cf. Exod. 24:18, 3 Kings 19:8, Matthew 4:2), caste et continenter a temporum delectatione vivere, hoc est quadraginta diebus ieiunare monemur. Many examples of Augustine's symbolical interpretation of the ten are to be found in his sermons; cf. Pontet, *Augustin prédicateur*, Index, s.v. *nombre*, 10. For the antithesis of the "spiritual" three and the "material" four cf. the interesting historical and psychological data given by C. G. Jung, *Psychology and Alchemy* (New York, 1953, translation of *Psychologie und Alchemie* [Zürich, 1944]).

numerically ordered multitude as a reflection of a unity, implies, first, a vindication of the corporeal world, but only insofar as it is ordered toward the spiritual (see immediately below); secondly, of the periods or "ages" of history insofar as they are a prelude to eternity (see Chapter V, 6); and thirdly, of the multitudinous and societal life of rational creatures on earth and in heaven insofar as the common good of this Civitas Dei is ordered toward the supreme good, God (see Chapter V, 7).

With regard to the first point, Augustine says in *De libero arbitrio*[17] that the mind, tired out by its search for the highest truth, "beaten" as it were by the wisdom beyond its grasp, might rest temporarily on the road in the beauty of those numbers which can be seen in things of nature and in works of art only to return refreshed to its quest for the supercorporeal sempiternal numbers. In corporeal things the beauty of numbers expresses itself not only arithmetically but also geometrically: in the proportion of parts to a whole or in symmetry between the parts of a whole (*partium congruentia*).[18] Since number tends toward unity, the simplest figures most equal in themselves—the

---

[17] See quotation above, p. 214, n. 3; cf. also above, p. 184, n. 45.

[18] Recalling his work *De pulchro et apto*, which was lost even then, Augustine says in *Confessiones* IV, 13, 20, Skutella 69: . . . videbam in ipsis corporibus aliud esse quasi totum et ideo pulchrum, aliud autem quod ideo deceret, quoniam apte acconmodaretur alicui, sicut pars corporis ad universum suum. . . . For equality or similitude and proportion of parts as numerical relations see *De musica* VI, 13, 38, *PL* XXXII, 1183 f., *De ordine* II, 11, 34 and 18, 47 ff., *CSEL* LXIII, 171 f. and 179 ff. In *De civitate Dei* XXII, 19, *Corp. Christ., Ser. Lat.* XLVIII, 838, Augustine uses the Ciceronian definition of corporeal beauty: Omnis enim corporis pulchritudo est partium congruentia cum quadam coloris suavitate (cf. Cicero, *Tusc.*, IV, 31; for the origin in Greek philosophy of the Ciceronian combination of proportion and color see K. Svoboda, *L'esthétique de saint Augustin et ses sources* [Opera Facult. Phil. Universitatis Masarykianae Brunensis XXXV, Brno, 1933] 53 f., E. Panofsky, "*Idea*" [Studien der Bibliothek Warburg V, Leipzig, Berlin, 1924] 14 and n. 57). The origin of the aesthetic of proportion, symmetry, and equality is Platonic; cf. Plato's *Laws* 667E f. and *Sophist* 235D–236A. In Augustine also, as in Plato, the works of art are inferior to those of nature, because the former are twice removed from the realm of the divine (cf. p. 111, n. 10). See Augustine, *De diversis quaestionibus* LXXXIII, *quaest.* LXXVIII: *De pulchritudine simulacrorum*, *PL* XL, 89 f.: Ars illa summa omnipotentis Dei, per quam ex nihilo facta sunt omnia, quae etiam sapientia eius dicitur, ipsa operatur etiam per artifices, ut pulchra atque congruentia faciant. . . . Sed ideo isti non possunt de nihilo aliquid fabricare, quia per corpus operantur, cum tamen eos numeros et lineamentorum convenientiam, quae per corpus corpori imprimunt, in animo accipiant ab illa summa sapientia, quae ipsos numeros et ipsam convenientiam longe artificiosius universo mundi corpori impressit, quod de nihilo fabricatum est. . . .

square, the equilateral triangle, and the circle, in this ascending order of rank—are the most perfect and a line is more perfect than a surface, let alone a solid, while the point is the most perfect of all.[19]

More perfect than any geometrical figure or than any number to be found in the realm of bodies are the numbers in the soul or mind from and through which it is possible to ascend to the numbers of reason or wisdom (*numeri rationales* or *intellectuales*)[20] which though created are very close to God.

The soul . . . becomes better if it lacks those numbers which it receives through the body, when it turns away from the carnal senses and is reformed by the divine numbers of wisdom.[21]

. . . and so through a definite regress from all wanton movements, in the exercise of which the soul shows a defect of its essence, the delight in the numbers of reason is restituted and our life is converted to God thus giving to the body numbers of sanity without enjoying them for their own sake; and this we shall achieve if, while our outward man is corrupted (cf. 2 Cor. 4:16), it is changed into something better.[22]

The realm of numbers then is instrumental in man's reform, but not all kinds of numbers are of equal value in this respect.

Toward the end of *De musica*, Augustine therefore sums up the multi-partite hierarchy of "corporeal," "psychological," and "rational" numbers,[23] which he had developed in this work, in new terms which are of the greatest interest and importance. He now links those numbers

---

[19] See *De quantitate animae* 8, 13–12, 21, *PL* XXXII, 1042 ff. Cf. Plato, *Philebus* 51C.

[20] Cf. *De musica* VI, 17, 58, *PL* XXXII, 1193.

[21] See *De musica* VI, 4, 7, *PL* XXXII, 1167: Anima . . . istis, quae per corpus accipit, carendo fit melior, cum sese avertit a carnalibus sensibus et divinis sapientiae numeris reformatur. These numbers of wisdom, though also called *numeri rationis* or *rationales* in *De musica*, transcend the reasoning power of the individual mind; cf. *De libero arbitrio* II, 79–133, *CSEL* LXXIV, 56–71.

[22] *De musica* VI, 11, 33, *PL* XXXII, 1181: . . . atque ita certis regressibus ab omni lasciviente motu, in quo defectus essentiae est, animae delectatione in rationis numeros restituta ad Deum tota vita nostra convertitur, dans corpori numeros sanitatis, non accipiens inde laetitiam, quod corrupto exteriore homine et eius in melius commutatione continget.

[23] The many more classes of numbers discussed by Augustine in *De musica* are here thus summarized for the sake of simplicity. Among the "psychological" numbers, there are those of memory (*numeri recordabiles*, see *De musica* VI, 3, 4, also 4, 6, and 8, 22, *PL* XXXII, 1164 f., 1165 f., 1175 f.). There is not, however, in *De musica* a doctrine of memory comparable to that of the *Confessiones* or the *De Trinitate*, adumbrations of which are rather to be found in *De quantitate animae* 5, 9, *PL* XXXII, 1040.

which are characteristic of the corporeal world to space (*loci*),[24] and those which are characteristic of the soul to time, "because that beauty which is changeable only in time is superior to that which is changeable both in space and time."[25] This relatively high evaluation of time as compared to space[26] gives a first inkling of Augustine's later theory of time. Here, however, time is not yet psychological in the sense of the conception of time in the *Confessions*.[27] Augustine rather places the roots of time in a "movement of life" (*vitalus motus*) which one would suspect to be the Augustinian version of the Plotinian life of the world soul (identical for Plotinus with time, see above, pp. 206 f.), even if Augustine had not confirmed such interpretation by rejecting its validity and revising his own formulation in his *Retractationes*.[28]

[24] The ancient conception of space may be roughly defined as a conception of "places" (τόποι, *loci*) and the intervals between them; see, for instance, P. Duhem, *Le système du monde* I (reprinted Paris, 1954) 189 ff., 197 ff., E. Panofsky, "Die Perspektive als symbolische Form," *Vorträge der Bibliothek Warburg* 1924–1925 (Leipzig, Berlin, 1927) 270 f.

[25] See *De musica* VI, 14, 44, *PL* XXXII, 1186: Laboriosior est huius mundi amor (it is hard to satisfy love of real beauty on this earth). Quod enim in illo anima quaerit, constantiam scilicet aeternitatemque, non invenit: quoniam rerum transitu completur infima pulchritudo, et quod in illa imitatur constantiam, a summo Deo per animam traicitur: quoniam prior est species tantummodo tempore commutabilis quam ea quae et tempore et locis. This means that corporeal beauty, which is spatially extended and temporally unstable, becomes greater, if it is referred to the soul, whose subjection to mere temporal change absorbs, as it were, the lack of spatial integration which is particularly characteristic of bodies. There is a suggestion here also of Plato's doctrine in the *Timaeus* (37D) of time as an image of eternity and this is more clearly the case in an earlier chapter of *De musica* VI, i.e., in 11, 29, *PL* XXXII, 1179. See also below, p. 446, n. 17.

[26] See also *De quantitate animae* 14, 24, *PL* XXXII, 1048 f., about the fact that the soul is not subject to the three dimensions of space; corporeal spatial magnitude is there called *tumor* (see similarly *De musica* VI, 12, 34, *PL* XXXII, 1181: . . . illa [i.e., spatia locorum] tument), a typically Augustinian term which he uses all through his works to designate material greatness and pride.

[27] The most recent editors of *De musica*, G. Finaert, A.A., and F.-J. Thonnard, A.A., are probably right in maintaining that the sixth Book was written together with the first five (c. 386–388). If we really possess only a revised edition of Book VI (so Marrou, *Augustin* 580 ff.), this revision was probably not a very far-reaching one.

[28] See *De musica* VI, 17, 58, *PL* XXXII, 1192 f.: Ista certe omnia, quae carnalis sensus ministerio numeramus . . ., locales numeros qui videntur esse in aliquo statu, nisi praecedentibus intimis et in silentio temporalibus numeris, qui sunt in motu, nec accipere illos possunt nec habere. Illos itidem temporum intervallis agiles praecedit et modificat vitalis motus serviens Domino rerum omnium, non temporalia habens digesta intervalla numerorum suorum, sed tempora ministrante potentia. Supra quam rationales et intellectuales numeri beatarum animarum atque sanctarum legem ipsam Dei . . . nulla interposita natura excipientes usque ad terrena et inferna iura transmittunt. The following translation is

There he also tells us that the realm of the supracorporeal and supra-psychological *numeri rationales et intellectuales* (numbers of wisdom) is

given, because in the last English translation of *De musica* by R. C. Taliaferro (The Fathers of the Church in English Translation, New York, 1947), the rendering of this difficult passage does not seem to me quite satisfactory.

"Now all these things which we number with the help of the carnal senses . . ., can only receive and possess local numbers, which seemingly are in a stable condition, if they are preceded in a hidden inward and silent manner by temporal numbers, which are in motion. And these again, agile as they are in their temporal intervals, are preceded and controlled by a movement of life, which serves the Lord of all things, and this vital movement is not divided in its numbers according to temporal intervals, and yet has the times in its ministering power. And above it, the rational and intellectual numbers of the blessed and holy souls receive the law of God itself without any intermediary nature . . . and transmit it unto the law and order of the terrestrial and infernal realms."

It will be noted that according to this text a certain condition, a spatial status, of the corporeal world is preceded both in rank and "in time" by the temporal movement which brought about that status. See also *De musica* VI, 17, 57, *PL* XXXII, 1119 ff., where the precedence, in both senses, of temporal over spatial numbers, in an artist's work as well as in the origin and growth of God's creatures, is discussed in connection with the *creatio ex nihilo*. Augustine's *vitalis motus*, which no doubt is identical with the *vitalis intentio* of *Epist.* CLXVI, 2, 4, *CSEL* XLIV, 550 ff., and with the *motus* or *motio vitalis* of which he speaks in *De vera religione* 42, 79, *PL* XXXIV, 158, exists even beyond the realm of bodies and in a sense belongs to the *rationes seminales*; see *De vera religione* 42, 79, and cf. above, pp. 174 f. Just as the latter concept, so also the *motus vitalis* has antecedents in Stoicism (see v. Arnim, *Stoic. Veter. Fragm.* II, 549, 710, 718, and 1132, cf. Svoboda, *Esthétique* 102–112) and in Neoplatonism; the relationship to the concept of life-power, ζωτικὴ δύναμις, vis or *virtus vitalis* (Posidonian and non-Stoic according to Reinhardt, *Poseidonios* 242 ff., *idem*, *Kosmos und Sympathie* 329, and *idem*, article "Poseidonios," PW, *RE* XLIII, 648 f.) would require further investigation. It occurs, for instance, in Gregory of Nyssa (see above, p. 175, n. 23) and in Augustine's *Retractiones* I, X, 4, *CSEL* XXXVI, 54 f. Augustine's conception of a "vital movement" at any rate seems to have its closest relative in Plotinus' "life of the world soul": they both have a time function—comparable to that of Bergson's *élan vital* and *durée* (cf. Guitton, *Temps et éternité*)—from which the time intervals, measured by individual souls in the spatio-temporal corporeal world, are derived. While in his *Retractationes* Augustine does not explicitly deal with the *vitalis motus* of *De musica* IV, 17, 58, only with a *spiritualis vitalisque virtus*, serving God through the angels (cf. *Retractationes* I, X, 4), his revision there of *De musica* VI, 14, 44 (see note 25), is highly relevant in this respect. In *Retractationes* I, 10, 4, he says that this latter text of *De musica*, with its insistence on the mediatorship of the temporally unstable soul between God and spatio-temporal beauty, is correct only if understood of the beauty of *animated* beings; yet, his own expressions in *De musica* VI, 14, 44, would lead one, he says, to conceive of the whole world as an animated being (*animale*), as Plato (cf. *Timaeus* 30B) and many other philosophers had done, but as he now no longer dares to maintain. This revision confirms that also according to the mature thought of St. Augustine time is eminently in the soul, though no longer in the "world soul," but in the soul of man and in a sense also in the angelic mind (for the latter's relation to time see above, pp. 181 f. and Excursus III).

that of the angels who transmit them to the rest of creation.[29] Already in *De Genesi ad litteram* the proper mode of angelic existence had been defined as the nontemporal vision of these *rationes aeternae*.[30]

Thus St. Augustine's Civitas Dei, which includes the angels and the elect of God (see below), is reformed by the divine numbers of wisdom which the angelic citizens already possess forever and which are continuously transmitted to the human citizens so that they may finally share in the angelic life in heaven.

6. THE AGES OF THE WORLD AND OF MAN

Awareness of the reformative function of number as well as of time can contribute to a deeper understanding of history. Among the corporeal terrestrial refractions of the eternal numbers, there was for St. Augustine that of the six ages of the world, which began after the days of creation and will end before the general resurrection of mankind. To know this history can be useful, but dangerous too for those who have not the help of the Holy Spirit.[1] The ages of history can be understood only in conjunction with the days of creation, the sixth or Christian age, especially, only in its parallelism with the sixth day on which man was created, and the end of history only by analogy with God's rest on the seventh day and with Christ's

---

[29] See the last sentence of the text from *De musica* VI, 17, 58, quoted in the preceding note. Cf. *Retractationes* I, 10, 4, *CSEL* XXXVI, 55 f., where Augustine says that in spite of the incorrect use of the term *animae* for the angels, he had them in mind.

[30] Cf. above, Part Two, Chapter V, 2.

[1] *Epist.* CI, 2, *CSEL* XXXIV, 541: After having contrasted the liberal arts of his time and the defective idea of liberty, on which they were based, with Christian liberty Augustine says: Historia sane, cuius scriptores fidem se praecipue narrationibus suis debere profitentur, fortassis habeat aliquid cognitione dignum liberis, cum sive bona sive mala hominum, tamen vera, narrantur. Quamvis in eis cognoscendis qui Sancto Spiritu non adiuti sunt rumoresque colligere ipsa humanae infirmitatis condicione compulsi sunt, quem ad modum non fallerentur in plurimis omnino non video. Et tamen aliqua in eis propinquitas libertatis, si voluntatem mentiendi non habent nec homines fallunt, nisi cum ab hominibus humana infirmitate falluntur. Cf. *De doctrina christina* II, 44, *Flor. Patr.* XXIV, 39: Narratione autem historica cum praeterita etiam hominum instituta narrantur, non inter humana instituta ipsa historia numeranda est, quia iam quae transierunt nec infecta fieri possunt in ordine temporum habenda sunt, quorum est conditor et administrator Deus. Aliud est enim facta narrare, aliud docere facienda. Historia facta narrat fideliter atque utiliter.

Resurrection on Easter Sunday, the eighth day counted from the beginning of the week of His Passion.[2]

It was seen in the preceding chapter how Augustine combined ancient arithmology and Christian number symbolism with regard to the decadic structure of the sequence of natural numbers.[3] A similar observation can be made in respect to the numbers six, seven, and eight.[4] Six, the first "perfect" number arithmologically,[5] also symbolizes the hexaemeral perfection of the work of creation and its continuation in six ages of world history. Seven, the sum of the Trinitarian three and the cosmic four (which corresponds to the four elements, the four extensions of the world, the four seasons, etc.),[6] also represents God's rest on the seventh day of creation and the rest of the souls in God after the six ages. Eight, finally, which according to an old arithmological tradition signifies the plenitude of number in a special way, because it is the first cube of a number other than one (the third power of two, two itself being a symbol of linear extension)[7]—

---

[2] See the brief, but excellent synthesis of early Christian and mediaeval world age speculation in de Lubac, *Catholicisme* 117 ff., and the recent article by R. Schmidt, "Aetates mundi: Die Weltalter als Gliederungsprinzip der Geschichte," *Z. Ki. Gesch.* LXVII (1955–56) 288 ff., where the author also discusses the Augustinian, ultimately Pauline, conception of three ages (*ante legem, sub lege, sub gratia*) and non-Augustinian three, four, and five age ideologies, all of which, however important for mediaeval theology of history, are of lesser relevance as far as the history of the idea of reform is concerned.

[3] See above, pp. 215 ff.

[4] For the Neopythagorean background of patristic symbolism of the six, seven, and eight see the example from Clement of Alexandria, *Stromata* VI, 15, *GCS, Clem. Alex.* II, 499 ff., discussed in an important chapter of A. Delatte's *Littérature pythagoricienne* 231 ff. For the Gnostic ogdoas cf. R. Reitzenstein, *Poimandres* (Leipzig, 1904) 53 and 63, H. Leisegang, *Die Gnosis,* 4th ed. (Stuttgart, 1955), Index s.v. "Ogdoas," M. Pulver, "Jesus' Round Dance and Crucifixion according to the Acts of St. John," *Papers from the Eranos-Jahrbücher II: The Mysteries* (New York, 1955) 183 and 187 ff.

[5] Because it is the first which is the sum of its non-fractional parts ($6 = 1 + 2 + 3$). Cf. *De civitate Dei* XI, 30, *Corp. Christ., Ser. Lat.* XLVIII, 350; cf. A. Schmitt, "Zahlenmystik" 355 f., 364.

[6] For the "elemental" and cosmological symbolism of the four, see above, p. 217, n. 16, also Pontet, *Augustin prédicateur* 288 ff., A. Schmitt, "Zahlenmystik" 365.

[7] See F. J. Dölger, "Zur Symbolik des altchristlichen Taufhauses I: Das Oktogon und die Symbolik der Achtzahl . . .," *Ant. u. Chr.* IV (1934), especially 175–181, where Dölger rightly points to the "Pythagorean" origin of this doctrine; cf. Philo, *De specialibus legibus* II, 211 f., Cohn and Wendland V, 139; Clement of Alexandria, *Stromata* VI, 11, 84, 6, *GCS, Clem. Alex.* II, 473; Macrobius, *In somnium Scipionis* I, 5, 11 and 15–18, ed. F. Eyssenhardt (Leipzig, 1893) 493 ff. I do not find the idea of the *arithmological* perfection of the eight in Augustine.

eight also is a symbol of the Resurrection of Christ and of Christians and therefore of spiritual resurrection in baptism which in St. Augustine's age was usually given at Easter.

The allegorical interpretation of the six days of creation, of the seventh day of the Lord, and of Easter Sunday and every Sunday, as foreshadowing the ages of history and metahistory, goes back to the beginnings of patristic literature, to Ps.-Barnabas and Justin and Irenaeus to whom it came from Jewish sources.[8] It is related to millenarism,[9] an outline of which was given in Part One of this book. To recapitulate: the six days of creation and six historical ages of one thousand years each must correspond to one another; for according to 2 Peter 3:8 (based on Psalm 89:4)

. . . one day with the Lord is as a thousand years, and a thousand years as one day.

To the creational Sabbath day then there must correspond a seventh age of rest and bliss, the millennium of Apocalypse 20:2–6. This eschatological "Sabbath" again is the gateway as it were to the "eighth day" of another world.[10]

St. Augustine had at first adhered to a spiritualized form of millenarism[11] which had come to him from the earlier Judaeo-Christian

---

[8] Cf. A. Wikenhauser, "Die Herkunft der Idee des tausendjährigen Reiches in der Johannes-Apokalypse," *Röm. Quart.* XLV (1937) 1 ff.

[9] In this connection, cf. J. H. Waszink, "Tertullians eschatologische Deutung der Siebenzahl," *Pisciculi F. J. Dölger* 276 ff.

[10] See, for instance, Ps.-Barnabas, *Epistula*, esp. 15, 4 ff., *Flor. Patr.* I, 60 ff.: Προσέχετε, τέκνα, τί λέγει τὸ "συνετέλεσεν ἐν ἓξ ἡμέραις" (cf. Gen. 2:2 f.). Τοῦτο λέγει ὅτι ἐν ἑξακισχιλίοις ἔτεσιν συντελέσει Κύριος τὰ σύμπαντα· ἡ γὰρ ἡμέρα παρ' αὐτῷ σημαίνει χίλια ἔτη (and reference to Ps. 89:4 and 2 Peter 3:8). . . . "Καὶ κατέπαυσεν τῇ ἡμέρᾳ τῇ ἑβδόμῃ" (Gen. 2:2) τοῦτο λέγει· ὅταν ἐλθὼν ὁ Υἱὸς αὐτοῦ καταργήσει τὸν καιρὸν τοῦ ἀνόμου καὶ κρινεῖ τοὺς ἀσεβεῖς καὶ ἀλλάξει τὸν ἥλιον καὶ τὴν σελήνην καὶ τοὺς ἀστέρας, τότε καλῶς καταπαύσεται ἐν τῇ ἡμέρᾳ τῇ ἑβδόμῃ. . . . Ὁρᾶτε, πῶς λέγει· οὐ τὰ νῦν σάββατα ἐμοὶ δεκτά, ἀλλὰ ὃ πεποίηκα, ἐν ᾧ καταπαύσας τὰ πάντα ἀρχὴν ἡμέρας ὀγδόης ποιήσω, ὅ ἐστιν ἄλλου κόσμου ἀρχήν. Διὸ καὶ ἄγομεν τὴν ἡμέραν τὴν ὀγδόην εἰς εὐφροσύνην, ἐν ᾗ καὶ ὁ Ἰησοῦς ἀνέστη ἐκ νεκρῶν. . . . For this text and many others, especially for Clement of Alexandria's and Origen's interpretation of the eight as a symbol of eternal life, and for Gnostic symbolism of the eight cf. Dölger, "Oktogon" 171 ff.

[11] See, for instance, *Sermo* CCLIX, 2 (about 393), *PL* XXXVIII, 1197, where the seventh day still corresponds to the *quies futura sanctorum in hac terra*, even though the millenarian scheme is on the whole given up; see also *Sermo Mai* XCIV, 4, quoted below, pp. 226 f., n. 18; for other examples of Augustine's early millenarism, see F. E. Cranz, "The Development

tradition, as did his world age speculation in general.[12] But soon he gave up the millenarian scheme, though not the analogy with the creational days, and divided the ages of history as follows: from Adam to Noah, from Noah to Abraham, from Abraham to David, from David to the Babylonian Captivity, from the Captivity to Christ, from Christ to the world's end. These ages are not millennial and they are of unequal but definite length, except for the sixth and last which is of unknown duration.[13] The exact meaning of the seventh day and age in Augustine's new and mature conception of history and metahistory will be discussed presently.

Before inspecting Augustine's metahistorical seventh day and age more closely it is necessary to illustrate the fact that for Augustine as already for Origen, for the Cappadocians, and for St. Ambrose the six creational days and the Sabbath day taken together represented through their septenary number the temporal condition of the created and historical world, and especially the ever repeated series of the seven week days,[14] which delays the advent of the eighth day, that

of Augustine's Ideas on Society before the Donatist Controversy," *Harv. Theol. Rev.* XLVII (1954) 271. Cf. *De civitate Dei* XX, 7, *Corp. Christ.*, *Ser. Lat.* XLVIII, 709, where Augustine expressly says that his millenarism had been one of spiritual, not of material bliss and joy. In general cf. now G. Folliet, A. A., "La typologie du *sabbat* chez saint Augustin," *Rev. ét.'s aug.* II (1956) 371 ff., and O. Rousseau, O.S.B., "La typologie augustinienne de l'hexaéméron et la théologie du temps," *Festgabe Joseph Lortz* (Baden-Baden, 1958) 47 ff.

[12] Cf. above, pp. 27 f. See also H. Scholz, *Glaube und Unglaube in der Weltgeschichte: Ein Kommentar zu Augustins De civitate Dei* (Leipzig, 1911) 154 ff.; W. M. Green, *Augustine on the Teaching of History* (University of California Publications in Classical Philology XII, 18, Berkeley, Los Angeles, 1944) 315 ff.

[13] See *De civitate Dei* XXII, 30, *Corp. Christ.*, *Ser. Lat.* XLVIII, 865 f. (end of the whole work); *De diversis quaestionibus* LXXXIII, quaest. LVIII, 2, *PL* XL, 43; *De Genesi contra Manichaeos* I, 23, 35–41, *PL* XXXIV, 190 ff.; *Contra Faustum Manichaeum* XII, 8, *CSEL* XXV, 1, 336; *De catechizandis rudibus* 22, 39, *PL* XL, 338; *De Trinitate* IV, 4, 7, *PL* XLII, 892; *Sermo* CXXV, 4, *PL* XXXVIII, 692; *Sermo* CCLIX, 2, *PL* XXXVIII, 1197 f.; etc.

[14] See, for instance, Origen, *In Leviticum*, homil. VIII, 4, *GCS*, *Orig.* VI, 399, 12 ff.; Basil, *Hexaemeron*, homil. II, 8, *PG* XXIX, 49A ff. (for this text see below, p. 228); idem, *De Spiritu Sancto* 27, 66, *PG* XXXII, 192A f.; Gregory of Nyssa, texts quoted pp. 228 f., n. 21. For Ambrose, see *Explanatio Psalmi XXXVII*, 2, *CSEL* LXIV, 138: . . . in sabbatorum diebus, hoc est in hoc vitae istius tempore. Septem enim diebus ebdomada omnis concluditur . . .; *Expositio evangelii Lucae* VIII, 23, *CSEL* XXXII, 401: . . . cum septimo die requieverit Deus ab omnibus operibus suis, post ebdomadam istius mundi quies nobis diuturna promittitur. . . . For Augustine, see, for instance, *Sermo* LXXXIII, 6, 7, *PL* XXXVIII, 518, *Sermo* XCV, 2, *PL* XXXVIII, 581, *Sermo* CXIV, 1, *PL* XXXVIII, 652, *De consensu evangelistarum* II, 4, 13, *CSEL* XLIII, 94, *In Johannis evangelium tractatus* CXXII, 6, *Corp. Christ.*, *Ser. Lat.* XXXVI, 671.

is eternity.[15] Augustine, Ambrose, and most of the Greek Fathers are in unison also in their conception of an increase of perfection from the seventh to the eighth "day," the latter corresponding to Easter day and Sunday, counted as eighth from the first day of the Old Testament week.[16] They all stress the superiority of Easter and of the dominical *ogdoas* of the new dispensation over the sabbatial *hebdomas* of the Old Law.[17] Thus Augustine insists that Sunday, the resurrectional "eighth day," which is also the first of a new week, symbolizes not only a return to the impermanent sabbatial rest of the *prima vita* of Paradise but something more: a rest of eternal duration and imperishable beatitude.[18] Ambrose indicates that ever since Christ's Resurrection on

---

[15] These symbolical interpretations are indebted to Neopythagorean and Gnostic speculations on the "temporal" seven and the "supratemporal" eight (see A. Delatte, *Littérature pythagoricienne* 231 ff., J. Daniélou, S.J., "La typologie de la semaine au IVe siècle," *Rech.'s sc. rel.* XXXV (1948) 382 ff.; cf. pp. 223 f., nn. 4, 7, 10).

[16] So already Justin, *Dialogus* 41, 4, ed. E. J. Goodspeed, *Die ältesten Apologeten* (Göttingen, 1914) 138, and *ibid.* 138, 1, Goodspeed 260. In general, see Daniélou, "Semaine au IVe siècle"; also *idem*, "Semaine dans le christianisme primitif" 1 ff.

[17] Also Augustine, in spite of U. Grossmann's remarks in her valuable article "Zahlensymbolik" 33 ff. For Philo, of course, the seven of the Sabbath had still been the number of supreme excellence; cf. *De opificio mundi* 30 ff. (89 ff.), Cohn and Wendland I, 31 ff.

[18] In the early *Sermo* CCLIX (c. 2, *PL* XXXVIII, 1198), which still has some millenarian connotations (cf. p. 228, n. 11), the transition from the seventh to the eighth day or age is conceived as a restoration of the state of Paradise, though the eighth, symbolizing immortality regained through baptism, is exalted over the seventh, which symbolizes the terrestrial millennium. (For the African custom, to which Augustine refers in this sermon, of baptizing infants not later than the eighth day after their birth, see also *Contra duas epistulas Pelagianorum* IV, 23, *CSEL* LX, 546 f., with a long quotation from Cyprian, *Epist.* LXIV, *ad Fidum.*) *Sermo Mai* XCIV of uncertain, but probably still rather early date and *Epist.* LV, written about the year 400, show how Augustine's thought gradually evolved to greater clarity, toward a resurrectional symbolism of the ogdoas, superior to a merely sabbatial symbolism which remains bound up with the septenarian structure of this world between creation and the end. See *Sermo Mai* XCIV, *de dominico die octavarum sanctae Paschae*, 3, Morin, *Aug. Serm.*, *Miscell. Agost.* I, 335: Octonario itaque numero praefigurantur quae ad futurum saeculum pertinent, ubi nullo volumine temporum seu deficit seu proficit aliquid, sed stabili beatitudine iugiter perseverat. Et quoniam istius saeculi tempora septenario numero dierum per circuitum repetito dilabuntur, recte ille tamquam octavus dicitur dies, quo post labores temporales cum pervenerint sancti, nulla vicissitudine lucis et noctis actionem requiemve distingunt. . . . *Ibid.* 4, Morin 336: . . . sabbatum quod septimo die significatur, quamvis eodem dierum temporali contineatur volumine, habet utique requiem quae in hac terra sanctis promissa est (this millenarian allusion points to the relatively early date of this sermon). . . . Sed propterea ille dies iam non habet vesperam quia sine ullo incursu atque obnubilatione tristitiae . . . traicit sanctos in octavum diem, hoc est beatitudinem sempiternam. Aliud est enim inter ipsa adhuc tempora requiescere in

the day after the Sabbath (*prima sabbati*, cf. Matthew 29:1) Sunday,
that "eighth" and "first" day has become the holy day *par excellence*
and the symbol for man's striving for similarity with God.[19] Among the

Domino, quod die septimo, id est sabbato, significatur; aliud autem transcendere omnia
tempora et in artificem temporum sine ullo iam fine componi, quod octavo significatur
die, qui non volvendo cum ceteris aeternitatis indicium se habere declarat. . . . *Ibid.* 5,
Morin 336 f.: Et in his quidem diebus (i.e., in time) . . . idem invenitur octavus qui
primus est—nam ipse dicitur prima sabbati (after Matthew 28:1: first day after the seventh,
i.e., after the Sabbath day) dominicus dies (the Sunday)—sed ipse primus (Sunday) secundo
(Monday) succedente decedit. In illa revera (i.e., in eternity), quam iste octavus primusque
significat, et prima est aeternitas, quam in origine primorum parentum peccando deserentes
in istam mortalitatem devenimus; et ultimam quasi octavam, quam post resurrectionem
novissima inimica morte destructa repetimus. . . . Non ergo immerito etiam ipse Dominus
noster primo eodemque octavo die dominico demonstrare dignatus est in carne sua etiam
corporalis resurrectionis exemplum. . . . See furthermore *Epist.* LV, 9, 17, *CSEL* XXXIV,
188: Quia ergo per requiem ad primam vitam reditur, unde anima lapsa est in peccatum,
propterea sabbato requies significatur. Illa autem prima vita, quae a peregrinatione redeuntibus et primam stolam accipientibus (cf. Luke 15:22) redditur, per unam sabbati, quem
diem dominicum dicimus, figuratur. Quaere septem dies, Genesim lege: invenies septimum
sine vespere, quia requiem sine fine significat. Prima ergo vita non fuit sempiterna peccanti:
requies autem ultima sempiterna est ac per hoc et octavus sempiternam beatitudinem
habebit, quia requies illa, quae sempiterna est, excipitur ab octavo, non extinguitur:
neque enim esset aliter sempiterna. Ita ergo erit octavus qui primus, ut prima vita [non
tollatur], sed aeterna reddatur. On the resurrection or Easter symbolism of the number
eight, cf. also *Epist.* LV, 13, 23, *CSEL* XXXIV, 194 f., and *De civitate Dei* XXII, 30 (quoted,
p. 230, n. 28). For all these texts see also Daniélou, "Semaine au IVe siècle" 401 ff. and
cf. P. A. Underwood, "The Fountain of Life in Manuscripts of the Gospels," *Dumb. Oaks
Pap.* V (Cambridge, Mass., 1950) 80 ff., for the symbolism of the numbers six, seven, and
eight (especially in *Epist.* LV) in relation to the hexagonal and octagonal shapes of early
Christian baptisteries and fonts. For further Augustinian texts on the seventh and eighth
days, see Pontet, *Augustin prédicateur* 297, Dölger, "Oktogon" 169 f.

[19] See Ambrose, *Explanatio Psalmi XLVII*, 1 f., *CSEL* LXIV, 347 (with reference to the
title *Psalmus . . . secunda sabbati*, which Ambrose here treats as equivalent to *prima sabbati*):
Quid est enim secunda sabbati nisi dominica dies quae sabbatum sequebatur? Dies autem
sabbati erat dierum ordine posterior, sanctificatione legis anterior. Sed ubi finis legis
advenit . . . et [Christus] resurrectione sua sanctificavit octavam, coepit eadem prima
esse quae octava est, et octava quae prima, habens ex numeri ordine praerogativam et ex
resurrectione Domini sanctitatem. Unde et in evangelio legimus δευτερόπρωτον sabbatum
(cf. Luke 6:1), quod Latine dicitur secundoprimum. Ubi enim dominica dies coepit
praecellere qua Dominus resurrexit, sabbatum quod primum erat secundum haberi coepit a
primo; prima enim requies cessavit, secunda successit. . . . *Ibid.* 2, *CSEL* LXIV, 347: Nos
qui observantiam induimus spiritalem et ad similitudinem et requiem Dei cupimus nostram
formare militiam atque in illa civitate caelesti nostrum exhibere ministerium . . ., primam
dicimus sabbati, sicut est scriptum: "Vespere autem sabbati, quae lucescit in primam
sabbati" (Matthew 28:1). . . . See also Ambrose, *Epist.* XLIV, 16, *PL* XVI, 1189C:
Itaque septima mundi (here a symbolical expression for the not yet supranatural perfection

Greeks, St. Basil expresses the Platonic doctrine that time is an image of eternity in terms of the symbolism of the seven and eight when he says that the repetition of the seven day cycle of the week suggests a relationship to eternity, since the latter revolves around itself and is infinite, and that nevertheless there exists the more sublime eighth day of the Lord which is outside this time of weeks.[20] For Gregory of Nyssa the creational *hebdomas* represents time, whereas the resurrectional *ogdoas* is the beginning of the future *aion* toward which all virtuous life directs its gaze.[21] According to Gregory of Nazianzus

of the Old Testament Sabbath) conclusa est: octava illuxit gratia, quae fecit hominem iam non huius mundi esse, sed supra mundum . . .; *ibid.* 17, *PL* XVI, 1190A: Abiit ergo hebdomas, venit octava. Abiit heri, venit hodie: illud hodie quod promissum est. . . . Abiit ergo ille dies testamenti veteris, venit dies novus quo testamentum consummatum est novum. . . . For Ambrosian symbolical interpretations of the "eight" in the liturgy and for possible influence of Ambrosian octave symbolism on that of Augustine, cf. Dölger, "Oktogon" 160 ff., 170, and Pontet, *Augustin prédicateur* 297.

[20] Basil, *Hexaemeron*, homil. II, 8, *PG* XXIX, 49C–52B :. . . ὁ τὴν τοῦ χρόνου φύσιν κατασκευάσας Θεὸς μέτρα αὐτῷ καὶ σημεῖα τὰ τῶν ἡμερῶν ἐπέβαλε διαστήματα καὶ ἑβδομάδι αὐτὸν ἐκμετρῶν ἀεὶ τὴν ἑβδομάδα εἰς ἑαυτὴν ἀνακυκλοῦσθαι κελεύει ἐξαριθμοῦσαν τοῦ χρόνου τὴν κίνησιν, τὴν ἑβδομάδα δὲ πάλιν ἐκπληροῦν τὴν ἡμέραν μίαν ἑπτάκις αὐτὴν εἰς ἑαυτὴν ἀναστρέφουσαν. Τοῦτο δὲ κυκλικόν ἐστι τὸ σχῆμα ἀφ᾽ ἑαυτοῦ ἄρχεσθαι καὶ εἰς ἑαυτὸ καταλήγειν· ὃ δὴ καὶ τοῦ αἰῶνος ἴδιον εἰς ἑαυτὸν ἀναστρέφειν καὶ μηδαμοῦ περατοῦσθαι· διὰ τοῦτο τὴν κεφαλὴν τοῦ χρόνου οὐχὶ πρώτην ἡμέραν, ἀλλὰ μίαν ὠνόμασεν, ἵνα καὶ ἐκ τῆς προσηγορίας τὸ συγγενὲς ἔχῃ πρὸς τὸν αἰῶνα. . . . Ἐπεὶ ἀνέσπερον καὶ ἀδιάδοχον καὶ ἀτελεύτητον τὴν ἡμέραν ἐκείνην οἶδεν ὁ λόγος (i.e., Holy Scripture), ἣν καὶ ὀγδόην ὁ ψαλμῳδὸς προσηγόρευσε διὰ τὸ ἔξω κεῖσθαι τοῦ ἑβδοματικοῦ τούτου χρόνου· ὥστε κἂν ἡμέραν εἴπῃς κἂν αἰῶνα, τὴν αὐτὴν ἐρεῖς ἔννοιαν· εἴτε οὖν ἡμέρα ἡ κατάστασις ἐκείνη λέγοιτο, μία ἐστὶ καὶ οὐ πολλαί· εἴτε αἰὼν προσαγορεύοιτο, μοναχὸς ἂν εἴη καὶ οὐ πολλοστός. Ἵνα οὖν πρὸς τὴν μέλλουσαν ζωὴν τὴν ἔννοιαν ἀπαγάγῃ, μίαν ὠνόμασε τοῦ αἰῶνος τὴν εἰκόνα, τὴν ἀπαρχὴν τῶν ἡμερῶν, τὴν ὁμήλικα τοῦ φωτός, τὴν ἁγίαν κυριακὴν, τὴν τῇ ἀναστάσει τοῦ Κυρίου τετιμημένην. See also the similar text in Basil's *De Spiritu Sancto* 27, 66, *PG* XXXII, 192A ff. These texts, and the kindred Augustinian one from *Sermo Mai* XCIV, quoted pp. 226 f., n. 18, must, of course, not be interpreted in the pre-Christian sense of eternal recurrence of identical events. It would even be misleading to say—as Daniélou, "Semaine au IVe siècle" 388, does with regard to Basil and Pontet, *Augustin prédicateur* 292, does with regard to the Augustinian text—that time is here conceived as a cycle rather than as a straight line; it is rather eternity that is, so to speak, cyclical—time only in so far, as its God-made or man-made divisions imitate eternity (in the sense in which, for instance, O. Casel, O.S.B., *Das christliche Kultmysterium*, 2nd ed. [1935] interprets the ecclesiastical year), while time itself, whether physical or psychological, is, nevertheless, irreversibly directed from its creation to its return into eternity. For Basil, *Hexaem. II*, 8, cf. also J. F. Callahan, *Dumb. Oaks Pap.* XII (1958) 37 f.

[21] See Gregory of Nyssa, *In Psalmorum inscriptiones* 2, 5, *PG* XLIV, 504D ff.: . . . Συμβουλεύει τοίνυν ἡ ὑπὲρ τῆς "ὀγδόης" ἐπιγραφὴ μὴ πρὸς τὸν παρόντα βλέπειν χρόνον, ἀλλὰ πρὸς τὴν ὀνδόην ὁρᾶν. Ὅταν γὰρ ὁ ῥοώδης οὗτος καὶ παροδικὸς παύσηται χρόνος . . . στήσεται

the eighth day, the Christian Sunday, is even greater than the first day of creation, "higher than the high, more wonderful than the wonderful day";[22] nevertheless, the *ogdoas* (because it connotes eternity in which beginning and end are one) also suggests the return (*apocatastasis*) of all things to their original condition of perfection.[23] Extending the symbolism of the octave to the liturgical usage of conferring baptism at Easter Ambrose, therefore, can speak in the same breath of vocation to the Kingdom of Heaven and of return to Paradise:

... who ... on the eighth day (i.e., Sunday, and here especially Easter Sunday) receives the mysteries of regeneration is consecrated by grace and called to the inheritance of the heavenly Kingdom ... on the eighth day the grace of the Spirit has been freed to restore to Paradise those whom their guilt had made exiles. . . . The hebdomas of the Old Testament is the octave of the New when Christ arose and the day of new salvation shone for all,[24]

πάντως καὶ ἡ ἑβδομὰς ἡ ἐκμετροῦσα τὸν χρόνον καὶ διαδέξεται ἡ ὀγδόη ἐκείνη ἥτις ἐστὶν ὁ ἐφεξῆς αἰὼν ὅλος μία ἡμέρα γενόμενος, καθὼς φησί τις τῶν προφητῶν· "Μεγάλην ἡμέραν" (Joel 2:11) τὴν ἐλπιζομένην ὀνομάσας ζωήν. See also In sextum Psalmum, de octava, PG XLIV, 609B ff.: Ὁ τοῦ βίου τούτου χρόνος ἐν τῇ πρώτῃ δημιουργίᾳ τῆς κτίσεως διὰ μιᾶς ἑβδομάδος ἡμερῶν συνεπληρώθη. . . . Ἡ δὲ ἑβδόμη πέρας γενομένη τῆς κτίσεως ἐν ἑαυτῇ περιέγραψε τὸν συμπαρεκτεινόμενον τῇ κατασκευῇ τοῦ κόσμου χρόνον. . . . Καὶ . . . ὅτ᾽ ἂν ἐκμετρῶμεν ταῖς ἡμέραις τὸν χρόνον, ἀπὸ τῆς μιᾶς ἀρχόμενοι καὶ τῇ ἑβδόμῃ τὸν ἀριθμὸν κατακλείοντες, πάλιν ἐπὶ τὴν μίαν ἀναποδίζομεν ἀεὶ διὰ τοῦ κύκλου τῶν ἑβδομάδων ἀναμετροῦντες ὅλον τὸ τοῦ χρόνου διάστημα· ἕως ἂν παρελθόντων τῶν κινουμένων καὶ παυσαμένης ποτὲ τῆς ῥοώδους κινήσεως . . . ἔλθῃ τὰ μηκέτι σαλευόμενα . . . διότι τοῦ ἑβδοματικοῦ παυσαμένου χρόνου ἐνστήσεται ἡμέρα ὀγδόη μετὰ τὴν ἑβδόμην· ὀγδόη μὲν λεγομένη, ὅτι μετὰ τὴν ἑβδόμην γίνεται, οὐκέτι δὲ τὴν τοῦ ἀριθμοῦ διαδοχὴν ἐφ᾽ ἑαυτῆς δεχομένη. Μία γὰρ εἰς τὸ διηνεκὲς παραμένει, οὐδέποτε νυκτερινῷ διαιρονμένη ζόφῳ. Cf. Daniélou, "Semaine au IVe siècle" 393 ff.

²² Gregory Nazianzen, Oratio XLIV, in novam dominicam 5, PG XXXVI, 612C f.: . . . ὥσπερ ἡ πρώτη κτίσις τὴν ἀρχὴν ἀπὸ κυριακῆς λαμβάνει (i.e., creation took place on Sunday) . . . , οὕτω καὶ ἡ δευτέρα πάλιν ἐκ τῆς αὐτῆς ἄρχεται (i.e., redemptive second creation took place on Easter Sunday), πρώτη οὖσα τῶν μετ᾽ αὐτὴν καὶ ὀγδοὰς ἀπὸ τῶν πρὸ αὐτῆς, ὑψηλῆς ὑψηλοτέρα καὶ θαυμασίας θαυμασιωτέρα. Cf. Daniélou, "Semaine au IVe siècle" 392 f. and ibid. 390 f., for Oratio XLI, in Pentecosten, PG XXXVI, 429C ff. Cf. also Oratio XXXVIII, PG XXXVI, 325C f., where Gregory says that the Incarnation is more wonderful and more divine than even creation.

²³ Oratio XLIV, PG XXXVI, 613A: . . . τῆς ἐκεῖθεν ἀποκαταστάσεως. Similarly, Gregory of Nyssa, De beatitudinibus, or. VIII, PG XLIV, 1292A f.; cf. Daniélou, "Semaine au IVe siècle" 397.

²⁴ Ambrose, Epist. XLIV, 5, PL XVI, 1186B f.: . . . qui . . . octavo die regenerationis sortitur mysteria, consecratur per gratiam et ad haereditatem regni coelestis vocatur . . . octavo die soluta paradiso reddidit Spiritus gratia, quos extorres sua fecerat culpa. . . . Hebdomas veteris testamenti est octava novi, quando Christus resurrexit et dies omnibus novae salutis illuxit.

and in his early *Sermon* CCLIX[25] even Augustine, whose renewal terminology and ideology were as a rule less retrospective, sees the new life inherent in the "octave" as a return to the beginning.

In all these speculations the seventh age on the whole remained part of the time-bound world, though through its correspondence with God's Sabbath it could appear as transitional between God and creation, between history and eternity, so that there is no "evening" between the "seventh day" of rest in God and the "eighth day" of ultimate eternity. In this respect St. Augustine, after he had abandoned millenarism, expressed the clearest and most original views.[26] While maintaining the "temporal" symbolism of the seven[27] he transferred the seventh age itself beyond terrestrial life, but without taking it altogether out of time and history; for he identified it with the souls' rest in God before the final resurrection of the bodies—only then the eighth age of eternity will set in.[28] Furthermore, he made a suggestion

[25] See above, p. 226, n. 18.

[26] See the texts quoted pp. 226 f., n. 18. It may be recalled that in his interpretation of the work of creation in *De Genesi ad litteram* Augustine also pointed out that the seventh day has no evening; cf. above p. 179.   [27] Cf. pp. 225 f., nn. 14 and 18.

[28] *De civitate Dei* XXII, 30, *Corp. Christ., Ser. Lat.* XLVIII, 866: Post hanc (i.e., after the sixth age of which the duration is known only to God) tamquam in die septimo requiescet Deus, cum eundem diem septimum, quod nos erimus, in se ipso Deo faciet requiescere . . .; haec . . . septima erit sabbatum nostrum, cuius finis non erit vespera, sed dominicus dies velut octavus aeternus, qui Christi resurrectione sacratus est, aeternam non solum spiritus, verum etiam corporis requiem praefigurans. In this text the superiority of the eighth day or age over the seventh is linked to a difference between the rest in God of body and soul after the general resurrection and the merely spiritual rest in God, which is no doubt that of the souls after their death, but before the resurrection of the bodies. As well known, many of the Fathers assumed that after the resurrection of the bodies and the Last Judgment the just would reach a higher degree of closeness to, or vision of, God than they could have immediately after death (for the relation of such views to Jewish eschatological ideology of the late ancient period, see above, p. 65, n. 6). For various expressions of this conception by the Fathers, and later by St. Bernard of Clairvaux and by Pope John XXII (as a private theologian), see, for instance, E. Portalié, article "Augustin (Saint)," *DThC* I, 2, 2444 ff., E. Vacandard, article "Bernard (Saint)," abbé de Clairvaux," *ibid.* II, 1, 781 f., X. Le Bachelet, article "Benoît XII, constitution Benedictus Deus," *ibid.* II, 1, 657 ff.; also B. Bartmann, *Lehrbuch der Dogmatik* II, 8th ed. (Freiburg i. B., 1932) 474 ff., de Lubac, *Catholicisme* 92–104. It would seem that this conception forms the background not only of patristic speculations on the superiority of the resurrectional eight over the sabbatial seven, but also of the belief in return to Paradise as a preparation for entry into the Kingdom of God, which was held by some of the Fathers; see p. 143, n. 58, for Ambrose's paradisiacal *habitacula* or *promptuaria*, and also p. 144, n. 61, for his "first" and "second Kingdom of God"; cf. above, p. 65, n. 6, for Ephraem's "Pre-Paradise"; Origen's con-

regarding the sixth age which likewise amounted to a rejection of millenarism and was to become of the greatest influence in the mediaeval west: he identified the "thousand" years of relative peace on earth, revealed by Apocalypse 20:2–7, with the historical period of indefinite duration extending from the first coming of Christ (the first resurrection of Apoc. 20:5 f.) to His second coming (Apoc. 20:11 ff.), that is to say, with the sixth age rather than with any meta-historical millennium.[29] In the west this Augustinian identification was to be upset only centuries later by Joachism and utopian schemes of historical interpretation more or less related to it.[30]

ception of progress from Paradise to Kingdom of Heaven, on the other hand, had no direct relation, to say the least, to the resurrection of the bodies; it rather was part of his general belief in the return of all creation to a purely spiritual condition (cf. above, p. 72).

[29] De civitate Dei XX, 7–9, XXII, 30,   Corp. Christ., Ser. Lat. XLVIII, 708 ff.; Epistola CXCIX, 17, CSEL LVII, 247 f. In De civitate Dei XX, 7, Corp. Christ., Ser. Lat. XLVIII, 710, Augustine gives two alternatives for an interpretation of the millennium of the Apocalypse: aut quia in ultimis annis mille ista res agitur, id est sexto annorum miliario tamquam sexto die cuius nunc spatia posteriora volvuntur, secuturo deinde sabbato quod non habet vesperam, requie scilicet sanctorum, quae non habet finem, ut huius miliarii tamquam diei novissimam partem, quae remanebat usque ad terminum saeculi, mille annos appellaverit eo loquendi modo quo pars significatur a toto; aut certe mille annos pro annis omnibus huius saeculi posuit, ut perfecto numero notaretur ipsa temporis plenitudo. The first alternative fitted the interpretation of the sixth age in the early mediaeval west. It is interesting to compare Augustine's transformation of the millennium with the different way in which Ambrose had overcome millenarism. While he had interpreted the millennium of Apoc. 20 as inner-historical in the sense of the second of Augustine's alternative interpretations, he had understood the first resurrection of Apoc. 20:5 f. differently from Augustine: not as the coming of the Christian dispensation, but as the spiritual resurrection of the just after their death ("first Kingdom of Heaven") still to be completed by the resurrection of their bodies ("second Kingdom of Heaven"); see Expositio in evangelium Lucae V, 61, CSEL XXXII, 4, 206: Primum ergo regnum caelorum sanctis propositum est in absolutione corporis, secundum regnum caelorum est post resurrectionem esse cum Christo (cf. Phil. 1:23); cf. Explanatio Psalmi I, 54, CSEL LXIV, 46; cf. J. E. Niederhuber, Die Eschatologie des hl. Ambrosius (Forschungen zur christlichen Literatur-und Dogmengeschichte VI, 3, Paderborn, 1907) 74 ff., 197 ff., B. Botte, O.S.B., "Prima Resurrectio: Un vestige de millénarisme dans les liturgies occidentales," Rech.'s théol. a. m. XV (1948) 5 ff.

[30] See Part One, p. 29, n. 14. In the early Christian east, an identification of the six world ages with definite historical periods, comparable to that of St. Augustine, is not found; Eusebius' Chronicon, though it has a six or even seven-partite division of history, does not use the concept of world ages, cf. Schmidt, "Aetates mundi" 304 ff. Notwithstanding all calculations and speculations concerning the duration of the world before and after the coming of Christ, the pattern of the week itself was considered only as a symbol of time; cf. above, p. 225, n. 14, and see Daniélou, "Semaine dans le christianisme primitif,"

Augustine also combined the six world ages, which themselves correspond to the six days of creation, with a sequence of six ages of individual human life. This combination is found in works belonging to the first decades of years after his conversion and he still maintained it in his *Retractationes* written toward the end of his life.

In *De Genesi contra Manichaeos*, which is Augustine's earliest commentary on the Book of Genesis (c. 389), the corporeal and spiritual ages of man, *infantia, pueritia, adolescentia, iuventus, senioris aetas, senectus*, are compared in elaborate parallelism with the six days of creation and with the six ages of the world.[31] The fifth and sixth divisions may serve as examples:[32]

especially 16, also the other literature cited above, pp. 223 ff. However, it is interesting to see how in Byzantine eschatological texts of the seventh century, that is to say, after the traditional six thousand years from the presumed date of creation in 5500 B.C. had elapsed for some time, the seventh millennium, too, could be treated as historical and pre-eschatological; cf. E. v. Dobschütz, "Coislinianus 296," *Byz. Z.* XII (1903) 534 ff., especially 553 f., 566; A. A. Vasiliev, "Medieval Ideas of the End of the World: West and East," *Byzantion* XVI (1942–1943) 499 f. For somewhat different reasons, the mediaeval west after the great reawakening of historical speculation in the twelfth century tended to include a seventh age in his scheme of historical world ages; cf., for instance, A. Dempf, *Sacrum Imperium* (München, Berlin, 1929) 233 ff., for Rupert of Deutz, Otto of Freising, etc., 276, for Joachim of Flora, and 372 f., for St. Bonaventure.

    [31] See *De Genesi contra Manichaeos* I, 23, 25–35, 43, *PL* XXXIV, 190 ff. The parallelism is expressed, though in much less elaborate fashion, also in *De diversis quaestionibus LXXXIII*, *quaest.*, LVIII, 2 f., *PL* XL, 43 f. (this work was begun about 389); instead of *senioris aetas* Augustine here uses the term *gravitas*. It is obvious that Augustine's sixfold division of man's life signifies an adaptation of individual human development to the number of the six days of creation and of the six world ages. For the conception of six ages of individual man was very rare in Antiquity; the most common divisions were fourfold (still to be found in Ambrose, *De Abraham* II, 9, 65, *CSEL* XXXII, 1, 621), fivefold (still in Augustine, *Enarr. in Ps.* CXXVII, 15, Corp. Christ., Ser. Lat. XL, 1878), sevenfold and tenfold (for these two latter, see, for instance, Ambrose, *Epist.* XLIV, 12 f., *PL* XVI, 1189A ff., who, following Philo, in his long excursus on the number seven, *De mundi opificio* 30, 89 to 42, 127, Cohn and Wendland I, 31 ff., refers to Hippocrates' seven ages and to Solon's ten seven years' periods). Cf. A. Delatte, *Littérature pythagoricienne* 182 ff., Dobschütz, "Coislinianus 296," 563 ff., F. Boll, "Die Lebensalter," *Neue Jahrbücher für das klassische Altertum, Geschichte und deutsche Literatur* XXXI (1913) 89 ff., A. Hofmeister, "Puer, Iuvenis, Senex," *Papsttum und Kaisertum . . . Paul Kehr zum 65. Geburtstag* (München, 1926) 287 ff. Isidore of Seville, *Etymol.* XI, 2, ed. W. M. Lindsay II (Oxford, 1911), and *Differentiae* II, 19, *PL* LXXXIII, 81, has sixfold divisions of human life, which are on the whole identical with Augustine's scheme, and through Isidore such sixfold divisions became the most common ones in the mediaeval west (cf. Hofmeister 289 ff.).

    [32] For a translation of the full text relating to all six ages, see G. Boas, *Essays on Primitivism and Related Ideas in the Middle Ages* (Baltimore, 1948) 177 ff.

. . . and there was morning (i.e., the morning of the fifth day of creation, understood allegorically) [and there occurred] the transmigration to Babylon. . . . [33] And this age stretches out to the advent of our Lord Jesus Christ; this is the fifth age, a decline from early manhood (*iuventus*) to old age (*senectus*), not yet old age, but no longer early manhood, rather later manhood (*senioris aetas*), which the Greeks call πρεσβύτην, for an old man (*senex*) is called by them not πρεσβύτης, but γερών. And really, in the Jewish people, this age is bent down and broken in the same way, in which a man becomes an older man (*senior*) after his early manhood. And this age is well compared to that fifth day [of creation] on which the water animals and the birds of the air were made; [for] afterwards (i.e., in the fifth age of world history) those men among the nations began to live in the sea as it were and to have uncertain and unstable seats as the volatile birds. . . . The evening as it were of that day, that is to say, of that age, is the multiplication of sins in the Jewish people; for they were blinded to such an extent that they could not even acknowledge the Lord Jesus Christ. [34]

But there was morning through the preaching of the gospel by our Lord Jesus Christ and the fifth day ends. The sixth begins in which the old age (*senectus*) of the old man is seen. For in this age that carnal kingdom (i.e., the Kingdom of the Jews) was greatly weakened, when also the Temple was torn down and the sacrifices themselves stopped; and now that nation, as far as the strength of its kingdom is concerned, draws its last breath as it were. Yet in that age, in the old age of the old man as it were, the new man is born who already lives in the spirit. . . . At that time (i.e., on the sixth day of creation) man was made in the image and likeness of God, just as in the sixth age our Lord was born in the flesh. . . . And, as in that day [there were] male and female, so in this age [there is] Christ and the Church (cf. Eph. 5:22-33). [35]

---

[33] For Augustine's later exegesis of the mornings and evenings of the days of creation in *De Genesi ad litteram*, see above, pp. 179 f., n. 36.

[34] *De Genesi contra Manichaeos* I, 23, 39, *PL* XXXIV, 191 f.: 5ª aetas: Et fit mane transmigratio in Babyloniam. . . . Et porrigitur haec aetas usque ad adventum Domini nostri Iesu Christi, id est quinta aetas, scilicet declinatio a iuventute ad senectutem, nondum senectus, sed iam non iuventus: quae senioris aetas est, quem Graeci πρεσβύτην vocant. Nam senex apud eos non πρεσβύτης, sed γερών dicitur. Et revera sic ista aetas a regni robore inclinata et fracta est in populo Iudaeorum, quemadmodum homo a iuventute fit senior. Et bene comparatur illi diei quinto, quo facta sunt in aquis animalia et volatilia coeli, posteaquam illi homines inter gentes tanquam in mari vivere coeperunt et habere incertam sedem et instabilem sicut volantes aves. . . . Huius diei, hoc est huius aetatis, quasi vespera est multiplicatio peccatorum in populo Iudaeorum, quia sic excaecati sunt, ut etiam Dominum Iesum Christum non possent agnoscere.

[35] Cf. also below p. 238, n. 48.

And on that day man was set before the cattle and serpents and birds of the air, just as in this age Christ rules the souls who obey Him and who came to the Church in part from the gentiles and in part from the people of the Jews. . . . And as in that day man and the animals which are with him fed on seed-bearing herbs and fruit-bearing trees and green herbs, so in this age, as regards every spiritual man who is a good servant of Christ and imitates Him as best he can, he as well as the people with him are nourished spiritually by the food of the Holy Scriptures and by the divine law: this will result in part in their absorbing the fecundity of argument (*rationum*) and speech (*sermonum*) through the seed-bearing herbs as it were; in part in making the ways of human behavior useful (*ad utilitatem*) through the fruit-bearing trees as it were; in part in strengthening faith, hope, and charity directed toward life eternal, through the green, that is to say, the strong, herbs as it were. . . . But the evening of that age—may it not find us [here], if only it has not yet begun—is the one of which the Lord says: "But yet the Son of Man, when He cometh, shall He find, think you, faith on earth?" (Luke 18:8). . . .[36]

Thus far Augustine's exegesis has been historical and allegorical. In the following chapter he continues the interpretation of the work of the six days in a moral (tropological) sense, comparing them with the spiritual ages of man.

. . . on the fifth day he (i.e., man) made stronger by his acquaintance with these things (i.e., having become acquainted on the fourth day with spiritual intelligence and with its goal, the unchangeable truth, which are comparable to the stars and the sun, respectively, all of which were created on that fourth day), on the fifth day [then] man should begin to work in the most turbulent actions of the world, as if in the waters of the sea for the use of the society of his brethren . . . (*propter utilitatem fraternae societatis*).

But on the sixth day he should produce from the earth a living soul (*animam*

---

[36] *De Genesi contra Manichaeos* I, 23, 40 f., *PL* XXXIV, 192 f.: 6ª aetas: Mane autem fit ex praedicatione evangelii per Dominum nostrum Iesum Christum et finitur dies quintus: incipit sextus, in quo senectus veteris hominis apparet. Hac enim aetate illud carnale regnum vehementer attritum est, quando et templum deiectum est et sacrificia ipsa cessaverunt et nunc ea gens, quantum ad regni sui vires attinet, quasi extremam vitam trahit. In ista tamen aetate tanquam in senectute veteris hominis homo novus nascitur qui iam spiritualiter vivit. . . . Tunc fit homo ad imaginem et similitudinem Dei, sicut in ista sexta aetate nascitur in carne Dominus noster. . . . Et quemadmodum in illo die masculus et femina, sic et in ista aetate Christus et ecclesia (cf. Eph. 5:22–33). Et praeponitur homo in illo die pecoribus et serpentibus et volatilibus coeli, sicut in ista aetate Christus regit animas obtemperantes sibi, quae ad ecclesiam eius partim de gentibus partim de populo Iudaeorum venerunt. . . . Et sicut in illo die pascitur homo et animalia, quae cum ipso sunt, herbis seminalibus et lignis fructiferis et herbis viridibus, sic ista aetate spiritualis homo,

vivam), that is to say, out of the very stability of his mind (*mentis*), where it bears spiritual fruit, namely good thoughts, he should rule all the movements of his mood (*animi*), so that there be in him a living soul which serves reason and justice not temerity and sin. So also should man in the image and likeness of God become male and female: this means intellect (*intellectus*) and act (*actio*) and spiritual fetus from their copulation should fill the earth, that is to say, should subdue the flesh. . . .[37]

In his book *De vera religione*, written soon after *De Genesi ad Manichaeos* (c. 389–390), Augustine does not deal with the world ages but only with the physical and spiritual ages of man. Nevertheless, he retains the division of human life in six ages, *infantia*, *pueritia*, *adolescentia*, *iuventus*, *senior* (*aetas*), *deterior aetas*.[38] No doubt he wished to preserve the parallelism with the number of the world ages and of the creational days. The latter relationship is suggested by the characterization of the sixth age of man (old age) as a transition—later Augustine will say reform—to that perfect form of man which was made in the image and likeness of God.[39] The "seventh age" of man finally is

quicumque bonus minister est Christi et eum bene quantum potest imitatur, cum ipso populo spiritualiter pascitur sanctarum scripturarum alimentis et lege divina: partim ad concipiendam fecunditatem rationum atque sermonum tanquam herbis seminalibus, partim ad utilitatem morum conversationis humanae tanquam lignis fructiferis, partim ad vigorem fidei spei et charitatis in vitam aeternam tanquam herbis viridibus, id est, vigentibus. . . . *Ibid.* I, 23, 41, XXXIV, 193: 7ª aetas: Huius autem aetatis quasi vespera, quae utinam nos non inveniat, si tamen nondum coepit, illa est de qua Dominus dicit: "Putas cum veniet filius hominis inveniet fidem super terram?" (Luke 18:8). . . .

[37] *Ibid.* I, 25, 43, XXXIV, 194: Quarum rerum notitia fortior effectus incipiat quinto die in actionibus turbulentissimi saeculi tanquam in aquis maris operari propter utilitatem fraternae societatis et de corporalibus actionibus quae ad ipsum mare pertinent, id est, ad hanc vitam, producere animarum vivarum reptilia, id est, opera, quae prosint animis vivis, et cetos magnos, id est, fortissimas actiones, quibus fluctus saeculi dirumpuntur et contemnuntur, et volatilia coeli, id est, voces coelestia praedicantes. Sexto autem die producat de terra animam vivam, id est, de ipsa stabilitate mentis suae, ubi spirituales habet fructus, id est, bonas cogitationes, motu[s] omnes animi sui regat, ut sit in illo anima viva, id est, rationi et iustitiae serviens, non temeritati atque peccato. Ita fiat etiam homo ad imaginem et similitudinem Dei, masculus et femina, id est, intellectus et actio, quorum copulatione spiritualis fetus terram impleat, id est, carnem subiciat. . . .

[38] *De vera religione* 26, 48, PL XXXIV, 143 f. For the important role of this treatise in Augustine's spiritual development see below, pp. 263–265; cf. H. Dörries, "Das Verhältnis des Neuplatonischen und Christlichen in Augustins 'de vera religione'," Z. neutest. Wiss. XXIII (1924) 64 ff., Cranz, "Augustine's Ideas on Society," 266 ff.

[39] *De vera religione* 26, 49, PL XXXIV, 143 f.: Sextam [aetatem] omnimodae mutationis in aeternam vitam et usque ad totam oblivionem vitae temporalis transeuntem in perfectam formam quae facta est ad imaginem et similitudinem Dei.

identical with the seventh world age; for it is eternal rest and life itself, perpetual beatitude which does not know further ages.[40] Augustine does not here mention the eighth age, probably because in this treatise he was not concerned primarily with the historical and metahistorical world ages, but with man and his ages from birth to death.

Augustine then considered the progress of man through time not merely as a process of decay. To the ageing of individual man there corresponds his spiritual renewal, to the decline of the people of the Old Testament the coming of Christ, and above all to the creation of man on the last day of the six-day-work his reform in the last age of world history. Augustine never tires in saying it:

On the sixth day, in the book of Genesis, man is formed according to the image of God; in the sixth age of the world our reformation becomes manifest, in newness of the mind, according to the image of Him who created us, as the apostle says (cf. Col. 3:10).[41]

The comparatively external juxtaposition of the days of creation and of the world ages by the earlier Fathers thus receives a deeper meaning.

Looking, therefore, upon sin, upon mortality, upon time flying by, upon moaning and labor and sweat, upon ages succeeding one another without

---

[40] *Ibid.*, XXXIV, 144: Septima enim iam quies aeterna est et nullis aetatibus distinguenda beatitudo perpetua. Ut enim finis veteris hominis mors est, sic finis novi hominis vita aeterna.

[41] *Contra Faustum Manichaeum* XII, 8, *CSEL* XXV, 1, 336: Sexto die in Genesi formatur homo ad imaginem Dei: sexta aetate saeculi manifestatur reformatio nostra in novitate mentis secundum imaginem eius, qui creavit nos, sicut dicit apostolus (cf. Col. 3, 10). See further *De catechizandis rudibus* 22, 39, *PL* XL, 338: . . . ut hac sexta aetate mens humana renovetur ad imaginem Dei, sicut sexta die homo factus est ad imaginem Dei. See also *De Trinitate* IV, 4, 7, *PL* XLII, 892: . . . Deus sex diebus perfecit opera sua et sexto die factus est homo ad imaginem Dei. Et sexta aetate generis humani Filius Dei venit et factus est filius hominis, ut nos reformaret ad imaginem Dei; similarly *Enarr. in Ps. XCII*, 1, *Corp. Christ., Ser. Lat.* XXXIX, 1291, and in *In Johannis evangelium tractatus* IX, 6, *Corp. Christ., Ser. Lat.* XXXVI, 93 f.; with special reference to baptismal renovation, *Sermo* CCLIX, 2, *In die dominica octavarum Paschae*, *PL* XXXVIII, 1198: Et ideo quomodo formatus est homo in Genesi sexto die ad imaginem Dei, sic et in isto tempore quasi sexto die totius saeculi renovamur in baptismo, ut recipiamus imaginem conditoris nostri (on the other hand, baptism can be linked also to the symbolism of the eighth "day" or "age" of eternity, cf. pp. 224, 226 f.). Already Ambrose had said, *Expositio evangelii Lucae* V, 27, *CSEL* XXXII, 4, 191: Sexto autem die factus est homo, sexto igitur Christi opere reformatur iam non vetus sed nova creatura et quaedam forma peregrina.

rest, senselessly from infancy into old age—looking at these things, let us see in them the old man, the old day, the old canticle, the Old Testament. But, if we turn to the inward man, to the things that are to be renewed, let us find . . . a new man, a new day, a new canticle, the New Testament—and we shall love this newness so that we shall not fear there any oldness. . . . [42]

Augustine has described his own individual renewal as a history, in the *Confessiones*,[43] and he considers history itself as the interaction between God's ever renewing grace and mankind's individual efforts to make that grace fructify in reformation of character and circumstances. In collective as well as in personal history renewal must come from the innermost center of souls. All the more exasperating is the slowness of man's response to this crucial exigency of all reform.

Sero te amavi, pulchritudo tam antiqua et tam nova, sero te amavi. Et ecce intus eras, et ego foris et ibi te quaerebam et in ista formosa quae fecisti deformis inruebam. Mecum eras, et tecum non eram. [44]

This impassioned outcry, to which no translation can do full justice, concerns only an individual, Augustine himself. But it is related to the problem of the origins of Christian history as a whole: Why did Christ come so late and not immediately after man's fall? Augustine's answer links together the mysteries of individual and world history, which are both timeless in God's eternal present but for man exist in an order of succession.

For everything beautiful comes from the highest beauty, which is God; temporal beauty however is realized in those things which pass and succeed one another. Now, in all individual men every age from infancy to old age has its splendor (*decorem*) . . . and thus he is absurd who desires that there be only

[42] *Enarr. in Ps. XXXVIII*, 9, *Corp. Christ.*, *Ser. Lat.* XXXVIII, 410: Ergo ad peccatum, ad mortalitatem, ad praetervolantia tempora, ad gemitum et laborem et sudorem, ad aetates succedentes non manentes, ab infantia usque ad senectutem sine sensu transeuntes—ad haec adtendentes videamus hic veterem hominem, veterem diem, vetus canticum, vetus testamentum; conversi autem ad interiorem, ad ea quae innovanda sunt . . . inveniamus hominem novum, diem novum, canticum novum, testamentum novum—et sic amemus istam novitatem, ut non ibi timeamus vetustatem . . . (and this renovation will go on to the final resurrection of the bodies).

[43] Cf. R. Guardini, *Die Bekehrung des Aurelius Augustinus* (München, 1950) 15 f.

[44] *Confessiones* X, 27, 38, Skutella 23 f. Translation by E. B. Pusey: Too late loved I Thee, O Thou Beauty of ancient days, yet ever new! too late I loved Thee! And behold, Thou wert within, and I abroad, and there I searched for Thee; deformed I, plunging amid those fair forms, which Thou hadst made. Thou wert with me, but I was not with Thee.

one age in mankind itself as a whole; for it too has its ages as one man. And thus the Master through whose imitation mankind was to be formed toward its best moral state could not come from God, except at the time when it had reached the prime of manhood (*tempore iuventutis*).[45]

To this Augustine adds in his *Retractationes*:

But it might cause one to wonder why elsewhere[46] we have said that Christ came in the sixth age of the human race as if in its old age. Now, what was said about the age of manhood (*iuventus*) refers to the vigor and fervor of faith which operates by love and what was said about old age to the number (i.e., to the period) of time. . . .[47]

In the same way then in which the sixth day was the crowning of the work of creation, because man was then made in the image of God, are the old age of individual man and the sixth age of his history an end also in the sense of a new beginning. When Augustine, following St. Paul (Eph. 5:22–23), compares the creation of man as male and female on the sixth day with man's salvation by Christ and the Church in the sixth age,[48] it is seen that the sexual mode of propagation, which Gregory of Nyssa had considered only as a necessity foreseen by God in view of man's fall,[49] has become for Augustine a symbolical anticipation of the communal life of reformed man with Christ in the Church—which in its essence is the City of God.

---

[45] *De diversis quaestionibus LXXXIII*, quaest. XLIV, *PL* XL, 28: Quare tanto post venit Dominus Iesus Christus, et non in principio peccati hominis (chapter heading). Quia omne pulchrum a summa pulchritudine est, quod Deus est, temporalis autem pulchritudo rebus decedentibus succedentibusque peragitur. Habet autem decorem suum in singulis quibusque hominibus singula quaeque aetas ab infantia usque ad senectutem. Sicut ergo absurdus est qui iuvenilem tantum aetatem vellet esse in homine temporibus subdito . . ., sic absurdus est qui in ipso universo genere humano unam aetatem desiderat, nam et ipsum tanquam unus homo aetates suas agit. Nec oportuit venire divinitus magistrum, cuius imitatione in mores optimos formaretur, nisi tempore iuventutis.

[46] Cf. *De Genesi contra Manichaeos* I, 23, 40, *PL* XXXIV, 192; see also above, pp. 233 ff.

[47] *Retractationes* I, 25, 44, *CSEL* XXXVI, 121: Sed potest movere cur alibi dixerimus Christum in generis humani sexta aetate tamquam in senectute venisse. Hoc ergo quod de iuventute dictum est, ad vigorem fervoremque fidei refertur, quae per dilectionem operatur (cf. Gal. 5:6), illud autem de senectute ad temporum numerum. . . .

[48] See the text from *De Genesi contra Manichaeos*, quoted above, pp. 233 f., n. 36. This Augustinian linking of man's bisexuality to the image-likeness with God and its reform is more convincing than K. Barth's attempt to extend this relationship to an analogy with an inner-Trinitarian I-thou relationship; cf. above, p. 59, n. 49.

[49] See above, p. 175.

7. CIVITAS DEI

The significance of the Civitas Dei idea for the history of reform is bound up with its relation to the idea of the Church.[1] In order to elucidate this point it will be necessary to proceed methodically and to add another disquisition on the Augustinian Civitas Dei to the many already in existence.

For it is He Himself (i.e., God) who in the beginning founded the world, full of all good things, those visible and those intelligible; and in it He established nothing better than the spirits to whom He gave understanding (*intelligentia*) and granted the ability to contemplate Him and bound together in one society (*una societate*) which we call the holy and supernal city (*sanctam et supernam civitatem*). In it, that by which they (i.e., the spirits) are sustained and are happy is God Himself, their common life and nourishment as it were. . . .[2]

For St. Augustine, then, the best in creation is the society or community of the angels, to which are joined those men who are redeemed and are predestined for heaven,[3]

so that through them that part of the angels which has fallen away is made up for and restored by God and thus that beloved and supernal city is not

---

[1] Most of this chapter had been written before I became acquainted with the second volume of Mons. Charles Journet's work *L'église du verbe incarné* (Desclée de Brouwer, 1951), which in the chapter "Synonymes du nom d'église" (vol. II, pp. 50–92) contains an important theological and historical discussion of the ecclesiological terms *ecclesia, corpus, sponsa, regnum, communio sanctorum*, and *civitas*. Mons. Journet makes it abundantly clear that all these names designate the same reality, seen in its diverse aspects. The analysis of Augustine's *civitas* terminology, here attempted, only endeavors to illustrate the historical reasons for the significant role which the conception of the two cities assumed in Augustine's thought. The most important recent treatment of the subject is found in S. J. Grabowski, *The Church: An Introduction to the Theology of St. Augustine* (St. Louis, London, 1957); see references to this work in some of the notes to this chapter.

[2] *De civitate Dei* XXII, 1, *Corp. Christ., Ser. Lat.* XLVIII, 806: Ipse est enim, qui in principio condidit mundum plenum bonis omnibus visibilibus atque intellegibilibus rebus, in quo nihil melius instituit quam spiritus, quibus intellegentiam dedit et suae contemplationis habiles capacesque sui praestitit atque una societate devinxit, quam sanctam et supernam dicimus civitatem, in qua res, qua sustententur beatique sint, Deus ipse illis est tamquam vita victusque communis. . . .

[3] Gilson, *Augustin* 238, and also in his introduction to the translation of *De civitate Dei* by G. G. Walsh, S.J. (The Fathers of the Church in English Translation VIII, New York,

defrauded of the number of its citizens—nay, perhaps, may rejoice in an even larger number.[4]

The social character of the highest categories of Christian life is to St. Augustine a truth which he repeats ever so often:

For whence could this City of God . . . either originate or proceed on its run or reach its due end, if the life of the saints was not a social life?[5]

This origin, "process,"[6] and end Augustine has described in the twenty-two books of his great work *On the City of God*. It might also have been called "On the Two Cities":

Two loves then have made two cities, love of self unto contempt of God the earthly city, but love of God unto contempt of self the heavenly city. . . .[7]

These *civitates* are not cities or states; the term *civitas* is a "mystical"

1950), p. lxiii, rightly stresses the fact that membership in the City of God is ultimately dependent on divine predestination. See *De civitate Dei* XV, 1, *Corp. Christ., Ser. Lat.* XLVIII, 453: . . . duo genera . . ., unum eorum qui secundum hominem, alterum eorum qui secundum Deum vivunt; quas etiam mystice appellamus civitates duas, hoc est duas societates hominum, quarum est una, quae praedestinata est in aeternum regnare cum Deo, altera aeternum supplicium subire cum diabolo.

[4] *De civitate Dei* XXII, 1, XLVIII, 807: . . . ut inde [Deus] suppleat et instauret partem, quae lapsa est angelorum, ac sic illa dilecta et superna civitas non fraudetur suorum numero civium, quin etiam fortassis et uberiore laetetur. See also *Enchiridion* 29 (9), *PL* XL, 246. See pp. 326, n. 17, 329 f. for the special role in this repletion of the number of the angels of those who live the virginal *vita angelica*.

[5] *De civitate Dei* XIX, 5, *Corp. Christ., Ser. Lat.* XLVIII, 669: Nam unde ista Dei civitas . . . vel inchoaretur exortu vel progrederetur excursu vel adprehenderet debitos fines, si non esset socialis vita sanctorum? See also *De Genesi ad litteram* XI, 15, *CSEL* XXVIII, 1, 347 f.: . . . duo amores (for two loves as originators of the two cities, see also below, n. 7), quorum alter sanctus est, alter inmundus; alter socialis, alter privatus; alter communi utilitati consulens propter supernam societatem, alter etiam rem communem in potestatem propriam redigens propter adrogantem dominationem. . . . For the eminently social character of the concepts of the City of God and of the Church in the thought of St. Augustine, and not only of St. Augustine, see de Lubac, *Catholicisme* 85 ff., 290 ff.

[6] That *progredi* and similar Augustinian terms have nothing to do with progress in the modern sense of the term was rightly pointed out by T. E. Mommsen, "St. Augustine and the Christian Idea of Progress," *Jour. Hist. Ideas* XII (1951) 370 ff.

[7] *De civitate Dei* XIV, 28, *Corp. Christ., Ser. Lat.* XLVIII, 451: Fecerunt itaque civitates duas amores duo, terrenam scilicet amor sui usque ad contemptum Dei, caelestem vero amor Dei usque ad contemptum sui.

one, that is to say, a scripturally spiritual equivalent of the term society.[8] The two "cities" are societies of a special kind. The *Civitas Dei* is the society of the good angels and the predestined elect, past, present, and future. The *Civitas terrena* taken as its counterpart is identical neither with any particular political entity on earth, such as the Roman Empire, nor with any merely human society; it too is a "mystical" community, of the fallen angels and impious men.[9] To the City of Saints, the City of God, corresponds the City of the World, the City of the Devil. The only thing that according to Augustine really matters in the history of man is the conflict between these two cities or societies, the City of God and the City of the World—that is to say, of the world in so far as it disregards God—the one of the good, the other of the evil. This is a conflict which has lasted and will last from the revolt of Lucifer to the end of all things. During history the two cities are mixed physically, but separated morally; on the Day of Judgment they will be separated physically as well. On earth the City of God is a stranger and pilgrim (*peregrinans* or *in peregrinatione*),[10] but it exists also as the fatherland in heaven, Jerusalem, interpreted as *visio pacis*, the heavenly Jerusalem, which will descend to earth in the end, when heaven and earth are made new. Its counterpart is

---

[8] *Ibid.* XV, 1, XLVIII, 453 (text quoted p. 240, n. 3). J. Ratzinger, "Herkunft und Sinn der Civitas-Lehre Augustins," *Aug. Mag.* II, 971 n. 3, and H. I. Marrou, "Civitas Dei, civitas terrena: num tertium quid?," *Stud. Patr.* II, 343, have drawn attention to the fact that *mystice* here refers to the spiritual sense of Holy Scripture; see below, p. 242 and n. 11, about the heavenly Jerusalem and Babylon, the city of confusion, as the biblical "types" of the two cities.

[9] For the inclusion of the good and bad angels in the two cities see, for instance, *De civitate Dei* XV, 1, XLVIII, 453: ... de exortu earum (i.e., duarum civitatum) sive in angelis ... sive in duobus primis hominibus ...; also *De Genesi ad litteram* XI, 15, *CSEL* XXVIII, 1, 347 f.: Hi duo amores ... praecesserunt in angelis, alter in bonis, alter in malis ...; cf. Gilson's introduction to G. G. Walsh, S.J., translation of *De civitate Dei*, p. LVIII; also R. T. Marshall, *Studies in the Political and Socio-Religious Terminology of the De civitate Dei* (Washington, D.C., 1952) 12 f.

[10] See, for instance, *De civitate Dei* XV, 1, XLVIII, 453 f.: ... prior est natus civis huius saeculi, posterius autem isto peregrinus in saeculo et pertinens ad civitatem Dei, gratia praedestinatus, gratia electus, gratia peregrinus deorsum, gratia civis sursum. ... Superna est enim sanctorum civitas, quamvis hic pariat cives in quibus peregrinatur. ... The early Christian conception of ξενιτεία-*peregrinatio* could indirectly motivate ascetic flight into the desert, pilgrimages, and missions; cf. p. 67, n. 17, and the study of v. Campenhausen, quoted there.

seen prefigured by Babylon, interpreted as *confusio*, a symbol of the "worldly city."[11]

In St. Augustine's thought the concept of the City of God is distinguishable from that of the Kingdom of God.[12] Earlier it was pointed out that Origen, with his concept of *autobasileia*, expressed the doctrine of the Body of Christ in terms of the "Kingdom";[13] it is not without significance that Augustine can express it in terms of *civitas, societas, congregatio, communio*.[14]

The concept of any *civitas* or society for him implies multitude and number as well as unifying concord and peace;[15] and it is the essence of the idea of the Civitas Dei as one aspect of the Church, that through the increase in numbers of true Christians it grows, until it attains the fulness of Christ Himself (according to Eph. 4:10 ff. and 1:22 ff.).[16]

In order to understand the significance of Augustine's City of God it is necessary to trace briefly the principal phases of the history of that idea in earlier Christian literature. The origins are to be found in the Pauline Epistles and in the Apocalypse of St. John, and they rise from Old Testament foundations.[17] In the Letter to the Galatians and in the Letter to the Hebrews there is mention of "that Jerusalem which is

[11] For Augustine's translation of the names Jerusalem and Babylon as *visio pacis* and *confusio*, respectively, see the text from *De catechizandis rudibus* 20, 36 f., quoted below, p. 266, n. 111; also *Enarr. in Ps. LXIV*, 2, *Corp. Christ., Ser. Lat.* XXXIX, 823; the name of Jerusalem had been interpreted in this way already by Philo and Origen, see below, p. 246, n. 37. For Babylon, see also *De civitate Dei* XVI, 4, *Corp. Christ., Ser. Lat.* XLVIII, 504. Augustine himself mentions most of the sources of his concept of the *civitas Dei* (Ps. 86:3, Ps. 47:2 f. and 9, Ps. 45:5 f.) in *De civitate Dei* XI, 1, XLVIII, 321. See also *Enarr. in Ps. LXXXVI*, 6, *Corp. Christ., Ser. Lat.* XXXIX, 1204: Babylon civitas dicitur secundum saeculum. Quomodo una civitas sancta Ierusalem, una civitas iniqua Babylon. . . .

[12] See below, pp. 267 f.

[13] Cf. above, p. 116.

[14] *De civitate Dei, passim.*

[15] *De civitate Dei* I, 15, *Corp. Christ., Ser. Lat.* XLVII, 17: . . . cum aliud civitas non sit quam concors hominum multitudo. Cf. also *ibid.* II, 29, XLVII, 65 (where Augustine tries to dissuade the pagan Romans from worshipping their immoral gods): Quo igitur pacto deos, qui talibus delectantur obsequiis, haberi putas in numero sanctarum caelestium postestatum, cum homines, per quos eadem aguntur obsequia, non putasti habendos in numero qualiumcumque civium Romanorum? Incomparabiliter superna est civitas clarior, ubi victoria veritas, ubi dignitas sanctitas, ubi pax felicitas, ubi vita aeternitas.

[16] *Ibid.* XXII, 18, XLVIII, 836 f.

[17] For Augustine's use of the Psalms which mention the City of God, see the examples given above, n. 11.

above" and "is free: which is our mother,"[18] of "Mount Sion . . .
the City of the Living God, the heavenly Jerusalem . . . the company
(πανήγυρις) of many thousand angels . . . the Church (ἐκκλησία) of
the first born who are written in the heavens. . . ."[19] In this heavenly
city, according to the Letter to the Ephesians, Christians even now are
"fellow citizens with the saints, and the domestics of God,"[20] while
according to Hebrews they have "not here" (i.e., in this world) "a
lasting city."[21] For, as the Epistle to the Philippians expresses it, our
politeuma is in heaven, whence will also come He who will reform
our body in the resurrection.[22] In this life, therefore, Paul says in
Second Corinthians, "while we are in the body, we are absent
(ἐκδημοῦμεν, Vulgate: *peregrinamur*) from the Lord. . . . But we are
confident and have a good will to be absent rather from the body and
to be present with the Lord."[23]

In the Apocalypse St. John speaks of his vision of the renewal of
the world after the Last Judgment:

And I saw a New Heaven and a New Earth. . . . And I John saw the Holy
City, the New Jerusalem, coming down out of heaven from God, prepared
as a bride adorned for her husband.[24]

The Kingdom of God and the City of God then are in the New
Testament parallel, but not quite identical, concepts. Both have an
eschatological aspect, and at the same time the faithful may live in
them even here and now, though only "by faith, not by sight."[25]

---

[18] Gal. 4:26.   [19] Hebr. 12:22 f.
[20] Eph. 2:19.   [21] Hebr. 13:14.
[22] Phil. 3:21 f.   [23] 2 Cor. 5:6–8.

[24] Apoc. 21:1 f.; cf. also 21:9 ff. and 3:12; furthermore 14:8, 17:5, and 18:2 and
21, for Babylon as the city of evil.

[25] 2 Cor. 5:7. It seems that W. Bieder, *Ekklesia und Polis im Neuen Testament und in der
alten Kirche* (Zürich, 1941) in his polemic against Erik Peterson, underestimates the essential
continuity in the meaning of the concepts of *ecclesia* and *polis* through the entire early
Christian era. He and K. L. Schmidt, "Royaume, église, état et peuple . . .," *Le problème
du christianisme primitif* (Paris, 1938) 76 ff., and *Die Polis in Kirche und Welt* (Basel, 1939),
somewhat overestimate the influence of Platonism and Stoicism upon the patristic *polis*
idea. The idea of a terrestrial anticipation of heaven is scriptural, with regard to the
City of God as well as with regard to the Kingdom of God. There is no real opposition
between Phil. 3:20: ἡμῶν γὰρ τὸ πολίτευμα ἐν οὐρανοῖς ὑπάρχει and Luke 17:21: . . .
ἡ βασιλεία τοῦ Θεοῦ ἐντὸς ὑμῶν ἐστιν (though Bieder, *Ekklesia* 20 and K. L. Schmidt,
"Royaume" 90 and *Polis* 24, following M. Dibelius, are inclined to interpret the former

The subtle, but important, difference between these two New Testament concepts is simply that in the term *polis* (*civitas*) the social communal element is obviously stronger than in the term *basileia* (*regnum*), the meaning of which is rooted in the rule of God or Christ.[26]

Among the earliest works of the postapostolic age, it is above all the *Shepherd of Hermas* which develops the New Testament idea of the City of God. The City beyond the earth forms the subject of the so-called *First Similitude*. The special characteristic of this chapter is the antithetical juxtaposition of the πόλις ἡμῶν, that is to say, the "world," and the πόλις ταύτη, whose Lord is God.[27] The antithesis is almost Augustinian in its strength and precision and it is perhaps not altogether impossible that Augustine knew it.

In the theology of the second and third centuries, there is nothing that really matches the anticipations of "Hermas."[28]

Irenaeus, as pointed out earlier, believed that the heavens, that is to say, the Kingdom of Heaven or of God, Paradise, and the resplendent city, that is, the heavenly Jerusalem, which will descend to earth at the end of all things, are so many different mansions in the House of

verse only in the sense of a "colony of citizens of heaven"), similarly no contrast between 1 Peter 2:11: . . . ὡς παροίκους καὶ παρεπιδήμους and Eph. 2:19: οὐκέτι ἐστὲ ξένοι καὶ πάροικοι, ἀλλὰ ἐστὲ συμπολῖται τῶν ἁγίων καὶ οἰκεῖοι τοῦ Θεοῦ. See also K. L. Schmidt, *Polis* 108–110. Cf. below, pp. 278 ff., nn. 149 ff. For the continuity of the idea of the heavenly Jerusalem in Holy Scripture, patristic literature, and liturgy, see the series of articles "La Jérusalem céleste," *Vie spir.* LXXXVI (1952) 337 ff.

[26] For the relation between the Kingdom of God and the Kingdom of Christ, cf. above, pp. 115 f., n. 28.

[27] *Pastor Hermae*, simil. I, *GCS*, *Apostol. Väter* I, 46 ff.: ἐπὶ ξένης κατοικεῖτε ὑμεῖς οἱ δοῦλοι τοῦ Θεοῦ· ἡ γὰρ πόλις ὑμῶν μακράν ἐστιν ἀπὸ τῆς πόλεως ταύτης· εἰ οὖν οἴδατε . . . τὴν πόλιν ὑμῶν, ἐν ᾗ μέλλετε κατοικεῖν, τί ᾧδε ὑμεῖς ἑτοιμάζετε ἀγροὺς . . . καὶ οἰκήματα μάταια; Ταῦτα οὖν ὁ ἑτοιμάζων εἰς ταύτην τὴν πόλιν οὐ δύναται ἐπανακάμψαι εἰς τὴν ἰδίαν πόλιν. Ἄφρον καὶ δίψυχε καὶ ταλαίπωρε ἄνθρωπε, οὐ νοεῖς ὅτι ταῦτα πάντα ἀλλότριά εἰσι καὶ ὑπ' ἐξουσίαν ἑτέρου εἰσιν; Ἐρεῖ γὰρ ὁ Κύριος τῆς πόλεως ταύτης· "Οὐ θέλω σε κατοικεῖν εἰς τὴν πόλιν μου, ἀλλ' ἔξελθε ἐκ τῆς πόλεως ταύτης, ὅτι τοῖς νόμοις μου οὐ χρᾶσαι. . . . Ἡ τοῖς νόμοις μου χρῶ ἢ ἐκχώρει ἐκ τῆς χώρας μου." Σὺ οὖν τί μέλλεις ποιεῖν ἔχων νόμον ἐν τῇ σῇ πόλει; Ἕνεκεν τῶν ἀγρῶν σου καὶ τῆς λοιπῆς ὑπάρξεως τὸν νόμον σου πάντως ἀπαρνήσῃ καὶ πορεύσῃ τῷ νόμῳ τῆς πόλεως ταύτης; Βλέπε μὴ ἀσύμφορόν ἐστιν ἀπαρνῆσαι τὸν νόμον σου· ἐὰν γὰρ ἐπανακάμψαι θελήσῃς εἰς τὴν πόλιν σου, οὐ μὴ παραδεχθήσῃ. . . . Βλέπε οὖν σύ· ὡς ἐπὶ ξένης κατοικῶν μηδὲν πλέον ἑτοίμαζε σεαυτῷ εἰ μὴ τὴν αὐτάρκειαν τὴν ἀρκετήν σοι, καὶ ἕτοιμος γίνου, ἵνα, ὅταν θέλῃ ὁ δεσπότης τῆς πόλεως ταύτης ἐκβαλεῖν σε ἀντιταξάμενον τῷ νόμῳ αὐτοῦ, ἐξέλθῃς ἐκ τῆς πόλεως αὐτοῦ καὶ ἀπέλθῃς ἐν τῇ πόλει σου καὶ τῷ σῷ νόμῳ χρήσῃ ἀνυβρίστως ἀγαλλιώμενος.

[28] For Cyprian, cf. below, p. 247, n. 41, and p. 275, n. 142.

God, in which the just will dwell according to their merit.[29] It has been noted that he also could conceive of a spiritual anticipation of the return to Paradise even in this life through the Church[30] and, in a higher and more exceptional sense, in mystical rapture such as St. Paul experienced.[31] Yet the heavenly City does not play any role in this preeschatological doctrine of his, probably because St. John in whose tradition his work stands had set the time of its descent so definitely for the end of the world. It needed more allegorically minded exegetes to apply the image of the City of God to Christian life on this earth. This was done first in the School of Alexandria. Clement and Origen often use the idea of the City of God, both in conjunction with that of the Kingdom of God and separately. In the majority of cases the meaning is not purely eschatological and transcendent but ecclesiological—the πόλις is the Church—or, in Origen, also psychological—the πόλις is the soul.[32] Thus, Clement writes:

But I might pray to the spirit of Christ to be carried on wings to my Jerusalem. Indeed the Stoics too call heaven the true city, but what are here on earth, they say, are not yet cities [in the true sense]; they claim these are only called cities without being cities. Now the city and community of the good is a city-like complex (σύστημα) and multitude (πλῆθος) of men who live under law; and just so the Church lives under the Logos, an impregnable city on earth which cannot be tyrannized: the will of God on earth as in heaven.[33]

Here then the Church even on earth is compared with the heavenly Jerusalem. Elsewhere, Clement speaks of the true Christian as a citizen (πολίτης) of heaven, a tiller of Paradise; his sojourn on earth

---

[29] Irenaeus, *Adversus haereses* V, 36, 1, quoted above, p. 69, n. 27.

[30] *Ibid.* V, 10, 12, V, 20, 2; cf. above, pp. 69 f. nn. 29 and 31.

[31] *Ibid.* V, 5, 1; cf. above, p. 69, n. 30.

[32] For the close connection between the soul and the Church in patristic thought see the illuminating pages in de Lubac, *Catholicisme* 169 ff., for Origen, especially, 174 f.

[33] Clement of Alexandria, *Stromata* IV, 26, 172, 1 f., *GCS, Clem. Alex.* II, 324 f.: Ἐγὼ δὲ ἂν εὐξαίμην τὸ πνεῦμα τοῦ Χριστοῦ πτερῶσαί με εἰς τὴν Ἱερουσαλὴμ τὴν ἐμήν· λέγουσι γὰρ καὶ οἱ Στωϊκοὶ τὸν μὲν οὐρανὸν κυρίως πόλιν, τὰ δὲ ἐπὶ γῆς ἐνταῦθα οὐκέτι πόλεις· λέγεσθαι μὲν γάρ, οὐκ εἶναι δέ· σπουδαῖον γὰρ ἡ πόλις καὶ ὁ δῆμος ἀστεῖόν τι σύστημα καὶ πλῆθος ἀνθρώπων ὑπὸ νόμου διοικούμενον, καθάπερ ἡ ἐκκλεσία ὑπὸ Λόγου, ἀπολιόρκητος ἀτυράννητος πόλις ἐπὶ γῆς, θέλημα θεῖον ἐπὶ γῆς ὡς ἐν οὐρανῷ. Cf. ibid. VI, 14, 108, 1, II, 486: . . ."καταπαύσουσιν ἐν ὄρει ἁγίῳ Θεοῦ" (Ps. 15:1), τῇ ἀνωτάτω ἐκκλησίᾳ, καθ᾽ ἣν οἱ φιλόσοφοι συνάγονται τοῦ Θεοῦ, οἱ τῷ ὄντι Ἰσραηλῖται οἱ καθαροὶ τὴν καρδίαν. . . .

serves as his education and his instruction concerning the heavenly Father.[34]

Origen's heavenly Jerusalem too is not purely transcendent. In his later works, especially, he is increasingly definite in seeing in the terrestrial Church the medium of the soul's heavenly ascent,

. . . for in truth, there is no other ascension through which one may ascend to heaven, except by the Church of the multiform Wisdom of God,[35]

and he identifies the Church, which is the communion of all saints,[36] with the heavenly Jerusalem:

. . . for, truly, the Church is the City of God, the vision of peace; in it the peace which He [Christ] gave to us is made full and is seen, if only we are children of peace.[37]

Elsewhere, in an inversion of the metaphor, the souls themselves have become cities of God to Origen. He compares the slaying of the King of Jericho and of other enemies of Israel by Joshua with the destruction of sin in the city of our soul by Christ:

. . . so that after he has removed the king of sin from the city of our soul, our soul may become a City of God, and God may reign in it, and it may be said with regard to us: "lo, the Kingdom of God is within you" (cf. Luke 17:21).[38]

The last-quoted text is typical of the fact that the Greek Fathers on

---

[34] Protrepticus X, 92, 3, GCS, Clem. Alex. I, 68: ῍Η τίς οὐρανοῦ πολίτης εἶναι δυνάμενος ἔρεβος διώκει, ἐξὸν παράδεισον γεωργεῖν καὶ οὐρανὸν περιπολεῖν. . . . Paedagogus III, 12, 99, 1, GCS, Clem. Alex. I, 290: . . . πολιτεύεται μὲν ἐν οὐρανοῖς ἐπὶ γῆς παιδαγωγούμενος. . . .

[35] Origen, In Judices, homil. V, 5, GCS, Orig. VII, 495 12: . . . quia revera non est alia adscensio, qua adscendatur ad coelum, nisi per ecclesiam multiformis sapientiae Dei (cf. Eph. 3:10). Cf. Bieder, Ekklesia 126.

[36] Origen, In Cant. Cantic. I, GCS, Orig. VIII, 90, 4 f.: Ecclesia sit desiderans Christo coniungi; ecclesiam autem coetum omnium adverte sanctorum. Cf. Bieder, Ekklesia 115 f.

[37] In Jeremiam, homil. IX, GCS, Orig. III, 65, 21 ff.: . . . ἔστιν γὰρ ἡ πόλις τοῦ Θεοῦ ἡ ἐκκλησία, ἡ ὅρασις τῆς εἰρήνης, ἐν αὐτῇ [ἐστιν] ἡ εἰρήνη ἥν ἤγαγεν ἡμῖν, εἴγε ἐσμὲν τέκνα εἰρήνης, πληθύνεται καὶ ὁρᾶται. For the translation of the name Jerusalem as "vision of peace" see also Philo, for instance, De somniis II, 38, 250, Cohn and Wendland III, 298, for Augustine, see above, pp. 241 f.

[38] In Jesum Nave, homil. XIII, 1, GCS, Orig. VII, 371, 15 ff.: . . . ut posteaquam interemerit regem peccati de civitate animae nostrae, fiat anima nostra civitas Dei et regnet in ea Deus et dicatur ad nos quia "ecce regnum Dei intra vos est" (Luke 17:21); see also the rest of the homily.

the whole regarded the City of God and the Kingdom of God as identical ideas.[39]

The conception of the City of God, found in the Latin Fathers before St. Augustine, is more or less the same as that of the Greeks. For Tertullian it is either the supernal Jerusalem, essentially identical with the Kingdom of God in heaven, or it is another name for the Church.[40] Cyprian, without using the term *civitas Dei*, speaks of it in terms of the inhabitants of Paradise, of the heavenly fatherland and Kingdom.[41] Ambrose's use of the Civitas Dei concept is the most significant before Augustine, because the latter may well have been introduced by him to the symbolism of the City of God and because certain Ambrosian formulations foreshadow Augustine's *De civitate Dei* more directly than Greek or earlier Latin utterances concerning the divine city had done.

In his monographic commentaries to the Old Testament, in which he is very strongly dependent on Philo, Ambrose takes over the Philonian interpretation of the six cities of refuge of Genesis 16:6 ff. as six psychological conditions which the soul must attain in order to be cured from sin.[42] This is reminiscent also of Origen's

[39] See p. 124, n. 44, about the merging of the *basileia* and the *polis* concepts in Eusebius' view of the Church. For Greek patristic views of the heavenly *politeia* of virtue in the soul see also the texts from Basil the Great and Gregory of Nyssa quoted p. 80, nn. 70 and 72. In Ps.-Dionysius the Areopagite the concept of the heavenly and ecclesiastical *polis* and *politeia* is influenced, it seems, not so much by the scriptural heavenly Jerusalem as by the Platonic *politeia*; cf. R. Roques, *L'univers dionysien* (Théologie XXIX, Paris, 1954) 81 ff.

[40] See Tertullian, *De corona* 13, 4, *Corp. Christ.*, *Ser. Lat.* II, 1061: Sed tu peregrinus mundi huius et civis supernae Hierusalem—"noster," inquit, "municipatus in caelis" (cf. Phil. 3:20, note the translation of πολίτευμα by *municipatus*)—habes tuos census, tuos fastus, nihil tibi cum gaudiis saeculi . . .; *Adversus Marcionem* III, 23, 2, *Corp. Christ.*, *Ser. Lat.* I, 540: . . . ecclesiam, templum scilicet et domum et civitatem Dei.

[41] See Cyprian, *De mortalitate* 26, CSEL III, 313: Considerandum est . . . renuntiasse nos mundo et tamquam hospites et peregrinos hic interim degere. Amplectamur diem, qui adsignat singulos domicilio suo, qui nos paradiso . . . restituit et regno. . . . Patriam nos nostram paradisum conputamus. . . . Magnus illic nos carorum numerus expectat, parentum fratrum filiorum frequens nos et copiosa turba desiderat. . . . Qualis illic caelestium regnorum voluptas. . . . Illic apostolorum gloriosus chorus, illic prophetarum exultantium numerus, illic martyrum innumerabilis populus. . . .

[42] See Philo, *De fuga et inventione*, 17, 90 ff., Cohn and Wendland III, 128 ff., and cf. Ambrose, *De fuga saeculi* 2, 5–9 and 11–12, also 55–57, CSEL XXXII, 2, 165 ff., 171 f., 205 ff., *De Abraham* II, 9, 62, CSEL XXXII, 1, 615 f. (stranger on earth: citizen of heaven).

conception of the souls as cities of God.[43] Similarly, in his *Exposition to Psalm 118*, Ambrose says that Adam through his fall descended from the supernal Jerusalem and that we must be careful not to do the same by sinning;[44] in this same commentary he also says that the heavenly city is the Church.[45] In some of his letters he goes slightly beyond traditional formulations, when, for instance, in *Epistle* XXIX he calls the *civitas* the *vera gratia sanctorum*.[46] In *Epistle* LXIII, addressing the clergy of Vercelli, he admonishes them to leave this "terrestrial city," which is the "world," because their city is the supernal Jerusalem.[47]

It was St. Augustine who through his work *On the City of God* for all times reasserted and consolidated the idea of the Civitas Dei, the ideal of a Christian *civitas* or society, as an antithesis to the *civitas terrena* and as a supplement to the idea of the Kingship and Kingdom of God, the Regnum Dei or Regnum Christi. That Augustine could do so was undoubtedly in part due to the fact that he, as St. Ambrose, was a Roman and not a Greek, that even in these late imperial times he was able to think in the tradition of the *civitas* and *respublica*, whereas ever since Alexander the Great the spirit of the Greek polis had been almost completely absorbed by that of the Hellenistic Basileia.[48] Whosoever reads Augustine's letter to the Tribune Marcellinus, in which shortly after the capture of Rome by Alaric in 410 he replies to those who were wondering if the morality of the Sermon on the Mount had not undermined the strength of Rome, will notice how

[43] See above, p. 246, n. 38

[44] See Ambrose, *Expositio Psalmi CXVIII*, 21, 5, *CSEL* LXII, 476.

[45] *Ibid.* 15, 35, *CSEL* LXII, 349: Civitas Dei ecclesia est; ecclesia corpus est Christi. Peccat in caelum, qui caelestis civitatis iura contaminat et inmaculati corporis violat sanctitatem suorum conluvione vitiorum. Cf. *Apologia prophetae David* I, 17, 83, *CSEL* XXXII, 2, 353: . . . quisquis bona fide atque opere ingreditur ecclesiam, fit supernae illius civis et incola civitatis quae descendit de caelo.

[46] *Epist.* XXIX, 20, *PL* XVI, 1104B.

[47] *Epist.* LXIII, 104, *PL* XVI, 1269C: . . . et vos egredimini de hac terrena civitate, quia civitas vestra superior est Ierusalem. Ibi conversamini, ut dicatis: "Nostra autem conversatio in coelis est" (Phil. 3:20). Ideo Iesus exivit de civitate ut vos exeuntes de hoc mundo supra mundum sitis. Concerning the relevance of this text for the development of the "monastic" life of the clergy (*vita communis*) see p. 346, n. 18. For material on Ambrose's *civitas Dei* concept and for the relation of that concept to the Ambrosian antithesis between *regnum Dei* and *regnum huius mundi* see also J. E. Niederhuber, *Die Lehre des hl. Ambrosius vom Reiche Gottes auf Erden* (Forschungen zur christlichen Literatur-und Dogmengeschichte IV, 3–4, Paderborn, 1904) 47 ff., 84, 236.

[48] Similarly, Ratzinger, "Civitas-Lehre," *Aug. Mag.* II, 972.

naturally the concept of the Civitas Dei is linked with that of the *respublica Romana*, which *in abstracto*, though not in actual fact, is a *civitas terrena* in a neutral political sense; it need not have become a purely worldly and therefore bad *civitas terrena* or *diaboli*.[49]

In this reply, addressed to Marcellinus, who was a Christian Roman official and one of the most noble souls of the age, Augustine asks if the ancient Romans did not consider it a salutary deed to forgive injuries and he quotes Sallust and Cicero to show that they did. If divine authority, which prescribes that same forgiveness, was heard today, he says, it would

... stabilize, hallow, strengthen, and increase the state (*rem publicam*). For what is the state (*res publica*) but the affair of the people (*res populi*),[50] a common affair then, that is to say, an affair of the citizenry or city (*civitatis*)? But what is the "city" but a multitude of men who are brought together in some bond of concord ...?[51]

There is no telling, however, he continues, whither the evils accompanying life in society would finally have led the Roman state—which stands here for the social life of man after the fall—if the Cross of Christ had not been planted to hold up the collapsing mass:

... the heavenly authority had to come and to help, it had to persuade to voluntary poverty, continence, benevolence, justice, and concord, and true piety, and to the other life-giving luminous and powerful virtues: not only to

---

[49] For the *civitas diaboli*, cf. pp. 241, 269, n. 120. I doubt if W. Kamlah, *Christentum und Geschichtlichkeit* (Stuttgart, 1951) 166, is right when he says that Augustine chose the term *civitas Dei* in antithesis to the *civitas* Rome. Would it not then have been more natural for him to choose the term *imperium Dei*?

[50] After Cicero, *De republica* I, 25; see the following note.

[51] Augustine, *Epist.* CXXXVIII, 2, 10, *CSEL* XLIV, 135: [Divina auctoritas] si, ut dignum est, audiretur . . . constitueret, consecraret, firmaret augeretque rem publicam. Quid enim est res publica nisi res populi? Res ergo communis, res utique civitatis. Quid est autem civitas nisi hominum multitudo in quoddam vinculum redacta concordiae? Cf. *De civitate Dei* I, 1̄5̄, quoted above, p. 242, n. 15. See also Augustine's famous redefinition, directed against Cicero, of the concept of the *populus* in *De civitate Dei* XIX, 21–24, *Corp. Christ., Ser. Lat.* XLVIII, 687 ff. Cicero, *De republica* I, 25, had said: . . . populus . . . coetus multitudinis iuris consensu et utilitatis communione sociatus (cf. *De civitate Dei* XIX, 21, XLVIII, 687 f.). Augustine more realistically counters: Populus est coetus multitudinis rationalis rerum quas diligit concordi communione sociatus . . . (cf. *ibid.* 24, XLVIII, 695); for not every people can be defined by *ius* or *iustitia*, only that people which believes in the true God who can inspire it with true justice.

make possible the most ethical conduct of this life and the most harmonious social life (*societas*) of a terrestrial city, but the attainment of sempiternal salvation and of the celestial and divine state (*caelestem divinamque rem publicam*),[52] made up, as it were, of a sempiternal people—and in this state faith, hope, and charity admit us as citizens. Thus, as long as we are away from it (i.e., from the heavenly state or city) as pilgrims (*peregrinamur*), we should, if we cannot correct them, bear with those who wish that the state (*res publica*) remain unpunished in spite of its vices, that state which the first Romans set up and enlarged through their virtues, although they had not the true piety toward the true God who could have guided them also to the eternal city (*in aeternam civitatem*) through saving religion. Nevertheless, they maintained some probity of its own kind, which may have sufficed for the establishment, enlargement, and preservation of a terrestrial city. For God thus showed through the overopulent and famous Empire of the Romans how valuable are civic virtues even without the true religion and he did so in order that it be understood that, if the latter is added, men become citizens of the other city (*alterius civitatis*) whose king is truth, whose law is charity, whose mode of being is eternity.[53]

This letter was written shortly before Augustine began his work

---

[52] For *caelestis res publica* see also *De civitate Dei* II, 19 and 21, XLVII, 51 and 55; cf. Kamlah, *Christentum* 166, n. 128.

[53] *Epist.* CXXXVIII, 3, 17, *CSEL* XLIV, 143 ff.: Gratias Domino Deo nostro, qui contra ista mala misit nobis adiutorium singulare. Quo enim non tolleret, quem non involveret, in quod profundum non demergeret fluvius iste horrendae nequitiae generis humani, nisi crux Christi in tanta velut mole auctoritatis eminentius firmiusque figeretur, cuius adprehenso robore stabiles essemus, ne male suadentium vel in mala inpellentium tam vasto mundi huis abrepti gurgite sorberemur? In ista enim conluvie morum pessimorum et veteris perditae disciplinae maxime venire ac subvenire debuit caelestis auctoritas, quae voluntariam paupertatem, quae continentiam, benivolentiam, iustitiam atque concordiam veramque pietatem persuaderet ceterasque vitae luminosas validasque virtutes non tantum propter istam vitam honestissime gerendam nec tantum propter civitatis terrenae concordissimam societatem, verum etiam propter adipiscendam sempiternam salutem et sempiterni cuiusdam populi caelestem divinamque rem publicam, cui nos cives adsciscit fides, spes, caritas, ut quam diu inde peregrinamur feramus eos, si corrigere non valemus, qui vitiis inpunitis volunt stare rem publicam, quam primi Romani constituerunt auxeruntque virtutibus, etsi non habentes veram pietatem erga Deum verum, quae illos etiam in aeternam civitatem posset salubri religione perducere, custodientes tamen quandam sui generis probitatem, quae posset terrenae civitati constituendae augendae conservandaeque sufficere. Deus enim sic ostendit in opulentissimo et praeclaro imperio Romanorum quantum valerent civiles etiam sine vera religione virtutes, ut intellegerentur hac addita fieri homines cives alterius civitatis, cuius rex veritas, cuius lex caritas, cuius modus aeternitas.

On the City of God, which is likewise addressed to Marcellinus [54] and, as is well known, was meant among other things to answer the vital questions raised by Marcellinus and others and to account for the decline of a Roman Empire which had become Christian, a decline so frighteningly symbolized by the event of 410. In the letter some of the essential thoughts of the great work are already formulated, for instance, the idea of the two cities itself, the concept of the real but limited value of a virtuous terrestrial state, and a view of the Roman Empire according to which it could even at its best be no more than a foil for the City of God.

It will be well to pause here for a moment in order to consider Augustine's position with regard to the Empire and its Roman renewal ideology. His as well as Jerome's reaction to Alaric's sack of Rome—which broke the spirit of the "Theodosian Renaissance" as decisively as the *Sacco di Roma* of 1527 was to blight the mood of the Italian Renaissance—show very clearly their ambivalent attitudes toward Rome. St. Jerome, then an old man in his monk's cell at Bethlehem, was deeply shocked by the catastrophe, [55] but not unprepared spiritually. Had he not applied the old identification of the Great Harlot of the Apocalypse with Rome, the second Babylon, to the Christian Rome of his day [56] and bitterly spoken of "the impure dregs

---

[54] See *De civitate Dei*, preface; for Marcellinus see also below, p. 368.

[55] See Jerome, *Epist.* CXXVI, *ad Marcellinum et Anapsychiam*, 2, CSEL LVI, 144: Ezechielis volumen olim adgredi volui . . ., sed in ipso dictandi exordio ita animus meus occidentalium provinciarum et maxime urbis Romae vastatione confusus est, ut iuxta vulgare proverbium proprium quoque ignorarem vocabulum diuque tacui sciens tempus esse lacrimarum. See also *Epist.* CXXVII, *ad Principiam Virginem de Vita Sanctae Marcellae*, 12 f., CSEL LVI, 154 f.; *Comment. in Ezech.* I, III, VII, Prefaces, PL XXV, 15 ff., 79, 207 ff. Cf. also *Epist.* LX, *ad Heliodorum*, 16 f., CSEL LIV, 570 ff., in which as early as 396 Jerome calls his young friend Nepotianus, the nephew of Heliodorus, the companion of his own youth, happy because he did not live to see the misfortunes of the Roman Empire. Such passages are usually, and not without reason, interpreted as documents of Jerome's patriotism—see, for instance, J. Straub, "Christliche Geschichtsapologetik in der Krisis des römischen Reiches," *Historia* I (1950) 60 ff.—but cf. immediately below.

[56] *Interpretatio Libri Didymi Alexandrini de Spiritu Sancto, Praefatio,* PL XXIII, 107: Cum in Babylone (i.e., Rome) versarer et purpureae meretricis essem colonus et iure Quiritum viverem. . . . Pharisaeorum conclamavit senatus . . . omnis . . . adversum me . . . factio coniuravit. Illico ego velut postliminio Ierosolyman sum reversus et post Romuli casam et ludorum Lupercalia diversorium Mariae et Salvatoris speluncam aspexi. Cf. also *Epist.* XLVI, 11 ff., CSEL LIV, 341 ff.

of our time"?[57] Had he not made the destructions wrought by the barbarians, whose successes he considered a punishment for the vices of the Romans,[58] an occasion to deprecate second marriages, and marriage in general, and to extol virginity?[59] His attitude toward the collapse of the Roman world must be seen within the whole of his program for the reform of Christian society through monastic ideals —the program of most of the Fathers of the late fourth century, and above all St. Augustine's.[60]

[57] *Vita Malchi*, *PL* XXIII, 55, where St. Jerome says that he decided to start his Church History with the coming of Christ and to carry it on *usque ad nostram aetatem, id est . . . usque ad nostri temporis faecem*; he also says that the Church *postquam ad Christianos principes venerit, potentia quidem et divitiis maior, sed virtutibus minor facta sit*. This little known passage is quoted by Curtius, *European Literature* 410, n. 8, and by E. Seeberg, *Gottfried Arnold in Auswahl herausgegeben* (München, 1934) 16 (Introduction), where Seeberg rightly stresses the monastic nature of Jerome's view; see also the remarks of E. Seeberg, *Gottfried Arnold, Die Wissenschaft und die Mystik seiner Zeit* (Meerane, 1923) 257 ff., 275 ff., concerning such patristic views as starting points of mediaeval and modern sectarian and humanistic theories of decline as well as of reform (cf. V. Harris, *All Coherence Gone* [Chicago, 1949] for connections with early modern ideas on the decay of the universe). The relationship between the idea of reform and heretical or sectarian ideologies becomes very important only in the later Middle Ages; but see above, pp. 162–164, about the Pelagians and below, pp. 258 ff., 307 f., about the Donatists. Jerome's remark is significant in spite of the proverbial character of the phrase *usque ad faecem*; cf. A. Otto, *Die Sprichwörter und sprichwörtlichen Redensarten der Römer* (Leipzig, 1890) 130 f. See also Gregory of Nazianzus, *Carm.* II, I: *De seipso*, XI: *De vita sua* 20 ff., PG XXXVII, 1031. Later Augustine was to voice similar criticisms, cf. *Enarr. II in Ps. XXVI*, 19, *Corp. Christ., Ser. Lat.* XXXVIII, 165 and *Enarr. II in Ps. XXX*, 12, *Sermo* II, 6, XXXVIII, 206. But Jerome's, Gregory's, and Augustine's views had been anticipated even in the age of persecution by Origen who had reasserted the Pauline doctrine on the inner reformation of man according to Rom. 12:2 against the regrettable conformation to this world of many Christians in consequence of the increasing expansion of the Church. Cf. Origen, *Commentary to Matthew* XVII, 24, *GCS, Orig.* X, 652: Καὶ εἴ τίς γε κατανοῆσαι τὰ πολυάνθρωπα ἀθροίσματα τῶν . . . ἐκκλησιῶν καὶ ἐξετάσαι, πόσοι μὲν οἱ βιοῦντες ἐπιεικέστερον καὶ μεταμορφούμενοι τῇ ἀνακαινώσει τοῦ νοός, πόσοι δὲ οἱ ῥαθυμότερον πολιτευόμενοι καὶ συσχηματιζόμενοι τῷ αἰῶνι τούτῳ (cf. Rom. 12:2), ἴδοι ἂν ὅτι χρήσιμός ἐστιν ἡ λέγουσα τοῦ σωτῆρος φωνή· "πολλοὶ γάρ εἰσι κλητοί, ὀλίγοι δὲ ἐκλεκτοί" (Matthew 20:16); also *Commentar. in Epistulam Pauli ad Romanos* V, 8, PG XIV, 1040B: . . . apostolorum temporibus non, ut nunc fieri videmus, typus tantummodo mysteriorum his qui baptizabantur, sed virtus eorum ac ratio tradebatur . . . (these texts are cited by H. Chadwick, "The Evidences of Christianity in the Apologetic of Origen," *Stud. Patr.* II, 337).

[58] *Epist.* LX, 17, *ad Heliodorum*, *CSEL* LIV, 572: Nostris peccatis barbari fortes sunt, nostris vitiis Romanus superatur exercitus. . . .

[59] See, for instance, *Epist.* CXXIII, *ad Geruchiam de monogamia*, 15 f., *CSEL* LVI, 91 ff.

[60] See below, Part Three, Chapter II, 2.

Of St. Augustine, it cannot even be said that he was truly shocked by the calamity of 410: for in his view Rome was not really destroyed as long as men were alive in it who could turn to Christ.[61]

Quod custodit Christus, numquid tollit Gothus?[62]

To his fellow clerics and to all the people he sent a warning not to be upset by the upheavals of this world[63] and to Hesychius he wrote that he saw no reason why the Roman Empire should not rise again as it did before.[64] Similarly, in De civitate Dei, he speaks of the Roman Empire as stricken, but not changed. Why should one despair of its being restored (recreatum) as had happened on other occasions?[65]

---

[61] Sermo LXXXI, 9, PL XXXVIII, 505: Forte Roma non perit, si Romani non pereant. Non enim peribunt si Deum laudabunt. . . . Roma enim quid est nisi Romani? Non enim de lapidibus et lignis agitur, de excelsis insulis et amplissimis moenibus. It is possible that Augustine used here a phrase of Tacitus, Histor. I, 84: Quid? Vos pulcherrimam hanc urbem domibus et tectis et congestu lapidum stare creditis? Cf. M. Vogelstein, Kaiseridee-Romidee und das Verhältnis von Staat und Kirche seit Konstantin (Historische Untersuchungen VII, Breslau, 1930). See further Augustine's Sermo de urbis excidio, especially 6 ff., PL XL, 721 ff., where the topos of the city of citizens rather than of walls is raised to an even higher plane. Those just Romans who did not survive or escape and were killed during the capture of Rome have migrated to a better city, the City of God, and though they may not have escaped from the fires laid by the barbarians, they are safe from the fire of hell: An putatis civitatem in parietibus deputandam? Civitas in civibus est non in parietibus. . . . Nonne Deus pepercerat civitati quia civitas migraverat et perniciem illius ignis (i.e., the utterly destructive fire of Sodom which symbolizes hell) evaserat? . . . Migrarunt qui fugerunt, qui de corpore exierunt. . . . And finally: Appende cum Christo Romam, appende cum Christo totam terram, appende cum Christo coelum et terram. Nihil creatum cum creatore pensatur, nullum opus artifici comparatur. See also Sermo CV, 6, 8, PL XXXVIII, 621 f.: Ecce pereunt omnia christianis temporibus. Quid strepis? Non hoc promisit mihi Deus quod ista non peribunt. . . . Aeterna promisit aeternus. . . . Quid strepis, o munde immunde? . . . Quid avertere conaris? Tenere vis periens. Quid faceres si maneres?

[62] Sermo, Bibl. Casin. I, 133, Morin, Aug. Serm., Miscell. Agost. I, 409. For St. Augustine's sermons in general see Pontet, Augustin prédicateur, for their chronology above all A. Kunzelmann, "Die Chronologie der Sermones des hl. Augustinus," Miscell. Agost. II, 417 ff.

[63] See Epist. CXXII, fratribus conclericis et universae plebi, CSEL XXXIV, 2, 742 ff.

[64] Epist. CXCIX, De fine saeculi . . . fratri et coepiscopo Hesychio . . . , 10, 35, CSEL LVII, 274; see also 12, 46, LVII, 284 f., where the existence of pagans to whom the Gospel had yet not been preached—e.g., certain African tribes—is considered an indication that the end has not yet come.

[65] De civitate Dei IV, 7, Corp. Christ., Ser. Lat. XLVII, 104: . . . Romanum imperium adflictum est potius quam mutatum, quod et aliis ante Christi nomen temporibus ei contigit, et ab illa est adflictione recreatum, quod nec istis temporibus desperandum est. Quis enim de hac re novit voluntatem Dei?

Such passages show that Augustine was not really interested in "Christian Rome," but only in Christians who happened to be Romans. They express the serene detachment toward the Roman Empire as such, which is so characteristic of St. Augustine.[66] He was not hostile toward Rome, only toward Romans, emperors or citizens, who persecuted or corrupted Christianity. He even admitted Rome's greatness and accepted it as a basic fact of world history, but he saw all this in a merely relative perspective.[67]

When, therefore, Augustine can write *chorus Christi iam totus mundus est,*[68] and *pagani exstinguuntur et idola franguntur,*[69] if he speaks of the *pacata ecclesia,*[70] then he rejoices in the victory of Christianity over paganism and in the peace of the Church *in corde,*[71] but not in any glories of a Roman Empire reborn in Christian form, not in a new Golden Age. Where is the reign of Saturn—Virgil's or Claudianus'

[66] For instance, in the famous text, *De civitate Dei* V, 17, *Corp. Christ., Ser. Lat.* XLVII, 149: . . . quid interest, sub cuius imperio vivat homo moriturus, si illi qui imperant ad impia et iniqua non cogant.

[67] Cf. P. Gerosa, "S. Agostino e l'imperialismo Romano," *Miscell. Agost.* II, 977 f., Straub, "Geschichtsapologetik" 52 ff., *idem,* "Augustin's Sorge um die regeneratio imperii," *Hist. Jb.* LXXIII (1954) 36 ff., T. E. Mommsen, "Augustine" 346 ff., R. Arbesmann, O.S.A., "The Idea of Rome in the Sermons of St. Augustine," *Augustiniana* IV (1954) 305 ff. See also P. Brezzi, "Una 'Civitas terrena spiritualis' come ideale storico-politico di Sant Agostino," *Aug. Mag.* II, 915 ff., and V. Pöschl, "Augustinus und die römische Geschichtsauffassung," *Aug. Mag.* II, 957 ff., who seem to me somewhat to overrate Augustine's interest in the Roman Empire. E. v. Ivanka, "Römische Ideologie in der 'Civitas Dei,' " *Aug. Mag.* III, 411 ff., would appear to strike the right balance in his investigation of the Platonist origins of Augustine's view that Roman love of glory and resulting Roman rule were of real value as compared to cupidity and lust of domination, but, nevertheless, of relative value only. See now also H. I. Marrou, "Civitas Dei, civitas terrena: num tertium quid?," *Stud. Patr.* II, 342 ff., who rightly maintains against Mons. Journet that Augustine did not and could not conceive of a "third city of man" as a neutral or autonomous value beside his two cities (except *in abstracto,* cf. above, p. 249).

[68] *Enarr. in Ps. CXLIX,* c. 7, *Corp. Christ., Ser. Lat.* XL, 2183.

[69] *Enarr. in Ps. CXLIX,* c. 13, *Corp. Christ., Ser. Lat.* XL, 2186 f. See also *De divinatione daemonum* X, 14, *CSEL* XLI, 617 f.: isti irrisores nostri pauciores sunt hoc anno quam fuerunt priore anno. Ex quo enim "fremuerunt gentes . . ." (Is. 51:7 f.) . . . quando . . . fundebatur sanguis sanctorum et vastabatur ecclesia usque ad hoc tempus et deinceps quotidie minuuntur.

[70] *In Johannis evangelium tractatus* VI, 10, *Corp. Christ., Ser. Lat.* XXXVI, 58 f., on Christ as the "peacemaker" between the diverse languages of man, which had arisen because of the pride of the tower builders of Babel (Gen. 11:1 ff.).

[71] *Ibid.,* cf. above, n. 70. See similarly Jerome, *In Is.* IV, to Is. 11:6, and *In Is.* XVII, to Is. 60:10, *PL* XXIV, 151D and 616C f.

Golden Age? It is broken to make place for the Kingdom of Christ.[72]
The mission ascribed to Rome by Virgil in a famous verse of the
Aeneid

Parcere subiectis et debellare superbos [73]

is rejected in the book *On the City of God* as a usurpation of power
belonging to God, by men who, though they may rule others, are
dominated by their own lust of domination.[74] And Rome is not eternal, in spite of Virgil's

His ego nec metas rerum nec tempora pono
Imperium sine fine dedi. . . .[75]

Though Augustine speaks joyfully about "the cross on the brow of

[72] Cf. *Enarr. in Ps. XCVIII*, c. 14, *Corp. Christ.*, *Ser. Lat.* XXXIX, 1391; Augustine there
also mentions *Mercurii regnum*, referring, perhaps, to Hermetic mysticism.

[73] *Aeneid* VI, 853.

[74] *De civitate Dei*, I, Preface, *Corp. Christ.*, *Ser. Lat.* XLVII, 1. In other sections of *De
civitate Dei* Augustine's appreciation of the Virgilian verse is somewhat more positive;
cf. K. H. Schelkle, *Vergil in der Deutung Augustins* (Tübinger Beiträge zur Altertumswissenschaft XXXII, Stuttgart, Berlin, 1939) 73 ff.

[75] And, one might add, in spite of Prudentius' *didici contemnere finem* (cf. p. 17, n. 5) or
Rutilius Namatianus' *Quae restant nullis obnoxia tempora metis dum stabunt terrae, dum polus
astra feret* (cf. above, *ibid.*). The Augustinian spirit was not the Virgilian spirit of the
"Theodosian Renaissance" (see above, p. 20). Augustine quotes the famous verses of
Virgil, *Aeneid* I, 278 f., which inspired also Prudentius and Rutilius, in *Sermo* CV, 7, 10,
PL XXXVIII, 622 f. and adds: *Non plane ita respondet veritas*; further on, he cites Virgil
against Virgil by quoting *Georgica* II, 498: *Non res Romanae peritiuraque regna*. . . . Augustine
was, of course, not the first Christian to deny the eternity of Rome. For the fourth century
see, for instance, the Constantinian poet Juvencus, *Evangeliorum Libri* IV, *CSEL* XXIV, 1:

Immortale nihil mundi conpage tenetur,
Non orbis, non regna hominum, non aurea Roma,
Non mare, non tellus, non ignea sidera caeli.
Nam statuit genitor, rerum irrevocabile tempus
Quo cunctum torrens rapiat flamma ultima mundum.

With regard to the famous renewal and savior prophecy of Virgil's *Fourth Eclogue* (cf. above,
p. 12), Augustine credits the Sibyl of Cumae and not Virgil himself with prophetic
knowledge of Christ's coming, which he believed it expressed; see A. Kurfess, "Vergils
vierte Ekloge bei Hieronymus und Augustinus . . .," *Sacr. Erud.* VI (1954) 11; the author
also discusses Jerome's misrepresentation of Augustine's position; in general cf. Schelkle,
Vergil 16 ff., where the older literature is utilized; in addition see B. Altaner, "Augustinus
und die neutestamentlichen Apokryphen, Sibyllen und Sextussprüche," *Anal. Boll.* LXVII
(1949) 236 ff., and *idem.* "Augustinus und die griechische Patristik," *Rev. bén.* LXII
(1952) 201 ff.

kings,"[76] he also explains that the Christian emperors are rightly called blessed, not because of any successes gained by them, but only in so far as they were just and humble, *et se homines esse meminerunt*, and if they preferred the control of their evil desires to their government over nations.[77] God allowed Christian emperors such as Constantine the Great to obtain earthly power only because otherwise it might be thought that the worshippers of demons alone could achieve such things. This latter statement forms part of Augustine's answer, in his work *On the City of God*, to those who claimed that it was the Christian religion which had brought misfortune to the Romans.[78]

To return from Augustine's views on the Roman Empire to the relationship between Roman *civitas* and *respublica* ideology and the Augustinian concept of the two cities, it would certainly be wrong to overestimate the influence of the former on the latter. The idea of the City of God is clearly biblical and had already been developed by the earlier Fathers, as was shown by a few examples.[79] The close link to Holy Scripture is evident also in Augustine's conception of the two cities, above all in his countless identifications of the City of God with the heavenly Jerusalem and of the earthly or devilish city with Babylon.

In spite of the vast literature on Augustine's *De civitate Dei* two great questions remain, the first of which has never been answered in an entirely satisfactory manner, while the second in spite of its importance has hardly ever been raised. First, beside Roman *civitas* terminology and scriptural-patristic *polis* ideology, were there more immediate and special sources of Augustine's idea of two cities? Secondly, why did Augustine plan and compose the greatest of all his works around the concept of the City of God and not around any other related idea, such as the Kingdom of God, the Body of Christ, the Church?

[76] See *Enarr. in Ps. LXXIII*, 6 (v. 3), *Corp. Christ.*, *Ser. Lat.* XXXIX, 1010: Iam in frontibus regum pretiosius est signum crucis quam gemma diadematis.

[77] *De Civitate Dei* V, 24, *Corp. Christ.*, *Ser. Lat.* XLVII, 160. Cf. also Paulinus of Nola, *Epist.* XXVIII, 6, to Sulpicius Severus, *CSEL* XXIX, 247, where Paulinus says that he has written in praise of Theodosius the Great *ut in Theodosio non tam imperatorem quam Christi servum, non dominandi superbia, sed humilitate famulandi potentem, nec regno sed fide principem praedicarem*.

[78] *De Civitate Dei* V, 25 f., *Corp. Christ.*, *Ser. Lat.* XLVII, 160 ff., on the emperors from Constantine to Theodosius the Great.

[79] See above, pp. 244 ff.

The two questions are obviously interrelated and considered together have a bearing on Augustine's conception of reform. The first question has been answered in various ways. Manichean, Platonist, and Donatist influences have been adduced, not without some justification. Augustine had been a Manichean for nine years[80] and it is not impossible that some part of what as a Christian he must have considered a poison remained in his mind as an antidote to the superficial Christian optimism of the Theodosian age. Nevertheless, fundamentally the extreme dualism of the Manicheans, according to which good and evil were equally strong, was incompatible with Augustine's Christian faith and also with Platonism as understood by his contemporaries and by himself. Evil as such was for him only a defect, not anything that has being.[81] As regards the relationship of Augustine's Civitas Dei concept to Platonism, direct or indirect influence of Plato's ideal πολιτεία is certainly not improbable, since Augustine speaks of Plato as the man who had formed a theory of the city as it ought to be.[82] But, on the other hand, Platonism had little interest in tracing an entire history of the city of evil—or of the heavenly city on earth for that matter. A Platonist history of the terrestrial destinies of the heavenly *polis* and of its purely terrestrial and therefore evil counterpart is unthinkable, for the ultimate reason that a true Platonist sees the return from the world of becoming to that of stable being as a purely intellectual and psychological process and cannot be much

---

[80] For Augustine's Manichean period and his rejection of Manichaeism see P. Alfaric, *L'évolution intellectuelle de saint Augustin* (Paris, 1918).

[81] See above, p. 170, n. 10.

[82] See *De civitate Dei* II, 14, Corp. Christ., Ser. Lat. XLVII, 45: . . . Graeco Platoni . . ., qui cum ratione formaret, qualis esse civitas debeat. . . . Cf. E. Salin, *Civitas Dei* (Tübingen, 1926) 241, H. Scholz, *Glaube und Unglaube in der Weltgeschichte: Ein Kommentar zu Augustins De civitate Dei* (Leipzig, 1911) 74 ff. In this connection see H. I. Marrou's report at the *Congrès international augustinien* of 1954, "La théologie de l'histoire," *Aug. Mag.* III (1955) 200 ff., where M. Marrou rightly compares the concept of the *civitas Dei* to a Platonic idea or ideal (cf. now his article "Civitas Dei," in *Stud. Patr.* II, 343). For the "ideal" character of Augustine's Civitas Dei concept, see also below, p. 275. Scholz, *Glaube* 75 f., refers to the Stoics, and especially to Seneca, *De otio* IV, 1, where the great cosmic city of gods and men and the various terrestrial cities of men are contrasted with one another; but this is only a very superficial similarity. Philo's two cities ideology again and his conception of two races of men (cf. Scholz, *Glaube* 76) does not contain anything which Augustine could not have found expressed in a way more congenial to him in Holy Scripture (see especially below, pp. 264 ff., about St. Paul).

concerned with the spiritual-material composite of human history.[83] It is important to remember that Augustine's Civitas Dei is both an ideal *and* a reality arising out of the liturgical-juridical community of the historical Church.

Augustine's conception of the two cities owes more of its specific traits to the necessity of refuting the Donatists' doctrine of the Church than to the influence of Manicheans and Platonists. Donatism, which had originated in Augustine's own country almost a hundred years before his time, had this in common with early Pelagianism— from which it otherwise was quite different and which it preceded chronologically—that it, too, was originally a rigoristic movement against laxness in the Church. But while Pelagius was led to an exaggerated opinion and doctrine of man's moral strength, the concern of the *pars Donati* was mainly a practical one: they demanded the exclusion from the Church of all those who had weakened in the last great persecution of the Christians under Diocletian; baptisms and ordinations, conferred by such traitors, were declared invalid; at best the recipients of sacraments thus tainted could expect admission to penance and rebaptism or reordination.[84]

As the rest of the Church would not and could not go to such lengths, the Donatists of Africa considered themselves the only true and Catholic Church. Regardless of the truth or falsehood of the various accusations of the Donatists against the Catholics, their views and the fanatical violence of the way in which they tried to make them prevail were in flagrant contradiction to the letter and the spirit of charity of the New Testament. Had not Christ told the parable of the

[83] See the convincing refutation by F. E. Cranz, "De civitate Dei XV, 2, and Augustine's Idea of the Christian Society," *Speculum* XXV (1950) 215 ff., of H. Leisegang, "Der Ursprung der Lehre Augustins von der Civitas Dei," *Arch. Kult. Gesch.* XVI (1925) 127 ff., where the author attempted to prove the existence of a specific Neoplatonic pattern in *De civitate Dei* XV, 2.

[84] See also below, pp. 307 f. Especially, in the earliest phase of the history of Donatism, even *traditores* (originally those, who had handed over to the imperial officials the Holy Scriptures) themselves and, later on, *persecutores* (i.e., Catholics such as Augustine himself, who finally resorted to an appeal to imperial authority against the Donatists, see below, p. 465, n. 4) might, if they desired to become Donatists, be admitted to penance and to rebaptism or reordination; cf. K. Adam, *Die kirchliche Sündenvergebung nach dem hl. Augustin* (Paderborn, 1917) 75 f., W. H. C. Frend, *The Donatist Church* (Oxford, 1952) 20 and 195, L. Saltet, *Les réordinations* (Paris, 1907) 59 ff.

field of wheat in which an enemy had sown cockle which must, nevertheless, not be torn out prematurely,

. . . lest perhaps gathering up the cockle you root up the wheat also together with it. Suffer both to grow until the harvest, and in the time of the harvest I will say to the reapers: Gather up first the cockle and bind it into bundles to burn, but the wheat gather ye into my barn (Matthew 13:29 f.).

These Gospel verses were quoted by Augustine in his writings against the Donatists.[85]

And yet, the worldliness of the Church at the turn of the fourth century was too serious a problem that Augustine should not try to give a constructive answer to the Donatist outcry for a pure Church. It is not an accident that the idea of the two cities was first clearly formulated by St. Augustine about the time (c. 400) when he became engaged in his struggle with the Donatists.[86] It offers in any case a Catholic answer to Donatism. Both the City of God and the devilish City of the World (the terrestrial city in the pejorative sense of the term) traverse, as it were, the visible Church on earth. In essence this Church is the City of God, in those, that is to say, of its members who are the elect of God, whereas its bad members tend toward the City of the Devil and may be damned, though Augustine never despairs of their reform and salvation (see below, p. 279).

It is probable that Donatism had an even greater share in the origin of St. Augustine's doctrine of the two cities, that Ticonius, a Donatist who was in opposition to the majority of his own party, was the most immediate source of Augustine's ideology of the two cities.[87]

---

[85] See, for instance, De baptismo IV, 9, 13, CSEL LI, 237; cf. also De civitate Dei XX, 9, Corp. Christ., Ser. Lat. XLVIII, 715 f. (to Matthew 13:39 f.).

[86] In De catechizandis rudibus; see pp. 265 f., n. 111. For the influence of the Donatist problem in general on Augustine's concept of the two cities see now Frend, Donatist Church 201 ff. For an evaluation of this book see Excursus V.

[87] Cf. Scholz, Glaube 78 ff., P. Monceaux, Histoire littéraire de l'Afrique chrétienne depuis les origines jusqu'à l'invasion arabe V (Paris, 1920) 165 ff., J. N. Figgis, The Political Aspects of S. Augustine's 'City of God' (London, 1921) 46 f. and 127, n. 5, A. Pincherle, "L'ecclesiologia nella controversia donatista," Ric. rel. I (1925) 46 ff., idem, "Da Ticonio a Sant' Agostino," ibid. 413 ff., W. Kamlah, Apokalypse und Geschichtstheologie: Die mittelalterliche Auslegung der Apokalypse vor Joachim von Fiore (Berlin, 1935) 57 ff., idem, Christentum 143, E. Dinkler, article Ticonius, in PW, RE II, VI, 1, 853 ff., S. J. Grabowski, The Church: An Introduction to the Theology of St. Augustine (St. Louis, London, 1957) 551 ff., J. Ratzinger, "Beobachtungen zum Kirchenbegriff des Tyconius," Rev. ét.'s aug. II (1956) 173 ff.

Augustine thought highly of Ticonius' writings and could not understand that he had remained a Donatist. In *De doctrina christiana*[88] he discusses at length the one work of Ticonius which has survived in full,
the *Liber regularum*,[89] an attempt at a Christian hermeneutics. Fragments of Ticonius' *Commentary on the Apocalypse*,[90] which Augustine
briefly mentions in *De doctrina christiana*,[91] are preserved in a Turin
manuscript from Bobbio[92] and in several later commentaries.[93] It

[88] *De doctrina christiana* III, 30 ff., 42 ff., *Flor. Patr.* XXIV, 63 ff. For Ticonius see also
Gennadius, *De viris inlustribus* 18, ed. E. Richardson (Texte u. Untersuch. XIV, 1, 1896).

[89] *The Book of Rules of Tyconius*, ed. F. C. Burkitt (Texts and Studies III, 1, 1894).

[90] See now I. M. Gomez, O.S.B., "El perdido Comentario de Ticonio al Apocalipsis:
Principios de crítica literaria y textual para su reconstrucción," in *Miscellanea Biblica B.
Ubach* (Scripta et Documenta I, Montserrat, 1953) 387 ff.

[91] *De doctrina christiana* III, 30, 42, *Flor. Patr.* XXIV, 64.

[92] Cod. F IV 1 (Bobiensis 62) of the Library of Turin, ed. *Spicilegium Casinense Complectens
Analecta Sacra et Profana* III, 1 (Monte Cassino, 1897) 261 ff.

[93] The commentaries to the Apocalypse of the following pre-Carolingian authors depend
to a greater or lesser degree directly on Ticonius: Jerome's revision of Victorinus of Pettau
(ed. J. Haussleiter, *CSEL* XLIX); Primasius, early sixth century Bishop of Hadrumetum in
North Africa (*PL* LXVIII, 793 ff.; cf. J. García-Soriano, "Un codice visigotico del siglo
IX," *Boletin de la Academia de la Historia* CVI [1935] 442 ff., and J. Z. Cuevas, O.E.S.A.,
"El nuevo codice visigotico de la Academia de la Historia," *ibid.* 407 ff.); Caesarius, the
famous early sixth century Bishop of Arles (Morin, *Caesar. Arel. Opera* II, 210 ff. = Ps.-
Augustinus, *PL* XXXV, 2417 ff.; cf. Morin, "Le commentaire homilétique de s. Césaire
sur l'Apocalypse," *Rev. bén.* XLV [1933] 43 ff.); possibly Apringius, middle sixth century
Bishop of Beja in Portugal (ed. M. Férotin, O.S.B., *Apringius de Beja: Son commentaire de
l'Apocalypse* . . . [Paris, 1900]; Dom Férotin has seen that Beatus [see below] has incorporated the whole of Apringius; Dom Gomez, "Ticonio," and H. A. Sanders [in his
edition of Beatus] assert that Apringius has used Ticonius, as Beatus did; there is certainly
no "Ticonian" two cities ideology in Apringius); Cassiodorus (died 580), *Complexiones in
Apocalypsin* (*PL* LXX, 1405 ff.); Bede the Venerable (died 735), *Explanatio Apocalypsis* (*PL*
XCIII, 129 ff.); Ambrosius Autpertus (saec. VIII med.-ex.), *Commentary to the Apocalypse*
(*Maxima Bibliotheca Veterum Patrum* . . . XIII [Lyon, 1677] 403 ff., cf. S. Bovo, O.S.B.,
"Le fonti del commento di Ambrogio Autperto sull' Apocalisse," *Miscellanea Biblica et
Orientalia R. P. Athanasio Miller, O.S.B.*, . . . *Oblata* [Studia Anselmiana XXVII–XXVIII,
Roma, 1951] 372 ff.; also J. Winandy, O.S.B., "L'œuvre littéraire d'Ambroise Autpert,"
Rev. bén. LX [1950] 96 f.); Beatus, late eighth century priest of Liebana in Northern Spain
(ed. H. Florez, *Sancti Beati* . . . *in Apocalypsin* . . . *Commentaria* . . . [Madrid, 1770]; also
ed. H. A. Sanders, *Beati in Apocalipsin Libri Duodecim* [Papers and Monographs of the American Academy in Rome VII, Roma, 1930]). The reconstruction of Ticonius' commentary, in
so far as it is possible, remains an urgent desideratum in view of its importance for the
origins of Augustine's *De civitate Dei* (see also below, p. 263). Such a reconstruction is now
being prepared by Dom I. M. Gomez of Montserrat; see his article quoted on this page,
n. 90. Meanwhile cf. also J. Haussleiter, "Die Kommentare des Victorinus, Tichonius und
Hieronymus zur Apokalypse," *Zeitschrift für kirchliche Wissenschaft und kirchliches Leben* VII

must, however, be realized that the *Liber regularum* does not speak of *civitates* but of *corpora* and that Augustine has some reservations with regard to this work, which are of relevance for his conception of the two cities; furthermore, that the present state of investigation of the surviving fragments and excerpts from Ticonius' commentary to the Apocalypse does not yet permit a clear-cut decision as to what is Ticonian and what may be Augustinian.

In the *Liber regularum* the first rule speaks of *The Lord and His Body* (*De Domino et corpore eius*),[94] the second of *The Bipartite Body of the Lord* (*De Domini corpore bipartito*),[95] the seventh and last of *The Devil and His Body* (*De diabolo et corpore eius*).[96] Ticonius also deals with the bipartite Jerusalem, holy and eternal as well as cursed,[97] and elsewhere he expressly mentions two parts in the Church, one the abode of God, the other of the devil.[98] In the *Book of Rules* then Ticonius bases his distinction of a good and a bad part in the Church almost exclusively on the doctrine of the Church as the Body of Christ, which he calls bipartite. The Jerusalem metaphor is used in the same sense; there is no mention of *two* cities, but of the one Jerusalem which is bipartite.

Augustine, in commenting on Ticonius' second rule, *On the Bipartite Body of the Lord*, criticizes his notion of the *corpus bipartitum*:

. . . for that which will not be with the Lord for eternity is not truly the Body of the Lord. But he should have said: On the true and on the mixed, or on the true and on the simulated Body of the Lord or something of the kind. For not only in eternity, but even now hypocrites cannot be said to be with Him, although they may seem to be in His Church. Therefore this Rule could also have been called: On the mixed Church.[99]

(1896) 239 ff. (Haussleiter was wrong in assuming that the so-called *Summa dicendi* in Beatus' commentary represents Jerome's lost commentary to the Apocalypse), T. Hahn, *Tyconius-Studien* (Studien zur Geschichte der Theologie und Kirche VI, 2, Leipzig, 1900), W. Bousset, *Die Offenbarung Johannis* (Göttingen, 1906) 56 ff., H. Ramsay, O.S.B., "Le commentaire de l'Apocalypse par Beatus," *Revue d'histoire et de littérature religieuse* VII (1902) 418 ff., Pincherle, "Ticonio" 449 ff., M. de Alamo, O.S.B., "Los comentarios de Beato al Apocalipsis y Elipando," *Miscell. Mercati* II, 16 ff.

[94] Ticonius, *Book of Rules*, Burkitt 1 ff.

[95] *Book of Rules*, Burkitt 8 ff.   [96] Burkitt 70 ff.

[97] *Regula 5, Book of Rules*, Burkitt 63.   [98] *Regula 7*, Burkitt 73.

[99] *De doctrina christiana* III, 32, 45, *Flor. Patr.* XXIV, 65: . . . non enim re vera Domini corpus est quod cum illo non erit in aeternum, sed dicendum fuit: "De Domini corpore vero atque permixto" aut "vero atque simulato" vel quid aliud, quia non solum in aeter-

It is noteworthy that in this connection Augustine does not any more than Ticonius speak of two cities.

The terminology and ideology of the two cities does repeatedly occur in some of the commentaries to the Apocalypse in which Ticonius' lost commentary is incorporated, such as the commentaries of Primasius, Apringius, Caesarius of Arles, Bede, and especially Beatus. Even though Augustine's De civitate Dei did influence these post-Ticonian commentaries to some extent,[100] it is hardly possible to account for their antithetical use of the two cities terminology merely by that influence. For, while the conception of the two cities in De civitate Dei is of course not exclusively linked to the Apocalypse, the context in which the two cities concept occurs in the post-Ticonian commentaries is always that of the two apocalyptic cities, the "beloved city," the Heavenly Jerusalem of Apoc. 20:8 and 21, and its counterpart, Babylon, the great and evil city of Apoc. 14:8 and 16:9 to 19:2. In other words, the conception of the Civitas Dei and the Civitas Diaboli is here quite inseparable from the text of the Apocalypse. And above all, the terms in which the conception is expressed are in part very similar in the several commentaries, so that a common source must be assumed;[101] this source is not the De civitate

num, verum etiam nunc hypocritae non cum illo esse dicendi sunt, quamvis in eius esse videantur ecclesia. Unde poterat ista regula et sic appellari ut diceretur "de permixta ecclesia." Cf. S. J. Grabowski, "Sinners and the Mystical Body of Christ according to St. Augustine II," *Theol. Stud.* IX (1948) 48–58, idem, *The Church* 553 ff.

[100] So, for instance, Beatus has incorporated *De civitate Dei* XX, 19 (first half of the chapter) in Book VI of his commentary, where he deals with the Antichrist.

[101] Some of the correspondences between Primasius, Caesarius (= Ps.-Augustinian homilies), Bede, and Beatus, which prove their dependence on Ticonius, have been noted by Hahn, *Tyconius-Studien* 23 ff. Among these correspondences, there are a number of texts relating to the verses of the Apocalypse which speak of the two cities, Babylon and Jerusalem. To Apoc. 14:8 compare Beatus, *In Apocalipsin* VII, 1, 4 ff., Sanders, 515 f., with Primasius, *Commentarius in Apocalypsin* IV, 14, *PL* LXVIII, 887D f., and with Caesarius, *Expositio in Apocalypsim* XI, Morin, *Caesar. Arel. Opera* II, 246; to Apoc. 17:18, 21:10, and 21:24 compare Beatus, *In Apocalipsin* IX, 3, 10–12, Sanders 573 f., with Bede, *Explanatio Apocalypsis* III, 17, *PL* XCIII, 185A; to Apoc. 18:1 f. Beatus, *In Apocalipsin* X, 1, 2–4, Sanders 578, with Caesarius, *Expositio* XV, Morin, *Caesar. Arel. Opera*, II, 260, and with Bede, *Explanatio* III, 18, *PL* XCIII, 185B. Besides, there are many other relevant passages, especially in Beatus, which are probably taken from Ticonius, even though there are no parallels in the other commentaries. The Turin fragments of Ticonius' commentary (see above, p. 260) cover only Apoc. 2:18 to 4:1 and 7:16 to 12:6, chapters which are of relatively little importance for two cities ideology.

Dei, since the similar texts in question have no specific verbal parallels in Augustine's work (neither are such parallels found in Victorinus of Pettau's commentary on the Apocalypse of *c.* 300). The concept of the two cities, as it appears in Primasius', Apringius', Caesarius', Bede's and above all Beatus' commentaries, therefore, in all likelihood was taken from Ticonius himself whom all these works mention as one of their sources; it would appear then that Augustine could and did find this concept in Ticonius' commentary to the Apocalypse. A full clarification of the relationship between Augustine and Ticonius must await a new exhaustive study of the Ticonian commentary and its reconstruction, as far as this is possible.[102] Yet even now it would seem probable that Ticonius was the first to apply the apocalyptic terminology of the two cities to the problem of the Church's position in the world and that Augustine availed himself of this great idea of a man whom he esteemed. The magnitude, range, and depth of *De civitate Dei* nevertheless remain Augustine's own and many other elements beside the Ticonian motif have entered into the *magnum opus et arduum*.[103]

It has often been noted[104] that the idea of the two cities occurs in a rudimentary form in one of the earliest works of St. Augustine, in the book *On True Religion* (*De vera religione*) of c. 390, and this occurrence suggests a somewhat neglected[105] though obvious inspiration of

---

[102] Cf. also Pincherle, "Ticonio" 449 ff.

[103] Preface to *De civitate Dei*, Ccrp. Christ., Ser. Lat. XLVII, 1; cf. below, p. 273, n. 136. The two cities motif certainly did not for Ticonius have the very great significance which it had for Augustine. Not only in the *Book of Rules* (cf. above, p. 261), but also in the Turin fragments from the *Commentary on the Apocalypse*, the two *corpora* within the *ecclesia* have such an essential position in Ticonius' thought (see, for instance, *Spicil. Casin.* III, 316, to Apoc. 11:8, but also 291, about two *populi* in the Church, and 321, about two *aedificia* in the Church), that it is hard to imagine that in the lost portions of the commentary Ticonius would have developed the conception of the two cities of the Apocalypse in a way comparable to St. Augustine's great development in *De civitate Dei*.

[104] See, for instance, Scholz, *Glaube* 76, n. 1, F. Hofmann, *Der Kirchenbegriff des hl. Augustinus in seinen Grundlagen und in seiner Entwicklung* (München, 1933) 490, Kamlah, *Christentum* 312, G. Bardy, "La formation du concept de 'Cité de Dieu' dans l'œuvre de saint Augustin," *L'année théologique augustinienne* XIII (1952) 13 f., A. Lauras and H. Rondet, "Le thème des deux cités dans l'œuvre de saint Augustin," in: H. Rondet, M. Le Landais, A. Lauras, C. Couturier, *Etudes augustiniennes* (Paris, 1953) 101 f.

[105] Cf., however, F. E. Cranz, "The Development of Augustine's Ideas on Society before the Donatist Controversy," *Harv. Theol. Rev.* XLVII (1954) 255 ff.

Augustine's formulation of the two cities concept: St. Paul's conception of the old and new man.[106]

In studying Augustine's doctrine of the ages of man it was noticed that in *De vera religione* he speaks of corporeal and of spiritual ages.[107] Who lives according to the first

. . . is called the old man, the external, the earthly man, even though he may obtain what the people call felicity in a well constituted terrestrial "city" (*in bene constituta terrena civitate*). . . .

Yet there is also the spiritual man, who is born as the "old and external man," but is reborn internally, and who tends toward the heavenly laws; he is called "the new and interior and heavenly man." Now, just as individual man can either remain merely old and terrestrial or progress toward being new and celestial, so it is with the whole human race:

. . . all mankind (*universum genus humanum*), whose life from Adam to the end of this world is as that of one man, is administered by the laws of divine providence in such a way that it appears divided in two genera. In one genus, the crowd of the impious, who bear the image of the terrestrial man (cf. 1 Cor. 15:49), from the beginning of the world to its end, is contained; in the other the lineage (*series*) of the people dedicated to the one God (that is to say, of the Jews) . . . whose history is called the Old Testament, which—though it seemed to promise a terrestrial kingdom—is altogether nothing but the image (in the sense of prefiguration) of the new people (that is to say, the Christians) and of the New Testament, which promises the Kingdom of Heaven (*regnum caelorum*).[108]

---

[106] A second phase of Pauline influence on Augustine may be dated c. 396–397, in consequence of his becoming acquainted with the Ambrosiaster and with Ticonius; cf. E. Buonaiuti, "The Genesis of St. Augustine's Idea of Original Sin," *Harv. Theol. Rev.* X (1917) 159 ff., Pincherle, "Ticonio" 460 ff.

[107] See above, pp. 235 f.

[108] *De vera religione* 26, 48, *PL* XXXIV, 143: . . . haec est vita hominis viventis ex corpore et cupiditatibus rerum temporalium colligati. Hic dicitur vetus homo et exterior et terrenus, etiamsi obtineat eam quam vulgus vocat felicitatem in bene constituta terrena civitate. . . . *Ibid.* 26, 49, XXXIV, 143: Hunc autem hominem quem veterem et exteriorem et terrenum descripsimus . . ., nonnulli agunt totum ab istius vitae ortu usque ad occasum. Nonnulli autem istam vitam necessario ab illo incipiunt, sed renascuntur interius et caeteras eius partes suo robore spirituali et incrementis sapientiae corrumpunt et necant et in caelestes leges, donec post visibilem mortem totum instauretur, adstringunt. Iste dicitur novus homo et interior et coelestis, habens et ipse proportione non annis sed provectibus

The idea of the two cities appears here in its very first beginnings. Augustine speaks of two genera of men, of two peoples, of the *civitas terrena* and its relative value, and of the *regnum caelorum*, though not of the *civitas Dei*.[109] What matters most in this text is the way in which the terminology and ideology of the two genera of men or people grow out of the antithesis of the old and the new man; this is one of the first renderings and developments by St. Augustine of St. Paul's familiar teaching on the old and the new man, of the apostle's doctrine of the renewal of the first Adam through the second Adam, Christ.[110]

A decade later the conception of the two cities appears explicitly in *De catechizandis rudibus* of c. 400, and here again there are allusions to St. Paul, especially to the celestial free Jerusalem of Galatians 4:26. Of this city Christ is the King and David prefigured Him in the terrestrial Kingdom of Israel of which the earthly Jerusalem was the center.[111]

distinctas quasdam spirituales aetates suas. . . . *Ibid.* 27, 50, XXXIV, 144: Sicut autem isti ambo nullo dubitante ita sunt, ut unum eorum, id est veterem atque terrenum, possit in hac tota vita unus homo agere, novum vero et coelestem nemo in hac vita possit nisi cum vetere . . ., sic proportione universum genus humanum cuius tanquam unius hominis vita est ab Adam usque ad finem huius saeculi, ita sub divinae providentiae legibus administratur, ut in duo genera distributum appareat. Quorum in uno est turba impiorum terreni hominis imaginem (cf. 1 Cor. 15:45 ff.) ab initio saeculi usque ad finem gerentium. In altero series populi uni Deo dediti . . ., cuius historia vetus testamentum vocatur quasi terrenum pollicens regnum, quae tota nihil aliud est quam imago novi populi et novi testamenti pollicentis regnum coelorum. . . . It is of interest to compare these texts with Eusebius, *Demonstratio Evangelica* I, 8, *GCS, Euseb.* VI, 39 f., on δύοι βίων τρόποι in the Church of Christ; these two Eusebian "modes of life" have, however, another meaning than St. Paul's "two men" and Augustine's "two genera" and "two civitates": Eusebius speaks here on the one hand of the ὑπερφυής, the οὐράνιος, the ἱερώμενος, the perfect life of Christians (ὁ ἐντελὴς τῆς κατὰ τὸν χριστιανισμὸν πολιτείας τρόπος), referring to those who give up marriage and property, i.e., the monks, and to those who ἀποτελοῦσιν ἱερουργίαν, i.e., the priests, and on the other hand he speaks of the δεύτερος βαθμός of the ordinary Christians, who are married and engaged in the various professions of the "civic" life (πολιτικωτέρας ἀγωγῆς).

[109] In other texts, approximately contemporary or only slightly later, the biblical Civitas Dei, identified with the heavenly Jerusalem, does occur, but still without being explicitly contrasted with the earthly or devilish City; cf. Cranz, "Development" 272.

[110] See above, pp. 53 ff. About the same time, Augustine has similar Pauline formulations in *De libero arbitrio* I, 114, *CSEL* LXXIV, 34, and in *De diversis quaestionibus LXXXIII, quaest.* XXXV, 2, and LXIV, 2, *PL* XL, 24 f. and 55; cf. Cranz, "Development" 263, 273.

[111] *De catechizandis rudibus* 19, 31, *PL* XL, 333: Duae itaque civitates, una iniquorum, altera sanctorum, ab initio generis humani usque in finem saeculi perducuntur, nunc

It is clear then that Augustine developed the Pauline doctrine of the two modes of man into a theory of two cities, each under its own king, God and the devil.[112]

This leads to the second question mentioned above: How did it come about that Augustine's book on the City of God is centered in the *civitas Dei* and the *civitas terrena* rather than in the good and the

---

permixtae corporibus, sed voluntatibus separatae, in die vero iudicii etiam corpore separandae. . . . *Ibid.* 20, 36, XL, 336: . . . Ierusalem condita est, formosissima civitas Dei, serviens in signo liberae civitatis, quae coelestis Ierusalem dicitur (cf. Gal. 4:25 f.), quod verbum est Hebraeum et interpretatur visio pacis. Cuius cives sunt omnes sanctificati homines, qui fuerunt et qui sunt et qui futuri sunt, et omnes sanctificati spiritus etiam, quicumque in excelsis coelorum partibus pia devotione obtemperant Deo nec imitantur impiam diaboli superbiam et angelorum eius. Huius civitatis rex est Dominus Iesus Christus. . . . *Ibid.* 21, 37, XL, 337: Sicut autem Ierusalem significat civitatem societatemque sanctorum, sic Babylonia significat civitatem societatemque iniquorum, quoniam dicitur interpretari confusio. . . . Hoc autem totum (i.e., the Babylonian captivity of the Jews and their liberation) figurate significabat ecclesiam Christi in omnibus sanctis eius, qui sunt cives Ierusalem coelestis, servituram fuisse sub regibus huius saeculi . . ., quousque post tempus praefinitum . . . ab istius saeculi confusione tanquam de captivitate Babyloniae sicut Ierusalem liberetur ecclesia. Cf. Bardy, " 'Cité de Dieu' " 15 ff., Lauras and Rondet, "Deux cités" 102 ff. The last-mentioned authors give an excellent survey of the development of the theme of the two cities in Augustine's sermons, especially in the *Enarrationes in Psalmos*, after 400, i.e., before and alongside with the writing of *De civitate Dei*. In these sermons, too, Pauline ideas form an important element of Augustine's thought, in particular 1 Cor. 15:45 ff., with its antithesis of the earthly and the heavenly man; see *Enarr. in Ps. CXXXVI* and *Enarr. in Ps. LXI*, *Corp. Christ.*, *Ser. Lat.* XL, 1964 ff. and XXXIX, 772 ff., cf. Lauras and Rondet 124 and 133 f.

[112] As a less immediate background the conception of the "two ways" should be mentioned, both in its pagan and in its Jewish-Christian formulations: the "Pythagorean" *bivium* (symbolized by the letter Y) and the "choice of Hercules," as well as the broad and the straight way of Matthew 7:13 f., the ways of life and of death, of light and of darkness of *Didache* 1, 1 f., Bihlmeyer, *Apostol. Väter* 1, of the Latin *Doctrina XII apostolorum*, ed. J. Schlecht, *Die Apostellehre in der Liturgie der katholischen Kirche* (Freiburg i.B., 1901) 105, and of Ps.-Barnabas' *Epistle* 18 ff., *Flor. Patr.* I, 64 ff., the ways of righteousness and unrighteousness of the *Pastor Hermae*, *mandatum* 6, *GCS*, *Apostol. Väter* I, 31 ff. For the Jewish moral treatise on the "two ways," which in all probability formed the source of these Christian works, see now J. P. Audet, "Affinités littéraires et doctrinales du 'Manuel de discipline,' " *Rev. bibl.* LIX (1952) 219 ff., where the relationship to the sons of light and the sons of darkness in the *Manual of Discipline* of the "Dead Sea Scrolls" is discussed; see also M. Burrows, *The Dead Sea Scrolls* (New York 1955) 374 ff., 343 f. For the development of the combined ancient and Judaeo-Christian tradition of the two ways from Lactantius to the Renaissance, see E. Panofsky, *Hercules am Scheidewege und andere antike Bildstoffe in der neueren Kunst* (Studien der Bibliothek Warburg XVIII, Leipzig, Berlin, 1930), T. E. Mommsen, "Petrarch and the Story of the Choice of Hercules," *Journal of the Warburg and Courtauld Institutes* XVI (1953) 178 ff.

bad, the "wheat" and the "cockles" in the Church,[113] the Body of Christ and the Body of the Devil, the Kingdom of God and the Kingdom of This World?

The reason why Augustine did not write a work *De regno Dei* rather than *De civitate Dei*, will be evident to anyone who tries to substitute for the *civitas Dei peregrinans* an Eusebian terrestrial representation of the βασιλεία τοῦ Θεοῦ.[114] To Augustine who saw that after four hundred years of Christendom the Church still lived in precarious "pilgrimage," endangered internally by her own external victories, the imperial conception of the Kingdom of God on earth must have seemed incompatible with the exalted idea of the Regnum Dei. Rather than to veil the chasm between heaven and earth by a sacred symbolism and ritualism in which the border line between the ruler's and the priest's functions was constantly shifting, Augustine wanted to point up the difference between that which is essentially celestial and that which was all too terrestrial. For St. Augustine, therefore, the Regnum Dei was identical above all with the final stage of the Civitas Dei, when it will be reunited in heaven under its divine King.[115] He would occasionally say that the Church was the Regnum Dei: the Kingdom was somehow present even now in the rule of Christ and His saints, Christ who rules over the chaff as well as the wheat.[116] Yet the mode of

[113] See above, p. 259, n. 85, for Augustine's use of this scriptural parable.

[114] Since Erik Peterson's fundamental essay *Der Monotheismus als politisches Problem*, reprinted in *Theologische Traktate*, München, 1951, 45 ff., the contrast between Augustine's theology of history and "Eusebian" imperial ideology has been more and more fully realized; see, for instance, the articles by T. E. Mommsen, "Augustine," F. E. Cranz, "De civ. Dei XV, 2," and *idem*, "Kingdom and Polity in Eusebius of Caesarea," *Harv. Theol. Rev.* XLV (1952) 47 ff.; also Kamlah, *Christentum* 175 ff.

[115] See, for instance, Augustine, *De civitate Dei* XXII, 1, *Corp. Christ.*, *Ser. Lat.* XLVIII, 805 f.: . . . iste huis totius operis ultimus [liber] disputationem de civitatis Dei aeterna beatitudine continebit, quae . . . aeternitatis nomen accepit . . ., quem ad modum scriptum est in evangelio: "regni eius non erit finis" (Luke 1:33). . . .

[116] He did so in a famous and much discussed passage, in *De civitate Dei* XX, 9, *Corp. Christ.*, *Ser. Lat.* XLVIII, 715 f., where he speaks of the reign of the saints with Christ on earth during the thousand years of the devil's relative powerlessness, that is to say, during the sixth or Christian age, the last age of world history (see above, p. 231, n. 29). In this connection, commenting upon Matthew 25:34: "Venite, benedicti Patris mei, possidete paratum vobis regnum," he says: nisi alio aliquo modo longe quidem impari iam nunc regnarent cum illo sancti eius . . ., profecto non etiam nunc diceretur ecclesia regnum eius regnumve caelorum. Nam utique isto tempore in regno Dei eruditur scriba ille qui

life proper to Christians on earth remained that of the suffering stranger and pilgrim, and Augustine expressed it in terms of the *civitas* idea. The concept of the Regnum Dei has connotations of action, God's action of reigning over heavenly perfection and terrestrial imperfection; that of the Civitas Dei designates a status, the citizenry status of those who are actually or virtually God's people. The God of the Kingdom rules over all men, but the citizens of the City of God belong only to God. While, therefore, the Kingdom of God on earth in the Church cannot and need not be perfect, the concept of the City of God is perhaps somewhat closer to perfection, though on earth the full extent of the divine city is likewise not evident. The bond of love, hope, and faith, of concord and community between all those who love God[117] helps at any rate to make life on earth bearable for the fellow citizens of the Civitas Dei.

As to the Pauline concept of the Body of Christ, there was, it is true, little danger in the age of St. Augustine of its being drawn into the political sphere.[118] Far removed from all Constantinian-Eusebian

profert de thesauro suo nova et vetera (cf. Matthew 13:52). . . . Ergo et nunc ecclesia regnum Christi est regnumque caelorum. Regnant itaque cum illo etiam nunc sancti eius, aliter quidem quam tunc regnabunt; nec tamen cum illo regnant zizania, quamvis in ecclesia cum tritico crescant. . . . Postremo regnant cum illo, qui eo modo sunt in regno eius, ut sint etiam ipsi regnum eius. . . . For the interpretation of this text, see, especially, Gilson, *Augustin* 238, n. 2; cf. p. 282, n. 156. See also G. Bardy, "Définition de la Cité de Dieu," *L'année théologique augustinienne* XIII (1952) 124 f., H. de Lubac, S.J., *Méditation sur l'église*, 2nd ed. (Théologie XXVII, Paris, 1953) 54 f., and chapters 1–3, *passim*.

[117] Cf. *Enarr. in Ps. XCVIII*, 4, *Corp. Christ.*, *Ser. Lat.* XXXIX, 1381: Homines enim amantes se invicem et amantes Deum suum, qui in illis habitat, faciunt civitatem Deo. . . . See also *Epistola* CXXXVII, 17, *CSEL* XLIV, 3, 122, where Augustine imperceptibly changes over from the *salus reipublicae* to that of the *civitas Dei*: Hic etiam laudabilis rei publicae salus: neque enim conditur et custoditur optime civitas, nisi fundamento et vinculo fidei firmaeque concordiae, cum bonum commune diligitur, quod summum ac verissimum Deus est, atque in illo invicem sincerissime se diligunt homines, cum propter illum se diligunt. . . For the *vinculum societatis* or *communionis* or *concordiae* which unites the City of God, see, for instance, the references given by Marshall, *Studies* 10 f. Cf. also *Enchiridion* 56 (15), *PL* XL, 258 f., about the *vinculum caritatis* between the good men on earth and the angels.

[118] While on the one hand Graeco-Roman "body politic" ideology was one of the elements which entered into Pauline *corpus Christi* terminology (see, for instance, A. Wikenhauser, *Die Kirche als der mystische Leib Christi nach dem Apostel Paulus* [Münster i. W., 1937] 130 ff., W. Goossens, *L'église corps du Christ d'après saint Paul*, 2nd ed. [Paris, 1949] 80 ff., L. Cerfaux, *La théologie de l'église suivant saint Paul*, 2nd ed. [Unam Sanctam X, Paris, 1948] 276 ff.) and on the other hand from Constantine the Great onward the Christian *corpus* idea influenced Roman Law corporation concepts (cf. A. Ehrhardt, "Das Corpus

Basileia ideology, it was a genuinely Christian social and historical concept: ever since the coming of Christ His followers are its members and He is its Head. Augustine might in fact have followed Ticonius' terminology of a *corpus Christi bipartitum* which in its own way took account of the bad Christians in the Church. He did not do so, because he considered it wrong to conceive, as Ticonius had done, of a devilish as well as of a divine ecclesiological *corpus Domini*;[119] he preferred to see the *corpus* or *civitas diaboli*[120] as distinct from, though on earth mixed with, the *corpus Christi*, the *civitas Dei*. Hypocrites, "simulated" Christians are for Augustine not truly the Body of the Lord;[121] the Church itself is the true *corpus Christi* only in her essence, not necessarily in any one of her individual members who by right may belong to the Body of the Devil. On the other hand only those who are in the Church's communion can form the Body of Christ.[122] Thus the ecclesiological *corpus* is mysteriously one with the liturgical *corpus* in which Christ Himself together with His Church is offered again and again as a sacrifice to God on the altar during each Mass—this sacrifice being the one actual entry of eternity into our world of time and space.

Because both the *civitas Dei* and the *civitas terrena* or *diaboli* are characterized by the objects of their worship, the cult of the one true God and the many false gods, respectively,[123] Augustine can define the City of God as the great living sacrifice which is the *corpus Christi*.[124]

Christi und die Korporationen im spät-römischen Recht," *Sav. Z. R. Gesch.*, Rom. Abteil. LXX [1953] 299 ff., LXXI [1954] 25 ff), organological *political* theory, especially in the west, remained in a state of suspended animation in the early Middle Ages, that is to say, before John of Salisbury. It is true, though, that in the west, from the Carolingian period onward at least until the age of Gregory VII, the ecclesiological Body of Christ could be conceived of as including both *regnum* and *sacerdotium* (cf. my article, "Aspects of Mediaeval Thought on Church and State," *Rev. Pol.* IX [1947] 407 f.); but this development lies outside of Augustine's own conceptions of *corpus Christi*, *ecclesia*, and *civitas Dei*.

[119] See above, p. 261.

[120] For *corpus diaboli* cf. *De doctrina christiana* III, 37, 55, Flor. Patr. XXIV, 70 f. (with regard to Ticonius' seventh rule). For *civitas diaboli* see, for instance, *De civitate Dei* XVII, 20, XX, 11, and XXI, 1, Corp. Christ., Ser. Lat. XLVIII, 589, 720, and 758; cf. also above, p. 241.

[121] See above, p. 261. Cf. also Bardy, "Définition."

[122] Cf. Lauras and Rondet, "Deux cités" 154 f., especially n. 186.

[123] See especially *De civitate Dei* X, 1–20, Corp. Christ., Ser. Lat. XLVII, 271 ff.; cf. Ratzinger, "Civitas-Lehre," *Aug. Mag.* II, 977 ff.

[124] *De civitate Dei* X, 6, XLVII, 279, cf. Ratzinger, "Civitas-Lehre," and see below, pp. 280 f.

And still he chose the Civitas Dei and not the Corpus Christi as the key term of his theological interpretation of world history, no doubt because the concept of the City of God could more easily embrace also those men who with or without any fault of their own were not at a given time part of Christ's Body, but nevertheless would finally become a part of it because they belong to the elect of God. "St. Paul before his conversion is a typical example: he was not in the Church of Christ, but he was a predestined citizen of the City of God."[125] Thus Augustine's distinction between Corpus Christi and Civitas Dei, as well as that between Civitas Dei and Regnum Dei, are bound up with the most crucial terminological distinction appertaining to the idea of the City of God, with the distinction and the relationship between it and the Church.

Both the Civitas Dei and the Ecclesia are "social" ideas. *Nam unde ista Dei civitas . . . si non esset socialis vita sanctorum?*[126] How could there be a City of God, a citizenry of the saints, if their life was not a social one? The Church, too, is a social concept. She is the Christ-centered community: liturgical communion and even juridical institution; as such she includes for the time being also men who will ultimately be damned. While Augustine rejected Ticonius' *corpus Christi bipartitum*, he does not hesitate to speak of *Domini corpus permixtum*, of an *ecclesia permixta*.[127] The question arises whether for Augustine there exists a difference between the Civitas Dei and the Ecclesia in the sense that the City of God does not include the reprobate, even though they are temporarily a part of the Church. We read in *De civitate Dei*:

. . . so also, as long as she is on pilgrimage in the world, the City of God has with her men who belong to the number of her enemies, men who are connected to her through the communion of the sacraments, but will not be with her in the eternal lot of the saints. . . .[128]

---

[125] So Gilson in his introduction to the English translation of *De civitate Dei* by G. G. Walsh, S.J., p. LXIV; cf. also his *Augustin* 238. See *De civitate Dei* I, 35, XLVII, 33: Meminerit [peregrina civitas regis Christi] sane in ipsis inimicis latere cives futuros. . . .

[126] See above, p. 240.

[127] See above, pp. 261 f., n. 99. Cf. Grabowski, *The Church* 556 f.

[128] *De civitate Dei* I, 35, Corp. Christ., Scr. Lat. XLVII, 33 f. This passage is the continuation of the one quoted above, n. 125. The whole text reads as follows: Haec et alia, si qua uberius et commodius potuerit, respondeat inimicis suis redempta familia Domini Christi et peregrina civitas regis Christi. Meminerit sane in ipsis inimicis latere cives futuros, ne

Does the word *with* here infer that, while bad men can be *in* the Church, because, though hypocritically, they share in her sacramental communion—and elsewhere Augustine says expressly that there are *mali et ficti* in the Church[129]—these same men are not *in* but only *with* the Civitas Dei on earth? This is not impossible.[130] Yet,

infructuosum vel apud ipsos putet quod, donec perveniat ad confessos, portat infensos; sicut ex illorum numero etiam Dei civitas habet secum, quamdiu peregrinatur in mundo, conexos communione sacramentorum nec secum futuros in aeterna sorte sanctorum, qui partim in occulto, partim in aperto sunt, qui etiam cum ipsis inimicis adversus Deum, cuius sacramentum gerunt, murmurare non dubitant, modo cum illis theatra, modo ecclesias nobiscum replentes. De correctione autem quorundam etiam talium multo minus est desperandum, si apud apertissimos adversarios praedestinati amici latitant adhuc ignoti etiam sibi. Perplexae quippe sunt istae duae civitates in hoc saeculo invicemque permixtae, donec ultimo iudicio dirimantur. . . .

[129] See *De civitate Dei* XX, 19, *Corp. Christ., Ser. Lat.* XLVIII, 732: . . . de malis et fictis, qui sunt in ecclesia . . . (for the context cf. p. 278, n. 150); further *De catechizandis rudibus* 7, 11, also 25, 48, and 27, 54 f., *PL* XL, 317 f., 343 f., 346 f., *De baptismo* VI, 27, 52, *CSEL* LI, 325 f.; all these texts are quoted by Marshall, *Studies* 41.

[130] The crucial text in *De civitate Dei* I, 35, is interpreted in this sense by Etienne Gilson in his introduction to Father Walsh's translation of *De civitate Dei*, p. LXIII. f.: ". . . the Church is not identified with the City of God. The City of God . . . includes all those predestined to heavenly happiness, and only those. . . . No matter how strictly we conceive of the Church, there can still be men who will one day enjoy the vision of God, but who do not, as yet, belong to the Church. St. Paul before his conversion is a typical example: he was not in the Church of Christ, but he was a predestined citizen of the City of God. On the other hand, there are within the Church Christians who are not destined to heavenly happiness; these are members of the Church, but they are not citizens of the City of God. Nevertheless, just as certain peoples are incorporated into the earthly city because of their prevailing will, so the Church is . . . in the very essence of her will, the incarnation of the City of God" (cf. also Gilson, "Eglise et cité de Dieu . . . ," *Arch. hist. doct. litt. m.â.* XXVIII [1953] 23). The criticisms of Gilson by Cranz, "De civ. Dei XV, 2" 224, n. 22, and Marshall, *Studies* 88, are not conclusive with regard to this particular text; but see the text quoted in the following note. In his *Augustin* 238, Gilson mentioned as another difference between the Augustinian Civitas Dei and the Ecclesia the fact that "il y a manifestement eu des justes élus avant la constitution de l'Eglise du Christ," in the City of God, therefore, but not in the Church. In his introduction to Father Walsh's translation of *De civitate Dei*, Gilson does no longer speak of a difference in this respect, and with good reason; for Augustine on several occasions explicitly said that the just of the Old Testament and even some pagans already belonged to the Church. See, for instance, *Sermo IV, de Jacob et Esau* 11, 11, *PL* XXXVIII, 39: Ecclesiam autem accipite, fratres, non in his solis qui post Domini adventum et nativitatem esse coeperunt sancti, sed omnes quotquot fuerunt sancti ad ipsam ecclesiam pertinent; see also *De civitate Dei* XVIII, 51, *Corp. Christ., Ser. Lat.* XLVIII, 650, and other texts, quoted by Y. Congar, O.P., "Ecclesia ab Abel," *Abhandlungen über Theologie und Kirche: Festschrift für Karl Adam* (Düsseldorf, 1952), and by J. Beumer, S.J., "Die Idee einer vorchristlichen Kirche bei Augustinus," *Münchener Theologische Zeitschrift* III (1952) 161 ff.; cf. Cranz, "De civ. Dei XV, 2" 219 and n. 23, Journet, *Eglise* II, 1107 f.

elsewhere Augustine speaks very clearly of wicked men *in* the City of God during its terrestrial course, men who will either be corrected before their ends or will suffer eternal death.[131]

It is an undeniable fact that Augustine often simply identifies the concepts Ecclesia and Civitas Dei.[132] He does so in *De civitate Dei* as well as in other works,[133] particularly clearly in the *Enchiridion de*

---

and II, 34, n. 1 from p. 33, where Mons. Journet also vindicates the identity of the *final* status of the Church and of the City of God; for, "l'église future est précisément la société des élus"; Journet rightly refers to *Enarr. in Ps. IX*, 12, *Corp. Christ., Ser. Lat.* XXXVIII, 64 (to Ps. 9:12: Psallite Domino qui habitat in Sion): . . . Ipse (i.e., God) habitat in Sion, quod interpretatur "speculatio," et gestat imaginem ecclesiae, quae nunc est, sicut Ierusalem gestat imaginem ecclesiae, quae futura est, id est civitatis sanctorum iam angelica vita fruentium, quia Ierusalem interpretatur visio pacis. Praecedit autem speculatio visionem, sicut ista ecclesia praecedit eam, quae promittitur, civitatem immortalem et aeternam. Sed praecedit tempore, non dignitate. . . . Sed etiam ipsam, quae nunc est, ecclesiam, nisi Dominus inhabitaret, iret in errorem quamlibet studiosissima speculatio. . . .

[131] See *Enarr. in Ps. C*, 12, *Corp. Christ., Ser. Lat.* XXXIX, 1415 (to Ps. 100:8: In matutino interficiebam omnes peccatores terrae, ut disperderem de civitate Domini omnes operantes iniquitatem): Sunt ergo in civitate Domini operantes iniquitatem, et quasi parcitur eis modo. *Ibid.* 13, XXXIX, 1417: Nam quamdiu inter tentationes sumus, nox est. In ista nocte parcit Deus peccatoribus, ut non illos tollat; flagellat illos tentationibus, ut corrigantur; tolerat illos in civitate sua. . . . Tolerat, ut convertantur ad illum peccatores. Sed qui non se correxerint in isto tempore misericordiae, interficientur. Et quare interficientur? Ut dispergantur de civitate Domini, de societate Ierusalem, de societate sanctorum, de societate ecclesiae. I am indebted for this text to a former student of mine, the Rev. W. D. Lynn, S.J.; it is quoted also by Cranz, "De civ. Dei XV, 2" 224, n. 24. In general, see the excellent remarks by S. J. Grabowski, "Sinners and the Mystical Body of Christ according to St. Augustine," *Theol. Stud.* VIII (1947) 614 ff., IX (1948) 47 ff., especially, VIII, 655 ff., IX, 58 ff., *idem, The Church*, especially, 545 ff.

[132] This fact has been abundantly documented in the recent studies already mentioned, by Cranz, Marshall, Kamlah, and others; see also Hofmann, *Kirchenbegriff* 496 ff., Journet, *Eglise* II, 28 ff., 65 f., Grabowski, "Sinners," *Theol. Stud.* VIII, 614 ff., especially 655 ff., and the same author's justified criticism of earlier views (including my own) in his book *The Church* 531 ff.

[133] See, for instance, *De civitate Dei* VIII, 24, *Corp. Christ., Ser. Lat.* XLVII, 243: Aedificatur enim domus Domino civitas Dei, quae est sancta ecclesia . . .; *ibid.* XVI, 2, XLVIII, 500: ad Christum et eius ecclesiam, quae civitas Dei est . . .; *ibid.* XX, 11, XLVIII, 720: Haec enim erit novissima persecutio . . ., quam sancta ecclesia toto terrarum orbe patietur, universa scilicet civitas Christi, ab universa diaboli civitate . . .; *Enarr. in Ps. XCVIII*, 4, *Corp. Christ., Ser. Lat.* XXXIX, 1381: . . . quae est civitas Dei, nisi sancta ecclesia?; *Enarr. in Ps. C*, 13, quoted this page, n. 133. Augustine's concept of the Church comes very close to that of the *Civitas Dei* also in *De baptismo contra Donatistas*, where he speaks of bad Christians as only *seemingly* in the Church. See *De baptismo* VI, 2, 3, *CSEL* LI, 299: Item quisquis non habens caritatem et perditas vias morum ingrediens pessimorum intus videtur esse, cum foris sit . . .; *ibid.* VI, 3, 5, LI, 301: Quos (i.e., malos) non

fide spe et caritate, which is a little handbook on Christian doctrine and follows the order of the Creed. When Augustine reaches that part of the Creed which expresses the belief in the Church he speaks of her as the House, the Temple, the City of God and says that we must think of her not only in her terrestrial pilgrim's condition but also in her celestial part;[134] this heavenly Church or City of the Angels will at the end of all things have received fulness of its numbers through renewed men.[135] The terms *ecclesia* and *civitas Dei* then can mean the same. And yet, it cannot be an accident that Augustine wrote that incomparable work which he himself called his *magnum* and *ingens opus*, his *grande opus*,[136] around the concept of the City of God. Instead of speaking of the *civitas Dei caelestis* and *peregrinans*, Augustine might quite conceivably have used at all times and everywhere the terminology of the *ecclesia in gloria et pace* and the *ecclesia in via*, which corresponds to the later terms *ecclesia triumphans* and *ecclesia militans*.[137] Yet he did not do

pertinere ad sanctam ecclesiam Dei, quamvis intus esse videantur, ex hoc apertissime apparet, quia isti sunt avari, raptores, faeneratores, invidi, malivoli, et cetera huiusmodi, illa autem columba unica (cf. Cant. 6:8) pudica et casta, sponsa sine macula et ruga (cf. Eph. 5:27), hortus conclusus, fons signatus, paradisus cum fructu pomorum (Cant. 4:12 f.) et cetera, quae de illa similiter dicta sunt, quod non intellegitur nisi in bonis et sanctis et iustis . . . ; *ibid.* VII, 51, 99, LI, 370 f.: . . . puto me non temere dicere alios ita esse in domo Dei, ut et ipsi sint eadem domus Dei. . . . Alios autem ita dico esse in domo, ut non pertineant ad conpagem domus nec ad societatem fructiferae pacificaeque iustitiae, sed sicut esse palea dicitur in frumentis. Nam et istos in domo esse negare non possumus. . . .

[134] *Enchiridion* 56 (15), *PL* XL, 258: Rectus itaque confessionis ordo poscebat, ut Trinitati subiungeretur ecclesia tanquam habitatori domus sua et Deo templum suum et conditori civitas sua. Quae tota hic accipienda est, non solum ex parte, qua peregrinatur in terris . . . post captivitatem vetustatis cantans canticum novum, verum etiam ex illa, quae in coelis semper, ex quo condita est, cohaesit Deo. . . . Haec in sanctis angelis beata persistit et suae parti peregrinanti, sicut oportet, opitulatur, quia utraque una erit consortio aeternitatis et nunc una est vinculo charitatis. . . . In *Enchiridion* 111 (29), *PL* XL, 284, Augustine speaks only of the two cities, but this refers to their final state, after the Last Judgment.

[135] *Ibid.* 62 (16), XL, 261 quoted below, p. 278, n. 148.

[136] See preface to *De civitate Dei* I, *Corp. Christ.*, *Ser. Lat.* XLVII, 1; *ibid.* XXII, 30, XLVIII, 866; *Retractationes* II, 69, 1, *CSEL* XXXVI, 181.

[137] Augustine does not use the terms *ecclesia militans* and *ecclesia triumphans*, though he does speak occasionally of *regnum militiae* and *pacatissimum regnum*; see *De civitate Dei* XX, 9, *Corp. Christ.*, *Ser. Lat.* XLVIII, 716 f. It was only shortly after 1300 that the Augustinian Friar, Jacobus (Capocci) of Viterbo, in his *De regimine christiano* I, 1, ed. H. X. Arquillière, *Le plus ancien traité de l'église* (Etudes de théologie historique, Paris, 1926) 95 f., spoke of the *militaris ecclesia* (referring to Job 7:1) and of the *ecclesia triumphans*; yet it is clear from the context that by then these were current terms.

so. The reasons why the idea of the two cities was so essential to him are perhaps less difficult to discover than would at first appear and it is suggested that they are related to his desire for, to his concept of, reform.

First of all, the term *civitas Dei* was "freer" than the term *ecclesia*. It was not as the latter defined dogmatically, liturgically, juridically. The Ecclesia was and is primarily the Corpus Christi, the liturgical communion with and in Christ; on earth it is above all *communio sacramentorum*,[138] it is not yet fully identical with the *communio sanctorum*.[139] The Augustinian concept of the Civitas Dei is much closer to that of the *communio sanctorum*; it differs from the latter chiefly through the fact that in its terrestrial part it is still *in via*, still *peregrinans* and incomplete, whereas the Communion of the Saints envisages only those living and departed souls who at a given time already form a holy company with the angels.

The concept of the Civitas Dei thus could serve admirably to comprehend the heights and the depths of Christian life. St. Augustine saw that the Church of his time was deeply enmeshed in the imperfections of human existence; at the same time he knew that the essence of this same Church was holy and eternal. His idea of the Civitas Dei expressed the unity in this doubleness better than the concept Ecclesia itself does. The Ecclesia being the ever present Body of Christ was both too familiar and too sacred, its situation in the world too sensitive and too vital, to be made the key word of a theology of history, of history even in its relation to eternity;[140] and in fact, no *ex professo* treatise *De ecclesia* was written until the thirteenth century,[141] when the idea and reality of the Church had been securely established over a long period of time.

---

[138] See above, pp. 270 f., n. 128.

[139] But see also pp. 280–282, nn. 153 and 156. For the doctrine of the *communio sanctorum*, see J. P. Kirsch, *Die Lehre von der Gemeinschaft der Heiligen im christlichen Altertum* (Mainz, 1900).

[140] Cf. also Ratzinger, "Civitas-Lehre," *Aug. Mag.* II, 971: "Während ecclesia, dem Neuen Testament entnommen, offene Redeweise, sozusagen «Sachbegriff» ist, bleibt Civitas Dei immer allegorische Bildrede aus dem Alten Testament heraus, «locutio mystica». . . ."

[141] The first explicit treatise on the Church is that by Jacobus (Cappocci) of Viterbo, O.E.S.A., *De regimine christiano*, mentioned above. Gradually, as Gilson, "Eglise et cité de Dieu" 15, has formulated it, "la notion d'Eglise a pris une importance telle qu'elle a comme absorbé celle de Cité de Dieu, non d'ailleurs sans en avoir assimilé le contenu."

Another reason why Augustine wrote a *De civitate Dei* and not a *De ecclesia*, is no doubt to be found in the genesis and disposition of the work itself. Augustine's *De civitate Dei*, as his life's work in general, is animated not by one but by two main apologetic motives—not only by his well-known wish to defend Christianity against paganism and heresy, but also by the desire to hold up to the worldly Christians of his day a supreme ideal of life.[142] Augustine himself explains in the *Rectractationes* that, whereas the first ten books of *De civitate Dei* are chiefly a refutation of pagan Rome, the last twelve are an exposition of Christian doctrine in its own right.[143] It was natural, therefore, to start out in terminological and conceptual categories of Roman political thought—*respublica* and *civitas*—and gradually to proceed to an explicit or implicit, often almost casual, identification of Civitas Dei and Ecclesia.[144] In proceeding from the refutation of paganism

[142] This second motive is not yet found in Cyprian's great letter *Ad Demetrianum*, CSEL III, 1, 351 ff.; H. Koch, "La sopravvivenza di Cipriano nell' antica letteratura christiana," *Ric. rel.* VIII (1932) 317, exaggerates when he calls this letter a first sketch of Augustine's view of the world and of history.

[143] *Retractationes* II, LXIX, 1, CSEL XXXVI, 180 ff.: Interea Roma Gotthorum inruptione . . . eversa est. Cuius eversionem deorum falsorum multorumque cultores, quos usitato nomine paganos vocamus, in christianam religionem referre conantes solito acerbius et amarius Deum verum blasphemare coeperunt. Unde ergo exardescens "zelo domus Dei" (cf. Ps. 68:10, John 2:17) adversus eorum blasphemias vel errores libros de civitate Dei scribere institui. . . . Quorum quinque primi eos refellunt, qui res humanas ita prosperari volunt, ut ad hoc multorum deorum cultum, quos pagani colere consuerunt, necessarium esse arbitrentur, et, quia prohibentur, mala ista exoriri atque abundare contendunt. Sequentes autem quinque adversus eos loquuntur, qui . . . deorum multorum cultum . . . propter vitam post mortem futuram esse utilem disputant. . . . Sed ne quisquam nos aliena tantum redarguisse, non autem nostra asseruisse reprehenderet, id agit pars altera operis huius, quae libris duodecim continetur. . . . Duodecim ergo librorum sequentium primi quattuor continent exortum duarum civitatum, quarum est una Dei, altera huius mundi, secundi quattuor excursum earum sive procursum, tertii vero, qui et postremi, debitos fines.

[144] At times Augustine, almost in the way of an afterthought, adds the phrase *hoc est ecclesia* to the term *civitas Dei*, or vice versa; see, for instance, *De civitate Dei* XIII, 16 and XV, 26, *Corp. Christ.*, *Ser. Lat.* XLVIII, 396 and 493; cf. XVIII, 29, XLVIII, 619. It is hardly necessary to recall once more that πόλις-*civitas* was not only a "political" but also a metapolitical scriptural term, which in its application to heaven and in relation to God could assume a meaning even more "ideal" than that of *ecclesia* (see pp. 242 ff.). True, ever since the Pauline letters, the Christian ἐκκλησία stood against the profane ἐκκλησία, which was the assembly of the people of an earthly πόλις, just as the heavenly City stood against the terrestrial city, and the Kingdom of God against the kingdoms of this world (cf. E. Peterson, *Die Kirche* [1929], reprinted in *Theologische Traktate*, München, 1951, 422 f.,

to the apology and "self-criticism" of Christendom St. Augustine evidently did not consider it necessary or advisable to change the title and plan of the work or to modify the leading role of the City of God idea in it.

As with all his other writings so also with his books on the City of God Augustine undoubtedly wanted to help in bringing about a change to the better in the condition of the Church of his time. Yet there is also little doubt that to place the Ecclesia in the dead center of his great reckoning with Christians as well as pagans would have been as uncongenial to him as—to judge from earlier and later attempts —it would have been fruitless or disrupting. But, a work on the

most glorious City of God, be it in this temporal flow, while it is on pilgrimage among the impious and lives in faith (Habac. 2:4), be it in that stability of the eternal abode which it now expects with patience (cf. Rom. 8:25), "until justice be turned into judgment" (Ps. 93:15), and which it will afterwards attain eminently in the last victory and the perfect peace,[145]

a work in other words on those predestined to heavenly happiness and on their counterpart could and actually did set an inspiring standard and suggest that the troubles of Church history are only the heritage of human nature and that contrary to all other human societies the Church, insofar as it is the City of God, will not perish.[146]

---

idem, Von den Engeln [1935], reprinted ibid. 328 ff.). Nevertheless, already in the New Testament the Christian ecclesia and the heavenly city are not quite on the same level: the ecclesia is not wholly, but eminently an assembly or community on earth, though not of this world, whereas the heavenly city is eminently in heaven, though it has citizens on pilgrimage on earth (cf. p. 241, n. 10; also Peterson, Von den Engeln 377: "Niemals wird jemand— solange er in diesem Fleische lebt—durch seinen Eintritt in das himmlische Jerusalem aus der irdischen Ekklesia entlassen . . .").

[145] See De civitate Dei I, preface, Corp. Christ., Ser. Lat. XLVII, 1: Gloriosissimam civitatem Dei sive in hoc temporum cursu, cum inter impios peregrinatur ex fide vivens (cf. Habac. 2:4), sive in illa stabilitate sedis aeternae, quam nunc expectat per patientiam, quoadusque iustitia convertatur in iudicium (cf. Rom. 8:25, Ps. 93:15), deinceps adeptura per excellentiam victoria ultima et pace perfecta, hoc opere . . . defendere adversus eos, qui conditori eius deos suos praeferunt, . . . suscepi. . . .

[146] In this connection cf. Gilson, "Eglise et cité de Dieu" 23: "Augustin . . . a reconnu que, parfois, certains «citoyens de Babylone administrent la chose publique de la cité de Jérusalem» (Enarr. in Ps. LXI, 8, Corp. Christ., Ser. Lat. XXXIX, 778). On ne pouvait guère s'exprimer avec une indignation plus discrètement contenue, mais c'est probablement la vue de telles tristesses qui l'a retenu de conduire à son terme une identification [between Church and City of God] si bien préparée par lui."

A third reason, finally, for the predominant role of the Civitas Dei idea in Augustine's theology of history is most directly related to his conception of reform. Not any more than Christian Antiquity in general does Augustine know of a concept of "Church reform" as such.[147] Everything which pertains to reform is expressed in terms of personal renewal. At any given time the Church, insofar as it *truly was* the Church, was also the Civitas Dei and the *communio sanctorum*, essentially eternal and not in need of reform, whereas the reprobate in the Church—on its surface as it were—would not and could not be lastingly reformed. Yet, the individual elect of God, who on earth form the *civitas Dei peregrinans*, must be constantly reformed until the hour of their death. If then Augustine wanted to indicate the permanent need of reform in the Church, he must express this necessity in terms of a group of men capable of reform; these are the *cives* of the terrestrial Civitas Dei whose salvation will ultimately even "restore" the Kingdom of Heaven, in the sense that they will replenish the angelic hosts whose number was depleted by the fall of the rebel angels.

And certainly the holy angels taught by God . . . know how great a supplementary number the fulness of that city (i.e., the supernal City of God or the celestial part of the Church) expects out of mankind. Therefore, the apostle said: "To reestablish (*instaurare*) all things in Christ, that are in heaven and on earth, in Him" (Eph. 1:10). For, the things that are in heaven are reestablished when that which in the angels fell from heaven is made up (*redditur*) through men; and the things that are on earth are reestablished

---

[147] Notwithstanding the very ancient and important practice of ecclesiastical councils of renewing the "old canons" and the "doctrine of the Fathers" (see below, pp. 299–303), the idea of a reform of the whole Church itself does not seem to appear before the age of Gregory VII, when the Church begins to be defined also as an eminently sacerdotal, clerical quasi-corporation, in addition to being the liturgical communion of all the faithful; cf. my article, quoted above, p. 268, n. 118; also "The Concepts of «Ecclesia» and «Christianitas» . . .," *Sacerdozio e Regno da Gregorio VII a Bonifacio VIII* (Miscellanea Historiae Pontificiae XVIII, Roma, 1954) 51 ff., and "Two Gregorian Letters . . .," *Studi Gregor. V* (Roma, 1956) 224, 236 ff. "Church reform," when it is first clearly spoken of in the Hildebrandian age, is primarily reform of the *ecclesiastici*, in the sense of the clergy; only gradually the idea of a reform of the Church in its entirety evolves from there and even then it remains, in the Catholic Church, a reform "dans l'ordre de la *vie* de l'Eglise, non dans celui de sa *structure*: dogmes, sacrements, constitution hiérarchique" (Y. M.-J. Congar, O.P., *Vraie et fausse réforme dans l'eglise* [Unam Sanctam XX, Paris, 1950] 357).

when those same men themselves, who are predestined to eternal life, are renewed (*renovati*) from the oldness of corruption.[148]

Commenting in *De civitate Dei* upon the famous verses of the book Ecclesiastes (12:8) concerning the vanity of all things and considering the calamities, the errors of life, the ineluctable lapse of time, the apparent futility of the historical world of becoming Augustine concludes:

Yet, in the days of his vanity, it makes a very great difference whether [man] resists or obeys truth. . . . "Fear God," [Ecclesiastes] says, "and keep his commandments: for this is all man" (Eccl. 12:13). For, whosoever is, surely is this, a keeper of God's commandments, because he who is not this, is nothing, for, [such a one] is not reformed to the image of the truth and remains in the likeness of vanity.[149]

That there are in the Church on earth the *mali et ficti*, the wicked and the hypocrites, this may in Augustine's opinion be that *mysterium iniquitatis* of which St. Paul spoke.[150]

There are not wanting, in fact there are many within who by the loss of all morality torture the hearts of those who live piously, because by them the Christian and Catholic name is blasphemed; and the dearer that name is to

---

[148] *Enchiridion* 62 (16), *PL* XL, 261: Et utique noverunt angeli sancti docti de Deo . . . quanti numeri supplementum de genere humano integritas illius civitatis exspectet. Propter hoc ait apostolus: "instauravi omnia in Christo, quae in coelis sunt et quae in terris, in ipso" (Eph. 1:10). Instaurantur quippe quae in coelis sunt, cum id quod inde in angelis lapsum est ex hominibus redditur; instaurantur autem quae in terris sunt, cum ipsi homines qui praedestinati sunt ad aeternam vitam a corruptionis vetustate renovantur.

[149] *De civitate Dei* XX, 3, *Corp. Christ.*, *Ser. Lat.* XLVIII, 702: In diebus tamen vanitatis suae interest plurimum, utrum resistat an obtemperet veritati . . . "Deum," inquit, "time et mandata eius custodi, quia hoc est omnis homo" (Eccl. 12:13). Quicumque enim est, hoc est, custos utique mandatorum Dei; quoniam qui hoc non est, nihil est; non enim ad veritatis imaginem reformatur, remanens in similitudine vanitatis.

[150] *De civitate Dei* XX, 19, XLVIII, 732: After having mentioned the opinion of those who believed that 2 Thess. 2:7: ". . . tantum qui tenet nunc, teneat, donec de medio fiat," referred to the survival of the Roman Empire (an opinion which was to continue through the Middle Ages, cf. my article "Church and State" 419 f., n. 55), Augustine adds: Alii vero et quod ait: "Quid detineat scitis" (2 Thess. 2:6) et "mysterium operari iniquitatis" (cf. 2 Thess. 2:7) non putant dictum nisi de malis et fictis, qui sunt in ecclesia, donec perveniant ad tantum numerum, qui Antichristo magnum populum faciat; et hoc esse mysterium iniquitatis, quia videtur occultum; hortari autem apostolum fideles, ut in fide, quam tenent, tenaciter perseverent dicendo: "Tantum, qui modo tenet, teneat, donec de medio fiat," hoc est, donec exeat de medio ecclesiae mysterium iniquitatis, quod nunc occultum est.

those who want to live piously in Christ the more they bear pain that through bad men who are within it comes to be loved less than the minds of those who are pious desire. . . . But the pain itself which arises in the hearts of the pious, who are persecuted by the way of life of bad or false Christians, helps those who bear that pain, because it is derived from their charity in which they do not wish [the bad] to perish or to impede the salvation of others. Finally, great consolations arise also out of the correction [of the bad] (*de correctionibus eorum*) which permeates the souls of the pious with joy as great as had been the pain by which they had been tortured on account of their perdition. Thus, in this world, in these evil days (cf. Eph. 5:16) . . . until the end of this world, in between the persecutions of this world and the consolations of God, the Church takes its pilgrim's course.[151]

Correction, reformation of the human person is for Augustine the sole remedy against the evils of history. This means that even in the Church only the saint truly *is* and also that the Church exists truly only in its saints: this is, perhaps, the deepest meaning of the Augustinian City of God, which is the society of the angels and the elect.

Augustine, in *De civitate Dei* and elsewhere, has attempted a solution of the mystery of iniquity by showing that the same Church which has *mali* and *ficti* in her midst, is also the *Civitas Dei peregrinans* whose citizens must again and again be corrected and reformed by the grace of God, if they are to persevere, if they are to remain a part of that Church, of that Civitas which is holy and eternal.

It can never be emphasized too strongly that on the one hand every Christian concept of reform, and so also that of St. Augustine, is primarily individual, personal, and that on the other hand for Augustine, too, the *ecclesia sine macula aut ruga* (Eph. 5:27) exists and will exist notwithstanding the serious imperfections of a part of its

---

[151] *De civitate Dei* XVIII, 51, XLVIII, 649 f.: . . . non . . . desunt, immo multi sunt intus, qui corda pie viventium suis perditis moribus cruciant; quoniam per eos blasphematur Christianum et catholicum nomen; quod quanto est carius eis, qui volunt pie vivere in Christo, tanto magis dolent, quod per malos intus positos fit, ut minus, quam piorum mentes desiderant, diligatur. . . . Dolor autem ipse, qui fit in cordibus piorum, quos persequuntur mores Christianorum malorum sive falsorum, prodest dolentibus, quoniam de caritate descendit, qua eos perire nolunt nec impedire aliorum salutem. Denique magnae consolationes fiunt etiam de correctionibus eorum, quae piorum animas tanta iucunditate perfundunt, quantis doloribus de sua perditione cruciaverunt. Sic in hoc saeculo, in his diebus malis (cf. Ephes. 5:16) . . . usque in huius saeculi finem inter persecutiones mundi et consolationes Dei peregrinando procurrit ecclesia.

members. St. Augustine would no doubt have approved of the assertion that the Church is without sin, though there are sinners in it.[152]

In an important chapter of *De civitate Dei*, "On the True and Perfect Sacrifice," Augustine has established the identity of Christian reform, which is a willingness to make one's way of life a sacrifice to Christ, with the innermost life of the *ecclesia*, the *redempta civitas*, the *societas sanctorum*, the *unum corpus in Christo*, and he has done so with explicit reference to one of the Pauline key texts of all Christian reform ideology, Rom. 12:2:

A true sacrifice then is every work which is done in such a way that we may adhere to God in a holy society. . . . Thus man himself, consecrated in the name of God and devoted to God, is a sacrifice, in as much as he dies to the world so that he may live to God. . . . Our body . . . if we castigate it by temperance . . . is a sacrifice. The Apostle exhorts us to it when he says: "I beseech you, therefore, brethren, by the mercy of God that you present your bodies a living sacrifice, holy, pleasing unto God, your reasonable service" (Rom. 12:1). If then the body . . . is a sacrifice, how much more does the soul itself become a sacrifice, when it returns to God, so that, inflamed by fire of love for Him, it may lose the form of worldly concupiscence and, subject to His immutable form, may be reformed to Him and please Him because it has taken on something of His beauty. This very same thing the Apostle says when he continues and adds: "And be not conformed to this world; but be reformed in the newness of your mind . . ." (Rom. 12:2). Since, therefore, true sacrifices are works of mercy toward ourselves or toward our neighbors, which are referred to God . . . , it is actually brought about that this whole redeemed city, that is to say, the congregation and society of the saints, is offered to God as a universal sacrifice by the High Priest, who also offered Himself in His passion for us according to the form of a servant, so that we may be the body of such a head. . . . Thus, after the Apostle has exhorted us that we present our bodies a living sacrifice . . . (cf. Rom. 12:1) and that we be not conformed to this world, but reformed in the newness of our mind (cf. Rom. 12:2) . . . , he says: ". . . we being many are one body in Christ and every one members of one another" (Rom. 12:5). . . . This is the sacrifice of Christians: many are one body in Christ. And this the Church observes in the sacrament of the altar, known to the faith-

---

152 Journet, *Eglise* II, 1114, with Excursus VI, on the Church without spot or wrinkle (Eph. 5:27).

ful, where it is made clear to her that she herself is offered in that which she offers.[153]

This text explains how the City of God adheres to Him, because it truly offers the Corpus Christi in its twofold sense of the eucharistic sacrament and of the community of the faithful.

Just because ideally the City of God and the Church are identical and because Church reform is personal reform, St. Augustine also fervently desired that at least some of the Christians comprised by the terrestrial Church live in a Christian society on earth which, though "on pilgrimage," would correspond as closely as possible to the eternal Civitas Dei, to the Church in her essence. Already in the last book of the *Confessiones* he had asked how it was possible that the Christian world, which ostensibly observed God's precepts, was so far from being perfect. The rich young man of Matthew 19:16 ff., who stands here for the ordinary Christian, had claimed before Christ that he had kept all the commandments.

Whence then (asks St. Augustine) so many thorns, if the earth is fruitful? Go, root up the wooded thickets of avarice, sell what you have and be filled with fruit by giving to the poor and you will have treasure in heaven and follow the

---

[153] *De civitate Dei* X, 6, XLVII, 278 f.: Proinde verum sacrificium est omne opus quo agitur ut sancta societate inhaereamus Deo. . . . Unde ipse homo Dei nomine consecratus et Deo votus, in quantum mundo moritur ut Deo vivat, sacrificium est. . . . Corpus etiam nostrum, cum temperantia castigamus . . ., sacrificium est. Ad quod exhortans apostolus ait: "Obsecro itaque vos, fratres, per miserationem Dei, ut exhibeatis corpora vestra hostiam vivam, sanctam, Deo placentem, rationabile obsequium vestrum" (Rom. 12:1). Si ergo corpus . . . sacrificium est, quanto magis anima ipsa, cum se refert ad Deum, ut igne amoris eius accensa formam concupiscentiae saecularis amittat eique tamquam incommutabili formae subdita reformetur, hinc ei placens, quod ex eius pulchritudine acceperit, fit sacrificium! Quod idem apostolus consequenter adiungens: "Et nolite," inquit, "conformari huic saeculo; sed reformamini in novitate mentis vestrae . . ." (Rom. 12:2). Cum igitur vera sacrificia opera sint misericordiae sive in nos ipsos sive in proximos, quae referuntur ad Deum . . ., profecto efficitur ut tota ipsa redempta civitas, hoc est congregatio societasque sanctorum, universale sacrificium offeratur Deo per sacerdotem magnum, qui etiam se ipsum obtulit in passione pro nobis, ut tanti capitis corpus essemus, secundum formam servi. . . . Cum itaque nos hortatus esset apostolus, ut exhibeamus corpora nostra hostiam vivam . . . (cf. Rom. 12:1) et non conformemur huic saeculo, sed reformemur in novitate mentis nostrae (cf. Rom. 12:2) . . ., inquit ". . . multi unum corpus sumus in Christo; singuli autem alter alterius membra . . ." (Rom. 12:5). . . . Hoc est sacrificium Christianorum: multi unum corpus in Christo. Quod etiam sacramento altaris fidelibus noto frequentat ecclesia, ubi ei demonstratur, quod in ea re quam offert ipsa offeratur. Cf. also *De civitate Dei* XXII, 18, XLVIII, 836 f.

Lord if you want to be perfect (cf. Matthew 19:21) and associate yourself with those among whom He speaks wisdom (cf. 1 Cor. 2:6 f.). . . . But the barren earth was grieved and the thorns choked the word (cf. Matthew 13:7 and 22). But you, chosen generation, you weak in the world, who have forsaken all, that you may follow the Lord, go after Him and confound the strong (cf. 1 Peter 2:9, Matthew 19:21, 1 Cor. 1:27). . . .[154]

Perfection then is to be sought and found in giving up everything for Christ, in joining the company of those who have done so. Thus only will personal reform lead in some degree to a realization of the City of God on earth:

. . . and let them be a model (*forma*) to the believers by living before them and stirring them to imitation. . . . ". . . be not conformed to this world (Rom. 12:2), contain yourselves from it. . . ."[155]

Would Augustine find on earth those *perfecti*, those *sancti*, of whose life in a *vita socialis*, in communion with the saints and angels in heaven, he speaks in *De civitate Dei*?[156] If there ever had been such a society, how could it be restored? Through St. Augustine's whole life there runs the search for a perfect communal or societal way of

---

[154] *Confessiones* XIII, 19, 24, Skutella 347: Quaerebat dives ille a magistro bono, quid faceret, ut vitam aeternam consequeretur: dicat ei magister bonus . . . ut, si vult venire ad vitam, servet mandata (cf. Matthew 19:16 ff.) . . . ut appareat arida (i.e., *terra*, cf. Gen. 1:9: the appearance of dry land out of the sea was for Augustine a symbol of salvation). . . . Feci, inquit, haec omnia (cf. Matthew 19:20). Unde ergo tantae spinae, si terra fructifera est? Vade, extirpa silvosa dumeta avaritiae, vende, quae possides, et implere frugibus, dando pauperibus, et habebis thesaurum in caelis et sequere Dominum, si vis esse perfectus (cf. Matthew 19:21), eis sociatus, inter quos loquitur sapientiam (cf. 1 Cor. 2:6 f.) ille (i.e., Christus). . . . Sed contristata est terra sterilis et spinae suffocaverunt verbum (cf. Matthew 13:7 and 22). Vos autem genus electum, infirma mundi, qui dimisistis omnia, ut sequeremini Dominum, ite post eum et confundite fortia (cf. 1 Petr. 2:9, Matthew 19:21, 1 Cor. 1:27). . . .

[155] *Confessiones* XIII, 21, 30, Skutella 351: . . . et sint forma fidelibus vivendo coram eis et excitando ad imitationem . . . "Nolite conformari huic saeculo" (Rom. 12:2), continete vos ab eo. . . .

[156] See *De civitate Dei* XIX, 5, quoted above, p. 240, n. 5. See also Adam, *Sündenvergebung*, especially, 101 ff., 110 ff., where the unique importance of the *communio sanctorum* for Augustine's conception of the Church as a whole is demonstrated. As a Christian Augustine believed that the Church cannot lose its holiness altogether and that, therefore, in a sense it is already the *communio sanctorum*. This did not prevent him from distinguishing the *sancti* in the Church from the *mali* nor from reserving a special role and his special love to those who led the virginal *vita angelica* of asceticism and monasticism already on earth; cf. below, pp. 328–330.

Christian life.[157] In the days of his conversion he believed to have found it in the group of intellectually and religiously inclined friends who lived together in the country house of Verecundus at Cassiciacum;[158] later he found it more fully in a type of monasticism which was modelled after the common life of the Apostles in Jerusalem, described in the Acts of the Apostles.[159]

[157] That this need was felt also by others even outside the monastic sphere (cf. below, pp. 363–373, on lay *conversi* of Late Antiquity), seems to be indicated, for instance, by the name *Theopolis*, inspired no doubt by Augustine's *De civitate Dei* (perhaps, antithetically reminiscent also of Plotinus' *Platonopolis*?), which the former praetorian prefect of Gaul, Dardanus, a correspondent of Augustine and of Jerome, gave to his alpine estate in Southeastern France; see *C.I.L.* XII, no. 1524. Cf. Marrou, *Augustin, Retractatio* (Paris, 1949) 695, n. 14, and *idem*, "Un lieu dit 'Cité de Dieu,' " *Aug. Mag.* I, 101 ff.; also F. Chatillon, "Locus cui nomen Theopolis est . . .," *Bulletin de la Société des Etudes des Hautes-Alpes* 1943, 29 ff., where it is suggested that Dardanus, who disappears from the political scene toward the end of his life, led a quasi-monastic life in his foundation *Theopolis*. See Marrou's article on the hypothetical character of this assumption, which, however, may become more certain through further archaeological investigations for which M. Marrou has traced the way. I cannot follow M. Marrou (*Augustin, Retractatio* 696 ff.), when he draws a parallel between the idea of a *Theopolis* and the Christian Basileia of Byzantium.

[158] See *Confessiones* VIII and IX; cf. below, p. 353.

[159] Acts 2:44 and 4:32; for Augustine's monasticism and for monasticism in general as a vehicle of the idea of reform see below, Part Three. For the monks as *sancti*, see especially pp. 361 ff. It is significant that the Donatists who insisted on the sanctity of every member of the "empirical" Church, were hostile to monasticism even though the *Circumcelliones* had ascetic tendencies; cf. Augustine, *Enarr. in Ps. CXXXII*, 6, *Corp. Christ., Ser. Lat.* XL, 1931 (quoted by Frend, *Donatist Church* 320).

CHAPTER VI

THE IDEA OF REFORM IN THE EARLY CHRISTIAN LITURGY

The *Missale Romanum* contains the following oration:

Deus qui humanae substantiae dignitatem mirabiliter condidisti et mirabilius reformasti: da nobis per hujus aquae et vini mysterium ejus divinitatis esse consortes qui humanitatis nostrae fieri dignatus est particeps, Jesus Christus Filius tuus Dominus noster: Qui tecum vivit et regnat in unitate Spiritus Sancti Deus: per omnia saecula saeculorum. Amen.

O God, who hast marvellously created the dignity of human nature and more marvellously hast reformed it, grant us by the mystery of this water and wine to be sharers in the divinity of Him who deigned to become a participant of our humanity, Jesus Christ, thy Son, our Lord, who liveth and reigneth with Thee in the Unity of the Holy Spirit, one God, world without end. Amen.

Today this prayer is part of the *Ordo* of the Mass and is said by the priest, while he mixes water and wine in the chalice before offering it to God. Originally, however, a simpler form of the prayer (without reference to the eucharistic wine and water) belonged to the orations proper of the Old-Roman liturgy of Christmas; and in fact the antithesis, expressed in the prayer, of creation and of reformation, made possible by the Incarnation, is highly appropriate for the Feast of the Nativity. The oldest occurrence of this oration is in one of the Christmas masses in the unique manuscript, dating from the first half of the seventh century, of the so-called *Sacramentarium Leonianum*, now more correctly designated as *Sacramentarium Veronense*;[1] it also occurs in

---

[1] *Sacramentarium Veronense*, formula 1239, Mohlberg 157: Deus, qui in humanae substantiae dignitate et mirabiliter condedisti et mirabilius reformasti: da, quaesumus, nobis Iesu Christi filii tui [:eius:] divinitatis esse consortes, qui humanitatis nostrae fieri dignatus est particeps. . . . The text is corrupted; Dom Mohlberg conjectures: qui humanae substantiae dignitatem . . . ([:eius:] is an alternate reading furnished by the manuscript). Cf. J. A. Jungmann, S.J., *Missarum Sollemnia I* (Wien, 1952) 78 f.

the *Sacramentarium Gelasianum*,[2] very probably compiled in the second half of the seventh century,[3] and in the *Sacramentarium Gregorianum*.[4] A second oration almost identical in wording and meaning is found in another of the Christmas Masses of the *Sacramentarium Veronense*.[5] The tenor and style of these prayers have very close parallels in the *Sermons* of St. Leo the Great. These parallels have been collected by Dom P. de Puniet[6] and by Mons. C. Callewaert.[7]

The Pope often used sentences such as the following:

He, who gave much to man at his origin, since He made us according to His image, imparted far more to our reparation,[8]

[2] *Gelasian Sacramentary* I, 5, Wilson 5.

[3] Recently E. Bourque, *Etude sur les sacramentaires romains* (Studi di Antichità Cristiana XX, Città del Vaticano, 1949) 187–298, attempts again to support composition by Gelasius I (492–496), whereas H. Schmidt, S.J., "De lectionibus variantibus in formulis identicis sacramentariorum Leoniani, Gelasiani et Gregoriani," *Sacr. Erud.* IV (1952) 103 ff., comes to the same result as A. Baumstark, namely that the *Gelasian Sacramentary* was composed in Gaul shortly before or after Gregory the Great from Roman liturgical material of the second half of the sixth century. Abbot B. Capelle, O.S.B., argues for origin of the *Gelasian Sacramentary* in Rome during the second half of the sixth century in his article "Retouches gélasiennes dans le sacramentaire léonien," *Rev. bén.* LXI (1951) 3 ff.; cf. also *idem*, "Le sacramentaire romain avant s. Grégoire," *Rev. bén*, LXIV (1954) 157 ff. For the seventh century date see now A. Chavasse, *Le sacramentaire gélasien* (Tournai, 1957) 686.

[4] Ed. H. Lietzmann, *Das Sacramentarium Gregorianum nach dem Aachener Urexemplar* (Liturgiegeschichtliche Quellen III, Münster i.W. 1921) 13, no. 9, 6. The oration is found also in the Ambrosian pre-Christmas liturgy; see *Missale Ambrosianum Duplex*, Ratti and Magistretti 39.

[5] Formula 1258, Mohlberg 161: Deus, qui restaurationem condicionis humanae mirabilius operaris, quam substantiam condedisti: tribue, quaesumus, ut simul perficiatur in nobis et quod creavit Verbi tui divina generatio et quod eius hominis facti gloriosa nativitas reformavit. . . . For the use of the terms *reformare* and similar expressions such as *restaurare, reparare, renovare* in the *Sacramentary of Verona*, see Dom P. Bruylants, O.S.B., "Concordance verbale du sacramentaire léonien," *Arch. Lat. M. Ae.* XIX (1948) 251, 257 f. For the Roman liturgy in general see also W. Dürig, *Imago: Ein Beitrag zur Terminologie und Theologie der römischen Liturgie* (Münchener Theologische Studien II, V, 1952) 167 ff.: Excursus: "Renovatio ad imaginem Dei."

[6] Pierre de Puniet, O.S.B., "Intus reformari: Témoignages liturgiques sur le mystère de l'Emmanuel," *Ephem. Liturg.* LII (1938) 125 ff.

[7] C. Callewaert, "Saint Léon le Grand et les textes du Léonien," *Sacr. Erud.* I (1948) 35 ff., 105 ff. Cf. now A. P. Lang, S.V.D., *Leo der Grosse und die Texte des Altgelasianums* (Steyl, 1957) 47–89.

[8] Leo the Great, *Sermo XXIV*, 2, *PL* LIV, 204C: Qui cum origini humanae multum dederit, quod nos ad imaginem suam fecit, reparationi nostrae longe amplius tribuit.

or

more wonderful is the second generation of mankind than its first creation,[9]

or

merciful God wished to aid His creature, which had been made according to His image by Jesus Christ, His only begotten one, in such a way that the reparation of nature would not be outside of nature and that at the same time this second creation would go beyond the dignity of [man's] own origin. Happy [would man have been], if he had not fallen away from that [condition] which God made, but more happy [can he be], if he remains in that state which [God] remade. It meant much to have received form from Christ, but it means more to have in Christ [one's] substance.[10]

While the "Leonine" Sacramentary is only a private and probably non-Roman collection of liturgical texts, which dates from the seventh or late sixth century,[11] the bulk at least of these texts themselves is Roman and probably older. It is not impossible that some of the Masses contained in the *Sacramentarium Veronense*, and especially the Christmas orations quoted above, were composed by Leo the Great himself,[12] though in his sermons the Pope may have drawn on already extant liturgical prayers;[13] it is possible also that some of the Christmas Masses were composed by or for a later Pope.[14] The *Deus qui*

[9] Leo the Great, *Sermo* LXVI, 1, *PL* LIV, 365A: . . . mirabilior est secunda hominum generatio quam prima conditio.

[10] Leo the Great, *Sermo* LXXII, 2, *PL* LIV, 390 f.: . . . ita misericors Deus creaturae ad imaginem suam factae per unigenitum suum Iesum Christum voluit subvenire, ut nec extra naturam esset naturae reparatio et ultra propriae originis dignitatem proficeret secunda conditio. Felix, si ab eo non decideret quod Deus fecit, sed felicior, si in eo maneat quod refecit. Multum fuit a Christo recepisse formam, sed plus est in Christo habere substantiam. The last sentence refers to the Incarnation (cf. below, p. 287, n. 17). Note also the relation to the *felix culpa* motif, and cf. p. 287, n. 15.

[11] See, for instance, A. Stuiber, *Libelli Sacramentorum Romani: Untersuchungen zur Entstehung des sogenannten Sacramentarium Leonianum* (Theophaneia VI, Bonn, 1950); Bourque, *Sacramentaires* 146 ff.; H. Schmidt, "De lectionibus" 136; Chavasse, *Sacramentaire gélasien* 680 (c. 560).

[12] Cf. Callewaert, "Léon" and *idem*, "Le Communicantes et le Nobis quoque peccatoribus," *Sacr. Erud.* I (1948) 134 ff., 149 f.

[13] So F. L. Cross, "Pre-Leonine Elements in the Proper of the Roman Mass," *Jour. Theol. Stud.* L (1949) 191 ff.

[14] B. Capelle, O.S.B., "Messes du s. Pape Gélase dans le sacramentaire léonien," *Rev. bén.* LVI (1945–1946) 12 ff., C. Coeberg, "Le pape saint Gélase Ier auteur de plusieurs messes et préfaces du soi-disant sacramentaire léonien," *Sacr. Erud.* IV (1952) 46 ff., and A. Chavasse, "Messes du pape Vigile (537–555) dans le sacramentaire léonien," *Ephem.*

humanae substantiae oration and similar prayers originate at any rate in the early Christian period and, just as the kindred Leonine sermon texts, are centered in the idea that reform is something even more wonderful than creation. They thus exemplify that emphasis upon *reformatio in melius* which is characteristic of western patristic thought and especially of St. Augustine.[15]

Leo, the Pope of Chalcedon, is the great western doctor of the full reality of the Incarnation,[16] which alone can lead to the renewed God-likeness of man. Much as the Greek Fathers he sees the essence of redemption in the divinization of man, the possibility of which was brought about by Christ's taking on human nature,[17]

so that we are found in the nature of Him, whom we in our nature adore.[18]

Liturg. LXIV (1950) 161 ff., have shown that some of the liturgical texts of the so-called *Sacramentarium Leonianum* were composed by Pope Gelasius I and others by Pope Vigilius. According to Dom C. Coebergh, O.S.B., "Sacramentaire léonien et liturgie mozarabe," *Miscell. Mohlberg* II, 304, even the Christmas Masses of the Leonianum cannot according to their vocabulary be by Leo the Great, but may be by the African Gelasius I (Dom Coebergh does not, however, specifically deal with the oration *Deus qui humanae substantiae*); see also *ibid.* 299 f. and 304 about Augustinian influence on a preface for Pentecost in the "Leonianum," which may be by Gelasius I.

[15] See above, pp. 146 f., also p. 286, n. 10, for the concept of *felix culpa* and its liturgical use in the *Exultet* hymn. Cf. also the *Ordo agentibus publicam poenitentiam* in the *Gelasian Sacramentary* I, 38, Wilson 63 ff.: . . . nunc tamen et largior est per indulgentiam remissio peccatorum et copiosior per gratiam assumptio renascentium. Augemur regenerandis, crescimus reversis. Lavant aquae, lavant lacrimae. . . . Deus, humani generis conditor et benignissime reformator, qui hominem invidia diaboli ab aeternitate deiectum unici Filii tui sanguine redemisti vivifica itaque quem tibi nullatenus mori desideras et qui non derelinquis devium assume correctum . . . atque ab erroris via ad iter reversus iustitiae nequaquam ultra novis vulneribus saucietur, sed integrum sit ei atque perpetuum et quod gratia tua contulit et quod misericordia reformavit.

[16] Bourque, *Sacramentaires* 128 f., has noted that some of the Christmas Masses of the "*Leonianum*" reflect the theology of two natures in Christ, which is Chalcedonian (and Leonine); see also Callewaert, "Communicantes" 145 ff., with regard to the Leonine dyophysite character of the *Communicantes* prayer for Epiphany in the "*Leonianum.*"

[17] Cf. Jean Rivière, *Le dogme de la rédemption* (Paris, 1905) 265 ff., de Puniet, "Intus reformari" 128, n. 9.

[18] Leo the Great, *Sermo* XXVIII, 1, *PL* LIV, 222A: . . . ut . . . in ipsius inveniamur natura quem adoramus in nostra. Compare this with the Fourth Christmas Mass of the "*Leonianum*" or *Sacramentarium Veronense*, formula 1249, Mohlberg 159 f.: . . . ut . . . in illius inveniamur forma, in quo tecum est nostra substantia. . . . Cf. also Leo's *Sermo* LXXXII, 2, quoted above, p. 286, n. 10.

And yet, in his insistence upon the superiority of reform over original perfection,[19] Leo is a disciple of Augustine more than of the Greeks. He may have contributed to the blending of Greek and Augustinian elements also in the Roman liturgy.[20]

As far as the non-Roman western liturgies are concerned, the old-Spanish (Visigothic or Mozarabic) liturgy, as well known, contains both eastern and western elements; quite often it speaks of man's return to Paradise,[21] but stresses even more strongly his reform to the

[19] See above, pp. 285 ff.

[20] See also the oration for the consecration of virgins in the *Sacramentarium Veronense*, formula 1104, Mohlberg 138, (also in the *Gelasian Sacramentary* I, 103, Wilson 156, and in the *Ambrosian Pontificale* of the ninth century, ed. M. Magistretti, *Pontificale in Usum Ecclesiae Mediolanensis* [Monumenta Veteris Liturgiae Ambrosianae, Milano, 1897] 57), which may be of Leonine origin (cf. de Puniet, "Intus reformari" 134 ff., also *idem*, *Le pontifical romain* [Louvain, 1931] 167 ff., furthermore, Dom C. Coebergh, "Saint Léon le Grand auteur de la grande formule *Ad virgines sacras* du sacramentaire léonien," *Sacr. Erud.* VI [1954] 282 ff.): Deus, castorum corporum benignus habitator et incorruptarum, Deus, amator animarum; Deus, qui humanam subs⟨t⟩antiam in primis hominibus diabolica fraude vitiatam ita in Verbo tuo, per quod omnia facta sunt, reparas, ut eam non solum ad primae originis innocentiam revoces, sed etiam ad experientiam quorundam bonorum, quae in novo saeculo sunt habenda, perducas et obstrictos adhuc condicione mortalium iam ad similitudinem provehas angelorum. . . . Here return to primaeval innocence and acquisition of the even higher goods of the new dispensation are clearly combined; at the same time virginity implies similitude to the angels. Cf. *Sacramentarium Veronense*, formula 923, Mohlberg 116, where an admonition for fasting in September, in gratitude for the fruits of the earth, is based on the idea of man's, the divine image's, reform toward angelic similitude through the celestial *panis aeternus*. For the angel-likeness of the virginal and ascetic life, see also below, p. 326 and cf. above, pp. 124, n. 46, 126, nn. 51 f.

[21] For instance, *Liber Mozarabicus sacramentorum*, *Missa in diem sancti Clementis*, Benedictio, Férotin, *Liber Sacramentorum* 42: Clementie suo dono vos beatificet in hoc seculo et ab omni sorde purificatos restituat paradiso. Ibid., *Missa de VIa feria Pasche*, Inlatio, Férotin, *Liber Sacramentorum* 286: . . . humanum genus per hominem Deum paradiso, unde prevaricatione Ade eliminatum fuerat, restitutum. Ibid., *In XVo dominico de quotidiano*, Inlatio, Férotin, *Liber Sacramentorum* 640 f.: Dignum et iustum est . . . per Dominum nostrum Ihesum Christum Filium tuum, quem de celo mittens, carnem adsumit propter salutem nostram et crucem, quum ascendit, latroni adfixo peccata donavit, nobis omnibus paradisi ianuam reseravit. See also *Liber ordinum*, *Ordo baptismi* . . ., Férotin, *Liber Ordinum* 30: Redde quod in paradiso Adam perdidit. . . . Ablue terre squalentis ingluviem; discute paradisi maceriam flammeis obicibus fluctuantem. Pateat redeuntibus florei ruris ingressus. Recipiant ymaginem deitatis olim perditam livore serpentis. . . . *Liber ordinum*, *Ordo in finem hominis diei* . . ., Férotin, *Liber Ordinum* 115: . . . ut ab omni metu gehenne atque ab eterni iudicii pena absolutus inter electos tuos resurgere bonisque iungi concedas et Abrahe sinu receptus paradisi letitia fruatur et requiescat in secula sempiterna. Ibid., *Ordo ad consecrandum novum sepulcrum*, Oratio . . ., Antiph., Férotin, *Liber Ordinum* 123: Aperiat tibi Dominus paradisi ianuam; ut ad illam patriam revertaris, ubi mors non est, ubi dulce gaudium perseverat.

better.[22] The exact relationship of the Ambrosian liturgy to other liturgies, eastern and western, is still controverted; it might be observed at any rate that this ancient liturgy of Milan expresses the idea

[22] See, for instance, Liber Mozarabicus sacramentorum, Missa in Hilaria Pasche dicenda, Férotin, Liber Sacramentorum 254 f. : Amisit vetustas obproprium, mors aculeum. . . . Homo est qui perdidit : Deus homo factus est qui redemit. Maiorem tibi exegit, Domine, pietatem nostra calamitas, quam perdiderat prothoplaustorum effusa libertas. Tunc servi dicebamur futuri, nunc filii. . . . Tunc non licuit paradisum habere per culpam; nunc celum datur sperare per gratiam. Melius ergo, multoque melius, crevimus post ruinam (cf. p. 287, n. 15, for the idea of felix culpa). Ibid., Missa de diem sancte crucis, Férotin, Liber Sacramentorum 318 : . . . per hanc crucem hominem, quem transgressio precepti de paradyso expulit, confessio nominis Christi sine dubio reformavit. . . . Ibid., Inlatio, Férotin, Liber Sacramentorum 320 : Dignum et iustum est . . . de utriusque Ade, illius scilicet habitatoris paradisi, et istius redemptoris humani generis, exempla preponere. Ille quidem prior est, iste melior. . . . Ille transgressione legis paradisum amisit, iste per passionem crucis mundum adquisivit. . . . Tunc homo mandatum non custodiendo de paradyso pellitur, nunc latro Christum Dominum confitendo in paradyso introducitur. See also Liber ordinum, Ordo de missa unius penitentis, Inlatio, Férotin, Liber Ordinum 353 : Nam qui condideras cuncta bona, nimium erat opus bonum; sed quia adposuisti reparare humani generis lapsum, totum est excellentium omnipotentie tue indicium. . . . Ibid., Missa in fine hominis diei, Férotin, Liber Ordinum 391 (see also the nearly identical Missa in XVI° dominico de quotidiano, Liber Mozarabicus sacramentorum, Férotin, Liber Sacramentorum 642 ff.) : Omnipotentem Deum qui humanum genus condidit et post ruinam reparavit ad vitam, fratres karissimi, humiliter exoremus, ut famulo suo impleat reparationis perfectionem qui originis condidit dignitatem. (Cf. the famous oration Deus qui humanae substantiae, discussed above, p. 284.) Ibid., Inlatio, Férotin, Liber Ordinum. 391 f. : Dignum satis vere est et omni laude conspicuum tibi dare gloriam et honorem, omnipotens Deus Pater, qui cum Filio tuo et cum Spiritu Sancto unus in Trinitate equalis Deus existens unicum Filium tuum Dominum nostrum Ihesum Christum adsumtione carnis eiusdem persone restaurasti perditum hominem : reparator occurrens in eius occasu, qui bone conditionis perdiderat statum. . . . Nec proximans finis mundi reos secum ad interitum ducat nec brevitas vite nostre immundos nos usquequaque detineat. Sed et quos defecit dies in consolationem nostram renovata lux reparet et quod mundus tendit ad finem spes futuri confoveat. Et quod vivere nostrum resolutionis sue sustinet debitum, famuli tui transitus pacem et letitiam consequatur eterne beatitudinis : ut dum quicquid in occasu nostro est salutis, hec salutaris victima interne salutis statum reduxerit et in nos plenum maneat redemtionis nostre ministerium. . . . For possible Augustinian influence on the Mozarabic liturgy through a presumably Gelasian oration of the "Leonianum," see p. 396, n. 46. See also the strikingly Augustinian formula in the Liber ordinum, Férotin, Liber Ordinum 358 : in prima resurrectione que in hac vita consistit; this corresponds to Augustine's identification of the prima resurrectio and of the millennium of Apoc. 20: 5 f. with Christian history (see above p. 231, n. 29); cf. B. Botte, O.S.B. "Prima Resurrectio: Un vestige du millénarisme dans les liturgies occidentales," Rech.'s théol. a. m. XV (1948) 10 f., where it is shown that this Augustinian interpretation of prima resurrectio is not the one usually found in liturgical documents.

of reform to the better much as the Roman liturgy does.[23] The oldest
monuments of the Gallican and Celtic liturgies such as the *Missale
Gothicum*, *Mone's Masses*, and the *Stowe* and *Bobbio Missals* in their prayers
exultantly praise God for the renewal of man, with emphasis on restorative and redintegrative reform, an emphasis which is in conformity
with other eastern Christian elements in these liturgies.[24]

Among the eastern Christian liturgies only the Greek liturgy falls
within the scope of this study. Even with this restriction I can, in the
absence of critical editions of most of the Greek liturgical books,[25]
venture only a few tentative remarks concerning the reform ideology
expressed in them. The prayers and hymns of the Feast of the Nativity,
as found in the *Menaia*, which are still in use in the Greek liturgy,[26]
offer some material for comparison with the Roman Christmas liturgy
and the related Leonine sermons. It is true that in many cases the age
of these liturgical texts is uncertain;[27] yet, even though not a few
of them are from the Byzantine period, they most likely stand in the

[23] See above, p. 285, n. 4, for the occurrence of the oration *Deus qui humanae substantiae*
in the pre-Christmas liturgy of the *Missale Ambrosianum*, which also in the Easter Sunday Mass
for the newly baptized contains the following prayer (*Missale Ambrosianum Duplex*, Ratti and
Magistretti 249): Deus qui humanam naturam supra primae originis reparas dignitatem,
respice ad pietatis tuae ineffabile sacramentum: et quos regenerationis mysterio dignatus es
innovare, in his dona tuae perpetis gratiae benedictionisque conserva. Cf. above, p. 288,
n. 20, for the great Roman prayer of the consecration of virgins in the *Ambrosian Pontificale*.

[24] See, for instance, *Missale Gothicum*, *Missa in invencione sanctae crucis*, collect, Bannister
92, no. 318: . . . quosque transgressio praecepti de paradyso expulit, confessio nominis
Christi in paradyso reformit salvator; *Bobbio Missal*, Third Mass for Lent, Lowe 46, no.
148: . . . ut qui de paradyso non abstinendo cecidemus, eodem nunc ieiunando redeamus
(also *ibid.*, Lowe 50, no. 167), and *ibid.*, Fourth Sunday Mass, Lowe 145, no. 479: . . .
Deus qui . . . hominem . . . ad veniam vitamque revocasti, mittendum nobis unigenitum
tuum salvatorem nostrum, per quem . . . paradisi portas aperires, fidem innovaris, vita
mortuis redderis, Dei filius faceris et celestia rigna perduceris. . . .

[25] For old and new editions of the Greek liturgy, see the bibliography in E. Wellesz, *A
History of Byzantine Music and Hymnography* (Oxford, 1949) especially 332; cf. *ibid.* 18 f.,
about the publications of transcriptions of the text and music of Byzantine hymns in the
Monumenta Musicae Byzantinae. See also E. Mercenier and F. Paris, *La prière des églises de rite
byzantin* I, 2nd ed. (Chevetogne, 1937) xxxiv ff.

[26] Μηναῖα τοῦ ὅλου ἐνιαυτοῦ, comprising the offices of the feasts of the saints for all
twelve months of the year; cf. the edition of the Propaganda in Rome (1888–1901) and the
slightly more recent Athens edition.

[27] Cf. Wellesz, *Byzantine Music*, especially the list of hymnographers on pp. 342 ff. and
the literature mentioned there; also C. Emerau, "Hymnographi byzantini," *Echos d'orient*
XXI–XXV (1922–1926).

tradition of older Greek Christian liturgical literature and spirituality. If this is admitted, then the fourfold linking of the Incarnation to man's return to Paradise in the Greek liturgy of Christmas carries some weight:

Come, let us rejoice in the Lord and narrate this present mystery. The wall of separation has been dissolved (cf. Eph. 2:14), the flaming sword has turned back and the Cherubim have moved away from the tree of life; and I partake of the delight of Paradise from which I had been ejected because of disobedience.[28]

Today the Virgin gives birth to the maker of the Universe. The cave brings forth Eden, and the star makes known Christ, sun to those in darkness. . . .[29]

Rejoice, Jerusalem, and all of you who love Zion say praise. Today the age-old bond of Adam's condemnation has been untied. Paradise has been opened to us, the serpent has been crushed. . . . May then all creation dance and exult; for Christ has come to recall it and to save our souls.[30]

Bethlehem has opened Eden: come and let us see. In secret we find delight: come, let us receive in the cave that which is of Paradise.[31]

The return to Paradise is mentioned several times also in the liturgical services of the Easter season. The Crucifixion and Resurrection no less than the Incarnation can be seen as leading to the reopening of Paradise which in the Greek liturgy, incidentally, does not seem to be distinct from the Kingdom of God.[32] In the liturgy of

---

[28] Μηναῖα τοῦ ὅλου ἐνιαυτοῦ, Μὴν Δεκέμβριος (Athens, 1904) 300 f.: Vespers for Christmas day (sticheron, ascribed to Germanus, perhaps, the eighth century Patriarch of Constantinople): Δεῦτε ἀγαλλιασώμεθα τῷ Κυρίῳ, τὸ παρὸν μυστήριον ἐκδιηγούμενοι. Τὸ μεσότοιχον τοῦ φραγμοῦ διαλέλυται (cf. Eph. 2:14) ἡ φλογίνη ῥομφαία τὰ νῶτα δίδωσι, καὶ τὰ Χερουβὶμ παραχωρεῖ τοῦ ξύλου τῆς ζωῆς· κἀγὼ τοῦ παραδείσου τῆς τρυφῆς μεταλαμβάνω, οὗ προεξεβλήθην διὰ τῆς παρακοῆς.

[29] Ibid. 307: Σήμερον τίκτει ἡ πάρθενος τὸν ποιητὴν τοῦ παντός. Ἐδὲμ προσφέρει σπήλαιον, καὶ ἀστὴρ μηνύει Χριστόν, τὸν ἥλιον τοῖς ἐν σκότει.

[30] Ibid. 308: Εὐφράνθητι, Ἱερουσαλήμ, καὶ πανηγυρίσατε πάντες οἱ ἀγαπῶντες Σιών. Σήμερον ὁ χρόνιος ἐλύθη δεσμὸς τῆς καταδίκης τοῦ Ἀδάμ· ὁ παράδεισος ἡμῖν ἠνεῴχθη, ὁ ὄφις κατηργήθη. . . . Χορευέτω τοίνυν πᾶσα ἡ κτίσις καὶ σκιρτάτω· ἀνακαλέσαι γὰρ αὐτὴν παραγέγονε Χριστὸς καὶ σῶσαι τὰς ψυχὰς ἡμῶν.

[31] Ibid. 312: Τὴν Ἐδὲμ Βηθλεὲμ ἤνοιξε, δεῦτε ἴδωμεν· τὴν τρυφὴν ἐν κρυφῇ εὕρομεν, δεῦτε λάβωμεν τὰ τοῦ παραδείσου ἔνδον τοῦ σπηλαίου.

[32] See, for instance, an oration for Epiphany ascribed to the Patriarch Sophronius of Jerusalem (early seventh century), Μηναῖα τοῦ ὅλου ἐνιαυτοῦ, Μὴν Ἰανουάριος (Athens 1905) 105 f.; also the Good Friday liturgy in the Τριῴδιον (Athens, 1915) 550, where Christ's promise to the good thief that he will be with Him in Paradise (Luke 23:43) is

Good Friday, the Church is called a spiritual Paradise,[33] the side wound of Christ, its vivifying source, is as the waters of Eden,[34] and on Easter day, in the famous "Golden Canon" by St. John Damascene, Christ's rising from the tomb without breaking its seals is compared both to His virgin birth and to the opening of the gates of Paradise.[35] Thus a most intimate relationship between Christ's Incarnation and Resurrection and man's redemption and return to Eden is established. A triumphant sticheron[36] of the Easter Sunday liturgy, exulting in the great renewal of the world through the Resurrection, concludes with the invocation of man's return to Paradise and of his sanctification:

A sacred Pasch has been revealed to us today, a new holy Pasch, a mystical Pasch, a most august Pasch, a Pasch that is Christ the Redeemer, a Pasch without blame, a great Pasch, a Pasch of the faithful, a Pasch that opens to us the gates of Paradise, a Pasch that sanctifies all the faithful.[37]

The absence from all these texts of a Greek equivalent to the Latin *mirabilius reformasti*[38] is as notable as the relatively rare occurrence of the idea of the return to Paradise in the prayers of the early Latin sacramentaries.[39]

As to that other great complex of early Christian renewal ideas

held equivalent to his entry into the Kingdom of God. See also above, p. 65, n. 6, about St. Ephraem's views concerning Paradise and Kingdom of God; some of the Greek Fathers, and above all St. Ambrose, make a clear distinction between them.

[33] Cf. Irenaeus, quoted above, pp. 69 f.

[34] See Τριῴδιον (Athens, 1915) 551: Ἡ ζωηφόρος σου πλευρά, ὡς ἐξ Ἐδὲμ πηγὴ ἀναβλύζουσα, τὴν ἐκκλησίαν σου, Χριστὲ, ὡς λογικὸν ποτίζει παράδεισον ... See also the liturgy of the Feast of the Exaltation of the Cross, Matins, Ode 5, Μηναῖα τοῦ ὅλου ἐνιαυτοῦ, Μὴν Σεπτέμβριος (Athens, 1904) 138.

[35] Πεντηκοστάριον (Athens, 1892) 5: Easter Sunday, Ode 6: ... Φυλάξας τὰ σήμαντρα σῶα, Χριστὲ, ἐξηγέρθης τοῦ τάφου, ὁ τὰς κλεῖς τῆς παρθένου μὴ λυμηνάμενος ἐν τῷ τόκῳ σου καὶ ἀνέῳξας ἡμῖν παραδείσου τὰς πύλας. For the "Golden Canon" cf. Wellesz, *Byzantine Music* 176 ff.

[36] That is a troparion (stanza) independent from the odes which make up the canons, and corresponding to some extent to the western antiphones; cf. Wellesz 213 ff.

[37] Πεντηκοστάριον (Athens, 1892), Easter Sunday: Πάσχα ἱερὸν ἡμῖν σήμερον ἀναδέδεικται, Πάσχα καινὸν ἅγιον, Πάσχα μυστικόν, Πάσχα πανσεβάσμιον, Πάσχα Χριστὸς ὁ λυτρωτής, Πάσχα ἄμωμον, Πάσχα μέγα, Πάσχα τῶν πιστῶν, Πάσχα τὸ πυλὰς ἡμῖν τοῦ παραδείσου ἀνοῖξαν, Πάσχα πάντας ἁγιάζον πιστούς.

[38] See above, p. 284.

[39] There is a reference to the fall from Paradise and to a corresponding return to eternal beatitude in an oration for the Vigil of Pentecost in the *Sacramentarium Veronense* ("*Leon-ianum*"), formula 194, Mohlberg 25: Annue, misericors Deus, ut qui divina praecepta

which includes the reformation of the divine image in man, assimilation with God and purification of the soul, most of its variations are represented in the eastern as well as in the western liturgies.

So, for instance, in the *Liturgy of St. Basil*, which may on the whole be the work of the great Cappadocian bishop himself,[40] the anaphora speaks of man as first created in the divine image and then conformed again to the image of Christ's glory, after He had overcome sin and death by assuming human form.[41] This is somewhat reminiscent of a passage in St. Basil's longer monastic rules[42] and it corresponds to the old patristic idea, found already in St. Irenaeus, that man can more easily become like God since God had become man.[43] Similarly, a Christmas sticheron of Patriarch Sophronius of Jerusalem (early seventh century) says that Christ, having taken on our form, deified what he had assumed.[44]

In the west, the renewal formulae of the Leonine and Gelasian Sacramentaries in a few instances explicitly refer to the reformation of the divine image-likeness.[45] Of particular interest is one of the

---

violando paradisi felicitate decidimus, ad aeternae beatitudinis redeamus accessum per tuorum custodiam mandatorum. . . . Cf. also the *Gelasian Sacramentary* II, 18, *De inventione sanctae crucis*, Wilson 172: . . . lignum vitae, paradisique reparator, and the texts quoted above, p. 288, n. 21, p. 289, n. 24.

[40] Cf. Wellesz, *Byzantine Music* 108, F. Probst, *Die Liturgie des vierten Jahrhunderts und deren Reform* (Münster, 1893). St. Basil's "reform" of the liturgy seems to have consisted of an adaptation and abbreviation of earlier liturgical texts.

[41] See F. E. Brightman, *Liturgies Eastern and Western* I (Oxford, 1896) 324 ff.

[42] *Regulae fusius tractatae* II, 3, PG XXXI, 913B ff.

[43] See above, p. 84.

[44] Μηναῖα τοῦ ὅλου ἐνιαυτοῦ, Μὴν Δεκέμβριος (Athens, 1904) 285: . . . Θεὸς ἀνθρώποις ἐκ παρθένου πεφανέρωται, μορφωθεὶς τὸ καθ᾽ ἡμᾶς καὶ θεώσας τὸ πρόσλημμα. . . .

[45] The text from the *Sacramentarium Veronense*, formula 923, Mohlberg 116, quoted p. 288, n. 20, begins as follows: Vere dignum: quia tuae rationis imaginem mundanis regionibus constitutam, et humanis non desinis fovere subsidiis et reformare divinis. See also *Gelasian Sacramentary* III, 26, *Orationes pro caritate*, Wilson 247: Deus qui nos ad imaginem tuam sacramentis renovas et praeceptis, perfice gressus nostros in semitis tuis. . . . *Ibid.* I, 44, Prayer for the Benediction of the Baptismal Font on Holy Saturday, Wilson 86: Descendat in hanc plenitudinem fontis virtus Spiritus tui et totam huius aquae substantiam regenerandi fecundet effectu. Hic omnia peccatorum maculae deleantur. Hic natura ad imaginem tuam condita et ad honorem sui reformata principii cunctis vetustatis squaloribus emundetur, ut omnis homo hoc sacramentum regenerationis ingressus in vera innocentia, nova infantia renascatur. The same formula is found in the baptismal *Ordo* of the *Stowe Missal*, Warner, II, 30 f. For other formulations of the reform of the divine image see *Bobbio Missal*, Lowe 23 no. 63 (Third Advent Mass) and 24 no. 66 (Mass for the Vigil of Christmas).

Christmas orations of the *Gelasianum*, because it shows a reflection of the Greek patristic doctrine that the creational image-likeness is to be perfected by a virtuous life, here expressed as the fulfillment of the divine commandments.[46] The mystical elaborations, however, of the doctrine of assimilation to God which play such a considerable role in Greek patristic theology are not a salient trait of the liturgy either in the east or in the west. It seems that in the presence of the liturgical mysteries themselves radical divinization mysticism remained reverently silent.

Yet the same reverence which tempered the use of the *homoiosis-similitudo* ideology in the liturgical formulae, dwelt all the more insistently on the idea of *catharsis-puritas*, which in mystical theology is so closely linked to the assimilation to God. In the liturgy the idea of purity is, of course, intimately connected with penance and with the subsequent reception of the eucharistic sacrament. From the countless prayers for purification and for penitential and eucharistic renewal found in the early Greek and Latin liturgies it will suffice to select a few instances only.

One of these examples occurs as a postcommunion prayer in the *Veronense* and *Gelasianum* and modified through combination with another postcommunion has finally become part of the Canon of the Mass. The original form is:

Grant us, o Lord, we pray, through the intercession of thy saints that we may receive with a pure mind what we touch with our mouth.[47]

This prayer for a pure heart after reception of the *hostia pura* sums up the celebration of the purest sacrifice and it must be understood in conjunction with other orations in the same sacramentaries which testify to the belief in renewal by penance and by the eucharistic sacrament itself.

---

[46] *Gelasian Sacramentary* I, 5, Wilson 6: . . . Deus qui nativitatis tuae exordia pro nostra necessarium salvatione duxisti, respice nos propitius: et quos similes ad imaginem tuam fecisti, similiores observatione perfice mandatorum. See also the almost identical oration for the Second Mass of Christmas Day in *Missale Ambrosianum Duplex*, Ratti and Magistretti 44.

[47] *Sacramentarium Veronense*, formula 1207, Mohlberg 153: Presta nobis, Domine, quaesumus, intercedentibus sanctis tuis, ut quae ore contegimus, pura mente capiamus. . . . Cf. *Gelasian Sacramentary* II, 13, postcommunion, Wilson 168. See *Missale Romanum*, *Canon Missae*: Quod ore sumpsimus, Domine, pura mente capiamus: et de munere temporali fiat nobis remedium sempiternum.

Thus, for instance, a rubric at the end of the *Gelasian Sacramentary* stresses the renovating character of penitential purification by incorporating in the prayers said in the rite of the imposition of public penance Ps. 50[48] and the beginning of Ps. 102 down to the joyful verse

Thy youth shall be renewed like the eagle's [49]

and both the *Veronense* and the *Gelasianum* abound in such Mass prayers as the following collect:

May, o Lord, the performing of the celestial sacrament purify us and ever restore us through its divine effects, so that we can comprehend your greatness[50]

or this postcommunion:

Satiated, o Lord, by your salutary [gift] we beg and implore that we may be renewed by the effect of that in which we rejoice tasting it.[51]

A last example is taken from one of the earliest surviving documents of Christian liturgy, the so-called *Euchologium* of Bishop Serapion of Thmuis in Egypt, friend of St. Athanasius. The first part of a prayer for the Church in this collection of liturgical texts beautifully evokes purity which comes from God and exists in the angels and pure souls who serve God in the Church in the purest manner, through liturgical praise:

Lord God of the ages, God of the rational spirits, God of the pure souls and of all those who truly and purely call on Thee, you who in heaven appear to

---

[48] Cf. Ps. 50:12 and 14: ". . . renew a right spirit within my bowels. . . . Restore unto me the joy of thy salvation. . . ." See also above, p. 52, below, p. 312, n. 33.

[49] Ps. 102:5: Renovabitur ut aquilae iuventus tua. Cf. *Gelasian Sacramentary*, Wilson 314 f. (the rubric may be as late as the manuscript Cod. Vat. Reg. 316 of the *Gelasian Sacramentary*, i.e. saec. VIII in.). For the renewal ideology centered in verse 5 of Ps. 102, cf. pp. 45, 52, 312, 314. For penitential renewal in the liturgy cf. also p. 289, n. 22.

[50] *Sacramentarium Veronense*, formula 1041, Mohlberg 132 (cf. *Gelasian Sacramentary* I, 98, Wilson 150): Purificet nos, Domine, caelestis exsecutio sacramenti et ad tuam magnificentiam capiendam divinis effectibus semper instauret.

[51] *Sacramentarium Veronense*, formula 891, Mohlberg 112 (cf. *Gelasian Sacramentary* I, 17 and II, 60, Wilson 16 and 201): Salutari tuo, Domine, satia[s]ti supplices depraecamur, ut cuius laetamur gustu renovemur effectu.

the pure spirits and are known by them and who on earth are praised by the Catholic Church and dwell in it, who are served by the holy angels and the pure souls, you who even of the heavens have made a living choir to the glory and praise of the truth: grant that this Church be a living and pure Church, grant that it have divine powers and pure angels as servers, so that it may praise Thee in a pure manner. . . .[52]

The challenge of purity has at all times been a stimulus to reform, because only pure souls can rightly and truly approach God. "For one who is not pure, to touch what is pure—it is to be feared that this is not permissible," thus Plato said in the *Phaedo*;[53] and Apuleius' Lucius is but one of many adepts of ancient mystery cults, admitted to the *epoptia* of the god only after purification of body and mind.[54] The same holds true *a fortiori* for the relation between purity and liturgy in the Christian world,[55] where the liturgy culminates in a unique union between man and God. As compared to other ancient mystery religions, however, the Christian conception of purity and purification is the least ritualistic and of this fact the Christian concept of penance is an example. For a Christian who has lost baptismal purity there still remains "the second baptism," "the baptism of

[52] Serapion of Thmuis, *Euchologium* 10 (24), 1 f., Funk, *Didascal. et Constit. Apostol.* II, 168: Κύριε Θεὲ τῶν αἰώνων, Θεὲ τῶν λογικῶν πνευμάτων (cf. Ecclesiasticus 36 : 17 [Septuagint], Num. 16: 22), Θεὲ ψυχῶν καθαρῶν καὶ πάντων τῶν γνησίως σε καὶ καθαρῶς ἐπικαλουμένων, ὁ ἐν οὐρανῷ φαινόμενος καὶ γινωσκόμενος τοῖς καθαροῖς πνεύμασιν, ὁ ἐπὶ γῆς ὑμνούμενος καὶ κατοικῶν ἐν τῇ καθολικῇ ἐκκλησίᾳ, ὑπὸ ἀγγέλων ἁγίων λειτουργούμενος καὶ καθαρῶν ψυχῶν, ὁ ποιήσας καὶ ἐξ οὐρανῶν χορὸν ζῶντα εἰς δόξαν καὶ αἶνον τῆς ἀληθείας· δὸς τὴν ἐκκλησίαν ταύτην ζῶσαν καὶ καθαρὰν ἐκκλησίαν εἶναι, δὸς αὐτὴν ἔχειν θείας δυνάμεις καὶ καθαροὺς ἀγγέλους λειτουργούς, ἵνα δυνηθῇ καθαρῶς ὑμνεῖν σε. . . . With regard to purity as a condition of the eucharistic sacrifice, see *Didache* 14, 1 f., Bihlmeyer, *Apostol. Väter* 8, a text to which Dom Anselm Strittmatter, O.S.B., kindly drew my attention. The idea of the angels' invisible participation also in the terrestrial liturgy of the Church was greatly developed later, and not only in the Ps.-Dionysian parallelism of the celestial and ecclesiastical hierarchies; see, for instance, the *Cherubic Hymn*, probably from the sixth century, quoted below, p. 349, n. 32; in general, cf. E. Peterson, *Von den Engeln*, reprinted in *Theologische Traktate* (München, 1951) 343 ff.

[53] *Phaedo* 67B: μὴ καθαρῷ γὰρ καθαροῦ ἐφάπτεσθαι μὴ οὐ θεμιτὸν ᾖ. Cf. A.-J. Festugière, *Contemplation et vie contemplative selon Platon*, 2nd ed. (Paris, 1950), especially the chapter on *catharsis*, 123 ff.

[54] Apuleius, *Metamorphoses* XI, 23.

[55] See, for instance Cassian, *Institutiones* II, 13, *CSEL* XVII, 1, 28: . . . purificationem nostram nocturnis psalmis et orationibus adquisitam. . . .

tears." Penance, just as baptism, belongs to the foundations of the Christian reform idea. Being sacraments, both baptism and penance are of the realm of canon law as well as of those of theology and liturgy. As will be seen presently, the role of the reform idea in early Christian canon law and sacramental theology is even larger than has so far been suggested.

CHAPTER VII

THE IDEA OF REFORM IN EARLY CHRISTIAN CANON LAW AND SACRAMENTAL THEOLOGY

1. RENEWAL OF THE CANONS

The most general application of renewal ideology to the realm of canon law is in the renovation of old conciliar canons by subsequent councils.

It is unnecessary to adduce many examples for the well-known fact that from the beginnings of its history the Church strove to preserve its unadulterated tradition, in other terms, to prevent innovations contrary to that tradition. It is sufficient to refer back to Pope Stephen I's famous dictum:

Nihil innovetur nisi quod traditum est,

which was mentioned earlier, when the renewal doctrines of the pre-Augustinian Latin Fathers were discussed.[1] The early councils were satisfied with occasional references to the corroboration of ancient doctrine and discipline,[2] but gradually opportunities for deviations and need for corrections and amplifications increased and a terminology and ideology of renewal made its appearance in conciliar acts.

Already the Council of Elvira (saec. IV in.) speaks of the emendation *iuxta auctoritatem scripturarum* of an evil institution.[3] Later on, many councils thought it advisable, before dealing with the various necessities of the Church, to set down in corroboration the faith of the three hundred and eighteen Fathers of Nicaea. Thus at the Second General Council, of Constantinople (381), the Fathers according to

---

[1] See above, p. 139, also below, pp. 304 ff.

[2] Cyprian and the African bishops, when they emphasized the superiority of truth over custom in rejecting a particular tradition concerning the baptism of heretics, did of course not intend to invalidate the principle of doctrinary and disciplinary tradition in general; cf. above, pp. 138 f.

[3] Council of Elvira, can. 43, Bruns, *Can. Apostol. et Concil.* II, 7.

their address to Theodosius the Great first renewed (ἀνανεωσάμεθα, *renovavimus*) their mutual concord, then pronounced the validity of the faith of Nicaea, and finally defined canons for the good order of the churches.[4] The First Council of Toledo (398) threatened those who infringed upon the Nicene canons with excommunication, unless they mended their error.[5] The renewal function of a council could also be expressed in terms related to current Renaissance ideology: thus the synodal epistle of the semi-Arian Council of Ancyra of 357 could speak of the reflourishing (αὖθις ἀνθήσασα) faith of the (non-orthodox) bishops who had first attended and then deserted the Council of Sardica of 343–344.[6]

About the middle of the fifth century the ancient imperial acclamations found entrance into the quasi-ritualistic procedure of the councils as well as into the liturgy.[7] In both cases the main emphasis of the acclamations naturally shifted from the political to the ecclesiastical sphere. Besides vows and praises to God, Christ, the saints, the emperors, the senate, and the hierarchy, the conciliar acclamations could include various expressions of approval or disapproval of the conciliar decisions and aspirations of reform. Combinations of some of these elements are encountered, for instance, among the acclamations of the Council of Chalcedon (451). After the deposition of Dioscurus

the most pious oriental . . . bishops said: This is a just judgment. The most pious Illyrian . . . bishops said: We all erred, we all deserve the same sentence. . . . The most pious oriental . . . bishops said: Many years to the

---

[4] Second Ecumenical Council of Constantinople (381), Mansi, *Concil.* III, 557B f.

[5] First Council of Toledo, Bruns, *Canon. Apostol. et Concil.* I, 203: . . . constituta . . . concilii Nicaeni perpetuo esse servanda . . . si quis cognitis gestis concilii Nicaeni aliud quam statutum est facere praesumpserit . . . excommunicatus habeatur, nisi per correptionem fratrum emendaverit errorem.

[6] Council of Ancyra of 357, Mansi, *Concil.* III, 269B: . . . καὶ μετὰ ταῦτα κατὰ Σαρδικὴν καὶ τὴν ἐκεῖ αὖθις ἀνθήσασαν πίστιν. . . . However, as noted above (p. 26), the use of vitalistic renewal terms in a "reform" context is not a rare phenomenon; see, for instance, below, p. 302, n. 17 and n. 18, for *redivivus*.

[7] For the acclamations of the Christian emperors, and especially their acclamations by the councils, see, for instance, P. Battifol, *Etudes de liturgie et d'archéologie chrétienne* (Paris, 1919) 84 ff.: essay III: "Origine du règlement des conciles," E. Peterson, *ΕΙΣ ΘΕΟΣ* (Forschungen zur Religion und Literatur des Alten und Neuen Testaments XLI [Neue Folge XXI], Göttingen, 1926), especially 146 ff., E. H. Kantorowicz, *Laudes Regiae* (Berkeley, Los Angeles, 1946), especially 68 ff.

senate. Holy God, holy strong one, holy immortal one, have mercy on us. Many years to the emperors. The impious one always takes flight. . . . This is a just synod. . . .[8]

The famous Chalcedonian acclamations for Pope Leo the Great which were voiced at a later session of the council are kept in the same style:

This is the faith of the Fathers. This is the faith of the Apostles. We all believe thus. The orthodox believe thus. Anathema to him who does not thus believe. Petrus has expressed these things through Leo. . . .[9]
To the Archbishop Leo many years. Leo has passed judgment with God.[10]

These acclamations of the Council of Chalcedon have been quoted, even though they do not contain any explicit terms of reform, because the Greek synodal formulary very likely was not without influence upon the Roman conciliar *Laudes* of similar though not identical structure which do contain such terms. Their earliest occurrence in Rome seems to be at the Council of 465, held under Pope Hilarus, when, for instance, the assembled bishops and priests acclaimed letters received from the bishops of the province of Tarragona in Northern Spain in the following manner:

That these things be emended, we pray: said six times. That these things be cut down, we pray: said seven times. That the discipline be preserved, we pray: said eight times. That what is ancient be preserved, we pray: said five times. That the canons be observed, we pray: said seven times. . . . Hear us, Christ, to Hilarus life: said five times. Worthy Pope, worthy teacher: said eight times. . . . All the bishops said: We follow all the sentences of our brethren (that is to say, of the bishops of the province of Tarragona); all of them we confirm and decree to be observed. Hear us, Christ, to Hilarus life:

---

[8] Fourth Ecumenical Council, Chalcedon, 451, *Actio Prima*, Schwartz, *Acta Concil. Oecum.* II, I, 1, 195, no. 1069 ff.: Οἱ Ἀνατολικοὶ καὶ οἱ σὺν αὐτοῖς εὐλαβέστατοι ἐπίσκοποι ἐβόησαν· Αὕτη δικαία κρίσις. Οἱ Ἰλλυρικοὶ καὶ οἱ σὺν αὐτοῖς εὐλαβέστατοι ἐπίσκοποι εἶπον· Πάντες ἐσφάλημεν, πάντες συγγνώμης ἀξιωθῶμεν. Οἱ Ἀνατολικοὶ καὶ οἱ σὺν αὐτοῖς εὐλαβέστατοι ἐπίσκοποι εἶπον· Πολλὰ τὰ ἔτη τῆς συγκλήτου. Ἅγιος ὁ Θεός, ἅγιος ἰσχυρός, ἅγιος ἀθάνατος, ἐλέησον ἡμᾶς. Πολλὰ τὰ ἔτη τῶν βασιλέων. Ὁ ἀσεβὴς ἀεὶ φεύγει. . . . Αὕτη δικαία σύνοδος. . . .

[9] *Ibid.*, *Actio Tertia*, Schwartz, *loc. cit.*, II, I, 2, 81 [277], no. 23: Αὕτη ἡ πίστις τῶν πατέρων. Αὕτη ἡ πίστις τῶν ἀποστόλων. Πάντες οὕτω πιστεύομεν. Οἱ ὀρθόδοξοι οὕτω πιστεύομεν. Ἀνάθεμα τῷ μὴ οὕτω πιστεύοντι. Πέτρος διὰ Λέοντος ταῦτα ἐξεφώνησεν. . . .

[10] *Ibid.*, *Actio Nona*, Schwartz, *loc. cit.*, II, I, 3, 10 [369], no. 15: Τοῦ ἀρχιεπισκόπου Λέοντος πολλὰ τὰ ἔτη. Μετὰ τοῦ Θεοῦ Λέων ἐδίκασεν. . . .

said six times. Things wrongly admitted should be corrected by you: said eight times. What is not licit, must not be done: said eight times.[11]

The same type of conciliar acclamation appears in the same period under the Popes Gelasius I[12] and Symmachus; especially the latter's restitution to the papal see after the Laurentian schism was acclaimed in terms of lawful reform and amendment for scandal.[13]

A new conciliar reform motive comes to the fore in the latter part of the fifth and above all in the sixth century, in the acts of western synods held outside of Rome. It might, perhaps, be called the "interruption" motive and its emergence no doubt reflects the beginnings of the partial disorganization of ecclesiastical life which was a consequence of the Barbarian Invasions. By the middle of the eighth century this process had reached a stage where St. Boniface could rightly complain that the canons had not been renewed for eighty years.[14]

[11] Roman Council of 465, Mansi, Concil. VII, 963: Ut haec emendentur rogamus! dictum est sexies. Ut haec recidantur rogamus! dictum est septies. Ut disciplina servetur rogamus! dictum est octies. Ut antiquitas servetur rogamus! dictum est quinquies. Ut canones custodiantur rogamus! dictum est septies. . . . Exaudi, Christe! Hilaro vita! dictum est quinquies. Dignus papa, dignus doctor! dictum est octies. . . . Ab universis episcopis dictum est: Sententias fratrum omnes sequimur, omnes confirmamus et observandas esse decernimus. Exaudi, Christe! Hilaro vita! dictum est sexies. Quae male admissa sunt, per te corrigantur! dictum est octies. Quod non licet, non fiat! dictum est octies. . . . Cf. C. J. Hefele, Histoire des conciles, trans. by Dom H. Leclercq, II, 2 (Paris, 1908) 903 f.

[12] Roman Council of 495, Collectio Avellana 103, CSEL XXXV, 1, 487: . . . exaudi, Christe: Gelasio vita! dictum quindecies. Domine Petre, tu illum serva! dictum duodecies. Cuius sedem et annos! dictum septies. Vicarium Christi te videmus! dictum undecies. Apostolum Petrum te videmus! dictum sexies. Cuius sedem et annos! dictum septies trigesies. Cf. Hefele-Leclercq, Conciles II, 2, 944 .. Kantorowicz, Laudes 68, n. 14, M. Maccarrone, Vicarius Christi (Lateranum, Nova Series, XVIII, 1–4, Roma, 1952) 54.

[13] Roman Council of 499, Bruns, Can. Apostol. et Concil. II, 288: Ut fiat rogamus! dictum est decies. Ut scandala amputentur rogamus! dictum est novies. Cf. Hefele-Leclercq, Conciles II, 2, 947 ff., Kantorowicz, Laudes 68, n. 14.

[14] Boniface, Epist. 50, MGH, Epist. Selectae I, 82: . . . [Carlomannus] promisit se de ecclesiastica religione, que iam longo tempore, id est non minus quam per LX vel LXX annos calcata et dissipata fuit, aliquid corrigere et emendare vellet. . . . Franci enim, ut seniores dicunt, plus quam per tempus octuginta annorum synodum non fecerunt nec archiepiscopum habuerunt nec aecclesiae canonica alicubi fundabant vel renovabant. Cf. Concilium Germanicum of 743, MGH, Leg. III, Concil. II, 1, 2 ff.: Ego Karlmannus, dux et princeps Francorum . . . episcopos . . . congregavi . . ., ut mihi consilium dedissent, quomodo lex Dei et aecclesiastica relegio recuperetur, que in diebus preteritorum principum dissipata corruit. . . . Statuimus per annos singulos synodum congregare, ut nobis

But, already in 461 the First Council of Tours has this introduction to its canons:

. . . because through long carelessness the rule concerning matters of ecclesiastical discipline had been somewhat corrupted, they (i.e., the council) wished to confirm their definition, which is in accordance with the authority of the Fathers, by issuing this present document: not dwelling on those things which were illicitly allowed in former times, but taking care of the welfare of all for the future: so that with the observance of the statutes of the Fathers, according to the evangelical precepts and the apostolic doctrine, the Church of the Lord may remain pure and immaculate.[15]

In a similar vein, the Council of Vannes of c. 465 speaks of sanctions against omissions and presumptions with regard to the *priora patrum statuta*.[16]

In the sixth century, such conciliar statements were to multiply. In 517, at the Council of Epaone, Avitus of Vienne demands greater frequency of synods, which in his words would mean "a wholesome revival of an interrupted custom."[17] The Second Council of Toledo of 531, for instance, states:

If, however, the decrees of former councils have so far been neglected through the abuse of the times, they must now receive the censure of a revival of order[18]

presentibus canonum decreta et aecclesiae iura restaurentur et relegio christiana emendetur. . . . (For the date 743, not 742, see Th. Schieffer, "Angelsachsen und Franken," *Abhandlungen der Akademie der Wissenschaften und Literatur in Mainz* 1950, 20 [1951] 22 ff.)

[15] First Council of Tours, Bruns, *Can. Apostol. et Concil.* II, 139: . . . ut quia per longam incuriam in aliquo de rebus ecclesiasticae disciplinae regula fuisset vitiata, definitionem suam, quae cum patrum auctoritate concordat, praesentis scripturae emissione firmarent: non quae prius illicite admissa sunt revolventes, sed in posterum universorum utilitate prospicientes; ut secundum evangelica praecepta et apostolicam doctrinam patrum statuta servantes ecclesia Domini pura et immaculata permaneat.

[16] *Concilium Veneticum* of c. 465, Bruns, *Can. Apostol. et Concil.* II, 142. Cf. Hefele-Leclercq, *Conciles* II, 2, 904 f.

[17] Council of Epaone of 517, *MGH Leg.* III, *Concil.* I, 17, Letter of Avitus of Vienne: . . . supplicat per me . . . ecclesia Viennensis, poscit intermissae consuetudinis rediviva salubritas, quod hactenus infrequentatum torpuit, excitari. . . .

[18] Second Council of Toledo, Bruns, *Can. Apostol. et Concil.* I, 207: . . . ut si qua in antiquis canonibus minime commemorata sunt, salubri tractatu ac diligenti consideratione instituantur; si qua vero in anterioribus conciliis sunt decreta, sed abusione temporum hactenus sunt neglecta, redivivae ordinationis censuram obtineant. . . .

and the Third Council of Orléans of 538:

> . . . concerning those things which for a long time have not been observed and were interrupted we preserve the tenor of the earlier canons and we have renewed the old statutes in these present norms and have found it necessary to add new ones according to the condition of times and cases.[19]

There are many more texts of the same kind to be found in the acts of sixth and seventh century western councils. The realization of the necessity of almost perpetual conciliar reform proved to be of great importance to the history of Church reform in the west and was to come to the foreground again in all great reform periods, for instance, in the so-called Carolingian Renaissance and in the Hildebrandian Reform.

2. THE PROBLEMS OF REBAPTISM, REORDINATION, AND PENANCE

These problems, though of less general a nature than the concern for the renovation of conciliar canons, reach down to even deeper layers of Christian reform ideology. They first made themselves felt in the third century, largely in consequence of three more or less simultaneous developments in Christendom: the heresies, the weakness of not a few Christians in the great persecutions, and the increase of serious sins among Christians which accompanied the numerical growth of the Christian community itself. Humanly speaking, the survival of the Church amongst these dangers and difficulties was due not only to the almost unbelievable heroism of the martyrs and confessors, but also to the wisdom of those leaders of the Church who succeeded in steering a middle course between the extremes of laxness and rigorism. How difficult a course this was, may be briefly illustrated by St. Cyprian's somewhat contradictory attitudes with regard to penance on the one hand and to the sacraments administered by heretical, schismatic, or unworthy priests on the other.

In spite of his aversion to making readmission to the Church too

---

[19] Third Council of Orleans, *MGH, Leg.* III, *Concil.* I, 73: . . . de his, quae per longum tempus observatione cessante fuerant intermissa, priorum canonum tenore servato praesentibus regulis vetera statuta renovavimus et nova pro causarum vel temporum condicione addenda credidimus.

easy for the *lapsi* of the Decian persecution of 250–251,[1] Cyprian held against Novatianus and his followers—who, as the Montanists, rejected the possibility of forgiveness of the capital sins by the Church—that within the Church any sin, even the gravest, could be remitted by the Church after sincere and severe penance.[2] Penance for Cyprian is in a sense a second baptism, though here remission of sins is no longer free, but must be earned; in this respect he is in conformity with the general doctrine of the Church.[3] Yet with regard to his teaching on baptism and ordination, matters are much more complex. Here he maintained staunchly—and in spite of the conflict with Pope Stephen I, which thus arose[4]—that the defect inherent in the sacrament of baptism conferred by a heretic or schismatic could not be cured merely through penance and through absolution by episcopal imposition of hands and invocation of the Holy Spirit.[5] To Cyprian baptism by a heretic or schismatic, and likewise ordination in a sect, were not true sacraments, because not given within the Church, "out-

---

[1] See Cyprian, De lapsis, CSEL III, 237 ff., Epist. XIX, CSEL III, 525 f.; cf. A. d'Alès, La théologie de saint Cyprien (Paris, 1922) 282 ff., B. Poschmann, Paenitentia Secunda: Die kirchliche Busse im ältesten Christentum bis Cyprian und Origenes (Theophaneia I, Bonn, 1940) 368 ff., J. Quasten, Patrology II (Westminster, Md., 1953) 348 f., 380 f.

[2] For the Montanists see Tertullian, De pudicitia, Corp. Christ., Ser. Lat. II, 1279 ff.; cf. Quasten, Patrology II, 332 ff., but see now also E. Langstadt, "Tertullian's Doctrine of Sin and the Power of Absolution in 'de pudicitia,'" Stud. Patr. II, 251 ff. For Novatianus see, for instance, Cyprian, Epist. LV, 24 ff., CSEL III, 642 ff.; cf. Quasten, Patrology II, 212 ff. For Cyprian himself see, for instance, De opere et eleemosynis, CSEL III, 374 ff.; cf. Quasten, Patrology II, 380 f. See also Testimon. III, 35, CSEL III, 147: Deum ad hoc patientem esse, ut nos paeniteat peccati nostri et reformemur. For Cyprian's doctrine of penance see, especially, K. Rahner, S.J., "Die Busslehre des hl. Cyprian von Karthago," Z. kath. Theol. LXXIV (1952) 257 ff., 381 ff.

[3] See the parallelism of the gratia, quae de baptismi sanctificatione percipitur, and the paenitentia, per quam curatur, in Cyprian's Epist. LIX, 13, CSEL III, 681 f. In general cf. Poschmann, Paenitentia Secunda, E. F. Latko, Origen's Concept of Penance (Diss., Faculté de Théologie, Université Laval, Quebec, 1949), P. Galtier, S.J., Aux origines du sacrement de pénitence (Analecta Gregoriana LIV, Ser. Fac. Theol., Sectio A [n. 6], Roma, 1951).

[4] Cf. above, p. 139.

[5] Cyprian, Epist. LXXII, to Stephen I, 1, CSEL III, 2, 775: . . . eos qui sunt foris extra ecclesiam tincti et apud haereticos et schismaticos profanae aquae labe maculati, quando ad nos . . . venerint, baptizari oportere eo, quod parum sit eis manum inponere ad accipiendum Spiritum Sanctum, nisi accipiant et ecclesiae baptismum . . .; cf. also Epist. LXIX, 11, CSEL III, 760. For the meaning of the ritual of imposition of hands and invocation of the Holy Spirit as both a perfecting of baptism and as penitential, according to the view of Stephen I, see A. Schebler, Die Reordinationen in der "altkatholischen" Kirche unter besonderer Berücksichtigung der Anschauungen Rudolph Sohms (Bonn, 1936) 34 f.

side of which there is no salvation." [6] Baptism, therefore, must be repeated or, in Cyprianic terms, be *truly* conferred for the first time. [7]
As to ordination, the fact of heresy or schism not only annuls it, but
taints the recipient to such a degree [8] that Cyprian does not even consider reordination, let alone reconciliation by the imposition of hands. [9]
St. Cyprian's views on rebaptism and the nonvalidity of heretical
ordination were not generally accepted in the ancient Church—
Rome, especially, held to the opposite tradition [10]—but they were
widely held. Tertullian had maintained the nonvalidity of the baptism
of heretics even before his Montanist period; Bishop Agrippinus of
Carthage, [11] and in Cyprian's own time the whole African episcopate, [12]
as well as some bishops of Asia Minor, especially Firmilianus of
Caesarea, [13] practiced or advocated their rebaptism. It was on the
occasion of the controversy about baptism and rebaptism of heretics
that Cyprian and the Council of Carthage of September 1, 256, took
up and developed so forcefully the Tertullianean antithesis of custom
and truth of which mention has been made. [14]

The attitude of these second and third century African and Asian
Fathers toward baptism and ordination expresses a very radical view
of reform in the Christian world, a view which explains the more
rigoristic of the two contrasting traditions concerning these sacraments in the ancient Church. These two traditions appear even side
by side in the First Oecumenical Council of Nicaea (325), which

---

[6] Cyprian, *Epist.* LXXIII, 21, *CSEL* III, 2, 795: . . . salus extra ecclesiam non est. . . .

[7] Cyprian, *Epist.* LXXI, 1, *CSEL* III, 771: Nos autem dicimus eos, qui inde (i.e., from
heresy) veniunt, non rebaptizari apud nos, sed baptizari. Neque enim accipiunt illic aliquid
ubi nihil est, sed veniunt ad nos, ut hic accipiant ubi et gratia et veritas omnis est.

[8] *Epist.* LV, 24, *CSEL* III, 643: Qui ergo nec unitatem Spiritus nec coniunctionem pacis
observat et se ab ecclesiae vinculo atque a sacerdotum collegio separat, episcopi nec
potestatem potest habere nec honorem, qui episcopatus nec unitatem voluit tenere nec
pacem; *Epist.* LXXII, 2, III, 776.

[9] See L. Saltet, *Les réordinations* (Paris, 1907) 10 and 28 ff., Schebler, *Reordinationen* 14.

[10] See the literature mentioned, in n. 9 and p. 306, n. 16.

[11] See Tertullian, *De baptismo* 15, 1 ff., *Corp. Christ.*, *Ser. Lat.* I, 290; for Agrippinus, see
Cyprian, *Epist.* LXXI and LXXIII, *CSEL* III, 774 and 780; cf. Saltet, *Réordinations* 12.

[12] See *Sententiae LXXXVII episcoporum*, ed. H. v. Soden, *Nachr. Gött.*, Philol.-Histor.
Klasse, 1909, 247 ff.

[13] See Firmilianus' letter to Cyprian, which is no. LXXV in the corpus of the latter's
Epistles, *CSEL* III, 810 ff.

[14] See above, p. 138.

prescribed the rebaptism and reordination of the followers of Paul of Samosata because of their antitrinitarian doctrine, but not the rebaptism of the Novatians.[15] It is unnecessary to enter here upon the entire history of the two traditions. While rebaptism was abandoned by the Church earlier than reordination, the underlying rigoristic principle, though clearly refuted by St. Augustine, was not completely eliminated even from Catholic theory and practice until the age of scholasticism.[16] Wherever and whenever this principle continued to be applied in its fulness to the sacraments of heretics or schismatics, it implied that wrong doctrine and discipline deprives priest and bishop of the capacity to confer baptism or holy orders validly, because they are not true ministers of Christ, not true instruments of the Holy Spirit. If they presume and pretend to act as such, the heretically or schismatically baptized or ordained must be made a Christian, a cleric all over again—not only for the sake of the recipients of these sacraments, but also for that of the whole Church, which would otherwise be corrupted.

For clarity's sake the foregoing remarks have been restricted to the baptism and ordination of heretics and schismatics, but it must be noted also that in Cyprian's view the personal integrity of a priest was an essential prerequisite for the exercise of his office.[17] Half a

---

[15] First Oecumenical Council of Nicaea (325), canons 8 and 19, Mansi, *Concil.* II, 671 f., 675 f.; cf. Hefele-Leclercq, *Conciles* I, 1, 576 ff. On different views concerning the council's decisions on Novatianist ordinations, see Saltet, *Réordinations* 35 ff., and Schebler, *Reordinationen* 44 ff.

[16] See Saltet, *Réordinations*. See also R. Sohm, "Das altkatholische Kirchenrecht und das Dekret Gratians," *Festschrift der Leipziger Juristenfakultät für Dr. Adolf Wach* . . . (München, Leipzig, 1918) 1–674, with rich material, very valuable in spite of Sohm's well-known untenable theory on the nature of early Canon Law.

[17] Cf. Cyprian, *Epist.* LXVII, 2, *CSEL* III, 736: . . . in ordinationibus sacerdotum non nisi immaculatos et integros antistites eligere debemus . . . ; *Epist.* LXXII, 2, III, 777: . . . oportet enim sacerdotes et ministros, qui altari et sacrificiis deserviunt, integros atque immaculatos esse. . . . The question of the validity of sacraments administered by unworthy or heretical and schismatic priests is, of course, different from the other one whether they personally may continue their sacerdotal or episcopal functions or are to be deposed and restricted to lay communion; the latter practice was as a rule adhered to by the ancient Church in the case of unworthy clerics and of those clerics who were personally responsible for their heretical or schismatic status. Yet a milder practice was sometimes followed, for instance, in the case of the Donatists; see Augustine, *Epist.* CLXXXV, 10, 44, *CSEL* LVII, 38 f.; cf. E. Vacandard, article "Déposition et dégradation des clercs," *DThC* IV, 1, 451 ff.

century after Cyprian's death as a martyr this more general rigorism was to become the core of Donatism, which made systematic and fanatical intolerance of really or allegedly unworthy clerics the foundation of its claim to be the only true Church.[18] The Donatists most emphatically denied the validity of all sacraments received from priests or bishops who were not in the state of grace, who were contaminated in any way by grave sins. This, according to them, was the condition to which, with the exception of themselves, the entire Church had fallen, because it had condoned temporary apostasy and suffered even among its clergy traitors to Christ (such as the *traditores* of the holy scriptures during the persecution of Diocletian and other compromisers). In the course of the long history of Donatism there were phases in which Catholics who went over to the Donatists were rebaptized, and in the case of clerics, reordained by them, whereas in other phases the imposition of hands in *poenitentiam* was considered sufficient to discredit the validity of the Catholic sacraments and to reconcile the converts.[19] In his struggle with the Donatists, Augustine refuted both the Cyprianic and the Donatist conceptions of sacramental validity as allegedly dependent on orthodoxy or on personal worthiness. He showed that repetition of baptism and ordination, far from protecting the sacredness of these sacraments, was on the contrary sacrilegious, because based on the belief that man rather than God was their grantor.[20] While claiming to safeguard the orthodox

---

[18] For Donatism, see above all P. Monceaux, *Histoire littéraire de l'Afrique chrétienne depuis les origines jusqu'à l'invasion arabe* IV–VII (1912–1923), and the recent book of W. H. C. Frend, *The Donatist Church* (Oxford, 1952); this latter work is particularly important for the continuity between Tertullianean and Cyprianic ideas and Donatism. For useful comparisons of Montanism and Donatism with later heresies, such as that of the Anabaptists, Quietists, Jansenists, see R. A. Knox, *Enthusiasm* (Oxford, 1950).

[19] For Donatist rebaptism, see Saltet, *Réordinations* 59 ff., Frend, *Donatist Church* 167 f., 189, 195 f., etc.; for Donatist reordination, Saltet, *Réordinations* 59 ff., where it is also shown how the imposition of hands upon a cleric could be interpreted by the Donatists as stamping him a penitent and as thus incapacitating him for the clerical status. The imposition of hands *sub imagine poenitentiae* according to Pope Innocent I (*Epist.* XXIV, *PL* XX, 549 ff.) was, of course, used also by the Catholics in the reconciliation of heretics. Recently J. Macdonald, "Imposition of Hands in the Letters of Innocent I," *Stud. Patr.* II, 49 ff., has defended the controversial view that this amounted to reconfirmation.

[20] For Augustine and Donatism, see, beside Monceaux, *Histoire littéraire*, F. van der Meer, *Augustinus der Seelsorger* (German translation of *Augustinus de Zielzorger*, 2nd ed., Köln, 1953) 98 ff., and F. Hofmann, *Der Kirchenbegriff des hl. Augustinus* (München, 1933) 124 ff., and, especially, K. Adam, *Die kirchliche Südenvergebung nach dem hl. Augustinus* (Forschungen zur

faith and to guarantee a pure Church and an irreproachable clergy, the rigoristic principle which stands behind the repetition of baptism and ordinations was a dangerous one, not least because the continuation of sacramental life in the Church was thus made dependent upon arbitrary decisions on truth or falseness, worth or unworth of Christians, priests, bishops.[21]

In spite of Augustine's theoretical solution of these problems, attempts at solving doctrinal and moral crises in the history of the Church through rebaptism and reordination did not come to an end with the patristic age but were to recur in later moments of crisis. Without going beyond the earlier Middle Ages, one might refer to the famous trial against the corpse of Pope Formosus (died 896), which was based on the belief that the posthumous declaration of the invalidity of his elevation to the papacy could invalidate also the ordinations performed by him;[22] or to the defence of the reordination of simonist clerics by Cardinal Humbert of Silva Candida, Hildebrand's great though impetuous contemporary, and by other spiritual descendents of St. Cyprian in the age of Gregory VII.[23]

christlichen Literatur- und Dogmengeschichte XIV, 1, Paderborn, 1917) 75–118. Of particular importance is Augustine's first anti-Donatist work of c. 400, De baptismo, CSEL LI, because of the detailed discussion of the Cyprianic baptismal controversy which was constantly used for their cause by the Donatists (cf. also above, p. 307, n. 18). See, for instance, De baptismo V, 12, 14, CSEL LI, 275: Per quemlibet enim ministrum detur, illius est baptismus de quo dictum est: "Hic est qui baptizat" (John 1:33); ibid. VI, 4, 6, LI, 301 f.: Nam cum malus tradit bono, id est in unitatis vinculo veraci conversione mutato, inter bonum sacramentum, quod traditur, et bonum fidelem, cui traditur, tradentis malitia superatur. See furthermore Augustine's Contra litteras Petiliani I, 6, 7, CSEL LII, 7: . . . sive a fideli, sive a perfido dispensatore sacramentum baptismi quisque percipiat, spes ei omnis in Christo sit, ne sit "maledictus qui spem suam ponit in homine" (cf. Jer. 17:5), quoted by Adam, Sündenvergebung 100. Cf. also Frend, Donatist Church 227 ff.: ch. XV: "St. Augustine and the Donatists"; Frend, however, does not seem to consider sufficiently that, in spite of all his respect for Cyprian, Augustine criticizes and re-interprets his doctrine of the sacraments and distinguishes in it what is close to the Donatists from the Catholic point of view; see, for instance, Epist. XCIII, 10, 38, CSEL XXXIV, 2, 482 f., Contra Cresconium II, 31, 39, PL XLIII, 489 f. Cf. also J.-B. Bord, "L'autorité de saint Cyprien dans la controverse baptismale, jugée d'après saint Augustin," Rev. hist. ecclés. XVIII (1922) 445 ff.

[21] Augustine, Contra litteras Petiliani II, 5, 11, CSEL LII, 25: . . . quis enim homo de homine securus est . . . ? (quoted by Adam, Sündenvergebung 99).

[22] On this episode, see, for instance, Histoire de l'église, edd. A. Fliche and V. Martin, VII: E. Amann and A. Dumas, L'église au pouvoir des laïques (888–1057) (Paris, 1948) 15 ff.

[23] See Schebler, Reordinationen 229 ff.

Whereas such extreme solutions were to prove so many dead end roads in the history of the Christian reform idea, a certain radicalism belongs to the signature of early Christian sacramental law and theology and this appears very clearly in the history of the sacrament of penance.

The principal form of early Christian penance for capital sins, such as idolatry, apostasy, murder, adultery, was public, severe, and was considered as nonrepeatable.[24] Even with this severity, admission to penance was considered a great concession; the feeling was that a Christian's commission of such serious sins was almost unthinkable. No doubt, such sins were rare in the first two centuries; but the emergence of rigoristic sects, from Montanism to Donatism, would alone be sufficient to prove a deterioration of ethical standards at least from the third century onward and more definitely after the external victory of the Church over paganism. In the Theodosian age the great Church Fathers expressed their misgivings over the moral state of the Church in no uncertain words.

It was in the same period—late fourth and early fifth century—that a new concept and practice of penance began to prevail. Public penance was not given up officially; but, because of the length and severity of the penitential practices imposed and above all because of the nonrepeatable character of the sacrament and its humiliating aspect and disabling consequences, there was a strong tendency to postpone it until proximity of death seemed to urge it and at the same time to preclude occasions for further sin. These considerations were similar to those which often caused the delay of baptism. It is not necessary to enter into the controversial question as to how early so-called private penance was introduced in the Church.[25] It is probable at any rate

[24] Cf. B. Poschmann, *Die abendländische Kirchenbusse im Ausgang des christlichen Altertums,* (München, 1928), idem, *Die abendländische Kirchenbusse im frühen Mittelalter* (Breslau, 1930), idem, *Paenitentia Secunda,* Adam, *Sündenvergebung,* idem, *Die geheime Kirchenbusse nach dem heiligen Augustin* (Münchener Studien zur historischen Theologie II, München, 1921), R. C. Mortimer, *The Origins of Private Penance in the Western Church* (Oxford, 1939), P. Galtier, S.J., *L'église et la rémission des péchés aux premiers siècles* (Paris, 1932), idem, "A propos de la pénitence primitive: Méthodes et conclusions," *Rev. hist. ecclés.* XXX (1934) 517 ff., 797 ff., idem, "Pénitents et 'convertis': De la pénitence latine à la pénitence celtique," *ibid.* XXXIII (1937) 5 ff., 277 ff., idem, *Origines de pénitence,* idem, *De Paenitentia: Tractatus Dogmatico-Historicus,* 2nd ed. (Rome, 1950).

[25] See K. Rahner, "Busslehre" 425 ff., about the conceptual and historical difficulties of the problem. From the point of view of modern terminology it would seem that K. Adam

that St. Basil, St. Augustine, and other Fathers of that time had the inadequacies of public penance in mind, when they insisted so strongly on the biblical and earlier ascetic conception that a true spirit of penance should extend far beyond gross sin to everything which is not pleasing to God.[26] And this was one of the great functions of monasticism: to demonstrate in practice that spiritual perfection and complete detachment from sin are ultimately one and the same thing, that the safest way and perhaps the only way to cease being a sinner is to become a saint. It is in the ascetic-monastic milieu, therefore, that the beginnings of what today is called private penance, and even repeatable confession and absolution, are to be found.[27]

and P. Galtier are right against Poschmann in asserting that the beginnings of private ecclesiastical penance, as distinct from merely monastic confession (see below), reach back far into the early history of the Church; see also J. Grotz, S.J., *Die Entwicklung des Busstufenwesens in der vornicänischen Kirche* (Freiburg i. B., 1955).

[26] For Basil see K. Holl, *Enthusiasmus und Bussgewalt im griechischen Mönchtum* (Leipzig, 1898) 258 and 261 ff. Very characteristic are the following passages from *De iudicio Dei* 7, *PG* XXXI, 669A f. (quoted by Holl, *loc. cit.*): "Ἆρά γε ἠπάτησεν ἡμᾶς ἡ κακίστη συνήθεια· ἆρα κακῶν αἰτία ἡμῖν μεγάλων γέγονεν ἡ διεστραμμένη τῶν ἀνθρώπων παράδοσις, τὰ μὲν παραιτουμένη δῆθεν τῶν ἁμαρτημάτων, τὰ δὲ ἀδιαφόρως αἱρουμένη· καὶ κατὰ μέν τινων σφοδρῶς ἀγανακτεῖν προσποιουμένη, οἷον φόνου καὶ μοιχείας καὶ τῶν τοιούτων· τὰ δὲ οὐδὲ ψιλῆς γοῦν ἐπιτιμήσεως ἄξια κρίνουσα, οἷον ὀργὴν ἢ λοιδορίαν ἢ μέθην ἢ πλεονεξίαν καὶ ὅσα τοιαῦτα, καθ' ὧν ἁπάντων καὶ ἀλλαχοῦ ἔδωκε τὴν αὐτὴν ἀπόφασιν ὁ ἐν Χριστῷ λαλῶν Παῦλος, εἰπὼν ὅτι "οἱ τὰ τοιαῦτα πράσσοντες ἄξιοι θανάτου εἰσίν" (cf. Rom. 1:32). See also *ibid.* 4, XXXI, 661A f.: Εὑρίσκω τοίνυν, ἀναλαβὼν τὰς θείας γραφὰς, ἐν τῇ παλαιᾷ καὶ καινῇ διαθήκῃ, οὔτε ἐν τῷ πλήθει τῶν ἁμαρτανομένων οὔτε ἐν τῷ μεγέθει τῶν ἁμαρτημάτων, ἐν μόνῃ δὲ τῇ παραβάσει οὑτινοσοῦν προστάγματος σαφῶς κρινομένην τὴν πρὸς Θεὸν ἀπείθειαν καὶ κοινὸν κατὰ πάσης παρακοῆς τοῦ Θεοῦ τὸ κρίμα. ... Cf. Dom David Amand (de Mendieta), *L'ascèse monastique de saint Basile* (Maredsous, 1948) 152 ff. See also Holl, *Enthusiasmus* 270 f., for Gregory of Nyssa. For Augustine see Adam, *Sündenvergebung* 143 ff.: ch. 4, §14: "Die neue Einteilung der Sünden," and *idem*, *Kirchenbusse* 72 ff.: ch. 3: "Die Einteilung der Sünden." See, especially, Augustine's *Speculum* 29, *CSEL* XII, 199 f.: nonnulli putant tria tantum crimina esse mortifera: idolatriam et homicidium et fornicationem. ... Quasi non sint mortifera crimina quaecumque alia . . ., quae a regno Dei separant . . .; cf. also *Sermo* CCCLI, 3, 3 ff., *PL* XXXIX, 1537 ff.; *Sermo* CCLXXVIII, 12, 12, *PL* XXXVIII, 1273.

[27] Already Origen had spoken of the possibility of repeated, though probably not yet of sacramental repeated, penance for "common" sins, by which he means sins which are not of the utmost gravity; see *In Leviticum, homil.* XV, 2, *GCS, Orig.* VI, 489: . . . si forte aliqui . . . lapsus acciderit, semper est recuperandi facultas . . . si nos aliqua culpa mortalis invenerit, quae non in crimine mortali, non in blasphemia fidei, quae muro ecclesiastici et apostolici dogmatis cincta est, sed vel in sermonis vel in morum vitio consistat. . . . In gravioribus enim criminibus semel tantum poenitentiae conceditur locus; ista vero communia, quae frequenter incurrimus, semper poenitentiam recipiunt et sine intermissione redimuntur (quoted by Galtier, *Paenitentia* 248, §295; cf. Latko, *Penance* 115 ff.).

This is particularly true for the east. Ever since St. Basil, eastern coenobites had to reveal their secret sins and faults to a monastic spiritual director who was not necessarily a priest[28] and gradually the same type of spiritual direction and of supervision of penance came to be exercised by the monasteries with regard to laymen also.[29]

In the west the development is in some respects the same, in others different. The differences are bound up with the relationship of monasticism to the Church at large, which is not quite the same in the Christian east and west. St. Augustine, for instance, is no less inspired by the monastic-ascetic ideal than St. Basil or St. Gregory of Nyssa, but he made it fructify more directly for episcopal concerns of pastoral care;[30] he was followed on this path later by St. Gregory the Great. With regard to the spiritualization of penance Augustine is in unison with the Greeks,[31] whose conception of Christ as the great physician and of penance as medicine he further develops, but he stresses ascetic perfection less and elementary satisfaction for guilt more than they.[32]

[28] For Basil's introduction of obligatory confession in his monasteries, see Holl, *Enthusiasmus* 261 ff.; for the ascetic spirituality, which forms the background of Basil's doctrine of penance, see Amand, *Ascèse* 164 ff.

[29] Cf. also above, p. 125, n. 47. But see Holl, *Enthusiasmus* 312 ff., also 274 ff. and 326 ff., for the fact that non-monastic public ecclesiastical penance did never completely disappear from the Greek Church and for the other one that, with the consolidation of the sacramental character of penance under western influence after the union of 1274, monastic influence upon confession and penance was curtailed, though not abolished. Cf. H. Delehaye, S.J., "Byzantine Monasticism," in *Byzantium*, edd. N. H. Baynes and H. St. L. B. Moss (Oxford, 1948), especially, 163 f.

[30] See below, pp. 350–365.   [31] See p. 310 and this page.

[32] For the therapeutic connotations of the early Christian concepts of penance and conversion and of reform and salvation and for their peculiar development, according to St. Augustine, toward the central idea of Christ, the *medicus humilis*, see R. Arbesmann, O.S.A., "The Concept of 'Christus medicus' in St. Augustine," *Traditio* X (1954) 1 ff. Cf. also Adam, *Sündenvergebung*, especially, 43–49, and *ibid.* 31–42 for guilt and satisfaction. Augustine also saw the eucharistic sacrament as life-restoring medicine, first, because it stipulates and presupposes previous conversion, regeneration, reform, penance, second, because the ever repeated participation in the sacrifice of Christ is for Christians a "daily bread" which gives them the spiritual health and strength for further progress in their reformation toward God. Cf. K. Adam, *Die Eucharistielehre des hl. Augustin* (Forschungen zur christlichen Literatur-und Dogmengeschichte VIII, 1, Paderborn, 1908), where Adam, for instance, quotes (p. 156) Augustine's *Sermo* CXXXI, 1, *PL* XXXVIII, 729: . . . de corpore ac sanguine suo dedit nobis salubrem refectionem. . . . Illud manducare refici est; sed sic reficeris ut non deficiat unde reficeris. . . . Manduca vitam, bibe vitam. . . . See also G. Lecordier, *La doctrine de l'eucharistie chez saint Augustin* (Thèse, Université de Strasbourg, Faculté de Théologie Catholique, Paris, 1930).

Even before he was forced in his struggle with the Pelagians to emphasize the insufficiency of the human will and the primary need of divine grace, Augustine knew only too well about the permanently endangered spiritual condition, in this terrestrial life, of every baptized Christian. He therefore attributes relatively more importance to the ever-present therapeutic exigencies of postbaptismal corrective *conversio* or *reformatio*[33] than to divine assimilation and perfection.[34]

Augustine's late anti-Pelagian treatise *De correptione et gratia* confirms the general naturè of his teaching on penance[35] by developing a theory of admonition and censure within the doctrine of grace and perseverance.[36] Writing to the monks of Hadrumetum, who apparently believed that their superiors should only pray for them, so that they might obtain the grace of obedience, rather than admonish and censure

[33] See *Enarr. in Ps. CII*, 5, *Corp. Christ.*, *Ser. Lat.* XL, 1454 f. (quoted by Arbesmann, " 'Christus medicus' " 20): . . . (to Ps. 102:3–5: ". . . sanat omnes languores tuos . . . Qui redimit de corruptione vitam tuam . . . Renovabitur sicut aquilae iuventus tua"). . . . Non enim cessavit vocare aut vocatum neglexit instruere aut instructum cessavit perficere aut perfectum neglexit coronare. Quid dicis? Quia es peccator? Convertere et accipe retributiones istas. . . . Post remissionem peccatorum corpus informum geris . . . adhuc quibusdam perturbationibus etiam ipsa anima quatitur . . . adhuc in periculis tentationum versatur. . . . Languor est: "sanat" et "omnes languores tuos". . . . Magni sunt, inquies: sed maior est medicus. . . . Deus fecit corpus tuum, Deus fecit animam tuam; novit quemadmodum recreet quod creavit, novit quemadmodum reformet quod ipse formavit. . . . See also *Enarr. in Ps. LXXVIII*, 4, *Corp. Christ.*, *Ser. Lat.* XXXIX, 1101: . . . multos paenitentia reparavit. . . . Paenitentis enim vox est: "Et a delicto meo munda me" (Ps. 50:4) et "Cor mundum crea in me, Deus, et spiritum rectum innova in visceribus meis" (Ps. 50:12).

[34] That the remedial aspects of postbaptismal reform were generally emphasized in the west can be seen very clearly from the studies of C. Vogel, *La discipline pénitentielle en Gaule des origines à la fin du VIIe siècle* (Paris, 1952) and "La discipline pénitentielle en Gaule des origines au IXe siècle. Le dossier hagiographique," *Rev. sc. rel.* XXX (1956) 1 ff., 157 ff.

[35] The question whether and in how far Augustine and his age thought that penance might be repeatable is answered in the affirmative by Adam, *Sündenvergebung* 151 ff.: ch. 4, §15: "Die Wiederholbarkeit der Privatbusse." The opposite view is held, not convincingly in my opinion, by B. Poschmann, for instance, in a note to Augustine's *Epist.* CLIII: see Poschmann's anthology, *S. Aurelii Augustini episcopi Hipponensis textus selecti de paenitentia*, *Flor. Patr.* XXXVIII, 36, n. 1. It is probable that in Christian Antiquity *relapsi* in the sense of lapse after public penance were not admitted again to penance by the Church; but this did not necessarily apply to those whose sins did not require public penance; cf. Galtier *Paenitentia* 267–274; cf. also the text from Origen, quoted above, p. 310, n. 27.

[36] For Augustine's doctrine in *De correptione et gratia* of the perseverance of the elect as opposed to the corruptible innocence of Adam see above, p. 159.

them, Augustine points out that they misunderstand the relationship between divine grace and human effort; on this occasion he says:[37]

... you must be admonished and censured (corripiendus[38] es) also for the reason that you do not want to be. For, you do not wish to have your vices demonstrated to you, you do not want them to be pricked so that you may suffer useful pain and look for a physician. You do not want to be shown to yourself, lest seeing yourself deformed (deformem) you may wish for one who will reform you (reformatorem), and may submit to him in order not to remain in that shameful state.

Here the connection between Augustine's concepts of reform and of exhortation to penance is very clear. At other times, he stresses more the relationship between penitential and baptismal conversion. So he describes in Sermo XCVIII the change of mind which must precede the acceptance of ecclesiastical penance and forgiveness of sins as a resurgere and reviviscere, terms reminiscent not only of eschatological, but also of baptismal terminology.[39]

---

[37] Augustine, De correptione et gratia 5, 7, PL XLIV, 919: ... etiam propterea corripiendus es, quia corripi non vis. Non vis enim tibi tua vitia demonstrari, non vis ut feriantur fiatque tibi utilis dolor quo medicum quaeras. Non vis tibi tu ipse ostendi, ut cum deformem te vides reformatorem desideres eique supplices ne in illa remaneas foeditate. This thought is carried further in the following paragraph, 5, 8, XLIV, 920: Tunc autem correptione proficit homo, cum miseretur atque adiuvat qui facit, quos voluerit, etiam sine correptione proficere. Sed quare isti sic, illi aliter atque alii aliter diversis et innumerabilibus modis vocentur ut reformentur, absit ut dicamus iudicium luti esse debere, sed figuli.

[38] The term and concept corripere is very important in the history of penance, especially for the controversial origins of private penance (see in particular Augustine's Sermo LXXXII, PL XXXVIII, and the works of Adam, Poschmann, and Galtier, quoted above, p. 309, n. 24). The Christian concept of correptio, with its link to ecclesiastical penance, is of biblical origin. See Matthew 18:15 ff.: Si autem peccaverit in te frater tuus, vade et corripe (ἔλεγξον) eum inter te et ipsum solum. ... Si autem te non audierit, adhibe tecum adhuc unum vel duos. ... Quod si non audierit eos, dic ecclesiae. ... In 2 Tim. 3:16 the corripere of the Vulgate translates ἐπανόρθωσις, a setting right or correcting, and is followed by erudire, which is a translation of παιδεία, a term so replete with educational connotations (for the relation between paideia and reform in general cf. above, p. 46, and especially, pp. 60 f., with reference to Werner Jaeger's Paideia and other works of his). The basic meaning of corripere is that of reproof and admonition. Nevertheless, the boundary line to censure and even punishment is not a sharp one; see, for instance, Augustine, Contra litteras Petiliani II, 85, 189, CSEL LII, 117: Quisquis igitur in ecclesia non invenitur, iam non interrogetur, sed aut correctus convertatur aut correptus non conqueratur; see also below, p. 414, for the use of corripere by Caesarius of Arles.

[39] Augustine, Sermo XCVIII, 6, 6, PL XXXVIII, 595: Nonne post obiurgationes, post increpationes dimittuntur homines cogitationibus suis et incipiunt secum volvere quam

Both in the early Christian east and west the relationship between penance and the ideology of renewal in general is very close[40] (whether penance be linked more closely to baptism or to postbaptismal reform). This can be seen, for instance, from patristic exegesis of Psalm 102:5, a beautiful verse in which renovation of the soul is compared to an eagle's rejuvenation.[41] The Fathers in their interpretations are here largely dependent upon the *Physiologus*, a work in which age-old animal lore has become part of Christian symbolism, especially in illustration of man's struggle against the passions.[42] The *Physiologus* exists in several Greek recensions and was translated into Latin and many other languages. From it the Fathers received not a few stories about animals and among them various legends of the eagle: it was believed, for instance, to suffer in its old age from increasing heaviness of its wings and from blindness, also to be threatened by starvation because of the growing projection of its upper mandible over the lower, which finally would prevent it from opening its beak.[43] Beside the phoenix legend,[44] to which, too, the *Physiologus* devotes a chapter, it was no doubt Ps. 102:5 which encouraged the divers redactors of the *Physiologus* to spin their tales around the eagle's supposed rejuvenation and to make the great bird enter upon a new cycle of life by burning its heavy plumage, by curing its sight through plunges into a fountain which rises toward the sun,

---

malam vitam gerant . . . ? Deinde displicentes sibi mutare vitam instituunt. Resurrexerunt isti; revixerunt quibus displicet quod fuerunt, sed reviviscentes ambulare non possunt (this is a reference to the Gospel story of Lazarus [John 11:44], who after having been resuscitated by Jesus had to be freed from his funeral shroud before he could walk). Haec sunt vincula ipsius reatus. Opus est ergo ut qui revixit solvatur et ire permittatur. Hoc officium discipulis dedit quibus ait: "Quae solveritis in terra, soluta sunt et in coelo" (Matthew 18:18).

[40] Cf., for instance, the *apocatastasis* terminology of penitential reconciliation in the *Apostolic Constitutions*, cited above, p. 76, n. 55.

[41] Ps. 102:5: Renovabitur ut aquilae iuventus tua; cf. above, p. 21, n. 21, and p. 45. Cf. above, p. 295, for the use of this verse in the liturgy, also p. 423, n. 93.

[42] See above all B. E. Perry, article "Physiologus," PW, *RE* XX, 1 (XXXIX), 1074 ff., also E. Peterson, "Die Spiritualität des griechischen Physiologus," *Byz. Z.* XLVII (1954) 60 ff., J. Hubaux and M. Leroy, *Le mythe du Phénix dans les littératures grecque et latine* (Bibliothèque de la Faculté de Philosophie et Lettres de l'Université de Liège LXXXII, 1939) 136 ff., A. Grillmeier, S.J., *Der Logos am Kreus* (München, 1956) 81 ff.

[43] As recognized already by F. Lauchert, *Geschichte des Physiologus* (Strassburg, 1889) 10, the beak-and-starvation motif can be traced to Aristotle, *Historia animalium* IX, 32, 619, 16 ff.

[44] Cf. above, pp. 21 and 134.

by breaking its cumbersome beak on a rock. While one recension of the *Physiologus* and patristic texts dependent on it interpret the eagle's bath in the well and the shedding of the old plumage in the sense of baptismal renovation, with a clear allusion to the putting off of the old and the putting on of the new man according to Eph. 4:22 ff. and Col. 3:8 ff., the beak-and-rock variant of the eagle story according to the *Physiologus* tradition symbolically identifies the rock on which the eagle breaks its beak as faith, the beak's excessive protuberance representing sinfulness, and connects the whole process of the rejuvenation with penance and with man's renewal in general.[45]

The chapters which follow, on monasticism as a principal means of realizing the idea of reform, will further elucidate the relations between penance and various aspects of Christian renewal ideology; conversion to a monastic or quasi-monastic way of life was often part of the penitential renovation of a Christian.

---

[45] Among the three main variants of the eagle story which are found in Sbordone's three main recensions of the Greek *Physiologus* two are of importance in the present context: one in the first recension, c. 6, F. Sbordone, *Physiologus* (Milano, etc., 1936) 22 ff., where the emphasis lies on the cure of the eagle's old eyes and old wings—the "old man"—by means of the sun of justice and of the baptismal bath, the other in the so-called Byzantine recension, c. 8, Sbordone, 191 ff., where the rejuvenation of the eagle includes the breaking of the "excessive" beak on the rock of orthodox faith and where the fountain and the sun are interpreted as the tears and fervor of repentance. Augustine knew this variant of the *Physiologus* story about the eagle (perhaps already extant in Latin translation), for he used it in his *Enarr. in Ps. CII*, 9, *Corp. Christ., Ser. Lat.* XL, 1459, where the rock however is Christ and the eagle's rejuvenation an intimation of man's resurrection; in *Enarr. in Ps. LXVI*, 10, *Corp. Christ., Ser. Lat.* XXXIX, 867 f., this rejuvenation is simply a symbol of man's renovation through Christ.

PART THREE

MONASTICISM AS A VEHICLE OF THE CHRISTIAN IDEA OF REFORM IN THE AGE OF THE FATHERS

PART THREE

MONASTICISM AS A VEHICLE OF THE
CLERICAL IDEA OF REFORM IN THE
GREGORIAN...

CHAPTER I

MONASTICISM AS THE EXEMPLARY CHRISTIAN
WAY OF LIFE

Both in the Christian east and in the Christian west and ever since the very beginnings of Christianity, reform was regarded as an important and indispensable supplement to prebaptismal conversion and to baptismal regeneration. In a Church which had become very big and very mixed the ever present need for individual and social reform had to be satisfied through special members and organisms within the whole of the Church's body. This is not to say that postbaptismal conversion to an ascetic and quasi-monastic life had not existed much earlier than the Church's external victory in the fourth century.[1] Nevertheless, the origins of Christian monasticism in the strict sense coincide approximately with the moment in the history of the Church in which she was confronted by the new tasks and dangers resulting from her having become a power not only in the spiritual, but also in the material order;[2] and from that time onward those who in one way or another followed the monastic, the "religious," way of life,

[1] For premonastic Christian asceticism, see, for instance, M. Viller and M. Olphe-Galliard, article "Ascèse, Ascétisme III: L'ascèse chrétienne," in DSpir I, 960 ff. It seems hardly necessary to enter here upon the problem of how far late ancient pagan and Jewish asceticism influenced the beginnings of Christian asceticism and monasticism. The character of the latter is in any case so well defined that one is justified in treating it as a phenomenon sui generis, regardless of undoubted, but secondary, external influence. A good survey of the problem is found in K. Heussi, Der Ursprung des Mönchtums (Tübingen, 1936). Much light has recently been shed on pre-Christian Jewish asceticism by the discovery of the Dead Sea Scrolls; cf., for instance, M. Burrows, The Dead Sea Scrolls (New York, 1955). For late antique pagan Greek asceticism and its relation to early Christian asceticism, see the judicious remarks of W. Jaeger, Two Rediscovered Works of Ancient Christian Literature: Gregory of Nyssa and Macarius (Leiden, 1954) 70 ff.

[2] Heussi, Mönchtum 110 ff., goes, I believe, too far in denying that monasticism was in part a reaction against worldliness in the Church. He is right, however, in stressing (pp. 67 ff.) that only with the increasing strength and the more secure position of the Church did and could the ascetics leave the ordinary Christian communities for the desert.

were the principal agents of reform in the Christian world. This must not be misunderstood. The monks went to the desert not only because they sought a moral perfection which was hard to attain in the world. Their desire was rather to lead already on earth that radically Christian life of which the perpetual praise of God by the angels and saints in heaven is the great prototype.[3] It was seen in previous chapters that the early Christian reformation of man to the image of God far transcended the ethical sphere and was meant to lead him to deification through the unitive contemplation of God in and through His Son and to the building of the divine Kingdom and City among men. Monasticism was eminently and concretely directed toward these two goals which ideally were those of every Christian.

The following chapters are focused on those aspects of asceticism and monasticism which have a special bearing upon the development of the ideology and reality of reform.

1. THE QUESTION: "WHAT SHALL I DO?"

When the rich young man had asked Jesus: "What good shall I do that I may have life everlasting?"[1] and had assured Him that he had kept all the commandments of God, Jesus finally answered: "If thou wilt be perfect, go sell what thou hast and give to the poor, and thou shalt have treasures in heaven; and come follow me."[2]

These counsels of perfection include voluntary poverty and followership of Christ. The first counsel is clear cut, the second contains many things. What exactly did "follow me" mean or what was the best way to follow Christ? That this question was not easily answered can be seen from the ever-repeated plea of the early monks to their spiritual superiors: "What shall I do? Give me a word."[3] They had

---

[3] For the *vita angelica* see below, p. 326, n. 17, and cf. Agnès Lamy, "Bios Angelikos," *Dieu vivant* VII (s.a.) 66.

[1] Matthew 19:16; cf. Mark 10:17, Luke 18:18.

[2] Matthew 19:21; cf. Mark 10:21, Luke 18:22.

[3] See *Apophthegmata patrum, PG* LXV, passim; *Vitae patrum* V: *Verba seniorum, PL* LXXIII, 855 ff., passim. For the *status quaestionis* concerning the various versions of the *Apophthegmata patrum* and related collections of sayings of the Desert Fathers, such as the *Sententiae patrum, Historia monachorum, Historia Lausiaca*, etc., see Heussi, *Mönchtum* 133 ff., H. Dörries, "Die Vita Antonii als Geschichtsquelle," *Nachr. Gött.*, Philol.-Histor. Klasse, 1949, 14, 373 ff., n. 24 (with discussion of the older studies by Bousset, Reitzenstein, etc.).

taken the counsel of poverty very seriously and in a radical reaction against both the opulence and the misery of late ancient city civilization, Christian as well as pagan, had withdrawn to the deserts of Egypt, Palestine, Syria. But there their troubles had not come to an end, they had only been brought into focus more sharply.[4] The coping with the fundamental urges of human nature became now of immense importance to them. The control of hunger and thirst,[5] sleep[6] and sexual desire,[7] and of all the subtle motions of the soul connected with these urges and their control provoked a sophistication of asceticism which matched the sophistication of some of the excesses of late ancient society. Personal sin, or at least the lack of personal virtue, even laxity in its more pardonable forms, were recognized as the root of all social evils. The prostitute, especially, became one of the symbols of both personal and social deficiency.[8] And yet it was not so that even the most heroic acts of continence and abnegation with regard to the natural instincts could be considered sure means to any degree of perfection. For they could be accompanied by vicious thoughts, words, and acts, of malevolence, pride, and despair, and by the specific enemy of the monks, *acedia* or tedium of life.[9] No wonder then that the early monks asked so often: "What shall I do?" and that the answers of the great Fathers of monasticism, as they survive in the *Apophthegmata Patrum* and in other collections of their sayings, constitute an elaborate code of ascetic

[4] Cf. *Apophthegmata patrum: De abbate Theodoro Phermensi* 2, PG LXV, 188B: Φύσει ἔχω ἐν τῷ σχήματι ἑβδομήκοντα ἔτη καὶ οὐδὲ μίαν ἡμέραν εὗρον ἀνάπαυσιν. . . .

[5] See, for instance, Jerome, *Vita S. Hilarionis* 11, PL XXIII, 33 f., for the amazing diet of this hermit.

[6] *Vitae patrum* V: *Verba seniorum* IV, 3, PL LXXIII, 865A: Sufficit monacho si dormierit unam horam, si tamen pugnator est.

[7] Cf. Heussi, *Mönchtum* 226 ff. The famous account, however, of St. Anthony's temptations in his *Vita* by St. Athanasius constitutes according to Dörries, "Vita Antonii," a conscious idealization, with the purpose of extolling the true Christian's Christ-inspired power against death-bearing demonic forces; but see also L. v. Hertling, S.J., "Studi storici antoniani negli ultimi trent' anni," *Antonius Magnus Eremita, 356–1956* (Studia Anselmiana XXXVIII, Roma, 1956) 13 ff., and B. Steidle, O.S.B., "«Homo Dei Antonius»," *ibid.* 148 ff.

[8] See the series of lives of saints (Mary, Thais, Pelagia, Mary of Egypt) who had been prostitutes, but were converted, in *Vitae patrum* I, PG LXXIII, 651D ff.

[9] See, for instance, Cassian, *Institutiones* X: *De spiritu acediae*, CSEL XVII, 172 ff.; cf. G. Bardy, article "Acedia," *DSpir* I, 166 ff., A. Vögtle, article "Acedia," *RLAC* I, 62 f.

practice and monastic behavior. Before monasticism could become a transforming force for the Church as a whole the Christian individual in almost complete seclusion, a conscious deserter in the desert, withdrawn not only from society, but also from the Church, not only from ecclesiastical organization, but at times even from the bond of the liturgy,[10] *solus ad solum*,[11] alone with God, had to work out his own salvation as an example for all times.

2. VIRGINITY

The greatest and essentially the most difficult monastic renunciation was the giving up of marriage, that is absolute continence or virginity.[1] In the Gospel of St. Matthew Christ's recommendation of virginity is

[10] As a rule, the Egyptian hermits assembled on Saturday and Sunday for the liturgy; see, for instance, *Historia monachorum* 23, 3, ed. E. Preuschen, *Palladius und Rufinus* (Giessen, 1897) 84, ll. 7 ff., also the Latin translation by Rufinus, c. 22, *PL* XXI, 444C ff. (cf. now A. J. Festugière, "Le problème littéraire de l'Historia monachorum," *Hermes* LXXXII [1955] 257 ff.); these hermits might, however, withdraw into absolute solitude for years— cf. Athanasius, *Vita S. Antonii* 14, *PG* XXVI, 864B—and receive holy communion from visiting priests—cf. *Historia monachorum* 151, Preuschen 69, ll. 16 ff., and Rufinus' translation, *PL* XXI, 434A—or consume the consecrated host alone—for this·latter practice, see Basil, *Epist.* XCIII, *PG* XXXII, 484B f., where, it is true, Basil does not speak of hermits in particular, but of monks in general. For the liturgical practice of the Egyptian *coenobia* as well as of the settlements of hermits see Dom C. Butler's edition of *The Lausiac History of Palladius* II (Texts and Studies VI, 2, Cambridge, 1904) 207 ff., n. 53; also R. Reitzenstein, *Historia Monachorum und Historia Lausiaca* (Göttingen, 1916) 188 f., Heussi, *Mönchtum* 186.

[11] This formula or similar ones occur both in the Latin and the Greek versions of the sayings of the Desert Fathers; see, for instance, *Apophthegmata patrum: De abbate Alonio* 1, *PG* LXV, 133A: Εἶπεν ὁ ἀββᾶς Ἀλώνιος· " Ἐὰν μὴ εἴπῃ ἐν τῇ καρδίᾳ αὐτοῦ ἄνθρωπος ὅτι «Ἐγὼ μόνος καὶ ὁ Θεὸς ἐσμὲν ἐν τῷ κόσμῳ», οὐκ ἕξει ἀνάπαυσιν." Cf. also the text printed by F. Nau, "Histoires des solitaires égyptiens (ms. Coislin 126, fol. 158 ff.)," *Revue de l'orient chrétien* XII (1907), 401 no. 89: Ἠρωτήθη γέρων ποῖον δεῖ εἶναι τὸν μόναχον, καὶ εἶπεν· " Ἐὰν ὡς κατ' ἐμὲ μόνος πρὸς μόνον." Cf. the Latin version in Dom A. Wilmart, O.S.B., "Le recueil latin des apophtegmes," *Rev. bén.* XXXIV (1922) 196, n. 1: Inquisitus senex, cuius modi deberet esse monachus, respondit: Si quantum in me est, solus ad solum. In a different sense, both metaphysical and mystical, the formula was used also by Plotinus, *Ennead* VI, 9, 11: Φυγὴ μόνου πρὸς μόνον, cf. J. Maréchal, S.J., *Etudes sur la psychologie des mystiques* II (Museum Lessianum, Sect. Philos. XIX, Bruxelles, Paris, 1937) 49 ff.: "Le 'seul à seul' avec Dieu dans l' extase d'après Plotin," and E. Peterson, "Herkunft und Bedeutung der *ΜΟΝΟΣ ΠΡΟΣ ΜΟΝΟΝ*-Formel bei Plotin," *Philologus* LXXXVIII (1933), where also the earlier history of the phrase is discussed.

[1] In the New Testament—for instance, Acts 24:25, Gal. 5:23, 1 Cor. 7:9—ἐγκράτεια, ἐγκρατεύεσθαι can be understood both as absolute continence and as chastity (the Vulgate has *castitas* in Acts 24:25, *se continere* in 1 Cor. 7:9, and both *continentia* and *castitas* in Gal.

separated from the exhortation to follow Him only by His promise of the Kingdom of Heaven to such who are like little children.[2] Also in refuting the Sadducees' pseudo-problem concerning the resurrection of the woman who had had seven husbands He spoke of the difference between "the children of this world who marry and are given in marriage" and "the children of the resurrection" who "shall neither be married nor take wives" and who cannot "die any more: for they are equal to the angels and are the children of God."[3] In the Apocalypse of St. John, the Lamb of God, Christ, stands on Mount Zion (in the heavenly Jerusalem) adored by those "who were not defiled with women: for they are virgins. These follow the Lamb whithersoever He goeth."[4] In the First Letter to the Corinthians St. Paul made it very clear that he considered marriage good, but virginity better. The reason he gives is that the time left to mankind before the end of the world has become very short and that the unmarried can make the best use of it, being solicitous only "for the things that belong to the Lord," while the married man "is divided" between his wife and God, and so the married woman between God and her husband.[5]

The term virgin ($\pi\acute{\alpha}\rho\theta\epsilon\nu\sigma$) was used both for men and women by St. Paul[6] and by the early Fathers. But soon it came to be used chiefly for women who had dedicated their virginal lives to God. This development is connected with the application to virginity of the Pauline doctrine of the Church as the bride of Christ. In the Letter to the Ephesians Paul had compared a husband to Christ and a wife to the

---

5:23). The Greek Fathers as a rule used the term $\dot{\epsilon}\gamma\kappa\rho\acute{\alpha}\tau\epsilon\iota\alpha$ in the sense of absolute continence or virginity; see the treatise on virginity, attributed to St. Athanasius, *De virginitate* 24, ed. E. v. d. Goltz (Texte u. Untersuch. XXIX, 1905) 59 (for the probable inauthenticity of the treatise and for genuine Athanasian texts on the virginal life see now M. Aubineau, S.J., "Les écrits de saint Athanase sur la virginité," *Rev. ascét. myst.* XXXI [1955] 140 ff.). The name of the sect of the Encratites, who wanted to make virginity obligatory for every Christian, is derived from $\dot{\epsilon}\gamma\kappa\rho\acute{\alpha}\tau\epsilon\iota\alpha$, understood in this sense (cf. G. Bareille, article "Encratites," in *DThC* V, 1, 4 ff.). See also K. Müller, *Die Forderung der Ehelosigkeit für alle Getauften in der alten Kirche* (Sammlung gemeinverständlicher Vorträge und Schriften aus dem Gebiet der Theologie und Religionsgeschichte CXXVI, Tübingen, 1927).

[2] Matthew 19:11 ff.
[3] See Matthew 22:23 ff., Mark 12:18 ff., Luke 20:27 ff.
[4] Apoc. 14:4.　　　　[5] 1 Cor. 7:25 ff.　　　　[6] 1 Cor. 7:25 ff.

Church,[7] but in the Second Corinthians he also had spoken of the Church of Corinth as "a chaste virgin" whom he had espoused to Christ.[8]

Bridal metaphors for the relationship between Christ and His Church, between Christ and the Christian soul, are of the essence of all Christian mysticism. But it is clear that they will apply especially to the God-dedicated virginal woman who has no other bridegroom than Christ. Tertullian seems to have been the first to make such comparisons.[9] Origen soon followed.[10] Ever since, the mystical marriage with Christ has been the highest aspiration open to a Christian woman, the priesthood being the prerogative of men.

But is not, according to Christian doctrine, motherhood an equally great glory of the female sex, since its exemplar is the Mother of God? Furthermore, had not God said to man: "Increase and multiply, and fill the earth . . ."?[11]

The first question was answered in the sense that both in Mary, the virginal mother of Jesus, and in the Church, the bride of Christ and the mother of Christians, virginity and motherhood are indeed identical.[12] With regard to the second question, however, if referred to individual Christians, the consensus of the Fathers was that the world was now full enough and that therefore the command to multiply physically was superseded or had to be understood in a spiritual sense.[13] Thus St. Cyprian could say that the true fecundity of the

[7] Eph. 5:22 ff.

[8] 2 Cor. 11:2.

[9] See, for instance, De virginibus velandis 16, 4, Corp. Christ., Ser. Lat. II, 1225: Nupsisti enim Christo, illi tradidisti carnem tuam, illi sponsasti maturitatem tuam . . . (a similar passage is found already in De oratione 22, 9, Corp. Christ., Ser. Lat. I, 271). Cf. P.-Th. Camelot, O.P., Virgines Christi (Paris, 1944) 53 ff. (also in Vie spir. LXX [1944] 30 ff., 110 ff.).

[10] See Origen, In Genes., homil. III, 6, GCS, Orig. VI, 47, ll. 8 ff. (of Christ and the Church); ibid. X, 4, GCS, Orig. VI, 98, ll. 4 ff. (of Christ and the soul).

[11] Gen. 1:28.

[12] For Mary as virgin and mother see, for instance, Ambrose, De virginibus II, 2, 6–18, Cazzaniga 36 ff. For the Church see ibid. I, 6, 31, Cazzaniga 16: Sic sancta ecclesia immaculata coitu, fecunda partu, virgo est castitate, mater est prole. . . . See also immediately below.

[13] See, for instance, Tertullian, De exhortatione castitatis 6, 1 ff., Corp. Christ., Ser. Lat. II, 1023 f.; Cyprian, De habitu virginum 23, CSEL III, 203 f.; Jerome, Epist. XXII, ad Eustochium 21, CSEL LIV, 171 ff.

Church lay in its bringing forth a great number of virgins.[14] St. Methodius could hold that Genesis 1:28 adumbrated the spiritual increase of the Church, the virgins being the mates of the Divine Logos and the less perfect Christians the children. Methodius in this connection develops a threefold typological parallelism, which contains elements of postbaptismal ascetic as well as of baptismal and of basic soteriological renewal ideology. For, the shaping of Eve from Adam's side prophetically foreshadows the origin of the Church from Christ's side wound and this again points to the rebirth of the soul in baptism which recapitulates the passion and death of Christ. Adam's sleep and Christ's death are mystically conceived as ecstasies and the side of Adam, the side of Christ, have become types of the Holy Spirit: in the symbolic death of baptismal *palingenesia* the life-giving force of the Spirit, typified by Adam's rib and Christ's side wound, initiates the great renewal (ἀνανέωσις, ἀνακαινισμός, ἀναπλάσσειν) of man, whose soul, if it strives for perfection with all its strength, will then, as a new and better Eve, become the virginal bride of Christ, the same Christ in whom and from whom it was reborn.[15]

---

[14] See Cyprian, *De habitu virginum* 3, *CSEL* III, 189: nunc nobis ad virgines sermo est. . . . Flos est ille ecclesiastici germinis . . . Dei imago respondens ad sanctimoniam Domini. . . . Gaudet per illas adque in illis largiter floret ecclesiae matris gloriosa fecunditas, quantoque plus copiosa virginitas numero suo addit, gaudium matris augescit; see also *ibid.* 23, *CSEL* III, 204, to 1 Cor. 15:47 f.: hanc imaginem [eius qui de caelo est] virginitas portat.

[15] Methodius, *Symposium* III, 8, 70 ff., *GCS, Method.* 35 ff.: Ὅθεν ὁ ἀπόστολος εὐθυβόλως εἰς Χριστὸν ἀνηκόντισε τὰ κατὰ τὸν Ἀδάμ. Οὕτως γὰρ ἂν μάλιστα ἐκ τῶν ὀστῶν αὐτοῦ καὶ τῆς σαρκὸς τὴν ἐκκλησίαν συμφωνῆσαι γεγονέναι, ἧς δὴ χάριν . . . κατῆλθεν ὁ Λόγος προσκολληθησόμενος τῇ γυναικὶ (i.e., to the Church) καὶ ὕπνωσε τὴν ἔκστασιν τοῦ πάθους. . . . Ταύτῃ γὰρ καὶ τό "αὐξάνεσθε καὶ πληθύνεσθε" (cf. Gen. 1:28) πληροῦται προσηκόντως, εἰς μέγεθος καὶ κάλλος καὶ πλῆθος αὐξανομένης καθ' ἡμέραν αὐτῆς (i.e., the Church) διὰ τὴν σύνερξιν καὶ τὴν κοινωνίαν τοῦ Λόγου. . . . Οὐ γὰρ ἂν ἄλλως ἡ ἐκκλησία συλλαβεῖν τοὺς πιστεύοντας καὶ ἀναγεννῆσαι διὰ τοῦ λουτροῦ δύναιτο τῆς παλιγγενεσίας (cf. Tit. 3:5), ἐὰν μὴ καὶ δι' αὐτοὺς ὁ Χριστὸς κενώσας ἑαυτὸν . . . πάλιν ἀποθανῇ καταβὰς ἐξ οὐρανῶν καὶ προσκολληθεὶς τῇ ἑαυτοῦ γυναικί, τῇ ἐκκλησίᾳ, παράσχοι τῆς πλευρᾶς ἀφαιρεῖσθαι τῆς ἑαυτοῦ δύναμίν τινα . . . πλευρὰν δὲ τὸ Πνεῦμα τῆς ἀληθείας τὸ Παράκλητον (cf. John 15:26). . . . Ἀδύνατον δὲ τοῦ Πνεύματος τοῦ ἁγίου μετασχεῖν τινα καὶ μέλος καταλεχθῆναι Χριστοῦ, ἐὰν μὴ πρότερον καὶ ἐπὶ τούτου συγκατελθὼν ὁ Λόγος ἐκστῇ κοιμηθείς, ἵνα τὴν ἀνανέωσιν καὶ τὸν ἀνακαινισμὸν συνεξαναστὰς τοῦ ὕπνου τοῦ κεκοιμημένου καὶ αὐτὸς μεταλαβεῖν δυνήθη Πνεύματος ἀναπλησθείς . . . ἀφ' οὗ ὁ Θεὸς μετὰ τὴν ἔκστασιν τοῦ Χριστοῦ, ὅ δή ἐστι μετὰ τὴν ἐνανθρώπησιν καὶ τὸ πάθος, τὴν βοηθὸν αὐτῷ κατασκευάζει (cf. Gen. 2:18), λέγω δὲ τὰς ἡρμοσμένας αὐτῷ καὶ νενυμφευμένας ψυχάς. . . . Οἱ μὲν γὰρ κρείττονες καὶ τρανότερον σπάσαντες ἤδη τὴν ἀλήθειαν, οὗτοι διὰ τὴν τελείαν κάθαρσιν καὶ πίστιν ἀποστερωθέντες τῶν τῆς σαρκὸς ἀτοπημάτων ἐκκλησία γίνονται καὶ βοηθὸς τοῦ Χριστοῦ, παρθένος ὥσπερ κατὰ τὸν ἀπόστολον (cf. 2 Cor. 11:2) αὐτῷ καθηρμοσμένοι τε καὶ νενυμφευμένοι. . . .

There was no doubt, above all, that Christ Himself and the greatest of saints, Mary, John the Baptist, John the Evangelist, and many others, had lived in the virginal state. In order to follow and imitate Christ, therefore, it was best to do the same. Also, from Christ's word that after the resurrection man will no longer marry and will be equal to the angels[16] one could plausibly conclude that virginity dedicated to God could lead close to an angelic state of life even on earth. In justifying virginity St. Jerome says that Christ wanted angels on earth who together with the angels in heaven would adore Him. St. Athanasius, St. Ambrose, and St. Leo the Great, too, speak of the virgins as of angelic beings and according to St. Gregory of Nyssa ascetics and monks seek the angelic life even on earth.[17]

Οἱ δὲ ἀτελεῖς ἔτι καὶ ἀπαρχόμενοι εἰς σωτηρίαν τῶν μαθημάτων ὠδίνονται καὶ μορφοῦνται ὥσπερ ὑπὸ μητράσι πρὸς τῶν τελειοτέρων, ἔστ' ἂν ἀποκυηθέντες ἀναγεννηθῶσιν εἰς μέγεθος καὶ κάλλος ἀρετῆς, καὶ πάλιν αὖ κατὰ προκοπὴν ἐκκλησία καὶ οὗτοι γεγονότες εἰς ἑτέρων τόκον ὑπουργήσωσι τέκνων καὶ ἀνατροφήν. . . . For this whole passage, see M. Bonwetsch, "Die Theologie des Methodius von Olympus," *Abhandl. Gött.*, Philos.-Histor. Klasse, Neue Folge VII, 1 (1903) 14, and the annotated translation of H. Musurillo, S.J., *St. Methodius, The Symposium* (Ancient Christian Writers XXVII, Westminster, Md., 1958) 65 ff., 200 ff. Cf. J. Farges, *Les idées morales et religieuses de Méthode d'Olympe* (Paris, 1929) 137 ff., J. C. Plumpe, *Mater Ecclesia* (Catholic University of America Studies in Christian Antiquity V, Washington, D.C., 1943) 111 ff., J. Daniélou, S.J., *Sacramentum Futuri* (Paris, 1950) 37 ff., also H. Rahner, S.J., "«Mysterium Lunae» II: Die gebärende Kirche," *Z. kath. Theol.* LXIV (1940) 71 ff. Methodius' sleep and death mysticism about Adam, Christ, and the Church had been anticipated to some extent by Tertullian, *De anima* 43, 10, Waszink 60: Si enim Adam de Christo figuram dabat, somnus Adae mors erat Christi dormituri in mortem, ut de iniuria perinde lateris eius vera mater viventium figuraretur ecclesia. Cf. Daniélou, *Sacramentum Futuri*, for the continuation of these ideas by Hilary of Poitiers and other western Fathers.   [16] See Matthew 22 : 23 ff.

[17] Jerome, *Epist.* XXII, *ad Eustochium* 21, CSEL LIV, 173: Statim ut Filius Dei ingressus est super terram, novam sibi familiam instituit, ut qui ab angelis adorabatur in caelo, haberet angelos et in terris; cf. *Adversus Iovinianum* I, 36, PL XXIII, 273A. See also Athanasius, *Apologia ad Constantium imperatorem* 33, PG XXV, 640: . . . εἰκόνα τῆς τῶν ἀγγέλων ἁγιότητος . . . ἐπὶ γῆς τὴν παρθενίαν, cf. Camelot, *Virgines* 31; Ambrose, *De virginibus* I, 8, 52, Cazzaniga 27: Castitas (in the sense of virginal continence) etiam angelos fecit . . . , cf. the immediately preceding and following parts of ch. 8; Gregory of Nyssa, *De instituto christiano*, Jaeger, *Greg. Nyss. Opera* VIII, 1, 70, l. 19: . . . τὸν τῶν ἀγγέλων ἐπὶ τῆς γῆς ζήσεσθε βίον. For John Chrysostom cf. above, pp. 126 f., for Leo the Great and the liturgy see p. 288, n. 20. Many more patristic examples of the belief that the virginal, the ascetic, the monastic life is angel-like might be adduced. Cf. for instance Evagrius Ponticus (Ps.-Nilus), *De oratione* 113, PG LXXIX, 1192D (cf. I. Hausherr, S.J., "Le traité de l'oraison d'Evagre le Pontique (Pseudo Nil)," *Rev. ascét. myst.* XV [1934] 144 f.): Ἰσάγγελος γίνεται μοναχὸς διὰ τῆς ἀληθοῦς προσευχῆς. See also Lamy, "Bios angelikos," Steidle, "«Homo Dei Antonius»" 173 ff., J. Leclercq, O.S.B., *La vie parfaite* (Turnhout, Paris, 1948) 19 ff.

From another point of view, virginity was close to martyrdom through which Christians gave their lives for Christ's sake. The early Christian hierarchy of values recognized the fact that beside life itself there is in the natural order of the world nothing higher than the physical and spiritual union of love. To give it up could be a preparation and even a substitute for martyrdom.[18]

For all these reasons virginity came to be considered as eminently helpful in the reformation of the image of God in man. The Greek Fathers, especially, connected virginity with the assimilation of man to God. So, for instance, in an *Ascetical Discourse* attributed to St. Basil of Caesarea the author in speaking of the recovery of the lost likeness to God through the overcoming of the passions (ἀπάθεια) says that virginity is an ally of those who wish to achieve this aim.[19] The author of the treatise *On the True Integrity of Virginity*, probably Basil of Ancyra, bases the praise of virginity on the conception that if uncorrupted it will make man similar to incorruptible God. The virgin will experience even on this earth a rapture to the Paradise of the third heaven as did St. Paul.[20] St. Gregory of Nyssa in his book *On Virginity*, which is such a characteristic document of Greek patristic reform ideology,[21] asserts that the incorruption and purity of virginity have their prototype in the Trinity itself, in the passionless generation of the Son and the incorruptible purity of the Spirit. As a consequence of the Incarnation of God in the Virgin Mary the power of virginity is so great that it can be at the same time with the Father in heaven and attend to the salvation of man on earth; it can bring God down to communion with human life and give man wings of desire for heaven; thus

---

[18] See Athanasius, *De incarnatione* 48, PG XXV, 181B, where virginity and martyrdom are linked together; see also Methodius, *Symposium* VIII, 12 f., 203 f., GCS, *Method.* 96 ff. Many other examples are cited by E. E. Malone, O.S.B., "The Monk and the Martyr," *Antonius Magnus Eremita,* 356–1956 (Studia Anselmiana XXXVIII, 1956) 201 ff.

[19] *Sermo asceticus* 1 f., PG XXXI, 872A (St. Basil's authorship is improbable, according to Amand, *Ascèse* XXVI): Εἰ οὖν διὰ τῆς ἀπαθείας τὴν εἰκόνα τοῦ Θεοῦ πάλιν ἀναλαμβάνομεν . . . ταύτης γενώμεθα τῆς σπουδῆς, ὥστε μηδένι πάθει μηδέποτε καταδυναστευθῆναι ἡμῶν τὴν ψυχὴν . . . Τῆς δὲ τοιαύτης σπουδῆς συνεργός ἐστιν ἡ παρθενία. . . .

[20] Basil of Ancyra, *De vera virginitatis integritate* 2, PG XXX (appendix to the works of St. Basil of Caesarea) 672B: Μέγα μὲν γὰρ . . . παρθενία, τῷ ἀφθάρτῳ Θεῷ . . . ἐξομοιοῦσα τὸν ἄνθρωπον. Ibid. 66, XXX, 804B: reference to 2 Cor. 12:3. Cf. Camelot, *Virgines* 59 f. For the attribution of the treatise to Basil of Ancyra, see F. Cavallera, article "Basile d'Ancyre," in *DSpir* I, 1283.

[21] Cf. above, pp. 76 f.

it becomes a link (σύνδεσμός) which assists man in attaining familiarity with God.[22]

In the treatises on virginity written by the Latin Fathers, such as the ones by Tertullian, Cyprian, and Ambrose, already mentioned, and above all in Augustine's De Sancta Virginitate one finds comparatively little of this assimilation ideology, but together with the ubiquitous topos of the vita angelica[23] a simple insistence that the virginal life is an imitation of that of Christ and His Mother, a full dedication to God.

In De sancta Virginitate St. Augustine comments on the words of St. John,[24] the virginal Apostle, about the virgins who follow the Lamb of God wheresoever He goes:

Where do we believe this Lamb to go whither none dares or is able to follow Him except you (i.e., the virgins)?... To what pastures and meadows? Where, I believe, [His] pastures are joys, not the vain joys of this world... nor the joys, which in the Kingdom of God itself will be had [even] by those who are not virginal, but such as will be distinct from all other joys. The joy of the virgins of Christ will be of Christ, in Christ, with Christ, after Christ, through Christ, because of Christ.... Go toward these [joys], follow the Lamb, because the flesh of the Lamb is in truth virginal.... Rightly do you follow Him through virginity of heart and flesh whithersoever He goes. For

---

[22] Gregory of Nyssa, De virginitate, Cavarnos, in Jaeger, Greg. Nyss. Opera VIII, 1, 253: ... ἐν Πατρὶ παρθενίαν εὑρίσκεσθαι τῷ καὶ Υἱὸν ἔχοντι καὶ δίχα πάθους γεννήσαντι.... Καὶ πάλιν τὸ ἴσον παράδοξον Υἱὸς διὰ παρθενίας νοούμενος. Ἐνθεωρεῖται δὲ ὡσαύτως καὶ τῇ τοῦ ἁγίου Πνεύματος φυσικῇ καὶ ἀφθάρτῳ καθαρότητι· τὸ γὰρ καθαρὸν καὶ ἄφθαρτον ὀνομάσας ἄλλῳ ὀνόματι τὴν παρθενίαν ἐσήμανας.... Ibid. 254: ... (the divine nature) τὴν ζωὴν ἐχαρίσθη, ἵνα καταβληθεῖσαν τὴν ἀνθρωπίνην φύσιν ὑπὸ τῆς ἐμπαθοῦς διαθέσεως, ὥσπερ τινὰ χεῖρα τὴν τῆς καθαρότητος μετουσίαν ὀρέξασα, πάλιν ὀρθώσῃ καὶ πρὸς τὰ ἄνω βλέπειν χειραγωγήσῃ. Διὰ τοῦτο γὰρ οἶμαι καὶ τὴν πηγὴν τῆς ἀφθαρσίας αὐτὸν τὸν Κύριον ἡμῶν Ἰησοῦν Χριστὸν μὴ διὰ γάμου εἰσελθεῖν εἰς τὸν κόσμον, ἵνα ἐνδείξεται διὰ τοῦ τρόπου τῆς ἐνανθρωπήσεως τὸ μέγα τοῦτο μυστήριον, ὅτι Θεοῦ παρουσίαν καὶ εἴσοδον μόνη καθαρότης ἱκανή ἐστι δέξασθαι, ἣν ἄλλως οὐκ ἔστι πρὸς ἀκρίβειαν πᾶσαν κατορθωθῆναι, εἰ μὴ παντελῶς τις ἑαυτὸν τῶν τῆς σαρκὸς παθημάτων ἀλλοτριώσειεν. Ὅπερ γὰρ ἐν τῇ ἀμιάντῳ Μαρίᾳ γέγονε σωματικῶς..., τοῦτο καὶ ἐπὶ πάσης ψυχῆς κατὰ λόγον παρθενευούσης γίνεται.... Ibid. 255: Ἐπεὶ οὖν τοσαύτη ἐστὶ τῆς παρθενίας ἡ δύναμις, ὡς καὶ ἐν τοῖς οὐρανοῖς παρὰ τῷ Πατρὶ τῶν πνευμάτων μένειν... καὶ τῆς ἀνθρωπίνης σωτηρίας ἐφάπτεσθαι, τὸν μὲν Θεὸν δι' ἑαυτῆς πρὸς τὴν τοῦ ἀνθρωπίνου βίου κοινωνίαν κατάγουσα, τὸν δὲ ἄνθρωπον ἐν ἑαυτῇ πρὸς τὴν τῶν οὐρανίων ἐπιθυμίαν πτεροῦσα καὶ οἱονεὶ σύνδεσμός τις γινομένη τῆς ἀνθρωπίνης πρὸς τὸν Θεὸν οἰκειώσεως..., τίς ἂν εὑρεθείη δύναμις λόγων συνανιοῦσα τῷ μεγέθει τοῦ θαύματος; cf. Jaeger, Rediscovered Works 24 ff.

[23] Cf. above, p. 326, n. 17.

[24] Apoc. 14: 4 (Vulgate): Hi sunt qui cum mulieribus non sunt coinquinati; virgines enim sunt. Hi sequuntur agnum quocumque ierit. ...

what is to follow if not to imitate? . . . Him [Christ] each follows in that in which he [or she] imitates Him. And not in so far as He is the One Son of God by whom all things are made, but in so far as He is the Son of Man did He show what must be imitated in Him. And many things in Him are offered to all for imitation, but the virginity of the flesh not to all. For those in whom it has already been brought about that they are not virgins, cannot bring it about that they be virgins. May, therefore, the rest of the faithful, who have lost the virginity of the body, follow the Lamb, not whithersoever He goes, but as far as they can. . . . But lo, that Lamb walks on the virginal path. How will those go after Him who have lost what they can in no manner receive back? You then go after Him, [you] His virgins. You go after Him even there (i.e., to the realm of virginity), for because of this one thing (i.e., virginity) you [may] follow Him whithersoever He goes. For we can exhort married people to follow Him to every other gift of sanctity, but not to the one which they have irreparably lost. [25]

It seems clear then that for St. Augustine those who lead the virginal life, those who can follow Christ wheresoever He goes, those who already in this "terrestrial mortality meditate the heavenly and angelic life," [26] are the citizens par excellence of the City of God, which had

[25] Augustine, *De sancta virginitate* 27–29, CSEL XLI, 264–266: Quo ire putamus hunc agnum, quo nemo eum sequi vel audeat vel valeat nisi vos? . . . In quos saltus et prata? Ubi credo sunt gramina gaudia; non gaudia saeculi huius vana . . . nec gaudia qualia in ipso regno Dei ceteris non virginibus, sed a ceterorum omnium gaudiorum sorte distincta: gaudia virginum Christi, de Christo, in Christo, cum Christo, post Christum, per Christum, propter Christum. . . . Ite in haec, sequimini agnum, quia et agni caro utique virgo. . . . Merito eum sequimini virginitate cordis et carnis quocumque ierit. . . . Hunc in eo quisque sequitur in quo imitatur: non in quantum ille Filius Dei est unus, per quem facta sunt omnia, sed in quantum Filius hominis, quia oportebat, in se praebuit imitanda. Et multa in illo ad imitandum omnibus proponuntur, virginitas autem carnis non omnibus; non enim habent quid faciant ut virgines sint, in quibus iam factum est ut virgines non sint. Sequantur itaque agnum ceteri fideles, qui virginitatem corporis amiserunt, non quocumque ille ierit, sed quousque ipsi potuerint. . . . Sed ecce ille agnus graditur itinere virginali. Quomodo post eum ibunt, qui hoc amiserunt quod nullo modo recipiunt? Vos ergo, vos, ite post eum, virgines eius; vos et illuc ite post eum, quia propter hoc unum quocumque ierit sequimini eum. Ad quodlibet enim aliud sanctitatis donum, quo eum sequantur, hortari possumus coniugatos praeter hoc quod inreparabiliter amiserunt. For an analysis of Augustine's treatise see J. Heerinckx, O.F.M., "Divi Augustini tractatus «De sancta virginitate»," *Antonianum* VI (1931) 37 ff.

[26] Augustine, *De sancta virginitate* 24, CSEL XLI, 260: . . . caelestem et angelicam vitam in terrena mortalitate meditantes. . . . It is not without interest that Augustine does not speak of angel-likeness in the strict sense, but of meditation of the angelic life; see also *Confessiones* XIII, 19, Skutella . . .: perfectorum, sed nondum sicut angelorum.

been diminished by the fall of the rebel angels, but is being replenished by the elect.[27]

The Roman liturgy and St. Leo the Great fused western and eastern Christian thought on virginity and bound it up with the ideology of regeneration and reform.[28] Christ, Leo says, was born from a virgin, so that virginity, which could not be preserved in generation, would now become a thing capable of imitation through rebirth in Christ.[29]

3. CONTEMPLATION AND CHARITY

The difference between eastern and western patristic ideas of reform is reflected also in two distinct attitudes toward asceticism and toward the monastic life. The Greek conception of assimilation to God, as vision of God through the purified soul which thus returns to its original Paradise,[1] favored the contemplation of God even over an active life of charity for God and man, which seemed to flow more naturally from the Augustinian idea of the reformation of the Trinitarian image in the soul through memory, intelligence, and love.[2] The very subtle differences involved are not absolute contrasts. It must never be forgotten that in practice something of each attitude was contained in the other. It has recently been pointed out that in the Christian east too the emphasis on contemplation is not equally strong everywhere and at all times. Love for God, imitation of God, dedication to God could be translated into a life of prayer, of charity to one's fellow man, and of renunciation of self without any conscious attempt to experience practically, without any intention to circumscribe theoretically, the vision of God on earth.[3]

As was seen in an earlier chapter,[4] the blending of Greek philosophical speculation on the contemplative (theoretical) and the active

---

[27] Cf. above, pp. 239 f., 282, n. 156.   [28] See above, p. 288.

[29] Leo the Great, Sermo XXII, 2, PL LIV, 196A: . . . ut virginitas quae in aliis non poterat salva esse generando, fieret et in aliis imitabilis renascendo (aliis-aliis is untranslatable).

[1] See above, pp. 63 ff. and 83 ff.   [2] See above, pp. 196 ff.

[3] Cf. A. J. Festugière, "Ascèse et contemplation," Vie spir., Supplément, 1939, December, 165 ff. (also in L'enfant d'Agrigent [Paris, 1950]), I. Hausherr, S.J., "Les grands courants de la spiritualité orientale," Orientalia Christiana Periodica I (1935) 114 ff., idem, "L'imitation de Jésus-Christ dans la spiritualité byzantine," Mélanges Cavallera 231 ff. See also above, pp. 155 f.

[4] See above, pp. 98 ff., nn. 61–63.

(practical or political) life with Christian scriptural thought was the work of the School of Alexandria, above all of Origen, whose ideas were most deeply developed by Gregory of Nyssa and most effectively popularized among the monks by Evagrius Ponticus. Origen seems to have been the first also to interpret the New Testament story of Martha's active concern for Jesus and of her sister Mary's quiet attention to His word, for which she received higher praise,[5] as signifying the higher value of the contemplative life.[6]

Nevertheless, the πρᾶξις or πρακτικὴ φιλοσοφία of the Greek and oriental Fathers and ascetics does not correspond to practical life in the modern sense, but only to those activities which are directly conducive to that *catharsis* which is indispensable for the higher stages of the ascent to God. It is very important to realize that their thought on the active and the contemplative life does not conceive of the former as a life of action directed toward the world outside the soul. For Origen, for Evagrius, and for eastern Christian asceticism and monasticism in general the πρακτική consists in the struggle against vice and for virtue; this alone can prepare for θεωρία or θεολογία or θεογνωσία, which comprise the true understanding of God's works and word, and ultimately the vision of God through similarity with Him.[7] In this conception the active or practical life does not refer to action, understood in the ordinary meaning of the word, although such activity may be good in itself. Even to actions of charity which are definitely Christ-like and apostolic it seems to apply only indirectly.[8]

Eastern Christian doctrine on the contemplative and active life is therefore eminently ascetic and monastic and this can still be felt strongly from the account given of it by the great transmitter of eastern

---

[5] Luke 10:38–42.

[6] See Origen, *In Lucam*, fragm. XXXIX, GCS, *Orig.* IX, 252; *Commentary to the Gospel of St. John*, fragm. LXXX, GCS, *Orig.* IV, 547: Εἴπερ δὲ σύμβολόν ἐστι Μαρία μὲν τοῦ θεωρητικοῦ βίου, Μάρθα δὲ τοῦ πρακτικοῦ. . . .

[7] See the references and bibliography above, pp. 99 f., nn. 61 and 63.

[8] See, for instance, Evagrius Ponticus, *Rerum monachalium rationes* 3, PG XL, 1253D, on hospitality toward visitors to the monastery, which is deprecated with a reference to Martha and Mary in Luke 10:38 ff.; also Evagrius, *Centuriae* I, 11, Frankenberg 57, where he says that though those who engage in such activities will rule in the world to come, those who even now "acquire spiritual bodies," i.e. strive for the contemplation of God, already βασιλεύουσιν ἐν τοῖς γενομένοις αἰῶσιν, that is to say, possess the Kingdom even on earth; cf. above, p. 112, n. 13, for the full text.

monastic spirituality to the west in the age of St. Augustine, St. John Cassian, whose dependence on Evagrius Ponticus was very close.[9] He treats both kinds of life in the sense of monastic "sciences" or "disciplines" (religionis disciplina or professio or scientia, as opposed to other scientiae, disciplinae, and artes).[10] Though among the ways in which the πρακτική is carried out Cassian can include the life of the hermits, who "adhere to God most intimately through the science of solitude,"[11] hermits are above all bent upon theoria (contemplatio Dei)[12] and therefore not the true representatives of praxis; these are the coenobites who live in communities of monks, in monasteries.[13] But he also knows other forms of the active life: the care of strangers in hospices (such as the xenodochium of Macarius of Alexandria) and of the sick, intercession for the poor and oppressed, the teaching of Christian doctrine, alms giving.[14] While Cassian follows Evagrius and the Greek

[9] See S. Marsili, O.S.B., Giovanni Cassiano ed Evagrio Pontico (Studia Anselmiana V, Roma, 1936) 77 ff.; O. Chadwick, John Cassian (Cambridge, 1950) 82 ff. For Evagrius see also above, pp. 98–100.

[10] See Cassian, Conlationes XIV, 1, 3, CSEL XIII, 398 f.: . . . religionis nostrae disciplina atque professio . . . duplex scientia . . .: prima πρακτική, id est actualis, quae emendatione morum et vitiorum purgatione perficitur; altera θεωρητική, quae in contemplatione divinarum rerum et sacratissimorum sensuum cognitione consistit.

[11] Ibid. XIV, 4, 1 ff., CSEL XIII, 400 f.: Haec igitur πρακτική . . . erga multas professiones studiaque dividitur. Quidam enim summam intentionis suae erga heremi secreta et cordis constituunt puritatem, ut in praeteritis Heliam et Helisaeum nostrisque temporibus beatum Antonium . . . familiarissime Deo per silentium solitudinis cohaesisse cognoscimus.

[12] See Conlationes, Praefatio 4, CSEL XIII, 4.

[13] Ibid. XIV, 4, 2, CSEL XIII, 400: Quidam erga institutionem fratrum et pervigilem coenobiorum curam omnem studii sui sollicitudinem dediderunt. . . . For identification of the coenobitic with the active and of the hermitic with the contemplative life see Conlatio XVIII: De tribus generibus monachorum, especially XVIII, 4, 2, CSEL XIII, 509: . . . anachoretarum, qui prius in coenobiis instituti iamque in actuali conversatione perfecti solitudinis elegere secreta . . .; also ibid. XIX: De fine coenobiotae et heremitae, especially XIX, 8 f., CSEL XIII, 542 f. Cassian's distinction between the practical or actual coenobitic and the theoretical or contemplative hermitic life is connected with his conception of three abrenuntiationes in Conlationes III, 6, CSEL XIII, 73, the first being corporalis and involving aversion from the world and conversion to the monastic life, the second, since it consists in rejection of former habits and vices, corresponding to actualis conversatio, which is eminently coenobitical, the third, which detaches the mind from all present and visible things, leading to contemplation, which is eminently hermitic; for the relation between the terms and concepts conversio and conversatio, see below, pp. 345 f.

[14] Ibid. XIV, 4, 2 f., CSEL XIII, 400 f.: Quosdam xenodochii et susceptionis pium delectat obsequium, per quod etiam in praeteritis Abraham patriarcham et Loth Domino placuisse et nuper beatum Macarium . . ., qui xenodochio ita apud Alexandriam praefuit,

tradition in setting Mary's part, the *summum* or *principale bonum* of *theoria* or *contemplatio divina*, high above that of Martha, above the *actuale quamvis laudabile opus*,[15] his combination of monastic ascesis with a medley of non-monastic occupations under the heading of active or practical life does constitute a transition between Christian Antiquity and the Middle Ages as well as between the Christian east and west.[16] Also, his conception of the θεωρητική,[17] while derived from the mystical tradition of the Greek Fathers, does no longer comprise all aspects of their thought. Cassian distinguishes two degrees of θεωρία, corresponding both to the distinction between the literal (historical) and the spiritual (tropological, allegorical, anagogical) understanding of Holy Scripture and to that between the φυσική and the θεολογική, as defined by Evagrius;[18] moreover, he agrees with the latter in

ut nulli eorum, qui solitudinis secreta sectati sunt, inferior sit credendus. Quidam eligentes aegrotantium curam, alii intercessionem, quae pro miseris atque obpressis inpenditur, exsequentes aut doctrinae instantes aut elemosynam pauperibus largientes inter magnos ac summos viros pro affectu suo ac pietate viguerunt.

[15] *Conlationes* I, 8, 3, *CSEL* XIII, 15; see also *ibid.* XXIII, 3, 1, XIII, 642; cf. above, p. 331, nn. 6, 8, for Origen and Evagrius.

[16] Marsili, *Cassiano* 110 f., and Chadwick, *Cassian* 105 f., perhaps, do not sufficiently consider that Cassian does not always exactly follow Evagrius' conception of the πρακτική; this emerges clearly from a comparison for instance, of the Evagrian texts referred to above, p. 331, n. 8, with *Conlationes* XIV, 4, *CSEL* XIII, 400 f., and the continuation *ibid.* XIV, 5–7, XIII, 401 ff. The text *Conlationes* I, 10, 5, XIII, 17, quoted by Marsili, *Cassiano*, 111, contrasts the practical with the theoretical life and not the πρακτική as self-improvement with the πρακτική, as charitable works; of the latter Cassian says significantly (*Conlationes* I, 10, 4, XIII, 17): . . . opera pietatis ac misericordiae necessaria sunt in hoc tempore, dum adhuc inaequalis diversitas dominatur; quorum ne hic quidem expectaretur operatio, nisi inopum, indigentum infirmorumque pars maxima redundaret, quae iniquitate hominum facta est. . . . It remains true, of course, that Cassian does not approve of work for others which would involve the monk in a nonmonastic way of life; see *Conlationes* XXIII, 3 ff., XXIV, 9 and 13, *CSEL* XIII, 677 ff., 683 f. and 688 ff., quoted by Chadwick, *Cassian* 105 f. Cf. also above, p. 78, for Basil the Great's attitude.

[17] See Marsili, *Cassiano* 25 ff., on Cassian's terminology and conception of contemplation, also 23 f. on image-likeness, assimilation, imitation, perfection, and 38 ff. on the relation between active and contemplative life.

[18] See *Conlationes* XIV, 8, 1, *CSEL* XIII, 404: . . . θεωρητικὴ vero in duas dividitur partes, id est in historicam interpretationem et intelligentiam spiritalem. . . . Spiritalis autem scientiae genera sunt tria: tropologia, allegoria, anagoge (of which the first, since it is *moralis explanatio*, belongs both to the *actualis* or πρακτική and to the *theoretica*; cf. H. Caplan, "The Four Senses of Scriptural Interpretation . . .," *Speculum* IV [1929] 282 ff., H. de Lubac, S.J., "«Typologie» et «allégorisme»," *Rech.'s sc. rel.* XXXIV [1947] 180 ff., idem, "Sur un vieux distique: La doctrine du «quadruple sens»," *Mélanges Cavallera*

identifying the highest summit of θεωρία with contemplative prayer;[19] but there is in his writings relatively little speculation on the deification of man.[20]

St. Augustine's teaching on the *vita activa* and the *vita contemplativa*[21] differs more from that of the Greeks than Cassian's, though the distinction between the two lives is sharply formulated by Augustine, too, for instance, in his work *On the Consensus of the Evangelists* (about 400):

. . . because two virtues are set before the human soul, one active, the other contemplative, the first the road, the second the goal, and because through the first one toils so that the heart is purified for the vision of God and in the second he is at rest and sees God: [therefore] the first is contained in the precepts for the practice of the temporal life, the second in the doctrine of sempiternal life beyond. And therefore the first [kind of virtues] works, the second rests, because the former consists in the purgation of sins, the second in the light of the purified. And therefore in this mortal life the first exists in the working out of good habits (*in opere bonae conversationis*), the second rather in faith and, in a very few, in some partial vision of the unchangeable truth as "through a glass in a dark manner" (1 Cor. 13:12).[22]

347 ff.). See on the other hand *Conlationes* I, 15, 1, *CSEL* XIII, 25: Contemplatio vero Dei multifarie concipitur. Nam Deus non sola inconprehensibilis illius substantiae suae admiratione cognoscitur, quod tamen adhuc in spe promissionis absconditum est (this corresponds to Evagrius' θεολογική), sed etiam creaturarum suarum magnitudine . . . pervidetur (corresponding to Evagrius' φυσική); see also the other Cassianic and Evagrian texts quoted and discussed in Marsili, *Cassiano* 121 ff.

[19] On this point, see Hausherr, "Le traité de l'oraison d'Evagre le Pontique (Pseudo Nil)," *Rev. ascét. myst.* XV (1934) 34 ff., 113 ff., and Marsili, *Cassiano* 145 ff., Chadwick, *Cassian* 141 ff.

[20] This has been noted also by Chadwick, *Cassian* 148, who, *ibid.* 88, remarks on the fact that even the mere act of translation into Latin was bound to remove certain aspects of Greek ascetic and mystic ideology. On the question, whether or not and in what sense Cassian considered the vision of God possible in this life, see Marsili, *Cassiano* 61 ff., and for the problem in general, see above, pp. 102 f., n. 73. Particularly important is the continuation of the text from *Conlationes* I, 15 (quoted above, n. 18), *CSEL* XIII, 26, where Cassian qualifies the impossibility of seeing God and remaining alive (Ex. 33:20) by applying it to the man who still lives for the world and for terrestrial desires.

[21] See in general F. Cayré, A.A., *La contemplation augustinienne*, 2nd ed. (Bibliothèque augustinienne, Paris, 1954).

[22] Augustine, *De consensu evangelistarum* I, 5, 8, *CSEL* XLIII, 7 f.: . . . cum duae virtutes propositae sint animae humanae, una activa, altera contemplativa, illa qua itur, ista qua pervenitur, illa qua laboratur, ut cor mundetur ad videndum Deum, ista qua vacatur et videtur Deus: illa est in praeceptis exercendae vitae huius temporalis, ista in doctrina vitae illius sempiternae. Ac per hoc illa operatur, ista requiescit, quia illa est in purgatione

He goes on to explain that the three evangelists of the synoptic Gospels—Matthew, Mark and Luke—have related chiefly the deeds of Christ and those words of His which were most valuable for this present life, whereas St. John, flying as an eagle over the clouds of human infirmity, gazes with the sharp and steadfast eyes of the heart upon the light of unchangeable truth.[23]

In this text both the influence of Greek conceptions and their development in Augustine's own thought are perceptible. Both ways of life are seen in terms of virtue, with the vision of God as the ultimate aim. But active virtue is clearly extended to cover all temporal life, whereas the apex of contemplation is considered as something quite exceptional and in any case incomplete on earth.

Augustine's thought on the active and the contemplative life can be studied also in his *Sermons*, in connection with his exegesis of the Gospel episode of Martha and Mary, which had been paradigmatic in this respect also for Origen, Evagrius, and Cassian.

Christ had said to Martha:

Martha, Martha, thou art careful, and art troubled about many things, but one thing is necessary. . . .[24]

St. Augustine begins his interpretation by saying that Jesus' words

admonish us that there is a certain one thing (*unum aliquid*) toward which we should tend while we labor in this multitudinous world. But we still tend [toward it] like pilgrims, not yet dwelling in it; still on the road, not yet in our fatherland, still in desire, not yet in fruition. Nevertheless, let us tend [there] and let us do so without laziness and interruption that we may some time arrive there.[25]

peccatorum, ista in lumine purgatorum. Ac per hoc in hac vita mortali illa est in opere bonae conversationis, ista vero magis in fide et aput perpaucos per speculum in enigmate (cf. 1 Cor. 13:12) et ex parte in aliqua visione incommutabilis veritatis. See also *ibid.*, *CSEL* LXIII, 8, and *Contra Faustum* XXII, 52 ff., *CSEL* XXV, 1, 645 ff., for Leah and Rachel as types of the active and contemplative lives, For Augustine's doctrine of the vision of God see above pp. 190 ff.

[23] *De consensu evangelistarum* I, 6, 9, *CSEL* XLIII, 9 f.

[24] Luke 10:41 f.

[25] Augustine, *Sermo* CIII, 1, 1, *PL* XXXVIII, 613: Verba Domini nostri Iesu Christi . . . admonent nos esse unum aliquid quo tendamus, quando in huius saeculi multitudine laboramus. Tendimus autem adhuc peregrinantes, nondum manentes; adhuc in via, nondum in patria; adhuc desiderando, nondum fruendo. Tamen tendamus et sine pigritia et sine intermissione tendamus, ut aliquando pervenire valeamus.

The task (*officium*) of Martha as well as that of Mary are good, but that of Mary is better. Why?

Because one thing is necessary, that highest one, the one in which the Father, the Son, and the Holy Spirit are one. . . . True, our God is a Trinity. The Father is not the Son, the Son is not the Father, the Holy Spirit is neither Father nor the Son, but Spirit of both. And yet these three are not three Gods, not three almighties, but one almighty God, the Trinity itself one God. "But one thing is necessary." And He does not lead us to this one, except if we many are of one heart.[26]

This text shows that for Augustine the goal of contemplation is not so much assimilation to God the Father through Christ and the Holy Spirit, but rather union with the whole one Trinity. The road goes from and through multitudinous active life to unified contemplative life. Martha, too, occupied as she is in her many meritorious ministrations, seeks through them nothing but rest in God. That this is so, St. Augustine says, becomes evident as soon as one realizes that in heaven there will no longer be the stranger, the hungry, the thirsty to be cared for, no longer the warring to be placated, the dead to be buried. All this will not be there. What will be there? That which Mary elected as the better part even on earth: the Word of God.[27]

[26] *Ibid.* 3, 4, *PL* XXXVIII, 614 f.: Quia unum est necessarium, unum illud supernum, unum ubi Pater et Filius et Spiritus Sanctus sunt unum. . . . Certe Trinitas est Deus noster. Pater non est Filius, Filius non est Pater, Spiritus Sanctus nec Pater est nec Filius, sed amborum Spiritus: et tamen ista tria non tres dii, non tres omnipotentes, sed unus Deus omnipotens, ipsa Trinitas unus Deus: quia unum necessarium est. Ad hoc unum non nos perducit, nisi multi habeamus cor unum. See also *Sermo Guelferbyt.* XXIX, Morin, *Aug. Serm.* (*Miscell.* Agost. I) 543 ff. (*Sermo* CIV, Lambot, *Aug. Serm. Sel.*, *Strom. Patr. et Med.* I, 54 ff.); *Sermo* CLXIX, 14, 17, *PL* XXXVIII, 925 f.; *Sermo* CLXXIX, 3, 3 to 6, 6, *PL* XXXVIII, 967 ff.

[27] *Sermo* CIII, 5, 6, *PL* XXXVIII, 615: Caeterum tu, Martha, pace tua dixerim, in bono ministerio benedicta, pro isto labore tuo mercedem quaeris quietem. Modo occupata es circa multum ministerium, pascere vis mortalia corpora, licet sanctorum: numquid, cum veneris ad illam patriam, invenies peregrinum quem suscipias hospitio, invenies esurientem cui panem frangas, sitientem cui potum porrigas, aegrum quem visites, litigantem quem concordes, mortuum quem sepelias? Omnia ista tibi non erunt: sed quid ibi erit? Quod Maria elegit . . . hoc ibi erit plenum atque perfectum, quod hic elegit Maria: de illa mensa opulenta, de verbo Domini, micas colligebat. . . . See also the distinction between the active and the contemplative life, carried out in terms of the difference between the Apostles Peter and John, in Augustine's *In Johannis evangelium tractatus* CXXIV, 5 ff., *Corp. Christ.*, *Ser. Lat.* XXXVI, 685 ff. For the rest see the excellent essay by A.-M. la Bonnardière, "Marthe et Marie, figures de l'église," *Vie spir.* LXXXVI (1952) 404, where also the other antithetical types of the active and contemplative life such as Leah and Rachel, etc., are considered.

Once again the antithesis between the divine and the earthly is expressed in terms of unity and multiplicity, a terminology so characteristic of St. Augustine.[28] It is obvious that this manner of thinking will grant relatively more to the active life than can be allowed to it when the concepts of similarity and dissimilarity are used antithetically. Ordered multiplicity (number) can have relative value, dissimilarity cannot.[29]

From these premises Augustine's position with regard to the evaluation of the active and the contemplative life and more specifically with regard to the relationship between monasticism and the Church at large can be understood.

The close connection between Augustine's monastic ideal and his ideas on reform emerges clearly from his life and work. His very conversion in the garden outside Milan was insolubly bound up with his hearing for the first time of Christian monasticism as a radical program of Christian life.[30] It was the example thus given which threw him into the inner crisis which lead to his moral liberation. From that day onward monasticism was for him, too, the perfect form of Christianity.[31] On the other hand, many of Augustine's writings eloquently express his conviction that the true contemplative life, which is a life for God, must flow over into a life of love for man, must issue above all into the apostolic effort of bringing others to the love of God. The City of God, he says, is concerned with man's choice between the different ways of life only in so far as it matters how much each takes for himself by love of truth (*amore veritatis*), how much he gives to others by duty of love (*officio caritatis*).[32]

But none must be in leisure (*otiosus*) in such a way that in that leisure he does not ponder what is useful for his neighbor or be so active (*actuosus*) that he does not seek out the contemplation of God. . . . Love of truth (*caritas veritatis*) therefore seeks holy leisure; necessity of charity (*necessitas caritatis*) accepts just business. . . . And yet, the delight in truth must not thus be given

---

[28] See above, pp. 212 ff.

[29] See above, p. 188, n. 8, about Augustine's concept of the *regio dissimilitudinis*.

[30] See *Confessiones* VIII, 6, 14 ff., Skutella 164 ff.; cf. below, p. 354.

[31] See below, pp. 353 ff.

[32] *De civitate Dei* XIX, 19, Corp. Christ., Ser. Lat. XLVIII, 686.

up altogether lest that sweetness [of truth] be taken away and lest that necessity [of charity] become oppressive.[33]

On earth then there will necessarily be conflict, but a fruitful conflict, between contemplation and the service for others.

For if the minister [of God] is not on fire when he preaches he does not set afire him to whom he preaches.[34]

I for my part . . . like it better to learn than to teach. In this sense we also are admonished by the Apostle James when he says: "And let every man be swift to hear, but slow to speak" (James 1:19). The sweetness of truth then should invite us to learn, the necessities of charity should force us to teach. Yet in this connection it is rather to be wished that this necessity through which man teaches something to man may pass away and we may all become the disciples of God (docibiles Dei); though we really are this [already] if we learn those things which appertain to true piety, even when a man seems to teach them.[35]

An explicit application of Augustine's teaching on action and contemplation to the relation between monastic and nonmonastic Christian life is found in the letter he wrote as a bishop to the abbot and monks of Capraria.

[33] Ibid., XLVIII, 686 f.: Nec sic esse quisque debet otiosus ut in eodem otio utilitatem non cogitet proximi, nec sic actuosus ut contemplationem non requirat Dei. . . . Quam ob rem otium sanctum quaerit caritas veritatis, negotium iustum suscipit necessitas caritatis . . . ; sed nec sic omni modo veritatis delectatio deserenda est ne subtrahatur illa suavitas et opprimat ista necessitas. Augustine here anticipates the later concept of the "mixed life" which is both active and contemplative. His terminology is dependent on Varro and through him on the Cynic elaboration of the contrast between the contemplative and the active ways of life in the sense of a distinction of three ways, the third being ex utroque compositum; see De civitate Dei XIX, 19, Corp. Christ., Ser. Lat. XLVIII, 686: Unde illam quam Varro adhibuit ex Cynicis differentiam, si nihil turpiter atque intemperanter agat, omnino non curat. Ex tribus vero illis vitae generibus, otioso, actuoso et ex utroque composito, quamvis salva fide quisque possit in quolibet eorum vitam ducere et ad sempiterna praemia pervenire, interest tamen quid amore teneat veritatis, quid officio caritatis inpendat.

[34] Augustine, Enarr. in Ps. CIII, sermo II, 4, Corp. Christ., Ser. Lat. XL, 1493: Nisi enim ardeat minister praedicans, non accendit eum cui praedicat.

[35] Augustine, De octo Dulcitii quaestionibus, quaest., 9, 3, 6, PL XL, 160 f.: Ego enim . . . plus amo discere quam docere. Nam hoc admonemur etiam dicente apostolo Iacobo: "Sit autem omnis homo velox ad audiendum, tardus autem ad loquendum" (James 1:19). Ut ergo discamus, invitare nos debet suavitas veritatis; ut autem doceamus, cogere necessitas charitatis. Ubi potius optandum est, ut transeat ista necessitas qua hominem docet aliquid homo, et simus omnes docibiles Dei; quamvis et hoc simus, cum ea quae ad veram pietatem pertinent discimus, etiam quando illa docere videtur homo.

When we think of your tranquility which you have in Christ we, too, though involved in variegated and arduous labors, rest in your charity. For we are one body under one head so that you, too, are busy (*negotiosi*) in us and we are at rest (*otiosi*) in you [in accordance with St. Paul's teaching on the Church as the Body of Christ (1 Cor. 12:26)].

He therefore asks for their prayers; for his own are often weakened by the darkness and the tumult of secular activities into which he as a bishop is drawn to such an extent that he can hardly breathe.

But you, brethren, we exhort in the Lord that . . . if the Church, your mother, should desire your help you do neither accept it with avid elation nor reject it in bland slothfulness, but obey God with a humble heart. . . . And do not prefer your state of rest to the necessities of the Church. For if none of the good were willing to minister to her who gives birth you would not find any way in which you could be born (that is to say, reborn by the Church).[36]

On other occasions Augustine gave further reasons why even in the monastic state full peace and rest are impossible. True, the desert is full of servants of God who if they had liked it among men would not have fled there. And still, even in the desert, others will congregate around the man who wants to be alone, will seek the desert with him, will affect his way of life. Charity will oblige him to allow these to stay with him. Thus he will still be with others among whom there will be those who will try his patience. For in any congregation there will be bad men with whom it is necessary to bear, as Christ bore even with Judas. Thus certain virtues of the active life which are needed by Christian society in general, by the whole terrestrial Church, are after all required also in the monastic state.

[36] Augustine, *Epist.* XLVIII, 1 f., *CSEL* XXXIV, 2, 137 f.: Quando quietem vestram cogitamus, quam habetis in Christo, etiam nos, quamvis in laboribus variis asperisque versemur, in vestra caritate requiescimus. Unum enim corpus sub uno capite sumus, ut et vos in nobis negotiosi et nos in vobis otiosi simus. . . . Admonemus ergo et petimus et obsecramus . . ., ut nostri memores sitis in sanctis orationibus vestris . . .; nostras enim sauciat et debilitat caligo et tumultus saecularium actionum . . ., ut vix respirare possimus, credentes tamen quod ille (that is to say, God) . . . perseverantes nos in eo ministerio, in quo conlocare dignatus est cum promissa mercede, adiuvantibus orationibus vestris ab omni angustia liberabit. Vos autem, fratres, exhortamur in Domino, ut . . . si qua opera vestra mater ecclesia desideraverit, nec elatione avida suscipiatis nec blandiente desidia respuatis, sed miti corde obtemperetis. . . . Nec vestrum otium necessitatibus ecclesiae praeponatis cui parturienti, si nulli boni ministrare vellent, quo modo nasceremini non inveniretis.

For you cannot be separated from the human kind, as long as you live among men.[37]

Such arguments are evidence that for Augustine true monasticism is coenobitical, not hermitical, and also that it is apostolic or, in modern terminology, mixed rather than purely contemplative.

Something of this Augustinian attitude survived in the truly charitable spirit of the early mediaeval western monks—in St. Severin, for instance[38]—and this spirit no doubt helped in converting the barbarian tribes and in the often quite as arduous task of preserving Christianity among the Romans.[39]

[37] See Augustine, Enarr. in Ps. LIV, 9, Corp. Christ., Ser. Lat. XXXIX, 663 f.: Unde enim putatis . . . servis Dei impleta esse deserta? Si bene illis esset inter homines, recederent ab hominibus? Et tamen quid faciunt et ipsi? Ecce elongant fugientes, manent in deserto (cf. Ps. 54:8): sed numquid singillatim? Tenet eos caritas, ut cum multis maneant: et de ipsis multis exsistunt qui exerceant. Quia in omni congregatione multitudinis necesse est, ut inveniantur mali. Deus enim . . . novit . . . necessarium esse nobis, ut feramus malos. . . . Quo iturus es, quo volaturus, ubi requieturus? . . . In quo deserto? Ubicumque fueris, congregabunt se ceteri, desertum tecum petent, affectabunt vitam tuam, tu repellere non potes societatem fratrum, miscentur tibi etiam mali, adhuc tibi exercitatio debetur. . . . Non enim a genere humano separatus esse poteris, quamdiu in hominibus vivis. Adtende potius consolatorem illum Dominum et regem, imperatorem et creatorem nostrum creatum etiam inter nos; adtende quia duodecim suis miscuit unum quem pateretur (i.e., Judas). See also Enarr. in Ps. XCIX, 9, Corp. Christ., Ser. Lat. XXXIX, 1398: Sed quo se separaturus est christianus, ut non gemat inter falsos fratres . . ., and the rest of this sermon.

[38] For the great apostle of late fifth century Noricum, St. Severin, see now the remarkable book by F. Kaphahn, Zwischen Antike und Mittelalter (München, s.a.) 92 ff., also I. Zibermayr, Noricum, Baiern und Österreich (München, Berlin, 1944) 41 ff., R. Noll's introduction to his reprint of Mommsen's edition with German translation of the Vita S. Severini: Eugippius, Das Leben des hl. Severin (Linz a.D., 1947) and E. K. Winter, "The Byzantine Millennium of Vienna," Medievalia et Humanistica X (1956) 7 ff., where more special Severin studies by the author are quoted. Cf. below, p. 382, n. 18.

[39] Cf. also below, pp. 359–365, about Augustine's synthesis of monasticism and the clericate.

CHAPTER II

MONKS, PRIESTS, CONVERSI

1. Hermits, Coenobites, Clerics

The epochal role of St. Pachomius as the founder of coenobitical monasticism has been rightly stressed in recent times.[1] Nevertheless, it remains true that St. Basil the Great laid even deeper spiritual foundations for the common life of monks, as distinct from hermitical monasticism.[2] His reasons for valuing and propagating the ideals of community monasticism were much the same as those given later by St. Augustine under different circumstances:[3]

. . . Christ's precept of charity does not permit the individual to consider [only] what appertains to him. . . .

. . . if all we, who are united in the one hope of our calling,[4] are one body with Christ as our head and are all of us members of one another,[5] if then we were not joined together by union in the Holy Spirit in the harmony of one body, but if each of us should choose to live in solitude and would not serve the common good in a manner pleasing to God but would be fulfilling his own passion of self-satisfaction—how then could we, split off and separated, save the relation and assistance of members to one another or the submission to our head who is Christ? . . .

Consider further that the Lord was not satisfied with instruction by word alone, but so as to transmit to us clearly and exactly the example of humility in the perfection of charity girded Himself and washed the feet of the disciples. Whom, therefore, will you wash, to whom will you minister, compared to whom will you be the lowest, if you live alone? . . .

An arena for combat, a good path of progress, a continual discipline, and a practicing of the Lord's commandments: all this is the dwelling together of brethren in a community. This kind of life has as its goal the glory of God according to the precept of our Lord Jesus Christ who has said: "So let your

---

[1] Cf. H. Bacht, "L'importance de l'idéal monastique de s. Pacôme pour l'histoire du monachisme chrétien," *Rev. ascét. myst.* XXVI (1950) 309 ff.

[2] Cf. also above, pp. 126 f.   [3] See below, pp. 355 ff.

[4] Cf. Eph. 4:4.   [5] Cf. 1 Cor. 12:12.

light shine before men that they may see your good works and glorify your Father who is in heaven" (Matthew 5:16); [this life] maintains also the character traits of the saints whose history the Acts [of the Apostles] relate and about whom it is written: "And all they that believed were together and had all things common" (Acts 2:44) and again: "And all the multitude of believers had but one heart and one soul; neither did anyone say that aught of the things which they possessed was his own, but all things were common unto them" (Acts 4:32).[6]

It would seem that the inner motives of Basil's praise of communal asceticism were connected not only with his higher evaluation of the life of coenobites as compared to that of hermits. Dom J. Gribomont has shown[7] that the ascetics of Asia Minor, such as Eustathius of Sebaste, whom Basil regarded as his master in the ascetic life, and at first even Basil himself, were not yet monks and organizers of monasticism in the sense of St. Anthony and St. Pachomius, but represented a movement of more general radical reform which demanded of all Christians fullest adherence to the evangelical-apostolic way of life.

---

[6] This whole text is contained in Basil's *Longer Rules*. See *Regulae fusius tractatae* VII, 1, PG XXXI, 928D f.: . . . ὁ τῆς ἀγάπης τοῦ Χριστοῦ λόγος οὐκ ἐπιτρέπει τὸ ἴδιον σκοπεῖν ἕκαστον. . . . *Ibid.* VII, 2, XXXI, 929C: Εἰ δὲ καὶ πάντες, οἱ ἐν μιᾷ ἐλπίδι τῆς κλήσεως προσληφθέντες, ἓν σῶμά ἐσμεν, κεφαλὴν ἔχοντες τὸν Χριστόν, ὁ δὲ καθεὶς ἀλλήλων μέλη, ἐὰν μὴ ἐκ συμφωνίας πρὸς ἑνὸς σώματος ἁρμολογίαν ἐν Πνεύματι ἁγίῳ συναρμοσθῶμεν, ἕκαστος δὲ ἡμῶν τὴν μόνωσιν αἱρῆται, μὴ κατὰ τὸ εὐάρεστον τῷ Θεῷ πρὸς τὸ κοινῇ συμφέρον τῇ οἰκονομίᾳ δουλεύων, ἀλλὰ τὸ ἴδιον τῆς αὐταρεσκείας πάθος πληροφορῶν· πῶς δυνάμεθα ἀπεσχισμένοι καὶ διῃρημένοι σώζειν τὴν τῶν μελῶν πρὸς ἄλληλα σχέσιν τε καὶ ὑπηρεσίαν ἢ τὴν ὑποταγὴν πρὸς τὴν κεφαλὴν ἡμῶν ἥτις ἐστιν ὁ Χριστός; *Ibid.* VII, 4, XXXI, 933A ff.: 'Ιδοὺ γὰρ ὁ Κύριος δι' ὑπερβολὴν φιλανθρωπίας οὐκ ἠρκέσθη τῇ ἐκ τοῦ λόγου διδασκαλίᾳ μόνον, ἀλλ' ὥστε ἀκριβῶς καὶ ἐναργῶς ἡμῖν παραδοῦναι τὸ ὑπόδειγμα τῆς ταπεινοφροσύνης ἐν τῇ τελειότητι τῆς ἀγάπης, αὐτὸς περιζωσάμενος ἔνιψε τοὺς πόδας τῶν μαθητῶν. Τίνα οὖν ἀπονίψεις, τίνα θεραπεύσεις, τίνος ἔσχατος ἔσῃ, αὐτὸς καθ' ἑαυτὸν διάγων; . . . Στάδιον οὖν ἀθλήσεως καὶ προκοπῆς εὐοδίᾳ καὶ διηνεκὴς γυμνασία καὶ μελέτη τῶν τοῦ Κυρίου ἐντολῶν καὶ ἐπὶ τὸ αὐτὸ κατοίκησίς ἐστι τῶν ἀδελφῶν· σκοπὸν μὲν ἔχουσα τὴν δόξαν τοῦ Θεοῦ κατ' ἐντολὴν τοῦ Κυρίου ἡμῶν Ἰησοῦ Χριστοῦ εἰπόντος· "Οὕτω λαμψάτω τὸ φῶς ὑμῶν ἔμπροσθεν τῶν ἀνθρώπων ὅπως ἴδωσιν ὑμῶν τὰ καλὰ ἔργα καὶ δοξάσωσι τὸν Πατέρα ὑμῶν τὸν ἐν τοῖς οὐρανοῖς" (Matthew 5:16)· χαρακτῆρα δὲ σώζουσα τῶν ἐν ταῖς Πράξεσιν ἱστορουμένων ἁγίων περὶ ὧν γέγραπται· "Πάντες δὲ οἱ πιστεύοντες ἦσαν ἐπὶ τὸ αὐτὸ καὶ εἶχον ἅπαντα κοινά" (Acts 2:44)· καὶ πάλιν· "Τοῦ δὲ πλήθους τῶν πιστευσάντων ἦν ἡ καρδία καὶ ἡ ψυχὴ μία· καὶ οὐδὲ εἷς τι τῶν ὑπαρχόντων αὐτῷ ἔλεγεν ἴδιον εἶναι, ἀλλ' ἦν αὐτοῖς ἅπαντα κοινά" (Acts 4:32). See also Dom David Amand (de Mendieta), *L'ascèse monastique de saint Basile* (Maredsous, 1948), 120, 122, 124, 127, 128 ff.

[7] J. Gribomont, O.S.B., "Le monachisme au IVe s. en Asie Mineure: de Gangres au Messalianisme," *Stud. Patr.* II, 400 ff., and *idem*, "Les Règles Morales de saint Basile et le Nouveau Testament," *Stud. Patr.* II, 416 ff.

It may be recalled that only a little later St. John Chrysostom tried to reform the Christian societies of Antioch and Constantinople from the same basis; he failed, probably because he attempted to reach out too far beyond the ascetic sphere of influence.[8] But with Basil the ascetic ideal remained foremost and gradually assumed those more institutionalized monastic forms with which we are familiar from the printed text of his ascetical writings.[9] Nevertheless, the less strictly monastic origins of his asceticism make it more easily understandable that he linked his coenobitical idea to the primitive Christian community of Jerusalem, the Church of the Apostles. From St. Basil onward the derivation of coenobitical monasticism from the community of the Apostles was at any rate an important element of early Christian and mediaeval monastic ideology.[10]

John Cassian, for instance, in his eighteenth *Conference* gives an elaborate historical sketch of the development of monasticism which is centered in the *topos* of apostolic origins:

. . .the discipline of the coenobites has its origins in the times of the preaching of the Apostles. . . . The whole Church was then in such a condition as can be found now only with difficulty in a very few, in monasteries (*coenobiis*).[11]

After the death of the Apostles, Cassian continues, the faithful began to become less fervent, not least because of the influx of converted pagans. The belief then arose that concessions made to the weakness of the latter held good for all Christians.

But those in whom the apostolic fervor was still alive remembered that pristine perfection. They left their cities and the company of those who

---

[8] See above, pp. 125–130.

[9] For successive stages in the corpus of Basil's ascetical writings and for the manuscripts which represent this development cf. J. Gribomont, O.S.B., *Histoire du texte des Ascétiques de s. Basile* (Bibliothèque du Muséon XXXII, Louvain, 1953) 323 ff.

[10] As such it appears already in a work of John Chrysostom, still belonging to his early, monastic, phase (cf. above, p. 126, n. 51); in a development inverse to that of Basil, Chrysostom was later to hold up the life of the Apostles as a model for the whole Church; see above, p. 128.

[11] Cassian, *Conlationes* XVIII, 5, 1 f., *CSEL* XIII, 509 f.: Itaque coenobiotarum disciplina a tempore praedicationis apostolicae sumpsit exordium. Nam talis extitit in Hierosolymis omnis illa credentium multitudo, quae in Actibus Apostolorum ita describitur . . . (there follow quotations from Acts 4:32, 2:45, 4:34 f.). . . . Talis, inquam, erat tunc omnis ecclesia, quales nunc perpaucos in coenobiis invenire difficile est. Cf. also *Institutiones* VII, 17, *CSEL* XVII, 140 ff.

believed that the negligence of a relaxed life was allowed to them and to the Church of God. They began to dwell in suburban and more hidden places and to practice privately and for themselves what they remembered to have been instituted by the Apostles for the entire body of the Church generally. . . . Gradually, in the course of time, these, segregated from the crowd of believers, were named monks (*monachi*) or μονάζοντες from their obligation to an isolated (*singularis*) and solitary life, since they abstained from marriage and had separated themselves from the company of their relatives and the way of life of the world. As a further consequence, they were called coenobites (*coenobiotae*) from their common life and their cells and dwelling places *coenobia*. This alone, therefore, was the oldest genus of monks, which is the first not only in time, but also in grace. . . .[12]

From the number of these perfect men and from this most prolific root as it were there came forth later the flowers and fruit of the anchorites or hermits.[13]

[12] *Conlationes* XVIII, 5, 2 ff., *CSEL* XIII, 510 f.: Sed cum apostolorum excessu tepescere coepisset credentium multitudo, ea vel maxime quae ad fidem Christi de alienigenis ac diversis gentibus confluebat, a quibus apostoli pro ipsis fidei rudimentis et inveterata gentilitatis consuetudine nihil amplius expectabant nisi "ut ab inmolaticiis idolorum et fornicatione et suffocatis et sanguine" (cf. Acts 15:29) temperarent, atque ista libertas, quae gentibus propter infirmitatem primae credulitatis indulta est, etiam illius ecclesiae perfectionem, quae Hierosolymis consistebat, paulatim contaminare coepisset et crescente cotidie vel indigenarum numero vel advenarum primae illius fidei refrigesceret fervor, non solum hi, qui ad fidem Christi confluxerant, verum etiam illi, qui erant ecclesiae principes, ab illa districtione laxati sunt. Nonnulli enim existimantes id, quod videbant gentibus pro infirmitate concessum, sibi etiam licitum, nihil se detrimenti perpeti crediderunt, si cum substantiis ac facultatibus suis fidem Christi confessionemque sequerentur. Hi autem, quibus adhuc apostolicus inerat fervor, memores illius pristinae perfectionis discedentes a civitatibus suis illorumque consortio, qui sibi vel ecclesiae Dei remissioris vitae negligentiam licitam esse credebant, in locis suburbanis ac secretioribus conmanere et ea, quae ab apostolis per universum corpus ecclesiae generaliter meminerant instituta, privatim ac peculiariter exercere coeperunt: atque ita coaluit ista, quam diximus, discipulorum, qui se ab illorum contagio sequestraverunt, disciplina. Qui paulatim tempore procedente segregati a credentium turbis, ab eo quod a coniugiis abstinerent et a parentum se consortio mundique istius conversatione secernerent, monachi sive μονάζοντες a singularis ac solitariae vitae districtione nominati sunt. Unde consequens fuit, ut ex communione consortii coenobiotae cellaeque ac diversoria eorum coenobia vocarentur. Istud ergo solummodo fuit antiquissimum monachorum genus, quod non solum tempore, sed etiam gratia primum est quodque per annos plurimos inviolabile usque ad abbatis Pauli vel Antoni duravit aetatem: cuius etiam nunc adhuc in districtis coenobiis cernimus residere vestigia.

[13] *Ibid.* XVIII, 6, 1, XIII, 511: De hoc perfectorum numero et, ut ita dixerim, fecundissima radice sanctorum etiam anachoretarum post haec flores fructusque prolati sunt. . . .

In the following *Conference* Cassian discusses the end and value of both the coenobitical and the anchoretic or hermitical life. The essence of the latter state he calls here *theoretica puritas*, that purity which is the presupposition for the vision of God and for the union of the mind with Christ. With regard to the former, he mentions especially the full renunciation of the monk's own will, that mortification and crucifixion of the will which is inseparable from the communal monastic life, which is here significantly called *conversatio communis* rather than *actualis*.[14] Though Cassian does not mention it here, it is quite clear that in the monastic way of life the highest grade: *theoretica puritas* or the hermit's contemplation, and the second highest grade: *conversatio actualis* or *communis* or the practical life of the coenobites, can follow only after a first step, *conversio* to monasticism, has been taken. *Conversio, converti* in this sense occur in the *Conlationes* on several occasions.[15] In Cassian's time these words as well as the expression *conversus* are just beginning to assume the meaning of monastic or near-monastic reform terms.[16] In Cassian's third *Conference* there is clear correspondence between the three steps of conversion, praxis, theoria, and

---

[14] *Ibid.* XIX, 8, 3 f., XIII, 542 f.: Finis quidem coenobiotae est omnes suas mortificare et crucifigere voluntates ac secundum evangelicae perfectionis salutare mandatum nihil de crastino cogitare. . . . Heremitae vero perfectio est exutum mentem a cunctis habere terrenis eamque quantum humana inbecillitas valet sic unire cum Christo. . . . *Ibid.* XIX, 9, 1 f., XIII, 543 f.: . . . in utraque professione per omnia consummatum invenire difficile est, quia nec anachoreta ἀκτημοσύνην, id est contemptum ac privationem materialem rerum, nec coenobiota theoreticam ad integrum potest adsequi puritatem . . . (with the exception, however, of some great monks of whom it could be doubted *utrum in illa heremitica puritate an in ista conversatione communi magnanimitas eorum mirabilius aptaretur*). For the term *conversatio communis* see immediately below.

[15] See especially *Conlationes* XXIV, 1, 3, XIII, 675, and 13, 4–6, XIII, 689 f. I cannot agree with F. Friedrich, O.S.B., "Conversatio Morum: Das zweite Gelübde des Benediktinermönches," *Studien und Mitteilungen zur Geschichte des Benediktiner-Ordens und seiner Zweige* LIX (1941) 224 ff., when he asserts that Cassian never spoke of *conversio*, always of *conversatio*; it is true that the evidence of the manuscripts and the sense of the text should often have led the editor of the *Conlationes* in *CSEL* to choose *conversatio* rather than *conversio* in establishing the text.

[16] Cf. L. Th. A. Lorié, S.J., *Spiritual Terminology in the Latin Translations of the Vita Antonii* (Latinitas Christianorum Primaeva XI, Nijmegen, 1955) 94 ff. As well known, the increasing vogue of the term *conversio* in the sense of *monastic* conversion brought about the substitution of *conversio* for *conversatio* in crucial parts of the *Rule of St. Benedict* at least since the eighth century. Cf. Dom C. Butler, O.S.B., *Benedictine Monachism* (London, etc., 1924) 134 ff, Dom C. Chapman, O.S.B., *Saint Benedict and the Sixth Century* (New York, etc., 1929) 207 ff., Dom J. McCann, O.S.B., *Saint Benedict* (London, 1938) 149 ff.

the three monastic *abrenuntiationes* of which the first means a renouncing of the "world" with its riches and opportunities, the second a renouncing of all evil habits and inclinations of body and mind, the third a renouncing of everything present and visible in concentrated desire for the invisible celestial things to come.[17]

These Cassianic texts not only show an adaptation to monastic reform ideology of such basic Christian concepts as conversion and contemplation, but also significantly combine the idea of the practice of virtues (*conversatio actualis*, πρακτική) with that of the common life in the term *conversatio communis*. The elements of this composite expression are scriptural *conversatio*, meaning in most instances "way of life,"[18] and the *communia* of the Acts of the Apostles, meaning community of goods and of life.[19] While one part of this combination, *conversatio*, was to become of utmost importance for Benedictine monastic reform ideology, since the *Rule of St. Benedict* in one of its three vows demands *conversatio morum*, "a life of virtue,"[20] the other part, which may be designated as *vita communis*, essential already for St. Basil's conception of the coenobitic life, also formed the core of the monastic idea of St. Augustine, who, furthermore, as a bishop extended the ideal of the common life to his clergy.

[17] See *Conlationes* III, 6, *CSEL* XIII, 73 f., and cf. above, p. 332, n. 13.

[18] Of special importance for ascetic-monastic and mystical ideology is the Pauline text Phil. 3:20: *nostra autem conversatio* (πολίτευμα) *in caelis est*. See, for instance, Ambrose, *De virginitate* 10, 59, Cazzaniga 28: . . . te docuit quemadmodum in caelo stare possis, cum dicit: "Nostra autem conversatio in caelis est," conversatio morum, conversatio factorum, conversatio fidei (quoted by Friedrich, "Conversatio Morum" 259). Cassian, *Conlationes* III, 6, 4, *CSEL* XIII, 74, has a non-Vulgate translation for πολίτευμα: *municipatus* instead of *conversatio* (cf. also Tertullian, *De corona* 13, 4, *Corp. Christ.*, *Ser. Lat.* II, 1061); this is of interest in connection with the development of western *civitas Dei* ideology; cf. p. 247, n. 40. Where Cassian uses the term *conversatio*, he derives it no doubt from other scriptural texts, e.g. 1 Tim. 4:12, Hebr. 13:7, 1 Peter 3:1 (where *conversatio* is translation of ἀναστροφή).

[19] See above, p. 343, n. 11.

[20] *S. Benedicti Regula* 58, 26, Linderbauer 64; see also *ibid*. 58, 2, Linderbauer 63. For the meaning of the term cf. Friedrich, "Conversatio Morum" 200 ff., where the older studies of Abbot I. Herwegen and Dom Rothenhäusler are discussed; see also Ph. Schmitz, O.S.B., article "Conversatio (conversio) morum," *DSpir*, fasc. XIV–XV, 2206 ff., and P. Hörger, O.S.B., "«Initium Conversationis»," *Benedictus, der Vater des Abendlandes*, 547–1947 (München, 1947) 213 ff. Cf. Ph. Oppenheim, O.S.B., "Mönchsweihe und Taufritus: Ein Kommentar zur Auslegung bei Dionysius dem Areopagiten," in *Miscell. Mohlberg* I, 259 ff., for the relation between monastic and baptismal renewal.

In the closely related *Sermons* CCCLV and CCCLVI, *On the Life and Behavior of His Clergy*,[21] St. Augustine quotes at length and discusses fully the entire text from the fourth chapter of the Acts of the Apostles,[22] in which the life of the primitive Christian community of Jerusalem is described. These sermons, apart from the fact that they are among the most personal and stirring monuments of the saint's preaching, are very interesting also because they show how the Bishop Augustine used the example of apostolic Jerusalem to impose the monastic way of life on the clergy of his Church. They mark an event of prime importance in the history of monasticism: they are documents of the "monastization" of the clergy.

In order to appreciate this development, which will be studied in the next chapter, especially from these sermons and from some other writings of St. Augustine, it is necessary to realize clearly that early monasticism, whether coenobitical or hermitical, was essentially a monasticism of lay people, that is to say, of men not in clerical orders[23] and of consecrated virgins or nuns. This can be seen from every page of the lives and histories of the early monks. Whether intentionally or merely as a matter of fact, this state of affairs was to some extent a reaction against increasing worldliness in the Church, the clergy not excluded.[24]

A change came with some of the great bishops of the late fourth century who had been monks before they accepted, often very reluctantly, the responsibilities of the priesthood and the episcopate, which were

---

[21] See below, pp. 359–361.   [22] Acts 4:31–35.

[23] Cf. H. Bacht, S.J., "Die Rolle des orientalischen Mönchtums in den kirchenpolitischen Auseinandersetzungen um Chalkedon (431–519)," in *Das Konzil von Chalkedon*, edd. A. Grillmeier, S.J., and H. Bacht, S.J., II (Würzburg, 1953) 300 ff., L. Ueding, "Die Kanones von Chalkedon und ihre Bedeutung für Mönchtum und Klerus," *ibid.* 573. The percentage of priests and clerics in fourth and fifth century eastern Christian monasteries, though not negligible (cf. Bacht, "Orientalisches Mönchtum" 301 ff.), remained relatively small. On the other hand see below, p. 348, for the establishment of a semi-clerical status of the monks by the Council of Chalcedon.

[24] See, for instance, Jerome, *Epist.* XIV, *ad Heliodorum*, 9, CSEL LIV, 57 f., where he warns of the dangers of the clerical state and says: Non omnes episcopi episcopi. . . . Probet se unusquisque et sic accedat. Non facit ecclesiastica dignitas Christianum. . . . Cf. the text from Cassian, quoted above, p. 344, n. 12; see also his famous sentence in *Institutiones* XI, 18, CSEL XVII, 203: . . . haec est antiquitus patrum permanens nunc usque sententia . . . omnimodis monachum fugere debere mulieres et episcopos. Neuter enim sinit eum, quem semel suae familiaritati devinxerit, vel quieti cellae ulterius operam dare vel divinae theoriae per sanctarum rerum intuitum purissimis oculis inhaerere.

particularly grave and complex in that period. Basil of Caesarea is one of the first in the east and one of the most imposing of these ascetics on episcopal thrones who tried to maintain as far as possible a monastic way of life even as bishops. And yet, St. Basil's monasteries were for lay men; clerics within a monastic community were to remain exceptions for a long time to come. Only a short time after St. Basil, another monk and bishop, St. John Chrysostom, in his widely read work *On the Priesthood* presupposes that a monk is not ordinarily a priest and indeed sets the priest and bishop high above all other members of the Church, even above the monks.[25]

The distinct functions of monks and clerics were in any case recognized and maintained at least theoretically in the west as well as in the east, notwithstanding the western tendency toward "monastization" of the clergy, which will be discussed more fully later. "For different is the cause of the monks from that of the clerics," says St. Jerome.[26] The monastic legislation of the Council of Chalcedon treats the monastic state as semiclerical, as distinct from both the clerical and the lay condition.[27]

Ps.-Dionysius the Areopagite continued the glorification of both priests and monks. There is no longer any question but that the priesthood has the higher and the episcopate the highest rank in the ecclesiastical hierarchy, which in its entirety tends toward the familiar terminus of Greek patristic thought: the deification ($\theta \acute{\epsilon} \omega \sigma \iota \varsigma$) of man, consisting in his assimilation ($\acute{o}\mu o \acute{\iota} \omega \sigma \iota \varsigma$) to, and union ($\acute{\epsilon} \nu \omega \sigma \iota \varsigma$) with,

[25] See above, p. 126.

[26] Cf. Jerome, *Epist.* XIV, *ad Heliodorum*, 8, CSEL LIV, 55: Sed alia . . . monachi causa est, alia clericorum.

[27] Council of Chalcedon, canon 4, Schwartz, *Acta Concil. Oecum.* II, I, 2, 159 (355): Οἱ ἀληθῶς καὶ εἰλικρινῶς τὸν μονήρη μετιόντες βίον τῆς προσηκούσης ἀξιούσθωσαν τιμῆς· ἐπειδὴ δὲ τινὲς τῷ μοναχικῷ κεχρημένοι προσχήματι τάς τε ἐκκλησίας καὶ τὰ πολιτικὰ διαταράτ-τουσι πράγματα περιιόντες ἀδιαφόρως ἐν ταῖς πόλεσιν, οὐ μὴν ἀλλὰ καὶ μοναστήρια ἑαυτοῖς συνιστᾶν ἐπιτηδεύοντες, ἔδοξεν μηδένα μὲν μηδαμοῦ οἰκοδομεῖν μηδὲ συνιστᾶν μοναστήριον ἢ εὐκτήριον οἶκον παρὰ γνώμην τοῦ τῆς πόλεως ἐπισκόπου, τοὺς δὲ καθ᾽ ἑκάστην πόλιν καὶ χώραν μονάζοντας ὑποτετάχθαι τῷ ἐπισκόπῳ καὶ τὴν ἡσυχίαν ἀσπάζεσθαι καὶ προσέχειν μόνῃ τῇ νηστείᾳ καὶ τῇ προσευχῇ, ἐν οἷς τόποις ἀπετάξαντο, προσκατερούντας, μήτε δὲ ἐκκλησιαστικοῖς μήτε βιωτικοῖς παρενοχλεῖν πράγμασιν ἢ ἐπικοινωνεῖν καταλιμπάνοντας τὰ ἴδια μοναστήρια, εἰ μή ποτε ἄρα ἐπιτραπεῖεν διὰ χρείαν ἀναγκαίαν ὑπὸ τοῦ τῆς πόλεως ἐπισκόπου . . . τὸν μέντοι ἐπίσκοπον τῆς πόλεως χρὴ τὴν δέουσαν πρόνοιαν ποιεῖσθαι τῶν μοναστηρίων. See also T. P. McLaughlin, C.S.B., *Le très ancien droit monastique de l'occident* (Archives de la France monastique XXXVIII, Ligugé and Paris, 1935) 112 f., 130 ff.

God within the limits of the possible.[28] This is the aim of monks as well as of priests and bishops and indeed of all Christians. Yet, while the monastic state is the most perfect only among those who are to be sanctified,[29] the episcopal is the most perfect among those who sanctify, the clergy.[30] The very fact that the making of a monk is conceived of as a *mysterion*, as a quasi-sacramental ordination,[31] makes him subject to the ecclesiastical hierarchy in which his position must at least in theory be below that of the cleric.[32] One might say that in eastern

[28] Ps.-Dionysius, *De ecclesiastica hierarchia* I, 3, *PG* III, 373C–376A: . . . οὗτως ἱεράρχην ὁ λέγων δηλοῖ τὸν ἔνθεόν τε καὶ θεῖον ἄνδρα, τὸν πάσης ἱερᾶς ἐπιστήμονα γνώσεως, ἐν ᾧ καὶ καθαρῶς ἡ κατ᾽ αὐτὸν ἱεραρχία πᾶσα τελεῖται καὶ γινώσκεται. . . . Ἡ δὲ θέωσίς ἐστιν ἡ πρὸς Θεὸν ὡς ἐφικτὸν ἀφομοίωσίς τε καὶ ἕνωσις. . . .

[29] *De ecclesiastica hierarchia* VI, 1, 3, *PG* III, 532C f.: Ἡ δὲ τῶν τελουμένων ἁπασῶν ὑψηλοτέρα τάξις ἡ τῶν μοναχῶν ἐστιν ἱερὰ διακόσμησις, πᾶσαν μὲν ἀποκεκαθαρμένην κάθαρσιν . . . καὶ ταῖς τῶν ἱεραρχῶν τελειωτικαῖς δυνάμεσιν ἐγχειριζομένη καὶ ταῖς ἐνθέοις αὐτῶν ἐλλάμψεσι καὶ . . . ἱερῶν τελετῶν ἱερουργίαις καὶ πρὸς τῆς ἱερᾶς αὐτῶν ἐπιστημῆς ἀναλόγως εἰς τελειοτάτην ἀναγομένη τελείωσιν. Ἔνθεν οἱ θεῖοι καθηγεμόνες ἡμῶν ἐπονυμῶν αὐτοὺς ἱερῶν ἠξίωσαν. . . . Cf. also *ibid*. VI, 3, 2, III, 533D ff.

[30] *Ibid.* V, 1, 5, III, 505A f.: Οὐκοῦν ἡ θεία τῶν ἱεραρχῶν τάξις πρώτη μὲν ἔστι τῶν θεοπτικῶν τάξεων ἀκροτάτη δὲ καὶ ἐσχάτη πάλιν ἡ αὐτή, καὶ γὰρ εἰς αὐτὴν ἀποτελεῖται καὶ ἀποπληροῦται πᾶσα τῆς καθ᾽ ἡμᾶς ἱεραρχίας ἡ διακόσμησις. Ὡς γὰρ ἅπασαν ἱεραρχίαν ὁρῶμεν εἰς τὸν Ἰησοῦν ἀποπεραιουμένην, οὗτως ἑκάστην εἰς τὸν οἰκεῖον ἔνθεον ἱεράρχην.

[31] *Ibid.* VI, 2, III, 533A f., chapter heading: Μυστήριον μοναχικῆς τελειώσεως. For the relation between monks and clerics and the "sacrament of monastic consacration" according to Ps.-Dionysius cf. R. Roques, *L'univers dionysien* (Théologie XXIX, Paris, 1954) 176 ff., 187 ff., 284 ff. See also K. Holl, *Enthusiasmus und Bussgewalt beim griechischen Mönchtum* (Leipzig, 1898) 205 ff., J. Hörmann, *Untersuchungen zur griechischen Laienbeicht* (Donauwörth, 1913) 70 ff., Oppenheim, "Mönchsweihe" 259 ff., about entry into the monastic state as a *mysterion*, as a second baptism (cf. also below, pp. 350 ff., about monastic *conversio* in the west).

[32] Cf. Roques 191, Holl 209 ff., especially with regard to Ps.-Dionysius, *De ecclesiastica hierarchia* VI, 3, 1, *PG* III, 533C, and *Epist.* VIII, *ad Demophilum*, 2, *PG* III, 1092B–D. While the ancient tradition of the angelic life of the virgins, ascetics, and monks (see above, p. 326) was not lost, the Ps.-Dionysian parallelism of the ecclesiastical and celestial hierarchies could not fail to shed angelic lustre on the clergy. This probably is also the meaning of the beautiful *Cherubic Hymn*, sung in the Byzantine liturgy at the Great Entrance of the clergy since the late sixth century: Οἱ τὰ χερουβὶμ μυστικῶς εἰκονίζοντες καὶ τῇ ζωοποιῷ Τριάδι τὸν τρισάγιον ὕμνον προσᾴδοντες πᾶσαν τὴν βιωτικὴν ἀποθώμεθα μέριμναν. Ὡς τὸν βασιλέα τῶν ὅλων ὑποδεξόμενοι ταῖς ἀγγελικαῖς ἀοράτως δορυφορούμενον τάξεσιν ἀλληλούϊα, ἀλληλούϊα, ἀλληλούϊα (cf. F. E. Brightman, *Liturgies Eastern and Western* I [Oxford, 1896] 377 ff., E. Wellesz, *A History of Byzantine Music and Hymnography* [Oxford, 1949] 139). Already St. John Chrysostom had compared the priests to angels (see above, p. 126, n. 52). For the history of the idea of the angelic character of the priesthood cf. F. Baethgen, "Der Engelspapst," *Schriften der Königsberger Gelehrten Gesellschaft*, Geisteswiss. Klasse, X, 2 (1933) 114 ff.

Christendom by the middle of the fifth century monasticism itself had become "hieraticized" and that this development was made only more apparent by the practice of choosing bishops mostly from the ranks of the monks.[33]

2. St. Augustine's Conception of the Monastic and the Clerical Life

In the west, on the contrary, from the late fourth century onward, one meets with efforts toward "monastization" of the clergy, and this in spite of considerable resistance to monasticism on the part of a number of bishops and priests.[1] It is not only that monk-bishops such as Martin of Tours, Paulinus of Nola, and Augustine himself continued their ascetic or monastic habits of life after having become bishops,[2] as Basil of Caesarea did in the east;[3] even more important is the emergence of the "common life," *vita communis*, of bishops, priests, and clerics at certain churches.[4] This way of life, though not monastic

[33] See Bacht, "Orientalisches Mönchtum" 302 ff., Ueding, "Chalkedon" 592, n. 104. Cf. below, pp. 354, 392. ff., also for the somewhat different development in the west, even though there, too, monks were often raised to the episcopate.

[1] Thus, for instance, St. Martin of Tours encountered considerable antagonism to his combination of the episcopate with the monastic life (on which cf. p. 351); see Sulpicius Severus, *Vita S. Martini* 9, 3, CSEL I, 119. In general, cf. A. Hauck, *Kirchengeschichte Deutschlands* I (Leipzig, 1922) 54 ff., Helen R. Bitterman, "The Beginning of the Struggle between the Regular and the Secular Clergy," in *Medieval and Historiographical Studies in Honor of James Westfall Thompson* (Chicago, 1938) 19 ff. Well known are Helvidius' and Jovinian's attacks against ascetics and monks, to which St. Jerome reacted so vigorously.

[2] See in general E. Spreitzenhofer, O.S.B., *Die Entwicklung des alten Mönchtums in Italien von seinen ersten Anfängen bis zum Auftreten des heil. Benedict* (Wien, 1894); for Paulinus of Nola, cf. P. Fabre, *Saint Paulin de Nole et l'amitié chrétienne* (Bibliothèque des Ecoles Françaises d'Athènes et de Rome CLXVII, Paris, 1949) 39 ff. Pope Innocent I (died 417) made it a law that a monk who was ordained to clerical rank must continue his monastic way of life; cf. *Epist.* II, to Victricius of Rouen, 10 f. (13) PL XX, 477A. See now also P. R. Oliger, O.F.M., *Les évêques réguliers* (Museum Lessianum, Sect. Histor. XVIII, Paris, Louvain, 1958).

[3] For St. Basil, see Gregory Nazianzen, *Oratio* XLIII, 60–62, PG XXXVI, 573C ff.

[4] This is probable for Eusebius of Vercelli and certain for Augustine; see below. For Paulinus of Nola, cf. Spreitzenhofer 21, Fabre 47. Perhaps, a remark by St. Jerome about the clergy of Aquileia also belongs in this context, cf. his *Chronicon*, GCS, *Euseb.* VII (2nd ed.) 247: Aquileienses clerici quasi chorus beatorum habentur. There is a possible reference to clerics living in *vita communis* in *Epist.* I, 6, 7 of Pope Siricius, to Bishop Himerius of Tarragona, of 385, PL XIII, 1137C.

in the technical sense, often approached the monastic status to a high degree.[5]

In order to understand the efforts of the bishop Augustine to fuse the monastic and clerical ways of life at his cathedral church of Hippo, they must be seen against the background of the remotely related, but not identical, attempt of his older contemporary St. Martin of Tours and of the more closely similar antecedent of Vercelli.

St. Martin, the great Gallic bishop and saint of Roman military and eastern hermitical origins, could not bear life in the episcopal residence at Tours. He retired as often as he could to a hermit's cell outside the city, where gradually other monks joined him.[6] Thus the equivalent of an eastern Christian "Laura" was formed;[7] but it seems that this monastic colony had no direct relation to the urban clergy of the cathedral of Tours, even though not a few of the Martinian monks became priests and bishops.[8] This is quite in keeping with the situation in the east. Though it was not rare that monks were ordained priests or became bishops, there is no indication that St. Basil or, with one exception, any other eastern bishop introduced the monastic ideal among their diocesan clergy; neither on the other hand did any of them successfully subordinate the monastic purpose to the way of life of the whole

[5] For the fact that clerical and monastic institutions were not always clearly distinct from one another in Christian Antiquity and the early Middle Ages, see also below, pp. 386 ff.

[6] See Sulpicius Severus, *Vita S. Martini* 10, 2 ff., CSEL I, 120: . . . ita . . . inplebat episcopi dignitatem, ut non tamen propositum monachi virtutemque desereret. Aliquandiu ergo adhaerenti ad ecclesiam cellula usus est; dein, cum inquietudinem se frequentantium ferre non posset, duobus fere extra civitatem milibus monasterium sibi statuit. Qui locus tam secretus et remotus erat, ut eremi solitudinem non desideraret . . . ipse ex lignis contextam cellulam habebat multique ex fratribus in eundem modum. . . . Discipuli fere octoginta erant, qui ad exemplum beati magistri instituebantur. Nemo ibi quicquam proprium habebat, omnia in medium conferebantur (cf. Acts 4 : 32 and 4 :34). Non emere aut vendere, ut plerisque monachis moris est, quicquam licebat. . . .

[7] The monastery of Marmoutier grew later out of it.

[8] See Sulpicius Severus, *Vita S. Martini* 10, 9, CSEL I, 120: . . . pluresque ex eis postea episcopos vidimus. Quae enim esset civitas aut ecclesia quae non sibi de Martini monasterio cuperet sacerdotem? Pope Siricius did not oppose this development, but in his letter (quoted above, p. 350, n. 4) c. 13, 17, PL XIII, 1144 f., warns that monks should not ascend to the episcopate *saltu*, but remain in the lower ranks of the clergy for the periods prescribed.

Church.[9] The exception is the clerico-monastic community founded in the early fourth century by the monk-bishop Melas of Rhinokurura in Southern Palestine, where according to Sozomenus the clerics "had in common their dwelling, their table, and everything else."[10]

Whether or not Bishop Eusebius of Vercelli, who usually is considered the initiator of the clerico-monastic life in the west, knew of the eastern example, St. Ambrose's enthusiastic description of that saint's way of life leaves little doubt that he lived in *vita communis* with his clergy.[11] Of Ambrose himself it is certain that he founded monasteries and directed one of them: the one which Augustine mentions as flourishing *sub Ambrosio nutritore*;[12] since, however, this monastery was outside the walls of Milan, it probably was not closely connected with the bishop's church and there is no definite evidence that it was clerical. While the possibility that Augustine's conception of a mo-

---

[9] For St. John Chrysostom's attempts in that direction cf. pp. 127 ff. For an extreme example of separateness of the monastic life from the Church see a letter probably wrongly attributed to St. Basil: *Epist.* XLII, 4 f., *PG* XXXII, 353C ff. (the content seems to deny Basil's authorship and to indicate a hermitic milieu; so also W. K. L. Clarke, *St. Basil the Great* [Cambridge, 1913] 111; in one manuscript this piece is said to be ascribed by some to Nilus of Ancyra; cf. R. J. Deferrari, *Saint Basil: The Letters* [Loeb Classical Library, London, 1926] I, 240 f., also for the inclusion of this "letter" in manuscripts of Basil's homilies, which links the question of its authenticity to the manuscript tradition of the homilies); in this text, quoted by Holl, *Enthusiasmus* 169, the hermit is advised not to be deceived by the pretence of spiritual advantage, which he may hope to gain from sharing in the πνευματικαὶ πανηγύρεις of the bishops' churches. See also the pithy remarks of Cassian, quoted above, p. 347, n. 24. For the fact that, nevertheless, priests and above all bishops were often taken from the monks, both in the east and in the west, cf. Ueding, "Chalkedon," 575 f., 592, also above, pp. 347 f., 350, and below, pp. 354, 392 ff.

[10] Sozomenus, *Historia ecclesiastica* VI, 31, ed. R. Hussey, II (Oxford, 1860) 645. The rareness of the *vita communis* among the eastern Christian clergy is no doubt connected with the fact that contrary to the west the east did not insist on general clerical celibacy, though it became the rule for bishops and higher clergy.

[11] See Ambrose, *Epist.* LXIII, 66, *PL* XVI, 1258B ff.: . . . in Vercellensi ecclesia, ubi duo pariter exigi videntur ab episcopo, monasterii continentia et disciplina ecclesiae. Haec enim primus in occidentis partibus diversa inter se Eusebius sanctae memoriae coniunxit; ut et in civitate positus instituta monachorum teneret et ecclesiam regeret ieiunii sobrietate. Multum enim adiumenti accedit ad sacerdotis gratiam, si ad studium abstinentiae et ad normam integritatis iuventutem astringat et vernantes intra urbem abdicet usu urbis et conversatione. See also *ibid.* 71 ff., XVI, 1260C ff., where Ambrose compares with one another and praises the clerical office and the monastic institute, not without the usual reference to the angelic character of the ascetic life. Cf. also below, p. 362, n. 61.

[12] See Augustine, *Confessiones* VIII, 6, 15, Skutella 165.

nastic clergy was influenced by St. Ambrose and through him by St. Eusebius of Vercelli cannot be excluded, such an assumption is not necessary. For Augustine's whole life since his conversion was in one sense a "monastic itinerary"[13] and the monastic impulse of his nature must have been a very personal one. A good deal of it was due to Augustine's strong need for friendship, for the sharing of the deepest interests of his soul with like-minded friends. This urge goes back to the time of his early youth in Carthage[14] and it reached its first maturity in the intellectually and spiritually fruitful days of Cassiciacum.[15] The Cassiciacum dialogues—*Adversus academicos*,[16] *De beata vita*,[17] *De ordine*[18]—are documents not only of Augustine's own thought, but also of the give and take of minds in a circle of friends which really existed.[19] The same is true of most of the works written soon after Augustine's baptism, in Milan, Rome, and during his first African years: *De musica*,[20] *De quantitate animae*,[21] *De libero arbitrio*,[22] and *De magistro*.[23] All these writings are comparable in this respect to the great prototype of such works, the Platonic dialogues.[24] The inner relation to them goes beyond the literary (dialogue) form and beyond the intellectual influence of Platonism on St. Augustine. In *De ordine*, especially, one finds a mood not unlike Plato's philosophical ἔρως and μανία. In all these Augustinian dialogues there is a human and humanistic element of mutual inspiration and spiritual contact between master and disciples, ordered as in Plato toward the pursuit of the highest

[13] Cf. M. Mellet, O.P., *L'itinéraire et l'idéal monastique de saint Augustin* (Paris, 1934), P. Monceaux, "Saint Augustin et saint Antoine," *Miscell. Agost.* II, 61 ff., U. Moricca, "Spunti polemici di Sant' Agostino contro i nemici e i falsi interpreti del suo ideale monastico," *Miscell. Agost.* II, 933 ff., A. Zumkeller, O.E.S.A., *Das Mönchtum des heiligen Augustinus* (Würzburg, 1950).

[14] *Confessiones* IV, 8, 13 f., Skutella 63 f.

[15] *Confessiones* VIII and IX, Skutella 152 ff., 179 ff.

[16] *CSEL* XLIII, 3 ff.   [17] *CSEL* LXIII, 89 ff.

[18] *CSEL* XLIII, 121 ff.

[19] Cf. F. Poulsen, "Saint Augustin et ses élèves," *Hommages à Joseph Bidez et à Franz Cumont* = Collection Latomus II (Bruxelles, s. a.) 271 ff. The dialogues may nevertheless be in part fiction; cf. J. J. O'Meara, "The Historicity of the Early Dialogues of Saint Augustine," *Vigil. Christ.* V (1951) 150 ff.

[20] *PL* XXXII, 1081 ff.   [21] *PL* XXXII, 1035 ff.

[22] *CSEL* LXXIV.   [23] *PL* XXXII, 1193 ff.

[24] In the early African works the dialogue form, though still extant, gradually becomes less important for the structure of the treatises. Even before his return to Africa Augustine wrote the *Soliloquia* (in 387), *PL* XXXII, 869 ff., where he is alone with himself and with God.

good,[25] only for Augustine and his friends this highest good was the Christian God. For, Cassiciacum directly followed Augustine's conversion and was followed in turn by his baptism and in a relatively short time by his elevation to the priesthood and the episcopate. This development was shared by a number of his friends who returned to Africa with him and became priests and bishops as Augustine himself.[26] For Augustine and no doubt at least for some of his companions their awakening to a fully Christian life was insolubly bound up with the Cassiciacum experience of a common life of seekers of God.

As is well known, the most immediate of the causes which had brought about the conversion of Augustine (and of his friend Alypius) had been the example of the eastern monks and, especially, of St. Anthony.[27] In the years following Cassiciacum the Christian monastic factor became much stronger than the element of philosophic friendship, but the latter was not altogether lost, it rather assumed a

---

[25] Cf. the article by Poulsen, quoted in n. 19; also E. Salin, *Civitas Dei* (Tübingen, 1926) 160 ff., as far as I know, the only work on St. Augustine in which the connection between his ideal of friendship and his monastic ideal is pointed out clearly; some remarks also in Zumkeller, *Mönchtum* 24, and in V. (F.) Nolte, O.E.S.A., *Augustins Freundschaftsideal in seinen Briefen* (Würzburg, 1939) 119. There is no evidence that the Augustine of the Cassiciacum period was influenced by the tradition of the old-Pythagorean brotherhood; but, since he was acquainted with the Neopythagorean literature of his time, it is not impossible that he had heard also of that tradition. For "Pythagorean" influence on the formulation of Acts 4:32, a text which was of the greatest importance for the monastic ideal of St. Augustine (cf. below, pp. 359–360) as well as of other Fathers (cf. pp. 126 ff., 342, 343, n. 11, on John Chrysostom, Basil, and Cassian, respectively), see H. v. Schubert, "Der Kommunismus der Wiedertäufer und seine Quellen," *Sitzungsberichte der Heidelberger Akademie der Wissenschaften*, Philos.-histor. Klasse, 1919, 11, 35 ff., who refers to Plato, *Republic* 449C, and above all to the surprisingly close parallels to Acts 4:32 in Jamblichus, *De vita pythagorica* 30, 168.

[26] Cf. Possidius, *Vita S. Augustini episcopi* 11, *PL* XXXII, 42: Proficiente porro doctrina divina sub sancto et cum sancto Augustino in monasterio Deo servientes ecclesiae Hipponensi clerici ordinari coeperunt. Ac deinde innotescente et clarescente de die in diem (cf. 2 Cor. 4:16) ecclesiae catholicae praedicationis veritate sanctorumque servorum Dei proposito, continentia et paupertate profunda ex monasterio, quod per illum memorabilem virum et esse et crescere coeperat, magno desiderio poscere atque accipere episcopos et clericos pax ecclesiae atque unitas et coepit primo et postea consecuta est. Nam ferme decem, quos ipse novi, sanctos ac venerabiles viros continentes et doctissimos beatus Augustinus diversis ecclesiis nonnullis quoque eminentioribus rogatus dedit. Similiterque et ipsi ex illorum sanctorum proposito venientes Domini ecclesiis propagatis et monasteria instituerunt; et studio crescente aedificationis verbi Dei caeteris ecclesiis promotos fratres ad suscipiendum sacerdotium praestiterunt.

[27] *Confessiones* VIII, 6, 14, Skutella 164 f.

new form.[28] Though Augustine had heard of monasticism first in the form of the anchoretic life, it seems that he never thought of becoming a hermit himself; he was much more attracted by the coenobitic type of monastic life.[29] It was the communal type of monasticism which he began to imitate as soon as he had returned to his native country. As in Cassiciacum, so also in the monastery founded by Augustine in his home town Thagaste, intellectual interest and work no doubt played a great role, but they were now more strictly centered in the meditation of Holy Scripture.[30] At Thagaste and later at Hippo, where Augustine having become a priest founded and directed a monastery near the cathedral (intra ecclesiam),[31] in the garden which Bishop Valerius had given him for that purpose,[32] the Christian-Platonic circle of the Cassiciacum period was absorbed by an exemplar which had already inspired St. Basil and other great admirers of the coenobitic ideal,[33] by the example of the apostolic community of Jerusalem.[34] After having become Bishop of Hippo, Augustine must soon have formed the conviction that the two highest aspects of the Christian life—the way of the monk and the office of the priest and bishop—should be welded into unity of perfection. Clerics and priests, together with their bishop, should live as monks, having everything in common as the apostles, and monks should be capable and willing, if needed, to serve the Church as priests and bishops. This was the spiritual community

[28] Cf. H.-U. v. Balthasar, Augustinus: Das Antlitz der Kirche (Einsiedeln, Köln, 1942) 25.

[29] For Augustine's praise of, and attitude to, the various forms of monasticism, see De moribus ecclesiae catholicae I, 31, 65 ff. and 33, 70 ff., PL XXXII, 1337 ff.

[30] See Possidius, Vita S. Augustini episcopi 3, PL XXXII, 36: Ac placuit ei (i.e., to Augustine) percepta gratia cum aliis civibus et amicis suis Deo pariter servientibus ad Africam et propriam domum agrosque remeare. Ad quos veniens et in quibus constitutus ferme triennio et a se iam alienatis curis saecularibus cum iis qui eidem adhaerebant Deo vivebat ieiuniis, orationibus bonisque operibus in lege Domini meditans die ac nocte (cf. Ps. 1 : 2). Et de iis, quae sibi Deus cogitanti atque oranti intellecta revelabat, et praesentes et absentes sermonibus ac libris docebat.

[31] See Possidius, text quoted below, n. 34.

[32] See Sermo CCCLV, 2, Lambot, Aug. serm. sel., Strom. Patr. et Med. I, 125.

[33] See above, p. 354, n. 25.

[34] See Possidius, Vita S. Augustini episcopi 5, PL XXXII, 37: [Augustinus] Factus ergo presbyter monasterium intra ecclesiam mox instituit et cum Dei servis vivere coepit secundum modum et regulam sub sanctis apostolis constitutam, maxime ut nemo quidquam proprium in illa societate haberet, sed eis essent omnia communia et distribuerentur unicuique, sicut opus erat (cf. Acts 4 : 32); quod iam ipse prior fecerat, dum de transmarinis ad sua remeasset (i.e., in Thagaste).

of Augustine's youth transposed to the highest Christian level and many of his friends, associates, and disciples carried out the new ideal with him, either in *vita communis* at the bishop's house in Hippo or by ascending to priesthood and episcopate elsewhere from the Augustinian monasteries.[35]

The principal documents of Augustine's conception of monasticism and of a quasi-monastic clerical life are the *Augustinian Rule*, the little book *On the Work of the Monks*,[36] *Sermons* CCCLV and CCCLVI,[37] and the *Vita S. Augustini* by Possidius.[38] The controversy of the last twenty years concerning the *Augustinian Rule* has somewhat clarified the problem of its origin.[39] Above all there can be little doubt that Augustine

---

[35] See Possidius, *Vita S. Aug. ep.* 24 f., *PL* XXXII, 53 ff., especially 25, XXXII 54: Cum ipso semper clerici una etiam domo ac mensa sumptibusque communibus alebantur et vestiebantur. Above all, see *Sermones* CCCLV and CCCLVI, quoted below.

[36] *De opere monachorum*, *CSEL* XLI.

[37] For them, see below, pp. 359–360.

[38] See the passages quoted above, pp. 354 ff., nn. 26, 30, 34 f.

[39] Best edition in R. Arbesmann, O.S.A., and W. Hümpfner, O.S.A., *Jordani de Saxonia, O.E.S.A., Liber Vitasfratrum* (New York, 1943) 491 ff.; the older editions and literature are listed there and the critical problems concerning the Augustinian Rule are thoroughly discussed and largely clarified. See also W. Hümpfner, O.S.A., "Die Mönchsregel des heiligen Augustinus," *Aug. Mag.* I, 241 ff., M. Verheijen, O.E.S.A., "Remarques sur deux textes rejetés de la «Regula ad servos Dei»," *Année théol. aug.* 1951, 345 ff., idem, "La Regula Sancti Augustini," *Vigil. Christ.* VII (1953) 27 ff., idem, "Les Sermons 355–356 de saint Augustin et la Regula Sancti Augustini," *Rech.'s sc. rel.* XLI (1953) 231 ff., idem, "Remarques sur le style de la 'Regula Secunda' de saint Augustin: Son rédacteur," *Aug. Mag.* I, 255 ff., idem, "Les manuscrits de la «Lettre CCXI de saint Augustin»," *Revue du moyen âge latin* VIII (1952) 97 ff., idem, "La «Regula Puellarum» et la «Regula Sancti Augustini»," *Augustiniana* IV (1954) 258 ff. According to P. Verheijen the text which used to be called St. Augustine's *Regula Secunda* and is now called *Disciplina monasterii* or *Ordo monasterii*, constituting according to P. Mandonnet, O.P., *Saint Dominique* II (Paris, 1937) 107–162, and according to P. Hümpfner the first Rule of St. Augustine (see immediately below), was redacted by Augustine's friend and disciple Alypius. As to the text which once was wrongly called St. Augustine's *Regula tertia*, but is more correctly known as his *Regula ad servos Dei*, the long held view that it was originally written by Augustine for nuns, together with *Epist.* CCXI, *CSEL* LVII, 356 ff., and not for monks, was shaken by P. Mandonnet in his book on St. Dominic, mentioned above (the Dominican historian here followed the tracks of the eighteenth century historian of the Augustinian Canons Regular, E. Amort). The attempt by C. Lambot, O.S.B., "Saint Augustin a-t-il rédigé la règle pour moines qui porte son nom?," *Rev. bén.* LIII (1941) 41 ff., to reassert the older view has been refuted by N. Merlin, O.E.S.A., "Exemple typique d'un préjugé littéraire," *Anal. Praem.* XXIV (1948) 1 ff., by L. Cilleruelo, "Nuevas dudas sobre la Regula ad Servos Dei de San Agustin," *Archivo Agustiniano* XLIV (1950) 85 ff., and by Verheijen "Remarques."

wrote a rule for monks and not for nuns and that this rule has been preserved in the so-called *Regula ad servos Dei*; the female adaptation of
the rule, which in many manuscripts and printed editions is combined
with Augustine's *Epist.* CCXI addressed to nuns, is of later origin and,
perhaps, was made in sixth or seventh century Spain.[40] In the following remarks on the *Augustinian Rule* the authorship of St. Augustine at
least for the *Regula ad servos Dei* (once incorrectly called *Regula tertia*)
will be taken for granted; Augustine's authorship of the so-called
Ordo monasterii (or *Disciplina monasterii*, once wrongly called *Regula
secunda*), which in almost all of the oldest manuscripts immediately
precedes Augustine's *Regula ad servos Dei*, forming an introductory
first part to it, is nevertheless not certain, the style being rather different from Augustine's. If the *Ordo monasterii* is not by Augustine
himself, it did, however, almost certainly originate in his age and in

[40] See Augustine, *Epist.* CCXI, *CSEL* LVII, 356 ff. To this letter, supposedly written by
Augustine to African nuns, is added in relatively late manuscripts the female redaction of
the *Augustinian Regula ad servos Dei*; there is, however, one manuscript, Cod. Escuraliensis
a. I. 13 (probably saec. IX), where a combination of fragments from *Epist.* CCXI and of the
female version of the *Augustinian Regula ad servos Dei* also includes a female version of the
Augustinian Ordo monasterii. For date, locality and authorship of these female adaptations
and of *Epist.* CCXI, see A. C. Vega, O.E.S.A., "Una adaptación de la 'Informatio regularis'
de San Agustín anterior al siglo IX para unas virgines españoles . . .," *Miscell. Mercati* II,
34 ff., Hümpfner, "Mönchsregel" 251 ff., Verheijen, "Manuscrits," *idem*, "«Regula
Puellarum»," and *idem*, "Regula Sancti Augustini" 45 ff. P. Hümpfner, "Mönchsregel"
250 f. thinks that the female version of the combined *Augustinian Ordo monasterii* and *Regula
ad servos Dei* as well as *Epist.* CCXI, attributed to Augustine, are the work of St. Fructuosus
of Braga. Yet it would seem that P. Verheijen, "Regula Sancti Augustini" 48–54, has
proved that about half a century before Fructuosus the female adaptation had been used by
St. Leander of Seville in his *De institutione virginum* and by St. Isidore of Seville in his *Regula
monachorum* (cf. also below, p. 384, nn. 26 ff., Hümpfner's suggestion that Fructuosus had
used Isidore's *Regula* in addition to the *Augustinian Rule* seems to be less convincing,
especially as it ignores the relation to Leander). The oldest manuscript of the female
adaptation, Cod. Escural. a. I. 13, has a passage which textually corresponds with canon
11 of the Fourth Council of Toledo of 633 (cf. Vega, "Adaptación" 50, §11); though
this council was presided over by Isidore, it seems more likely that the *Augustinian Rule*, as
it appears in the Escuraliensis, used the conciliar canon than that the canon used the rule;
the passage in question may be a later addition to the female adaptation of the *Augustinian
Rule*. The *Regula consensoria monachorum*, Arbesmann and Hümpfner, *Liber Vitasfratrum* 485 ff.
(also *PL* XXXII, 1447 ff.), which used to be called the *Regula prima* of St. Augustine, is
certainly not by the Bishop of Hippo and by most authors is now considered as late seventh
century Spanish in origin, probably from the milieu of St. Fructuosus of Braga; cf. C. J.
Bishko, "The Date and Nature of the Spanish Consensoria Monachorum," *Amer. Jour.
Philol.* LXIX (1948) 377 ff.

an Augustinian milieu. I shall call it the *Augustinian Ordo monasterii*, since together with the *Augustinian Regula ad servos Dei* it was from an early date part of the *Augustinian Rule* (though except for its first sentence it was to be eliminated as largely inapplicable in the course of the Middle Ages).[41]

The Augustinian character of the rule is confirmed by its content and, as far as the *Regula ad servos Dei* is concerned, also by its style. This emerges from comparisons[42] with such Augustinian works as *De moribus ecclesiae catholicae*,[43] *De opere monachorum*,[44] *Sermons* CCCLV and CCCLVI.[45] It is not necessary to discuss various attempts to connect the *Ordo monasterii* and the *Regula ad servos Dei* with either one or the other of the Augustinian monasteries at Thagaste and in the garden at Hippo;[46] of greater consequence is the strong probability that at

[41] In the edition of the *Augustinian Ordo monasterii* and of the *Augustinian Regula ad servos Dei* by Arbesmann and Hümpfner, *Liber Vitasfratrum* 491 ff., the former is called *Regula Sancti Augustini prima*, the latter *Regula Sancti Augustini secunda*. For the almost complete elimination of the *Ordo monasterii* from the *Rule of St. Augustine* in the twelfth century, see Mandonnet, *Dominique* II, 151 ff., Hümpfner, "Mönchsregel" 242 ff.

[42] Carried out by Verheijen, "Regula Sancti Augustini," *idem*, "Sermons," and Hümpfner, "Mönchsregel" 244 ff.; see also A. Zumkeller, O.E.S.A., "Regeln des heiligen Augustinus: Zum geistigen Gehalt der Augustinerregel," v. Balthasar, *Grosse Ordensregeln* 113 ff. (notes), and now above all T. van Bavel, O.E.S.A., "Parallèles, vocabulaire et citations bibliques de la «Regula Sancti Augustini»," *Augustiniana* IX (1959) 12 ff.

[43] See, especially, *De moribus ecclesiae catholicae* I, 31–33, *PL* XXXII, 1337 ff., also other passages, quoted by Hümpfner, "Mönchsregel" 244 f.

[44] For the relevant texts from *De opere monachorum*, *CSEL* XLI, see Hümpfner, "Mönchsregel" 245–246; cf. below, pp. 362 ff.

[45] For these *Sermons*, see pp. 359 f.

[46] W. Hümpfner, O.E.S.A., in his introduction to Arbesmann and Hümpfner, *Liber Vitasfratrum*, p. lxxviii, and in his introduction to the *Rule of St. Augustine*, "Die Regeln des heiligen Augustinus: Zur Überlieferung der Augustinerregel," v. Balthasar, *Grosse Ordensregeln* 101 f., holds that both the *Augustinian Ordo monasterii* and the *Augustinian Regula ad servos Dei* were written by Augustine himself, the former for the monastery at Thagaste, the latter for that in the garden at the bishop's house at Hippo; P. Verheijen, "Regula Sancti Augustini" 44, believes that the *Ordo monasterii*, too, belonged to the monastery in the garden at Hippo, and, contrary to the *Regula ad servos Dei*, was written not by Augustine himself, but by Alypius (cf. above, p. 356, n. 39), though inspired and approved by Augustine. It should be mentioned that the late Cardinal Ildefonso Schuster, O.S.B., *Saint Benedict and His Times* (transl. by G. J. Roettger, O.S.B., St. Louis, London, 1951) 244 ff., thought that both the *Augustinian Ordo monasterii* and the *Augustinian Regula ad servos Dei* are the work of Eugippius, who was the biographer of St. Severin, the apostle of Noricum. It is known from Isidore of Seville, *De viris illustribus*, that Eugippius wrote a monastic rule, and his Augustinianism is beyond doubt (see below, p. 382, n. 18); yet Cardinal Schuster's hypothesis is not supported by the manuscript tradition.

least the *Regula ad servos Dei* was later used by Augustine and his quasi-monastic clergy in their common life in the bishop's house.[47]

How the bishop Augustine tried to combine his monastic ideal with the clerical life is known chiefly from the aforementioned *Sermons* CCCLV and CCCLVI (held in December, 425, and January, 426, respectively)[48] concerning his clergy.[49] In these sermons the aged bishop gives an account to the Christian people of Hippo of his own way of life and that of his clergy, a very few of whom had apparently been unwilling to give up all personal property.

You know (Augustine says in *Sermon* CCCLV) . . . that we live in that house which is called the house of the bishop in such a manner that we imitate as well as we can those saints of whom the Acts of the Apostles speak: "none of them said that anything was his own, but all things were common unto them" (Acts 4:32).[50]

He states that in doing so he and those who share his purpose only continue their earlier monastic way of life.[51] And indeed, the *Augustinian Rule* (*Regula ad servos Dei*) forbids any personal property on the strength of the same text from the Acts of the Apostles and adds that it is the purpose of the common life to live together in harmony and to have one heart and one soul in God (cf. Acts 4:32 and 35).[52]

[47] This is suggested by *Sermons* CCCLV and CCCLVI; cf. Hümpfner, "Mönchsregel" 248 f.

[48] Cf. A. Kunzelmann, "Die Chronologie der Sermones des hl. Augustinus," *Miscell. Agost.* II, 509, and above all Dom Lambot's edition, cited immediately below.

[49] Cf. P. Grech, O.E.S.A., "The Augustinian Community and the Primitive Church," *Augustiniana* V (1955) 459 ff.

[50] *Sermo* CCCLV, 2, Lambot, *Aug. Serm. Sel., Strom. Patr. et Med.* I, 124: . . . nostis . . . sic nos vivere in domo ea quae dicitur domus episcopi, ut quantum possumus imitemur eos sanctos, de quibus loquitur liber Actuum Apostolorum: "Nemo dicebat aliquid proprium, sed erant illis omnia communia" (Acts 4:32).

[51] *Sermo* CCCLV, 2, Lambot 124 ff.: Ego, quem Deo propitio videtis episcopum vestrum, iuvenis veni ad istam civitatem. . . . Quaerebam ubi constituerem monasterium et viverem cum fratribus meis. . . . Veni ad istam civitatem propter videndum amicum, quem putabam me lucrari posse Deo, ut nobiscum esset in monasterio. . . . Apprehensus presbyter factus sum. . . . Et quia hoc disponebam esse in monasterio cum fratribus . . ., beatae memoriae senex Valerius (Augustine's predecessor as Bishop of Hippo) dedit mihi hortum illum, in quo est nunc monasterium. . . .

[52] *Augustinian Regula ad servos Dei* 1, Arbesmann and Hümpfner, *Liber Vitasfratrum* 494: Primum propter quod in unum estis congregati, ut unanimes habitetis in domo et sit vobis "anima una et cor unum" (Acts 4:32) in Deo. Et non dicatis aliquid proprium, sed

Sermon CCCLV continues:

And I wished to have in this house of the bishop a monastery of clerics. This then is how we live. No one in the society is allowed to have anything of his own. But perhaps some have. It is allowed to none: if some have they do what is not allowed.[53]

. . . if one has undertaken [to live in] the society of the common life which is praised in the *Acts of the Apostles* and then deserts it he falls: he falls away from his vow, he falls away from a holy profession. . . .

A cleric professes two things, sanctity as well as the clerical state: at any rate sanctity—for the clericate God layed upon his neck because of His people and it is rather a burden than an honor. . . . So he professed sanctity: then he has professed a society of life in common. . . .

If [a cleric] is prepared to be nourished by God through His Church, not to have anything of his own, but either to give it to the poor or to the community then he may remain with me. Who does not want this has freedom [to go]. But let him see whether he can [thus] gain eternity of happiness.[54]

At the beginning of *Sermon* CCCLVI, Augustine makes the Deacon Lazarus[55] read the pertinent text from the Acts of the Apostles

sint vobis omnia communia et distribuatur unicuique vestrum a praeposito vestro victus et tegumentum, non aequaliter omnibus, quia non aequaliter valetis omnes, sed potius unicuique sicut cuique opus fuerit. Sic enim legitis in Actibus apostolorum, quia "erant eis omnia communia" (Acts 4:32) et "distribuebatur unicuique sicut cuique opus erat" (Acts 4:35). The quotations from the Acts of the Apostles are not taken from the Vulgate, but from one of the older Latin versions.

[53] *Sermo* CCCLV, 2, Lambot 125 f.: Perveni ad episcopatum: vidi necesse habere episcopum exhibere humanitatem adsiduam quibusque venientibus sive transeuntibus, quod si non fecisset episcopus, inhumanus diceretur. Si autem ista consuetudo in monasterio missa esset, indecens esset. Et volui habere in domo ista episcopi monasterium clericorum. Ecce quomodo vivimus. Nulli licet in societate habere aliquid proprium. Sed forte aliqui habent. Nulli licet: si qui habent, faciunt quod non licet.

[54] *Sermo* CCCLV, 6, Lambot 130: . . . cadit qui societatem communis vitae iam susceptam, quae laudatur in Apostolorum Actibus, deserit: a voto suo cadit, a professione sancta cadit . . . clericus duas res professus est, et sanctitatem et clericatum: interim (the Maurinians emended this to *interius*) sanctitatem—nam clericatum per populum suum Deus imposuit cervicibus ipsius: magis onus est quam honor . . . ergo professus est sanctitatem: professus est communiter vivendi societatem. . . . Si paratus est pasci a Deo per ecclesiam ipsius, non habere aliquid proprium, sed aut erogare pauperibus aut in commune mittere, maneat mecum. Qui hoc non vult, habeat libertatem; sed videat, utrum habere possit felicitatis aeternitatem.

[55] It is not impossible that Augustine chose a deacon of this name because of the parable of Lazarus and the rich man (Luke 16:19 ff.).

(4:31–35). Or rather he has him read only half and then repeats the lesson himself.

For more does it delight me to read this word than to argue in my own words.[56]

He then declares that he has found all his brethren and clerics who live with him, priests, deacons, and subdeacons, as he wanted to find them, that is to say, poor. Nevertheless, he discusses some individual cases, in part exemplary, in part doubtful; the latter, however, have, he says, been settled to his satisfaction.[57] Finally, he once more sharply reasserts his firm resolve not to tolerate in his Church any cleric who does not truly lead the "social life" (*vitam nostram socialem*), who, in other words, pretends to, but does not, conform with the "monastization" of the clericate.

May such a one appeal against me to a thousand councils, may he set sail against me wheresoever he wishes, may he in fact be wheresoever he can: the Lord will help me so that, where I am bishop, he cannot be cleric.[58]

These sermons are the most important evidence of St. Augustine's insistence on a way of life equivalent to monastic status for his clergy. They also form a striking parallel to the definition of the City of God in *De civitate Dei*, where he says: *nam unde esset ista civitas . . ., si non esset socialis vita sanctorum*.[59] It is quite clear that the common life of Augustine's clerics, the *vita nostra socialis*, is the ideal life of the citizens of the *civitas Dei* on earth. For on the one hand he who professes sanctity, according to Augustine, professes *societatem vitae communis*,[60] on the

[56] *Sermo* CCCLVI, 1, Lambot, *August. Serm. Sel., Strom. Patr. et Med.* I, 133: Plus enim me delectat huius verbi esse lectorem quam verbi mei disputatorem.

[57] *Ibid.* 3–15, Lambot 134–143.

[58] *Ibid.* 14, Lambot 141: Ecce dico, audistis, audiunt. Qui habere voluerit aliquid proprium et de proprio vivere et contra ista nostra praecepta facere, parum est ut dicam, non mecum manebit, sed clericus non erit. Dixeram enim, et scio me dixisse, ut si nolint suscipere socialem vitam mecum, non illis tollerem clericatum; seorsum manerent, seorsum viverent, quomodo possint Deo viverent. Et tamen ante oculos posui, quantum mali sit a proposito cadere. . . . Quo modo (Lambot: *Quomodo*) ergo, quicumque voluisset extra manere et de suo vivere, non ei tollerem clericatum, ita modo, quia placuit illis Deo propitio socialis haec vita, quisquis cum hypocrisi vixerit, quisquis inventus fuerit habens proprium, non illi permitto ut inde faciat testamentum, sed delebo eum de tabula clericorum. Interpellet contra me mille concilia, naviget contra me quo voluerit, sit certe ubi potuerit: adiuvabit me Dominus, ut ubi ego episcopus sum ille clericus esse non possit. . . .

[59] See above, p. 240.   [60] See above, p. 360, n. 54.

other hand the *Augustinian Rule* speaks of the monastic community as of a *sancta societas*.[61] On earth these *sancti* are the members *par excellence* of the City of God.[62]

The treatise *De opere monachorum*,[63] conversely, shows that among all those who live as monks Augustine considers clerics to hold the highest spiritual rank and privilege.[64]

St. Augustine wrote that book because certain apparently somewhat arrogant and lazy monks refused to perform manual labor.[65] Appealing to Christ's parable in the Gospel of St. Matthew,[66] they rather rashly and almost comically claimed the privilege of the lilies of the field which neither labor nor spin. In refuting these monks Augustine developed his own conception of monasticism as an imitation of the life of the apostles. They indeed did carry out manual as well as spiritual work, even though they would, St. Augustine says with St. Paul, have been entitled to dispense with physical work because of their

---

[61] Augustinian *Regula ad servos Dei* 2, Arbesmann and Hümpfner, *Liber Vitasfratrum* 495. Ambrose had anticipated Augustinian *civitas Dei* terminology, admonishing the clerics of the Cathedral of Vercelli to continue the monastico-clerical life, which Bishop Eusebius had instituted (cf. also p. 352, n. 11); see the passage of *Epist.* LXIII, 104, *PL* XVI, 1269C, quoted above, p. 248, n. 47, and to be cited again here because of its significance: . . . et vos egredimini de hac terrena civitate, quia civitas vestra superior est Ierusalem. Ibi conversamini, ut dicatis: "Nostra conversatio in coelis est" (Phil. 3:20). Ideo Iesus exivit de civitate, ut vos exeuntes de hoc mundo supra mundum sitis.

[62] Salvianus, too, *De gubernatione Dei* I, 2 f., especially I, 2, 7, *CSEL* VIII, 6, calls the "true Christians" *sancti*; these are the *religiosi* (cf. *ibid.* I, 2, 8 f. and I, 3, 13, *CSEL* VIII, 6 f. and 9) who, if not exclusively, at least frequently, are identified by Salvianus with monks, cf. *ibid.* V, 10, 52, *CSEL* VIII, 118 f., on the occasion of his denunciation of false *religiosi* . . . qui . . . non conversatione alii, sed professione nomen tantum demutavere non vitam . . . , vestem tantummodo exuere non mentem.

[63] Augustine, *De opere monachorum*, *CSEL* XLI, 529 ff.

[64] He was aware of the fact that not all monks make good clerics; cf. *Epist.* LX, 1, *CSEL* XXXIV, 2, 221 f.: . . . aliquando etiam bonus monachus vix bonum clericum faciat, si adsit ei sufficiens continentia et tamen desit instructio necessaria aut personae regularis integritas.

[65] It has recently been suggested in an interesting article by G. Folliet, A.A., "Des moines euchites à Carthage en 400–401," *Stud. Patr.* II, 386 ff., that these monks were Messalians. "Lazy" monks of a similar type are mentioned about the same time also in the Christian east; cf., for instance, Cyril of Alexandria (?), *Adversus anthropomorphitas*, PG LXXVI, 1076A ff. (quoted by H. du Manoir de Jouaye, S.J., *Dogme et spiritualité chez saint Cyrille d'Alexandrie* [Etudes de théologie et d'histoire de la spiritualité II, Paris, 1944] 405).

[66] Matthew 6:28, Luke 12:27.

spiritual tasks and had every right to be supported by the faithful.[67] The same rule must be applied to the monks. It is wrong to interpret 2 Thess. 3:10: "who does not wish to work, should not eat," to spiritual work only.[68] Neither Christ nor St. Paul had meant that monks should not work physically if they can.

If complete absorption in prayer and in the word of God did necessarily prevent monks from performing manual work, then they ought not even to be able to find time for eating or the preparation of food.[69] Is it not possible to pray and meditate while working physically?[70] It is different with monks who are at the same time clerics. Ministers of the word of God are entitled to live *ex evangelio*, they may "eat their bread gratuitously," receiving it from those to whom they preach "gratuitous grace." Even though it would be best if they too did manual work at certain times and thus earned their bread, as St. Paul did, this is often impossible.[71] Augustine exemplifies from his own experience as a bishop:

I invoke the Lord Jesus. . . . as witness over my soul that as regards my own convenience I should much rather every day at certain hours work at something with my hands . . . and have the remaining hours free for reading and praying or for some activity connected with Holy Scripture (*divinis litteris*) than suffer the most tumultuous perplexities of the causes of strangers concerning the business of the world, which I must untangle through judgment or stop by intervention. . . . And yet, we accept this labor not without the

---

[67] *De opere monachorum* 16, 17, *CSEL* XLI, 558 ff.

[68] *Ibid*. 1, 2 f., XLI, 534 ff.　　　　　　[69] *Ibid*. 17, 20, XLI, 564.

[70] *Ibid*., XLI, 564 f. See also *ibid*. 25, 33, XLI, 580: . . . neque enim propterea christiana militia ad pietatem divites humiliantur, ut pauperes ad superbiam extollantur. Nullo modo enim decet, ut in ea vita, ubi senatores fiunt laboriosi, ibi fiant opifices otiosi, et quo veniunt relictis deliciis suis, qui fuerant praediorum domini, ibi sint rustici delicati; similarly *Augustinian Regula ad servos Dei* 5 and 2, Arbesmann and Hümpfner, *Liber Vitas-fratrum* 496 and 495. Augustine holds that monks who had come from the lower strata of society and had worked physically before entering the monastery should be even more willing to do manual work than those whose social origin had not accustomed them to physical labor. Also he warns the former not to envy the latter, if these receive finer food, clothing, and bedding, because their previous habits of life have made them physically delicate; cf. *Augustinian Regula ad servos Dei*, 5, Arbesmann and Hümpfner 496 ff., and *De opere monachorum* 21, 25 ff., *CSEL* XLI, 570 ff. As to the type of manual work performed in the monastery Augustine does not state exactly in what it consisted; it was hardly agricultural on a large scale; cf. also above, p. 78.

[71] Cf. *De opere monachorum* 7, 8 ff., XLI, 542 ff., and 15, 16 ff., XLI, 556 ff.

consolation of the Lord. . . . For we are servants of His Church and mostly of [her] weaker members. . . .[72]

Such servants then, monks who are clerics as well as clerics who live monastically, are for St. Augustine the leaders of the Church, because they have chosen the exemplary apostolic life. If a great citizen of pagan Rome could prefer the common weal to his own to such an extent that he did not even have a dowry to give to his daughter,

what other intention should the citizen of that city which is the heavenly Jerusalem have toward his commonwealth (res publica) but that he have in common with his brother that which he produces with his own hands and that if his brother lack of something he supply it from that which is common [to all]; thus he can say with him whose precept and example he has been following: "As having nothing, and possessing all things" (2 Cor. 6:10).[73]

Augustine did not mean to say that every Christian must lead the monastic life—it is very significant that, while he demanded the apostolic vita communis from his own monks and clergy, he considered heretical the self-styled Apostolici who declared that Christians who do not give up property and marriage have no hope for salvation.[74] Yet it remains true that in Augustine's view monastic or quasi-monastic life in common was the fullest realization of the City of God on earth. In that life physical work is important, but a special place is reserved for those who do the spiritual work of God. The distinctive characteristics or principles of St. Augustine's conception of the monastic life in that wider sense which embraces also the vita communis of the clergy

[72] Ibid. 29, 37, XLI, 587 f.: . . . Dominum Iesum . . . testem invoco super animam meam, quoniam, quantum ad meum adtinet commodum, multo mallem per singulos dies certis horis . . . aliquid manibus operari et ceteras horas habere ad legendum et orandum aut aliquid de divinis litteris agendum liberas quam tumultuosissimas perplexitates causarum alienarum pati de negotiis saecularibus vel iudicando dirimendis vel interveniendo praecidendis. . . . Quem tamen laborem non sine consolatione Domini suscipimus. . . . Servi enim sumus eius ecclesiae et maxime infirmioribus membris. . . . See also above, pp. 334–340, about Augustine's conception of the active, the contemplative, and the "mixed" lives.

[73] Ibid. 25, 32, XLI, 579: . . . quo animo esse debet in republica sua civis aeternae illius civitatis Hierusalem caelestis, nisi ut illud ipsum, quod propriis manibus elaborat, in commune habeat cum fratre et, si quid ei defuerit, de communi suppleat, dicens cum illo, cuius praeceptum exemplumque secutus est: "quasi nihil habentes et omnia possidentes" (2 Cor. 6:10).

[74] See Augustine, De haeresibus 40, PL XLII, 32.

thus remained essentially the same from the time of his catechumenate at Cassiciacum (where philosophical-theological discussions had alternated with a certain amount of work on Verecundus' estate) to that of his episcopate at Hippo. These principles were mainly two: the gathering of a group of intellectually gifted men for the service of God—after St. Augustine's baptism and ordination more clearly defined as service for the Church—and the formation of small groups who wanted to live the apostolic life, outside, as far as possible, of the social and economic framework of the rest of the world, but working for the spiritual interest of that world nevertheless. In discussing St. Paul's account of his apostolic labors, St. Augustine also transferred the Pauline idea and term of the *miles Christi*, the soldier of Christ,[75] to the ascetic and monastic life. He was not the first to do so. Origen, Athanasius, and above all Basil the Great, the true founder of Greek monastic community life, had preceded him; Jerome and Cassian were akin to him in this as in other points of monastic theory and practice.[76] Even so, St. Augustine's constant use of the terms *militia Christi*, *militia christiana*, *militia divina* for the monastic communities shows that he considered them as advance-guards, as an elite among the Christians.[77] On the other hand, the *clericatus militia* has even higher rank,[78] and there can be no doubt that monasticism and clericate combined constituted in Augustine's eyes the highest form of the Christian life.[79]

[75] See 2 Cor. 10:4, 1 Tim. 1:18.

[76] For the concept of the *militia Christi* see A. Harnack, *Militia Christi* (Tübingen, 1905); also H. Emonds, O.S.B., "Geistlicher Kriegsdienst. Der Topos der militia spiritualis," *Heil. Überlief.* 21 ff., P. Antin, O.S.B. "Le monachisme de saint Jérôme," *Mélanges bénédictines* (Abbaye Saint Wandrille, 1947) 87 f.

[77] *De opere monachorum, passim.*

[78] Augustine, *Epist.* LX, *CSEL* XXXIV, 2, 221 f. See also *De opere monachorum* 16, 19, *CSEL* XLI, 563 f.: . . . non cessavit apostolus . . . exhortari fideles, qui haberent huius modi substantiam, ut nihil deesset necessitatibus servorum Dei, qui celsiorem sanctitatis gradum in ecclesia tenere voluerunt, ut spei saecularis vincula cuncta praeciderent et animum liberum divinae militiae dedicarent. . . . Cf. also the examples given for Augustine's use of the term *miles Christi* for the priests in B. Poschmann, *S. Aurelii Augustini . . . textus selecti de paenitentia*, Flor. Patr. XXXVIII, 20, l. 25 and n. 1.

[79] See, for instance, *De catechizandis rudibus* 23, 43, *PL* XL, 341, where it is said that the earliest Christian communities of the Holy Land, the great models of the monastic life for St. Augustine, supported the ministers of the Word of God, *milites Christi*, who lived in the same poor and ascetic way as the rest of the faithful. . . . [Paulus] ecclesias . . . constituens per omnes gentes, qua evangelium seminabat, impense praecipiebat, ut, quoniam

3. POSTBAPTISMAL CONVERSI IN THE WEST FROM THE FOURTH TO THE SIXTH CENTURY

Beside the strictly monastic elite, there existed another, considered as an elite also by St. Augustine. This was the class of the post-baptismal "converts," *conversi* in one of those technical meanings of the word which did not refer to prebaptismal conversion.[1] The terms *converti*, *conversio*, ·*conversi* in their postbaptismal meaning could, as mentioned, refer to entry into the monastic life,[2] but they also could be applied to a fairly large group of men and women who, unable to enter monasteries because of their domestic or public responsibilities in the world, nevertheless, decided to detach themselves as fully as possible from worldly goods and pleasures, and thus to follow Christ. Many of them had been very wealthy, since they came from the senatorial aristocracy whose estates covered vast portions of the Roman Empire. They either gave everything away or made at least

ipsi ex idolorum cultu venientes et ad unum Deum colendum rudes non facile poterant rebus suis venditis et distributis servire Deo, oblationes facerent in pauperes sanctorum, qui erant in ecclesiis Iudaeae, quae Christo crediderant: ita illos tanquam milites, illos autem tanquam stipendiarios provinciales apostolica doctrina constituit, inserens eis Christum velut lapidem angularem . . . in quo ambo quasi parietes de diverso venientes, de Iudaeis videlicet atque gentibus, germana claritate copularentur (cf. Ps. 117:22, Eph. 2:14 and 20, etc.). For Augustine's view that those who lived monastically formed an elite in the Church see also *Contra Faustum* V, 9, *CSEL* XXV, 1, 281 f., a text significant both for monks and for lay *conversi* (for the latter, see following section). Quam multi autem in nostra communione veraciter faciunt ista sublimiora praecepta evangelica. . .! Quam multi homines utriusque sexus ab omni concubitu puri atque integri, quam multi experti et postea continentes, quam multi rerum suarum distributores et relictores, quam multi ieiuniis . . . corpus servituti subicientes! Quam multae fraternae congregationes, nihil habentes proprium, sed omnia communia, et haec nonnisi ad victum et tegumentum necessaria, unam animam et cor unum in Deum caritatis igne conflantes (cf. Acts 4:32 and 35). . .! In quorum societate quasi dispares adparent, sed tamen eadem caritate copulantur, qui propter aliquam necessitudinem secundum apostoli exhortationem habent uxores tamquam non habentes et emunt tamquam non tenentes et utuntur hoc mundo tamquam non utentes (cf. 1 Cor. 7:29 ff.). See also the rest of the paragraph. Cf. F. van der Meer, *Augustinus der Seelsorger* (German translation of *Augustinus de Zielzorger*), 2nd ed. (Köln, 1953) 216, 232, 245, Zumkeller, "Regeln" 114 f. With regard to these and other Augustinian texts see also H. Rondet, "Richesse et pauvreté dans la prédication de saint Augustin," *Rev. ascét. myst.* XXX (1954), especially 196 ff.: "La pauvreté des moines et des clercs," furthermore Grech, "Augustinian Community" and D. Sanchis, O.S.B., "Pauvreté monastique et charité fraternelle chez saint Augustin," *Augustiniana* VIII (1958) 5 ff.

[1] See also Part One, pp. 32 f.   [2] See above, p. 345.

part of it over to a religious establishment or, if they had to carry on in the world, they made only the most restricted use of their possessions and privileges. In a sense, these nonmonastic *conversi* are spiritual descendants of the premonastic ascetics of early Christianity.[3]

Postbaptismal *conversio*, be it monastic or "secular," was first of all a type of *paenitentia*.[4] And indeed, what greater penance could there be for great and small sinners than to give up wealth and human love for ever and to enter either into a monastery or, perhaps even more difficult, upon an ascetic way of life among the good things of this world, which these penitents and *conversi* were to use as if not using them.[5] *Conversio* as an entering upon a life of penance in the midst of the world is advocated very clearly in certain documents of the fifth century, such as Gennadius' *Ecclesiastica dogmata*,[6] some of the letters of Bishop Faustus of Riez,[7] and a sermon *De paenitentia*, formerly ascribed to Faustus, but probably by a Paulinus (of Bordeaux?).[8] A

---

[3] Cf. M. Viller and M. Olphe-Galliard, article "Ascèse," *DSpir* I, 964 ff., especially 976. For the connection between these nonmonastic *conversi* and the mediaeval monastic *conversi* as well as the lay brothers, who from the eleventh century onward were known as *conversi*, see now the fundamental study of K. Hallinger, O.S.B., "Woher kommen die Laienbrüder?," *Analecta Sacri Ordinis Cisterciensis* XII (1956) 1 ff., in which most of the older literature is critically discussed.

[4] Cf. P. Galtier, "Pénitents et «convertis»: De la pénitence latine à la pénitence celtique," *Rev. hist. ecclés.* XXXIII (1937) 5 ff. and 277 ff., idem, article "Conversi," *DSpir*, fasc. XIV–XV, 2218 ff.; also C. Vogel, *La discipline pénitentielle en Gaule des origines à la fin du VIIᵉ siècle* (Paris, 1952), especially 128 ff., and idem, "La discipline pénitentielle en Gaule des origines au IXᵉ siècle: Le dossier hagiographique," *Rev. sc. rel.* XXX (1956) 174 ff. A beautiful résumé of early Christian thought on conversion and penance was given by St. Isidore of Seville, *Sententiae* II, 7–10, *PL* LXXXIII, 606 ff.

[5] Cf. 1 Cor. 7: 31: ... καὶ οἱ χρώμενοι τὸν κόσμον ὡς μὴ καταχρώμενοι, . . . et qui utuntur hoc mundo tamquam non utantur. Cf. above, p. 127, n. 55, for John Chrysostom. See also Augustine, *De nuptiis et concupiscentia* I, 15, *CSEL* XLII, 227; *Contra Iulianum* V, 60, *PL* XLIV, 817; *Enarr. in Ps. CXLVII*, 4, *Corp. Christ.*, *Ser. Lat.* XL, 2141 f.; *De doctrina christiana* I, 4, 4, *Flor. Patr.* XXIV, 5.

[6] Gennadius, *Liber sive diffinitio ecclesiasticorum dogmatum* 22, ed. C. Turner, *Jour. Theol. Stud.* VII (1906) 94; cf. Galtier, "Pénitents" 6 ff.

[7] Faustus of Riez, *Epist.* VI, IX, and X, *CSEL* XXI, 195 ff., 208 ff.; cf. Galtier, "Pénitents" 16 ff. For Faustus, see also below, pp. 406 ff.

[8] *PL* LVIII, 875 and *PL* CIII, 699; cf. B. Poschmann, *Die abendländische Kirchenbusse im Ausgang des christlichen Altertums* (Münchener Studien zur historischen Theologie VII, München, 1928) 128, n. 4, Galtier, "Pénitents" 7 ff. For the manuscript tradition, under the title *Sententia Paulini ad monachos de paenitentia*, see Morin, *Caesar. Arel. Opera* I, 1, *Corp. Christ.*, *Ser. Lat.* CIII, p. xxxvi.

conception of nonmonastic, or at least not immediately monastic, change of life had inspired already the famous conversions of Roman patricians, brought about or encouraged by St. Jerome, and still formed the background of Cassiodorus' relinquishing of office and honors.

There can be little doubt that Augustine counted the *conversi* and *conversae*, who remained in the world, among the *sancti*, who form the *civitas Dei* on earth. It is hardly an accident that he dedicated his work on the City of God to a high official of the Roman Empire, Marcellinus, who was such a man.[9] After Marcellinus' execution, which may have been the result of Donatist intrigues as well as of political disturbances, Augustine writes admiringly about his life;[10] he also says that Marcellinus, though he would have loved to give up all worldly business and to receive the belt of the *militia Christi*, was prevented from doing so by the tie of marriage, with which he was already bound when he began to long for better bonds—he was not allowed to dissolve that former tie, even though it was an inferior one.[11] Similarly, the few good Christians, in whom Salvianus sees the sole hope of the world, include men and women in secular life as well as monks and nuns.[12]

---

[9] See also Augustine, *Epist.* CXXXVIII, *ad Marcellinum, CSEL* XLIV, 126 ff., mentioned pp. 248 ff., nn. 51, 53, and *Epist.* CXXXIII, CXXXIX, CXLIII. To Marcellinus, Augustine also dedicated his first anti-Pelagian works, *De peccatorum meritis et remissione* and *De spiritu et littera*. See the excellent brief character sketch of Marcellinus in van der Meer, *Augustinus* 209 f.

[10] There can be little doubt that he considered him a saint; cf. also van der Meer, *Augustinus* 209: "ein Heiliger trotz der *chlamys* und der Sporen."

[11] Augustinus, *Epist.* CLI, 8, *CSEL* XLIV, 388 f.: Quae illi vero probitas in moribus, in amicitia fides, in doctrina studium, in religione sinceritas, in coniugio pudicitia, in iudicio continentia, erga inimicos patientia, erga amicos affabilitas, erga sanctos humilitas, erga omnes caritas, in beneficiis praestandis facilitas, in petendis pudor, in recte factis amor, in peccatis dolor! . . . Quantus in eo contemptus rerum praesentium, quanta spes et desiderium bonorum aeternorum! Ne relictis omnibus saecularibus actionibus susciperet cingulum militiae christianae, vinculum praepediebat uxorium, quo iam innodatus coeperat concupiscere meliora, quando iam non licebat illa quamvis inferiora disrumpere. For the concept of the *militia Christi, christiana* or *divina*, which for Augustine here and elsewhere means monasticism, see above, p. 365.

[12] Salvianus, *De gubernatione Dei* IV, 13, 62, *CSEL* VIII, 87: . . . excipio enim primum omnes religiosos, deinde nonnullos etiam saeculares religiosis pares aut, si id nimis grande est, aliqua tamen religiosi honestorum actuum probitate consimiles . . .; see also *ibid.* VII, 3, 14, *CSEL* VIII, 159, where Salvianus alludes to Paulinus of Nola's renunciation of wealth and worldly life: . . . exceptis tamen perpaucis ferme sanctis atque insignibus

Because of the combination of worldly eminence and sanctity in many of these converts, the penitential character of *conversio* not infrequently receded to the background and was even superseded by a tendency to make use of their gifts and sincerity by elevating them to the priestly and episcopal office, without extended clerical preparation.[13] Within the great senatorial families St. Paulinus of Nola[14] is the most famous example in the late fourth and St. Apollinaris Sidonius[15] in the late fifth century among many similar cases of *conversi*-bishops.

Pontius Meropius Paulinus, the immensely rich scion of one of the great Gallo-Roman families, was the pupil and friend of the poet Ausonius[16] who was one of the most typical figures of the so-called "Theodosian Renaissance." Paulinus himself belonged to the very class, the very officialdom, the very cultural milieu—whether pagan or more or less superficially Christian—in which that Renaissance movement had taken root.[17] Yet he and his wife left it all for the

---

viris, qui, ut quidam de numero ipsorum ait, "sparsis redemerunt crimina nummis" . . . ; cf. C. Weyman, "Analecta II: Salvianus und Paulinus von Nola," *Hist. Jb.* XV (1894) 372 f., who has proved that Salvianus here quotes a hexameter, belonging to an inscription composed by Paulinus, who in it refers to himself; see Paulinus' *Epist.* XXXII, 3, *CSEL* XXIX, 278, 9.

[13] See Galtier, "Pénitents" 23 ff., 283.

[14] For Paulinus of Nola and his friend Sulpicius Severus, the biographer of St. Martin of Tours, see now above all Fabre, *Paulin de Nole*, also the recent article on Paulinus by Helm, in PW, *RE* XXXVI, 3 (XVIII, 4). For Paulinus' literary importance cf. M. Schanz, *Geschichte der römischen Literatur* IV, 1, 2nd ed. (Handbuch der klassischen Altertumswissenschaft VIII, München, 1914) 273 ff. and F. J. E. Raby, *A History of Christian Latin Poetry from the Beginnings to the Close of the Middle Ages* (Oxford, 1927) 101 f.

[15] For Apollinaris Sidonius see, for instance, Schanz, IV, 2 (1920) 43 ff., §1024–1026, Raby, *A History of Secular Latin Poetry in the Middle Ages* I, 2nd ed. (Oxford, 1957) 73 ff., P. Courcelle, *Les lettres grecques en occident. De Macrobe à Cassiodore*, 2nd ed. (Bibliothèque des Ecoles Françaises d'Athènes et de Rome, CLIX, Paris, 1948) 235 ff., idem, *Histoire littéraire des grandes invasions germaniques* (Paris, 1948) 138 ff., A. Loyen, *Sidoine Apollinaire et l'esprit précieux en Gaule aux derniers jours de l'empire* (Collection d'études latines . . ., Série scientifique XX, Paris, 1943).

[16] Cf. the famous exchange of poetic epistles between the aged Ausonius and Paulinus whom the old teacher unsuccessfully tried to bring back to a worldly life (Paulinus, *Carm.* X and XI, *CSEL* XXX, 24 ff., 39 ff.).

[17] For the "Theodosian Renaissance" see above, pp. 17–20. Paulinus, too, wrote a panegyric for Theodosius the Great, which is lost; he himself tells us that he celebrated *non tam imperatorem quam Christi servum* (cf. *Epist.* XXVIII, 6, *CSEL* XXIX, 247); this anticipates Augustine's attitude in *De civitate Dei* (cf. above, p. 256).

monastic way of life and his poetry rings a tone[18] very different even from that of Prudentius, with the exception, it is true, of the latter's beautiful hymns in the *Cathemerinon*.[19] He was elected Bishop of Nola in Campania in 409.

Half a century later Apollinaris Sidonius, who died as Bishop of Clermont Ferrand in 479, was one of the principal representatives of what has recently been called the "Renaissance of 470."[20] His elevation to the episcopate was due probably more to the force of external circumstances than to internal reasons. Yet it is not necessary to doubt the sincerity of his conversion to a new way of life, though even as a bishop the Christian humanism of his epistolography is of a much more precious[21] kind than the serene piety of Paulinus' letters and poems.

Whether or not these converts were great literary figures, whether they became bishops or monks and nuns or remained in the "secular" state, their history from the fourth to the sixth century documents the spiritual vitality of the upper strata of Christian Roman society.[22]

---

[18] The crystalline clarity and serenity of Paulinus' poems has not yet been fully appreciated. He has neither the brilliance of Prudentius nor his exaggerations. See, for instance, Paulinus' *Carmen* XXXII, *CSEL* XXX, 329, which begins as follows: Discussi fateor sectas, Antonius, omnes; / plurima quaesivi, per singula quaeque cucurri, / sed nihil inveni melius quam credere Christo; or the beginning of the epithalamium, *Carmen* XXV, *loc. cit.*, 238: Concordes animae casto sociantur amore, / virgo puer Christi, virgo puella Dei.

[19] The question of Prudentius' conversion is complicated by a literary problem. The chronology of his poems is uncertain and controversial. It is generally assumed that the *Contra Symmachum* (cf. p. 17, n. 5, pp. 147, n. 70) was written 402–403, that is to say, before Prudentius' spiritual conversion and resolve to dedicate his remaining years to Christian poetry of which he speaks in the preface to his poems. Even though most modern critics believe that all of Prudentius' works were written before the preface, it would not seem impossible that at least the truly religious *Cathemerinon* (*CSEL* LXI, 1 ff.) dates from the time after his conversion. For literature on the problem see B. M. Peebles, *The Poet Prudentius* (New York, 1951).

[20] Cf. Courcelle, *Lettres grecques* 221 ff.; he connects the "Renaissance of 470" with the reign of the Greek Anthemius as emperor in the west (467–472).

[21] Loyen, *Sidoine Apollinaire*, sees Apollinaris Sidonius too exclusively from the literary side and therefore is of the opinion that his true personality is found only in that part of his life which lies before his conversion and episcopate. Courcelle, *Grandes invasions* 138 ff., rightly stresses his remarkable and courageous activity as a bishop.

[22] W. H. C. Frend, *The Donatist Church* (Oxford, 1952) 328 ff., considers the fact that Augustine and the Catholic Church in general accepted the prevailing social order (though they extolled those who transcended it) as a defect and as a principal cause of failure in permanently winning over the Donatists whose revolt was both social and religious. While

Beside the development of patristic theology, of liturgy, and canon law, and beside monasticism in the strict sense, the movement of lay *conversio* showed what Christianity could achieve within ancient civilization. It was important that the highly civilized disciples and friends of St. Jerome, St. Paulinus of Nola, and St. Augustine—the Melanias and Marcellas, Paulas and Paulinas, Blesillas and Eusto-chiums and Demetrias', the Pammachius and Pinianus, Ponticianus, Romanianus, and Marcellinus, and many others[23]—became models of an inner reform of Christian society, though some of them retained permanently, others for a long time, a nonmonastic way of life.[24] As

this explanation of the tenacious resistance of the Donatists against the Catholics no doubt contains much that is true, the problem is really a wider one and involves the whole relationship between wealth, culture, and religion: while Christianity demands social justice, it is to say the least doubtful if it demands abolition of wealth and even more doubtful, if even a Christian culture can exist without it. See also below, pp. 463–467, Excursus V.

[23] A comprehensive study of the noble lay converts of this period would be very much worth while; for the background see now the interesting article of A. Chastagnol, "Le sénateur Volusien et la conversion d'une famille de l'aristocratie romaine au bas-empire," *Revue des études anciennes* LVIII (Annales de la Faculté des Lettres de Bordeaux, Ser. IV, LXXVIII, 1956) 241 ff.; on the "Volusiani" (Ceionii) cf. also H. Bloch, "A New Document of the Last Pagan Revival in the West," *Harv. Theol. Rev.* XXXVIII (1945) 212 f. For Jerome's spiritual guidance of Marcella, Paula and her daughters, his relation to Pammachius, etc., see F. Cavallera, *Saint Jérôme* I, 1 and 2 (Spicilegium Sacrum Lovaniense I and II, Louvain, Paris, 1922). For various degrees of asceticism among the members of great Roman families who were friends and correspondents of St. Augustine's cf. van der Meer, *Augustinus* 208 ff.; for Augustine's letters and treatises, addressed to Paulina (not the daughter of Paula), Proba, Juliana, Italica, Laurentius, etc., see below, pp. 376, n. 11. For Ponticianus, the high imperial official through whom Augustine heard for the first time of the monastic life, see *Confessiones* VIII, 6, 14, Skutella 164 (cf. above, p. 354; for Romanianus see *Confessiones* VI, 14, 24, Skutella 121. For Gallic lay *conversi* of the late fifth, sixth, and seventh centuries see Galtier, "Pénitents" 277 ff., also Nora K. Chadwick, *Poetry and Letters in Early Christian Gaul* (London, 1955). For the Christian east one may recall the names of the Empresses Galla Placidia, St. Pulcheria, Athenais-Eudoxia; see also Gregory of Nyssa's funeral orations for Flacilla, the wife of Theodosius the Great, and for his daughter, the first Pulcheria; cf. p. 124, n. 45. See p. 127, on John Chrysostom's ideal of the Christian life in the world according to 1 Cor. 7:29 ff. Ascetics who lived in the world and some times formed associations of their own were in the Christian east from the later fourth to the seventh century known as the "zealous," σπουδαῖοι, and later as φιλόπονοι or under still other names; cf. S. Pétridès, "Spoudaei et Philopones," *Echos d'orient* VII (1904) 341 ff.

[24] Within this whole group of people the border line between an ascetic life in the world and the strictly monastic life remains fluid. No doubt Jerome thought of all of them when he wrote to the senator and ascetic Pammachius, in *Epist.* LXVI, 4, 3, *CSEL* LIV, 651, that

a group, they were the first to give a valid answer to the everpresent question whether a fully Christian life is possible outside the monastery for people who are in possession of all the material and cultural advantages of their age. Their experience was that it is possible, although difficult. It involved not only a change of personal *habitus* (which could be understood both in the literal and in the metaphorical sense),[25] but it also must lead to a new conception of the content and form of civilization. A transformation of those pre-Christian or imperfectly Christian cultural ideals and educational materials, which were still current in the Theodosian age, was taking place. By c. 400, in the west, at least St. Ambrose and St. Paulinus of Nola, to some extent also Prudentius, and in the east, St. Gregory Nazianzen and Synesius, had shown what the Christian spirit could make of the old forms of poetry; and the masters of church architecture and liturgical

in the beginnings of Church history rare indeed were the wise, powerful, and noble among the Christians, whereas now many monks come from the ranks of these same wise, powerful, and noble—no need to point out that he speaks here in social terms, not in terms of spiritual wisdom, etc. For Jerome and the ascetic-monastic life in general see Cavallera, *Jérôme, passim*, Antin, "Monachisme" 69 ff., and (Cardinal) Ildefonso Schuster, O.S.B., "L'influenza di S. Girolamo sui primordi della vita monastica in Roma," *Miscellanea Geronimiana* (Roma, 1920) 115 ff.

[25] For literal change of dress, see the material collected by Galtier, "Pénitents," 13 ff. See, especially, Paulinus of Nola, *Epist.* XXIX, 12, *CSEL* XXIX, 259, on the meeting of Melania the Elder, dressed in old, black clothes, with her family, the great Valerii, after her return from the Holy Land: Vidimus dignam Deo huius mundi confusionem, purpuream sericam auratamque supellectilem pannis veteribus et nigris servientem. See also Jerome, *Epist.* LXVI, 6, 1, *CSEL* LIV, 654, about Pammachius to whom the letter is addressed: Quis hoc crederet, ut consulum pronepos et Furiani germinis decus inter purpuras senatorum furva tunica pullatus incederet, ut non erubesceret oculos sodalium, ut deridentes se ipse rideret? On the other hand the common ascetic *topos* that change of *mores* is more important than change of *vestimenta* could be applied also to lay conversion. See the following passage from Caesarius of Arles' *Sermo* LVI, 3, *Corp. Christ.*, *Ser. Lat.* CIII, 250, which is interesting also for the combination of recall *ad sanitatem pristinam* and conversion *ad meliora*: Nec nos hoc dicimus . . . ut iuvenes, qui coniugia habere videntur, habitum magis quam mores debeant conmutare. Quid enim homini uxorem habenti nocet, si mores perditos voluerit ad opera bona vel honesta convertere, si peccatorum suorum vulnera elemosynis, ieiuniis et orationibus ad sanitatem pristinam studeat revocare? Vera enim conversio sine vestimentorum commutatione sufficit sibi: vestimenta vero religiosa sine bonis operibus non solum remedium habere non poterunt, sed etiam iustum Dei iudicium sustinebunt. Convertamur ergo ad meliora, dum in nostra sunt potestate remedia. . . . For the antithesis of *vestem mutasse* and *mores bonos retinere*, as applied to nuns and monks, cf., for instance, Caesarius, *Ad sanctimoniales epist.* II, 2, Morin, *Caesar. Arel. Opera* II, 135 f., and *idem*, *Regula monachorum*, Morin 154, l. 30, 155, ll. 7 f.

music, of mosaic and of manuscript illumination had begun to create
a great Christian style in building, imagery, and chant. In the intellectual sphere, it was above all St. Augustine who, beside St. Jerome's
more specialized scriptural scholarship, endeavored to set up new
standards of education in knowledge and wisdom.

4. St. Augustine's Program of Education and Its Relation to the Ascetic Reform Ideal

It was upon the monks, the monastically living clerics, and the *conversi* that Augustine no doubt set his hopes in drawing up his famous
program of Christian learning and teaching in the four books of *De
doctrina christiana*.[1]

In this work Augustine gives "precepts" which will be helpful,
first, in the discovery of truth from the Scriptures, and then, in the
teaching of this truth to others.[2] The novelty of his concept of
Christian teaching and learning lies in the resolute subordination of
all knowledge still to be gained in the schools about the year 400 to
Christian sacred knowledge and wisdom, that is to say, to the understanding of Holy Scripture and to the Christian life resulting from
it. While this point of view does not exclude the more "technical"
types of knowledge needed by all who live in the society of man, it
admits the liberal arts (in the wider sense of the term) as a legitimate
object of study for Christians only in so far as they have some bearing
upon *doctrina christiana* or are of definite help in its acquisition—as is,
for instance, the case with the mastery of the languages of the Bible
or the right interpretation of the mathematical, astronomical, minera-
logical, botanical, zoological, geographical, and historical terms which
occur in it or the methods of logical reasoning without which no
intellectual activity is possible.[3] On such premises and only on such

---

[1] Augustine, *De doctrina christiana*, Flor. Patr. XXIV.

[2] *Ibid.*, *Prologus*, Flor. Patr., XXIV, 1 : Sunt praecepta quaedam tractandarum scripturarum,
quae studiosis earum video non incommode posse tradi, ut non solum legendo alios, qui
divinarum litterarum operta aperuerunt, sed et aliis ipsi aperiendo proficiant.

[3] *Ibid.* II, 39, 58, *Flor. Patr.*, XXIV, 45 : Quamobrem videtur mihi studiosis et ingeniosis
adolescentibus et timentibus Deum beatamque vitam quaerentibus salubriter praecipi, ut
nullas doctrinas, quae praeter ecclesiam Christi exercentur, tamquam ad beatam vitam
capessendam secure sequi audeant, sed eas sobrie diligenterque diiudicent. . . . Illa vero

premises the liberal arts of the classical course of study and their sub-
sidiary disciplines are in Augustine's eyes both useful and indispensable.
Thus a system of intellectual culture is built up which has a definitely
Christian scope and, while potentially including any kind of knowledge,
stresses the necessity for a Christian to pursue knowledge only in view
of the ultimate goal.[4]

The entire first three books of De doctrina christiana are taken up
with "the method of discovery of what we are to understand"; only
in the fourth and last book Augustine turns to "the method of teaching
what has been understood."[5] There he shows that the three styles of
Ciceronian eloquentia—submisse, temperate, and granditer[6]—are directed
ultimately toward "a change of life" (mutatio vitae).[7]

instituta hominum, quae ad societatem conviventium valent, pro ipsa huius vitae necessitate
non neglegant. In ceteris autem doctrinis, quae apud gentes inveniuntur, praeter historiam
rerum vel praeteriti temporis vel praesentis ad sensus corporis pertinentium, quibus
etiam utilium artium corporalium experimenta et coniecturae annumerantur, et praeter
rationem disputationis et numeri nihil utile esse arbitror. For the linking of the various
types of knowledge to the understanding of Holy Scripture, see ibid. II, 39, 59, also
II, 16, 24, II, 28, 42, II, 29 f., 46 f., II, 31, 48–50, II, 34 f., 52 f., II, 38, 56 f., Flor. Patr.
XXIV, 45, 30 f., 38 f., 40 f., 41 f., 43, 44 f. Most of these texts are cited and discussed
by E. Gilson, Introduction à l'étude de saint Augustin, 3rd ed. (Paris, 1949) 161.

[4] Cf. H.-I. Marrou, Saint Augustin et la fin de la culture antique (Paris, 1949), especially
339–356. Augustine's most famous definition of the Christian intellectual's attitude to
pagan secular culture is contained in his elaborate simile of "the spoiling of the Egypt-
ians" in De doctrina christiana II, 40, 60 ff., Flor. Patr. XXIV, 46. There, he says that
Christians may and should take over whatever is true in pagan philosophy, because all truth
is rightfully theirs—just as according to Ex. 3:22, 11:2, and 12:35, God had permitted
to the Israelites, and even admonished them, to take away with them Egyptian gold and
silver vessels and vestments. Cf. E. A. Quain, S.J., "The Medieval Accessus ad Auctores,"
Traditio III (1945) 223 f.

[5] De doctrina christiana I, 1, 1, Flor. Patr. XXIV, 4: Duae sunt res quibus nititur omnis
tractatio scripturarum: modus inveniendi quae intellegenda sunt et modus proferendi
quae intellecta sunt . . ., cf. ibid. IV, 1, 1, XXIV, 71 f.

[6] Ibid. IV, 12, 27, XXIV, 83: Dixit ergo quidam eloquens (i.e., Cicero, Orator 21, 69),
et verum dixit, ita dicere debere eloquentem, "ut doceat, ut delectet, ut flectat" . . .;
ibid. IV, 17, 34, XXIV, 87: Ad haec enim tria, id est, ut doceat, ut delectet, ut flectat,
etiam tria illa videtur pertinere voluisse idem ipse Romani auctor eloquii, cum itidem
dixit: "is igitur erit eloquens, qui poterit parva submisse, modica temperate, magna
granditer dicere" (Cicero, Orator 29, 101). . . .

[7] Ibid. IV, 24, 53, XXIV, 98, where Augustine relates how by preaching granditer at
Caesarea in Mauretania he stopped the traditional yearly "riot" (caterva) during which two
parties fought one another with much bloodshed: . . . egi quidem granditer quantum
valui, ut tam crudele atque inveteratum malum de cordibus et moribus eorum avellerem
pelleremque dicendo. Non tamen egisse aliquid me putavi, cum eos audirem acclamantes,

Modern historians have expressed some surprise that Augustine did not make any concrete suggestions as to how the principles of Christian education laid down in De doctrina christiana should be realized in a Christian scholastic organization. Neither St. Augustine nor any of the other Fathers, it is said, took any steps toward overcoming the most serious handicap of Christian education in patristic times: the all but nonexistence of Christian schools on the elementary and secondary level for children who were destined for life in the world.[8]

Perhaps, one may assume that the Fathers simply did not consider the way in which the fundamentals of knowledge were to be acquired by those who lived in the world a specifically Christian or ecclesiastical concern. This knowledge had to be gained by all who needed or wanted it, both lay men and clerics, and it was permissible as well as necessary to obtain it within the framework of domestic and public education

sed cum flentes viderem. Acclamationibus quippe se doceri et delectari, flecti autem lacrimis indicabant. Quas ubi adspexi, immanem illam consuetudinem a patribus et avis longeque a maioribus raditam, quae pectora eorum hostiliter obsidebat vel potius possidebat, devictam antequam re ipsa id ostenderent credidi. Moxque sermone finito ad agendas Deo gratias corda atque ora converti. Et ecce iam ferme octo vel amplius anni sunt, propitio Christo, ex quo illic nihil tale tentatum est. Sunt et alia multa experimenta, quibus didicimus homines, quid in eis fecerit sapientis granditas dictionis, non clamore potius quam gemitu, aliquando etima lacrimis, postremo vitae mutatione monstrasse. See also ibid. IV, 4, 6, XXIV, 74: . . . maioribus dicendi viribus opus est . . . quaecumque . . . valent ad commovendos animos. . . . Such high estimate of rhetoric explains to some extent the boasting of personified Rhetorica in Ennodius of Pavia's so-called Paraenesis didascalica (Opusc. 6), MGH, AA VII, 313 f.: post apicem divinitatis ego illa sum quae commuto si sunt facta vel facio. One might also refer to Hilarius of Arles' Vita S. Honorati 3, 17, PL L, 1258B ff., where the disciple of the founder of the monastery of Lérins says that Honoratus, ministering the word of Christ, changed (permutatio) "animals" into men, not as Circe men into animals. This may be a retort to Rutilius Namatianus, De reditu I, 525 f., Vessereau and Préchac 27, who had attacked monasticism in this manner:

Non, rogo, deterior Circeis secta venenis?
Tunc mutabantur corpora, nunc animi.

For Augustine's transformation of the Ciceronian styles of eloquence, cf. E. Auerbach, "Sermo Humilis," Romanische Forschungen LXIV (1952) 304 ff.

[8] Cf. Marrou, Augustin 399 ff., idem, Histoire de l'éducation dans l'antiquité (Paris, 1948) 419 ff. See also M. L. W. Laistner, "Pagan Schools and Christian Teachers," Liber Floridus: Mittellateinische Studien Paul Lehmann . . . gewidmet (Erzabtei St. Ottilien, 1950) 47 ff., G. Bardy, "Les origines des écoles monastiques en orient," Mélanges Joseph de Ghellinck (Gembloux, 1951) 293 ff., idem, "Les origines des écoles monastiques en occident," Sacr. Erud. V (1953) 86 ff., idem, "L'église et l'enseignement en occident au Ve siècle," Mélanges Cavallera 191 ff.

as it still existed in the Graeco-Roman world.[9] The only thing that mattered from the Christian point of view was its integration with "Christian Doctrine." That meant above all that if pagan authors had to be studied it must be clearly understood that their value for a Christian was at its best relative.

It would seem that the deeper reason for this critical rather than constructive attitude toward basic and intermediate education was the conviction that a Christian reform of the ancient educational system could only come "from the top." A program of *doctrina Christiana*, of Christian learning and teaching, had to be realized at first by those who were willing to lead the exemplary Christian life. And these for Augustine were first of all the true followers of the Apostles: the monks, the clerics who lived in *vita communis*, and the *conversi*. It is from this point of view that one must understand Augustine's special concern for the monks who were clerics in *De opere monachorum*[10] and also his extensive correspondence as a spiritual director of laymen who were interested in the intellectual foundations of their religion.[11] Perhaps the program of *De doctrina christiana* could and would have expanded more quickly and more widely to nonmonastic, nonclerical Christian society in the west had Roman civilization not collapsed. On the other hand it was just the decline of secular educational institutions which caused monasteries, episcopal churches, and even parish churches to take over to some extent the teaching of children destined for the life of the world beside the instruction of those who would presumably become monks and priests.

[9] Thus with regard to rhetoric which, as just observed, was so important to Augustine even within the framework of *doctrina christiana* he, nevertheless, says, *De doctrina christiana* IV, 1, 2, *Flor. Patr.* XXIV, 72: . . . rhetorica . . . a me non exspectentur. . . . Non quod nihil habeant utilitatis, sed quod si quid habent seorsum discendum est, si cui fortassis bono viro etiam haec vacat discere. . . .

[10] Cf. above, pp. 362–365. See also *Augustinian Ordo monasterii* 3, Arbesmann and Hümpfner, *Liber Vitasfratrum* 491, where daily reading (from Sext to None) is made one of the tasks of the monks.

[11] Cf. above, pp. 248 ff., for the correspondence with Marcellinus; see also, for instance, the letters and treatises addressed to Paulina (*Epist.* CXLVII, *de videndo Deo*), Juliana (*Epist.* CL, CLXXXVIII, treatise *De bono viduitatis*), Proba (*Epist.* CXXX, CXXXI), Italica (*Epist.* XCII, XCIX), etc. One might also mention the books *De octo quaestionibus ad Dulcitium* (tribune in Africa) and *Enchiridion* or *De fide, spe, et caritate ad Laurentium* (Dulcitius' brother), and several others. Cf. van der Meer, *Augustinus* 261 ff.

Augustine's program of a *doctrina christiana* was closely bound up with his ideal of a monastic or quasi-monastic life for clerics and laymen. This mode of life was the principal practical vehicle through which the Augustinian idea of reform was carried into effect. The monk-priests and *conversi* were the *sancti* of the *Civitas Dei* on its earthly pilgrimage, whose teaching and example should bring about a *mutatio vitae*.[12] The end of this "change of life" may be safely identified with the key idea of patristic reform ideology: *reformatio ad imaginem Dei*.[13] The Augustinian road then leads from *doctrina christiana*, the receiving of "Christian instruction," to prebaptismal conversion, to baptismal regeneration, to reformation and postbaptismal conversion, to a monastic or at least ascetic way of life in the City of God on earth, and through it all back to *doctrina christiana*, the giving of "Christian instruction" within the *Civitas Dei*.[14]

---

[12] See Possidius, *Vita S. Augustini episcopi* 11, *PL* XXXII, 42, about the role of Augustine's monks and clerics as well as of his writings in the propagation of Christian doctrine. Cf. also above, p. 355, n. 30, another text from Possidius.

[13] Cf. *De doctrina christiana* I, 18, 17 to 22, 20, *Flor. Patr.* XXIV, 10, where *conversio*, *reformari in melius*, and *configurari veritati* through penance and mortification are based on the doctrine of man's creation *ad imaginem et similitudinem Dei*.

[14] See also the remarks of Ernst Hoffmann, "Platonism in Augustine's Philosophy of History," *Philosophy and History: Essays Presented to Ernst Cassirer* (Oxford, 1936) 188 f.: "Thus through Augustine there comes into Christianity the motive of labouring at the cultivation of the mind . . ., not for the sake of the cultivation of the mind, but for the sake of the divinely willed fact that God is surrounded by the *Civitas divina* as his eternal company. . . . We can bring home to the earthly city the consciousness that there is a divine city. . . . And we can establish Christian learning in order, by interpreting the Word, to labour along with the working of the divine Word."

CHAPTER III

THE TRANSMISSION OF AUGUSTINIAN MONASTICISM TO EARLY MEDIAEVAL EUROPE

In the west the apostolic and pedagogical aspects of the Augustinian monastic ideal survived as important realizations of the patristic idea of reform,[1] until they were temporarily and partially overshadowed by the ascendency of Benedictine and Celtic monasticism in the age of Gregory the Great. The present chapter is concerned with their survival during the last phase of Late Antiquity and with their transmission to the Middle Ages. The reform ideas of St. Benedict, St. Columbanus, St. Gregory the Great, though they, too, are rooted in the patristic tradition, are above all initial elements of mediaeval history itself; they must, therefore, be left for a continuation of this study.

1. THE INFLUENCE OF THE AUGUSTINIAN RULE[2]

St. Augustine died in 430 during the siege of Hippo by the Vandals and in the following one hundred years the Church of North Africa suffered greatly, chiefly because of the hostility of the Arian conquerors to Catholicism. Bishop Victor of Vita and other sources of the fifth and sixth centuries give facts and figures hardly to be gainsaid about murders and atrocities, hideous tortures and concentration

---

[1] See in general L. Cilleruelo, O.S.A., "Influencia de S. Agustin en la espiritualidad cristiana hasta la edad media," *Revista de Espiritualidad* XIV (1955) 125 ff., who in this connection rightly quotes Possidius, *Vita S. Augustini episcopi* 31, PL XXXII, 64: Clerum sufficientissimum et monasteria virorum ac feminarum continentibus cum suis praepositis plena ecclesiae dimisit, una cum bibliothecis libros et tractatus vel suos vel aliorum sanctorum habentibus, in quibus dono Dei qualis quantusque in ecclesia fuerit noscitur et in his semper vivere a fidelibus invenitur. See also the texts from Possidius, quoted above, p. 354, n. 26, and p. 355, n. 30.

[2] For the problems of the *Augustinian Rule*, see above, pp. 356–359.

camps, destructions and confiscations, and the exile or emigration of many African bishops, priests, and monks.[3] The exiles and refugees were scattered all over the Mediterranean area. Yet only in a few instances do we have definite information on the settlement of these Africans in Europe; only rarely can anything be ascertained about the later history of their monastic foundations or their influence in general on the ecclesiastical life of their adopted countries.

Of the African bishops who were deported or left voluntarily in the second half of the fifth and in the early sixth century many went to Sardinia.[4] St. Augustine's body itself was translated there.[5] The great monk-bishop and heir to the Augustinian tradition, St. Fulgentius of Ruspe, spent more than twenty years on the island until he could permanently return to Africa a few years before the reconquest by Justinian.[6] Yet nothing is known about a lasting effect of this "Augustinian" phase of Sardinian Church history.

About the year 440 Bishop Gaudiosus of Abitine in Africa Proconsularis, who had fled Vandal persecution, founded a monastery at Naples[7] which may well have followed the *Augustinian Rule*. Later, during the Byzantine period, two African abbots went to Spain and

[3] See Victor of Vita, *Historia persecutionis Africanae provinciae* I, 5–18, CSEL VII, 4 ff. Cf. P. Courcelle, *Histoire littéraire des grandes invasions germaniques* (Paris, 1948) 151 ff.

[4] See the principal data in Courcelle 157, 162 ff.

[5] Cf. the treatise of W. Bonjour, O.S.A. (died 1714), quoted below, p. 380, n. 11. Because of the invasion of Sardinia by the Moslems the remains of St. Augustine were transferred a second time, to Pavia, in the early eighth century; see the treatise of P. Bonjour, pp. 491 ff.

[6] See Ferrandus, *Vita S. Fulgentii*, PL LXV, 117 ff. For Fulgentius, see G.-G. Lapeyre, *Saint Fulgence de Ruspe* (Paris, 1929); the edition of the *Vita S. Fulgentii* by Lapeyre (Paris, 1929) was not available to me. Cf. O. Bardenhewer, *Geschichte der altkirchlichen Literatur* V (Freiburg i. B., 1932) 303 ff. For the Sardinian Catholic exiles from Vandal North Africa see also Ch. Courtois, *Les Vandales et l'Afrique* (Paris, 1955) 189.

[7] According to the *Vita et miracula* of St. Agnellus of Naples (saec. VI) by the Subdeacon Peter (only in part edited by B. Capasso, *Monumenta ad Neapolitani Ducatus Historiam Pertinentia* I [Società Napoletana di Storia Patria, Monumenti Storici, Ser. I, I, Napoli, 1881] 307 ff., cf. *ibid.* 22, n. 2, for Gaudiosus' monastery), which it is true dates only from the ninth century; on manuscripts of this work and other sources for St. Gaudiosus see H. Delehaye, S.J., "Hagiographie napolitaine," *Anal. Boll.* LVII (1939) 28 and LIX (1941) 23 ff., 32 f.; also D. Mallardo, *Ordo ad Ungendum Infirmum ex Cod. Neapol. saec. XII–XIII* (Napoli, 1938) and *idem, Il Calendario Lotteriano del secolo XIII* (Napoli, 1940), both not available to me.

Portugal with a number of monks:[8] Donatus founded the *monasterium Servitanum* in Castil[9] and Nanctus established his community in the diocese of Merida.[10] It is probable that further emigrations of African monks and clerics to Europe took place at the time of the Moslem invasions.

This is about all the concrete direct information which is available at present concerning African ecclesiastical and, especially, monastic influence upon Europe.[11] All the more important are traces of the use of the *Augustinian Rule* by other monastic legislators. During the fifth and sixth centuries such traces are found in France, Italy, and Spain.

Even though there is no evidence of direct African affiliation, the use of the *Augustinian Rule* is significant in itself. At Arles, still under Gothic domination, St. Caesarius' *Regula virginum*, first written about 512, revised and completed by 534, clearly shows acquaintance with

[8] P. B. Gams, *Die Kirchengeschichte von Spanien* II, 2 (Regensburg, 1874) 55 ff., and J. Perez de Urbel, O.S.B., *Los monjes españoles en la edad media*, 2nd ed., I (Madrid, 1945) 202 ff., assume that these emigrations were caused by the incursions of the Berbers, whereas C. W. Barlow, "The Literary Heritage of Spain," *Folia* I (1946) 105 thinks of depradations by some Vandal tribe.

[9] See Ildephonse of Toledo, *De viris illustribus* 4, *PL* XCVI, 200. This monastery was probably situated in the former diocese of Arcávica the location of which may have been at Cabeza del Griego in the region of Cuenca. Cf. A. Lambert, O.S.B., article "Arcavica," *DHGE* III, 1514 ff.

[10] See *Vitas sanctorum patrum Emeretensium* III, 1 (III, 7), Garvin 156 and commentary 341 ff. Cf. also below, p. 393, n. 32.

[11] In 1211 the *fratres* of Fontaine-Géhard (Fons Gyardi or Gehardi, Département Mayenne) whose monastery had been given to the Benedictines of Marmoutier by Bishop William of Le Mans in 1147, and then again by Bishop Hamelin in 1203, protested to Pope Innocent III that they had observed the rule of St. Augustine from the beginning of their foundation and wished to be reformed to their original status. See Innocent III to Marmoutier and to the Bishop of Angers, July 14, 1211 (*JL* 4280 and 4281); cf. Cottineau, *Répert.* I, 1172 f., L. Celier, *Catalogue des actes des évêques du Mans jusqu'à la fin du XIIIᵉ siècle* (Paris, 1900) 60 no. 84, 164 no. 320, 165 no. 322, F. Roth, O.E.S.A., "Cardinal Richard Annibaldi, First Protector of the Augustinian Order, 1243–1276," *Augustiniana* II–IV (1952–1954) 38. According to Guillaume Bonjour, O.S.A. (1670–1714), Fontaine-Géhard was founded in the first half of the sixth century. Yet, the sources adduced by Bonjour speak only of hermits and do not mention the rule of St. Augustine. Cf. W. Bonjour, "De loco obitus S. Augustini, de sepultura et translatione eiusdem Iᵃ et IIᵃ, de Augustinianorum in Gallia continua successione," published in *Analecta Augustiniana* II (1907–1908) 351 ff., 376 ff., 401 ff., 440 ff., and especially 487–491.

Augustine's rule; [12] the same is true, though to a much lesser extent, also for Caesarius' earlier short *Regula monachorum*.[13] Caesarius came from the famous island monastery of Lérins off the coast of Southern Gaul, a sphere in which eastern ascetic influence, so obvious in the writings of John Cassian of Marseilles, prevailed and where Semi-Pelagian opposition to Augustine's doctrine of grace had developed.[14] Yet, Caesarius was an Augustinian in spite of his Lerinian background and it was he who terminated Semi-Pelagianism at the Council of Orange of 529.[15]

As to the fact that St. Benedict used the *Augustinian Rule*, beside those of St. Pachomius, St. Basil, the works of Cassian, and other patristic sources, it is touched here only in passing, since it can be appropriately discussed only in a full treatment of Benedictine monasticism.

About twenty-five years ago Dom Morin discovered that the *ordo* of the divine office prescribed by Cassiodorus for his monks of Vivarium is the same as that of the *Augustinian Ordo monasterii*, which may be the first rule of St. Augustine and in any case almost certainly comes from an Augustinian monastic milieu.[16] It would therefore seem very probable that the *Augustinian Rule* was known at Vivarium; it may well have come there from Africa through Gaudiosus' monastic foundation at Naples of which in Cassiodorus' time the great St. Agnellus was abbot.[17]

[12] Caesarius of Arles, *Regula virginum*, Morin, *Caesar. Arel. Opera* II, 99 ff. Cf. C. Lambot, O.S.B., "La règle de s. Augustin et s. Césaire," *Rev. bén.* XLI (1929) 337 f., and M. Verheijen, O.E.S.A., "La Regula Sancti Augustini," *Vigil. Christ.* VII (1953) 32, for the use of both *Ordo monasterii* and *Regula ad servos Dei* by Caesarius. The fact that Caesarius used Augustine's rule in the male rather than in the female version for his monastery of nuns confirms the probable later date of that latter version; cf. above, p. 357, n. 40.

[13] Caesarius of Arles, *Regula monachorum*, Morin, *Caesar. Arel. Opera* II, 149 ff.; cf. Lambot, "Règle de s. Augustin et s. Césaire" 338 f. Through the rules of Caesarius, elements of the *Augustinian Rule* have found entrance also in the *Regula ad monachos* (*PL* LXVIII, 385 ff.) and the *Regula ad virgines* (*PL* LXVIII, 399 ff.) of Aurelianus of Arles (Caesarius' second successor 546–551) and in the *Regula ad virgines* (*PL* LXXXVII, 273 ff.) of Bishop Donatus of Besançon (died 660).

[14] See below, pp. 403 ff.   [15] See below, p. 413.

[16] G. Morin, O.S.B., "L'ordre des heures canoniales dans les monastères de Cassiodore," *Rev. bén.* XLIII (1931).

[17] In the article, quoted in the preceding note, Dom Morin (p. 151) suggests that Cassiodorus derived the liturgical *ordo* of Vivarium (with which the *Augustinian Ordo monasterii* corresponds) from the African monastic tradition in South Italy, represented by such men as Gaudiosus and Agnellus; he does not take the further step of identifying the *Ordo monasterii* with a rule of St. Augustine himself.

It is not improbable also that the monastery of St. Severin at Castellum Lucullanum (Pizzofalcone, Naples), founded by Eugippius (fl. c. 509), the disciple and biographer of the great Danubian apostle Severin and the first "florilegist" of Augustine's works, followed the *Augustinian Rule* or a rule based on it;[18] but all that we know in this respect (from Isidore of Seville) is that Eugippius wrote a rule which is lost.[19]

The early mediaeval anonymous *Rule of St. Paul and St. Stephen*, which seems to be of Northern Spanish (Gallegan) origin, has clearly used the *Augustinian Regula ad servos Dei*; what is suggested about the necessity of attending to the words rather than to the melodious modulations of the psalmody is taken over textually from Augustine's rule to which explicit reference is made.[20] A slight indication of

[18] For Eugippius, his *Vita* or *Commemoratorium de vita S. Severini* (ed. Th. Mommsen, *Scriptores rerum Germanicarum*, 1898) and his *Excerpta ex operibus S. Augustini* (CSEL IX, 1 ff.) see Wattenbach-Levison I, 44 ff., I. Zibermayr, *Noricum, Baiern und Österreich* (München, Berlin, 1944) 41 ff., F. Kaphahn, *Zwischen Antike und Mittelalter* (München, s.a.) 92 ff., W. Bulst, "Eugippius und die Legende des hl. Severin," *Die Welt als Geschichte* X (1950) 18 ff. For Severin see also E. K. Winter, "The Byzantine Millennium of Vienna," *Medievalia et Humanistica* X (1956) 7 ff.

[19] Isidore of Seville, *De viris illustribus* 26, 34, *PL* LXXXIII, 1097A. There does not seem to be any direct evidence from the sources for the assumption of some modern historians that Eugippius' rule was identical with the *Augustinian Rule* and that it was later adopted by the Italian St. Victorianus when he founded the monastery of San Martin d'Asan in the Pyrenees early in the sixth century (so Arbesmann and Hümpfner, *Liber Vitasfratrum*, p. lxxxii, n. 88, cf. Perez de Urbel, *Monjes* I, 496 and 247 f.; see also above, p. 358, n. 46, on Cardinal Schuster's hypothesis that Eugippius was the author of the *Augustinian Ordo monasterii*). The alleged influence of the *Augustinian Rule* on the monastery of San Martin d'Asan (Arbesmann and Hümpfner, *Liber Vitasfratrum*, cf. Perez de Urbel, *Monjes* I, 179) rests only on the shaky basis of an allusion to Acts 4:32 in the relatively late *Life of St. Victorianus*, for which see A. Lambert, O.S.B., article "Asan," *DHGE* IV, 867 ff. For Victorianus see now also A. Mundò, O.S.B., "Il monachesimo nella penisola Iberica fino al sec. VII," *Il monachesimo nell' Alto Medioevo e la formazione della civiltà occidentale* (Settimane di Studio del Centro Italiano di Studi sull'Alto Medioevo IV, Spoleto, 1957) 89 ff.

[20] *Regula SS. Pauli et Stephani* 14, *PL* LXVI, 954A.: Et ea cantare debemus quae, sicut beatus Augustinus dicit, ita scripta sunt ut cantentur, quae autem non ita scripta sunt, non cantamus. Cf. *Augustinian Regula ad servos Dei* 3, Arbesmann and Hümpfner, *Liber Vitasfratrum* 495: Et nolite cantare nisi quod legistis esse cantandum; quod autem non ita scriptum est ut cantetur, non cantetur. For the *Regula SS. Pauli et Stephani*, which is contained in St. Benedict of Aniane's *Codex regularum*, see U. Berlière, O.S.B., "La règle des SS. Etienne et Paul," *Mélanges Paul Thomas* (Bruges, 1930) 39 ff. Dom Berlière stresses correspondence with the *Rule of St. Benedict* and remains undecided about time and provenance. C. J. Bishko, "Spanish Monasticism in the Visigothic Period" (Unprinted Ph.D.

possible dependence upon the *Augustinian Rule* has been noticed in the
treatise *De districtione monachorum*, written by a disciple of the above-
named Abbot Donatus, Eutropius, who was his successor as abbot of
the *monasterium Servitanum* and later became bishop of Valencia.[21] The
Augustinian Rule has a much larger share in the composition of the so-
called *Regula Tarnatensis*:[22] in fact almost the entire text of the *Augustinian Regula ad servos Dei* has been incorporated in the second part
of that rule (c. 14 ff.) and the *Augustinian Ordo monasterii* is used
in the first part.[23] The *Regula Tarnatensis* is of uncertain origin and
date, but shows some similarity to the monastic *Rule of St. Isidore of
Seville*.[24] Isidore's older brother, St. Leander of Seville (died 600),
who was a monk before he became bishop, in his *Liber de institutione
virginum et contemptu mundi*, written for nuns,[25] and Isidore himself in

---

Diss., Harvard University, Cambridge, Mass., 1937) 189 ff., and "The Date and
Nature of the Spanish Consensoria Monachorum," *Amer. Jour. Philol.* LXIX (1948)
380, 388, assumes Northern Spanish (Gallegan) origin in the last quarter of the seventh
century.

[21] See Verheijen, "Regula Sancti Augustini" 55 f., on textual correspondence with both
the *Augustinian Regula ad servos Dei* and the *Augustinian Ordo monasterii*. For the treatise
De districtione monachorum, see also below, p. 416, n. 69.

[22] *Regula Tarnatensis*, PL LXVI, 977 ff.

[23] Cf. *Regula Tarnatensis* c. 11 and c. 13 with *Augustinian Ordo monasterii* c. 4: . . .
apostolicam enim vitam optamus vivere, and c. 10: Si quis autem non omni virtute . . .,
Arbesmann and Hümpfner, *Liber Vitasfratrum* 492.

[24] Cf. Perez de Urbel, *Monjes* I, 493 ff., A. E. Anspach, "Das Fortleben Isidors im VII.
bis IX. Jahrhundert," in *Miscell. Isidor.* 326. The textual relationship between *Regula
Tarnatensis* 4 and canon 42 of the Fourth Council of Toledo, alleged by Perez de Urbel,
Monjes I, 494, and Anspach, 326, is too vague to prove dependence either way. The opinion,
even now current in the literature, that the *Regula Tarnatensis* belonged to the monastery
of Acaunum near St. Maurice-en-Valais has been refuted by Bishop Marius Besson as early
as 1911: the *monasterium Acaunense*, founded in 515 by the Burgundian King Sigismund, had
nothing to do with the church which in the fourth century had existed at Acaunum and
conceivably could have been served by clerics who lived in *vita communis* similar to that
practiced by Eusebius of Vercelli or Augustine and their clerics; furthermore, though St.
Maurice was called Tarnadae in the fourth century, the sources never speak of a *monasterium
Tarnatense*. Cf. M. Besson, "Regula Tarnatensis," *Zeitschrift für Schweizerische Kirchengeschichte* V (1911) 296 ff., idem, *Monasterium Acaunense* (Fribourg, 1913), not available to me,
J.-M. Theurillat, "L'abbaye de Saint-Maurice d'Agaune. Des origines à la réforme canoniale, 515-830," *Vallesia* (1954).

[25] PL LXXII, 873 ff. See also A. C. Vega, O.S.A., El *"De institutione virginum"* de San
Leandro de Sevilla, con diez capitulos e medios ineditos (El Escorial, 1948), J. Madoz, S.J.,
"Una nueva transmision del «Libellus de institutione virginum» de San Leandro de Sevilla
. . .," *Anal. Boll.* LXVII= *Mélanges Paul Peeters* I (1949) 407 ff.

his *Regula monachorum*[26] have both used the female adaptation of the *Augustinian Rule*, Isidore in addition also oriental rules, Cassian, and, perhaps, the *Rule of St. Benedict*, and the lost rule of the Spaniard John of Biclaro.[27]

More important even than the textual relationship of these later rules to that of St. Augustine, is the Augustinian "flavor" which is more pronounced in them than in the *Rule of St. Benedict*. Their spirit is that of the *cor unum et anima una in Deo* of the Acts of the Apostles and of the Augustinian Rule.[28] At the same time one may observe in them a certain lack of precise regulations with regard to many details of monastic life.[29] All this is typically Augustinian and forms a con-

[26] *PL* LXXXIII, 867 ff.

[27] For Leander, see W. S. Porter, "Early Spanish Monasticism," *Laudate* X (1932) 9 ff., J. Madoz, S.J., "Varios enigmas de la «Regla» de San Leandro decifrados por el estudio de sus fuentes," *Miscell. Mercati* I, 265 ff., Verheijen, "Regula Sancti Augustini" 53 f. Cf. p. 357, n. 40. For Isidore's *Regula monachorum* and its sources cf. Porter, "Spanish Monasticism," Laudate X, 66 ff., S. McKenna, "The Monastic Rules of Visigothic Spain" (M. A. Diss., Catholic University of America, Washington, D.C., 1935) 33 f., Bishko, "Spanish Monasticism," and above all Sr. P. J. Mullins, O.P., *The Spiritual Life according to Saint Isidore of Seville* (Catholic University of America Studies in Medieval and Renaissance Latin, Language, and Literature XIII, Washington, D.C., 1940) 68 ff., where the considerable dependence of St. Isidore's rule on that of St. Augustine is well illustrated. For the perusal of the female adaptation of the *Augustinian Rule* (both *Ordo monasterii* and *Regula ad servos Dei*) by the *Rule of St. Isidore*, though the latter is written for monks, see Verheijen, "Regula S. Augustini" 48 ff.; about P. Hümpfner's different view, see above, p. 357, n. 40. P. Verheijen, in his article "La «Regula Puellarum» et la «Regula Sancti Augustini»," *Augustiniana* IV (1954) 267 f., wishes to prove by textual comparison that Isidore has used also the male form of Augustine's rule; but this seems to be less convincing. For the rest, P. Verheijen himself rightly suggests that Isidore's perusal of the female adaptation is best explained by the fact that he knew it through his brother, St. Leander, who had used it in his *Liber de institutione virginum*, which was addressed to their sister, the nun Florentia.

[28] See above, pp. 359–361, for the *Augustinian Rule* and for Augustine's *Sermons* CCCLV and CCCLVI. The Augustinian spirit is particularly striking in the *Rule of St. Isidore*. For the ideal of the apostolic common life according to Acts 4:32–35 Isidore's *Regula monachorum* 3, 1 and 12, 1, *PL* LXXXIII, 870B and 882A, should be compared with the *Augustinian Regula ad servos Dei* 1, Arbesmann and Hümpfner, *Liber Vitasfratrum* 494. Isidore in his rule also uses Augustine's *De moribus ecclesiae catholicae* I, 31, 67, *PL* XXXII, 1338, and *De opere monachorum* 17, 20, *CSEL* XLI, 564; cf. Sr. P. J. Mullins, *Isidore* 73.

[29] Cf. the remarks of W. Hümpfner, O.E.S.A., "Die Regeln des heiligen Augustinus: Zur Überlieferung der Augustinerregel," v. Balthasar, *Grosse Ordensregeln* 106, A. Zumkeller, O.E.S.A., "Regeln des heiligen Augustinus: Zum geistigen Gehalt der Augustinerregel," v. Balthasar, *Grosse Ordensregeln* 119, Zumkeller, *Das Mönchtum des heiligen Augustinus* (Würzburg, 1950) 219. See also F. van der Meer, *Augustinus der Seelsorger* (German translation of *Augustinus de Zielzorger*), 2nd ed. (Köln, 1953) 254, for Augustine's relative lack of interest

trast to St. Benedict's, the great lawgiver's, rule, which, too, is pervaded by the spirit of fraternal charity, but on the whole expresses it implicitly rather than explicitly[30] and pays much more attention to organization.

The Augustinian spirit of monastic charity was extended by Augustine and his disciples to the *vita communis* of the clergy;[31] also, Augustine made it clear by word and deed that lay monks must heed the call to the priesthood and episcopate if they were needed for the service of the Church as a whole.[32] While this is quite different from St. Benedict's much stricter distinction of the clerical and monastic orders, close contacts between monasticism and the clericate were continued in various forms, with or without direct Augustinian influence, in the post-Augustinian west.

2. MONASTIC LIFE OF CLERICAL COMMUNITIES IN THE POST-AUGUSTINIAN AGE

If St. Augustine's emphasis on a common clerical life without individual property was neither quite isolated nor absolutely novel,[1] it was still he who expressed the idea with such ethical and spiritual force that it was probably never forgotten and in any case was repeatedly revitalized during the history of the Church in the west. The *vita communis* and *apostolica* of the clergy was a very effective means of its reform, since it acted as a definite check on personal wealth and excluded noncelibatarian clerics, thus removing two great obstacles

in administrative and organizational detail; his attitude seems to have been based on the feeling that these things could take care of themselves with a minimum of intervention on his part, if he was only able to inculcate the right spirit. See also below, p. 416, about the different cultural atmosphere of the following century, which required a different approach.

[30] The most typically Augustinian quotation from Acts 4:32-35: *anima una et cor unum* (*Augustinian Regula ad servos Dei* 1, Arbesmann and Hümpfner, *Liber Vitasfratrum* 494) does not occur in the *Rule of St. Benedict*; in chapters 34 and 55, Linderbauer 46 and 62, only the verse Acts 4:35, containing the practical application of the principle of fraternal love, is quoted: *dividebatur* or *dabatur singulis prout cuique opus erat*, in chapter 33, Linderbauer 46, only the last part of the verse Acts 4:32: *omniaqua . . . sint communia* and *nec quisquam . . . suum aliquid dicat.*

[31] See above, Part Three, Chapter II, 2.

[32] See above, pp. 339, 355 f.

[1] See above, pp. 350-353.

to a spiritual conception of the clericate. This then was another of those productive Augustinian ideas which were destined to be taken up anew in later periods of Church reform.

The sources concerning the existence and circumstances of clerical *vita communis* in Late Antiquity and the early Middle Ages are scarce.[2] But there is little doubt that it did exist in some churches of the west and that in a number of instances, though certainly not always, it did descend from the clerico-monastic way of life of the Augustinian age. This does not mean that the eleventh century clerical reform or the twelfth century Augustinian Canons Regular and related clerico-monastic groups can be derived in unbroken line from St. Augustine's clergy in the bishop's house at Hippo. Between the sixth and the eleventh century there is in fact no definite evidence that the clerical *vita communis*, where it was practiced, was based on the *Augustinian Rule*. It is rather the continuity of a monastically or quasi-monastically living clergy which is of interest, a specific realization and heritage of the reform ideology not only of St. Augustine himself, but of the Augustinian age as a whole. The following brief survey of what is known about the *vita communis* of the clergy in the fifth and sixth centuries will, therefore, include more than those instances in which a connection with St. Augustine and Africa can be surmised.

At the beginning of any such account the observation must be made that in late patristic and early mediaeval times the distinction between monks and clerics was in practice not anyway as clear cut as some of the legislative and literary sources of the time would lead one to believe.[3] In spite of the fact that many important documents of the period, such as St. Jerome's *Epistle to Heliodorus*, the acts of the Council of Chalcedon, the *Rule of St. Benedict*, the canons of the Council of Carthage of 525, a letter of St. Columbanus, stress the difference

---

[2] Cf. L. Hertling, S.J., "Kanoniker, Augustinusregel und Augustinerorden," *Z. kath. Theol.* LIV (1930) 334 ff., Ch. Dereine, S.J., article "Chânoines," *DHGE* XII, 353 ff., also *idem*, "Vie commune, règle de saint Augustin et chânoines réguliers au XIe siècle," *Rev. hist. ecclés.* XLI (1946) 365 ff., and A. Smith, article "Chanoines réguliers," *DSpir*, fasc. VIII, 463 ff., J. C. Dickinson, *The Origins of the Austin Canons and Their Introduction into England* (London, 1950), id., "Aux origines de la vie commune dans le clergé," *Vie spir.*, Suppl. VI (1953) 63 ff.

[3] See also Hertling, "Kanoniker," and the article series "Réguliers et séculiers" by F. Petit, O. Praem., J. Winandy, O.S.B., etc., in *Vie spir.* LXXX (1949) 9 ff.

between clerics and monks,[4] it is at times hard to see in what way the common life of the clergy attached to a *basilica*, that is to say, to a cathedral church or to a church founded over the relics of a saint, differed from the monastic life, except, of course, that in a monastery there were at that time very few priests and clerics or none at all.[5] The lack of distinctness between the two ways of life is indicated to some extent by early mediaeval terminology itself. The matter has been clarified especially with regard to Merovingian France, by L. Levillain, whereas the development in other countries has not yet been studied to the same extent.[6]

[4] For St. Jerome and the Council of Chalcedon, see p. 347 f., nn. 24, 27. St. Benedict makes it very clear that the reception of priests into the monastery is exceptional, even though his rule envisages the ordination of one or several priests and deacons for the monastery; see *Sancti Benedicti Regula* 60 and 62, Linderbauer 65 f. and 67. For the Council of Carthage of 525 see Mansi, *Concil.* VIII, 656: Erunt igitur omnia omnino monasteria, sicut semper fuerunt, a conditione clericorum modis omnibus libera sibi tantum et Deo placentia. . . . See also Columbanus, *Epist.* II (utilizing Jerome's *Epist.* XIV, *ad Heliodorum*, cf. above, p. 347, n. 24), *Scriptores Latini Hiberniae* II (Dublin, 1957) 20: Alia enim sunt et alia clericorum et monachorum documenta, ea et longe ab invicem separata. Cf. in general T. P. McLaughlin, *Le très ancien droit monastique de l'occident* (Archives de la France monastique XXXVIII, Ligugé, Paris, 1935) 111 ff.

[5] Cf. the preceding note for the *Rule of St. Benedict*; also, for instance, St. Aurelianus of Arles, *Regula ad monachos* 46 (cf. p. 381, n. 13), *PL* LXVIII, 392C: Nullus honorem presbyterii aut diaconatus accipiat praeter abbatem, si voluerit ordinari presbyterum et unum diaconum et subdiaconum, quo ipse voluerit et quando voluerit, ordinandi habeat potestatem....

[6] Cf. L. Levillain, "Etudes sur l'abbaye de Saint-Denis à l'époque mérovingienne II," *Bibliothèque de l'Ecole des Chartes* LXXXVI (1925) 5 ff. See also Margaret Deanesly, "Early English and Gallic Minsters," *Trans. R. Histor. Soc.*, Ser. IV, XXIII (1941) 25 ff. In general, cf. the excellent, but in this respect not exhaustive, work of A. Pöschl, *Bischofsgut und Mensa Episcopalis* I (Bonn, 1908), and Dereine, "Chânoines." For Rome in particular, see the pertinent remarks in the work of Abbot (later Cardinal) Ildefonso Schuster, O.S.B., *The Sacramentary* (*Liber Sacramentorum*): *Historical and Liturgical Notes on the Roman Missal*, trans. from the Italian by A. Levelis-Marke, III (New York, etc., 1927), with regard to the early mediaeval monasteries at the Lateran and Vatican Basilicas, etc., and for the symbiosis of monks and clerics there and their share in the liturgical service in those basilicas; see, especially, p. 69 f. on the mixed monastic-clerical character of the Pope's "Bishop's House," the Lateran Palace: "the Popes . . . surrounded themselves in the palace of the Lateran Patriarchate with secular priests and with monks indifferently, for they were both equally attached to the service of the *Episcopium*. These latter were in the habit of residing with the Pontiff at the Lateran, as soon as they had been chosen to the subdiaconate. . . . Those Popes who came originally from monasteries were disposed to lead within the palace of the Patriarchate the same life as they had led in the cloister . . . they surrounded themselves preferably with monks, so that the episcopal palace assumed the appearance of a monastery. St. Gregory [the Great] did this . . . and many years previously in Italy, at Milan and at Vercelli, also in Africa, through the influence of St. Martin [of Tours], St.

The term *abbas* (*abbates*), so familiar from mediaeval monastic history, was in sixth and seventh century France applied also to the head and sometimes to the members of communities of priests and clerics who served such important *basilicae* as St. Martin of Tours, St. Hilary of Poitiers, St. Rémi of Reims, St. Germain of Auxerre, St. Denis.[7] Members of these basilican communities were also designated as *custodes, clerici, fratres, pauperes*, and even as *monachi*; but they were obviously not monks in the sense of the theoretical distinction between the monastic and the clerical lives, even though the *fratres, monachi*, etc., also included lay personnel attached to the Church.[8] The basilican clerics and "monks," though they did not before c. 650 follow the rules of St. Benedict or of St. Columbanus or another definitely monastic rule,[9] did live according to certain norms which in the

Ambrose, St. Eusebius, and St. Augustine, many episcopal dwellings were turned into monasteries." Cf. also Cardinal I. Schuster's *Saint Benedict and His Times*, trans. G. J. Roettger, O.S.B. (St. Louis, London, 1951) 375 ff., G. Ferrari, O.S.B., *Early Roman Monasteries* (Studi di Antichità Cristiana XXIII, Città del Vaticano, 1957) 242 ff., 363 ff., 377 ff. Canons Regular in the proper sense, who lived according to the rule of St. Augustine, existed at the Lateran at least since the bull of Anastasius IV of December 30, 1153, cf. JL 9793 and P. F. Kehr, *Italia Pontificia* I (Berlin, 1906) 28, no. 19. Attempts toward the *vita communis* of the Roman clergy had been made even before the time of Hildebrand, who was instrumental in strengthening these efforts; see Hildebrand's speech at the Roman Synod of 1059, ed. A. Werminghoff, in *Neues Archiv* XXVII (1902) 669 ff., and the literature mentioned below, p. 401, n. 63, also Kehr, *loc. cit.* 25, no. 7, about Alexander II's lost privilege for *canonici* of the Lateran. That the African Pope Gelasius I (492–496) instituted Canons Regular of St. Augustine at the Lateran seems to be mentioned first by the great antiquarian Onophrius Panvinius, O.E.S.A., in his annotations to Platina's *Historia de vitis pontificum Romanorum* (Venezia, 1562) 52 f. Panvinius refers to the archives of the Lateran Basilica. While Gelasius I can of course not have instituted Augustinian Canons Regular of the mediaeval type at the Lateran, he might as an African conceivably have transferred to the Lateran Basilica the Augustinian *vita communis* of the clergy, which would have lapsed in the early Middle Ages, since Hildebrand speaks of a renewal.

[7] Cf. Levillain, "Saint-Denis" 44 ff., 52 ff., McLaughlin, *Droit monastique* 30 ff., Deanesly, "Minsters" 37 ff. Gregory of Tours accordingly does not sharply distinguish the terms *clericus* and *monachus*; cf. McLaughlin 122.

[8] See Levillain, "Saint-Denis," especially 62 ff. Levillain, *ibid.* 52, would like to call such establishments "basiliques à laure," to distinguish them from the basilicas, i.e., from the church buildings, of monasteries. Yet, with the possible exception of St. Martin of Tours, there does not seem to be any evidence of oriental influence on these basilicas, which, as Levillain rightly says, "participent . . . au double caractère de la collégiale et du monastère." An interesting instance of the long survival of such mixed basilican communities is quoted for Arezzo from the *Historia custodum Aretinorum* of the late eleventh century (*MGH, SS* XXX, 2, 1471 ff.) by R. W. Southern, *The Making of the Middle Ages* (New Haven, 1953) 128 ff.

[9] Cf. Levillain, "Saint-Denis" 77 ff.

sources are usually termed *canonum regula* or the like;[10] such terms may simply refer to adherence to the liturgical canon and the canon law, governing ecclesiastical institutions,[11] but as will be seen presently this *vita canonica* did in some cases probably include *vita communis* without individual property.

It will perhaps always remain uncertain whether and to what extent the example of the apostolic common life of the Augustinian clergy of Africa contributed to the survival or emergence of similar phenomena in early mediaeval Europe.[12] There are a few indications, however, which would seem to make it probable that the Augustinian *vita communis* did have a share in such developments of the early mediaeval centuries. This question is not identical with that of the influence of the *Augustinian Rule*: the latter, though used by the clergy of Hippo and probably by other clerical communities, was by its origin monastic in the stricter sense; moreover, Augustine's institution of the common life of the clergy could be propagated also by personal filiation and by the literary transmission of *Sermons* CCCLV and CCCLVI and other relevant writings of his.[13]

In the second half of the fifth century the African rhetor Julianus Pomerius, a true "Augustinian" in his literary work, appeared in Southern France; at Arles St. Caesarius was his pupil.[14] Pomerius

---

[10] See, for instance, First Council of Orléans, of 511, can. 17, *MGH, Leg.* III, *Concil.* I, 6; cf. Levillain, "Saint-Denis" 73; for the continued use of this terminology in later times, see Dereine, "Vie commune" 366 ff., 388 ff.

[11] Cf. below, p. 390 f., n. 21.

[12] While the great sixteenth, seventeenth, and eighteenth century historians of the Augustinian Canons Regular and of the Augustinian Hermits, such as Panvinio, Pennotto, Lupus, and Amort, were all in favor of continuity, the Benedictine Mabillon expressed grave doubts. For a good critical discussion by the Bollandists, see *AA. SS., October,* Vol. IX, 598 f., 730 ff.

[13] It is characteristic of the manuscript tradition of the *Augustinian Rule* that it is often found together with extracts from Augustine's *Sermons* CCCLV and CCCLVI on the common life of the clergy (for these sermons see above, pp. 359–361) and with other relevant patristic texts as well as with other rules; cf. Ch. Dereine, S.J., "Enquête sur la règle de saint Augustin," *Scriptorium* II (1948) 28 ff.

[14] For Pomerius' life, the Augustinian character of his literary work, and his influence on St. Caesarius of Arles see the convenient résumé and bibliography in the English translation of his work *The Contemplative Life* by Sr. M. J. Suelzer (Ancient Christian Writers IV, Westminster, Md., 1947); also Cilleruelo, "Influencia" 131 f. and M. L. W. Laistner, "The Influence during the Middle Ages of the Treatise *De vita contemplativa* . . .," *Miscell. Mercati* II, 344 ff.

became a priest in Gaul; the title *abbas* by which he was addressed does, as pointed out above, not necessarily make him the head of a monastery, but perhaps the superior of clerics living in *vita communis*.[15] And indeed, a large section of his treatise *De vita contemplativa* is devoted to the proposition that ideally priests and clerics should not retain personal property and should live in common.[16] His approach to the subject is strongly reminiscent of Augustine's *Sermons* CCCLV and CCCLVI.[17] Augustinian also is his concern to prove that bishops and priests can and ought to live the contemplative life in the midst of pastoral cares.[18] It is true that while Augustine had altogether rejected for his own Church clerics who were unwilling to share in the *vita communis*, Pomerius, who deals with the problem in a general way, also considered those who are "too weak to renounce their possessions." He is willing to admit that these can be without sin if they are content with what they own and do not claim anything from the Church.[19] The great principle is: "What the Church owns she has in common with all those who have nothing. . . ."[20]

It must be repeated that generally in this period and in the whole early Middle Ages clerics could live in so-called *vita canonica* without living also in *vita communis*: *canonici* did not necessarily renounce their own property. Contrary to the *vita communis*, canonical life (the *ordo canonicus*) meant primarily performance in common of the liturgical office in the cathedral or basilica to which the *canonici* were attached, not infrequently also common meals and common domicile. Much more rarely no doubt was a *vita communis* of the Augustinian type joined to the *vita canonica*; it may be that in the early Middle Ages the combination more often than not remained an ideal postulate.[21]

---

[15] Cf. Sr. M. J. Suelzer, in her translation of Pomerius' work, pp. 4 and 173 f., G. Fritz, article "Pomère," *DThC* XII, 2, 2537 ff. Cilleruelo, "Influencia" 132, thinks that Pomerius actually introduced the concept of the "canonical" life of clerics into Gaul, but does not prove this.

[16] See Pomerius, *De vita contemplativa* II, 9 to 16, *PL* LIX, 453B ff.

[17] Cf. above, pp. 359–361.

[18] See *De vita contemplativa* I, 13, *PL* LIX, 429A ff., and cf. the Augustinian texts, quoted above, pp. 337 ff.

[19] *De vita contemplativa* II, 12, LIX, 455D f.

[20] *Ibid.* II, 9, LIX, 454A: Quod habet ecclesia, cum omnibus nihil habentibus habet commune. . . .

[21] All this has been made quite clear by Pöschl, *Bischofsgut*, especially 48 ff., also by Hertling, "Kanoniker" 335 ff., and "Die professio der Kleriker und die Entstehung der

It is almost certain, nevertheless, that the Augustinian synthesis of clericate and monasticism did survive. There is good evidence for post-Augustinian Africa in Ferrandus' *Vita* of the sixth century Bishop St. Fulgentius of Ruspe, who has already been mentioned as a transmitter to Europe of African influence. When Fulgentius became a bishop he did not cease to be a monk.[22] He did not want to be without the company of monks and built a monastery near the cathedral.[23] There and in the monasteries which he founded in Sardinia, at and near Cagliari, during his exile, he lived with his monks in the Augustinian manner in full community of possessions according to the Acts of the Apostles.[24]

drei Gelübde," *Z. kath. Theol.* LVI (1932), especially 160 ff. Dereine, in his various studies, quoted above, does not always sufficiently consider the practical distinctness of *vita communis* and *vita canonica*, while Pöschl, on the other hand, *Bischofsgut* 58, denies all connection between the two, hardly with good reason. The expression *canonicus* originates from the Greek term κανών which has a long, complicated, and interesting history; cf. H. Oppel, "*KANΩN*, Zur Bedeutungsgeschichte des Wortes und seiner lateinischen Entsprechungen (regula-norma)," *Philologus*, Suppl. Bd. XXX, 4 (1937), L. Wenger, "Canon in den römischen Rechtsquellen und in den Papyri," *Sitz. Ber. Wien* CCXX, 2 (1942). Of the various ecclesiastical meanings of canon the liturgical—signifying psalmody or other liturgical prayer (cf. Pöschl, *Bischofsgut* 52 f.)—and the juridical—especially regarding clerical life (cf. Hertling, "Kanoniker" 338 ff.)—are here particularly important.

[22] Ferrandus, *Vita S. Fulgentii* 18, 37, *PL* LXV, 135D f. (the edition of G.-G.Lapeyre, Paris, 1929, was not accessible to me): Nec ita factus est episcopus ut esse desisteret monachus; sed accepta pontificis dignitate professionis praeteritae servavit integritatem. For Fulgentius, see also below, pp. 408 f., and the biography of Lapeyre, quoted there.

[23] Ferrandus, *Vita S. Fulgentii* 19, 39, *PL* LXV, 136D ff.; see in this connection also *ibid.* 11, 23, LXV, 128D f., where Ferrandus narrates that Bishop Eulalius of Syracuse, whom Fulgentius had visited in his youth, had a *monasterium proprium, cui semper adhaerebat quoties ab ecclesiasticis actibus vacabat.*

[24] Cf. *ibid.* 19, 39 and 29, 57 f., LXV, 137A and 146 D ff.; also *ibid.* 20, 43, LXV, 138C f. (about the first monastic settlement at Cagliari of Fulgentius and his fellow exiles from Africa): . . . similitudinem magni cuiusdam monasterii monachis et clericis adunatis sapienter effecit. Erat quippe eis communis mensa, commune cellarium, communis oratio simul et lectio. Nullus se super alterum insolenter efferebat neque propriis fratribus amplius aut peculiarius consulebat, nisi quod magis illi monachi, qui beatum Fulgentium sequebantur, districtioris abstinentiae regulam custodientes nihil omnino proprium possidebant nec inter alios clericos clericorum more vivebant; *ibid.* 27, 51, LXV, 143B f. (about the second Sardinian monastery, near Cagliari): principaliter hoc observandum monachis tradens, ut nullus eorum quidquam proprium sibi vindicaret, sed essent omnibus omnia communia (cf. Acts 4:32); the rest of the paragraph, too, is Augustinian in spirit and at the same time perhaps influenced by the *Rule of St. Benedict*, c. 33 f., Linderbauer 46 f., cf. J. Chapman, O.S.B., *Saint Benedict and the Sixth Century* (New York, etc., 1929) 115.

In the Augustinian manner, too, he valued those monks highest who showed love for "spiritual" science and chose his clerics chiefly from their midst.[25] One can therefore hardly doubt that Fulgentius and his clergy followed the example of Augustine's *episcopium* at Hippo in a *vita communis* without individual property.

It is possible that the Augustinian combination of *domus episcopi* and monastery was fused with the eastern practice of elevating monks to the episcopate in the sphere of influence of the great island monastery of Lérins where Augustinian as well as oriental trends of thought were active, notwithstanding the strong Semi-Pelagian reaction against Augustine's doctrine of grace.[26] The *paradisus Lerinensis* has with good reason been called a "nursery of bishops."[27] Not a few of these bishops continued to live as monks and reformed or founded monasteries, for which they wrote rules and from which they allowed bishops to be taken.[28] There is no certain evidence that the clergy of their

[25] Ferrandus, *Vita S. Fulgentii* 17, 52, *PL* LXV 144A f.: Laborantes fratres et opera carnalia indefessis viribus exercentes, lectionis autem studium non habentes, minus diligebat nec honore maximo dignis iudicabat. In quo autem fuisset scientiae spiritalis affectus, etiamsi virtute corporis destitus operari manibus numquam posset, ab eo peculiariter habebatur dilectus et gratus; see also *ibid.* 29, 57 ff., LXV, 146B ff., about the relationship between monks and clerics at Ruspe after Fulgentius' final return from exile.

[26] See below, pp. 404 ff.

[27] By A. Cooper-Marsdin, *The History of the Islands of Lerins* (Cambridge, 1913); cf. P. de Labriolle, *Histoire de la littérature latine chrétienne*, 3rd ed. by G. Bardy, II (Paris, 1947) 649. For Lérins see also L. Cristiani, *Lérins et ses fondateurs* (Paris, 1946) and Nora K. Chadwick, *Poetry and Letters in Early Christian Gaul* (London, 1955) 142 ff. For the conception of Lérins as a Paradise in the wider context of the Paradise-likeness of the hermitical life see Eucherius of Lyons, *De laude heremi*, especially 42, *CSEL* XXXI, 192; for the expression *Lirinensis insulae paradisus* in the *Vita S. Hilarii Arelatensis*, see p. 413, n. 55. Bishops who had been monks at Lérins were, for instance, St. Honoratus of Arles, St. Hilarius of Arles, St. Caesarius of Arles, St. Eucherius of Lyons, St. Valerian of Cimiez, Faustus of Riez; cf. also Eucherius, *De laude heremi*.

[28] For Caesarius of Arles' monastic rules see above, pp. 380–381. For his predecessor as bishop, Hilarius, see Reverentius (saec. VI), *Vita S. Hilarii Arelatensis* 7 (for this biography see also p. 413, n. 55), *PL* L, 1229A: (after having become bishop) Hilarius, quem pax longa nutrierat (i.e., at Lérins), congregationem subito [instituerit] secreti cupidam, continentiae virtute crescentem, quam suo non minus pene imbuit exemplo quam formavit eloquio. . . . It is possible that this refers not to a monastery in the strict sense, but to common life of the clergy at the bishop's cathedral, cf. Cristiani, *Lérins* 133. The monastic rule of Caesarius' successor Aurelianus of Arles (cf. p. 381, n. 13) envisages the possibility that bishops will be taken from the monastery; see his *Regula ad monachos* 46, *PL* LXVIII, 392: Si vero Deo propitio ita proficeretis, ut aliquis ex vobis ad episcopatum expetatur, ipse solus egrediatur.

dioceses lived in *vita communis*, though one would be inclined to think so, at least in the case of Arles under St. Caesarius,[29] who was influenced by Augustine in drawing up his monastic rules[30] and also in writing his sermons.

As to Spain, direct and indirect oriental influence on its early monastic institutions, though no doubt extant, has perhaps been somewhat exaggerated and the same holds true for the influence of the *Rule of St. Benedict*;[31] there are at any rate some traces also of a blending of the clerical and the monastic life. The Fourth Council of Toledo of 663 assumes that the clerics of episcopal churches normally live together *in conclavi episcopi*.[32] This community of domicile may or may not indicate *vita communis* without individual property. St. Isidore of Seville, who presided over the council, was not a monk, but as well known he was greatly influenced by St. Augustine; how fully he may have tried to realize the latter's conception of the clerical life we do not know.[33] The bent of the Visigothic councils was in general favorable to ascetic ideals. Thus the Third Council of Toledo of 589 legislated that a bishop may give property of his church to a monastery,[34] may even constitute a Church of his diocese as a *monachorum regulariter congregatio*, and may endow it from the substance of the bishop's

---

[29] Cf. also A. Malnory, *Saint Césaire, évêque d'Arles 503–543* (Bibliothèque de l'Ecole des Hautes Etudes, Sciences philosophiques et historiques, CIII, Paris, 1894) 26 ff.

[30] See above, pp. 380 f.

[31] See, for instance, Perez de Urbel, *Monjes*. Cf. W. Hümpfner, O.S.A., in his introduction to Arbesmann and Hümpfner, *Liber Vitasfratrum*, and Mullins, *Isidore* 68 ff.

[32] Fourth Council of Toledo, can. 23 f., Bruns, *Can. Apost. et Concil.* I, 230 f.: can. 23: Non aliter placuit ut quemadmodum antistite ita presbyteres atque levitae, quos forte infirmitas aut aetatis gravitas in conclavi episcopi manere non sinit, ut et iidem in cellulis suis testes vitae habeant . . .; can. 24: . . . si qui in clero puberes aut adolescentes existunt, omnes in uno conclavi atrii commorentur . . . deputati probatissimo seniori, quem et magistrum doctrinae et testem vitae habeant. . . . Qui autem his praeceptis reluctaverint, monasteriis deputentur. . . . See also the seventh century *Vitas sanctorum patrum Emeretensium* I, 1 (I, 1), Garvin 138 and 273 ff., where the *domus* of St. Eulalia is the establishment in which the Bishop of Merida lived together with his clerics and *pueri* ("seminarians"). Cf. above, p. 380, for the monastery of the African Nanctus in Merida.

[33] Cf. J. Perez Llamazares, "¿San Isidoro de Sevilla, monje?," *Miscell. Isidor.* 39 ff., for the *vita canonica* (but not necessarily *vita communis*) of St. Isidore and of early mediaeval Spanish cathedral clergy in general.

[34] Third Council of Toledo, can. 3, Bruns, *Can. Apost. et Concil.* I, 213: . . . si quid vero quod utilitatem non gravet ecclesiae pro suffragio monachorum ad suam parochiam pertinentium dederint, firmum maneat. Cf. McLaughlin, *Droit monastique* 143.

Church if this will not be detrimental to the latter.[35] The spiritual basis of such legislation is stated by the Fourth Council of Toledo when it compares the clerical life as such with the monastic state in the following manner: "The monks desire a better life" (quia meliorem vitam sequi cupiunt).[36]

The early seventh century Bishop St. Braulio of Saragossa wrote a life of the great hermit St. Millan (Aemilianus) of Cogolla who died in 574 at the age of a hundred years. We know from this source that as an old man Millan was ordained to the priesthood and after a short phase as a parish priest withdrew to an oratory which became the nucleus of the famous monastery of San Millan de Cogolla. The Vita also mentions that at the time of his death Millan called to his side the priest Asellus cum quo habebat collegium.[37] This expression makes it appear possible that St. Millan's oratory was an establishment somewhat similar to St. Martin of Tours' "Laura" and to the half-monastic, half-collegiate churches of Merovingian Gaul mentioned above.

Such an interpretation seems to be confirmed by the close relationship between monastery and episcopate in sixth century Braga in Suevian Galicia under St. Martin of Dumium and Braga (died 579).[38] This namesake and Pannonian fellowcountryman of St. Martin of Tours founded the monasterium Dumiense just outside the city of Braga of which he later became the metropolitan.[39] Yet even as bishop and archbishop

---

[35] Ibid., can. 4, Bruns I, 213: Si episcopus unam de parochitanis ecclesiis suis monasterium dicare voluerit, ut in ea monachorum regulariter congregatio vivat, hoc de consensu concilii sui habeat licentiam faciendi; qui etiam, si de rebus ecclesiae pro eorum substantia aliquid quod detrimentum ecclesiae non exhibeat eidem loco donaverit, sit stabile. . . . Cf. McLaughlin, Droit monastique 143 f.

[36] Fourth Council of Toledo, can. 50, Bruns I, 235: Clerici, qui monachorum propositum appetunt, quia meliorem vitam sequi cupiunt, liberos eis ab episcopo in monasteriis largiri oportet ingressus, nec interdici propositum eorum, qui ad contemplationis desiderium transire nituntur. Cf. McLaughlin, Droit monastique 143, Mullins, Isidore 14.

[37] Braulio of Saragossa, Vita S. Aemiliani 28, 34, PL LXXX, 712C (the edition of J. Cazzaniga in Bollettino del Comitato per la preparazione dell' edizione nazionale dei classici greci e latini, N.S., fasc. 2 [Roma, Accademia Nazionale dei Lincei, 1955] was inaccessible to me). See C. H. Lynch, Saint Braulio, Bishop of Saragossa (631–651) (Catholic University of America, Washington, D.C., 1938) especially 220 ff.

[38] For St. Martin of Braga, see now the introduction to C. W. Barlow's edition of his works, Martini Episcopi Bracarensis Opera Omnia (New Haven, 1950).

[39] Cf. Barlow, Martini Bracar. Opera 3 ff.; also C. P. Caspari, Martin von Bracara's Schrift De correctione rusticorum . . . (Christiania, 1883), Introduction, X–XVIII.

he was the head of the monastery of Dumium; for Isidore of Seville calls him *Dumiensis monasterii sanctissimus pontifex*[40] and *monasterii Dumiensis episcopus*.[41] It is not impossible that the *monasterium* was a laura-like settlement of hermits as in the case of St. Martin of Tours;[42] but since Martin of Braga's episcopal dignity is mentioned in so close a connection with the monastery the latter may well have included the community of his diocesan clerics.[43] It is significant, perhaps, that *clerici*, but not *monachi*, are mentioned in the canons of the First and Second Councils of Braga, which were held in Martin's time and possibly drafted by him.[44]

In the seventh century, under St. Fructuosus of Braga (died c. 665), and in the two generations following his death an attempt was made to "monasticize" the entire Church of Galicia under abbot-bishops and

[40] Isidore of Seville, *De viris illustribus* 35, 45, *PL* LXXXIII, 1100.

[41] *Idem, Historia Gothorum, Wandalorum, Sueborum, MGH, AA* XI, 302 f. For St. Martin's immediate successors as bishops of the *monasterium Dumiense*, see H. Florez, O.S.A., *España Sagrada* XVIII (Madrid, 1764) 38 ff.

[42] Oriental influence was no doubt strong, for Martin of Braga and his disciple Paschasius translated parts of the *Sententiae* and *Vitae* of the Egyptian "Desert Fathers" from the Greek into Latin (perhaps, from a manuscript brought to Spain from the east by St. Martin); for the place of these collections in the *Apophthegmata Patrum* literature see the introduction to Barlow's edition of Martin's *Sententiae patrum Aegyptiorum, Martini Bracar. Opera* 11 ff.

[43] Paschasius in the dedication to his own translation of *Vitae patrum* addresses Martin as *presbyter et abbas*. Before his elevation to the episcopate Martin may have been in a similar position with regard to the monastery of Dumium as St. Augustine had been with regard to the "monastery in the garden" at Hippo, when he was priest but not yet bishop. Perhaps, Martin, as Augustine, continued a quasi-monastic life with his clergy as bishop. In this connection, see the *Pactum* attributed to St. Fructuosus of Dumium and Braga (died c. 665), a supplement to the so-called *Regula communis* likewise attributed to Fructuosus; the *Pactum* has the form of a treaty between abbot and monks and grants the monks the right to appeal to an *episcopus qui sub regula vivit*; he may perhaps have been the Abbot-Bishop of Dumium and Metropolitan of Braga who in the era of Fructuosus seems to have been also the head of a "congregation" of monasteries; cf. I. Herwegen, O.S.B., *Das Pactum des hl. Fruktuosus von Braga* (Kirchenrechtliche Abhandlungen XL, Stuttgart, 1907) 56 f.; also Porter, "Spanish Monasticism" *Laudate* X (1932) 161 ff., and the recent study of A. Mundò, O.S.B., "Il monachesimo nella penisola Iberica fino al sec. VII," *Il monachesimo nell' Alto Medioevo e la formazione della civiltà occidentale* (Settimane di Studio del Centro Italiano di Studi sull' Alto Medioevo IV, Spoleto, 1957) 103 ff., also 81, where other monk-bishops of sixth and seventh century Spain are mentioned. According to Bishko, "Spanish Monasticism" 186 f., *Regula communis* and *Pactum* were certainly not written by or for Fructuosus himself, but by several successive writers of the later seventh century.

[44] Cf. First Council of Braga, of 561, Barlow, *Martini Bracar. Opera* 105 ff.; Second Council of Braga, of 572, Barlow 116 ff.

monastically living priests.[45] Martin of Braga's position as "monastic bishop" and the subsequent development of monasticism in Galicia makes one wonder whether there may be at least parallelism between such Spanish phenomena[46] and the abbot-bishops of fifth, sixth, and seventh century Britain and Ireland. Could the monastic organization of the Irish Church, still rather enigmatic as to its origins, be a peculiarly inverted adaptation to Celtic rural clan society of the western Mediterranean and Gallic, originally urban, fusion of monasticism and clericate which has been discussed in this chapter? In other words, was the leadership of monks, especially in the Irish Church, a last

[45] Cf. Bishko "Spanish Monasticism" 299 ff. This development can be studied, for instance, from the *Regula communis* attributed to Fructuosus; from c. 1 and c. 2, *PL* LXXXVII, 1111 ff., it would appear that the process of "monastization" of the clergy was a reaction against a quasi-monastic "synoecism" of secular priests and lay *conversi*, cf. Bishko, "Spanish Monasticism" 257 ff., and for these Spanish *conversi*, who kept their possessions at least in part, also K. Hallinger, O.S.B., "Woher kommen die Laienbrüder?," *Analecta Sacri Ordinis Cisterciensis* XII (1956) 67 f.

[46] For the concept of "Spanish phenomena" in late ancient and early mediaeval palaeography, literature, art, liturgy, and theology and for their transmission to seventh and eighth century England and from there to Merovingian and Carolingian Francia, see L. Traube, *Einleitung in die lateinische Philologie des Mittelalters*, ed. P. Lehmann, in: L. Traube, *Vorlesungen und Abhandlungen*, ed. F. Boll, II (München, 1911) 59 ff., 126; E. A. Lowe, *Codices Latini Antiquiores* VI (Oxford, 1953) where several manuscripts of Spanish provenance, now in France, are discussed; G. Morin, O.S.B., "L'origine du symbole d'Athanase," *Jour. Theol. Stud.* XII (1911) 355; W. Neuss, *Die Apokalypse des hl. Johannes in der altspanischen und altchristlichen Bibel-Illustration* (Spanische Forschungen der Görres-Gesellschaft, Reihe I, II and III, Münster i. W., 1931), a study which proves African influence on the text and the illustration of the Apocalypse in Spain; E. Bishop, "Spanish Symptoms," *Liturgica Historica* (Oxford, 1918) 198; G. Manz, *Ausdrucksformen der lateinischen Liturgiesprache bis ins elfte Jahrhundert* (Texte und Arbeiten, herausgegeben durch die Erzabtei Beuron, Abteilung I, Beiheft I, 1941), a study which pays special attention to old-Spanish elements in all extant early mediaeval liturgical manuscripts; L. Eizenhöfer, O.S.B., "Nochmals «Spanish Symptoms»," *Sacr. Erud.* IV (1952) 31–45; C. Coebergh, O.S.B., "Sacramentaire léonien et liturgie mozarabe," *Miscell. Mohlberg* II, 295 ff. (these last two studies discuss the relationship—apparently effective both ways—between the liturgy represented by the *Sacramentarium Veronense*, i.e., the "*Sacramentarium Leonianum*," and the old-Spanish liturgy); J. A. Jungmann, S.J., "Die Abwehr des germanischen Arianismus und der Umbruch der religiösen Kultur im frühen Mittelalter," *Z. kath. Theol.* LXIX (1947), especially 55. It may be assumed that on not a few occasions the existence and transmission of "Spanish symptoms" are themselves symptomatic of the spreading of Augustinian influence; cf. in this connection Coebergh, "Sacramentaire léonien et liturgie mozarabe," *Miscell. Mohlberg* II, 295 ff., for the influence of an Augustinian sermon upon an oration of the *Sacramentarium Veronense*: this same oration, composed perhaps by the African Pope Gelasius I, has left traces also in the Mozarabic liturgy of Spain.

consequence, however devious, of that development toward "monastization" of the clergy which had been started by St. Eusebius of Vercelli and St. Augustine and of which the phenomenon of the Gallegan Church of the last two pre-Islamic centuries was another late and peculiar offshoot? Of the abbots who ruled the Irish Church during the sixth and seventh centuries about half were at the same time bishops, the other half priests; the latter had in their monasteries bishops who exercised episcopal powers of order, but not of jurisdiction.[47] This situation seems to have developed gradually out of the monastic bent within the episcopal organization of the Irish Church by St. Patrick, some of whose helpers at least seem to have been monastically living bishops and priests.[48] St. Patrick had perhaps spent a number of years of his early manhood in Auxerre under the great St. Germanus, to whose episcopal Church a clerico-monastic community of the Gallic basilican type was quite probably attached and who had built a monastery near Auxerre to which he withdrew whenever possible.[49]

[47] Cf. J. Ryan, *Irish Monasticism: Origins and Early Development* (Dublin, Cork, 1931) 167 ff., L. Gougaud, O.S.B., *Christianity in Celtic Lands* (London, 1932) 220 ff.

[48] See the story about the two *pueri Patricii*, who were at the same time bishops and monks, in the *Book of Armagh* and in *Ms. Cotton Otho E. XIII* of the British Museum, ed. L. Bieler, "Libri Epistolarum Sancti Patricii Episcopi I," *Classica et Mediaevalia* XI (1950) 104 (reissued by the Irish Manuscript Commission [Dublin, 1952]; both texts are discussed in L. Bieler's translation of *The Works of St. Patrick* [Ancient Christian Writers XVII, Westminster, Md., London, 1953] 48 and 94 f.; cf. Bieler, *The Life and Legend of St. Patrick* [Dublin, London, 1949] 33 and 129). See also Ryan, *Irish Monasticism* 93 ff., who holds that the Patrician clerics, while not monks in the strict sense, did not differ much from monks in their way of life, which must have been similar to that of the clerics of Eusebius at Vercelli and of Augustine at Hippo.

[49] The early life of St. Patrick is full of uncertainties; see J. Carney, *Studies in Irish Literature and History* (Dublin, 1955) 324 ff., Nora K. Chadwick, etc., *Studies in the Early British Church* (Cambridge, 1958) 26, 115. For Patrick's possible stay at Auxerre cf. R. Louis, "Le séjour de saint Patrice à Auxerre," *Mélanges Halphen* 445 ff., P. Grosjean, S.J., "Notes chronologiques sur le séjour de S. Patrice en Gaule," *Anal. Boll.* LXIII (1945) 73 ff., especially 117, where it is suggested that St. Germanus of Auxerre was surrounded by a semi-regular community of clerics and monks, much as St. Martin of Tours had been; cf. also P. Grosjean, "Notes d'hagiographie celtique 27: S. Patrice à Auxerre sous s. Germain: Le témoignage des noms gaulois," *Anal. Boll.* LXXV (1957) 158 ff. For St. Germanus' monastic "refuge" see Constantius, *Vita Germani episcopi Autissiodorensis* (saec. V ex.) 6, *MGH, Scriptores Rerum Merovingicarum* VII, 254: Itaque vir beatissimus . . . inter frequentias populorum solitudinis vitam et heremum in saeculi conversatione servavit.

Patrick also had as models of the combined episcopal and monastic ways of life St. Martin of Tours[50] and those early fifth century bishops of Gaul who had been monks at Lérins.[51] In the post-Patrician period the monastic trend of the Irish Church was reinforced not only by the continued absence of cities—so that the bishop's monastery became his *civitas* (Irish: *cathair*)[52] and the monastic territory his *parochia* (*paruchia*)[53]—but also, perhaps, by the influence of some of the great apostles of Britain, such as St. Ninian of Candida Casa (Whithorn) in Galloway[54] and St. David of Menevia in Wales.[55] Also, in late fifth and sixth century Gaul Salvianus of Marseille and the Breton Abbot St. Gildas of Rhys extolled the monks and some *saeculares religiosis pares* as the only remaining representatives of a really Christian life at the

Qui duplicem viam Christo ad profectum religionis instituens in conspectu oppidi interposito Icauna flumine (i.e., the Yonne) monasterium conlocavit, ut ad fidem catholicam populi et congregationibus monachorum et ecclesiastica gratia raperentur; see also *ibid.* 9, MGH, *Script. Rer. Merov.* VII, 256. This monastery had been dedicated to St. Cosmas and St. Damian by St. Germanus, but later had St. Marianus, one of its own monks, as patron; it is not identical with the great quasi-monastic basilica of St. Germain (cf. above, p. 388) which had grown out of a sanctuary likewise founded by Germanus and consecrated by him in honor of St. Mauritius and his companions; since Germanus was buried there, he became the patron saint; see the Carolingian *Gesta episcoporum Antissiodorensium* I, 8, PL CXXXVIII, 226A f., cf. Cottineau, *Répert.* I, 216 and 219. For Germanus see also Nora K. Chadwick, *Poetry and Letters in Early Christian Gaul* (London, 1955) 240 ff., and *Saint Germain et son temps*, edd. G. Le Bras and E. Gilson (Auxerre, 1950), not accessible to me.

[50] For Martinian influence on Patrick see Ryan, *Irish Monasticism* 94 f., especially with regard to the probability that Patrick knew and brought to Ireland Sulpicius Severus' works on St. Martin.

[51] Whether or not Patrick had been at Lérins has long been a controversial question. There is no proof of his stay there; cf. Bieler, *Works of St. Patrick* 95 f.; Grosjean, "S. Patrice" 92 f., thinks it possible that Patrick spent some time on the Island of Capraria, where Martin of Tours had dwelt, and on the Hyères Islands near Marseilles, which were inhabited by hermits to whom Cassian dedicated Books XVIII to XXIV of his *Conlationes*; see also Louis, "Saint Patrice" 445 ff.

[52] Cf. Ryan, *Irish Monasticism* 88.

[53] Meaning diocese; cf. Ryan, *Irish Monasticism* 87, Gougaud, *Christianity* 222, Deanesly, "Minsters" 30–34.

[54] See Ryan, *Irish Monasticism* 105 ff. For St. Ninian cf. now above all P. Grosjean, S.J., "Les Pictes apostats dans l'épître de s. Patrice," *Anal. Boll.* LXXVI (1958) 354 ff., also W. D. Simpson, *Saint Ninian and the Origins of the Christian Church in Scotland* (Edinburgh, London, 1940), Nora Chadwick, *Early British Church* 60 f.

[55] Cf. Ryan, *Irish Monasticism* 113 f., 160 ff., A. W. Wade-Evans, *Welsh Christian Origins* (Oxford, 1934) 146 ff., Chadwick, *Early British Church* 130 ff.

expense of bishops and priests; there may well have been repercussions of their views in Ireland.[56]

The questions alluded to fall outside the scope of this volume and so do the problems of early Anglo-Saxon monasticism. Yet one may here at least recall the famous *Responsa* allegedly sent by Pope Gregory the Great to Archbishop Augustine of Canterbury; even if these instructions in their present form should date from the early eighth century,[57] they would still offer evidence on the relationship between monasticism and the clerical life among the Anglo-Saxons since the time of their conversion as well as after the renewed influence of Rome and Mediterranean Christendom through Archbishop Theodore of Canterbury (died 690) and his helpers, especially Abbot Hadrian who was African by origin. If in *Responsum* I Gregory the Great says that Bishop Augustine being a monk must live in common life with his clergy and adds a clear reference to Acts 4:32,[58] it is more than likely that this reflects conditions at Roman basilicas and, especially, at the Lateran Church and

[56] Salvianus, *De gubernatione Dei* VII, 14, 58, *CSEL* VIII, 173: Exceptis enim paucissimis Dei servis, quid fuit totum Africae territorium quam domus una vitiorum . . .; IV, 13, 62, *CSEL* VIII, 87: . . . excipio enim primum omnes religiosos, deinde nonnullos etiam saeculares religiosis pares aut, si id nimis grande est, aliqua tamen religiosis honestorum actuum probitate consimiles . . .; see also the texts quoted p. 362, n. 62; for Salvianus' opinion of the African clerics and priests of his time, cf. *ibid.* VII, 17, 74, *CSEL* VIII, 179; but see also *ibid.* V, 10, 52, VIII, 118 f., about false *religiosi* (cf. above, p. 362, n. 62). Gildas, *De excidio et conquestu Britanniae* 65, *MGH, AA* XIII, 61 f., very probably means the monks when he says: quorum vitam non solum laudo, verum etiam cunctis mundi opibus praefero cuiusque me, si fieri possit, ante mortis diem esse aliquamdiu participem opto et sitio. . . . In the following paragraph, *MGH, AA* XIII, 62, he contrasts them with the *sacerdotes insipientes*, the *ministri impudentes*, etc. Ryan, *Irish Monasticism* 164 ff., perhaps overestimates the influence of Gildas, who was not a monk but a cleric (cf. O. Chadwick, "Gildas and the Monastic Order," *Jour. Theol. Stud.*, New Ser. V [1954] 78 ff.), on the monastic organization of the Irish Church. For the Christian and pre-Christian motives which created the peculiar forms of Irish ecclesiastical and monastic life see J. F. Kenney, *The Sources for the Early History of Ireland* I (New York, 1929) 291–303.

[57] See S. Brechter, O.S.B., *Die Quellen zur Angelsachsenmission Gregors des Grossen* (Beiträge zur Geschichte des alten Mönchtums und des Benediktinerordens XXII, Münster i. W., 1941); cf. Margaret Deanesly and P. Grosjean, S.J., "The Canterbury Edition of the Answers of Pope Gregory I to St. Augustine," *Journal of Ecclesiastical History* X (1959) 1 ff.

[58] Gregory the Great, *Responsa ad Augustinum, Registrum epistularum* XI, 56 a, *MGH, Epist.* II, 333: Sed quia tua fraternitas monasterii regulis erudita seorsum vivere non debet a clericis suis, in ecclesia Anglorum, quae auctore Deo nuper adhuc ad fidem perducta est, hanc debet conversationem instituere, quae initio nascentis ecclesiae fuit patribus nostris, in quibus nullus eorum ex his, quae possidebant, aliquid suum esse dicebat, sed erant eis omnia communia (cf. Acts 4:32 ff.).

the adjacent papal *episcopium*[59] in which clerics and monks, and monks who had become clerics, lived side by side in a kind of common life.[60]

In conclusion, the monastic reformers of the Carolingian period and of subsequent centuries—and many modern historians as well—were somewhat biased or mistaken when they drew too sharp a line between the monastic life and the clerical life of the early mediaeval west.[61] The

[59] It is probably significant that the Cathedral at Canterbury, "Christ Church," was dedicated to the Holy Savior (*Sancti Salvatoris*), as the Lateran Church originally was; see also W. Levison, *England and the Continent in the Eighth Century* (Oxford, 1946) 34 f.

[60] Cf. p. 387 f., n. 6. See also Deanesly, "Minsters," especially 41: "In England in the seventh century, as in Gaul, the line between clerical and ascetic minsters is thin; the life is largely communal in both . . ."; cf. Miss Deanesly's older article, "The Familia of Christ Church, Canterbury, 597–832," *Essays in Medieval History Presented to Thomas Frederick Tout* (Manchester, 1925) 1 ff., where it is denied that either Gregory the Great's monastery of St. Andrew, from which Augustine came, or Christ Church at Canterbury were Benedictine. Cf. D. Knowles, O.S.B., *The Monastic Order in England* (Cambridge, 1940) 17 and 21: St. Augustine of Canterbury's "conception of the monastic life was therefore probably something between that of the Rule [of St. Benedict] and that of the basilical monasteries of the City [of Rome]." Miss Deanesly and P. Grosjean, in the article quoted in n. 57, have I believe shown against Dom S. Brechter that *Responsum* I (cf. p. 399, n. 58) is Gregorian in substance. A. M. Zimmermann, O.S.B., *Kalendarium Benedictinum* I (Metten, 1933) LIII ff., concludes from the text of *Responsum* I that Augustine of Canterbury must have been a Benedictine monk; yet it is at least equally probable that Gregory the Great or the redactor of the *Responsa* meant by the phrase *tua fraternitas monasterii regulis erudita seorsum vivere non debet a clericis suis* the way of life of the Roman basilicas, which had been taken up in England by the non-Benedictine forerunners of the later Benedictine English "cathedral-monasteries" (cf., for instance, Knowles, *Monastic Order in England* 45, 619 f., 696 f., F. M. Stenton, *Anglo-Saxon England* [Oxford, 1943] 148 f., Brechter, *Quellen zur Angelsachsenmission* 67 f.). The question whether or not Gregory the Great's and Augustine's monastery of St. Andrew on the Coelian Hill in Rome itself was Benedictine, is answered in the negative by Dom Kassius Hallinger, O.S.B., "Papst Gregor der Grosse und der hl. Benedikt," *Commentationes in Regulam S. Benedicti* (Studia Anselmiana XLII, Roma, 1957) 231 ff.

[61] See Levillain, "Saint-Denis" 35 ff., for the struggle over the monastic or canonical origin and status of the Abbey of St. Denis at the time of Louis the Pious. Charlemagne may have had an inkling of the truth when in *Capitulare* LXXI of 811, c. 12, MGH, Leg. II, *Capitularia Regum Francorum* I, 161 f., he ordered an inquiry on the following subject: De conversatione monachorum et utrum aliqui monachi esse possint praeter eos, qui regulam sancti Benedicti observant. Inquirendum etiam, si in Gallia monachi fuissent priusquam traditio regulae sancti Benedicti in has parroechias pervenisset; cf. also *Capit.* LXXII, 12, MGH, Leg. II, Capit. Reg. Franc. I, 164, a text from which it would appear that Charlemagne was thinking less of the *vita communis* of clerics than of pre-Benedictine monks, such as St. Martin of Tours and his disciples. However, already in 801 or 802 Charlemagne in a famous

bias, it is true, had some foundation, not only in theory and legislation, but in practice as well, because, as pointed out, there existed
a clerical *vita canonica* which was not *vita communis* and, even more
important, because the way of life of the clergy had gradually deterio-
rated and by the middle of the eighth century had indeed fallen to a low
estate. In spite of all their efforts toward reform not only of monks, but
also of clerics, the Carolingians succeeded only in restoring canonical
life, not clerical *vita communis*.[62] Common life of the clergy was not
restored on a significant scale until the Hildebrandian and post-
Hildebrandian ages.[63] By the eleventh century the complete breakdown,
under the influence of feudalism, of the Augustinian and generally

letter to Alcuin and the religious of the Abbey of St. Martin of Tours had somewhat
impatiently remarked that the latter at various times had asserted to be monks or canons or
neither; see *Alcuini Epist.* CCXLVII, *MGH, Epist.* IV, 400. About the same time Alcuin
wrote to Archbishop Arn of Salzburg that there was a *tertium genus* between monks and
canons which should not be condemned; see *Alcuini Epist.* CCLVIII, *MGH, Epist.* IV, 416.
The late mediaeval and early modern dispute between the Canons Regular of St. Augustine
(who as such first appear in the twelfth century) and the Augustinian Hermits (who became
a religious order through union of several monastic groups in 1256) as to whose way of life
was more truly derived from St. Augustine's was based to some extent on an anachronistic
strict distinction between the monastic and canonical life. For the history of the Canons
Regular see beside the literature quoted above, p. 386, n. 2, Ch. Dereine, S.J., "L'élaboration du statut canonique des chânoines réguliers . . ." *Rev. hist. ecclés.* XLVI (1951) 534 ff.,
G. Schreiber, "Religiöse Verbände in mittelalterlicher Wertung," *Hist. Jb.* LXII–LXIX
(1949) 284 ff., with references to further studies by the author and others; several German
studies, for instance, J. Wirges, *Die Anfänge der Augustinerchorherren* (Betzdorf, 1928), were
not available to me. For the Augustinian Hermits see beside Arbesmann and Hümpfner,
Liber Vitasfratrum, also R. Arbesmann, O.S.A., "Jordanus of Saxony's Vita S. Augustini
. . .," *Traditio* I (1943) 341 ff., idem, "Henry of Friemar's «Treatise on the Origins and
Development of the Order of the Hermit Friars . . .»," *Augustiniana* VI (1956) 37 ff.,
Roth, "Annibaldi" 36 ff.: ch. 2: "The Augustinian Order in the Thirteenth Century. . . ."

[62] See E. Morhain, "Origine et histoire de la Regula Canonicorum de saint Chrodegang,"
Miscellanea Pio Paschini I (Rome, 1948) 173 ff., A. Werminghoff, "Die Beschlüsse des
Aachener Konziles im Jahre 816," *Neues Archiv* XXVII (1902) 669 ff., Hertling, "Kanoniker"
347 ff., E. Delaruelle, "En relisant le «De institutione regia» de Jonas d'Orléans,"
Mélanges Halphen 177 ff.

[63] See G. Morin, O.S.B., "Règlements de Grégoire VII pour les chanoines réguliers,"
in Dom Morin's *Etudes, textes, découvertes* I (Anecdota Maredsolana, Ser. II, Maredsous,
Paris, 1913) 457 ff. (also in *Rev. bén.* XVIII [1901] 177 ff.), Hertling, "Kanoniker" 349 ff.,
idem, "Professio" 164 ff,. Dereine, "Statut," idem, "Vie commune" 399 ff., idem, "Le
problème de la vie commune chez les canonistes d'Anselme de Lucques à Gratien," *Studi
Greg.* III (1948) 287 ff., G. Bardy, "Saint Grégoire VII et la réforme canoniale au XIe
siècle," *Studi Greg.* I (1947) 48 ff.; for St. Peter Damian in particular see now F. Dressler,
Petrus Damiani: Leben und Werk (Studia Anselmiana XXXIV, Roma, 1954).

western *vita communis* of the clergy had come to be felt as no less a calamity than the corruption of the monastic order. Its restoration, wherever possible, became then an important point of the reformers' program, bound up as it was with the struggle against clerical avarice and incontinence and all their concomitants.[64]

3. VARIATIONS OF THE AUGUSTINIAN REFORM IDEA IN THE PRINCIPAL MONASTIC MILIEUS OF THE LATE ANCIENT WEST

In his work *On Christian Doctrine* St. Augustine, as was seen above,[1] quotes an example of how the Christian rhetor and teacher may bring about a "change of life" (*mutatio vitae*) in his hearers, even may succeed in abolishing a particularly horrid inveterate custom (*immanem consuetudinem longeque a maioribus traditam*).[2] In *De civitate Dei* he compares the spiritual progress (*proficere*) of the entire City of God on earth to the effect which *recta eruditio* has upon the individual: both in the

---

[64] This renewal of the clerical *vita communis* of the Augustinian type from the eleventh century onward is connected with a renewed concept of the *vita apostolica* as the model of both the monastic and the clerical state. The new conception of *vita apostolica* inspired a missionary lay element as well as the best part of the clergy and of the monks and produced a religious movement of great variety which ranged from predominantly clerical monastic orders to sectarian and heretical travesties of the life of the Apostles (see above, p. 364, n. 74, about heretical *Apostolici* already in the age of St. Augustine). Among the new orders the Canons Regular, the Premonstratensians, the Dominicans followed the "rediscovered" *Augustinian Rule*, as did certain semihermitical and missionary groups some of which finally coalesced into the Hermits of St. Augustine. For the later stages of the *vita communis et apostolica* see above all the excellent surveys by H. Grundmann, "Neue Beiträge zur Geschichte der religiösen Bewegungen im Mittelalter," *Arch. Kult. Gesch.* XXXVII (1955) 129 ff. (cf. his older book *Religiöse Bewegungen im Mittelalter* [Historische Studien CCLXVII, Berlin, 1935]) and by M. D. Chenu, O.P., "Moines, clercs, laïcs au carrefour de la vie évangélique (XII siècle)," *Rev. hist. ecclés.* XLIX (1954) 59 ff.; also J. v. Walter, *Die ersten Wanderprediger Frankreichs* (Leipzig, 1903–1906), L.-M. Dewailly, "Notes sur l'histoire de l'adjectif «apostolique»," *Mélanges de science religieuse* V (1949) 141 ff., L. Spätling, *De Apostolicis, Pseudoapostolis, Apostolinis* (Diss., Antonianum, München, 1947, not available to me), Ch. Dereine, S.J., "Les origines de Prémontré," *Rev. hist. ecclés.* XLII (1947) 352, G. Schreiber, "Prämonstratenserkultur des 12. Jahrhunderts," *Anal. Praem.* XVI–XVII (1940–1941), *idem*, "Gregor VII, Cluny, Citeaux, Prémontré zu Eigenkirche, Parochie, Seelsorge," *Z. R. Gesch.*, Kanonist. Abteil. XXXIV (1947) 31 ff., P. Mandonnet, O.P., *Saint Dominique* II (Paris, 1937) 103 ff.

[1] See Part Three, Chapter II, 4.

[2] *De doctrina christiana* IV, 24, 53, *Flor. Patr.* XXIV, 98; cf. above, pp. 374 f., n. 7.

human person and in the human race it is the rise from temporal to eternal, from visible to invisible things which achieves progress gradually in accordance with the ages of man and history—if only man is aware of his submission to the true (verus) creator and lord of his soul.[3]

A glance backward[4] will suffice to establish the connection between these Augustinian reasonings and Tertullian's, Cyprian's, and Ambrose's ideas on a proficere, a reformari in melius, on the problem of the relation between veritas and consuetudo.

It is perhaps characteristic of Augustine that he makes mutatio vitae issue from the right use of rhetoric, understood as a part of doctrina christiana, and that he links progress, understood in a Christian spiritual sense, to eruditio. This shows a certain amount of intellectual optimism and of practical educational rationalism on his part. Such tendencies were balanced in St. Augustine by that far-reaching ethical pessimism and corresponding trust in divine grace alone which he had developed in his own struggle with sin and confirmed in his controversies with the Pelagians, thus moving away to some extent from the mystical divinization theology of the Greek Fathers.[5]

The approximately one hundred years from Augustine's controversy with the monks of Hadrumetum—De gratia et libero arbitrio and De correptione et gratia (written 426–427)[6]—to the Second Council of Orange in Southern France (529) are the century of so-called Semi-Pelagianism. The theological and anthropological ways and deviations of Christian thought comprised under this name had originally little

---

[3] De civitate Dei X, 14, Corp. Christ., Ser. Lat. XLVII, 288: Sicut autem unius hominis, ita humani generis, quod ad Dei populum pertinet, recta eruditio per quosdam articulos temporum tamquam aetatum profecit accessibus, ut a temporalibus ad aeterna capienda et a visibilibus ad invisibilia surgeretur; ita sane ut etiam illo tempore, quo visibilia promittebantur divinitus praemia, unus tamen colendus commendaretur Deus, ne mens humana vel pro ipsis terrenis vitae transitoriae beneficiis cuiquam nisi vero animae creatori et domino subderetur. . . . Optime igitur anima humana adhuc terrenis desideriis infirma ea ipsa, quae temporaliter exoptat bona infima atque terrena vitae huic transitoriae necessaria et prae illius vitae sempiternis beneficiis contemnenda, non tamen nisi ab uno Deo expectare consuescit, ut ab illius cultu etiam in istorum desiderio non recedat, ad quem contemptu eorum et ab eis aversione perveniat.

[4] See above, pp. 134 ff., 138 f. 149 f.

[5] See above, Part Two, Chapter V, 1.

[6] Cf. K. Rahner, S.J., "Augustin und der Semipelagianismus," Z. kath. Theol. LXII (1938) 171 ff.

to do with the heresy of Pelagius, but were meant by their initiators and propagators in the ascetic circles of the South of Gaul to vindicate the Eastern Christian conception of the relation between God and man against the Augustinian doctrine of grace, free will, and predestination. In the discussion which followed, John Cassian of Marseilles and the monastic theologians of Lérins, especially St. Vincent of Lérins and Faustus, Bishop of Riez, tried to reserve for man himself a much larger role in the process of his reassimilation and reformation to God than Augustine, the Augustinians such as St. Prosper of Aquitaine and St. Fulgentius of Ruspe, and, under Augustinian influence, the Popes of the period were willing to allow.[7] In a geographically limited sphere and within the context of the doctrine of grace, the Semi-Pelagian controversy brought into the open the latent contrast between Eastern Christian and Augustinian thought on deification discussed in previous chapters,[8] even though the Semi-Pelagians were consciously anti-Augustinian only with regard to Augustine's doctrine of grace and predestination[9] and were indebted to his thought in not a few other respects. Cassian and the Lerinians sincerely disclaimed Pelagianism,[10] while their opponents equally sincerely and not without some reason feared its recrudescence in a mitigated form. The true concern of the

[7] For a comprehensive account of Semi-Pelagianism see E. Amann, article "Sémi-Pélagiens," DThC XIV, 2, 1796 ff. Cf. also the studies of F. Wörter, Beiträge zur Dogmengeschichte des Semipelagianismus (Paderborn, 1898) and Zur Dogmengeschichte des Semipelagianismus (Kirchengeschichtliche Studien V, 2, Münster i. W., 1899); furthermore G. Weigel, S.J., Faustus of Riez (Philadelphia, 1938) ch. II: "Lérins (424–433)," idem, "El concepto de la fe segun los Semipelagianos: Un análisis de las doctrinas de Fausto de Riez," Revista Universitaria XXV, 1 (Universidad Catolica de Chile, Anales de la Facultad Pontificia de Teologia I, 1940) 35 ff.

[8] Cf. above, pp. 106 f., 194 ff. W. Jaeger, in his recent book, Two Rediscovered Works of Ancient Christian Literature: Gregory of Nyssa and Macarius (Leiden, 1954) 88 ff., has drawn very interesting parallels between Semi-Pelagianism and Greek patristic "synergism." He rightly says (p. 98, n. from p. 97): "The historical relationship of Semipelagianism to the eastern fathers and to Gregory of Nyssa in particular deserves a new examination. . . ."

[9] See, for instance, Prosper of Aquitaine, Epist. ad Augustinum 9, PL LI, 74A: . . . unum eorum praecipuae auctoritatis et spiritualium studiorum virum, sanctum Hilarium Arelatensem episcopum, sciat beatitudo tua admiratorem sectatoremque in aliis omnibus tuae esse doctrinae. . . .

[10] In other matters too they adhered to a considerable stock of older Augustinian and common patristic doctrine. For Faustus of Riez cf. Weigel, Faustus 132. See also below, op. 409 f., for St. Vincent of Lérins who wrote both "Augustinian" and "anti-Augustinian" treatises.

Semi-Pelagian monks of Southern Gaul was centered in the legitimacy and effectiveness of ascetic efforts toward assimilation to God while Augustine and the Augustinians insisted upon the fact that in the reformation of the divine image man cannot do anything whatsoever by himself.

Augustine had said:

We could deform the image of God in us, but we cannot reform it.[11]

His loyal follower Prosper of Aquitaine said the same with different words:

Without God's instigation (*Deo non impellente*) man could fall (*corruere*), but he cannot rise (*consurgere*) if God does not raise him up (*Deo non erigente*).[12]

This text is taken from Prosper's tract against the *Collator* who of course is none other than Cassian, the author of the *Conlationes*. Prosper treats him not as a heretic, but as a respected though gravely mistaken brother. His treatise is directed especially against *Conlatio* XIII which had then just been completed (about 428). In spite of considerable emphasis on the necessity of divine grace for man's conversion, progress, and salvation Cassian also stressed, in contrast to Augustine, the possibility that at times man might on his own take the first small step (*ortum quendam bonae voluntatis*) toward receptivity of divine grace.[13] An important motive of Cassian's attitude here and in similar texts is no doubt his fear that if the will is made absolutely dependent on grace this might in some men lead to relaxation of spiritual effort and to slothfulness,[14] a fear which however in the opinion of Augustine and his followers is based on a misunderstanding: if persons acted in such manner they would do so only because they did not have God's

[11] Quoted above, p. 194.

[12] Prosper of Aquitaine, *De gratia et libero arbitrio contra Collatorem* 9, 3 (19). *PL* LI, 238A: . . . non sicut potuit Deo non impellente corruere, ita potest Deo non erigente consurgere.

[13] See Cassian, *Conlationes* XIII, 8, 3 f., *CSEL* XIII, 371; cf. O. Chadwick, *John Cassian* (Cambridge, 1950) 126 ff., 120 ff.

[14] See, for instance, *Conlationes* XIII, 13, 1, *CSEL* XIII, 382 f.: Et ita semper gratia Dei nostro in bonam partem cooperatur arbitrio atque in omnibus illud adiuvat, protegit ac defendit, ut nonnumquam etiam ab eo quosdam conatus bonae voluntatis vel exigat vel expectet, ne penitus dormienti aut inerti otio dissoluto sua dona conferre videatur, occasiones quodammodo quaerens, quibus humanae segnitiae torpore discusso non inrationabilis munificentiae suae largitus videatur. . . .

grace or conversely, if they had it, they could and would not act in such manner.[15]

Augustine had said comprehensively:

If you could not make yourself, how can you remake yourself?[16]

Prosper, therefore, without denying free will, does not grant Cassian even the small unaided step without God:

Free will remains, since God indeed created it with man himself; but having descended into vanities and cupidities through the neglect of God's law, it (i.e., the will) cannot be changed by itself, but only by the creator; so that whatever is made better in it (*in melius reficitur*) is not without Him who heals, not without Him who cures, whose new creature, whose new formation (*figmentum*) we are, created in Christ Jesus in good works which God has prepared so that we should walk in them (cf. Eph. 2:10).[17]

For human nature is reformable to Him who formed it. . . .[18]

In the second phase of the Semi-Pelagian reaction to Augustinianism, Faustus of Riez, though admitting the necessity of divine grace both in the beginning and in the progress of spiritual life, nevertheless claims, just as Cassian had done, that at times free will to the good may precede God's grace.[19] Faustus' relatively high estimate of man's ability to work for his perfection is no doubt connected with his dis-

[15] This is the gist of Augustine's *De correptione et gratia*; cf. above, p. 159, nn. 19 f. See also, for instance, the Augustinian Fulgentius of Ruspe's *De veritate praedestinationis* III, 6, 9, *PL* LXV, 656B f.: Pessimum est autem dicere, quia, si est praedestinatio, non debemus orare nec vigilare, sed facere omnes voluntates carnis, eo quod iam praedestinati fuerimus. Cum utique illa gratia, quae nobis divina praedestinatione fuit praeparata, ad hoc nobis detur, ut vigilemus et oremus. . . . Quomodo enim fieri potest, ut gratiam quisque accipiat et opera gratiae ipsa gratia in se operante non faciat? See also the text from Fulgentius, quoted below, p. 409, n. 30.

[16] Quoted above, p. 195.

[17] Prosper, *De gratia et libero arbitrio contra Collatorem* 12, 4 (26), *PL* LI, 246C f.: Manens enim liberum arbitrium, quod utique cum ipso homine Deus condidit, a vanitatibus et cupiditatibus suis, in quas neglecta Dei lege defluxit, non a seipso sed a creatore mutatur; ut quidquid in eo in melius reficitur nec sine illo sit, qui sanatur, nec nisi ab illo sit, qui medetur; cuius sumus nova creatura novumque figmentum creati in Christo Iesu in operibus bonis, quae praeparavit Deus, ut in illis ambulemus (cf. Eph. 2:10).

[18] *Ibid.* 13, 2 (27), *PL* LI, 248A: Reformabilis enim est natura humana formatori suo. . . .

[19] Faustus of Riez, *De gratia* II, 10, *CSEL* XXI, 83 f.: Ne in hoc quidem videbor incautus, si profitear, quod aliquotiens in dispositionibus nostris, non quidem in vitae nostrae primordiis, sed dumtaxat in mediis, gratias speciales et ex accedenti largitate venientes voluntas nostra Deo ita ordinante praecedat.

tinction between image and similitude in man's relation to God: the former is common to all men, even the bad, and includes imperishable freedom of choice and immortality of the soul, but the latter is reserved for good men only and will make them more similar to God in proportion to their increase in virtues.[20] Faustus is here closer not only to Cassian, but also to Greek patristic *homoiosis* ideology,[21] than he is to Augustine who had rejected the distinction between image and similitude[22] and had placed less emphasis on the idea of man's deification even by grace.[23] With reference to Gal. 4:9: "But now, after that you have known God, or rather are known by God: how turn you again to the weak and needy elements, which you desire to serve again," Faustus states:

He (i.e., St. Paul) did not say: you cannot be good, but: you want to be bad. If they had not been able to remain corrected they would not be blamed for having lapsed to the worse. And again, he (that is to say, St. Paul) tells them: "My little children, of whom I am in labor again, until Christ be formed in you" (Gal. 4:19). Behold . . . , he asserts that they can still be reformed to the image of Christ and . . . he teaches that the ruined can be repaired. . . .[24]

The whole context and other similar Faustian texts as well leave no doubt that Faustus allots a large share to man's own effort in the shaping

[20] *Ibid.* II, 9, CSEL XXI, 78 f.: Imago ergo Dei homo dicitur, quia ei indulgenter ac dignanter inseruit veritas iustitiam, ratio sapientiam, perennitas aeternitatem. De imagine Dei est, quod intellegit, quod rectum sapit, quod inter malum et bonum iudicio examinante discriminat. Et cum Deus bonitas, misericordia, patientia atque iustitia sit, quanto quisque magis iustus ac patiens invenitur, tanto magis Deo similis adprobatur, cuius utique similitudo non in vultibus sed in virtutibus possidetur. . . . Solum vero arbitrium et inmortalitas, quae etiam malis insita est, non aufertur, licet dignitas et beatitudo inmortalitatis possit auferri. Quantum ergo ad libertatem arbitrii et inmortalitatem pertinet, imaginem Dei licet a se et in se decoloratam etiam mali habere possunt, similitudinem nisi boni habere non possunt. . . .

[21] Wörter, *Zur Dogmengeschichte* 59, rightly points out that Faustus must have conceived of the *similitudo* as given to man only potentially in creation and as to be made real through man's effort. Cf. above, pp. 87 f., for Origen's similar view.

[22] See above, p. 186.   [23] See above, pp. 194 f.

[24] Faustus of Riez, *De gratia* I, 12, CSEL XXI, 42 f.: Non dixit: boni esse non potestis, sed: mali esse vultis. Nisi bono potuissent stare correcti, non arguerentur ad deteriora prolapsi. Ad quos iterum dicit: "Filioli mei, quos iterum parturio, donec formetur Christus in vobis" (Gal. 4:19). Ecce istos, qui fide geniti facti fuerant abortivi, asserit adhuc posse ad Christi imaginem reformari et, dum perditos adhuc filios vocat, praevaricationem sine desperatione condemnat docens et reparari perdita et auferri posse conlata.

of his spiritual life. Though he recognizes that through Christ everything has been "repaired to the better" and though he "immeasurably
prefers" redemption even to creation, he nevertheless extols the
Restorer as Creator in the sense that His creational gifts to man have
preserved a certain autonomy of their own.[25] At times he pursues his
ascetic ethical optimism so far that he weakens God's power by making
His foreknowledge of man's ultimate end dependent on man's *profectus* or *defectus*.[26]

It is interesting to see how differently this whole complex of questions is approached by Fulgentius of Ruspe in his criticism of Faustus
and of other more extreme anti-Augustinians. Fulgentius, a monk-
bishop as Faustus, was as ascetically-minded as the latter or Cassian,
yet Augustine was the model not only of his life,[27] but also of his
thought. So, for instance, Fulgentius introduces Jeremiah's *Lamentations* 5:21, "Convert us, o Lord, to thee, and we shall be converted: renew our days as from the beginning" by the reminder that
this *conversio* or *renovatio* must not be assigned to human free will
(*arbitrio*).[28] Free will exists in the sense that we please God only if
we have the will to please Him; but it is He who grants us that will
and, if God does not change the will of man to the good, he will either
seek evil or not seek the good in the right way.[29] And yet, one must

---

[25] *Ibid.* II, 10, *CSEL* XXI, 83 : Cum vero ipse sit conditor, qui reparator, unus idemque in
utriusque operis laude benedicitur. . . . Iure itaque utriusque rei munus assero, quia me illi
scio debere, quod natus sum, cui debeo, quod renatus sum. Et propterea non ideo negabo
conditoris dona, quia perdidi, sed priora ideo sequentibus non exaequabo, quia multipli-
citer in melius reparata suscepi. Extollam beneficia creantis, sed in inmensum praeferam
redimentis.

[26] *Ibid.* II, 2, *CSEL* XXI, 62 : Sed adhuc dicis, quia opera ac voluntates hominum de nutu
et inpulsu praescientiae caelestis incipiant. Non ita est. Hoc potius agnosce, quod
praescientia Dei de materia humanorum actuum sumat exordium. Quid de nobis praescire
ac praeordinare debeat Deus, quantum pertinet ad futurum, in profectu hominis defectuque
consistit.

[27] See above, pp. 379, 391 f.; G.-G. Lapeyre, *Saint Fulgence de Ruspe* (Paris, 1929).

[28] Fulgentius of Ruspe, *De veritate praedestinationis et gratiae Dei ad Joannem et Venerium* II,
6, 9, *PL* LXV, 631D: Verumtamen ne conversio vel renovatio nostra humano assignetur
arbitrio, utramque nobis a Deo sanctus Ieremias deposcit his verbis: "Converte nos ad te
et convertemur; renova dies nostros sicut antea" (Lament. 5:21).

[29] *Ibid.* II, 5, 8, *PL* LXV, 631B: Deo igitur non placemus, nisi velimus; sed ab ipso
nobis tribuitur, ut velimus, a quo nisi voluntas hominis mutetur, ut bona sit, aut semper
appetit malum aut nunquam bene appetit bonum. . . .

not abuse the benefices of divine grace by sluggishness in good works,[30] a warning in which Fulgentius is a faithful disciple of Augustine. His great master had also said that the freedom of those redeemed by Christ and predestined to heaven is greater even than that of Adam in Paradise.[31] Similarly Fulgentius says:

A greater grace is given now when free will is repaired by faith; and while by the infused gift of faith and charity God repairs the freedom of our will, he thus perfects in us virtue within weakness. . . . Man's (i.e., Adam's) virtue, possessing [only] a lesser grace, fell, defeated on its own accord; and the weakness of man, through greater assistance of grace, receives the victory which it lost. . . .[32]

While thus the Augustinians in their counterattack against the Semi-Pelagians upheld the principles of *reformatio in melius* and *felix culpa*,[33] the Semi-Pelagian milieu produced a significant statement on the relation of tradition and renovation to truth, or more concretely, to the deposit of faith, a problem which in various ways had already occupied Tertullian, Cyprian, Ambrosius, and Augustine.[34] It was Vincent of Lérins who raised the question anew in his famous *Commonitorium*.[35] Vincent, as other Semi-Pelagians, is close to Augustine in matters other than grace and predestination. He even compiled excerpts from his writings, relating to the doctrines of the Trinity and of the Incarnation, and he introduced and concluded this work with

---

[30] *Ibid.* II, 14, 23, *PL* LXV 639A f.: Neque sic putemus abutendum beneficiis gratiae, ut absque bonis operibus torpeamus. Ab iis enim gratia profecto discedit, quorum caritas refrigescit. . . . Non nobis est a sancto labore cessandum, quibus divinae gratiae non solum merces promittitur, sed et auxilium suffragatur. The whole paragraph is important for the Augustinian doctrine that full acknowledgement of divine grace does not take away the basis of man's own effort; cf. above, pp. 165 ff., 405 f.

[31] See above, p. 159.

[32] *Ibid.* III, 17, 27, *PL* LXV, 665C f.: Maior ergo nunc datur gratia, dum per fidem liberum reparatur arbitrium: et cum dono fidei atque caritatis infuso arbitrii nostri Deus reparat libertatem, sic in nobis perficit in infirmitate virtutem. . . . Virtus itaque hominis, quae minorem habuit gratiam, sponte victa cecidit; et infirmitas hominis maiore adiutorio gratiae victoriam recipit, quam amisit.

[33] Cf. above, pp. 156, 146.

[34] Cf. above, pp. 136–139, 147–150.

[35] Vincent of Lérins, *Commonitorium*, Moxon.

elaborate praise of the great doctor of the Church.[36] In the *Commoni-*
torium, however, the scales of his judgment are loaded to the disad-
vantage of an Augustinian ideology of renewal because of an unavowed
bias in this treatise: the supposition of an excessive novelty of
Augustine's doctrine on grace.[37] Some of Vincent's formulations are
ultraconservative and resemble in this respect certain propositions
of Tertullian in *De praescriptione haereticorum*.[38] Among his three famous
criteria of orthodoxy: *quod ubique, quod semper, quod ab omnibus creditum*
est or *universitas, antiquitas, consensio*[39] the argument from antiquity
is reminiscent of Tertullian's assertion of the *principalitas* (priority)
of truth before error. Such arguments are clearly not without danger,
since antiquity and priority can be made to serve custom rather than
truth, as was done, for instance, by Symmachus in his defence of
paganism, which Ambrose refuted by a rejection of the value of
antiquity as such.[40] In Vincent's case the ever recurrent *antiquitas*
argument shows above all concern for the preservation of the deposit
of faith—on the basis of the oft-repeated verse I Tim. 6:20: "O
Timothy, keep that which is committed to thy trust (*depositum custodi*),
avoiding the profane novelties of words (*profanas vocum nóvitates*) . . ."[41]
—but also a rather shortsighted attitude toward the possibilities of
evolution of dogma from an implicit to an explicit stage, an attitude
aimed concretely against Augustine's elaboration of a doctrine of grace
and predestination.[42] Vincent interprets Pope Stephen I's celebrated

---

[36] Cf. J. Madoz, S.J., "Un tratado desconocido de San Vicente de Lerins: «Excerpta
sancte memorie Vincenti Lirinensis insule presbiteri ex universo beate recordationis Augustini in unum collecta»," *Gregorianum* XXI (1940) 75 ff.

[37] It can hardly be doubted that Vincent's *Commonitorium* is directed against Augustine's
doctrine of grace and predestination, even though neither the doctrine nor its author are
mentioned; that the anti-Augustinian *Obiectiones Vincentianae* are by the same Vincent is
almost certain; see, for instance, H. Koch, *Vincenz von Lerin und Gennadius* (Texte u.
Untersuch. XXXI, 2 [1907] 37 ff.) and J. Madoz, S.J., *El Concepto de la Tradicion en S.*
Vicente de Lerins (Analecta Gregoriana V, Roma, 1933).

[38] See above, p. 137.   [39] Vincent of Lérins, *Commonitorium* 1, 3, Moxon 10.
[40] See above, p. 150.   [41] See, especially, *Commonitorium* 21 ff., Moxon 83 ff.
[42] That the development of dogma from the implicit to the explicit is often related to
the refutation of heresies had been made clear by Augustine, *De praedestinatione sanctorum* 14,
27, *PL* XLIV, 980, *De dono perseverantiae* 20, 53, *PL* XLV, 1026, *Enarratio in Ps.* LIV, 22,
Corp. Christ., Ser. Lat. XXXIX, 672 f. (quoted by Wörter, *Beiträge* 19, n. 1). It is very
interesting also to see how in his answers to the earliest Semi-Pelagian criticisms of his
doctrine of grace Augustine refuses to be identified with what he may have taught earlier

dictum against Cyprian: *Nihil innovandum nisi quod traditum est*[43] in the most narrowly traditionalist sense and does not stop to consider that this sentence does not exclude innovation, if it is founded upon tradition.[44]

It is true that in one section of his treatise Vincent, just as on occasion Tertullian,[45] attempts to transcend a merely static conception of the truths of Christianity. He tries to define desirable dogmatic progress, *profectus* as opposed to objectionable *permutatio*, he speaks of a fruitful *amplificare* as opposed to a destructive *transvertere*.[46] But his Semi-Pelagian background, his opposition to the Augustinian explications of implicit dogma, make him adhere rigidly to conceptual categories which significantly evoke Greek patristic ideology of identity between end and beginning,[47] of reform as return to Paradise, of progress as purification. It is not an accident that he so vehemently opposes all difference between "first" and "last" developments, between the *prima* and the *extrema*, in the Church's spiritual history,[48]

in his life; for with the grace of God his doctrine has progressed; he thus will not be tied to what is obsolete or "old" in his own work; see *De dono perseverantiae* 21, 55, *PL* XLV, 1028: . . . proficienter me existimo Deo miserante scripsisse, non tamen a perfectione coepisse (cf. Wörter, *Beiträge* 11). To show this, of course, was also one purpose of his *Retractationes*.

[43] See above, p. 139.

[44] See also n. 36 on p. 139.

[45] See above, pp. 137 f.

[46] *Commonitorium* 23, 28 f., Moxon 88 ff.: Sed forsitan dicit aliquis: Nullusne ergo in ecclesia Christi profectus habebitur religionis? Habeatur plane et maximus. . . . Sed ita tamen ut vere profectus sit ille fidei, non permutatio. Si quidem ad profectum pertinent ut in semetipsum unaquaeque res amplificetur, ad permutationem vero ut aliquid ex alio in aliud transvertatur. Crescat igitur oportet et multum vehementerque proficiat tam singulorum quam omnium, tam unius hominis quam totius ecclesiae aetatum ac saeculorum gradibus intellegentia scientia sapientia, sed in suo dumtaxat genere, in eodem scilicet dogmate eodem sensu eodemque sententia. Imitetur animarum religio rationem corporum: quae licet annorum processu numeros suos evolvant et explicent, eadem tamen quae erant permanent . . . ut nihil novum postea proferatur in senibus quod non in pueris iam ante latitaverat. . . . Ita etiam christianae religionis dogma sequatur has decet profectuum leges, ut annis scilicet consolidetur, dilatetur tempore, sublimetur aetate, incorruptum tamen inlibatumque permaneat. . . .

[47] Cf. above, p. 73.

[48] *Commonitorium* 23, 30, Moxon 91 f.: . . . hoc rectum et consequens est ut primis atque extremis sibimet non discrepantibus de incrementis triticeae institutionis (this is the evangelic "wheat" [cf. Matthew 13:24 ff.] sown in the beginnings of Christianity) triticei quoque dogmatis frugem demetamus. . . .

which he sees in terms of an unchanging spiritual Paradise,[49] that he
can envisage at best a "filing out," a *limare* or *polire*, of the deposit
of faith,[50] but not new, hitherto unrecognized aspects of inexhaustible
revealed truth. Vincent's thought reaches a high level where he pas-
sionately defends the purity of dogma, but it fails where he refuses to
admit progress of dogma from the implicit to the explicit, where he
insists that, notwithstanding all possible propagation, growth, and
elaboration of the Christian faith, for which he makes allowance, dogma
must still always remain identically the same.[51] He does not seem to
realize fully that a considerable evolution of Christian doctrine had
actually taken place within orthodoxy during the four Christian centuries that had preceded his own age, which was also that of St.
Augustine, a development which was definitely an explication of formerly only implicit doctrinal content and therefore went beyond the
mere "clarification" and "consolidation" which Vincent considers
alone permissible.

Vincent of Lérins' *Commonitorium* does not solve the problem of renewal in the innermost precinct of the Christian faith. However, with
the gradual weakening of the great heretical impulses of Late Antiquity
the dogmatic aspect of renewal ideology receded altogether into the
background and did not come to the fore again until the twelfth century when it was taken up under entirely new circumstances and with

---

[49] *Ibid.* 23, 30, Moxon 92 f.: Absit . . . ut in isto spirituali paradiso de cinnamomi et
balsami surculis lolium repente atque aconita proveniant. Quodcumque igitur in hac ecclesia,
Dei agricultura (1 Cor. 3:9), fide patrum satum est, hoc idem filiorum industria decet
excolatur et observetur, hoc idem floreat et maturescat, hoc idem proficiat et perficiatur.

[50] *Ibid.* 23, 30, Moxon 93: Fas est etenim, ut prisca illa caelestis philosophiae dogmata
processu temporis excurentur, limentur, poliantur, sed nefas est, ut commutentur, nefas,
ut detruncentur, ut mutilentur. . . . *Ibid.* 23, 32, Moxon 94 f.: Christi vero ecclesia . . .
si qua sunt . . . antiquitus informata et incohata, accuret et poliat, si qua iam expressa et
enucleata, consolidet et firmet, si qua iam confirmata et definita, custodiat. . . .

[51] So also Madoz, *Tradicion* 99 ff.; cf. the Vincentian texts quoted in nn. 48–50.
Some historians of theology believe that Vincent did admit a development of dogma from
the implicit to the explicit, but even though his formulations at times seem to favor such an
interpretation the over-all impression is to the contrary. For the relation of the *Commonitorium* to the theological problem involved, see, for instance, T. Spácil, S.J., *Doctrina
theologiae orientis separati: De revelatione, fide, dogmate* II (Orientalia Christiana Analecta CIV,
Roma, 1935) 184 ff.; for the difficulties of Vincent's rule of orthodoxy see also John
Henry Cardinal Newman, *An Essay on the Development of Christian Doctrine*, thirteenth ed.
(London, 1906) 10 ff., especially 27.

new connotations both within orthodoxy—for instance, by Anselm of Havelberg[52]—and at its fringe—by Joachim of Flora.[53]

As far as the main problems of Semi-Pelagianism are concerned, St. Caesarius of Arles, a former monk of Lérins and, at the same time, through Pomerius and in his own right heir to the full Augustinian tradition, has the merit of closing the controversy peacefully at the Second Council of Orange of the year 529, the *Acts* of which were confirmed by Pope Boniface II.[54] It was a victory for Augustinian theology and anthropology, but no censure was passed on the persons or the ascetic ideals of the monastic circles of Southern Gaul.[55] Cassian and Augustine could thus both remain active forces in western spirituality.[56]

[52] Cf. M. van Lee, "Les idées d'Anselme de Havelberg sur le développement des dogmes," *Anal. Praem.* XIV (1938) 5 ff., J. J. Heneghan, *The Progress of Dogma according to Anselm of Havelberg* (New York, 1943); see also A. Dempf, *Sacrum Imperium* (München, Berlin, 1929) 241 ff., J. Beumer, S.J., "Ein Religionsgespräch aus dem zwölften Jahrhundert," *Z. kath. Theol.* LXXIII (1951) 465 ff., J. Spörl, *Grundformen hochmittelalterlicher Geschichtsanschauung* (München, 1935) 18 ff., W. Kamlah, *Apokalypse und Geschichtstheologie: Die mittelalterliche Auslegung der Apokalypse vor Joachim von Fiore* (Historische Studien, Berlin, 1935) 64 ff., G. Schreiber, "Studien über Anselm von Havelberg," *Anal. Praem.* (1942) 5 ff., idem, "Anselm von Havelberg und die Ostkirche," *Z. Ki. Gesch.* LX (1941), idem, "Religiöse Verbände in mittelalterlicher Wertung," *Hist. Jb.* LXII–LXIX (1949) 284 ff., K. Fina, "Anselm von Havelberg: Untersuchungen zur Kirchen- und Geistesgeschichte des 12. Jahrhunderts," *Anal. Praem.* XXXII–XXXIV, especially XXXIV (1958) 13 ff. See also below, p. 423, n. 93.

[53] Cf. above, p. 29.

[54] Cf. Second Council of Orange, Bruns, *Can. Apost. et Concil.* I, 2, 176 ff., and for Boniface II's confirmation JL 881. For Caesarius of Arles and his theology see Malnory, *Césaire*, cf. F. Arnold, *Caesarius von Arles und die gallische Kirche seiner Zeit* (Leipzig, 1894).

[55] Reverentius' early sixth century *Vita* of the former Lerinian monk and later Archbishop of Arles Hilarius (cf. B. Kolon, O.F.M., *Die Vita S. Hilarii Arelatensis* [Rhetorische Studien XII, Paderborn, 1925]) shows how the Lerinian tradition could be adapted to the Augustinian conception of "reform to the better" through grace. See *Vita S. Hilarii Arelatensis* 4, 6, *PL* L, 1225: . . . quemadmodum humanum arbitrium divina praecedens gratia commutaret in melius, [Hilarius] digna conversationem sermone, mente habituque demonstrans . . . (cf. p. 372, n. 25, for Caesarius of Arles' *ad sanitatem pristinam revocare* and *converti ad meliora*); interesting also is the antithetical use of the ideas of Paradise and Kingdom of God, ibid. 5, 7, *PL* L 1226: [Hilarius] . . . ingreditur Lirinensis insulae paradisum, non unde more primi Adae in huius vitae mitteretur exilium, sed unde iure victoris ad coelestia postmodum regna raperetur. For the relationship between Paradise and heavenly Kingdom in patristic literature, cf. above, pp. 65, 230.

[56] For Cassianic and Augustinian influence on the *Rule of St. Benedict* see, for instance C. Butler, O.S.B., *Benedictine Monachism*, second ed. (London, etc., 1924) 165 f., also his edition of the *Rule of St. Benedict: Index Scriptorum*, s. v. *Cassianus*. Cf. C. Vagaggini, O.S.B., "San Benedetto e la questione semipelagiana," *Studia Benedictina* (Studia Anselmiana XVIII–XIX, Roma, 1947) 17 ff. Cf. above, p. 381.

Not any more than Augustine himself did Caesarius depreciate the reality of free will[57] and the necessity of human effort for salvation. His sermons are truly Augustinian in their insistence both on divine grace and on "progress in good works" (*profectus in operibus bonis*). Just as Augustine so also Caesarius says that baptism is not enough, though it "frees" from all evil; for by leading a good life with the grace of God man is expected to be "filled" to his full capacity with everything good (*repleri omnibus bonis*).[58]

Caesarius is very sure that reform means not only *ad sanitatem pristinam revocare*, but also *converti ad meliora*.[59] The ideology of Paradise and of the angelic life merges into that of the City of God, composed of angels and men under Christ the King.[60]

With regard to discipline and penance in the monastic life St. Caesarius stresses the necessity of *correptio*, that is to say, of admonition and censure as much as St. Augustine[61] and that of punitive correction—*severius corrigi, districtione severissima feriri, legitimam disciplinam*

---

[57] For Augustine, cf. above, pp. 164 f., 405 f.

[58] See Caesarius of Arles, *Sermo* XV, 3 f., *Corp. Christ.*, *Ser. Lat.* CIII, 74 f.: . . . grave malum est, si profectum non habuerit in operibus bonis . . . doleat, si se ipsum ex eo tempore, quo in Christo renatus est, nihil profecisse cognoverit . . . quomodo nos volumus, ut quicquid ad nos pertinet, sive in gregibus sive in quibuscumque agrorum fructibus, in omni bono crescant atque proficiant, hoc sine dubio et Deus noster de nobis et desiderat et expectat. . . . Totis ergo viribus fratres carissimi, operemur quod bonum est; nec nobis sufficiat, si tales sumus, quales fuimus eo tempore, quo baptismi sacramenta accepimus. Per baptismum enim vacuati sumus omnibus malis, sed cum Dei gratia bene agendo debemus repleri omnibus bonis. . . .

[59] See the passage from *Sermo* LVI, quoted above, p. 372, n. 25.

[60] Cf. Caesarius, *Sermo* CLI, 2, *Corp. Christ.*, *Ser. Lat.* CIV, 618: Patria nostra paradisus est, civitas nostra Hierusalem est illa caelestis; cives nostri angeli sunt, parentes nostri patriarchae sunt et prophetae, apostoli et martyres, rex noster Christus est (cf. Cyprian, *De mortalitate* 26, CSEL III, 1, 313, reference of Dom Morin in this edition of Caesarius' sermons; the text is quoted above, p. 247, n. 41).

[61] For Augustine see above, p. 313; for Caesarius, for instance, *Regula sanctarum virginum* 13, Morin, *Caesar. Arel. Opera* II, 104: Quae pro qualibet culpa ammonetur, castigatur, corripitur, arguenti respondere penitus non praesumat. . . . *Ibid.* 24, Morin II, 107: Si quam vero liberius quam decet agere videritis, secretius corripite ut sororem (cf. Augustinian *Regula ad servos Dei* 7, Arbesmann and Hümpfner, *Liber Vitasfratrum* 498 f.); Caesarius, *Sermo* CCXXV, 3, *Corp. Christ.*, *Ser. Lat.* CIV, 890: Si subdita et inferior tibi persona est quae non facit quod iustum est, castiga, increpa: si praevales, etiam cum severitate distringe (emendation to *non praevales* would seem reasonable).

accipere—more.[62] Caesarius' monastic rules provide for corporeal punishment,[63] for separation from common prayer as well as from common meals,[64] and in cases of extreme recalcitrance for monastic excommunication, that is to say, removal from the community until such time as willingness to do penance was forthcoming. This meant confinement in a separate place apart from the rest of the congregation,[65] a measure remotely anticipating the penitential imprisonments

[62] See Caesarius, *Regula sanctarum virginum* 32, Morin *Caesar. Arel. Opera* II, 109: . . . interversores rerum monasterialium severius corrigantur; *ibid.* 33, Morin II, 110: Quaecumque convicio vel maledicto vel etiam criminis obiectu laeserit sororem suam, meminerit culpam satisfactione purgare. Quod vitium si iterare praesumpserit, districtione severissima feriatur . . . (see also *ibid.* 46, Morin II, 114); *ibid.* 26, Morin II, 107: . . . si forte . . . aut furtum faciant aut in se invicem manus mittant, iustum est, ut legitimam disciplinam accipiant. . . . See also *ibid.* 25, Morin II, 107: . . . gravius emendetur; the whole passage is taken over from the Augustinian *Regula ad servos Dei* 7, Arbesmann and Hümpfner, *Liber Vitasfratrum* 499 f.

[63] *Regula sanctarum virginum* 26, Morin, *Caesar. Arel. Opera* II 107 f., also *Regula mona-chorum*, *ibid.* 151, l. 1 f.; the Augustinian *Ordo monasterii* considered corporeal punishment only for those of immature age (Arbesmann and Hümpfner, *Liber Vitasfratrum* 493); Basil never seems to mention corporeal punishment, his theory and practice are based on a "medical" concept of correction ((διόρθωσις, cf. *Regulae fusius tractatae* LI–LIII, *PG* XXXI, 1040 ff.), in general see E. F. Morison, *St. Basil and His Rule* (London, etc., 1913) 54 ff. and 107. St. Caesarius' contemporary, St. Benedict, thought corporeal punishment necessary for those who could not be corrected even by monastic excommunication; see *Sancti Benedicti Regula* 23 and 28, Linderbauer 41 and 43 f.

[64] *Regula sanctarum virginum* 13, Morin, *Caesar. Arel. Opera* II, 104: . . . a communione orationis vel a mensa secundum qualitatem culpae sequestrabitur; see also *ibid.* 12, Morin II, 104. Cf. *Sancti Benedicti Regula* 23–25, Linderbauer 41 ff. There is a certain amount of interdependence between the Benedictine and the Caesarian rules, but it is hard to tell whether Caesarius borrowed from Benedict or vice versa; cf. Chapman, *Benedict.* 75 ff.

[65] *Regula sanctarum virginum* 34, Morin II, 110: Si qua vero pro quacumque re excom-municata fuerit, remota a congregatione in loco, quo abbatissa iusserit, cum una de spiritualibus sororibus resideat, quo usque humiliter paenitendo indulgentiam accipiat; *ibid.*, *recapitulatio* 65, Morin II, 119: Et si forte . . . fuerit aliqua de filiabus nostris tam pertinax animo, quae huius regulae recapitulationem . . . inplere contempnat, a sanctae congregationis vestrae conventu eam . . . removete; et tamdiu in cella salutatorii (a place for the reception of visitors, no doubt outside the monastic enclosure) sit remota, quamdiu dignam paenitentiam agens humiliter veniam petat; et donec ad regulae instituta se corrigat, intus non regrediatur. For excommunication and confinement as well as corporeal punish-ment in the monasteries of St. Pachomius cf. K. Lehmann, "Die Entstehung der Freiheits-strafe in den Klöstern des heiligen Pachomius," *Sav. Z.R. Gesch.*, Kanonist. Abteil. XXXVII (1951) 1 ff., and in general the studies by F. Kober quoted there.

so characteristic of Irish monasticism of the following century. On the whole the *Rules of St. Caesarius*, as also the *Rule of St. Benedict*, place somewhat greater emphasis on the enforcement of monastic discipline than the *Augustinian Rule*. It is remarkable also how often St. Caesarius thinks it necessary to repeat entreaties and solemn invocations of God and His angels so that his rules may be strictly observed and their content neither changed nor violated.[66] Such emphasis and such reiteration were no doubt required in consequence of the progressive barbarization of the west which must have affected the monastic as well as the nonmonastic population.[67] Two sixth century Spanish treatises, written by monk-bishops, the *De correctione* (or *castigatione*) *rusticorum* by St. Martin of Braga[68] and the *Epistola de districtione monachorum et ruina monasteriorum* by St. Eutropius of Valencia[69] (disciple of that African St. Donatus who had founded the *monasterium Servi-*

[66] See *Regula sanctarum virginum* 47, Morin II, 114 f., and *ibid.*, *recapitulatio* 48 f., Morin II, 115, also 62–65, *loc. cit.*, 118 ff.

[67] In general see C. Vogel, *La discipline pénitentielle en Gaule des origines à la fin du VIIe siècle* (Paris, 1952) 79 ff., 157 ff., 199 ff., idem, "La discipline pénitentielle en Gaule des origines au IXe siècle. Le dossier hagiographique," *Rev. sc. rel.* XXX (1956) 6 ff., 23.

[68] Martin of Braga (cf. above, pp. 394 f.), *De correctione rusticorum*, Barlow, *Martini Bracar. Opera* 159 ff. In the oldest manuscript (Kassel, Landesbibliothek, Theol., Q. 10 [cf. Barlow, 168 f.]), the title is *Pro castigatione rusticorum*, taken apparently from ch. 1 of the work (see Barlow, 183). Martin's little treatise is modelled in part after Augustine's *De catechizandis rudibus* (cf. Barlow, 163 ff.), but it is very significant that while Augustine's *rudes* had been catechumens, Martin's *rustici*, with all their pagan superstitions, are baptized Christians. For influence of Caesarius of Arles on Martin of Braga see Morin, "Symbole d'Athanase" 340, and Barlow, 164.

[69] Eutropius of Valencia, *Epistula de districtione monachorum et ruina monasteriorum*, PL LXXX, 16B f.: Si autem a Deo nobis creditum gregem et exhortando et increpando saepius a diaboli laqueis et perverso voluerimus opere revocare, immites et asperi multorum ore dicemur. Sed quamvis hoc a multis . . . saepe dicatur, tenenda est tamen discretio et sanctae regulae institutio, ut quae patres instituerunt, etiam successores et filii integra illibataque custodiant et observent. Nam si in aliquo a sanctorum patrum institutione et tramite deviandum nec pro culpae suae quis qualitate et opere increpandus est, quis quaeso malorum hoc audit, qui nunc saltem propter supplicia terreantur, qui non, quaecumque voluerit, agat et praeceps feratur ad vitia. Et propterea divinae potentiae ordo et ineffabilis dispositio praecipit, ut sit in saeculo princeps, in ecclesia pastor et pontifex praeficiatur et in monasteriis pater, ut nefario operi et actibus scelestis et impiis obsistere et contra humani generis mores perpetratum facinus districtionis et severitatis possit gladio vindicare. Sanctus Augustinus praeclarus, ut optime nosti, ecclesiae doctor, quae in octavo Civitatis Dei libro dicit, adverte (this probably refers to Augustine's refutation of the worship of demons in *De civitate Dei* VIII). For Eutropius, cf. also above, p. 383.

tanum) illustrate by the very titles which they received the type of reform that was needed both for monks and for lay men.[70]

A very different transformation of the Augustinian synthesis of monastic and educational ideals, and one of the most important, took place in late sixth century Italy, where Ostrogoth rule had left the framework of ancient civilization relatively intact. And so this book may close with the evocation of the great though somewhat indistinct shadow of Cassiodorus.

He has already been mentioned as one of the eminent lay *conversi* of Late Antiquity[71] and as the founder of Vivarium, which may have followed the *Augustinian Rule* and certainly did adopt its liturgical *Ordo*.[72] A comparison between some of the letters which Cassiodorus wrote in the name of Theodoric the Great during his long term of high office and characteristic passages from those works, religious in the widest sense of the word, which he wrote after his resignation, will be illuminating. This comparison will reveal very little about the inner motives of Cassiodorus' conversion.[73] They were probably much more mixed than those of a St. Augustine or a St. Paulinus of Nola two centuries earlier. And yet, the great change in Cassiodorus' life is highly significant for western ideology of reform: it symbolizes a radical (though never quite final) parting of ways between the ideals of the Roman Empire and of Christianized ancient ruler worship on the one hand and of the Augustinian Civitas Dei idea on the other.

The excerpts here juxtaposed are taken from Cassiodorus' *Variae*, his own collection of Theodorician "state papers," which had been composed by him for the king, and from his *Institutiones divinarum et*

---

[70] In seventh century Spain this situation has become even clearer, as can be seen from the *Pactum*, attributed to St. Fructuosus of Braga (cf. p. 395, n. 43), which envisages confinement in a dark cell with restriction to bread and water and seventy-two blows of the whip for recalcitrant monks as well as *correptio* of an unjust abbot; see Herwegen, *Pactum* 3 f.

[71] See above, p. 368.

[72] Cf. above, p. 381.

[73] A. van de Vyver, "Cassiodore et son œuvre," *Speculum* VI (1931) 244 ff., and *idem*, "Les *Institutiones* de Cassiodore et sa fondation à Vivarium," *Rev. bén.* LIII (1941) 59 ff., has proved that Cassiodorus' *conversio*, which he mentions in *De orthographia*, Preface, Keil, *Gramm. Lat.* VII, 144, l. 1, was not entry into the monastic state. He remained a *grand seigneur* who founded a monastery on his estate and supervised its religious and cultural life.

saecularium litterarum, written after his withdrawal from public life.[74]
Variae I, 28: Theodoric speaks to Goths and Romans:

A worthy thing is the activity of building in a city; by it regal care commends
itself. For the reparation of old cities is the praise of the ages: through it
adornments of peace are acquired and at the same time the necessities of wars
are taken care of.[75]

With this compare *Institutiones divinarum litterarum* 32, 3, an admonition
to the abbot and monks of Vivarium:

To you then, citizens of religion (*cives religiosi*), is given your own city, as it
were, and, if with the assistance of the Lord you live in it in concord and in a
spiritual manner, you will already rejoice in a prefiguration of the heavenly
fatherland.[76]

Another significant text is *Variae* III, 31: Theodoric to the Senate of the
City of Rome:

Although we desire to bestow untiring care upon our whole commonwealth
(*rei publicae*) and, if God is favorable, will attempt to call all things back to
their pristine state (*ad statum pristinum cuncta revocare*), we are, nevertheless,
more strongly committed to the increase of the city of Rome.[77]

---

[74] See the somewhat similar comparison between *Variae* and *Institutiones* in the recent
study by W. Freund, *Modernus und andere Zeitbegriffe des Mittelalters* (Neue Münstersche
Beiträge zur Geschichtsforschung IV, Köln, Graz, 1957) 27 ff.

[75] Cassiodorus, *Variae* I, 28, *MGH, AA* XII, 29 f.: Universis Gothis et Romanis Theodericus rex. Digna est constructio civitatis, in qua se commendet cura regalis, quia laus est
temporum reparatio urbium vetustarum: in quibus et ornatus pacis adquiritur et bellorum
necessitas praecavetur. . . .

[76] Cassiodorus, *Institutiones I: Divinarum litterarum* XXXII, 3, Mynors 80: Data est itaque
vobis quaedam urbs propria, cives religiosi, in qua, si concorditer et spiritaliter Domino
praestante transigitis, caelestis iam patriae praefiguratione gaudetis. . . . Cf. above, pp.
116 f., for the concept of the heavenly fatherland on earth in the *Epistle to Diognetus* and in
Origen, p. 241, for the concept of the *civitas Dei peregrinans* in Augustine. The text from
Cassiodorus continues with the evocation of an intellectual and spiritual Paradise: Praesto
vobis sunt sanctarum scripturarum instrumenta dogmatica cum expositoribus suis, qui vere
sunt floriferi campi, caelestis paradisi poma suavia. . . .

[77] *Variae* III, 31, *MGH, AA* XII, 95 f.: Senatui urbis Romae Theodericus rex. Quamvis
universae rei publicae nostrae infatigabilem curam desideremus impendere et Deo favente
ad statum studeamus pristinum cuncta revocare, tamen Romae civitatis sollicitiora nos
augmenta constringunt. . . .

Hold against this *Institutiones saecularium litterarum*, Conclusion, 7:

. . . for it is an inestimable good to apprehend the Creator by whom lives whatever is vital, from whom receive knowledge all those who exist, by whom is administered whatever is created, by whom is repaired whatsoever arises restored to the better (*in melius instaurata*). [78]

These texts are interesting because they antithetically represent the ideals of terrestrial rulership and of the monastic commonwealth which anticipates the heavenly fatherland. Such idealizations could, however, have been formulated in a similar manner also by a Greek ascetic writer [79]—even though the Rome ideology of the *Variae* is of course western and the term *cives religiosi* sounds Augustinian. More characteristic is in any case the contrast between the retrospective reform ideology of Cassiodorus' Theodorician phase and the prospective, ameliorative reform idea which he propagated at Vivarium. The idea of an *instauratio in melius* owes more to western and Augustinian than to Greek patristic tradition and the program of Cassiodorus' *Institutiones* is in part dependent on *De doctrina christiana*,[80] even though much of the content, especially of Book II which deals with the *saeculares litterae*, is derived from the Greek-speaking east.[81]

Greek, and especially Platonic and Neoplatonic, elements are much stronger in Cassiodorus' great contemporary and colleague during

---

[78] *Institutiones II: Saecularium litterarum*, *Conclusio* 7, Mynors 162: . . . inaestimabile quippe donum est conspicere creatorem, unde vivunt quaecumque vitalia sunt, unde sapiunt quaecumque subsistunt, unde amministrantur quaecumque creata sunt, unde reparantur quaecumque in melius instaurata consurgunt. . . .

[79] See p. 69, n. 27, p. 116, n. 29, especially for the combination of *civitas* and *patria* ideology with that of Paradise, a combination which is generally patristic and found even in Augustine, in spite of the special character of his *civitas* concept.

[80] See the *Index Auctorum* in Mynors' edition for Cassiodorus' references to, and quotations from, *De doctrina christiana* and other works of St. Augustine. Among Cassiodorus' exegetical works, especially the *Commenta Psalterii*, *PL* LXX, 9 ff., owe much to Augustine's *Enarrationes in Psalmos*, as Cassiodorus himself states (*PL* LXX, 9A f.).

[81] Cf. Courcelle, *Lettres grecques* 321 ff. The first book of the *Institutiones*, concerning *divinae litterae*, was influenced also by the example of the *Instituta regularia divinae legis* of the Quaestor Palatii Junilius, a North African, whom Cassiodorus probably had met during his stay in Constantinople and whom he mentions in *Institutiones* I, 10, Mynors 34; cf. van de Vyver, "*Institutiones*" 84 f. Junilius' work was a Latin adaptation of a Greek manual by Paul of Persia who had taught at the famous Christian school of higher learning at Nisibis; cf. Courcelle, *Lettres grecques* 336.

his Theodorician phase, Boethius,[82] in spite of his opposition to the Ostrogothic version of the Byzantine Basileia ideal. Even though the Augustinian Civitas Dei probably appears in Boethius' *De consolatione philosophiae*,[83] his reform ideology seems to remain confined within the limits of a *reparatio in pristinum*.[84] Boethius, who died for the

---

[82] Cf. Courcelle, *Lettres grecques* 257 ff., especially 300 ff.

[83] Boethius, *De consolatione philosophiae* I, pros. 5, *CSEL* LXVII, 15, 4 f.: Si enim cuius oriundo sis patriae reminiscare, non uti Atheniensium quondam multitudinis imperio regitur, sed εἷς κοίρανός ἐστιν, εἷς βασιλεύς (Homer, *Iliad* II, 204 f.), qui frequentia civium, non depulsione laetetur, cuius agi frenis atque obtemperare iustitiae libertas est. An ignoras illam tuae civitatis antiquissimam legem qua sanctum est ei ius exsulare non esse quisquis in ea sedem fundare maluerit? The conception of liberty as obedience may also be Augustinian. For Augustine's influence on Boethius, suggested by Boethius himself (cf. *De Trinitate*, Preface, Stewart and Rand, *Boeth. Theol. Tract.* 4), see R. Carton, "Le christianisme et l'augustinisme de Boèce," *Mélanges augustiniens publiés à l'occasion du XVe centenaire de saint Augustin* (Paris, 1931) 243 ff., also the criticism of Courcelle, *Lettres grecques* 301 f., and above all E. T. Silk, "Boethius's Consolatio Philosophiae as a Sequel to Augustine's Dialogues and Soliloquia," *Harv. Theol. Rev.* XXXII (1939) 19 ff.; for Boethius' position between Plato and Augustine with regard to conversion and memory and with regard to the eternity or temporality of the world, cf. F. Klingner, *De Boethii Consolatione Philosophiae* (Philologische Untersuchungen XXVII, Berlin, 1921) 32 ff., 108 ff., K. Büchner, "Bemerkungen zum dritten Buche von des Boethius Trost der Philosophie," *Hist. Jb* LXII–LXIX (1949) 31 ff.; but see also Courcelle, *Lettres grecques* 295 ff. Boethius' authorship of *De fide catholica* which contains a reference to Augustine's *superna civitas* (cf. *De fide catholica*, Stewart and Rand, *Boeth. Theol. Tract.* 70, with Augustine's *De civitate Dei* XXII, 1, Corp. Christ., Ser. Lat. XLVIII, 807) is not beyond doubt. Cf. E. K. Rand, "Der dem Boethius zugeschriebene Traktat De Fide Catholica," *Jahrbücher für classische Philologie*, Suppl. Bd. XXVI (1901) 401 ff., especially 420 ff. Rand, who later admitted the authenticity of the treatise, had in this study shown its dependence on Augustine.

[84] For the resurrection of the bodies as *reparatio in statum pristinum* cf. *De fide catholica*, Stewart and Rand 70. For the return of all things to their beginning and the consolation to be gained from this, see *De consolatione philosophiae* III, metr. II, 34 ff., *CSEL* LXVII, 50:

> Repetunt proprios quaeque recursus
> redituque suo singula gaudent
> nec manet ulli traditus ordo
> nisi quod fini iunxerit ortum
> stabilemque sui fecerit orbem.

This is clearly the old Greek cyclical ideology (cf. above, p. 73, nn. 41 ff., about Origen's oft-repeated saying: *semper enim similis est finis initiis*). See also *De consolatione philosophiae* III, metr. IX, and IV, metr. VI, *CSEL* LXVII, 63 f. and 102 ff. For Greek ideology of assimilation to God or divinization in Boethius see *De consolatione philosophiae* I, pros. 4, 38 f., LXVII, 12: Instillabas . . . Pythagoricum illud ἕπου θεῷ. Nec conveniebat vilissimorum me spirituum praesidia captare, quem tu in hanc excellentiam componebas, ut consimilem Deo faceres; also *ibid.* III, pros. 10, 23 ff., LXVII, 66 f.: Nam quoniam beatitudinis adeptione fiunt

superiority of personal over royal "political" God-likeness, who in his prison wrote so beautifully of the eminence of the heavenly before the earthly city,[85] was probably a greater character than Cassiodorus. But the survivor had the saving grace of a very long life which led him to fructifications of his *conversio* denied to Boethius.

Cassiodorus' resumption of Augustine's ideal of Christian intellectual culture[86] as an essential part of man's way back to God is all the more admirable as his life and work in Vivarium reached far down into an age which had entered upon a deep cultural retrenchment. Already Caesarius of Arles had found it necessary to express himself in what he calls *sermo simplex, pedestris, rusticus* in order to be understood[87] and by the time of Gregory of Tours, who died about the same time as Cassiodorus, it would appear that the *sermo rusticus* had come to reflect the "vulgarization" of the Latin language and a definite break in the ancient school tradition of continental western Europe, with

homines beati, beatitudo vero est ipsa divinitas, divinitatis adeptione beatos fieri manifestum est. Sed uti iustitiae adeptione iusti, sapientiae sapientes fiunt, ita divinitatem adeptos deos fieri simili ratione necesse est. Omnis igitur beatus Deus, sed natura quidem unus; participatione vero nihil prohibet esse quam plurimos.

[85] See above, p. 420, n. 83.

[86] See *Institutiones* I: *Divinarum litterarum* XXX, 1, Mynors 75: Ego tamen fateor votum meum, quod inter vos quaecumque possunt corporeo labore compleri antiquariorum mihi studia, si tamen veraciter scribant, non immerito forsitan plus placere. . . . This is followed by a famous text concerning the transcription of manuscripts: Tot enim vulnera Satanas accipit quot antiquarius Domini verba describit. . . . Audiunt populi unde se a prava voluntate convertant et Domino pura mente deserviant. Cf. S. Esposito, S.J., "Cassiodoro, la Bibbia e la cultura occidentale," *Divus Thomas* (Piacenza, 1958) 193 ff.

[87] Caesarius of Arles, *Sermo* I, 20, *Corp. Christ.*, *Ser. Lat.* CIII, 16: Unde magis simplici et pedestri sermone, quem totus populus capere possit, debent dominici mei sacerdotes populis praedicare . . . ; cf. also *ibid.* 1, CIII, 1, and *ibid.* 13, CIII, 10; see furthermore *Sermo* LXXXVI, 1, CIII, 353: . . . rogo humiliter, ut contentae sint eruditae aures verba rustica aequanimiter sustinere, dummodo totus grex Domini simplici et, ut ita dixerim, pedestri sermone pabulum spiritale possit accipere . . . ; *Sermo* CXIV, 2, CIII, 474 f.: Et haec quidem secundum litteram, sicut in libris sanctorum scriptum invenimus, caritati vestrae rustico et simplici sermone, quem toti intellegere possint, insinuanda credidimus. . . . E. Auerbach, "Sermo humilis," *Romanische Forschungen* LXIV (1953) 343 ff., rightly stressed that in spite of Caesarius' apologies for his lack of literary culture (for the "author's modesty" *topos* cf. E. R. Curtius, *European Literature and the Latin Middle Ages* [trans. from the German by W. R. Trask, Bollingen Series XXXVI, New York, 1953] 83 ff.) his *sermo rusticus* represents a conscious effort toward simplification of style.

the exception perhaps of Italy.[88] It may be symptomatic of this development that even Cassiodorus, who about 535 had still dreamt of a school of higher learning at Rome,[89] wrote his last work on the subject of orthography and punctuation, for the benefit of his monks at Vivarium who had complained that it did not profit them to know the works of the ancients and Cassiodorus' own contributions if they were to remain ignorant of how to write down properly what they had learned.[90] No wonder that he, too, especially in the second edition of his *Institutiones saecularium litterarum*, finds it advisable to make concessions to the *simplicitas fratrum*.[91] And yet, to the very last he tried to maintain the continuity and universality of the heritage which he had received from the Fathers and the ancients.

No doubt the work of such intentional simplifiers of ancient Christian civilization as St. Benedict, St. Gregory the Great, and St.

[88] See in general H. I. Marrou, *Histoire de l'éducation dans l'antiquité* (Paris, 1948) 448 ff.; for Gaul cf. M. Roger, *L'enseignement des lettres classiques d'Ausone à Alcuin* (Paris, 1905) 89 ff., 155 ff.; for Gregory of Tours in particular, Wattenbach-Levison I, 99, with bibliography, also J. M. Wallace-Hadrill, "The Work of Gregory of Tours in the Light of Modern Research," *Trans. R. Histor. Soc.*, Ser. V, I (1951), especially 29 f., Auerbach, "Sermo humilis" 357 ff. For Spain see, for instance, Martin of Braga, *De correctione rusticorum* 1, Barlow, *Martin Bracar. Opera*, 183: . . . cibum rusticis rustico sermone condire. Barlow, too, in his introduction, p. 16, considers that the term *sermo rusticus* is in this period not just a rhetorical affectation, but corresponds to a real "vulgarization" of language and style.

[89] Cf. H. I. Marrou, "Autour de la bibliothèque du pape Agapit," *Mélanges d'archéologie et d'histoire* XLVIII (1931) 124 ff.

[90] See the significant complaint of the monks according to Cassiodorus' *De orthographia*, Preface, Keil, *Gramm. Lat.* VII, 143: . . . monachi mei subito clamare coeperunt: "Quid prodest cognoscere nos, vel quae antiqui fecerunt, vel ea, quae sagacitas vestra addenda curavit nosse diligenter, si quem ad modum ea scribere debeamus, omnimodis ignoremus?" The treatise was written c. 578, when Cassiodorus was ninety-three years old.

[91] *Institutiones* II, ⟨*De grammatica*⟩, Mynors 94, 9 ff.: . . . nobis tamen placet in medium Donatum deducere, qui et pueris specialiter aptus et tyronibus probatur accommodus . . . (the rest of the paragraph probably belongs to Cassiodorus' second recension of his work). Sed et sanctum Augustinum propter simplicitatem fratrum breviter instruendam aliqua de eodem titulo scripsisse repperimus. . . . See also *Institutiones* I, 21, *De sancto Hieronymo* 2, Mynors, 60, 14 ff. (the following text, too, is probably a late Cassiodorian addition, cf. van de Vyver, "Institutiones" 62 ff.): Nobis vero fuit causa diversa, primum quod ad fratres simplices et impolitos scripsimus instruendos, ut per multos auctores . . . caelestium scripturarum plenitudine compleantur. . . . Sed ne aliquid eis deesse possit, qui ad studia huius saeculi non fuerunt, tam de artibus quam de disciplinis saecularium litterarum . . . breviter credidimus ammonendos, ut simplicibus viris famuletur et mundanarum peritia litterarum. . . .

Columbanus, as St. Isidore of Seville and Venantius Fortunatus,[92] was very great and very necessary—their epochal role in the history of the mediaeval reform idea between Justinian and Charlemagne would fittingly introduce another volume. Yet it is memorable also that at least one man, who lived long enough to be their contemporary, succeeded in transmitting some of the more complex elements of the great religious culture of Antiquity to later ages.

In this tradition the idea of reform was an important element theologically, ascetically, and culturally. It was to remain the self-perpetuating core, the inner life spring of Christian tradition through lesser and greater times. In the age of the Fathers the scriptural reform idea had been elaborated intellectually and spiritually into an ideal postulate for the individual Christian conscience and had been made a living reality above all in the monastic sphere. To carry reform according to the image of God beyond personal and communal sanctity had seemed to be unnecessary. It was left to a later phase of mediaeval history, to the age of Gregory VII, to formulate clearly and to initiate courageously a reform of the *Ecclesia*, of the Church herself as the mystical and hierarchical Body of Christ,[93] and to the still later age of Innocent III

[92] Venantius Fortunatus' position in this historical process at the same time foreshadows the character of the cultural renewal which was to begin a century and a half later; he was not by accident a favorite model of the Carolingian authors. Fortunatus had spent his youth and received his education in the "Romania" of Gothic-Justinianean Italy. He "simplified" the culture which he had absorbed by the very cumulation of its elements, when he transmitted it to the Galloroman-Merovingian milieu. So, for instance, he externalized the Augustinian concept of *dulcedo* as the inner sweetness of friendship, above all between man and God and secondarily between human friends (cf. *Confessiones, passim*), by adapting it to the "courtly" conventions of sixth century Gaul (cf. R. Koebner, *Venantius Fortunatus* [Beiträge zur Kulturgeschichte des Mittelalters und der Renaissance XXII, Leipzig, Berlin, 1915], R. B. Bezzola, *Les origines et la formation de la littérature courtoise en occident, 500–1200*, I [Bibliothèque de l'Ecole des Hautes Etudes, Sciences historiques et philogiques, CCLXXXVI, Paris, 1944] especially 50 ff.: "Les grands dignitaires laïques mérovingiens et l'idéal de la *dulcedo*," Adele M. Fiske, R.S.C.J., "The Survival and Development of the Ancient Concept of Friendship in the Early Middle Ages" [Unprinted Fordham University Ph.D. Diss., New York, 1955]). On the other hand, if one compares Venantius Fortunatus' religious poetry with that of the fourth century, of St. Paulinus of Nola, for instance, the increasing penetration of the classical forms of expression by a mystical content emerges clearly.

[93] In the post-Gregorian age, therefore, Anselm of Havelberg can apply Ps. 102:5: Renovabitur ut aquilae iuventus tua (cf. above, pp. 21, 45, 295, 314) to the Church as a

and Thomas Aquinas to extend this reform to the whole *Christianitas*,[94] to the political, socio-economic, and cultural milieu of life, which the Church had helped to form and hoped to perfect.

whole; see his *Dialogi*, I: *De unitate fidei et multiplicitate vivendi . . .*, PL CLXXXVIII, 1149: Sancta ecclesia pertransiens per diversos status sibi invicem paulatim succedentes usque in hodiernum diem sicut iuventus aquilae renovatur et semper renovabitur. For Anselm of Havelberg see also above, p. 413, n. 52.

[94] For the relationship between *Ecclesia* and *Christianitas* cf. J. Rupp. *L'idée de chrétienté dans la pensée pontificale des origines à Innocent III* (Paris, 1939), E. Gilson, *La philosophie au moyen âge des origines patristiques à la fin du XIVᵉ siècle*, 2nd ed. (Paris, 1947) 252 ff., F. Kempf, S.J., *Papsttum und Kaisertum bei Innocenz III.* (Miscellanea Historiae Pontificiae XIX, Roma, 1954) 280 ff., also my article "The Concepts of «Ecclesia» and «Christianitas» . . .," *Sacerdozio e Regno da Gregorio a Bonifacio VIII* (Miscell. Hist. Pont. XVIII, Roma, 1954) 49 ff.

EXCURSUS I

THE DEFINITION OF AN IDEA[1]

As pointed out in the Introduction, there can be no doubt concerning the existence of reform ideas in early Christian and mediaeval times. Foundation *in re* of the idea of reform may be taken for granted. On this basis a "real," not merely nominal, definition of the idea of reform, as held in certain historical times and places, has been attempted.

As all nonmathematical definitions and, especially, every definition of historical facts—which are the least exhaustively and definitively known among all facts—a definition of the idea of reform is, to repeat it again, provisional, because incomplete on principle. It must be controlled over and over again by the evidence of the historical sources as to the existence or nonexistence of facts which correspond to this definition.

The fundamental importance of all definitions which are not assignments of names only is stated by A. N. Whitehead in this manner: ". . . if we abandon the strictly logical point of view, the definitions —though in form they remain the mere assignment of names—are at once seen to be the most important part of the subject. The act of assigning names is in fact the act of choosing the various complex ideas which are to be the special object of study. The whole subject depends

---

[1] The problem of the definition of ideas which occur within history has never been treated exhaustively and constructively. A few suggestive remarks are found in Crane Brinton, *The Anatomy of Revolutions* (New York, 1938) Chapter 1: "The Comparative Study of Revolutions." H. Rickert, in his famous book, *Die Grenzen der naturwissenschaftlichen Begriffsbildung*, 5th ed. (Tübingen, 1929) 48 ff., 54 ff., has a good discussion of definitions in general which, however, surprisingly is not carried over into his treatment of historical conceptualization. More important are the considerations concerning historical concepts and definitions by R. Aron, *Introduction à la philosophie de l'histoire* (Paris, 1938) 131 ff., 135 ff.; Aron deals with the difficult problem of historical conceptualization in general rather than with the comparatively simple case of the definition of specific and well-formulated historical ideas. The point of view taken in the present Excursus is in some respects not unlike that of K. Mannheim in his *Ideology and Utopia*, trans. L. Wirth and E. Shils (New York, Harvest Books, reprint of 1936 edition) 197 and 202.

on such a choice."[2] This holds true for nonmathematical definitions even more strongly than for the definitions of mathematics[3] and mathematical logic.[4] Nonmathematical definitions, including also definitions of historical facts, may be conceived of in at least two different ways.

One not followed in this study may be termed a nominalism of experience. It is the way of the positivist wing of mathematical or symbolical logic[5] and of the ideal-typical method in sociology; this way is subjective-empiricist as well as quasi-mathematical. In both cases definitions are constituted as independent from reality, though empirical facts can be compared with them.

According to the point of view of positivistic symbolic logic, an early exposition of which can be found in R. Carnap's *Der logische Aufbau der Welt*,[6] a definition is a rule which states how to reduce a proposition concerning some "subject-matter" to a proposition about a basic sense experience. The question whether or not there is anything real outside the experiencing subject has no scientific meaning for such logicians who therefore believe that they stand above the alternative realism-nominalism.[7]

For the ideal-typical mode of conceptualization and definition formulated by Max Weber "the ideal-typical concept . . . *is* no hypothesis but it offers guidance to the construction of hypotheses. . . . An ideal

---

[2] A. N. Whitehead, *The Axioms of Projective Geometry* (Cambridge, 1906) 2.

[3] For mathematical definition and abstraction see H. Weyl, *Philosophy of Mathematics and Natural Science* (Princeton 1949) 8 ff.

[4] For definition in mathematical or symbolic logic see, for instance, A. Tarski, *Introduction to Logic and to the Methodology of Deductive Sciences* (New York, 1941) 33 f.

[5] Above all in the former "Vienna Circle."

[6] R. Carnap, *Der logische Aufbau der Welt* (Berlin, 1928) 51, 85 ff.

[7] Cf. Carnap, *Der logische Aufbau der Welt* 27, also idem, *Scheinprobleme in der Philosophie* (Berlin, 1928) 36, idem, *The Logical Syntax of Language* (London, 1937) 301. In his more recent works Carnap, following A. Tarski, has turned from the mere study of the rule of logical "syntax" to problems of meaning, to logical "semantics" (cf. *Introduction to Semantics* [Cambridge, Mass., 1942]). But this new approach does not, it seems, entail a modification of the basic nominalism and positivism which is also adhered to by other members of the former "Vienna Circle" such as Philip G. Frank (cf. his *Modern Science and Its Philosophy* [Cambridge, Mass., 1949]) and K. R. Popper (see especially *The Open Society and Its Enemies* [London, 1945]). For A. J. Ayer's positivistic phase see the interesting criticism of C. B. Daly, "Logical Positivism, Metaphysics and Ethics, II," *The Irish Theological Quarterly* XXIV (1957) 32 ff.

type is formed by the one-sided *accentuation* of one or more points of view. . . . It is a utopia; it has the significance of a purely ideal *limiting* concept with which the real situation is *compared*. . . ."[8] According to Weber "a 'definition' of . . . synthetical historical terms according to the scheme of *genus proximum* and *differentia specifica*[9] is . . . nonsense" because of the difficulty of deciding which components of the concept are essential for the definition. Therefore "there remains only the ideal-type."[10]

Another conception of definition, here adhered to, is based on the Aristotelian-Thomistic realism of being combined with nonpositivistic elements in modern philosophy of science. It is founded on the assumption that concepts and their definitions are somehow connected with an existing reality. Their connection to that reality is a hypothetical one in the sense of Maritain's statement that a definition "does not form a whole or a finished structure";[11] a "second operation of the mind" is needed, a judgment as to (possible or actual) existence or

[8] Cf. Max Weber, "Die 'Objektivität' sozialwissenschaftlicher und sozialpolitischer Erkenntnis," *Archiv für Sozialwissenschaft und Sozialpolitik* XIX (Neue Folge I, 1904) 22 ff., trans. in *Max Weber on the Methodology of the Social Sciences*, edd. E. A. Shils and H. A. Finch (Glencoe, Ill., 1949) 90, 93. For Weber's nominalism see especially *From Max Weber: Essays in Sociology*, trans. and edd. H. H. Gerth and C. W. Mills (New York, 1946), Introduction 55, 59. Popper, *The Open Society* 278, is surely wrong when he asserts that Weber's ideal types correspond to the essences of Aristotle and Husserl.

[9] This is one type of definition in Aristotelian-Thomistic logic; cf. J. Gredt, *Elementa Philosophiae Aristotelico-Thomisticae* I (Freiburg, 1926) 32 f., 33.

[10] Cf. *Max Weber on the Methodology of the Social Sciences* 93.

[11] Jacques Maritain, *Formal Logic*, trans. of *Eléments de philosophie* II, I (New York, 1946) 78. Cf. Etienne Gilson, *L'être et l'essence* (Paris, 1948) 277, 281, 286 ff., Rickert, *Grenzen der naturwissenschaftlichen Begriffsbildung* 57 ff. See also Maritain, *Formal Logic* 19: ". . . since our ideas are the result of abstraction . . . the object which we lay hold of in them is always presented as abstracted from actual existence . . . it is not presented as an actually existing being, but only as a possible being, as a being that can exist . . ."; E. Gilson, *Being and Some Philosophers* (Toronto, 1949) 182: ". . . essential possibility is no sufficient reason for existential possibility. . . ." Essential possibility must here be understood more or less in the sense of potentiality, i.e., as the contrary not of essential necessity, but of existential actuality. In fact conceptualized essences, because they are universals and not particulars, are at the same time necessary and not contingent as seen from the essential order and possible and not actual as seen from the existential order. In other words all concepts, because they cannot envisage fully the particulars of an actually existent, have to some extent the character of universals with the latter's connotations of essentiality and necessity.

nonexistence.[12] Similarly Einstein distinguished two primary cognitive steps: first, the formation of concepts which are not identical with the totality of sense experience; second, the attribution of "real existence" to concepts.[13] It is true that there is little agreement on how exactly concepts and, especially, the "higher" concepts of any scientific system are related to reality. Aristotelians and Thomists believe that even concepts of the latter type can be abstracted by the mind from reality;[14] A. N. Whitehead's method of "extensive abstraction" is akin to this assumption.[15] Einstein and the majority of natural scientists on the contrary consider such concepts "of the second level"[16] as free inventions of the human mind, as hypotheses independent on principle from reality, though the possibility of correspondence with extramental reality is inherent in them.[17] Perhaps this rejection of the theory of abstraction, this insistence on the complete freedom of hypotheses, is of a methodological and practical rather than of a metaphysical nature.[18] For all concepts of

[12] See Maritain, *Les dégrès du savoir*, 4th ed. (Paris, 1946) 779 ff., *idem, Existence and the Existent* (New York, 1948) 17, Gilson, *Being and Some Philosophers* 187 ff., *idem, L'être et 'essence* 286 ff.

[13] Albert Einstein, "Physik und Realität," *Journal of the Franklin Institute* CCXXI (1936) 314.

[14] Cf. J. Maritain, *An Introduction to Philosophy* (trans. of *Eléments de philosophie* I, New York, 1930) 170 ff., *idem, Les degrès du savoir* 238 ff.; see also Felix Kaufmann, *Methodology of the Social Sciences* (Oxford, New York, 1944) 16, from Husserl's phenomenological point of view which is in this respect Aristotelian. Cf. E. Husserl, *Logische Untersuchungen*, 3rd. ed., II (Halle, 1922), part II, on abstraction. See also Kaufmann's remarks on definition (p. 34) which imply rejection of a mere correlation or correspondence theory.

[15] A. N. Whitehead, *An Enquiry Concerning the Principles of Natural Knowledge* (Cambridge, 1919) 101 ff., *idem, The Concept of Nature* (Cambridge, 1920) 80 f., *idem, Science and the Modern World* (Pelican Book Edition, 1938) 184 ff.

[16] Cf. Einstein, "Physik and Realität" 316 f.

[17] On these premises it becomes indeed not only wonderful, but a "miracle" and "beyond conception" that "the world of our sense experience can be conceptualized" (so Einstein, "Physik und Realität" 315 f.).

[18] In the sense of Goethe's dictum that "the whole of [the] inner life of thought proved to be a vital instrument of discovery (*eine lebendige Heuristik*)—first having the intimation of an unknown law, then striving to find it in the outer world and establish it there" (from *Maximen und Reflektionen* [*Schriften der Goethe-Gesellschaft* XXI (Weimar, 1907) 61, no. 328], quoted by E. Cassirer, *The Problem of Knowledge* [New Haven, 1950] 233). Cf. A. Einstein, *The World As I See It* (New York, 1934) 36 f.: ". . . we can discover by means of purely mathematical constructions the concepts and the laws connecting them with each other, which furnish the key to the understanding of natural phenomena. Experience may

actually existent things are "idealizations" open to reality and logically different from the constructs of mathematics and mathematical logic, from constituted concepts or from ideal types.[19] It is the task of every scientific investigation of reality to perform and to connect logically existential judgments at some stage of its progress. In this respect history does not differ from natural science.[20]

suggest the appropriate mathematical concepts, but they most certainly cannot be deduced from it." I believe that P. G. Frank, "Einstein, Mach and Logical Positivism," *Albert Einstein: Philosopher-Scientist* (The Library of Living Philosophers VII, Evanston, Ill., 1949) 271 ff., exaggerates the positivistic element in Einstein's philosophy of science. See Einstein, *The World As I See It* 37: "In a certain sense, therefore, I hold it true that pure thought can grasp reality, as the ancients dreamed"; also *ibid.* 60: "The belief in an external world independent of the perceiving subject is the basis of all natural science," and ". . . our notions of physical reality can never be final. We must always be ready to change these notions . . . in order to do justice to perceived facts. . . ." See also F. S. C. Northrop, "Einstein's Conception of Science," *Albert Einstein: Philosopher-Scientist* 390, 393, 401, 404. The connection between the method of modern natural science and the original philosophical, sociological, and scientific positivism of the nineteenth century has in any case become rather remote. Auguste Comte's "law of three stages" (*Cours de philosophie positive*, 3rd ed., I [Paris, 1869] 8, *idem*, *Discours sur l'esprit positif* [Paris, 1844] 2 ff.) envisaged a comparatively simple transition from the second metaphysical or abstract to the third scientific or positive stage—whereas the ulterior development of science itself has revived in a new sense the problem of the relation between scientific fact and scientific hypothesis. Cf., for instance, Henri Poincaré, *Science et méthode* (Paris, 1908), P. Duhem, *La théorie physique*, 2nd ed. (Paris, 1914), especially 33 (end of page), and Cassirer, *The Problem of Knowledge* 111 ff., on Poincaré and Duhem.

[19] Cf. Einstein, *Mein Weltbild*, 2nd ed. (Amsterdam, 1934) 177: Like the physicist, the historian, too, groups "*das tatsächliche Geschehen . . . um Ideale, die er sich bezüglich der menschlichen Gesellschaft gebildet hat*," a statement which holds true not only for "ideals" but also for conceptual "idealizations" in history as well as in physics. For "idealization" in this sense see also N. Bohr, *Atomic Theory and the Description of Nature* I (Cambridge, 1934) 5, *idem*, "Wirkungsquantum und Naturbeschreibung," *Die Naturwissenschaften* XVII (1929) 484 f.: "In den eigentlichen Naturwissenschaften (as distinct from mathematics) kann . . . von keinen streng abgeschlossenen Anwendungsgebieten der logischen Prinzipien die Rede sein, da wir immer mit neu hinzukommenden Tatsachen rechnen müssen, deren Einordnung in den Rahmen der früheren Erfahrungen eine Revision unserer begrifflichen Hilfsmittel verlangen kann." See also L. de Broglie, *Matière et lumière* (Paris, 1937) 307 ff., Chapter VI: "Réalité physique et idéalization."

[20] These facts are obscured in Rickert's *Grenzen der naturwissenschaftlichen Begriffsbildung*. The reason for this is his denial of all universality to concepts in historical inquiry (not only to historical facts) and his affirmation that they are gained only and always by relating facts to values. This value relation is for Rickert a purely formal one; that is to say, contrary to Humboldt, Ranke, and his school, he is not primarily interested in the historian's ability to recognize concrete values crystallized in ideas, but in the wider problem of historical knowledge in general which he believes possible only by identifying the cognition of the

For the purpose of this study then, definition is defined as the setting forth in terms "already known and whose meanings are beyond doubt"[21] of essential characteristics which are gained by comparing specific and general traits.[22] It is possible to define the idea of reform, to assume provisionally that the definition corresponds to reality, and to modify it if historical evidence demands, without for that reason denying that otherwise the idea of reform is valid as defined.[23]

---

essential with that of value *in abstracto*. An excellent criticism of Rickert's theory and a sound reassertion of the possibility of conceptualizing and knowing historical facts is given by M. Mandelbaum, *The Problem of Historical Knowledge: An Answer to Relativism* (New York, 1938) 119 ff., 177 ff.

[21] Tarski, *Introduction to Logic* 33 f. This applies chiefly to nominal definitions.

[22] This applies to that type of *definitio realis* which in Aristotelian-Thomistic logic is called *definitio essentialis metaphysica*, i.e., *per genus proximum et differentiam specificam* (cf. above, p. 429), and is considered the most perfect definition. See also Rickert, *Grenzen der naturwissenschaftlichen Begriffsbildung* 297, on historical concepts through which the historically essential is "lifted" and "gathered" out of history.

[23] The following striking rebuttal of nominalist logic by H. Poincaré (in other respects far removed from a realism of being) seems to apply here (see *Science et méthode* 190 f.): If, he asks, somebody discovered that phosphorus, defined as a substance which melts at 44 degrees centigrade, actually melts at 43.9 degrees should we conclude that what we call phosphorus is not true phosphorus or that phosphorus melts at 43.9 degrees? We could adopt either definition, but to opt for the first would be stupid, "*parce qu'on ne peut pas changer le nom d'un corps toutes les fois qu'on détermine une nouvelle décimale de son point de fusion.*"

EXCURSUS II

METAHISTORICAL PRECONCEPTIONS

At the end of Part One a second methodological problem was briefly touched upon. The essential characteristics of a historical idea may be unambiguous as factual constituents of that idea, but it does not follow implicitly that they may be taken at their face value. In concrete terms: the reform idea may on principle be considered as "beyond doubt" for those who held it, but its validity and efficacy are not "beyond doubt" from the point of view of the logic of historical knowledge.

It was a weakness of Wilhelm von Humboldt's and Ranke's great doctrine of historical ideas that they simply assumed the validity and efficacy of ideas which they considered as driving forces in history. They rightly saw ideas at work in history,[1] but they did not ask

---

[1] The nature of Humboldt's and Ranke's "ideas"—which have hardly anything in common with Hegelian idealism—stands in the middle between historical ideas in the strict sense, i.e., ideas expressed by men in history, and Platonist-Christian ideas in the mind of God. See W. v Humboldt, *Über die Aufgabe des Geschichtsschreibers*, in *Gesammelte Werke* I (Berlin, 1841) 19: "Die Idee äussert sich aber auf zwiefachem Wege, einmal als Richtung, die anfangs unscheinbar, aber allmählig sichtbar, und zuletzt unwiderstehlich, Viele, an verschiedenen Orten und unter verschiedenen Umständen ergreift; dann als Krafterzeugung, welche in ihrem Umfang und in ihrer Erhabenheit nicht aus den begleitenden Umständen herzuleiten ist." Ideas of the latter kind in their purest form are the eternal archtetype ideas, "*die ewigen Urideen alles Denkbaren*," which are intimations of God's government of the world (p. 23). See also L. v. Ranke, *Politisches Gespräch* (of 1836), trans. by T. H. v. Laue, in *Leopold Ranke: The Formative Years* (Princeton, 1950) 159: "The idea that inspires and dominates the whole, the prevailing tendency of the minds, and conditions in general, these are what determine the formation and the character of every institution"; cf. also v. Laue, *Leopold Ranke: The Formative Years* 47, for "the combination of human and divine elements" in Ranke's concept of ideas. On the theory of historical ideas cf. E. Cassirer, *The Problem of Knowledge* (New Haven, 1950) Chapter XIII, and H. Holborn, "The Science of History," *The Interpretation of History* (Princeton, 1943) 71 ff. Hegelian and related theories according to which the history of ideas itself unfolds according to an autonomous "impersonal" determination are not considered in this study, which holds to a Rankian and at the same time Aristotelian-Thomistic persuasion: that within human history ideas exist only in individual minds and in their extramental expressions or productions. Cf. J. Wach, *Das Verstehen: Grundzüge einer Geschichte der hermeneutischen Theorie im 19. Jahrhundert* III (Tübingen, 1933) 92, on Ranke: "Die Reflexion gibt sich bei ihm so gut wie immer als Abstraktion aus der Konstatierung des Faktischen. . . ." In the study of the idea of reform, and of reform

themselves persistently enough how far specific ideas corresponded to other ideological and nonideological realities, whether they did not represent one part of reality only, and perhaps even obscured other aspects.[2] A one-sided theory of historical ideas thus provoked the rise of equally one-sided doctrines of historical positivism and materialism.[3]

itself, it is quite evident that such historical phenomena result from individual thoughts and actions and not from any ghostlike dialectical process (a perversion of the Platonic doctrine of ideas). See in this connection the interesting remarks of D. Bidney, "The Concept of Meta-Anthropology and Its Significance for Contemporary Anthropological Science," *Ideological Differences and World Order*, ed. F. S. C. Northrop (New Haven, 1949) especially 323 ff. The study of the idea of reform, then, is the study of a concrete "unit-idea" in the sense of A. O. Lovejoy's terminology; cf. his Introduction, "The Study of the History of Ideas," to *The Great Chain of Being* (Cambridge, Mass., 1936) 15 ff., also "The Historiography of Ideas," *Essays in the History of Ideas* (Baltimore, 1948) 8 f.

[2] G. Fueter, *Geschichte der neueren Historiographie*, 3rd ed. (München, Berlin, 1936) 426 f., correctly criticizes the historians of the early ideological school for being incapable of recognizing, for instance, the economic and sociological aspects of political movements. Yet Humboldt (*Über die Aufgabe des Geschichtsschreibers* 15 ff.) saw clearly at least the principle of complementary existence of causally determined "mechanical" or "natural" chains of events and of free ideas in history. Similarly, Wilhelm Dilthey, *Der Aufbau der geschichtlichen Welt in den Geisteswissenschaften* (*Gesammelte Schriften* VII [Leipzig, Berlin, 1927] 260), envisages both the positing of ends by man and his psychological motives in doing so and he considers it as impossible and unnecessary to explain the former by the latter. Friedrich Meinecke saw (efficient) "causality" and "value" ("ideas" and "ideals," "teleology") as equally essential forces in history. See, especially, his "Kausalitäten und Werte in der Geschichte," first published in 1925, reprinted in *Schaffender Spiegel: Studien zur deutschen Geschichtsschreibung und Geschichtsauffassung* (Stuttgart, 1948) 56 ff., also the introduction to *Die Idee der Staatsräson*, 3rd ed. (München, Berlin, 1929); cf. E. N. Anderson, "Meinecke's Ideengeschichte and the Crisis in Historical Thinking," *Medieval and Historiographical Essays in Honor of James Westfall Thompson* (Chicago, 1938) 361 ff. For complementarity of "subjective" ideas and "objective" causes, of final and efficient causality, see below, pp. 437 ff.

[3] See the *Communist Manifesto* (1848, ed. H. J. Laski, London, 1948) 105: ". . . man's ideas, views, and conceptions, in one word, man's consciousness, changes with every change in the condition of his material existence, in his social relations and in his social life. . . . When people speak of ideas that revolutionise society, they do but express the fact that within the old society the elements of a new one have been created, and that the dissolution of the old ideas keeps even pace with the dissolution of the old conditions of existence." See also Karl Marx, *Zur Kritik der politischen Ökonomie* (1859, English trans. by N. I. Stone, New York, 1904) 11 f.: "It is not the consciousness of men that determines their existence but, on the contrary, their social existence determines their consciousness." A rejection of all teleology, in favor of efficient causality, and of all indeterminism and the assertion of absolute dependence of ideas on matter were stated with iron consistency by N. Bukharin, *Historical Materialism*, trans. from 3rd ed. (New York, 1925) 19 ff., 33 ff., 53 ff.; but on the whole, Marxist-Leninist philosophy does admit final causality for the realm of human life, though not for nonhuman nature; cf. G. A. Wetter, *Der dialektische Materialismus* (Wien, 1952) 400 ff.

It is necessary to raise the methodological question whether it is at least possible that "reforms," observable in history, are the outcome of reform ideas rather than the result of other ideological or nonideological forces which may find a more truthful expression, for instance, in the ideas of mere change or recurrence, of evolution or revolution. Even before any systematic approach to his historical material a historian can, on ultimately metahistorical grounds, become convinced that reform ideas are either deceptions and illusions or ineffectual or both and, therefore, while not denying the existence of the idea of reform in history reject the validity of the concept of reform itself.

If on the other hand a historian considers it at least possible to extract from the reform ideas given to him in his sources a concept of reform which to a considerable extent corresponds with these ideas, if further he holds that reform thus conceived *can* at least have played an effective role in the course of historical events, then he, too, must admit that such views depend in part on metahistorical preconceptions. To state these explicitly is almost a necessity of methodological integrity, whereas the type of objectivity postulated by positivistically inclined historians does not exist.[4]

The present study, as its very title indicates, assumes the possibility of influence exercised by the early Christian idea of reform on civilization, that is to say, of a spiritual influence on a partly material phenomenon. Consequently it also assumes the possibility of reform itself, understood in the sense of the early Christian idea, in other words, the validity of a concept of reform corresponding to the early Christian idea of it.

The most essential "differences" which distinguish the early Christian reform idea from other ideas of change are value, freedom, intentionality, perfectibility, and multiplicity.[5] It is obvious that such concepts, as soon as they are transposed from the history of ideology to the history of preterideological existence, must become metahistorical preconceptions which can be supported or weakened, but never proved or disproved by historical study alone.

While then a definition of the reform idea is founded on the belief

[4] Cf. the excellent remarks on the subject by H. I. Marrou, *De la connaissance historique* (Paris, 1956), especially 153 and 240.

[5] See Part One, Chapter II.

in the possibility of conceptual abstraction from an actually existent ideological reality, a concept of reform which is germane to this ideology is based on even more fundamental preconceptions. It presupposes the possibility at least that from the very depth of his dependence on God man can form something that he had possessed only potentially: new form, through an act of reform not reducible to its efficient causes alone.

Reform does exist in history and it is the subject matter of this study. But there is also change which is not reform and the latter must be seen against the background of the former. While it is assumed that the concept of reform is more than a logical *ens rationis* or an ideal-typical construct, that it has a possible foundation in reality, it is also recognized as representing only one possible complementary aspect of reality. There is *fundatio in re* not only of the reform concept and its inherent characteristics, but also of their complementary "opposites." This means that there are valid concepts also of material change, of recurrence indifferent to values, of determination through efficient causality, of absoluteness reflecting unity.

Does a relationship exist between this fundamental complementarity obtaining in the field of history and the complementarity which quantum physics has discovered in the realm of microphysical phenomena[6] and which has brought about a new world view in the truest sense of the word?

A distinction must here be made between the epistemological, or more exactly psychological, and the more general ontological level of the problem of complementarity as it presents itself in history.

The quantum-physical theory of complementarity has been applied to psychology by the founder of the theory, Niels Bohr, and by W. Pauli. They have pointed out, for instance, that conscious reflection is an act comparable in its disturbing effect to the act of measuring[7]

[6] A detailed and very clear exposition of the basic quantum-physical facts underlying the complementarity theory is given by W. Pauli, "Raum, Zeit und Kausalität," *Scientia* LIX (1936). Similarly, the essays by Niels Bohr, the founder of the physical complementarity theory, gathered in his book *Atomic Theory and the Description of Nature* I (Cambridge, 1934), can be understood by the nonphysicist.

[7] Pauli, "Raum, Zeit und Kausalität" 68 ff., explains how exactly the finiteness and indivisibility of the quantum of action (Planck's famous constant h) causes the impossibility of fully eliminating the influence of the measuring apparatus upon the microphysical object measured.

in microphysics and that for this reason the concept of consciousness "demands . . . a cut between subject and object, the *existence* of which is a logical necessity, while it remains to a certain degree arbitrary *where* this cut is made." [8] It is possible to extrapolate and absolutize either objectivity or subjectivity,[9] but the true solution is complementarity.

Such views are of general interest to the historian in whose field objectivist or subjectivist extrapolations, the ideal of absolute historical objectivity and a subjectivism in the manner of Croce, are still competing with one another and contaminating rather than complementing one another.[10] Yet on the epistemological level analogy with microphysical complementarity is not proper to history, but exists for all human events; on the other hand there is no possibility of immediate application of quantum-physical or psychological concepts to a problem of ontological historical complementarity such as that of reform and of change.

The situation of the historian differs from that of the psychologist in that historical investigation, the forming of historical concepts and preconceptions, do not affect the phenomena observed as introspection does in psychology (or measuring in microphysics), but only the historian's judgment. Historical facts remain unchanged, regardless of whether or not we observe them, and no matter how well we know their full reality.

The assumption of a historical complementarity, such as that of reform with its teleological element and of "mere" change determined by efficient causality, can therefore not be linked directly to psychological or physical complementarity and must rest on metahistorical preconceptions of a metaphysical nature. Complementarity of liberty and necessity, individuality and universality, multiplicity and unity has been recognized by many philosophers through the ages, by all those

[8] W. Pauli, "Die philosophische Bedeutung der Komplementarität," *Experientia* VI (1950) 74. Cf. Bohr, *Atomic Theory and the Description of Nature* I, 99 f. See also E. Wind, "Some Points of Contact between History and Natural Science," *Philosophy and History: Essays Presented to Ernst Cassirer* (Oxford, 1936) 255 ff.; Wind however deals with the "Intrusion of the Observer" in history as well as in physics in a general way, without special reference to the complementarity problem.

[9] Pauli, "Philosophische Bedeutung der Komplementarität," *Experientia* VI.

[10] Cf. the excellent account of the situation by C. M. Destler, "Some Observations on Contemporary Historical Theory," *The American Historical Review* LV (1950) 503 ff.

who adhered to a pluralist or perspectivist view of the natural world
and of our knowledge of it rather than to a metaphysical monism which
presupposes supramundane power of seeing all in one and one in all.[11]
Even though there is then only a remote analogy between historical
or metaphysical complementarity and the complementary conjuncts
of psychology and quantum physics, it is perhaps not meaningless for
the metaphysician to ask if quantum-physical and psychological complementarity reflect a complementary character of our knowledge in
general and of the structure of the world as a whole.[12]

It is from considerations such as these that a historian must, I believe,
evaluate Niels Bohr's application of the principle of complementarity
to what he calls the apparent antinomy between the psychological
experience of free will and the analysis of psychological situations
according to the principle of causality. Bohr expresses his view suc-
cinctly by stating that

. . . when we use the phrase "I will" we renounce explanatory argumentation.[13]

[11] From the point of view of a Christian pluralism-within-monism, *Deus omnia in omnibus*
will be a full reality only at the end of this world (1 Cor. 15:28). For the hierarchical and
analogical pluralism of Christian and, especially, Thomistic metaphysics see, for instance,
E. Przywara, S.J., *Analogia Entis* I (München, 1932), H. Meyer, *The Philosophy of St. Thomas
Aquinas*, trans. from the German by F. Eckoff (St. Louis, London, 1944) 141 ff., 244 ff.,
E. Gilson, *Le Thomisme*, 5th ed. (Paris, 1948) 150 ff., 182 ff., J. Maritain, *Science and
Wisdom*, trans. from the French by B. Wall (New York, 1940), especially 68 f., 86 ff.,
idem, *Humanisme intégral* (Paris, 1937) 175 ff. (especially for pluralism in the social realm).
It would lead much too far afield to trace even briefly the history of metaphysical pluralism
in general, of which the metaphysical complementarity here discussed is one aspect. I only
refer to the perspectivism of Whitehead's philosophy of nature, based on Leibnitz and
Spinoza (see A. N. Whitehead, *Science and the Modern World* [Pelican Edition, 1938] 87 f.),
to Mannheim's sociology of knowledge (see K. Mannheim, *Ideology and Utopia*, trans.
L. Wirth and E. Shils [New York, Harvest Books, reprint of 1936 edition] especially
147 ff.), and to Ortega y Gasset's philosophy of history (J. Ortega y Gasset, *El tema de
nuestro tiempo*, 5th ed. [Buenos Aires and Mexico, 1945] 142 ff.; cf. the characterization of
Ortega's perspectivism in Ernst R. Curtius, *Kritische Essays zur europäischen Literatur* [Bern,
1950] 264 ff.).

[12] Cf. J. Robert Oppenheimer, *Science and the Common Understanding* (New York, 1953)
76 ff.

[13] Cf. N. Bohr, "On the Notions of Causality and Complementarity," *Dialectica* II,
3–4 [7–8] (1948) 318: ". . . the place left for the feeling of volition is afforded by the
very circumstance that situations where we experience freedom of will are incompatible
with psychological situations where causal analysis is reasonably attempted. In other words,
when we use the phrase 'I will' we renounce explanatory argumentation."

This is clearly an extension of the psychological argument, quoted above, concerning self-observation and the complementarity of objectivity and subjectivity. A logical positivist, Philip Frank, objects that "in everyday life 'freedom' is never anything other than 'freedom from external coercion,' or at most 'freedom from intoxication and hypnosis'"; [14] consequently he rejects any application of complementarity to a more general idea of free will. In doing so he completely ignores a long intellectual tradition according to which the experience of human liberty is not only that of a lack of external coercion, etc., but also that of taking a confident stand above necessity, be it in Promethean defiance or in submission to a higher principle. [15]

It is true that from a metaphysical standpoint conclusions from psychological facts are inadequate to account for the full reality of free will as coexistent with causal determination. [16] Indeed this problem can hardly be approached successfully without considering at least the theological doctrine of predestination and its compatibility with that of free choice and without taking a stand concerning this mystery in one way or another. An inkling of a solution may then perhaps be gained and expressed in an approximative fashion in terms of a historical and metaphysical principle of complementarity or more exactly of two complementary aspects of time. Thus in studying the Augustinian idea of reform it is found that in the essentially historical realm of human life time can be envisaged under complementary aspects: as an implacably continuous determinant destructive of individuality— time the distracting *saeculum* according to early Christian terminology —or as a liberating movement of the inner life—time not only as

[14] Ph. Frank, *Modern Science and Its Philosophy* (Cambridge, Mass, 1949) 167.

[15] In the Christian tradition freedom from necessity (*liberum arbitrium*) is the presupposition for striving towards liberation from external (social) and internal (moral) pressure. See Bernard of Clairvaux, *De gratia et libero arbitrio* IV, 9 ff., *PL* CLXXXII, 1006–1008, for *libertas a necessitate* as presupposition for *libertas a peccato* (*liberum consilium*) and *libertas a miseria* (*liberum complacitum*); cf. E. Gilson, *La theologie mystique de saint Bernard* (Paris, 1947) 64–67, idem, *L'esprit de la philosophie médiévale*, 2nd ed. (Paris, 1944) 297 ff. For the Thomistic doctrine of freedom from constraint as based on the freedom of choice see J. Maritain, *De Bergson à Thomas d'Aquin* (New York, 1944), Chapters V and VI.

[16] Bohr himself has never claimed more than an analogy. Cf. also E. Cassirer, *Determinism and Indeterminism in Modern Physics* (trans. from the German by O. T. Benfey, New Haven, 1956) 197 ff.; Cassirer, however, failed to consider the connection of the problem with the psychology of the unconscious.

distentio but also as *intentio animae* which enables the individual to re-form the *ordo* of the person and of the world.[17] From St. Augustine and Boethius in the fifth and sixth centuries via St. Peter Damian in the eleventh to Maritain in the twentieth, the apparent antinomy between determination and freedom has been resolved in the fact that in God's eternity all successive moments of time are copresent, that therefore God can "at the same time" "foresee" man's acts and "fore-see" them as free.[18] This may mean that man in his "openness" to eternity is a complementary being, that in his power to choose he has his freely accepted formative and reformative "individual" time—the *kairos* of the Greeks, the *distentio* and *intentio animae* of St. Augustine—and that "at the same time" he is part of the space-time continuum and of the determined events in it.[19]

[17] See above, pp. 209 ff., Part Two, Ch. V, 4, for St. Augustine's conception of time. The "double" or complementary character of time here referred to has little to do with Bergson's distinction between time and duration; one might rather refer to certain ideas of Antoine Augustin Cournot and of Raymond Aron. See A. A. Cournot, *Traité de l'enchaîne-ment des idées fondamentales dans les sciences et dans l'histoire* (Paris, 1861; new edition, Paris, 1922) 207, 281 (cf. R. Levêque, *L'élément historique dans la connaissance humaine d'après Cournot* [Paris, 1938] 26), Raymond Aron, *Introduction à la philosophie de l'histoire* 8th ed. (Paris, 1948) 43, 102, 348. See also P. A. Sorokin, *Sociocultural Causality, Space, Time* (Durham, N. C., 1943) 158 ff., about "sociocultural time" which he considers as altogether different from physico-mathematical, biological, and psychological time (this seems to be going rather far). Sorokin uses the mediaeval terms *aeternitas*, *aevum* and *tempus* (see pp. 446 ff.), but in an unmediaeval sense; see also his *Social and Cultural Dynamics* II (New York, 1937) 413 ff., 421 ff.

[18] See Boethius, *De consolatione philosophiae*, end of last book, Petrus Damiani, *De divina omnipotentia in reparatione corruptae et factis infectis reddendis* 6, 8, PL CXLV, 604 ff., 607 ff.; cf. J. Maritain, *Existence and the Existent* (New York, 1948) 85 ff., idem, *On the Philosophy of History* (New York, 1957) 119 ff.

[19] Cf. Erich Frank, "Time and Eternity," *The Review of Metaphysics* II (1948) 39 ff., and idem, "The Role of History in Christian Thought," *The Duke Divinity Bulletin* XIV (1949) 66 ff., for similar views concerning the coexistence of creative time (*kairos*) and causally determined succession. Lynn White, Jr., in his stimulating essay "Christian Myth and Christian History," *Jour. Hist. Ideas* III (1942) 145 ff., tries to resolve much of the complementarity, discussed in this Excursus, in a bipolarity between myth and history, eternity and time. What he calls "mythical" and "eternal" is, however, historical through and through. The exposition in the text of the problem of free will is related to the Aristotelian-Thomistic distinction between final and efficient causality for which see Gredt, *Elementa Philosophiae Aristotelico-Thomisticae*, II, 154 ff., 169 ff., and E. Gilson, *L'esprit de la philosophie médiévale*, 2nd ed., 85 ff., Chapter V: *Analogie, causalité et finalité*. On finality see also N. Bohr, *Atomic Theory and the Description of Nature* I, 23. The "doubleness" of time is linked in Augustinian thought to a "doubleness" of number in its aspects of order and of multiplicity (see above, pp. 212 ff., and Excursus IV, 2 and 3).

If one posits as possible in history both free conscious reform and determined change, he admits that it is impossible to investigate and verify the realizations of both these concepts equally well at the same time.[20] There is only the choice of concentrating attention on "subjective" consciousness, liberty, intentionality, and the other characteristics of the reform concept or on that "objective" part of life which is material change, unconscious psychological flow, and determined continuity of causes and effects. To keep in mind and to describe as well as possible the interdependence of the two spheres remains, nevertheless, the task of the historian.[21]

Whether a historian follows more the one or the other of the two main complementary roads of historical investigation he not only studies history, but also makes it: the "subjectivity" of historical reflection necessarily adds something to physical, biological, psychological, and sociological "objects."

[20] The conception of complementarity in sociology and history is the subject of an article by Aline Lion, "The Social Phenomenon: The Notion of Complementarity and Historical Causality," *Dialectica* III, 3–11 (1949) 192 ff. Implicitly, and from different points of view, it is dealt with by F. J. Teggart, *Theory and Processes of History* (Berkeley, Los Angeles, 1941), who distinguished the study of "events" from that of "evolution" (pp. 141 ff.), and by Raymond Aron, *Introduction à la philosophie de l'histoire*, who stresses the (complementary) factors of (subjective) comprehension and (objective) causality (especially, pp. 246, 268 ff.).

[21] Attempts to explain historical events solely as a concatenation of causes and effects in space and time have with intrinsic logic led to historical or sociological statistics as far as individual events are concerned. For an early formulation (1869) of this statistic see A. Quetelet, *Sur l'homme et le développement de ses facultés ou essai de physique sociale* (Bruxelles, 1936). To what lengths a purely determinist and statistic inquiry into history may go can be seen from the famous example of H. T. Buckle's *History of Civilization in England* (first published 1857–1861) especially I, 13 ff., 164 ff., where Quetelet's method is used in an exclusive fashion. For Quetelet and Buckle see Cassirer, *Determinism and Indeterminism in Modern Physics* 209 ff. Material concerning the relationship between the statistical method and the investigation of (efficient and final) causes may be found in Aron, *Introduction à la philosophie de l'histoire* 208–215. It is interesting and has apparently never been noted by professional historians that Tolstoy in the second part of the epilogue to *War and Peace* (1886), especially in Chapters 8–12, puts forth a theory of history which is based to some extent on the complementarity of efficient causality and free will and which is greatly influenced by nineteenth century statistics. Tolstoy's conception of this complementarity is, however, not truly applicable to history because he seems to have believed that in historical studies the finding of statistical laws must replace completely the investigation of determined causes and of free actions (see Chapter 11, end, and Chapter 12). See in this connection the excellent criticism by Sorokin, *Sociocultural Causality, Space, Time* 38 ff., of all statistic, probabilistic attempts to explain human facts causally, i.e., according to efficient causality only.

Since reflective thought—and this leads back once more to the epistemological aspect of the complementarity problem—is part of the sphere of subjectivity, every act of reflecting, even if directed toward objectivity, increases the extension of subjectivity through the world. As history goes on ideas increase in number and cumulative strength, whereas the purely material elements of the world are ever the same, though their possible combinations will perhaps never be exhausted. Here lies the deeper reason why all historical ideas and concepts including our own not only interpret, but make history. A historical study of the reform idea thus becomes part of the history of that idea and the idea of reform itself has helped and will help in forming that complementary aspect of historical reality which is called reform.

SOME PATRISTIC DISTINCTIONS CONCERNING ETERNITY, AEVUM, AND TIME

The terminological and ideological problems concerning the relationship between time and eternity reflected in patristic texts originate in part in the ambiguous character of the Greek term αἰών. Its earliest meanings were "life force," "life time," "world time." [1] It was only Plato who in the *Timaeus* defined the αἰών as supratemporal eternity, of which time, χρόνος, is a moving image. [2] The question whether Plato's novel *aion* doctrine was influenced by the distinction between world time and eternity in Persian Zervan doctrine is controversial. [3] The fluctuations of *aion* terminology and ideology in the Hellenistic-oriental world during the centuries from Plato to Augustine [4] are connected with the complex history of personifications and deities of eternity or ever renewed time and not without relation to cosmological-vitalistic renewal ideas and to the idea of eternal Rome; [5] they include the emergence of a personal god *Aion* in Alexandria and

[1] Cf. A.-J. Festugière, "Le sens philosophique du mot αἰών . . .," *La Parola del Passato* XI (1949) 172 ff., *idem, La révélation d'Hermès Trismégiste* IV (Paris, 1954) 146 ff., 152 ff., 176 ff.

[2] Plato, *Timaeus* 37D: . . . εἰκὼ δ' ἐπενόει κινητόν τινα αἰῶνος ποιῆσαι, καὶ διακοσμῶν ἅμα οὐρανὸν ποιεῖ μένοντος αἰῶνος ἐν ἑνὶ κατ' ἀριθμὸν ἰοῦσαν αἰώνιον εἰκόνα, τοῦτον ὃν δὴ χρόνον ὠνομάκαμεν.

[3] Cf. A. D. Nock, "A Vision of Mandulis Aion," *Harv. Theol. Rev.* XXVII (1934) 78 ff., Festugière, *Révélation d'Hermès Trismégiste* IV, Lackeit, article "Aion," PW, *RE*, Suppl. Bd. III, 65 ff., H. Sasse, article "αἰών," *ThWbNT* I, 197 f., and *idem*, article "Aion" *RLAC* I, 193 ff. For the Iranian Zervan doctrine cf. H. Junker, "Über iranische Quellen der hellenistischen Aion-Vorstellung," *Vorträge der Bibliothek Warburg* 1921–22, I (1923) 125 ff., H. Corbin, "Cyclical Time in Mazdaism and Ismailism," *Man and Time: Papers from the Eranos Yearbooks* XXX, 3 (1957) 115 ff.

[4] Cf. Festugière, *Révélation d'Hermès Trismégiste* IV, 146–199.

[5] Cf. M. P. Charlesworth, "Providentia and Aeternitas," *Harv. Theol. Rev.* XXIX (1936) 107 ff.; cf. above, pp. 10 ff. and 16 ff.

elsewhere,[6] Gnostic speculations on *aiones* as divine or demonic forces
and habitats,[7] and lastly and most importantly for Christian thought
on eternity and time philosophical developments within Platonism,
especially in Philo and in Neoplatonism, in which the gap between
eternity and time is bridged by intermediate lower forms of eternity
or higher forms of time.[8]

Within Christendom, "world time" (that is to say, the time between creation and the end of the world), not eternity, is the basic
meaning of the New Testament term αἰών, the Vulgate translation of
which is *saeculum*, not *aeternitas*; through Christ, of course, the αἰών
of this world is already changing into the new αἰών μέλλων, which is
both present and to come. O. Cullmann in his famous book on Christ
and time[9] asserts that the New Testament does not know of supratemporal eternity and conceives of eternity only as limitless time.
However this may be,[10] it is certain that some of the Greek Fathers
on occasion made a distinction between αἰώνιος and ἀΐδιος, reserving the latter term or its equivalent προαιώνιος for the triune God
alone, whereas αἰών, αἰώνιος meant something like infinite time, a
still creaturely quasi-eternity which is not coeternal with God.[11] This
Greek patristic distinction inverts Neoplatonic terminology: for
Plotinus and his successors ἀϊδιότης, perpetuity or sempiternity, had

[6] Cf., especially, Nock, "Vision of Mandulis Aion" 83–99, D. Levi, *Antioch Mosaic Pavements* I (Princeton, 1947) 197 f., 253 ff. For the identity of the date of the feast of the Alexandrian *Aion* and that of Christian Epiphany, see, for instance, A. Strittmatter, O.S.B., "Christmas and the Epiphany . . .," *Thought* XVII (1942) 600 ff.

[7] Cf., for instance, H. Jonas, *Gnosis und spätantiker Geist* I (Göttingen, 1934) 98 ff., Nock, "Vision of Mandulis Aion" 89 f.

[8] Cf. H. Leisegang, *Die Begriffe der Zeit und Ewigkeit im späteren Platonismus* (Beiträge zur Geschichte der Philosophie des Mittelalters XIII, 4, Münster, i. W., 1913), P. Duhem, *Le système du monde* I (reprinted Paris, 1954) 246–275, especially 265, where Duhem points to the parallelism of late Neoplatonic intermediaries between time and eternity to the scholastic *aevum*; see below, p. 447.

[9] O. Cullmann, *Christus und die Zeit* (Zollikon–Zürich, 1946).

[10] On this point see the well-founded criticism of P. Gächter, S.J., in his review of Cullmann's book in *Z. kath. Theol.* LXIX (1947) 119 ff.

[11] See E. R. Redepenning, *Origines* II (Bonn, 1846) 294 f., H. Berkhof, *Die Theologie des Eusebius von Caesarea* (Amsterdam, 1939) 75 (Arians and near-Arians used the distinction to subordinate Christ to God the Father); cf. furthermore two Cappadocian texts (for which I am indebted to Professor Brooks Otis): Basil, *Adversus Eunomium* II, PG XXIX, 608C, and Gregory of Nyssa, *Contra Eunomium*, I, 359-361, Jaeger, *Greg. Nyss. Opera I*, 127; lastly, see Ps.-Dionysius, *De divinis nominibus* 10, 3, PG III, 938C, and 5, 10, PG III, 825B.

been inferior to the true eternity of the αἰών and the αἰώνιον;[12] such Greek patristic terminological inversion was due no doubt to the fact that in the New Testament αἰών, αἰώνιος indeed seem to designate ages of great length rather than eternity in the strict sense.

In the west, Hilary of Poitiers, Ambrose, Jerome, and Augustine were groping their way toward a Latin terminology of eternity and time that would adequately reproduce the two possible meanings of the terms αἰών, αἰώνιος, which can refer to a long time span or to eternity. Often the exegesis of scriptural passages was the occasion for their speculations in this direction. There was, for instance, the problem of the significance of Titus 1:2: *ante tempora aeterna* (old Latin translation of πρὸ χρόνων αἰωνίων), a phrase which Hilary of Poitiers simply interpreted as eternity.[13] Jerome's Vulgate translation has *ante tempora saecularia*, but in his *Commentarium in Epist. ad Titum* he renders the Greek πρὸ χρόνων αἰωνίων *ante saecula aeterna* and explains that *ante haec mundi tempora* there was an *aeternitas quedam saeculorum* which also might be called the "time" or rather the innumerable, infinite, and eternal "times" of God.[14] Ambrose, commenting on Ps. 118:89: *In aeternum, Domine, verbum tuum in caelo*, preferred the translation *in aeternum* for εἰς τὸν αἰῶνα to the other one, found in some manuscripts at his disposal: *in saeculum*; *saecula enim*, he says, *temporis sunt*.[15] As for Augustine, he went to much trouble in order to do justice to both meanings of αἰών, αἰώνιος[16] and at the same time to harmonize the scriptural and Platonic conceptions of eternity and time. One of the most important Augustinian texts is one already quoted in part, from *Enarr. in Ps. IX*. Here Augustine comments on Ps. 9:6: *Increpasti gentes et periit impius. Nomen eorum delesti in aeternum et in saeculum saeculi*:

What is the *saeculum saeculi* but that of which this world (*hoc saeculum*) is an

[12] See Plotinus, *Ennead* III, 7, 3 and 5; for the later Neoplatonists see P. Courcelle, *Les lettres grecques en occident*, 2nd ed. (Paris, 1948) 295 ff.

[13] Hilary of Poitiers, *De Trinitate* XII, 25–34, *PL* X, 448B ff.

[14] Jerome, *Commentar. in Epist. ad Titum*, to Tit. 1:2, *PL* XXVI, 594A ff.

[15] Ambrose, *Expositio Psalmi CXVIII* 12, 7, *CSEL* LXII, 255; see, however, *De Ioseph* 7, 39, *CSEL* XXXII, 2, 100, where the *saecula quae futura sunt* clearly are eternity.

[16] See, for instance, *De civitate Dei* XII, 20, *Corp. Christ.*, *Ser. Lat.* XLVIII, 376, on the *saecula saeculorum*; XVI, 26, XLVIII, 531, where Augustine points out that αἰών may signify a long period of time rather than eternity.

image or as it were a shadow? For the alternation of times which follow upon one another . . . constitutes a certain imitation of eternity. But the *saeculum* of this *saeculum* (i.e., the "world" or "age" which is the model of the terrestrial world or age) is that which exists in immutable eternity. . . . Thus the mode of being of this mutable *saeculum* is defined by that immutable *saeculum* which is called *saeculum saeculi*. . . . Or, perhaps, *saeculum saeculi* is said by way of repetition: in other words, after the term *in saeculum* had been used the term *in saeculum saeculi* may have been added, so that *in saeculum* would not be understood as that which is transitory. For the Greek original manuscripts read as follows: εἰς τὸν αἰῶνα καὶ εἰς τὸν αἰῶνα τοῦ αἰῶνος; this most Latins have translated not by *in saeculum et in saeculum saeculi*, but by *aeternum et in saeculum saeculi*, so that *in saeculum saeculi* explains *in aeternum*.[17]

Aἰών in the sense of saeculum thus is equivalent to *tempus*, *saeculum saeculi* (αἰὼν αἰῶνος) to eternity. In his interpretation of *ante aeterna tempora* of Titus 1:2, however, Augustine goes beyond the simple antithesis of eternity and time: in *De diversis quaestionibus LXXXIII*, quaest. LXXII, he suggests that the combination of the concepts of time and eternity in the expression *tempora aeterna* of Titus 1:2 corresponds to the concept *aevum* which, he says, differs from mutable time through its stability,[18] a stability which is not coeternity with God, as Augustine explicitly points out in his comments on Titus 1:2 in *De civitate Dei* XII, 17.[19] Augustine does not use the term *aevum* for the mode of

---

[17] *Enarr. in Ps. IX*, c. 7, *Corp. Christ., Ser. Lat.* XXXVIII, 61 f.: Quid est "saeculum saeculi," nisi cuius effigiem et tamquam umbram habet hoc saeculum? Vicissitudo enim temporum sibi succedentium . . . aeternitatis quaedam imitatio est. Sed huius saeculi saeculum est quod incommutabili aeternitate consistit. . . . Sic huius mutabilis saeculi modus ab illo incommutabili saeculo definitur quod dicitur saeculum saeculi. . . . Si tamen non repetitio est, ut postea quam dictum est "in saeculum," ne hoc acciperetur quod transit, subiceretur "in saeculum saeculi." Nam in Græcis exemplaribus sic est: εἰς τὸν αἰῶνα καὶ εἰς τὸν αἰῶνα τοῦ αἰῶνος. Quod Latini plerique interpretati sunt, non "in saeculum et in saeculum saeculi," sed "in aeternum et in saeculum saeculi": ut in eo quod dictum est "in saeculum saeculi," illud exponeretur quod dictum est "in aeternum."

[18] *De diversis quaestionibus LXXXIII*, quaest. LXXII, *PL* XL, 84: Quaeri potest quomodo ab ipso apostolo Paulo dictum sit "Ante tempora aeterna." Si enim tempora, quomodo aeterna? . . . An tempora aeterna aevum significavit? Inter quod et tempus hoc distat, quod illud stabile est, tempus autem mutabile.

[19] *De civitate Dei* XII, 17, *Corp. Christ., Ser. Lat.* XLVIII, 373: . . . non . . . dubito nihil omnino creaturae creatori esse coaeternum. Dicit etiam apostolus "tempora aeterna," nec ea futura, sed, quod magis est mirandum, praeterita. . . . Ecce dixit retro quod fuerint tempora aeterna, quae tamen non fuerint Deo coaeterna, si quidem ille ante tempora aeterna . . . erat. . . .

existence of angels or spiritual creatures, as the scholastics were to do, even though according to him their existence is neither properly temporal nor coeternal with God.[20] Not a few of the Greek Fathers did relate the angels to the αἰών, understood not as God's eternity but as an intermediate between eternity and time—for example, Justin, Irenaeus, Origen, Eusebius of Caesarea, Athanasius, Gregory Nazianzen, Gregory of Nyssa, and the Ps.-Dionysius, when they linked the πύλαι αἰώνιοι of Ps. 23:7–9 to the angels.[21] The fact that the angels are not coeternal with God meant for patristic thought, whether Augustinian or Greek, that being creatures they are not quite immutable and therefore not altogether without relation to time, yet except for the rebel angels never move away from God.[22] From this conception Thomistic angelology differs in so far as for it angels have immutable being as to their nature, but mutability as to choice, and as to understanding, affection, and place: *et ideo mensurantur aevo, quod est medium inter aeternitatem et tempus.*[23]

It may be noted that, while St. Thomas Aquinas could take over a

---

[20] See the text from *De civitate Dei* XII, 16, quoted above, pp. 180 f., n. 38.

[21] Cf. J. Daniélou, S.J., *Les anges et leur mission d'après les pères de l'église*, 2nd ed. (Collection Irénikon, Nouvelle Série V, Chevetogne, 1953) 51, 55 ff., on patristic exegesis of Ps. 23:9: Ἄρατε πύλας οἱ ἄρχοντες ὑμῶν καὶ ἐπάρθητε πύλαι αἰώνιοι καὶ εἰσελεύσεται ὁ βασιλεὺς τῆς δόξης. For Gregory of Nyssa, *In ascensionem Domini*, PG XLVI, 693A ff. (discussed by P. Daniélou also in "Notes sur trois textes eschatologiques de saint Grégoire de Nysse," *Rech.'s sc. rel.* XXX [1940] 352 f.) the πύλαι αἰώνιοι of Ps. 23:7 ff. can be the "eternal" doors either of heaven or of the subcelestial cosmos, guarded by the angels of heaven and of earth respectively and opened for Christ descending to earth in His Incarnation and ascending to heaven in His Ascension. For Ps.-Dionysius Areopagita, *De divinis nominibus* 5, 3 and 10, 3, PG III, 821D and 937C, cf. R. Roques, *L'univers dionysien* (Théologie XXIX, Paris, 1954) 162 f. In the Gallican liturgy of the seventh or eighth century (*Expositio brevis antiquae liturgiae Gallicanae*, cf. J. Quasten, "Oriental Influence in the Gallican Liturgy," *Traditio* I [1943] 60) the *portae aeternales* of Ps. 23 are the gates of hell the opening of which is demanded by the angels accompanying Christ in His descent to the infernal regions (so even much earlier the Greek *Physiologus*, cf. E. Peterson, "Die Spiritualität des griechischen Physiologos," *Byz. Z.* XLVII [1954] 70 f.).

[22] St. Basil and St. Gregory Nazianzen, therefore, call the angels δυσμετάθετοι or δυσκίνετοι rather than ἀκίνετοι; see the following texts (to which Professor Brooks Otis kindly drew my attention): Basil, *De Sancto Spiritu* 16, 38, PG XXXII, 137, less clearly, idem, *Homil. in Ps. XXXII*, c. 4, PG XXIX, 333D, Gregory Nazianzen, *Oratio* XXIX, 31, PG XXXVI, 72A–D, idem, *Oratio* XXXVIII, 11, ibid. 321A.

[23] Thomas Aquinas, *Summa Theologica* I, q. 10, a. 5. For the *aevum* doctrine of the scholastics and of the high and late mediaeval jurists see now E. H. Kantorowicz, *The King's Two Bodies* (Princeton, 1957) 275 ff.

famous definition of eternity from Boethius,[24] the latter had not used the term *aevum*. His terminology and ideology are in this respect quite un-Augustinian; in fact his distinction of the sempiternal or perpetual time of the world from eternity exactly reproduces the Neoplatonic distinction of ἀϊδιότης from αἰών or αἰώνιον.[25] In the Carolingian period Alcuin adopted the Augustinian interpretation of *tempora aeterna* as *aevum*;[26] of the two Carolingian translators of Ps.-Dionysius the Areopagite, Hilduin of St. Denis as a rule translated αἰών, αἰώνιος as *saeculum*, *saecularis*, John Scot Erigena, as *aeternum*, *aeternus*.[27]

[24] *Summa Theologica* I, q. 10, a. 1, quotes Boethius, *De consolatione philosophiae* V, *pros.* 6, 4, *CSEL* LXVII, 122: Aeternitas . . . est interminabilis vitae tota simul et perfecta possessio (for this cf. Plotinus, *Ennead* III, 7, 3).

[25] See *De consolatione philosophiae* V, *pros.* 6, 14, *CSEL* LXVII, 123: . . . Platonem sequentes Deum quidem aeternum, mundum vero dicamus esse perpetuum; also *De Trinitate* 4, 72 ff., Stewart and Rand, *Boeth. Theol. Tract.* 20 f.: . . . nostrum "nunc" quasi currens tempus facit et sempiternitatem, divinum vero "nunc" permanens neque movens sese atque consistens aeternitatem facit; cui nomini si adicias "semper," facies eius quod est nunc iugem indefessumque ac per hoc perpetuum cursum quod est sempiternitas; for the Neoplatonic background see pp. 444 f.

[26] Alcuin, *Epist.* CLXIII, *MGH*, *Epist.* IV, 263 f.

[27] Cf. *Dionysiaca: Recueil donnant l'ensemble des traductions latines des ouvrages attribués au Denys de l'Aréopage* . . ., 2 vols. (Paris, Roma, 1937), for instance, to *De divinis nominibus* 10 (*Dionysiaca* I, 482 ff.); however, in *De divinis nominibus* 5, 10, both Hilduin and John Scot translate αἰώνιος by *aeternaliter*, whereas the former has *aevum*, the latter *aeternum* for αὐτοαιών (*Dionysiaca* I, 366 f.).

EXCURSUS IV

POINTS OF CONTACT BETWEEN ST. AUGUSTINE AND MODERN MATHEMATICS AND SCIENCE[1]

1. FORMATION-REFORMATION AND INFORMATION

St. Augustine believed that creation included an act of formation through which almost nonexistent chaotic matter received form and order and only thus true being. Because of original sin, evil, decay, and death came into the world, all of them form-destroying forces. Through and in the great reformer Christ man can reform himself and the world.[2]

Modern science recognizes that in the world's relentless progress toward entropy, which in accordance with the second law of thermodynamics will finally through inexorable, irreversible degeneration of energy lead to random equilibrium, there are, nevertheless, "stages which . . . are of great significance for our purposes, for in them entropy does not increase and organization and its correlative, information, are being built up."[3] Information is a key term in the recently developed science of cybernetics, which is the study of messages as controlling agents. Information here means the transfer of a message, be it through the human brain itself or through a man-made machine. In both cases information is an element of order and thus constitutes an enclave of negative entropy or "negentropy," in other words an exceptional delaying phase in the world's tendency toward the most probable state of random equilibrium, which is both disorder and death.[4] On the human level the control of information

[1] I am aware of the sketchy character of this Excursus. The following remarks are meant only as tentative suggestions of possible methodological interest to historians of ideas.

[2] See above, Part Two, Chapter V.

[3] N. Wiener, *The Human Use of Human Beings: Cybernetics and Society*, 2nd ed. (Garden City, N.Y., 1954) 31.

[4] Cf. Wiener 12. For the concept of negentropy see, for instance, L. Brillouin, in *Journal of Applied Physics* XXII (1951).

involves a judgement as to whether or not the "incoming messages" have been properly used; this is not possible without memory to which in automatic machines the feedback mechanism to some extent corresponds.[5]

Not without good reason does N. Wiener compare the theories of entropy and information with the "Augustinian attitude toward order and conduct."[6] He also rightly points out that in both cases evil and death are seen as lack of order and being and not in a Manichaean way as forces in their own right.[7] The cybernetic concept of human and technological information thus becomes an ethical principle and its temporary defeats are due not to an opposing power but to our own weakness.[8] The individual human event has possibilities of reform, notwithstanding the fact that the world as a whole hurries toward its "most probable" state, toward an end which is formlessness. It may be added that St. Augustine would, perhaps, have derived the death of the world by entropy from the loss of its paradisiac state and might have reserved it to hell in contradistinction from that perfection of all information as well as reformation which is constituted by the beatific vision and by a new heaven and a new earth.

As to cosmogony, Augustine's theory of primaeval matter as formless, as timeless and spaceless,[9] is strangely congruent with one of the most imaginative contemporary hypotheses concerning the origin of the universe, that of G. Lemaître according to whom the universe may have begun with a single unstable (i.e., "unformed") giant atom (or atomic nucleus) the atomic weight of which was the mass of the entire universe. According to this hypothesis it was only with the explosive division of the "primitive atom" that space and time and

---

[5] See Wiener 58 f., and cf. above, pp. 201 ff., about Augustine's conception of memory.

[6] Wiener 27. One might also refer in this connection to A. Cournot's *Traité de l'enchaînement des idées fondamentales dans les sciences et dans l'histoire* (Paris, 1861; new edition, Paris, 1922) especially pp. 1-9, for emphasis on the related facts of order, form, and time.

[7] Wiener 34 f., 190 ff. It would seem, however, that Wiener somewhat underestimates the force of evil, though he is right in defining it as an absence of good.

8. Cf. Wiener 35. From the point of view of a historian the principles of information and negentropy vindicate to some extent and amplify the remarkable attempt of Henry Adams (and Brooks Adams) to interpret history on the basis of the second law of thermodynamics; see especially H. Adams, *A Letter to American Teachers of History* (written 1910), published by B. Adams in *The Degradation of the Democratic Dogma* (New York, 1920) 137 ff.

[9] See above, Part Two, Chapter V, 2.

thus the organization of the universe began.[10] The hypothesis has been combined with the theory of the expansion of the universe[11] and with the view that the differentiation of forms in it constitutes a partial negation of entropy.[12]

The difference between Augustinian primaeval matter and the "primitive atom" on the one hand and the entropy state of the world on the other consists in the unformed condition of the former as compared to the deformed condition of the latter.

2. TIME

Augustine greatly stresses the formative and reformative function of time, the former especially with regard to physical, the latter with regard to psychological time. Because time belongs not only to the physical world, but also to the nonspatial soul, it is of higher rank than space. Yet Augustine is also poignantly aware of the irreversible arrow

[10] See G. Lemaître, *L'hypothèse de l'atome primitif: Essai de cosmogonie* (Neuchâtel, 1946) especially 25 ff.: "Si le monde a commencé par un quantum unique, les notions d'espace et de temps n'auront absolument plus de signification au commencement même; mais elles acquerront progressivement quelque sens, quand le quantum originel se sera divisé en un nombre suffisant de quanta partiels"; also *idem, Rayons cosmiques et cosmologie* (Louvain, 1949) 36 ff.: "Devons nous essayer de remonter plus loin que l'atome primitif? Notre pensée peut-elle s'approcher, prise de vertige, de ce fond de l'espace-temps, de cet instant qui n'avait pas d'hier parce qu'hier il n'y avait pas d'espace?" Cf. Augustine, *Confessiones* XII, 7, 7, Skutella 298: . . . et ideo de nihilo fecisti caelum et terram, magnum quiddam et parvum quiddam . . . (*caelum* here refers to the realm of spirit and *terra* to unformed matter, cf. above, pp. 167 ff.).

[11] Cf. G. Gamow, *The Creation of the Universe* (New York, 1956) 21 ff., 53 ff.

[12] Beside Wiener, cf., for instance, C. F. v. Weizsäcker, *The History of Nature* (Chicago, 1949) 75 ff., especially the following passages on pp. 87–92, which are quoted here *in extenso* because of their obvious relevance for an Augustinian conception of "form" and "reform": "Visible form is not the only kind of order. . . . The gain in thermodynamic probability of the state brought about by [the] conversion [of energy into heat] is so immense that the small loss of probability connected with the formation of regular forms [negentropy!] is negligible in comparison. . . . A form is an improbable state because it is a kind of order. The Second Law [of thermodynamics] allows us to conclude from the existence of the form that something still more improbable has existed in the past, an energy, namely, capable of producing this form. . . . The end always is heat death. Most of the time, however, it consists not in a dissolution of forms, but rather in their hardening. From the moment on when no more energy is converted, forms can neither originate nor decay. . . . Decomposition is already a sign of new life, though of a lower order. All life

of time: every now is only a precariously held island in time's all-consuming stream which rushes on to the end.[1]

All three Augustinian insights in the problem of time, namely, first: that physical and psychological time are distinct from each other, second: that time for man has a more privileged character than space, and third: that time is irreversible, play a considerable role in modern science and philosophy, though in a different way and clearly without direct dependence on St. Augustine.

The irreversibility of time seems to be connected somehow with the increase of entropy in the world.[2] While the elementary laws of physics, especially quantum physics, affirm an absolute symmetry between past and future and thus seem to exclude the irreversibility of time, this becomes different as soon as the physicist includes in his observations large numbers of events and the statistic probability of their occurrence. In other words, as soon as the elementary physical event is taken out of its isolation, it becomes clear that the course of the world as a whole imposes upon it an irreversible direction. Thus it would seem that the psychological-biological arrow of time corresponds to the condition of the entropy-bound world of inanimate nature, taken in its entirety.[3] Our effort at coping with this situation, however, constitutes an element of negentropy.[4] While then the

in the universe, on a large scale or small, is the evolution of forms of ever greater differentiation, enclosed between the original chaos and the hardening of the end." See also the attempt at a synthesis of cosmological and of biological "organization" and order by François Meyer, *Problématique de l'évolution* (Bibliothèque de philosophie contemporaine, Logique et philosophie des sciences, Paris, 1954), where the author utilizes and modifies Frantappié's concept of "syntropy"; cf. furthermore H. F. Blum, *Time's Arrow and Evolution*, quoted this page, n. 2.

[1] See above, Part Two, Chapter V, 4.

[2] Cf. H. F. Blum, *Time's Arrow and Evolution*, 2nd ed. (Princeton, 1955) 16 and *passim*.

[3] Cf., for instance, C. F. v. Weizsäcker, *The History of Nature* (Chicago, 1949) 47–59, A. Grünbaum, "Time and Entropy," *American Scientist* XLIII (1955) 550 ff.

[4] Cf. O. Costa de Beauregard, "Quelques aspects de l'irréversibilité du temps dans la physique classique et quantique," *Revue des questions scientifiques* . . . (1952) 181: ". . . la flèche du temps biologique et psychologique représente une adaptation de la vie aux conditions dans lesquelles elle se trouve, en un point de la pente de la courbe de l'entropie voisine d'une fluctuation exceptionelle: sous peine d'être impossible, et même inconcevable, la vie est obligée d'explorer cette pente dans le sens qui fait croître l'entropie." I am greatly indebted to M. de Beauregard for his remarks on the subject in conversation and

distinctness of psychological and of physical time is a fact, they are not altogether separate entities.

Similar observations can be made with regard to the relation between time and space. Here again, the greater significance of time for the soul, so well pointed out by St. Augustine, is not without connection with physical facts. Modern physics illustrates the situation by an hourglass figure, symbolizing the double light cone of past and future, formed by the reception and emission of a light signal; the wide angles between the cone of the past and that of the future indicate that because of the finite and supreme velocity of light there are no simultaneous present-points which would lie on one horizontal line running through the here-and-now; only the one here-and-now point, where the cones meet, is the present, all other events may have been accessible in the past or may become accessible in the future, but in the present they are "absolutely elsewhere."[5] Thus every here-and-now has an immense past and future, but its present is limited to one point in space; with regard to every here-and-now time has the edge over space. Perhaps, Augustine felt this obscurely, when in a passage of De musica, where he does not speak of psychological but of physical time, he says that the temporal numbers are superior to the spatial ones.[6] Yet, in spite of the fact that in the macrocosmic space-time continuum physical time corresponds to psychological time through its irreversibility and through its very inseparability from any perception of space, it is only psychological time which for St. Augustine is a fulcrum of reform. Perhaps, it is not without significance that Augustine himself has not used the hourglass or double cone figure as a symbol of time, though it would at first glance seem to correspond so well to his conception of time as the precipitation of the future through the narrow gorge of the present into the depth of the past.[7] Actually, in his attempt to

correspondence. See also Blum's excellent discussion, Time's Arrow and Evolution 198–202, 154 f., of the ultimate validity of the second law of thermodynamics and of temporal irreversibility in biological evolution in spite of possible short term reversals on a small scale due to mutation and natural selection.

[5] The expression is that of A. S. Eddington, The Nature of the Physical World (New York, Cambridge, 1929) 48. For the hourglass figure see also H. Weyl, Philosophy of Mathematics and Natural Science (Princeton, 1949) 102.

[6] See above, p. 220.

[7] The hourglass figure is used in this sense by H. Eibl, Augustin und die Patristik (München, 1923) 326.

overcome temporal as well as spatial *distentio* through *extentio-intentio* toward God, Augustine is necessarily led to absorb the cone of the future into an already present concentration upon eternity; cf. *Confessiones* IV, 11, 16, Skutella 66: . . . et fluxa tua reformabuntur . . . et constringentur ad te (cf. above, p. 212, n. 40). More than the hourglass-shaped double light cone of modern physics, the single ascending and converging *cône du temps* of the late P. Teilhard de Chardin's biologically and suprabiologically oriented universe, culminating in a spiritualized humanity, would seem today to possess genuine affinity to Augustine's concepts of time and space.[8]

A conception of psychological and historical time, similar to that of St. Augustine, has in fact become a commonplace ever since Bergson's famous essays, and even more since the emergence of phenomenology[9] and "Gestaltpsychologie." Even though from an Augustinian point of view physical space-time is itself "form," it is justifiable to call psychological time "formed time" *par excellence*.[10] Psychological time is formed on a higher level; in Augustinian terms it is a time of reform, which can conquer the mundane spatiotemporal disgregation and distraction and to some extent even temporal distension through its intention toward eternity.[11]

3. NUMBER

The Augustinian conception of a universe ascending from formless matter to spatiotemporal order and to temporal and supratemporal life of the human soul is reflected also in Augustine's doctrine of numbers. Multiplicity as such is opposed to form and order, but number is not; on the contrary, it is the very form through which

---

[8] See P. Teilhard de Chardin, S.J., "L'esprit nouveau et le cône du temps," *Psyche* X (1955)= *Numéro spécial: Textes de Pierre Teilhard de Chardin*, pp. 48 ff.

[9] Cf. M. Heidegger, "Sein und Zeit I," *Jahrbuch für Philosophie und phänomenologische Forschung* VIII (1927) 1 ff., O. Becker, "Mathematische Existenz: Untersuchungen zur Logik und Ontologie der mathematischen Phänomene," *ibid.* VIII (1927) 439 ff., especially 637 ff., 660 ff.

[10] See S. Strasser, *Seele und Beseeltes* (Wien, 1955) 215 ff.: "Geformte Zeit als beseelte Zeit."

[11] See above, pp. 209 ff.

creation, always prone to relapse through formlessness toward the nothingness from which it was drawn, can maintain itself in being. There is an ascending hierarchy of numbers in everything that is, from corporeal to spatial, to temporal numbers, and higher up to the numbers of reason and to the spiritual numbers of the angels; only when the soul turns to the highest numbers, can it be truly reformed.[1]

On these premises, however, a difficult question arose for St. Augustine as for many thinkers before and after him; how, if numbers are an element of the divine order which tends toward unity, can there be an infinity of numbers? In this respect Augustine anticipated the problems of the modern dispute over the foundations of mathematics which developed out of G. Cantor's set theory. Cantor himself was clearly conscious of this anticipation and he rightly adduced a famous text from De civitate Dei XII, 19 in support of his theory of actually infinite (transfinite) numbers.[2]

St. Augustine's text reads as follows:

. . . while [numbers] are singly finite, they are collectively infinite. Does God, therefore, not know numbers on account of this infinity; and does His knowledge extend only to a certain height in numbers while of the rest He is ignorant? . . . The infinity of number, though there be no numbering of infinite numbers, is yet not incomprehensible to Him whose understanding is infinite. And thus, if everything which is comprehended is defined or made finite by the comprehension of Him who knows it, then all infinity is in some ineffable way made finite to God, for it is comprehensible by His knowledge. . . . God, whose knowledge is simply manifold and uniform in its variety, comprehends all incomprehensibles with so incomprehensible a comprehension that, though He willed always to make His later works novel and unlike what went before them, He could not produce them without order and foresight nor conceive them suddenly but by His eternal foreknowledge.[3]

---

[1] See above, Part Two, Chapter V, 5.

[2] G. Cantor, Gesammelte Abhandlungen, ed. E. Zermelo (Berlin, 1932) 403 ff., n. 3 to 401.

[3] Augustine, De civitate Dei XII, 19, Corp. Christ., Ser. Lat. XLVIII, 375 f. (the relevant text in its entirety): . . . [Numeros] quippe infinitos esse certissimum est; quoniam in quocumque numero finem faciendum putaveris, idem ipse, non dico uno addito augeri, sed quamlibet sit magnus et quamlibet ingentem multitudinem continens in ipsa ratione atque scientia numerorum non solum duplicari verum etiam multiplicari potest. Ita vero suis quisque numerus proprietatibus terminatur, ut nullus eorum par esse cuicumque alteri possit. Ergo et dispares inter se atque diversi sunt, et singuli quique finiti sunt, et omnes

Similarly, Augustine comments on Psalm 146:5: "Great is our Lord, and great is His power: and of His wisdom there is no number" in the following manner:

Who can explain this? . . . Is sand numbered? For us not, but for God yes, for Him the hairs of our head are numbered (cf. Matthew 10:30) and the sand is numbered. Whatever infinite, therefore, this world contains, though it is infinite for man, nevertheless, is not so for God—in fact it is numbered not only for God, but also for the angels. . . . His understanding is beyond all those who count by numbers, it cannot be numbered by us. And who shall number number itself? Whatever is numbered, is numbered by number . . . but number cannot be numbered in any way. What is it then in God from which and in which He made all things, He to whom it is said: ". . . thou hast ordered all things in measure, and number, and weight" (Wisdom 11: 21)? Or who can number or measure or weigh that very number, measure, and weight in which God ordered all things? . . . Let human voices be silent, let human thoughts be at rest; to the incomprehensible they must reach not as if understanding, but only as if participating: for we shall be partakers (cf. Hebrews 3:14). . . . And of what shall we be partakers, as if there were parts

infiniti sunt (already in *De musica* I, 11, *PL* XXXII, 1094, Augustine had said: Namque ista vis numero inest, ut omnis dictus finitus sit, non dictus autem infinitus; later in *De Trinitate* XI, 8, 12, *PL* XLII, 994: Dicimus enim innumerabilia non solum infinita, sed etiam quae ita finita sunt, ut facultatem numerantis excedant). Itane numeros propter infinitatem nescit omnes Deus et usque ad quandam summam numerorum scientia Dei pervenit, ceteros ignorat? Quis hoc etiam dementissimus dixerit? Nec audebunt isti contemnere numeros et eos dicere ad Dei scientiam non pertinere, apud quos Plato Deum magna auctoritate commendat mundum numeris fabricantem. Et apud nos Deo dictum legitur: "Omnia in mensura et numero et pondere disposuisti" (Wisdom 11:21); de quo et propheta dicit: "Qui profert numerose saeculum" (Is. 40:26) et Salvator in evangelio: "Capilli," inquit, "vestri omnes numerati sunt" (Matthew 10:30). Absit itaque ut dubitemus quod ei notus sit omnis numerus, "cuius intellegentiae," sicut in psalmo canitur, "non est numerus" (Ps. 146:6). Infinitas itaque numeri quamvis infinitorum numerorum nullus sit numerus, non est tamen inconprehensibilis ei cuius intellegentiae non est numerus. Quapropter si quidquid scientia conprehenditur, scientis conprehensione finitur: profecto et omnis infinitas quodam ineffabili modo Deo finita est, quia scientiae ipsius inconprehensibilis non est. Quare si infinitas numerorum scientiae Dei qua conprehenditur esse non potest infinita: qui tandem nos sumus homunculi, qui eius scientiae limites figere praesumamus dicentes quod, nisi eisdem circuitibus temporum eadem temporalia repetantur, non potest Deus cuncta, quae facit, vel praescire, ut faciat, vel scire, cum fecerit? Cuius sapientia simpliciter multiplex et uniformiter multiformis tam inconprehensibili conprehensione omnia inconprehensibilia conprehendit, ut quaecumque nova et dissimilia consequentia praecedentibus, si semper facere vellet, inordinata et inprovisa habere non posset, nec ea provideret ex proximo tempore, sed aeterna praescientia contineret.

in God? Who then can explain how the many may be partakers of the One who is simple?[4]

Cantor[5] was of the opinion that Augustine's view corresponded to his own theory of actually infinite numbers, whereas Origen's conception of numerical infinity corresponded only to the potentially infinite.[6] And indeed Augustine seems to suggest that the infinity of the set of all finite whole numbers, while it cannot be encompassed by the human mind, is a well-defined, completed quantity for God. In God there is no contrast between infinity and unity, between simplicity and multiplicity, *cuius sapientia simpliciter multiplex et uniformiter multiformis*.[7] In his correspondence with Cardinal Franzelin Cantor further explained that the actually infinite numbers belong to the realm of creation, whereas the eternal absolute and uncreated infinity of God stands above both actual infinity, which is formed, immutable, complete, and potential infinity, which is "improper" infinity, because mutable and augmentable on principle.[8]

---

[4] Augustine, *Enarr. in Ps.* CXLVI, 11, *Corp. Christ.*, *Ser. Lat.* XL, 2129 f.: . . . "Magnus Dominus noster et magna virtus eius, et intellegentiae eius non est numerus" (Ps. 146:5). Quis hoc exponat? . . . Numquid est numerus arenae? Nobis non est, Deo est, cui capilli capitis nostri numerati sunt (cf. Matthew 10:30) et arena numerata est. Quidquid ergo infinitum mundus iste complectitur, etiamsi homini, non tamen Deo, parum dico Deo, angelis numeratum est. "Intellegentiae eius non est numerus." Excedit omnes numerarios intellegentia eius, numerari a nobis non potest. Ipsum numerum quis numerat? Numero numerantur quaecumque numerantur . . . numeri non potest esse numerus, numerari numerus nullo pacto potest. Quid ergo est apud Deum unde fecit omnia et ubi fecit omnia, cui dicitur: "Omnia in mensura et numero et pondere disposuisti" (Wisdom 11:21)? Aut quis ipsam mensuram et ipsum numerum et ipsum pondus, ubi Deus omnia disposuit, aut numerare potest aut metiri aut appendere? . . . Conticescant humanae voces, requiescant humanae cogitationes; ad incomprehensibilia non se extendant quasi comprehensuri, sed tamquam participaturi: participes enim erimus (cf. Hebr. 3:14). . . . Et cuius rei participes erimus, quasi partes sint apud Deum aut per partes dividatur Deus? Quis ergo explicat quomodo sint participes unius simplicis multi? . . . "Intellegentiae eius non est numerus."

[5] Cantor, *Gesammelte Abhandlungen* 402 f.

[6] Origen, *De principiis* II, 9, 1, *GCS*, *Orig.* V, 164 f.: . . . non enim, ut quidam volunt, finem putandum est non habere creaturas, quia ubi finis non est, nec conpraehensio ulla vel circumscriptio esse potest. Quodsi fuerit, utique nec contineri vel dispensari a Deo quae facta sunt poterunt. Naturaliter nempe, quidquid infinitum fuerit, et inconpraehensibile erit; cf. Cantor, *Gesammelte Abhandlungen* 403; see also the parallel Greek and Latin fragments in Koetschau's edition, *GCS*, *Orig.* V 164, note.

[7] See above, p. 456, n. 3.

[8] Cantor, *Gesammelte Abhandlungen* 399 f.

From this point of view, time contrary to number does not belong to the realm of the actually infinite: the very limitless openness of its finite extension makes it only potentially or improperly infinite.[9] From the point of view, however, of the intuitionist school of modern mathematics, opposed to that of Cantor, the whole realm of mathematics, especially infinity, also the actually infinite, contains, in itself as a fundamental phenomenon, time; the actually infinite, in particular, comes into existence only in "human" time by the free and successive selection of the parts of which it is made up.[10] The Augustinian conception of time includes both these aspects: on the one hand, when time will have come to an end, it will clearly emerge as finite; on the other hand, for man, time is conducive to the eternal numbers, which dwell with God just as the angels and saints, though just as the latter they are not coeternal with God because created.

As well known, Cantor went far beyond the actually infinite set of the natural numbers and in a sense consolidated Dedekind's attempt at bridging the gap or at analytically explaining the relationship between natural numbers and the mathematical continuum (of real numbers).[11] Here the Augustinian point of view is transcended, since for Augustine numbers had their ultimate existence beyond the only form of the continuum which he envisaged, which was spatial and temporal continuity. For Augustine, as for Plato, the natural numbers in their

[9] Cf. Cantor, *Gesammelte Abhandlungen* 401.

[10] See L. E. J. Brouwer, "Intuitionism and Formalism," *Bulletin of the American Mathematical Society* XX (1913–1914) 85 f., *idem*, "Mathematik, Wissenschaft und Sprache," *Monatshefte für Mathematik und Physik* XXXVI (1929) 153 f., O. Becker, "Mathematische Existenz . . .," *Jahrbuch für Philosophie und phänomenologische Forschung* VIII (1927) 642, 660, 668 ff., 758 f.

[11] See Cantor, "Grundlagen einer allgemeinen Mannigfaltigkeitslehre," *Gesammelte Abhandlungen* 165 ff., especially 192: "Somit bleibt mir nichts anderes übrig, als mit Hilfe der . . . definierten reellen Zahlenbegriffe einen möglichst rein arithmetischen Begriff eines Punktkontinuums zu versuchen." Cf. H. Weyl, *Philosophy of Mathematics and Natural Science* (Princeton, 1949) 50, S. C. Kleene, *Introduction to Metamathematics* (New York, Toronto, 1952) 30. For the paradoxes or antinomies which arose from the arithmetization of analysis (i.e., of the mathematics of real numbers) and of Cantor's general set theory related to it, see, for instance, Kleene 36 ff.; also Kleene 46 ff. and 53 ff., for the reactions of intuitionism and of Hilbert's formalism, and 204 ff., for K. Gödel's "metamathematical" solution (in his famous paper "Über formal unentscheidbare Sätze der Principia Mathematica und verwandter Systeme I," *Monatshefte für Mathematik und Physik* XXXVIII [1931] 173 ff.).

ordered multiplicity remained a more direct revelation of divine unity than appears in the unity of a spatial or temporal continuum (or in the mathematical continuum of real, but irrational numbers).[12]

4. GENESIS 1 AND 2 AND EVOLUTION

As compared to Philo and St. Basil the novelty of Augustine's as well as of Gregory of Nyssa's interpretation of creation lies in the fact that for these two Fathers the "seminal" powers or reasons are effective not only in the reproduction in time of a species through its individuals, e.g. in the growth of a plant from seed to fruit, but with regard to species themselves. According to Gregory of Nyssa *all things*, even all the works of the "six days," were created simultaneously only in their *logoi spermatikoi*, to make their successive appearance in time later; according to Augustine this is true especially of *all living things*, the various species of the vegetable and animal realms: though mentioned separately in the six-day-account of the book of Genesis, they were really all created simultaneously, but only in their *rationes seminales*; according to both Gregory and Augustine this is true also for man as a psychosomatic being, in which respect he is the temporal realization of his seminal reason which had been created outside of time.[1]

---

[12] For Plato and Greek mathematical speculation on these matters see P.-H. Michel, *De Pythagore à Euclide* (Collection d'études anciennes publiée sous le patronage de l'Association Guillaume Budé, Paris, 1950).

[1] See above, Part Two, Chapter V, 2. It should be noted that the Septuagint uses the term γένος and the Vulgate (usually) *genus* for that which today is called a biological species (rather than genus). From Augustine's *De Genesi ad litteram* it is evident that he, too, interprets *genus* as biological species (see, for instance, *De Genesi ad litteram* III, 11 CSEL XXVIII, 1, 75); in fact, he uses *species* and *genus* indiscriminately (see, for instance, *De Genesi ad litteram* VI, 14, XXVIII, 1, 189, also *ibid.* V, 23, XXVIII, 1, 167). Much of Augustine's argument concerning simultaneous creation in *rationes causales* or *seminales* is based on Gen. 2:4–5, which in the old Latin version used by Augustine (and not essentially different in this case from the Vulgate) reads: Hic est liber creaturae caeli et terrae cum factus est dies, fecit Deus caelum et terram et omne viride agri antequam esset super terram et omne fenum agri antequam exortum est . . .; cf. *De Genesi ad litteram* V, 1 ff., and especially 4 ff., CSEL XXVIII, 1, 137 ff., 142 ff. Actually the Hebrew text is translated more correctly as follows: "This is the story of the heavens and the earth at their creation. When the Lord God made the earth and the heavens, there was not yet any field shrub on the earth nor had the plants of the field sprung up . . .," cf. B. Vawter, C.M., *A Path through Genesis* (New York, 1955) 50, also G. v. Rad, *Das erste Buch Mose: Genesis Kapitel 1–12*, 9, 2nd ed. (Das Alte Testament Deutsch, Neues Göttinger Bibelwerk, II, Göttingen, 1950) 58.

Do these patristic views suggest the possibility of evolution, after the completion of creation, of new species from older ones, through the agency of secondary causes? Gregory of Nyssa's and Augustine's theories about creation have been interpreted in the sense of an evolutionary doctrine by some theologians of the nineteenth and twentieth centuries.[2] With reference to such interpretations it has been rightly said that the seminal reasons are "principles of fixity and stability rather than novelty."[3] But this does not necessarily mean that in their realization in time secondary evolutionary causes cannot have played a role, much as they do, for instance, in the development of an individual plant from its seed. It is true that neither Gregory of Nyssa nor Augustine did envisage the evolution of one species from another.[4] Augustine's exegetical purpose, especially, was only to make understandable the appearance in time, subsequent to the initial timeless instant of simultaneous creation, of the various species, each of which has a seminal reason of its own.[5] But he does attribute to the liquid element, for instance, a contributory role in the emergence of

[2] Cf., for instance, J. A. Zahm, C.S.C., *Evolution and Dogma* (Chicago, 1896), H. de Dorlodot, *Le darwinisme au point de vue de l'orthodoxie catholique* (Bruxelles, Paris, 1921), E. C. Messenger, *Evolution and Theology* (New York, 1932).

[3] J. O'Toole, C.S.C., *The Philosophy of Creation in the Writings of St. Augustine* (Washington, D.C., 1944) 83; cf. E. Gilson, *Introduction à l'étude de saint Augustin*, 3rd ed. (Paris, 1949) 271; against an interpretation of Augustine's thought in the sense of evolutionary transformism also H. Meyer, *Geschichte der Lehre von den Keimkräften von der Stoa bis zum Ausgang der Patristik nach den Quellen dargestellt* (Bonn, 1914) 184 ff., H. Woods, S.J., *Augustine and Evolution* (New York, 1924), P. Schepens, "Num S. Augustinus patrocinatur evolutionismo?," *Gregorianum* VI (1925) 216 ff. For the position of Gregory of Nyssa see L. Rebecchi, "L'antropologia naturale di San Gregorio Nisseno," *Divus Thomas* XLVI (Piacenza, 1943) especially 309 ff.; cf. my article, quoted above, p. 176, n. 27. For the relation of patristic and late ancient thought in general to evolution ideology cf. also W. Zimmermann, *Evolution* (München, 1953) 63 ff. A fortiori there can, of course, be no question of biological evolution doctrine in the book of Genesis itself; cf. Vawter, *Genesis* 51 f.

[4] For Augustine cf. C. Boyer, S.J., "La théorie augustinienne des raisons séminales," *Miscell. Agost.* II, 795 ff. See Augustine, *De Genesi ad litteram* IX, 17, *CSEL* XXVIII, 1, 291: Unde fit ut de grano tritici non nascatur faba vel de faba triticum, vel de pecore homo vel de homine pecus. P. Boyer, "Raisons séminales" 817, rightly suggests, however, that Augustinian metaphors should not always be taken at their face value; also, the image used by Augustine in the text quoted is actually that of birth and has no direct relevance for the problem of evolution.

[5] Cf. Boyer, "Raisons séminales" 814 ff.

plants from the inanimate earth.[6] On Augustinian premises evolution of one species from another would not seem to be excluded, even though Augustine did not strictly consider it. Such evolution would mean realization of each original *ratio seminalis* through the agency or at least with the cooperation of secondary natural causes. As far as man is concerned, Augustine expressly says that at the stage represented by Gen. 1:26 ff. Adam's body was created only in its seminal reason and that it actually appeared only at the stage represented by Gen. 2:7.[7] Yet he also emphasizes that the actual appearance of the human body described in Gen. 2:7 in terms of formation from earth was a purely divine act in which no other than the divine nature operated.[8] No theory of evolution which posits even purely physical continuity between man and animal can, therefore, appeal to the cosmological and anthropological doctrines of St. Augustine himself.[9]

Under the impact of the facts ascertained by modern genetics and, especially, by the study of heredity and mutation some modifications of Darwin's theory of evolution do however come rather close to the Augustinian conception of the origin and history of life in general. If it is assumed that the origin of new species cannot be explained by natural selection alone, but presupposes unpredictable mutations,[10]

---

[6] See *De Genesi ad litteram* V, 7, XXVIII, 1, 151; cf. Boyer, "Raisons séminales" 803.

[7] See above, p. 183.

[8] See *De Genesi ad litteram* IX, 15, XXVIII, 1, 287 f., a text which deals chiefly with the creation of Eve, but incidentally also with that of Adam.

[9] Cf. P. Galtier, S.J., "Saint Augustin et l'origine de l'homme," *Gregorianum* XI (1930) 20 f.

[10] Cf. T. Dobzhansky, *Genetics and the Origin of Species*, 3rd ed. (New York, 1951) 78: ". . . the discovery of the origin of hereditary variation through mutation accounts for the presence in natural populations of the material upon which selection acts"; T. H. Morgan, *The Scientific Basis of Evolution* (New York, 1932) 130 f.: "The implication in the theory of natural selection, that by selecting the more extreme individuals of the population the next generation will be moved further in the same direction, is now known to be wrong. . . . Without this postulate, natural selection is impotent to bring about evolution. On the other hand, if variations arise, owing to genetic factors (mutants) that transcend the original limits, they will supply natural selection with materials for actual progressive changes. . . . Natural selection may . . . be invoked to explain the absence of a vast array of forms that have appeared, but this is saying no more than that most of them have not had a survival value. The argument shows that natural selection does not play the role of a creative principle in evolution"; see also G. G. Simpson, *The Meaning of Evolution* (New York, 1953) 98, F. Meyer, *Problématique de l'évolution* (Paris, 1954) 51 ff., H. F. Blum, *Time's Arrow and Evolution*, 2nd ed. (Princeton, 1955) 192 ff.

then the idea of evolution seems less incompatible with Augustine's conception of *rationes seminales* which combine creational origin and evolutionary novelty of species. Any newly emergent species could then be conceived as novel not with regard to God's original plan, but with regard to previous species.[11]

It must be remembered, of course, that within a Christian world view the human soul falls outside any evolutionary process and was created directly by God according to His image and likeness without any cooperation of secondary causes. This soul, created at the stage of Gen. 1:26, was and still is joined by God to the human body in an act corresponding to Gen. 2:7. Thus a completely new form of life was brought about in the creation of man and is still brought about in "every man that cometh into this world" (John 1:9). Human life is an "emergent" on an unprecedented level of evolution because it is open toward spiritual developments which in Christian terms are comprised in the reformation of man.

[11] There is no incompatibility between such an Augustinian conception and a view such as that of C. F. v. Weizsäcker, *The History of Nature* (Chicago, 1949) 135 f.: "In order to come into existence at all, every organic form must be physically possible. Darwinism presupposes that possibility . . . the monkey has existed potentially since the beginning of the world, because the laws of physics which have been in force since then permitted its existence. The forms that have arisen show how immeasurably rich in possibilities nature has always been. And the marvel of an actual form is hardly less than the marvel of a simple law containing in itself the possibility of this form, and of countless other forms besides."

ST. AUGUSTINE'S ATTITUDE TO THE SOCIOECONOMIC ORDER OF HIS TIME AND A RECENT BOOK ON DONATISM

St. Augustine did not envisage a reform of the socioeconomic order as such. In fact, since the Christianization of the Roman Empire not one of the Fathers seems to have doubted that it was possible to be a good Christian regardless of the fact that the framework of Roman society had remained basically the same; nor did any of them expect a universal change of economic and social conditions to result from the preaching of Christian morality. The existence above all of wealth and poverty was taken for granted; the only thing that mattered from the Christian point of view *sub specie aeternitatis* was a man's attitude toward these phenomena. While in conformity with the Gospel a poor man was considered to have the better chance to enter into the Kingdom of Heaven, the merit of a rich man who gave much or all of his possessions away was esteemed all the higher. While riches as such were not condemned, certain vices, such as avarice, pride, and above all injustice, were recognized as their almost regular concomitants. Luxury was thought of as a danger to the soul of him who enjoyed it and as a deprivation of the poor who could have benefited directly from the substance thus spent.

The Fathers did not expect a general disappearance of social in-justice on earth any more than they could hope for the complete extir-pation of sin before the end of the world. Yet this attitude of resignation with regard to human society as a whole was coupled with uncompromising insistence upon obedience to the Christian law for the individual; if realized fully such obedience would imperceptibly merge into sanctity.

Just as every man was expected to fulfil the divine commandments, so also the road to greater perfection was open to every one. Men and women were advised to take this road; if they did so they had to give up all individual possessions as a part of conversion to the monastic state or at least they must lead an ascetically frugal life in the world and practice almsgiving or make donations to the Church, the great trustee for the poor.

These generalities had to be recalled,[1] prior to any evaluation of a remarkable recent book, *The Donatist Church*, by W. H. C. Frend,[2] which both materially and methodologically has a bearing on the history of the idea and reality of reform in the Augustinian age. Illuminating as the book is on many aspects of Augustine's relation to Donatism, it does not seem to do full justice to his own ideas of reform in so far as they touch on the social and economic facts with which he was confronted.

Dr. Frend has used much of the geographical, archaeological, and historical evidence now available on pre-Roman, Roman, and early Christian North Africa[3] and has demonstrated that Donatism was at home above all on the frugal rural High Plains of Southern Numidia and Mauretania with their barely romanized Libyan population, whereas Catholicism remained strong among the upper and middle classes of the Roman cities of the Mediterranean coast and the adjoining river valleys. One might follow the author further, when he stresses Augustine's cooperation and social solidarity with the Roman officials and the great senatorial landowners (in so far as they were Christians or at least friendly to Christianity) and when he surmises that the Bishop of Hippo, who hardly knew the strongholds of the Donatists on

---

[1] See, for instance, I. Seipel, *Die wirtschaftsethischen Lehren der Kirchenväter* (Theologische Studien der Leogesellschaft XVIII, Wien, 1907), E. Troeltsch, *Die Soziallehren der christlichen Kirchen und Gruppen* (Gesammelte Schriften I, third ed., Tübingen, 1923) chapter I. Much useful material is found also in the two books by O. Schilling, *Reichtum und Eigentum in der altkirchlichen Literatur* (Freiburg i. B., 1908) and *Die Staats- und Soziallehren des hl. Augustinus* (ibid., 1910), though the interpretation of patristic texts is at times slightly colored by the influence of concepts which belong to a later phase of Church history. For John Chrysostom's somewhat special position among the Fathers, his relatively optimistic attitude with regard to a possible reform of the whole socioeconomic order through Christianity, see above, pp. 127 ff.

[2] W. H. C. Frend, *The Donatist Church: A Movement of Protest in Roman North Africa* (Oxford, 1952).

[3] See also the still more recent work of Ch. Courtois, *Les Vandales et l'Afrique* (Paris, 1955), which contains very important sections on Roman and Berber North Africa; see Courtois 135 ff. for the Donatists and the Catholic Church of North Africa.

the High Plains, had no real conception of their socioeconomic background and deceived himself when he thought that they could be converted by debates and treatises. It is true that Augustine finally appealed to the state's power and that nevertheless, and in part for that very reason, neither he nor African Catholicism in general were lastingly successful in the struggle against Donatism. Yet, in spite of the fact that in an emergency situation, where Augustine felt the fate of the Catholic Church in North Africa to hang in the balance, he went so far as to advocate legal suppression and consciously abandoned his earlier principles of toleration,[4] Frend's view of Augustine as an exponent of an alliance between ecclesiastical leaders and the imperial government, on the basis of "maintenance of the social *status quo*" and of "the romanized landowning interest,"[5] stands in contradiction to all that we know about Augustine's fundamental beliefs concerning the relationship between the Church and the Empire.[6] As far as the socioeconomic contrast between Donatists and Catholics is involved, Frend loyally lists numerous utterances by Augustine against the exploitation of the poor by the rich[7] as well as others which take not only inequality of socioeconomic status but also slavery for granted. While he is probably right in asserting that for Augustine the existing socioeconomic system was inviolate,[8] since it was legal,[9] it is hardly possible to link Augustine's admiration of saints who had been rich and had given up their wealth to an attitude of social conservatism and complacency.[10] On the contrary, one might argue (as I have tried to do)[11] that the ascetic self-denial and voluntary poverty of not a few

[4] See the good discussion of this question in the book by F. van der Meer, repeatedly mentioned, *Augustinus der Seelsorger* (Köln, 1953) 114; cf. also Courtois 136 ff.

[5] Frend, *Donatist Church* 327 and 329.

[6] Cf. above, pp. 251 ff.

[7] See also H. Rondet, "Richesse et pauvreté dans la prédication de saint Augustin," *Rev. ascét. myst.* XXX (1954) 201 ff., 212 ff.

[8] Frend, *Donatist Church* 330.

[9] Referring to Augustine's *Contra Gaudentium* I, 19, 20, CSEL LIII, 215, Frend, *Donatist Church* 330, asserts that for Augustine "a slave's relation to his master was divinely ordered," but the text speaks only of laws, not of divine or natural law; the contrary would be surprising, since the consensus of patristic opinion considered slavery a consequence of sin and not a part of the original *lex divina* or *naturae*.

[10] Frend, *Donatist Church* 328.

[11] See above, pp. 366 ff.

of the wealthy Roman aristocrats of Augustine's time and circle were among the best things which that age had to show. It is true that these rich and noble *conversi* were not very numerous and that the Church did not demand a complete renouncing of wealth, however strongly it counseled and praised such abnegation, however much it considered wealth in itself as vanity. If one assumes, as Frend does, that Augustine's and the Catholics' relative solidarity with the prevailing socioeconomic order was a principal cause of their failure in lastingly converting the Donatists, whose revolt was both social and religious, then it should also be admitted that the problem transcends the case of Donatism and extends to the whole relationship between wealth, culture, and religion. Though the Fathers themselves had comparatively little interest in external and material manifestations of a Christian culture, such as, for instance, the beautiful church mosaics of Rome or Ravenna, which for us are incomparable expressions of the early Christian spirit, but rather deprecated all splendor, it should be realized that even in a spiritual and intellectual event of such great consequence as the consummation of Augustine's conversion by baptism the retreat of Cassiciacum, provided for him by the generosity of his wealthy friend Verecundus, played its role. Similarly, Jerome's translation of the Bible would hardly have been accomplished, had not Paula established and maintained the monastery at Bethlehem where it was carried out. If then one believes in the value *ad maiorem Dei gloriam* of the great achievements of the human spirit, it seems impossible to ignore the testimony of history which would suggest that even a Christian culture cannot exist without accumulated wealth (not necessarily individual).[12] All such considerations must, of course, from a Christian point of view recede into the background as compared first with the exigencies of social justice and second of ultimate spiritual perfection. With regard to the latter, Frend is surely mistaken when he says: "Social inequalities were maintained in . . . monasteries," that is to say, in the African monasteries of Augustine's time.[13] This overlooks two important facts: first, that there were few

[12] In this connection cf. the excellent remarks of S. B. Clough in his book *The Rise and Fall of Civilization. An Inquiry into the Relationship between Economic Development and Civilization* (New York, etc., 1951).

[13] Frend, *Donatist Church* 328, n. 5.

things which concerned Augustine more than absolute absence of individual property in his monasteries and even among the clergy of his cathedral, and second, that the scarce privileges granted to monks who had come from an upper class milieu were granted only in a spirit of charity in order to make the transition from one life to another not too hard.[14] On a special occasion Augustine rejected a travesty of the monastic life where senators would work with their hands, while artisans were idle, and where farmers would indulge themselves, while former landowners had given up all their luxuries.[15] And yet, while he would consider it an injustice, if the rich were humbled only to make the poor proud,[16] he does not leave the shadow of a doubt that in the monastery, as in the world, those who need and have least in material advantages are truly the richest.[17]

Generally, one might well hold, in accordance with Karl Mannheim's theory of a sociology of knowledge, that "every point of view is particular to a certain definite [sociological] situation"[18]—in Augustine's case that of the Roman upper middle class of late ancient North Africa—without doubting, nevertheless, that a man of the intellect and faith of Augustine was able largely to control his social conditioning and to absorb, formulate, and act upon, transcendent truths.[19]

[14] See *Regula S. Augustini* (*ad servos Dei*) 5, Arbesmann and Hümpfner, *Liber Vitas fratrum* 496 ff.; also *De opere monachorum* 21, 25 ff., *CSEL* XLI, 570 ff. Cf. above, p. 363, n. 70.

[15] See the quotation from *De opere monachorum* 25, 33, p. 363, n. 70; cf. *Regula S. Augustini* 5 and 2, Arbesmann and Hümpfner 496 and 495.

[16] *De opere monachorum* 25, 33.

[17] *Regula S. Augustini* 5, Arbesmann and Hümpfner 497: Illos aestiment ditiores qui in sustinenda parcitate fuerint fortiores; melius est enim minus egere quam plus habere.

[18] K. Mannheim, *Ideology and Utopia*, trans. L. Wirth and E. Shils (New York, Harvest Books, reprint of 1936 edition) 89 f.

[19] Only after this Excursus was written, did I become acquainted with H.-J. Diesner, *Studien zur Gesellschaftslehre und sozialen Haltung Augustins* (Halle [Saale], 1954). The author, without knowing Frend's *Donatist Church*, comes to somewhat similar conclusions. However interesting some of his observations, his evaluation of Augustine's attitude toward both the upper and the lower strata of the North African population seems to me to be quite erroneous, because it presupposes and does not prove that Augustine must always be a friend of the rich.

ABBREVIATIONS and BIBLIOGRAPHY

A. DICTIONARIES AND MISCELLANEOUS

Aug. Mag. *Augustinus Magister* (Congrès International Augustinien, Paris, 21–24 Septembre 1954) 3 vols.

Cottineau, *Répert.* L. H. Cottineau, O.S.B., *Répertoire topo-bibliographique des abbayes et prieurés* (Mâcon, 1935—).

DACL *Dictionnaire d'archéologie chrétienne et de liturgie* (Paris, 1907—).

DBibl *Dictionnaire de la Bible* (Paris, 1895–1912).

DHGE *Dictionnaire d'histoire et de géographie ecclésiastique* (Paris, 1912—).

DSpir *Dictionnaire de spiritualité . . .* (Paris, 1932—).

DThC *Dictionnaire de théologie catholique* (Paris, 1909–50).

Heil. Überlief. *Heilige Überlieferung* (Beiträge zur Geschichte des alten Mönchtums und des Benediktinerordens, Erg. Bd., Münster, 1938).

JL *Regesta Pontificum Romanorum ab Condita Ecclesia ad Annum post Christum Natum MCXCVIII*, ed. Ph. Jaffé, 2nd ed. by W. Wattenbach, S. Loewenfeld, etc. (Leipzig, 1885–88) 2 vols.

LPG *Lexicon of Patristic Greek.*

Mélanges Cavallera *Mélanges offerts au R. P. Ferdinand Cavallera . . .* (Toulouse, 1948).

Mélanges Halphen *Mélanges d'histoire du moyen âge dédiés à la mémoire de Louis Halphen* (Paris, 1951).

Miscell. Agost. *Miscellanea Agostiniana: Testi e Studi pubblicati a cura dell'Ordine Eremitano di S. Agostino nel XV centenario della morte . . .* (Roma, 1930–31) 2 vols.

Miscell. Isidor. *Miscellanea Isidoriana* (Roma, 1936).

Miscell. Mercati *Miscellanea Giovanni Mercati* (Studi e Testi CXXI–CXXVI, Città del Vaticano, 1946).

Miscell. Mohlberg *Miscellanea Liturgica in Honorem L. C. Mohlberg* (Bibliotheca "Ephemerides Liturgicae," XXII–XXIII, Roma, 1948—).

Pisciculi *Pisciculi: Studien zur Religion und Kultur des Altertums Franz*
F. J. Dölger *Joseph Dölger zum sechzigsten Geburtstage dargeboten = Ant. u. Chr.*, Erg. Bd. I (1939).

Potthast	*Regesta Pontificum Romanorum inde ab A. post Christum Natum MCXCVIII ad A. MCCCIV*, ed. A. Potthast (Berlin, 1874–75) 2 vols.
PW,*RE*	Paulys *Real-Encyclopädie der classischen Altertumswissenschaft*, Neue Bearbeitung, edd. G. Wissowa, etc. (Stuttgart, 1894—).
RLAC	*Reallexikon für Antike und Christentum* (Stuttgart, 1950—).
Studies A. M. Friend	*Late Classical and Mediaeval Studies in Honor of Albert Mathias Friend, Jr.* (Princeton, 1956).
Studi Greg.	*Studi Gregoriani per la storia di Gregorio VII e della riforma Gregoriana* (Roma, 1947—).
Stud. Patr.	*Studia Patristica: Papers Presented to the Second International Conference on Patristic Studies . . .* , *Oxford, 1955* (Texte u. Untersuch. LXIII–LXIV, Berlin, 1957).
Texte u. Untersuch.	*Texte und Untersuchungen zur Geschichte der altchristlichen Literatur* (Leipzig-Berlin, 1883—).
ThLL	*Thesaurus Linguae Latinae.*
ThWbNT	*Theologisches Wörterbuch zum Neuen Testament* (Stuttgart, 1933—).
Varia Variorum	*Varia Variorum: Festgabe für Karl Reinhardt* (Münster, Köln, 1952).
Wattenbach-Levison	Wattenbach-Levison, *Deutschlands Geschichtsquellen im Mittelalter: Vorzeit und Karolinger* (Weimar, 1952—).

B. Periodicals

Abhandl. Gött.	*Gesellschaft der Wissenschaften zu Göttingen, Abhandlungen* (Göttingen).
Amer. Jour. Philol.	*American Journal of Philology* (Baltimore).
Anal. Boll.	*Analecta Bollandiana* (Bruxelles).
Anal. Praem.	*Analecta Praemonstratensia* (Averbode).
Année théol. aug.	*Année théologique augustinienne* (Paris).
Ant. u. Chr.	*Antike und Christentum* (Münster i. W.).
Anz. Gött.	*Göttingische Gelehrte Anzeigen* (Göttingen).
Anz. Wien	*Akademie der Wissenschaften in Wien, Anzeiger* (Wien).
Arch. hist. doctr. litt. m. â.	*Archives d'histoire doctrinale et littéraire du moyen âge* (Paris).
Arch. Kult. Gesch.	*Archiv für Kulturgeschichte* (Berlin, Leipzig).
Arch. Lat. M. Ae.	*Archivum Latinitatis Medii Aevi* (Bulletin Du Cange) (Paris).
Byz. Z.	*Byzantinische Zeitschrift* (Leipzig).
Class. Philol.	*Classical Philology* (Chicago).

Ephem. Liturg.	*Ephemerides Liturgicae* (Roma).
Harv. Theol. Rev.	*Harvard Theological Review* (Cambridge, Mass.).
Hist. Jb.	*Historisches Jahrbuch. Im Auftrage der Görresgesellschaft* . . . *herausgegeben* (München).
Jour. Hellen. Stud.	*Journal of Hellenic Studies* (London).
Jour. Hist. Ideas	*Journal of the History of Ideas* (Lancaster, Pa., New York).
Jour. Theol. Stud.	*Journal of Theological Studies* (London).
Mitt. Inst. Öst. Gesch. Forsch.	*Mitteilungen des Instituts für Österreichische Geschichtsforschung* (Wien).
Münch. theol. Z.	*Münchener theologische Zeitschrift* (München).
Nachricht. Gött.	*Gesellschaft der Wissenschaften zu Göttingen, Nachrichten* (Göttingen).
Nouv. rev. théol.	*Nouvelle revue théologique* (Tournai).
Rech.'s sc. rel.	*Recherches de science religieuse* (Paris).
Rech.'s théol. a.m.	*Recherches de théologie ancienne et médiévale* (Louvain).
Rev. ascét. myst.	*Revue d'ascétique et de mystique* (Toulouse).
Rev. bén.	*Revue bénédictine* (Maredsous).
Rev. bibl.	*Revue biblique* (Paris).
Rev. ét.'s aug.	*Revue des études augustiniennes* (Paris).
Rev. hist. ecclés.	*Revue d'histoire ecclésiastique* (Louvain).
Rev. hist. et philos. rel.	*Revue d'histoire et de philosophie religieuse* (Strasbourg).
Rev. hist. rel.	*Revue de l'histoire des religions* (Paris).
Rev. Pol.	*Review of Politics* (Notre Dame, Ind.).
Rev. sc. rel.	*Revue des sciences religieuses* (Strasbourg).
Ric. Rel.	*Ricerche Religiose* (Roma).
Röm. Quart.	*Römische Quartalschrift* (Freiburg i. B.).
Sacr. Erud.	*Sacris Erudiri* (Steenbrugge, etc.).
Sav. Z. R. Gesch.	*Zeitschrift der Savigny-Stiftung für Rechtsgeschichte* (Weimar).
Sitz. Ber. Bayer.	*Bayerische Akademie der Wissenschaften, Sitzungsberichte* (München).
Sitz. Ber. Preuss.	*Preussische Akademie der Wissenschaften, Sitzungsberichte* (Berlin).
Sitz. Ber. Wien	*Akademie der Wissenschaften in Wien, Sitzungsberichte* (Wien).
Theol. Stud.	*Theological Studies* (Woodstock Md.).
Trans. Amer. Philol. Ass.	*Transactions and Proceedings of the American Philological Association* (Lancaster, Pa., etc.).
Trans. R. Hist. Soc.	*Transactions of the Royal Historical Society* (London).

Vie spir.	*La vie spirituelle* (Paris).
Vigil. Christ.	*Vigiliae Christianae* (Amsterdam).
Z. kath. Theol.	*Zeitschrift für katholische Theologie* (Innsbruck).
Z. Ki. Gesch.	*Zeitschrift für Kirchengeschichte* (Stuttgart).
Z. neutest. Wiss.	*Zeitschrift für die neutestamentliche Wissenschaft* . . . (Giessen).

C. EDITIONS AND TRANSLATIONS

AA. SS. — *Acta Sanctorum* (Antwerp, etc., 1643—).

Arbesmann and Hümpfner, *Liber Vitasfratrum* — *Jordani de Saxonia Ordinis Eremitarum S. Augustini Liber Vitasfratrum*, edd. R. Arbesmann, O.S.A., and W. Hümpfner, O.S.A. (Cassiciacum I, American Series, New York, 1943), Appendices B and C: *Regula Sancti Augustini Episcopi*.

v. Arnim, *Stoic. Veter. Fragm.* — *Stoicorum Veterum Fragmenta*, ed. H. v. Arnim (Leipzig, 1903–24) 4 vols.

v. Balthasar, *Grosse Ordensregeln* — *Die Grossen Ordensregeln*, ed. H.-U. v. Balthasar (Menschen der Kirche VIII, Einsiedeln, Zürich, Köln, 1948).

Bannister — *Missale Gothicum I*, ed. H. M. Bannister (Henry Bradshaw Society LII, London, 1917).

Barlow, *Martini Bracar. Opera* — *Martini Episcopi Bracarensis Opera Omnia*, ed. C. W. Barlow (New Haven, 1950).

Beck, *Ephraems Hymnen über das Paradies* — E. Beck, O.S.B., *Ephraems Hymnen über das Paradies* (Studia Anselmiana XXVI, Roma, 1951).

Bieler, *Works of St. Patrick* — *The Works of St. Patrick*, trans. L. Bieler (Ancient Christian Writers XVII, Westminster, Md.).

Bihlmeyer, *Apostol. Väter* — *Die Apostolischen Väter*, ed. K. Bihlmeyer, I (Tübingen, 1924).

Bruns, *Can. Apost. et Concil.* — *Canones Apostolorum et Conciliorum Saec. IV, V, VI, VII*, ed. H. T. Bruns (Berlin, 1839) 2 vols.

Burkitt   *The Book of Rules of Tyconius,* ed. F. C. Burkitt (Texts and Studies III, I, Cambridge, 1894).

Cazzaniga   *S. Ambrosii Mediolanensis Episcopi De Virginibus Libri Tres,* ed. J. Cazzaniga (Corpus Scriptorum Latinorum Paravianum, Torino, etc., 1948).

CIL   *Corpus Inscriptionum Latinarum* (Berlin, 1863—).

Cohn and   *Philonis Alexandrini Opera Quae Supersunt,* edd. L. Cohn
Wendland   and P. Wendland (Berlin, 1896–1930) 7 vols.

Corp. Christ., Ser.   *Corpus Christianorum, Series Latina* (Turnhout, 1953—).
Lat.

CSEL   *Corpus Scriptorum Ecclesiasticorum Latinorum* (Wien, 1866—).

Daniélou   *Grégoire de Nysse, La vie de Moïse,* ed. and trans. J. Daniélou, S.J., 2nd ed. (Sources chrétiennes I bis, Paris, 1955).

Denzinger,   H. Denzinger (C. Bannwart), *Enchiridion Symbolorum,*
Enchir. Symb.   *Definitionum et Declarationum de Rebus Fidei et Morum,* 21st–23rd ed. by J. B. Umberg, S.J. (Freiburg i. B., 1937).

Diels,   *Die Fragmente der Vorsokratiker,* ed. and trans. H. Diels,
Vorsokratiker   6th ed. by W. Kranz, I (Berlin, 1952).

Dindorf   *Themistii Orationes . . . ,* ed. W. Dindorf (Leipzig, 1832).

Férotin,   *Le Liber Ordinum en usage dans l'église wisigothique et*
Liber Ordinum   *mozarabe d'Espagne du cinquième au onzième siècle,* ed. M. Férotin, O.S.B. (Monumenta Ecclesiae Liturgica V, Paris, 1904).

Férotin,   *Le Liber Mozarabicus Sacramentorum et les manuscrits*
Liber   *mozarabes,* ed. M. Férotin, O.S.B. (Monumenta Ecclesiae
Sacramentorum   Liturgica VI, Paris, 1912).

Finaert and   *Saint Augustin, La musique,* edd. and trans. G. Finaert,
Thonnard   A.A., and F.-J. Thonnard, A.A. (Bibliothèque Augustinienne, Oeuvres de saint Augustin, Sér. I, VII, Paris, 1947).

Flor. Patr.   *Florilegium Patristicum* (Bonn, 1911—).

Frankenberg

Evagrius Ponticus : Centuriae (Problemata Prognostica), trans. from the Syriac W. Frankenberg, *Abhandl. Gött.*, Philol.-histor. Klasse, Neue Folge, XIII, 2 (1912).

Funk,
Didascal. et Const.
Apostol.

Didascalia et Constitutiones Apostolorum, ed. F. X. Funk (Paderborn, 1905) 2 vols.

Funk,
Patres Apostol.

Patres Apostolici, ed. F. X. Funk, I (Tübingen, 1901).

Garvin

The Vitas Sanctorum Patrum Emeretensium, ed. J. N. Garvin, C.S.C. (Catholic University of America Studies in Medieval and Renaissance Latin Language and Literature XIX, Washington, D.C., 1946).

GCS

Die griechischen christlichen Schriftsteller der ersten Jahrhunderte (Berlin, Leipzig, 1897—).

Harvey

Sancti Irenaei Episcopi Lugdunensis Libros Quinque adversus Haereses ed. W. W. Harvey (Cambridge, 1857) 2 vols.

Jaeger,
Greg. Nyss. Opera

Gregorii Nysseni Opera, ed. W. Jaeger, I–II (Berlin, 1921), VIII, 1 (Leiden, 1952).

Keil,
Gramm. Lat.

Grammatici Latini, ed. H. Keil (Leipzig, 1855) 7 vols.

Koch

Claudii Claudiani Carmina, ed. J. Koch (Leipzig, 1893).

Lambot,
Aug. Serm. Sel.,
Strom. Patr. et
Med. I

Sancti Aurelii Augustini Sermones Selecti Duodeviginti, ed. C. Lambot, O.S.B. = *Stromata Patristica et Mediaevalia I* (Utrecht, Bruxelles, 1950).

Linderbauer

S. Benedicti Regula Monasteriorum, ed. B. Linderbauer, O.S.B. (*Flor. Patr.* XVII, 1928).

Lowe

The Bobbio Missal, Text, ed. E. A. Lowe (Henry Bradshaw Society LVIII, London, 1920).

Mansi,   *Sacrorum Conciliorum Nova et Amplissima Collectio*, ed. G. D.
Concil.   Mansi (Firenze, 1759–1927).

MGH   *Monumenta Germaniae Historica* (Hannover–Berlin,
                1826—).
    AA   *Auctores Antiquissimi*
    Concil.   *Concilia*
    Epist.   *Epistolae*
    Leg.   *Leges*

Mohlberg   *Sacramentarium Veronense*, ed. L. C. Mohlberg, O.S.B.
                (Rerum Ecclesiasticarum Documenta Cura Pontificii
                Athenaei Sancti Anselmi de Urbe Edita, Fontes I, Roma,
                1956)

Morin,   *Sancti Augustini Sermones post Maurinos Repertos*, ed. G.
Augustini Serm., Morin, O.S.B. = *Miscell. Agost.* I
Miscell. Agost. I

Morin,   *S. Caesarii Opera Omnia*, ed. G. Morin, O.S.B., II
Caesar. Arel. Opera (Maredsous, 1942).

Moxon   *The Commonitorium of Vincentius of Lerins*, ed. R. S. Moxon
                (Cambridge, 1915).

Mynors   *Cassiodori Senatoris Institutiones*, ed. R. A. B. Mynors
                (Oxford, 1937).

Nock and   *Corpus Hermeticum*, ed. A. D. Nock, trans. A.-J. Festu-
  Festugière,   gière, O.P. (Collection des Universités de France . . .
Corp. Herm.   Association Guillaume Budé, Paris, 1945) 2 vols.

Otto,   *Corpus Apologetarum Saeculi Secundi*, ed. J. C. T. Otto,
Corp. Apologet. VIII (Jena, 1861).

PG   *Patrologia Graeca*, ed. J. P. Migne (Paris, 1857–1912).

PL   *Patrologia Latina*, ed. J. P. Migne (Paris, 1844–1890).

Preuschen   E. Preuschen, *Palladius und Rufinus* (Giessen, 1897), with
                edition of the *Historia monachorum*.

Sabatier,
Bibliorum Versiones

P. Sabatier, O.S.B., *Bibliorum Sacrorum Latinae Versiones Antiquae* III (Reims, 1743).

Sanders

Beati in Apocalipsin Libri Duodecim, ed. H. A. Sanders (Papers and Monographs of the American Academy in Rome VII, Roma, 1930).

Schulte

S. Johannis Chrysostomi de Inani Gloria et de Educandis Liberis, ed. F. Schulte (Programm Gaesdonck DCXXVII, Münster, 1914).

Schwartz,
Acta Concil. Oecum.

Acta Conciliorum Oecumenicorum, ed. E. Schwartz (Berlin, Leipzig, 1914—).

Scott,
Hermet.

Hermetica, ed. W. Scott (Oxford, 1924–36) 4 vols.

Skutella

S. Aurelii Augustini Confessionum Libri Tredecim, ed. M. Skutella (Leipzig, 1934).

Spicil. Casin.

Spicilegium Casinense Complectens Analecta Sacra et Profana III, 1 (Monte Cassino, 1897).

Srawley

The Catechetical Oration of Gregory of Nyssa, ed. J. H. Srawley (Cambridge Patristic Texts, Cambridge, 1903).

Stewart and Rand,
Boeth. Theol. Tract.

Boethius: The Theological Tractates, edd. and trans. H. F. Stewart and E. K. Rand (Loeb Classical Library, London, Cambridge, Mass., 1946).

Terzaghi,
Synes. Cyren.
Hymni
Synes. Cyren.
Opuscula

Synesii Cyrenensis Hymni et Opuscula, ed. N. Terzaghi (Scriptores Graeci et Latini Consilio Academiae Lynceorum Editi, Roma, 1939–44) 2 vols.

Vessereau and
Préchac

Rutilius Namatianus: Sur son retour, edd. and trans. J. Vessereau and F. Préchac (Collection des Universités de France . . . Association Guillaume Budé, Paris, 1933).

Warner

The Stowe Missal, ed. G. F. Warner (Henry Bradshaw Society XXXI–XXXII, London, 1906–1915).

Waszink   *Quinti Septimii Florentis Tertulliani De Anima*, ed. J. H. Waszink (Amsterdam, 1947).

Wilson   *The Gelasian Sacramentary: Liber Sacramentorum Romanae Ecclesiae*, ed. H. A. Wilson (Oxford, 1894).

Wordsworth and   J. Wordsworth and H. J. White, etc., *Novum Testamentum*
White,   *Domini Nostri Jesu Christi Latine* II (Oxford, 1913–1941).
Novum Testamentum

D. Studies Cited in Abbreviation

Adam, E., *Die geheime Kirchenbusse nach dem heiligen Augustin* (Münchener Studien zur historischen Theologie II, München, 1921).

———— *Die kirchliche Sündenvergebung nach dem hl. Augustinus* (Forschungen zur christlichen Literatur-und Dogmengeschichte XIV, 1, Paderborn, 1917).

Allo, E. W., O.P., *Saint Paul: Seconde Epître aux Corinthiens* (Paris, 1937).

Amand (de Mendieta), D., *L'ascèse monastique de saint Basile* (Maredsous, 1948).

Amiot, F., *L'enseignement de saint Paul*, 2nd ed. (Paris, 1938).

Anastos, M. V., "Political Theory in the Lives of the Slavic Saints Constantine and Methodius," *Harvard Slavic Studies* II (1954) 17 ff.

Antin, P., O.S.B., "Le monachisme selon saint Jérôme," *Mélanges bénédictins* (Abbaye Saint Wandrille, 1947).

Arbesmann, R., O.S.A., "The Concept of 'Christus Medicus' in St. Augustine," *Traditio* X (1954) 1 ff.

Arnou, R., *Le désir de Dieu dans la philosophie de Plotin* (Paris, s. a.).

———— *ΠΡΑΞΙΣ* et *ΘΕΩΡΙΑ*: *Etude de detail sur le vocabulaire et la pensée des Ennéades de Plotin* (Paris, 1921).

Bacht, H., S.J., "Die Rolle des orientalischen Mönchtums in den kirchenpolitischen Auseinandersetzungen um Chalkedon (431–519)," *Das Konzil von Chalkedon*, edd. A. Grillmeier, S.J., and H. Bacht, S.J., II (Würzburg, 1953) 193 ff.

Balthasar, H. v., *Présence et pensée: Essai sur la philosophie religieuse de Grégoire de Nysse* (Paris, 1942).

Bardy, G., "Définition de la Cité de Dieu," *Année théol. aug.* XII (1942) 113 ff.

———— "La formation du concept de 'Cité de Dieu' dans l'œuvre de saint Augustin," *Année théol. aug.* XII (1952) 5 ff.

Barth, K., *Die kirchliche Dogmatik* I— (München and Zollikon, Zürich, 1932—).

Baur, C., O.S.B., *Der heilige Johannes Chrysostomus und seine Zeit* (München, 1929–30) 2 vols.

Baynes, N. H., "Eusebius and the Christian Empire," *Mélanges Bidez II* (Annuaire de l'Institut de Philologie et d'Histoire Orientales, Bruxelles, 1934) 13 ff.

Beck, E., O.S.B., *Ephraems Hymnen über das Paradies* (Studia Anselmiana XXVI, Roma, 1951).

Benz, E., *Marius Victorinus und die Entwicklung der abendländischen Willensmetaphysik* (Forschungen zur Kirchen-und Geistesgeschichte I, Stuttgart, 1932).

Berkhof, H., *Die Theologie des Eusebius von Caesarea* (Amsterdam, 1939).

———— *Kirche und Kaiser* (Zollikon, Zürich, 1947).

Bernard, R., *L'image de Dieu d'après saint Athanase* (Théologie XXV, Paris, 1952).

Bidez, J. and F. Cumont, *Les mages hellénisés* (Paris, 1938) 2 vols.

Bieder, W., *Ekklesia und Polis im Neuen Testament und in der alten Kirche* (Zürich, 1941).

Bishko, C. J., "Spanish Monasticism in the Visigothic Period" (Unprinted Ph.D. Diss., Harvard University, Cambridge, Mass., 1937).

———— "The Date and Nature of the Spanish Consensoria Monachorum," *Amer. Jour. Philol.* LXIX (1948) 377 ff.

Bloch, H., "A New Document of the Last Pagan Revival in the West," *Harv. Theol. Rev.* XXXVIII (1945) 199 ff.

Boas, G., *Essays on Primitivism and Related Ideas in the Middle Ages* (Baltimore, 1948).

Bourque, E., *Etude sur les sacramentaires romains* (Studi di Antichità Cristiana XX, Città del Vaticano, 1949).

Bousset, W., *Die Religion des Judentums im späthellenistischen Zeitalter*, 3rd ed. by H. Gressmann (Tübingen, 1926).

———— Hauptprobleme der Gnosis (Göttingen, 1907).

Boyer, C., S.J., "La théorie augustinienne des raisons séminales," *Miscell. Agost.* II, 795 ff.

Bréhier, E., *Les idées philosophiques et religieuses de Philon d'Alexandrie*, 3rd ed. (Etudes de philosophie médiévale VIII, Paris, 1950).

Bürke, G., S.J., "Des Origenes Lehre vom Urstand," *Z. kath. Theol.* LXXII (1950) 10 ff.

Burdach, K., *Vom Mittelalter zur Reformation* (Berlin, 1921–39).

———— "Sinn und Ursprung der Worte Renaissance und Reformation," *Reformation, Renaissance, Humanismus*, 2nd ed. (Berlin, Leipzig, 1926) 1 ff.

Callahan, J. F., *Four Views of Time in Ancient Philosophy* (Cambridge, Mass., 1948).

Callewaert, C., "Le Communicantes et le Nobis quoque peccatoribus," *Sacr. Erud.* I (1948) 131 ff.

—— "Saint Léon le Grand et les textes du Léonien," *Sacr. Erud.* I (1948) 35 ff.

Camelot, P.-TH., O.P., *Virgines Christi* (Paris, 1934).

Campenhausen, H. v., *Ambrosius von Mailand als Kirchenpolitiker* (Arbeiten zur Kirchengeschichte XII, Berlin, Leipzig, 1929).

—— *Die asketische Heimatlosigkeit im altkirchlichen und frühmittelalterlichen Mönchtum* (Sammlung gemeinverständlicher Vorträge und Schriften aus dem Gebiet der Theologie und Religionsgeschichte CXLIX, Tübingen, 1930).

Carcopino, J., *Virgile et le mystère de la IVe Églogue*, 2nd ed. (Paris, 1943).

Carney, E. J., O.S.F.S., *The Doctrine of St. Augustine on Sanctity* (The Catholic University of America Studies in Sacred Theology XCI, Washington, D.C., 1945).

Cavallera, F., *Saint Jérôme* I, 1 and 2 (Spicilegium Sacrum Lovaniense I and II, Louvain, Paris, 1922).

Cayré, F., A.A., *Initiation à la philosophie de saint Augustin* (Paris, 1947).

—— *La contemplation augustinienne*, 2nd ed. (Paris, 1954).

Chadwick, O., *John Cassian* (Cambridge, 1950).

Chaix-Ruy, J., *Saint Augustin: Temps et histoire* (Paris, 1956).

Chapman, J., O.S.B., *Saint Benedict and the Sixth Century* (New York, etc., 1929).

Cilleruelo, L., O.S.A., "Influencia de S. Agustin en la espiritualidad cristiana hasta la Edad Media," *Revista de Espiritualidad* XIV (1955) 125 ff.

Courcelle, P., *Histoire littéraire des grandes invasions germaniques* (Paris, 1948).

—— *Les lettre grecques en occident: De Macrobe à Cassiodore*, 2nd ed. (Bibliothèque des Ecoles Françaises d'Athènes et de Rome, CLIX, Paris, 1948).

Cranz, F. E., "De civitate Dei XV, 2, and Augustine's Idea of the Christian Society," *Speculum* XXV (1950) 220 ff.

—— "Kingdom and Polity in Eusebius of Caesarea," *Harv. Theol. Rev.* XLV (1952) 47 ff.

—— "The Development of Augustine's Ideas on Society before the Donatist Controversy," *Harv. Theol. Rev.* XLVII (1954) 255 ff.

Crouzel, H., S.J., *Théologie de l'image de Dieu chez Origène* (Théologie XXXIV, Paris, 1956).

Cullmann, O., *Königsherrschaft Christi und Kirche im Neuen Testament* (Theologische Studien X, Zollikon, Zürich, 1949).

Cumont, F., "La fin du monde selon les mages occidentaux," *Rev. hist. rel.* CIII (1931) 29 ff.

Curtius, E. R., *European Literature and the Latin Middle Ages*, trans. by W. R. Trask (Bollingen Series XXXVI, New York, 1953).

Daniélou, J., S.J., "La typologie de la semaine au IVe siècle," *Rech.'s sc. rel.* XXXV (1948) 382 ff.

———— "La typologie millénariste de la semaine dans le christianisme primitif," *Vigil. Christ.* II (1948) 1 ff.

———— *Origène* (Paris, 1948).

———— *Platonisme et théologie mystique : Essai sur la doctrine de saint Grégoire de Nysse*, 2nd ed. (Théologie II, Paris, 1953).

———— *Sacramentum Futuri : Etudes sur les origines de la typologie biblique* (Paris, 1950).

Deanesly, Margaret, "Early English and Gallic Minsters," *Trans. R. Hist. Soc.*, Ser. IV, XXIII (1941) 25 ff.

Delatte, A., *Etudes sur la littérature pythagoricienne* (Bibliothèque de l'Ecole des Hautes Etudes, Sciences historiques et philologiques, CCXVII, Paris, 1915).

Dereine, C., S.J., article "Chânoines," *DHGE* XII, 353 ff.

———— "L'élaboration du statut canonique des chânoines réguliers," *Rev. hist. ecclés.* XLVI (1951) 534 ff.

———— "Vie commune, règle de saint Augustin et chânoines réguliers au XIe siècle," *Rev. hist. ecclés.* XLI (1946) 365 ff.

Dey, J., *ΠΑΛΙΓΓΕΝΕΣΙΑ* (Neutestamentliche Abhandlungen XVII, 5, Münster, 1937).

Dinkler, E., *Die Anthropologie Augustins* (Forschungen zur Kirchen-und Geistesgeschichte IV, Stuttgart, 1934).

Dirksen, A. H., C.PP.S., *The New Testament Concept of Metanoia* (Diss., Catholic University of America, Washington, D.C., 1932).

Dobschütz, E. v., "Coislinianus 296," *Byz. Z.* XII (1903) 534 ff.

Dölger, F. J., "Zur Symbolik des altchristlichen Taufhauses I: Das Oktogon und die Symbolik der Achtzahl . . . ," *Ant. u. Chr.* IV (1934) 153 ff.

Downey, G., "Themistius and the Defence of Hellenism in the Fourth Century," *Harv. Theol. Rev.* L (1957) 259 ff.

Dürig, W., *Imago: Ein Beitrag zur Terminologie und Theologie der römischen Liturgie* (Münchener theologische Studien II, 5, München, 1952).

Dumbarton Oaks Papers (Cambridge, Mass., 1958).

Edelstein, H., *Die Musikanschauung Augustins nach seiner Schrift "De Musica"* (Diss. Freiburg i. B., Ohlau i. Schl., 1929).

Eliade, M., *Le mythe de l'éternel retour* (Paris, 1949).

Ensslin, W., "Die Religionspolitik des Kaisers Theodosius d. Gr.," *Sitz. Ber. Bayer.*, Philos.-Histor. Klasse, 1953, 2.

Fabre, P., *Saint Paulin de Nole et l'amitié chrétienne* (Bibliothèque des Ecoles Françaises d'Athènes et de Rome CLXVII, Paris, 1949).

Festugière, A.-J., O.P., *Contemplation et vie contemplative selon Platon*, 2nd ed. (Paris, 1950).

—— *La révélation d'Hermès Trismégiste* (Paris, 1950–54) 4 vols.

Frend, W. H. C., *The Donatist Church* (Oxford, 1952).

Frick, R., *Die Geschichte des Reich-Gottes-Gedankens in der alten Kirche bis zu Origenes und Augustin* (Beihefte zur Zeitschrift für die neutestamentliche Wissenschaft VI, Giessen, 1928).

Friedrich, F., O.S.B., "Conversatio Morum: Das zweite Gelübde des Benediktinermönches," *Studien und Mitteilungen zur Geschichte des Benediktiner-Ordens und seiner Zweige* LIX (1941) 200 ff.

Gaïth, J., *La conception de la liberté chez Grégoire de Nysse* (Etudes de philosophie médiévale XLIII, Paris, 1953).

Gall, A. v., *ΒΑΣΙΛΕΙΑ ΤΟΥ ΘΕΟΥ* (Heidelberg, 1926).

Galtier, P., S.J., *Aux origines du sacrement de pénitence* (Analecta Gregoriana LIV, Ser. Fac. Theol. Sect. A [n. 6], Roma, 1951).

—— *De Paenitentia : Tractatus Dogmatico-Historicus*, 2nd ed. (Roma, 1950).

—— *Le Saint Esprit en nous d'après les pères grecs* (Analecta Gregoriana XXV, Ser. Fac. Theol. Sect. A [n. 4], Roma, 1946).

—— "Pénitents et convertis: De la pénitence latine à la pénitence celtique," *Rev. hist. ecclés.* XXXIII (1937) 5 ff. and 277 ff.

Giet, S., *Les idées et l'action sociales de saint Basile* (Paris, 1941).

Gilson, E., "Eglise et cité de Dieu," *Arch. hist. doct. litt. m. â.* XXVIII, 1953 (1954) 5 ff.

—— *History of Christian Philosophy in the Middle Ages* (New York, 1955).

—— *Introduction à l'étude de saint Augustin*, 3rd ed. (Etudes de philosophie médiévale XI, Paris, 1949).

—— *La philosophie au moyen âge des origines patristiques à la fin du XIVe siècle*, 2nd ed. (Paris, 1947).

—— Introduction to *Saint Augustine, The City of God*, trans. by G. G. Walsh, S.J. (The Fathers of the Church in English Translation VIII, New York, 1950).

Gomez, I. M., O.S.B., "El perdido Comentario de Ticonio al Apocalipsis: Principios de crítica literaria y textual para su reconstrucción," *Miscellanea Biblica B. Ubach* (Scripta et Documenta I, Montserrat, 1953) 387 ff.

Gougaud, L., O.S.B., *Christianity in Celtic Lands* (London, 1932).

Grabowski, S.J., "Sinners and the Mystical Body of Christ according to St. Augustine," *Theological Studies* VIII (1947) 614 ff., IX (1948) 47 ff.

Grabowski, S.J., *The Church: An Introduction to the Theology of St. Augustine* (St. Louis, London, 1957).

Graf, A., *Miti, leggende e superstizioni del Medio Evo* (Torino, 1925).

Grech, P., O.E.S.A., "The Augustinian Community and the Primitive Church," *Augustiniana* V (1955) 459 ff.

Grosjean, P., S.J., "Notes chronologiques sur le séjour de s. Patrice en Gaule," *Anal. Boll.* LXIII (1945) 65 ff.

Gross, J., *La divinisation du chrétien d'après les pères grecs* (Paris, 1938).

Grossmann, Ursula, "Studien zur Zahlensymbolik des Frühmittelalters," *Z. kath. Theol.* LXXVI (1954) 19 ff.

Guitton, J., *Le temps et l'éternité chez Plotin et saint Augustin* (Paris, 1933).

Hahn, T., *Tyconius-Studien* (Studien zur Geschichte der Theologie und Kirche VI, 2, Leipzig, 1900).

Harnack, A., *Die Terminologie der Wiedergeburt und verwandter Erlebnisse in der ältesten Kirche* (Texte u. Untersuch. XLII, 2, 1917).

Hausherr, I., S.J., "L'imitation de Jésus-Christ dans la spiritualité byzantine," *Mélanges Cavallera* 231 ff.

Heer, F., "Die 'Renaissance'-Ideologie im frühen Mittelalter," *Mitt. Inst. Öst. Gesch. Forsch.* LVII (1949) 23 ff.

Hefele, C. J., *Histoire des conciles*, trans. by Dom H. Leclercq, II, 2 (Paris, 1908).

Heitmann, A., O.S.B., *Imitatio Dei: Die ethische Nachahmung Gottes nach der Väterlehre der zwei ersten Jahrhunderte* (Studia Anselmiana X, Roma, 1940).

Henry, P., S.J., *Plotin et l'occident* (Louvain, 1934).

Hertling, L., S.J., "Die professio der Kleriker und die Entstehung der drei Gelübde," *Z. kath. Theol.* LVI (1932) 148 ff.

———— "Kanoniker, Augustinusregel und Augustinerorden," *Z. kath. Theol.* LIV (1930) 334 ff.

Herwegen, I., O.S.B., *Das Pactum des hl. Fruktuosus von Braga* (Kirchenrechtliche Abhandlungen XL, Stuttgart, 1907).

Hess, W., O.S.B., "Imago Dei," *Benediktinische Monatsschrift* XXIX (1953) 371 ff.

Heussi, K., *Der Ursprung des Mönchtums* (Tübingen, 1936).

Hörmann, J., *Untersuchungen zur griechischen Laienbeicht* (Donauwörth, 1913).

Hofmann, F., *Der Kirchenbegriff des hl. Augustinus in seinen Grundlagen und in seiner Entwicklung* (München, 1933).

Holl, K., *Enthusiasmus und Bussgewalt beim griechischen Mönchtum* (Leipzig, 1898).

Hubaux, J. and M. Leroy, *Le mythe du Phénix dans les littératures grecque et latine* (Bibliothèque de la Faculté de philosophie et lettres de l'Université de Liège LXXXII, 1939).

Huby, J., S.J., *Mystiques paulinienne et johannique* (Paris, 1946).

Hümpfner, W., O.S.A., "Die Mönchsregel des heiligen Augustinus," *Aug. Mag.* I, 241 ff.

Ivanka, E. v., *Hellenisches und Christliches im frühbyzantinischen Geistesleben* (Wien, 1948).

Jaeger, W., *Aristotle* (Oxford, 1948).

——— *Paideia : The Ideals of Greek Culture*, trans. by G. Highet (New York, 1939–44) 3 vols.

——— *Two Rediscovered Works of Ancient Christian Literature : Gregory of Nyssa and Macarius* (Leiden, 1954).

Journet, C., *L'église du Verbe Incarné*, vol. I, 2nd ed. (Paris, 1955), vol. II (Paris, 1951).

Käsemann, E., *Leib und Leib Christi* (Beiträge zur historischen Theologie IX, Tübingen, 1933).

Kamlah, W., *Christentum und Geschichtlichkeit : Untersuchungen zur Entstehung des Christentums und zu Augustins "Bürgerschaft Gottes,"* 2nd ed. (Stuttgart, 1951).

Kantorowicz, E. H., "Deus per naturam, Deus per gratiam," *Harv. Theol. Rev.* XLV (1952) 253 ff.

——— "Kaiser Friedrich II. und das Königsbild des Hellenismus," *Varia Variorum* 171 ff.

——— *Laudes Regiae : A Study in Liturgical Acclamations and Mediaeval Ruler Worship* (University of California Publications in History XXXIII, Berkeley and Los Angeles, 1946).

——— *The King's Two Bodies: A Study in Mediaeval Political Theology* (Princeton, 1957).

Koch, H., "Das mystische Schauen beim hl. Gregor von Nyssa," *Theologische Quartalschrift* LXXX (1898) 397 ff.

Kraeling, H., *Anthropos and Son of Man : A Study in the Religious Syncretism of the Hellenistic Orient* (Columbia University Oriental Studies XXV, New York, 1927).

Kunzelmann, A., "Die Chronologie der Sermones des hl. Augustinus," *Miscell. Agost.* II, 417 ff.

Ladner, G. B., "Aspects of Mediaeval Thought on Church and State," *Rev. Pol.* IX (1947) 403 ff.

——— "The Concept of the Image in the Greek Fathers and the Byzantine Iconoclastic Controversy," *Dumb. Oaks Pap.* VII (Cambridge, Mass., 1953) 1 ff.

——— "The Philosophical Anthropology of St. Gregory of Nyssa," *Dumb. Oaks Pap.* XII (Cambridge, Mass., 1958).

Lampe, G. W. H., "Some Notes on the Significance of *ΒΑΣΙΛΕΙΑ ΤΟΥ ΘΕΟΥ, ΒΑΣΙΛΕΙΑ ΧΡΙΣΤΟΥ* in the Greek Fathers," *Jour. Theol. Stud.* XLIX (1948) 58 ff.

Lamy, Agnès, "Bios Angelikos," *Dieu vivant* VII (s.a.) 57 ff.

Latko, E. F., *Origen's Concept of Penance* (Diss., Faculté de Théologie, Université Laval, Québec, 1949).

Lauras, A. and H. Rondet, "Le thème des deux cités dans l'œuvre de saint Augustin," in: H. Rondet, M. Le Landais, A. Lauras, C. Couturier, *Etudes augustiniennes* (Paris, 1953) 97 ff.

Leisegang, H., *Die Begriffe der Zeit und Ewigkeit im späteren Platonismus* (Beiträge zur Geschichte der Philosophie des Mittelalters XIII, 4, Münster, 1913).

Lemaître, I., "La contemplation chez les grecs et autres orientaux chrétiens," *Rev. ascét. myst.* XXVI (1950) 121 ff.

Levillain, L., "Etudes sur l'abbaye de Saint-Denis à l'époque mérovingienne II," *Bibliothèque de l'Ecole des Chartes* LXXXVI (1925) 5 ff.

Leys, R., S.J., "La théologie spirituelle de Grégoire de Nysse," *Stud. Patr.* II, 495 ff.

—— *L'image de Dieu chez saint Grégoire de Nysse* (Museum Lessianum, Sect. Théol. XLIX, Bruxelles, Paris, 1951).

Lieske, A., S.J., "Die Theologie der Christusmystik Gregors von Nyssa," *Z. kath. Theol.* LXX (1948) 129 ff.

—— *Die Theologie der Logosmystik bei Origenes* (Münster, 1938).

Louis, R., "Le séjour de saint Patrice à Auxerre," *Mélanges Halphen* 445 ff.

Lubac, H. de, S.J., *Catholicisme: Les aspects sociaux du dogme* (Paris, 1947).

McLaughlin, T. P., C.S.B., *Le très ancien droit monastique de l'occident* (Archives de la France monastique XXXVIII, Ligugé, Paris, 1935).

Madoz, J., S.J., *El concepto de la tradicion en S. Vicente de Lerins* (Analecta Gregoriana V, Roma, 1933).

Malnory, A., *Saint Césaire, évêque d'Arles 503–543* (Bibliothèque de l'Ecole des Hautes Etudes, Sciences philosophiques et historiques, CIII, Paris, 1894).

Mandonnet, P., O.P., *Saint Dominique* (Paris, 1937) 2 vols.

Manoir de Juaye, H. du, S.J., *Dogme et spiritualité chez saint Cyrille d'Alexandrie* (Etudes de théologie et d'histoire de la spiritualité II, Paris, 1944).

Maréchal, J., S.J., *Etudes sur la psychologie des mystiques* (Museum Lessianum Sect. Philos. II and XIX, Bruxelles, Paris, 1924–37) 2 vols.

Marrou, H.-I., "Civitas Dei, civitas terrena: num tertium quid?", *Stud. Patr.* II, 342.

—— *Saint Augustin et la fin de la culture antique* and *Retractatio* (Bibliothèque des Ecoles Françaises d'Athènes et de Rome CXLV [bis], Paris, 1949).

Marshall, R. T., *Studies in the Political and Socio-Religious Terminology of the De Civitate Dei* (The Catholic University of America Patristic Studies LXXXVI, Washington, D.C., 1952).

Marsili, S., O.S.B., *Giovanni Cassiano ed Evagrio Pontico* (Studia Anselmiana V, Roma, 1936).

Mayer, A., O.S.B., *Das Gottesbild im Menschen nach Clemens von Alexandrien* (Studia Anselmiana XV, Roma, 1942).

Meer, F. van der, *Augustinus der Seelsorger*, trans. from *Augustinus de Zielzorger* by N. Grietemann, 2nd ed. (Köln, 1953).

Merki, H., O.S.B., *'ΟΜΟΙΩΣΙΣ ΘΕΩ̨: Von der platonischen Angleichung an Gott zur Gottähnlichkeit bei Gregor von Nyssa* (Paradosis VII, Freiburg i. d. Schweiz, 1952).

Meyer, H., *Geschichte der Lehre von den Keimkräften von der Stoa bis zum Ausgang der Patristik nach den Quellen dargestellt* (Bonn, 1914).

———— "Zur Lehre von der ewigen Wiederkunft aller Dinge," *Beiträge zur Geschichte des christlichen Altertums und der byzantinischen Literatur: Festgabe Albert Ehrhard* . . . (Bonn, Leipzig, 1922) 359 ff.

Meyer, L., "Perfection chrétienne et vie solitaire dans la pensée de saint Jean Chrysostome," *Rev. ascét. myst.* XIV (1933) 232 ff.

———— *Saint Jean Chrysostome, maître de perfection chrétienne* (Paris, 1933).

Mommsen, T. E., "Aponius and Orosius on the Significance of the Epiphany," *Studies A. M. Friend* 96 ff.

———— "St. Augustine and the Christian Idea of Progress," *Jour. Hist. Ideas* XII (1951) 346 ff.

Monceaux, P., *Histoire littéraire de l'Afrique chrétienne, depuis les origines jusqu'à l'invasion arabe* (Paris, 1901–23) 7 vols.

Morin, G., O.S.B., "L'origine du symbole d'Athanase," *Jour. Theol. Stud.* XII (1911) 161 ff., 337 ff.

Mullins, Sister P. J., O.P., *The Spiritual Life according to Saint Isidore of Seville* (Catholic University of America Studies in Medieval and Renaissance Latin Language and Literature XIII, Washington, D.C., 1940).

Niederhuber, J. E., *Die Eschatologie des hl. Ambrosius* (Forschungen zur christlichen Literatur-und Dogmengeschichte VI, 3, Paderborn, 1907).

———— *Die Lehre des hl. Ambrosius vom Reiche Gottes auf Erden* (Forschungen zur christlichen Literatur-und Dogmengeschichte IV, 3–4, Paderborn, 1904).

Nielen, J. M., "Die Kultsprache der Nachfolge und Nachahmung Gottes und verwandter Bezeichnungen im neutestamentlichen Schrifttum," *Heil. Überlief.* 59 ff.

Nock, A. D., *Conversion: The Old and the New Religion from Alexander the Great to Augustine of Hippo* (Oxford, 1933).

Nolte, V. (F.), O.E.S.A., *Augustins Freundschaftsideal in seinen Briefen* (Würzburg, 1939).

Oppenheim, Ph., O.S.B., "Mönchsweihe und Taufritus: Ein Kommentar zur Auslegung bei Dionysius dem Areopagiten," *Miscell. Mohlberg* I, 259 ff.

O'Toole, C. J., C.S.C., *The Philosophy of Creation in the Writings of St. Augustine* (Catholic University of America Philosophical Studies LXXXI, Washington, D.C., 1944).

Palanque, J. R., *Saint Ambroise et l'empire romain* (Paris, 1933).

Pépin, J., "Recherches sur les sens et les origines de l'expression *caelum caeli* dans le livre XII des *Confessions* de s. Augustin," *Arch. Lat. M. Ae.* XXIII (1953) 185 ff.

Perez de Urbel, J., O.S.B., *Los monjes españoles en la edad media*, 2nd ed. (Madrid, 1945) 2 vols.

Peterson, E., *Der Monotheismus als politisches Problem* (reprinted in *Theologische Traktate* [München, 1951] 45 ff.).

———— "Die Spiritualität des griechischen Physiologus," *Byz. Z.* XLVII (1954) 60 ff.

Pincherle, A., "Da Ticonio a Sant'Agostino," *Ric. Rel.* I (1925) 413 ff.

Plinval, G. de, *Pélage* (Lausanne, 1943).

Pöschl, A., *Bischofsgut und Mensa Episcopalis I* (Bonn, 1908).

Pontet, M., *L'exégèse de s. Augustin prédicateur* (Théologie VII, 1944).

Porter, W. S., "Early Spanish Monasticism," *Laudate* X–XII (1932–34).

Poschmann, B., *Paenitentia Secunda: Die kirchliche Busse im ältesten Christentum bis Cyprian und Origenes* (Theophaneia I, Bonn, 1940).

Prümm, K., S.J., *Christentum als Neuheitserlebnis* (Freiburg i. B., 1933).

Puech, A., *Un réformateur de la société chrétienne au IVe siècle: Saint Jean Chrysostome et les mœurs de son temps* (Paris, 1891).

Puech, H.-C., "Un livre récent sur la mystique d'Origène," *Rev. hist. et philos. rel.* XIII (1933) 508 ff.

Puniet, P. de, O.S.B., "Intus reformari: Témoignages liturgiques sur le mystère de l'Emmanuel," *Ephem. Liturg.* LII (1938) 125 ff.

Quasten, J., *Patrology* I and II (Westminster, Md., etc., 1951 and 1953).

Rahner, H., S.J., "Die Gottesgeburt: Die Lehre der Kirchenväter von der Geburt Christi im Herzen der Gläubigen," *Z. kath. Theol.* LIX (1935) 333 ff.

Rahner, K., S.J., "Die Busslehre des hl. Cyprian von Karthago," *Z. kath. Theol.* LXXIV (1952) 257 ff., 381 ff.

Ratzinger, J., "Herkunft und Sinn der Civitas-Lehre Augustins," *Aug. Mag.* II, 965 ff.

Rehm, W., *Der Untergang Roms im abendländischen Denken* (Leipzig, 1930).

Reinhardt, K., *Kosmos und Sympathie* (München, 1926).

—— *Poseidonios* (München, 1921).

Reitzenstein, R., *Das iranische Erlösungsmysterium* (Bonn, 1921).

—— *Die hellenistischen Mysterienreligionen*, 3rd ed. (Leipzig, Berlin, 1927).

—— *Historia Monachorum und Historia Lausiaca* (Göttingen, 1916).

—— and H. H. Schaeder, *Studien zum antiken Synkretismus aus Iran und Griechenland* (Studien der Bibliothek Warburg VII, Leipzig, Berlin, 1926).

Roques, R., *L'univers dionysien* (Théologie XXIX, Paris, 1954).

Rosenstock-Huessy, E., *Out of Revolution: Autobiography of Western Man* (New York, 1938).

Roth, F., O.E.S.A., "Cardinal Richard Annibaldi, First Protector of the Augustinian Order, 1243–1276," *Augustiniana* II (1952) 26 ff., 108 ff., 230 ff., III (1953) 21 ff., 283 ff., IV (1954) 5 ff.

Rüegg, A., *Die Jenseitsvorstellungen vor Dante und die übrigen literarischen Voraussetzungen der "Divina Commedia"* (Einsiedeln, Köln, 1945) 2 vols.

Ryan, J., *Irish Monasticism: Origins and Early Development* (Dublin, Cork, 1931).

Salin, E., *Civitas Dei* (Tübingen, 1926).

Saltet, L., *Les réordinations* (Paris, 1907).

Schebler, A., *Die Reordinationen in der "altkatholischen" Kirche unter besonderer Berücksichtigung der Anschauungen Rudolph Sohms* (Bonn, 1936).

Schelkle, K. H., *Vergil in der Deutung Augustins* (Tübinger Beiträge zur Altertumswissenschaft XXXII, Stuttgart, Berlin, 1939).

Schlier, H., *Christus und die Kirche im Epheserbrief* (Tübingen, 1930).

Schmidt, H., S.J., "De lectionibus variantibus in formulis identicis sacramentariorum Leoniani, Gelasiani et Gregoriani," *Sacr. Erud.* IV (1952) 103 ff.

Schmidt, K. L., *Die Polis in Kirche und Welt* (Basel, 1939).

—— "Royaume, église, état et peuple . . . ," *Le problème du christianisme primitif* (Paris, 1938).

Schmidt, R., "Aetates mundi: Die Weltalter als Gliederungsprinzip der Geschichte," *Z. Ki. Gesch.* LXVII (1955–56) 288 ff.

Schmitt, A., "Mathematik und Zahlenmystik," *Aurelius Augustinus: Festschrift der Görres-Gesellschaft zum 500. Todestage des heiligen Augustinus* (Köln, 1930) 353 ff.

Schneider, A., "Der Gedanke der Erkenntnis des Gleichen durch Gleiches in antiker und patristischer Zeit," *Beiträge zur Geschichte des Philosophie des Mittelalters*, Erg. Bd. II (Münster, 1923) 65 ff.

Scholz, H., *Glaube und Unglaube in der Weltgeschichte: Ein Kommentar zu Augustins De Civitate Dei* (Leipzig, 1911).

Seipel, I., *Die wirtschaftsethischen Lehren der Kirchenväter* (Theologische Studien der Leogesellschaft XVIII, Wien, 1907).

Setton, K. M., *Christian Attitude toward the Emperor in the Fourth Century* (New York, 1941).

Somers, H. M., S.J., "The Riddle of a Plural (Genesis 1, 26)," *Folia* IX (1955) 63 ff.

Stegmann, B. A., *Christ, the "Man from Heaven"* (The Catholic University of America New Testament Studies VI, Washington, D.C., 1927).

Steidle, B., O.S.B., "«Homo Dei Antonius»," *Antonius Magnus Eremita, 356–1956* (Studia Anselmiana XXXVIII, Roma, 1956) 148 ff.

Stolz, A., O.S.B., *The Doctrine of Spiritual Perfection*, trans. from *Theologie der Mystik* by A. Williams, O.S.B. (St. Louis, London, 1938).

Strack, H. L. and P. Billerbeck, *Kommentar zum Neuen Testament erläutert aus Talmud und Midrasch* (München, 1922–28) 5 vols.

Straub, J., "Christliche Geschichtsapologetik in der Krisis des römischen Reiches," *Historia* I (1950) 52 ff.

Struker, A., *Die Gottesebenbildlichkeit des Menschen in der altchristlichen Literatur der ersten zwei Jahrhunderte* (Münster, 1913).

Svoboda, K., *L'esthétique de saint Augustin et ses sources* (Opera Facultatis Universitatis Masarykianae Brunensis XXXV, Brno, 1933).

Swain, J. W., "The Theory of the Four Monarchies: Opposition History under the Roman Empire," *Class. Philol.* XXXV (1940) 1 ff.

Toumanoff, C., "Christian Caucasia between Byzantium and Iran: New Light from Old Sources," *Traditio* X (1954) 109 ff.

Toynbee, A. J., *A Study of History* (Oxford, 1934–54) 10 vols.

Treitinger, O., *Die oströmische Kaiser-und Reichsidee nach ihrer Gestaltung im höfischen Zeremoniell*, 2nd ed. (Darmstadt, 1956).

Trier, J., "Zur Vorgeschichte des Renaissance-Begriffs," *Arch. Kult. Gesch.* XXXIII (1950) 45 ff. (also in: *Holz: Etymologien aus dem Niederwald* [Münster, Köln, 1952] 144 ff.).

Ueding, L., "Die Kanones von Chalkedon und ihre Bedeutung für Mönchtum und Klerus," *Das Konzil von Chalkedon*, edd. A. Grillmeier, S.J., and H. Bacht, S.J., II (Würzburg, 1953) 569 ff.

Vawter, B., C. M., *A Path through Genesis* (New York, 1945).

Vega, A. C., O.E.S.A., "Una adaptacion de la 'Informatio regularis' de S. Agustin anterior al siglo IX para unas virgines españolas . . . ," *Miscell. Mercati* II, 34 ff.

Verheijen, M., O.E.S.A., "La «Regula Puellarum» et la «Regula Sancti Augustini»," *Augustiniana* IV (1954) 258 ff.

———— "La Regula Sancti Augustini," *Vigil. Christ.* VII (1954) 27 ff.

———— "Les manuscrits de la «Lettre CCXI de saint Augustin»," *Revue du moyen âge latin* VIII (1952) 97 ff.

———— "Les Sermons 355–356 de saint Augustin et la Regula Sancti Augustini," *Rech.'s sc. rel.* XLI (1953) 231 ff.

Völker, W., *Das Vollkommenheitsideal des Origenes* (Beiträge zur historischen Theologie VII, Tübingen, 1931).

———— *Der wahre Gnostiker nach Clemens Alexandrinus* (Texte u. Untersuch. LVII, Leipzig, 1952).

———— *Fortschritt und Vollendung bei Philo von Alexandrien* (Texte u. Untersuch. XLIX, 1, Leipzig, 1938).

———— *Gregor von Nyssa als Mystiker* (Wiesbaden, 1955).

———— *Kontemplation und Ekstase bei Pseudo-Dionysius Areopagita* (Wiesbaden, 1958).

Vogelstein, M., *Kaiseridee-Romidee und das Verhältnis von Staat und Kirche seit Konstantin* (Historische Untersuchungen VII, Breslau, 1930).

Vuippens, I. Ayer de, O.M. Cap., "Où plaça-t-on le paradis terrestre?," *Etudes franciscaines* XXXVI (1924) 117 ff., 371 ff., 561 ff., XXXVII (1925) 21 ff., 113 ff.

Vyver, A. van de, "Les *Institutiones* de Cassiodore et sa fondation à Vivarium," *Rev. bén.* LIII (1941) 59 ff.

Weigel, G., S.J., *Faustus of Riez* (Philadelphia, 1938).

Wellesz, E., *A History of Byzantine Music and Hymnography* (Oxford, 1949).

Wikenhauser, A., "Die Herkunft der Idee des tausendjährigen Reiches in der Johannes-Apokalypse," *Röm. Quart.* XLV (1937) 1 ff.

Wilson, R. McL., "The Early History of the Exegesis of Gen. 1.26," *Stud. Patr.* I, 420 ff.

Wörter, F., *Beiträge zur Dogmengeschichte des Semipelagianismus* (Paderborn, 1898).

———— *Zur Dogmengeschichte des Semipelagianismus* (Kirchengeschichtliche Studien V, 2, Münster, 1899).

Wolfson, H. A., *Philo* (Cambridge, Mass., 1947) 2 vols.

Zeller, E., *Die Philosophie der Griechen* I, 1, 6th ed. (Leipzig, 1919), III, 1, 5th ed. (Leipzig, 1923).

Zumkeller, A., O.E.S.A., *Das Mönchtum des heiligen Augustinus* (Würzburg, 1950).

———— "Zum geistigen Gehalt der Augustinerregel," v. Balthasar, *Grosse Ordensregeln* 113 ff.

ADDENDA TO THE
TORCHBOOK EDITION, 1967

Although it is impossible to attain completeness or perfection in a book, it may be useful to supply the following additions for this new edition, especially those references to important new publications which have appeared since 1959; cf. also my article "Erneuerung," *RLAC* VI (1964) 240 ff. Among critical reviews of the book, I should like to mention that of P. Levi, *Heythrop Journal* II (1961), 170 ff.; the reviewer rightly, regrets the scanty discussion in the book of the late ancient syncretistic antecedents of, or parallels with, the orthodox Christian ideology of renewal. While this intended limitation remains, I may refer, in order to illustrate my point of view, to a few remarks on Gnosticism in my recent article "Homo Viator: Mediaeval Ideas on Alienation and Order" *Speculum* XLII (1967) 233 ff. A full study of the very rich renewal ideology of the Gnostics·would be highly desirable; a short sketch is found in R. Roques, *Structures théologiques de la gnose à Richard de Saint-Victor* (Paris, 1962) 32 ff.

Pages 10–16, 68, 73, 203–12: For the ideologies of the Alpha and Omega and of the end which is like the beginning, and for their relation to the myth of eternal recurrence and to the phenomenon of time, cf. the illuminating remarks of V. Jankélévich, "La purification et le temps," *Archivio di Filosofia* 1958, 11 ff., esp. 13, also *id.*, "L'éternité et la première impureté," *ibid.* 1959, 25 ff.

Page 18, note 6: For the linking of the Roman *Renovatio* idea and the conception of the Incarnation as divine renewal in the *Hypapante* mosaic of S. Maria Maggiore in Rome of c. 430, see the posthumously published study of Ernst H. Kantorowicz, "Puer Exoriens," in *Perennitas . . . Beiträge . . . P. Thomas Michels O.S.B.* (Münster, 1963) 118 ff.; see also Kantorowicz, "Oriens Augusti—Lever du Roi," *Dumbarton Oaks Papers,* XVII (1963) 119 ff., where he discussed the continuity of the more cosmological solar aspects of imperial *renovatio* ideology. The cosmological-vitalistic concept of *palingenesia* too, could insert itself into this ideology; cf. J. Straub, "Παλιγ-γενεσία: Bemerkungen zu einem Papyrus (P. Lond. 878) aus der Zeit des Licinius," *Hist. JB.* LXXIV (1955) 653 ff.

Page 23, note 28: For the problem of the Renaissance cf. also the survey by F. Chabod in: *Machiavelli and the Renaissance* (London, 1958; New York, Harper Torchbooks, 1965) 149 ff.; furthermore P. O. Kristeller, *Renaissance Thought* I and II (New York, Harper Torchbooks, 1961 and 1965) and É. Gilson, "Notes sur une frontière contestée," *Archives d' histoire doctrinale et littéraire du moyen âge* XXXIII, 1958 (1959) 59 ff.

Page 32 f., note 7: For conversion cf. P. Aubin, S. J., *Le problème de la conversion: Etude sur un terme commun a l 'hellénisme et au christianisme des trois premiers siècles* (Paris, 1963).

Page 41 ff.: For the terminology of *reformare, renovare*, etc. in the Epistles of St. Paul, cf. now the great *Vetus Latina* work, edited by the Archabbey of Beuron, especially vol. XXIV, I: *Epistula ad Ephesios*, ed. H. J. Frede (Freiburg, 1962) 184 ff., to Eph. 4:23.

Page 43: For the term and concept of apocatastasis, cf. P. Siniscalco, "'Ἀποκατάστασις e ἀποκαθίστημι nella tradizione della Grande Chiesa fino ad Ireneo," *Stud. Patr.* III (Texte u. Untersuch. LXXVIII, Berlin 1961) 380 ff.

Page 63: Among the Greek Fathers whose renewal ideology is not treated in this book is Tatian; cf. now M. Elze, *Tatian und seine Theologie* (Göttingen, 1960), especially 91 ff., on Tatian's conception of the loss and restoration of man's image-likeness with God.

Pages 64–66, notes 5–12: For the location of the creational and eschatological Paradise in the East, cf. F. J. Dölger, *Sol Salutis*, 2nd ed. (Münster, 1925) 220 ff.

Pages 75 ff., 90 ff., etc.: Cf. the new editions of the works of Gregory of Nyssa, initiated by Werner Jaeger; *In Inscriptiones Psalmorum*, ed. J. McDonough, S. J., and P. Alexander, in Jaeger, *Greg. Nyss. Opera* V (1962); *In Canticum Canticorum*, ed. H. Langerbeck, *ibid.* VI (1960); *De vita Mosis*, ed. H. Musurillo, *ibid.* VII, I (1964).

Page 80: For St. Basil the Great's doctrine of deification and sanctification by the Holy Spirit, cf. A. Heising, O.S.B., "Der Heilige Geist und die Heiligung der Engel in der Pneumatologie des Basilius von Cäsarea," *Z. kath. Theol.* LXXXVII (1965) 257 ff.

Page 82 f., note 76: For Synesius cf. now also H. Strohm, "Zur Hymnen-dichtung des Synesios von Kyrene," *Hermes* XCIII (1965) 47 ff.

Page 82, note 76, page 171, note 12: Cf. Marius Victorinus, *Hymni*, ed. and trans. P. Henry and P. Hadot, in: *Marius Victorinus, Traités théologiques sur la Trinité*, 2 vols. (Sources chrétiennes LXVIII f., Paris, 1960). See especially II, 1083, to *Hymnus III*, 117–20, concerning *reformatio* by the Holy Spirit (relevant for p. 82, n. 76).

Pages 83 ff. and 185 ff.: For further literature on the *imago Dei* idea and on the doctrine of the reform of the divine image in man, cf. my articles "Eikon," *RLAC* IV, (1959) 771 f., and "Varia Archaeologica et Ideologica," *Traditio*, XVI (1960) 454 ff.; in addition, cf. J. Jervell, *Imago Dei: Gen. 1, 26 f. im Spätjudentum, in der Gnosis und in den paulinischen Briefen*, (Göttingen, 1960), P. Gerlitz, "Der mystische Bildbegriff (εἰκών und imago) in der frühchrist-lichen Geistesgeschichte," *Zeitschrift fur Religions – und Geistesgeschichte* XV (1963) 244 ff.; also my "Wimmer Lecture," *Ad imaginem Dei: The Image of Man in Medieval Art* (Latrobe, Pennsylvania, 1965).

Page 104 and note 85: For the Cappadocians' conception of the never ending desire for God and for the anticipation of this conception in Clement of Alexandria, cf. B. Otis, "Cappadocian Thought as a Coherent System," *Dumbarton Oaks Papers* XII (1958) 108.

Page 109, last two paragraphs: for the relationship between man's image-likeness to God and his rulership over the rest of creation, cf. Ladner, "Philosophical Anthropology of St. Gregory of Nyssa," *Dumbarton Oaks Papers* XII (1958) 67. Cf. also Ephraem, *In Genesim*, Sectio I, no. 29, ed. R.-M. Tonneau, *Corpus Scriptorum Christianorum Orientalium, Scriptores Syri* LXXII (Latin translation) (Louvain, 1955) 17 (I owe this reference to F. Pericoli Ridolfini, in his review of my book in *Rivista di Storia della Chiesa in Italia* XVII (1963) 325.

Page 125, note 49: See also R. J. H. Jenkins, "The Classical Background of the Scriptores post Theophanem," *Dumbarton Oaks Papers* VIII (1954) 23 and 30, for Constantine VII's conception of Basil I's life as Augustus-like, as νέος, καινούργιος, as a μεταβολή πρὸς τὸ κρεῖττον.

Page 130, note 63 and Exursus V: For the patristic attitude toward wealth, cf. the important work of E. F. Bruck, *Kirchenväter und soziales Erbrecht*

(Berlin, Göttingen, Heidelberg, 1956), to which Professor George H. Williams kindly drew my attention.

Page 147 ff.: For Q. Aurelius Symmachus and the affair of the Altar of Victory, cf. F. Paschoud, "Reflexions sur l' idéal religieux de Symmaque" (with further literature), *Historia* XIV (1965) 215 ff.

Page 162, note 29: For Pelagius and Pelagianism, cf. also J. Morris, "Pelagian Literature," *Jour. Theol. Stud.*, New Series, XVI (1965) 26 ff.

Page 167 ff.: For the six-day-work of creation in patristic and later Christian thought, cf. Y. M. J. Congar, O. P., "Le thème de *Dieu-Createur* et les explications de l'Hexaméron dans la tradition chrétienne," in: *L'homme devant Dieu: Mélanges offerts au Père Henri de Lubac* I (Paris, 1963) 189 ff.

Page 185 ff.: For the image of God in man according to St. Augustine, cf. also J. E. Sullivan, O.P., *The Image of God: The Doctrine of St. Augustine and Its Influence* (Dubuque, Iowa, 1963); R. A. Markus, "«Imago» and «similitudo» in Augustine," *Rev. ét.'s aug.* X (1964) 125 ff.

Pages 201, note 48, and 353, note 23: New edition of Augustine, *De magistro,* ed. G. Weigel, *CSEL* LXXVII (1961).

Page 203 ff.: For Augustine's conception of time, cf. O. Lechner, *Idee und Zeit in der Metaphysik Augustins* (Salzburger Studien zur Philosophie V, München, 1964), important especially for the fact that time for Augustine is not exhausted by its subjective mental aspect, and even less by its cosmological aspect, but can be understood only as a fundamental aspect of all created being in its relation to eternity. Cf. also L. Boros, "Les catégories de la temporalité chez saint Augustin," Archives de philosophie XXI (1958) 324 ff.

Page 220 f., note 28: The Augustinian concept of *motus vitalis* is metaphysical as well as vegetative-biological, an intermediary between the realms of intellect and sense (as are the *rationes seminales*). In John Scot it was to become a *copula* between mind and body foreshadowing the various psycho-physical intermediaries of the twelfth-century psychologist-theologians. Cf. Ladner, *Ad Imaginem Dei: The Image of Man in Medieval Art* (Latrobe, Pennsylvania, 1965).

Pages 221, note 28, 253 f. notes 38 ff., and 264 f., note 108: New edition of Augustine, *De Vera Religione,* ed. G. M. Green, *CSEL,* LXXVII (1961).

Page 222 ff.: For the Ages of the world in patristic thought, cf. A. Luneau, *L'histoire du salut chez les pères de l'église: La doctrine des âges du monde* (Paris, 1964).

Page 257: Among recent studies on the influence of Manicheeism on St. Augustine cf. especially W. H. C. Frend, "Gnostic-Manichaean Tradition in Roman North Africa," *The Journal of Ecclesiastical History* IV (1953) 13 ff., P. J. de Menasce, O.P., "Augustin Manichéen," in: *Freundesgabe für Ernst Robert Curtius* (Bern, 1956) 79 ff., A. Adam, "Das Fortwirken des Manichäismus bei Augustin," *Z. Ki. Gesch.* LXIX (1958) 1 ff.

Page 262 f., note 101 and 103: For Ticonius, cf. F. Lo Bue, *The Turin Fragments of Tyconius' Commentary on Revelation* (Cambridge, 1963).

Page 266, note 112: For the *Didache* cf. now J. P. Audet, *La Didachè: Instructions des Apôtres* (Paris, 1958). For the "two ways" cf. also F. J. Dölger, *Die Sonne der Gerechtigkeit und der Schwarze* (Münster, 1918) 124 ff.—For the germane subject of Christ as *the* way (John 14:6), cf. my article "Homo Viator," *Speculum* XLII (1967) 233 ff.; also M. Comeau, "Le Christ, chemin e terme de l'ascension spirituelle d'après saint Augustin," *Rech.'s sc. rel.* XL (1951–1952, Mélanges J. Lebreton) II, 80 ff.; L. Galati, *Cristo la via nel pensiero di S. Agostino* (Diss., Fac. Theol., Pontif. Università Gregoriana, Roma, 1957); T. Bavel, "L'humanité du Christ comme lac parvulorum et comme via dans la spiritualité de saint Augustin," *Augustiniana* VII (1957) 245 ff.

Page 270 ff. For the relationship between the City of God and the Church according to St. Augustine, cf. also Y. M. J. Congar, O.P., "«Civitas Dei» et «Ecclesia» chez saint Augustin. Histoire de la recherche: Son état présent," *Rev. ét's aug.* III (1957) 1 ff.; É. Lamirande, O.M.I., *L'église céleste selon saint Augustin* (Études augustiniennes, Paris, 1963).

Pages 284–99: For the chapter on the liturgy see also M. B. de Soos, O.S.B., "Présence du mystère du salut dans la liturgie d'après saint Léon," *Ephemerides Liturgicae* LXXIII (1959) 116 ff., concerning the renewal of the mysteries of salvation through their liturgical and sacramental repetition, and the same author's *Le mystère liturgique d'après Saint Léon le Grand* (Liturgiewissenschaftliche Quellen und Forschungen XXXIV, Münster, 1958) 61 ff., on *renovare* and *reparare* in Leo's Christmas sermons, in which the Pope speaks about the renewal of mankind through the Incarnation and its liturgical celebration.

Page 285 f., especially 286, note 12: For Leo the Great's influence on the liturgy cf. also E. Dekkers, O.S.B., "Autour de l'oeuvre liturgique de s. Léon le Grand," *Sacris Erudiri* X (1958) 363 ff., especially 385, for the oration *Deus qui humanae substantiae*.

Page 291 f.: For the motif of the return to Paradise in the Greek Christian liturgy cf. E. Timiadis, "«L'église le paradis retrouvé», selon l'hymnographie," in: *Studia Patristica* V, (Texte und Untersuch. LXXX, Berlin, 1962) 129 ff.

Page 288, note 20: Cf. also *Sacramentarium Veronense, Consecratio Presbyteri,* formula 954, Mohlberg 121: Domine, sancte pater, omnipotens aeterne Deus . . . per quem proficiunt universa; per quem cuncta firmantur, amplificatis semper in melius naturae rationabilis incrementis per ordinem congrua ratione dispositum (I owe this reference to Mons. Henry G. J. Beck, in his review of my book in the *American Historical Review* LXVI [1961] 428).

Pages 302 f. and 429: For the Gallic councils of the fifth and sixth centuries, cf. now *Concilia Galliae* A. 314- A. 506 (*Corp. Christ., Ser. Lat.* CXLVIII, 1963) 142 ff.: for Tours I of 461; 150 ff.: for Vannes of 461-91; *Concil. Gall.* A. 511-A. 695 (*Corp. Christ., Ser. Lat.* CXLVIII A, 1963) 3 ff.: for Orléans I of 511; 20 ff.: for Epaone of 517; 53 ff.: for Orange II of 529; 113 ff.: for Orléans III of 538.

Page 309 ff.: For the close relationship between penance and renewal ideology, cf. Aphraates, *Demonstratio* VII, ed. J. Parisot, *Patrologia Syriaca* (with Latin translation) I (Paris, 1894) 312 ff. (I owe this reference to F. Pericoli Ridolfini, in his review of my book in *Rivista di Storia della Chiesa in Italia* XVII (1963) 325.

Page 320, first note 3, and page 326, note 17: For the "angelic life" see also Uta Ranke-Heinemann, "Zum Ideal der vita angelica im frühen Mönchtum," *Geist und Leben* XXIX (1956) 347 ff.

Page 320, second note 3: For the *Apophthegmata Patrum* cf. also J.-C. Guy, *Recherches sur la tradition grecque des Apophthegmata Patrum* (Subsidia Hagiographica XXXVI, Bruxelles, 1962), and *id.* in *Rev. ascet. myst.* XLI (1965) 113 ff.

Page 322, note 10: For the *Historia Monachorum,* see now the critical edition of the Greek text by A.-J. Festugière, *Historia Monachorum in Aegypto* (Subsidia Hapiographica XXXIV, Bruxelles, 1961).

Pages 346, 385, 391, 415: Cf. the new edition of the Rule of St. Benedict, by R. Hanslik, *CSEL* LXXV (1960).

Page 346, note 18: For *conversatio* see also N. Alszeghi, *Nova Creatura: La nozione della grazia nei commentari medievali di S. Paolo* (Analecta Gregoriana LXXXI, Roma, 1956) 108 ff.

Page 349, notes 31 f.: For Ps.-Dionysius the Areopagite's conception of priesthood and monasticism, cf. also R. Roques, *Structures théologiques de la Gnose à Richard de Saint-Victor* (Paris, 1962) 198 ff.

Pages 350–65: For the role of monasticism in St. Augustine's life and work and for the Augustinian rule cf. A. Manrique, O.S.A., *La vida monastica en San Agustin,* (El Escorial, Salamanca, 1959). For the problem of pre-Augustinian monasticism in North Africa cf. J. M. del Estal, O.E.S.A., "Testimonio positivo de Petiliano sobre la inexistencia de monacato en Africa antes de S. Agustin," *Studia Monastica* III (1961) 123 ff., with good bibliographical notes, also *id.,* "Institucion monastica de San Agustin," *La Ciudad de Dios* CLXXVIII (1965) 201 ff. See also R. Lorenz, "Die Anfänge des abendländischen Mönchtums im 4. Jahrhundert," *Z. Ki. G.* LXXVII (1966) 1 ff., for early western monasticism in general, for the impulse given to it by St. Augustine, and (pp. 44 ff.) for the Augustinian Rule (with good bibliography.)

Page 353 ff.: For Augustine's road from the philosophical retreat of Cassiciacum to his African monasteries, cf. now R. J. Halliburton, "The Inclination to Retirement—The Retreat of Cassiciacum and the 'Monastery' of Tagaste," in: *Studia Patristica,* V (Texte u. Untersuch., Berlin, 1962) 329 ff.

Page 359 ff.: For Augustine's use of Acts 4: 32 ff. in the elaboration of his ideal of the monastic and clerical lives, cf. D. Sanchis, "Pauvreté monastique et charité fraternelle chez saint Augustin: Le commentaire augustinien de Actes 4, 32–35 entre 393 et 403," *Studia Monastica* IV (1962) 7 ff.

Page 382: For the *Rule of St. Paul and St. Stephen* cf. now J. E. M. Vilanova, *Regula Pauli et Stephani. Edicio critica i comentari* (Scripta et Documenta, XI, Montserrat, 1959).

Page 383: For the so-called *Regula Tarnatensis* cf. now L. R. Delasalle "Comparaison, datation, localisation relatives des règles monastiques de saint Césaire d' Arles, saint Ferréol d' Uzès et de la 'Regula Tarnantensis Monasterii'," *Augustiniana* XI (1961) 5 ff. See also G. Holzherr, O.S.B., "Die Regula Ferioli," *Commentationes in Regulam S. Benedicti* (Studia Anselmiana XLII, Roma, 1957) 223 ff., and id., *Regula Ferioli* (Einsiedeln, etc., 1961).

Page 387, note 6: For the influence of an Augustinian conception of the monastico-clerical life upon the life and liturgy of a Roman basilica of the seventh century, cf. also A. Chavasse, *Le sacramentaire gélasien* (Paris, etc., 1958) 508 f., 515 f.

Page 391 f.: For post-Augustinian monasticism in North Africa, and especially for St. Fulgentius of Ruspe, cf. J. J. Gavigan, O.E.S.A., *De Vita monastica in Africa septentrionali inde a temporibus S. Augustini usque ad invasiones Arabum* (Roma, Torino, 1962).

Page 397 f., note 49: For Germanus of Auxerre cf. now the introduction by R. Borius to his edition and French translation of the principal source: Constance de Lyon, *Vie de saint Germain d' Auxerre* (Sources Chrétiennes CXII, Paris, 1965).

Page 399, note 57: The authenticity of the *Responsa* has not been convincingly disproved; for this question cf. P. Meyvaert, O.S.B., "Les Responsiones de S. Grégoire le Grand à s. Augustin de Cantorbéry," *Revue d'histoire ecclésiastique* LIV (1959) 879 ff., and H. Farmer, O.S.B., "St. Gregory's Answers to St. Augustine of Canterbury," *Studia Monastica* I (1959) 419 ff.; also Margaret Deanesly, "The Capitular Text of the Responsiones of Pope Gregory I to St. Augustine," *Journal of Ecclesiastical History* XII (1961) 231 ff.

Page 400, note 60: For the question of Gregory the Great's Benedictinism cf. also O. M. Porcel, O.S.B., "San Gregorio Magno y el monacato," *Monastica* I (Scripta et Documenta XII, Montserrat, 1960) 1 ff. (versus Hallinger).

ADDENDA

Page 13, n. 26: For the Golden Age see also J. G. Griffiths, "Did Hesiod Invent the Golden Age," *Jour. Hist. Ideas* XIX (1958) 91 ff.

Page 65, n. 6, and pages 78 f.: For St. Ephraem's Hymns on Faith and on Paradise cf. now Dom E. Beck's edition and German translation in *Corpus Scriptorum Christianorum Orientalium* CLIV f. and CLXXIV f., *Scriptores Syri* LXXIII f. and LXXVIII f. (Louvain, 1955, 1957); for Ephraem's conception of the return to Paradise see also I. Ortiz de Urbina, S.J., "Le paradis eschatologique d'après saint Ephrem," *Orientalia Christiana Periodica* XX (1954) 476 ff.

Pages 83 ff.: For Greek patristic thought on the recovery of man's likeness to God see Hilda-C. Graef, "L'image de Dieu et la structure de l'âme d'après les pères grecs," *Vie spir.*, Suppl. V (1952) 331 ff.

Pages 84 f.: For St. Irenaeus' doctrine of man's image-likeness to God see also the important article by E. Peterson, "L'immaginè di Dio in S. Ireneo," *La Scuola Cattolica* LXIX (1941) 46 ff.

Page 112, n. 13, and page 331, n. 8: For control of Frankenberg's retranslation of Evagrius Ponticus' *Centuriae* from the Syriac to the Greek see now the new edition and French translation by A. Guillaumont, *Les six centuries des Kephalaia Gnostica d'Evagre le Pontique*, *Patrologia Orientalis* XXVIII, 1 (Paris, 1958).

Pages 136–139 and pages 409–412: For the early Christian concept of tradition cf. J. N. Bakhuizen van den Brink, "Traditio im theologischen Sinne," *Vigil. Christ.* XIII (1959) 65 ff.

Page 160, n. 22: For Theodore of Mopsuestia cf. also J. L. McKenzie, S.J., "Annotations on the Christology of Theodore of Mopsuestia," *Theol. Stud.* XIX (1958) 345 ff.

Page 188, n. 8: For the *Regio dissimilitudinis* see also P. Courcelle, "Tradition néo-platonicienne et traditions chrétiennes de la 'Région de dissemblance' (Platon, *Politique* 237d)," *Arch. hist. doctr. litt. m. â.* XXXII (1957) 5 ff.

Pages 350 ff.: For St. Augustine and monasticism see also A. Trapé, O.S.A., "San Agustin y el monacato occidental," N. Dominguez-del-Val, O.S.A., "Cultura y formación intelectual en los monasterios agustinianos de Tagaste, Cartago e Hipona," *La Ciudad de Dios* CLXIX (1956) 404 ff., 425 ff.; and other articles in the same volume.

Page 419, n. 81: For Junilius see also M. L. W. Laistner, "Antiochene

Exegesis in Western Europe during the Middle Ages," *Harv. Theol. Rev.* XL (1947) 23 ff.

Pages 420 f., nn. 83 ff., and page 448, nn. 24 f.: For the probability of the authenticity of Boethius' *De fide catholica* cf. W. Bark, "Boethius' Fourth Tractate, the So-Called *De fide catholica*," *Harv. Theol. Rev.* XXXIX (1946) 55 ff. In his new edition of Boethius' *De consolatione philosophiae*, *Corp. Christ.*, *Ser. Lat.* XCIV, 1 (1957), L. Bieler, in the preface, follows Rand's last opinion as well as those of Bark and of Dom. M. Cappuyns in accepting the authenticity of *De fide catholica*.

INDEX

Index references to footnotes often refer also to the appertaining text. The following abbreviations of authors' names, etc., are used in addition to conventional scriptural abbreviations:

Key Phrases

Χριστιανισμός ἐστι τῆς θείας φύσεως μίμησις, Christianity is an imitation of the divine nature (Greg. Nyss.): 91

Christus veritatem se, non consuetudinem cognominavit (Tert.): 138 n.28

Cor unum et anima una in Deo (Acts 4:32, Augustinian Rule): 359 n.52; 384; 385 n.30; cf. also 126 n.51, 128 (John Chrys.); 342 (Basil); 343 n.11 (Cass.)

Deus qui humanae substantiae dignitatem mirabiliter condidisti et mirabilius reformasti (liturgical prayer): 284

Ego creavi, ego recreo; ego formavi, ego reformo; ego feci, ego reficio (Aug.): 195 n.28

Fiunt, non nascuntur christiani (Tert.): 135

Ἰδοὺ γὰρ ἡ βασιλεία τοῦ Θεοῦ ἐντὸς ὑμῶν ἐστιν, Ecce enim regnum Dei intra vos est (Luke 17:21): 107

Imaginem in nobis Dei deformare potuimus, reformare non possumus (Aug.): 194 n.24

Μὴ συσχηματίζεσθε τῷ αἰῶνι τούτῳ, ἀλλὰ μεταμορφοῦσθε τῇ ἀνακαινώσει τοῦ νοός, Et nolite conformari huic saeculo, sed reformamini in novitate sensus vestri (Rom. 12:2): 53 n.19

Nihil innovetur nisi quod traditum est (Stephen I): 139; 298

Ὁμοίωσις θεῷ κατὰ τὸ δυνατόν (Plato): 83

Ὄρος ἐστὶ τῆς ἀνθρωπίνης μακαριότητος ἡ πρὸς τὸ θεῖον ὁμοίωσις, The definition of human beatitude is the assimilation to God (Greg. Nyss.): 90

Ποιήσωμεν ἄνθρωπον κατ᾽ εἰκόνα ἡμετέραν καὶ καθ᾽ ὁμοίωσιν, Faciamus hominem ad imaginem et similitudinem nostram (Gen. 1:26): 55 n.30

Praesens non habet spatium (Aug.): 203

Renovabitur ut aquilae iuventus tua (Ps. 102: 5): 52 n.14; 295; 314 n.41

Sexta aetate mens humana renovetur ad imaginem Dei, sicut sexta die homo factus est ad imaginem Dei (Aug.): 236 n.41

Θεὸν γενέσθαι (Basil): 80; 106

Unde ista Dei civitas . . . vel inchoaretur exortu vel progrederetur excursu vel adprehenderet debitos fines, si non esset socialis vita sanctorum (Aug.): 240 n.5

Measure, *Mensura, Modus:* 214 (Wisd. 11:
    21, Aug.); 215 n.6 (Aug.); 216 n.8:
    revocare (Aug.)
Medes. See Empires
Medicus. See God, Christ
Μείζων (see also Ἀνάγειν, Ἐπαυξάνειν):
    106 n.88: τῶν ἀεὶ μειζόνων ἀρχή (Greg.
    Nyss.)
Melania, the Elder (d. *c.* 410): 371; 372 n.25
Melania, the Younger, St. (d. 439): 371
Melas, St., Bishop of Rhinokurura (late
    4th cent.): 352
Melior, in melius (ad meliora). See *Commutare,
    Convertere, Crescere, Flectere, Instaurare,
    Mutare, Proficere, Referre, Reficere, Re-
    formare in melius, Renovare in melius,
    Reparare in melius, Restituere, Transire,
    Verti in melius, Vita melior*
Memory:
    Memoria: 197–199, 201f. n.54 (Aug.);
    192 n.20 (Aug.); 197, 201f.: Trini-
    tarian analogies (Aug.); 203f., 208, 211:
    time (Aug.); 219 n.23: numbers (Aug.);
    420 n.83 (Boeth.); 450
Mens: 173 n.19: man (Aug.); 197f. nn.38f.:
    Trinitarian analogies (Aug.)
Merida, Church of St. Eulalia (see also
    Nanctus): 393 n.32
Messalians: 362 n.65
Messianic, Messianism: 27: millenarian
    renewal ideas; 51: Israel; 108: kingdom
    (Jewish-Hellenistic expectations)
Μεταβάλλειν: 47 n.61: ἐπὶ τὸ βέλτιον
    (Plato); 48 n.63: πρὸς τὸν ἀμείνω [βίον]
    (Philo)
Μεταβολή: 71 n.38: ἐπὶ τὸ κρεῖττον (Clem.
    Alex.); 80, 161 n.25 (Basil); 162 n.28
    (Greg. Nyss.)
Metahistorical preconceptions: 35; 433–
    442
Μετακόσμησις: 47 n.59, 80, 161: ἐπὶ τὸ
    βέλτιον (Basil)
Metals (see also Golden Age, World ages):
    13 (Hesiod); 14 (Maguseans)
Metamorphosis, Μεταμόρφωσις, Μεταμορφοῦν
    (see also Μετασχηματίζειν, Transforma-
    tion, Transfiguration): 2; 39: *reformare*
    (Ovid); 40: *transformare* (Ovid, Virgil);

41: reform (Rom. 12:2, 2 Cor. 3:18);
    42 n.22: Transfiguration of Christ; 43;
    45; 47; 53 n.19 (Rom. 12:2, Matt. 17:2,
    Mark 9:2); 54 n.24 (2 Cor. 3:18); 92
    n.39: toward sin (Greg. Nyss.); 122
    n.42: of souls by king (Themist.)
Μεταμοσχεύειν: 70 n.35 (Clem. Alex.)
Metanoia, Μετανοεῖν, Μετάνοια (see also
    Change of Mind, Repentance, Conver-
    sion): 49; 50 n.4
Μεταπλάσσειν (Μεταπλάττειν): 47 n.58: ἐπὶ
    τὸ ἄμεινον (Cyr. Alex.); 86 n.12 (Clem.
    Alex.)
Μεταποιεῖν (ἐπὶ τὸ θειότερον): 48 n.64, 80
    n.72, 161f. n.28 (Greg. Nyss.)
Μεταστοιχειοῦν: 98 n.59 (Greg. Nyss.)
Μεταστρέφεσθαι: 49 n.2 (Plato)
Μετασχηματίζειν (see also Metamorphosis,
    Transfiguration): 41 (Plato, Phil. 3:
    20f.); 42; 43; 53 n.19: resurrection
    (Phil. 3: 20f.)
Μετάθεσις ἐπὶ τὸ βέλτιον: 47 n.62 (Polybius)
Μεταξύ (see also Dialectic): 95; 96
Μετατιθέναι: 70 n.35 (Clem. Alex.)
Metempsychosis (see also Reincarnation):
    12 n.17; 33 n.8
Μεθιστάναι: 122 n.41 (Euseb.); 124 n.45
    (Greg. Nyss.)
Methodius, St. (d. *c.* 311): 27 n.3; 325f.
    n.15: virginity;
    Symposium: III,8, 70ff.: 325 n.15;
    VIII,12f., 203f.: 327 n.18
Μεθόριος: 96 n.49: man (Greg. Nyss.)
Μετοικίζειν: 71 n.38 (Clem. Alex.)
Miles Christi: 365 (2 Cor. 10:4, 1 Tim. 1:
    18)
Militia Christi (christiana, divina, clericatus)
    (see also Monasticism, Clericate): 365,
    368 (Aug.)
Millan (Aemilianus) of Cogolla, St. (d. 574):
    394
Millenarism, Millenarian (see also Millen-
    nium): 27–31: millenarian renewal
    ideas; 66 n.15; 69 (Iren.); 140 (Lact.);
    224; 224f., 230, 231 n.29 (and Aug.);
    231 n.29 (and Ambr.)
Millennium(s) (see also World ages): 14:
    seventh (Magusean); 27f.: metahistorical

Selected titles: revised December, 1967

harper ✝ torchbooks

HUMANITIES AND SOCIAL SCIENCES

American Studies: General

American Studies: Colonial

American Studies: From the Revolution to 1860

American Studies: Since the Civil War

† The New American Nation Series, edited by Henry Steele Commager and Richard B. Morris.
‡ American Perspectives series, edited by Bernard Wishy and William E. Leuchtenburg.
* The Rise of Modern Europe series, edited by William L. Langer.
** History of Europe series, edited by J. H. Plumb.
¶ Researches in the Social, Cultural and Behavioral Sciences, edited by Benjamin Nelson.
§ The Library of Religion and Culture, edited by Benjamin Nelson.
Σ Harper Modern Science Series, edited by James R. Newman.
° Not for sale in Canada.
△ Not for sale in the U. K.

2

3

4

Christianity: The Roman and Eastern Traditions

Oriental Religions: Far Eastern, Near Eastern

Philosophy of Religion

Religion, Culture & Society

NATURAL SCIENCES AND MATHEMATICS

Biological Sciences

History of Science

Mathematics

Philosophy of Science

Physics and Cosmology